G000045318

R.V. Ishmael

Harhman V Heffew

Statement served late,
need good reason to need
person (Dri statements).

S.22. YJCEA.
   Admit s mdur witness who was
under 18 @ time of offence but over
18 now.

Blackstone's

Youth Court Handbook
2014–2015

Blackstone's
Youth Court
Handbook
2014–2015

Mark Ashford
Naomi Redhouse

Consultant Editor
Anthony Edwards

OXFORD
UNIVERSITY PRESS

OXFORD
UNIVERSITY PRESS

Great Clarendon Street, Oxford, OX2 6DP,
United Kingdom

Oxford University Press is a department of the University of Oxford.
It furthers the University's objective of excellence in research, scholarship,
and education by publishing worldwide. Oxford is a registered trade mark of
Oxford University Press in the UK and in certain other countries

© Mark Ashford, Naomi Redhouse, Anthony Edwards 2013

The moral rights of the authors have been asserted

First Edition Published in 2013

Impression: 1

All rights reserved. No part of this publication may be reproduced, stored in
a retrieval system, or transmitted, in any form or by any means, without the
prior permission in writing of Oxford University Press, or as expressly permitted
by law, by licence, or under terms agreed with the appropriate reprographics
rights organization. Enquiries concerning reproduction outside the scope of the
above should be sent to the Rights Department, Oxford University Press, at the
address above

You must not circulate this work in any other form
and you must impose this same condition on any acquirer

Crown copyright material is reproduced under Class Licence
Number C01P0000148 with the permission of OPSI
and the Queen's Printer for Scotland

Published in the United States of America by Oxford University Press
198 Madison Avenue, New York, NY 10016, United States of America

British Library Cataloguing in Publication Data

Data available

ISBN 978-0-19-967458-9

Printed by
L.E.G.O. S.p.A.–Lavis TN

Links to third party websites are provided by Oxford in good faith and
for information only. Oxford disclaims any responsibility for the materials
contained in any third party website referenced in this work.

Preface

We have written this book with the busy practitioner at the forefront of our minds. We hope that this includes solicitors, barristers, youth offending team staff, and other professionals working in the criminal justice system. Dealing with cases involving children and young people (referred to throughout the text as youths) presents a number of challenges. Our aim is to provide, in accessible form, all that is immediately necessary to deal with the day-to-day practice of the criminal courts where those defendants appear.

It has inevitably been necessary to select the material to be included from the wealth of information that could have filled a much larger volume. We hope that our choices will meet the requirements of the user of this text. We would like to thank our colleagues for raising questions which have assisted in those decisions.

We are particularly grateful to Roxanne Selby and Fiona Sinclair of OUP for their constant patience and support.

There are many others who have also contributed their ideas to this work but any mistakes are entirely our own.

We have stated the law as at 28 May 2013.

Any references to statutory guidance can be found on the CPS or Ministry of Justice websites.

Mark Ashford
Naomi Redhouse

Contents

Part A Offences

Part B Youth Justice System

Part C Decision to Prosecute and Diversion

Part D Procedure

Part E Case Management

Part F Sentencing

Contents

Part G Youths in the Adult Magistrates' Court

Part H Youths in the Crown Court

Part I Attaining 18

Part J Parents and Guardians

Appendices

Icons List

The following icons are used throughout this book:

DO	Dangerous Offender
EW	Either Way
🎚	Sentence
SO	Summary Only
GC	Grave Crime
IO	Indictable Only
📖	Cross reference to *Blackstone's Criminal Practice 2014*

Table of Cases

Table of Cases

Table of Cases

Table of Cases

Table of Cases

Table of Cases

Table of Cases

Table of Primary Legislation

Table of Primary Legislation

Table of Primary Legislation

Table of Primary Legislation

Table of Primary Legislation

Table of Primary Legislation

Table of Primary Legislation

Table of Secondary Legislation

Table of Secondary Legislation

Table of Conventions

Table of Practice Directions

Abbreviations

ABE	achieving best evidence
ACPO	Association of Chief Police Officers
ADHD	attention deficit hyperactivity disorder
A-G	Attorney General
ASBO	anti-social behaviour order
BA 1976	Bail Act 1976
CDA 1998	Crime and Disorder Act 1998
CJA 1988	Criminal Justice Act 1988
CJA 2003	Criminal Justice Act 2003
CJIA 2008	Criminal Justice and Immigration Act 2008
CPIA 1996	Criminal Procedure and Investigations Act 1996
Crim PR	Criminal Procedure Rules
CYPA 1933	Children and Young Persons Act 1933
CYPA 1963	Children and Young Persons Act 1963
CYPA 1969	Children and Young Persons Act 1969
CPS	Crown Prosecution Service
DPP	Director of Public Prosecutions
DTO	detention and training order
ECtHR	European Court of Human Rights
ISSP	Intensive Supervision and Surveillance Programme
LASPO 2012	Legal Aid Sentencing and Punishment of Offenders Act 2012
MCA 1980	Magistrates' Courts Act 1980
MDA 1971	Misuse of Drugs Act 1971
MHA 1983	Mental Health Act 1983
OAPA 1861	Offences Against the Person Act 1861
PACE 1984	Police and Criminal Evidence Act 1984
PCMH	plea and case management hearing
PCCSA 2000	Powers of Criminal Courts (Sentencing) Act 2000
POA 1986	Public Order Act 1986
POCA 2002	Proceeds of Crime Act 2002

Abbreviations

RTA 1988	Road Traffic Act 1988
RTOA 1988	Road Traffic Offenders Act 1988
SGC	Sentencing Guidelines Council
SOA 2003	Sexual Offences Act 2003
STI	sexually transmitted infection
TA 1968	Theft Act 1968
TIC	taken into consideration
YJB	Youth Justice Board
YJCEA 1999	Youth Justice and Criminal Evidence Act 1999
YOI	Young Offender Institution
YOT	Youth Offending Team
YRO	youth rehabilitation order

Part A
Offences

A1 **Offences against the Person**

A1.1 **Assault and battery**

All assaults and batteries are offences contrary to the CJA 1988 s 39.

The CDA 1998 s 29 creates a racially or religiously aggravated form of this offence. For the meaning of 'racially or religiously aggravated' see **F19**.

SO

EW If racially or religiously aggravated

DO If racially or religiously aggravated

⊞ 6 month DTO (24 month DTO if racially or religiously aggravated)

A1.1.1 *Sentencing*

There is no sentencing guideline specific for youths for this offence. The definitive sentencing guideline *Assault* (2010) provides guidance for sentencing **adult** offenders:

STEP ONE: Determining the offence category

The court should determine the offence category using the table below.

Category 1	Greater harm (injury or fear of injury must normally be present) and higher culpability
Category 2	Greater harm (injury or fear of injury must normally be present) and lower culpability; or lesser harm and higher culpability
Category 3	Lesser harm and lower culpability

The court should determine the offender's culpability and the harm caused, or intended, by reference **only** to the factors below (as demonstrated by the presence of one or more). These factors comprise the principal factual elements of the offence and should determine the category.

Factors indicating greater harm	Factors indicating lesser harm
Injury or fear of injury which is serious in the context of the offence (must normally be present) Victim is particularly vulnerable because of personal circumstances	Injury which is less serious in the context of the offence

A1 Offences against the Person

Sustained or repeated assault on the same victim	**Factors indicating lower culpability**
Factors indicating higher culpability	Subordinate role in group or gang
Statutory aggravating factors:	A greater degree of provocation than normally expected
Offence motivated by, or demonstrating, hostility to the victim based on his or her sexual orientation (or presumed sexual orientation)	Lack of premeditation
	Mental disorder or learning disability, where linked to commission of the offence
	Excessive self-defence
Offence motivated by, or demonstrating, hostility to the victim based on the victim's disability (or presumed disability)	
Other aggravating factors:	
A significant degree of premeditation	
Threatened or actual use of weapon or weapon equivalent (eg, shod foot, headbutting, use of acid, use of animal)	
Intention to commit more serious harm than actually resulted from the offence	
Deliberately causes more harm than is necessary for commission of offence	
Deliberate targeting of vulnerable victim	
Leading role in group or gang	
Offence motivated by, or demonstrating, hostility based on the victim's age, sex, gender identity (or presumed gender identity)	

STEP TWO: Starting point and category range

Having determined the category, the court should use the corresponding starting points to reach a sentence within the category range below. The starting point applies to all offenders irrespective of plea or previous convictions. A case of particular gravity, reflected by multiple features of culpability in step one, could merit upward adjustment from the starting point before further adjustment for aggravating or mitigating features, set out below.

Offence Category	Starting Point (*Applicable to all offenders*)	Category Range (*Applicable to all offenders*)
Category 1	High level community order	Low level community order—26 weeks' custody
Category 2	Medium level community order	Band A fine—High level community order
Category 3	Band A fine	Discharge—Band C fine

The table below contains a **non-exhaustive** list of additional factual elements providing the context of the offence and factors relating to the offender. Identify whether any combination of these, or other relevant factors, should result in an upward or downward adjustment from the starting point. In some cases, having considered these factors, it may be appropriate to move outside the identified category range.

Factors increasing seriousness	Factors reducing seriousness or reflecting personal mitigation
Statutory aggravating factors: Previous convictions, having regard to (a) the nature of the offence to which the conviction relates and its relevance to the current offence; and (b) the time that has elapsed since the conviction Offence committed whilst on bail **Other aggravating factors include:** Location of the offence Timing of the offence Ongoing effect upon the victim Offence committed against those working in the public sector or providing a service to the public Presence of others including relatives, especially children or partner of the victim Gratuitous degradation of victim In domestic violence cases, victim forced to leave their home Failure to comply with current court orders Offence committed whilst on licence An attempt to conceal or dispose of evidence Failure to respond to warnings or concerns expressed by others about the offender's behaviour Commission of offence whilst under the influence of alcohol or drugs Abuse of power and/or position of trust Exploiting contact arrangements with a child to commit an offence Established evidence of community impact Any steps taken to prevent the victim reporting an incident, obtaining assistance, and/or from assisting or supporting the prosecution Offences taken into consideration (TICs)	No previous convictions or no relevant/recent convictions Single blow Remorse Good character and/or exemplary conduct Determination and/or demonstration of steps taken to address addiction or offending behaviour Serious medical conditions requiring urgent, intensive, or long-term treatment Isolated incident Age and/or lack of maturity where it affects the responsibility of the offender Lapse of time since the offence where this is not the fault of the offender Mental disorder or learning disability, where not linked to the commission of the offence Sole or primary carer for dependent relatives

Section 29 offences only:
The court should determine the appropriate sentence for the offence without taking account of the element of aggravation and then make an addition to the sentence, considering the level of aggravation involved. It may be appropriate to move outside the identified category range, taking into account the increased statutory maximum.

Additional steps:

Consider any factors which indicate a reduction, such as: assistance to the prosecution; reduction for guilty plea; dangerousness; totality principle; compensation and ancillary orders; reasons; consideration for remand time.

A1.1.2 Key points

- An assault is the causing of another to apprehend immediate unlawful violence (*R v Ireland* [1998] AC 147).
- Battery or assault by beating is the inflicting of unlawful force.
- An assault or battery must be committed intentionally or with subjective recklessness.
- Words or a gesture (eg using fingers to imitate a gun being fired or a slashing action across the throat) could amount to an assault.
- Conditional threats such as telling a person 'Get out of my house or I will hurt you' can amount to an assault.
- Creating a danger can amount to an assault, for example, if a prisoner knows that he has a needle secreted on him and dishonestly does not inform a police officer carrying out a search, he may be liable if the officer injures himself on that needle, such a risk being reasonably forseeable (*DPP v Santana-Bermudez* [2003] EWHC 2908 (Admin)).
- As the violence must be unlawful it is open to the accused to raise the fact that he was acting in self-defence, to protect property, or to prevent a crime.
- Consent to an assault may be a defence. Where consent is in issue, the prosecution must disprove it (*R v Donovan* [1934] 2 KB 498). Where the victim does not attend court to give evidence, lack of consent can be inferred from other evidence in the case (eg CCTV recording of the attack) and need not come from the complainant (*DPP v Shabbir* [2009] EWHC 2754 (Admin)).
- Consent to rough and undisciplined play where there is no intention to cause injury is a defence to a charge of assault. Even if that consent is absent, genuine belief by a defendant that consent was present would be such a defence. If the belief is genuinely held, it is irrelevant whether it is reasonably held or not (*R v Jones* (1986) 83 Cr App R 375).
- This is an offence of basic intent. Voluntary intoxication cannot be a defence.

📖 See *Blackstone's Criminal Practice 2014* **B2.1–B2.21**

A1.2 Assault with intent to resist or prevent arrest

Offences Against the Person Act 1861 s 38

Whosoever shall assault any person with intent to resist or prevent the lawful apprehension or detainer of himself or of any other person for any offence, shall be guilty of [an offence].

 24 month DTO

A1.2.1 *Sentencing*

There is no sentencing guideline specific for youths for this offence. The definitive sentencing guideline *Assault* (2010) provides guidance for sentencing **adult** offenders:

STEP ONE: Determining the offence category

The court should determine the offence category using the table below.

Category 1	Greater harm **and** higher culpability
Category 2	Greater harm **and** lower culpability; or lesser harm **and** higher culpability
Category 3	Lesser harm **and** lower culpability

The court should determine the offender's culpability and the harm caused, or intended, by reference **only** to the factors identified in the table below (as demonstrated by the presence of one or more). These factors comprise the principal factual elements of the offence and should determine the category.

Factors indicating greater harm	**Factors indicating lesser harm**
Sustained or repeated assault on the same victim	Injury which is less serious in the context of the offence
Factors indicating higher culpability	**Factors indicating lower culpability**
Statutory aggravating factors:	Subordinate role in group or gang
Offence racially or religiously aggravated	Lack of premeditation
Offence motivated by, or demonstrating, hostility to the victim based on his or her sexual orientation (or presumed sexual orientation)	Mental disorder or learning disability, where linked to commission of the offence

A1 Offences against the Person

Offence motivated by, or demonstrating, hostility to the victim based on the victim's disability (or presumed disability)	
Other aggravating factors:	
A significant degree of premeditation	
Use of weapon or weapon equivalent (eg, shod foot, headbutting, use of acid, use of animal)	
Intention to commit more serious harm than actually resulted from the offence	
Deliberately causes more harm than is necessary for commission of offence	
Leading role in group or gang	
Offence motivated by, or demonstrating, hostility based on the victim's age, sex, gender identity (or presumed gender identity)	

STEP TWO: Starting point and category range

Having determined the category, the court should use the corresponding starting points to reach a sentence within the category range below. The starting point applies to all offenders irrespective of plea or previous convictions. A case of particular gravity, reflected by multiple features of culpability in step one, could merit upward adjustment from the starting point before further adjustment for aggravating or mitigating features, set out below.

Offence Category	Starting Point (*Applicable to all offenders*)	Category Range (*Applicable to all offenders*)
Category 1	26 weeks' custody	12 weeks–51 weeks' custody
Category 2	Medium level community order	Low level community order–High level community order
Category 3	Band B fine	Band A fine–Band C fine

The table below contains a **non-exhaustive** list of additional factual elements providing the context of the offence and factors relating to the offender. Identify whether any combination of these, or other relevant factors, should result in an upward or downward adjustment from the starting point. In some cases, having considered these factors, it may be appropriate to move outside the identified category range.

Factors increasing seriousness	Factors reducing seriousness or reflecting personal mitigation
Statutory aggravating factors: Previous convictions, having regard to (a) the nature of the offence to which the conviction relates and its relevance to the current offence; and (b) the time that has elapsed since the conviction	No previous convictions or no relevant/recent convictions Single blow Remorse Good character and/or exemplary conduct
Offence committed whilst on bail **Other aggravating factors include:** Location of the offence Timing of the offence Ongoing effect upon the victim Gratuitous degradation of victim Failure to comply with current court orders Offence committed whilst on licence An attempt to conceal or dispose of evidence Failure to respond to warnings or concerns expressed by others about the offender's behaviour Commission of offence whilst under the influence of alcohol or drugs Established evidence of community impact Any steps taken to prevent the victim reporting an incident, obtaining assistance, and/or from assisting or supporting the prosecution Offences taken into consideration (TICs)	Determination and/or demonstration of steps taken to address addiction or offending behaviour Serious medical conditions requiring urgent, intensive, or long-term treatment Isolated incident Age and/or lack of maturity where it affects the responsibility of the offender Lapse of time since the offence where this is not the fault of the offender Mental disorder or learning disability, where not linked to the commission of the offence Sole or primary carer for dependent relatives

Additional steps:

Consider any factors which indicate a reduction, such as: assistance to the prosecution; reduction for guilty plea; dangerousness; totality principle; compensation and ancillary orders; reasons; consideration for remand time.

A1.2.2 Key points

• The arrest or detention must be lawful (*R v Self* [1992] 3 All ER 476).

A1.3 Assault occasioning actual bodily harm

Offences Against the Person Act 1861 s 47

Any assault occasioning actual bodily harm shall be liable to

A1 Offences against the Person

The CDA 1998 s 32 creates a racially or religiously aggravated form of this offence. For the meaning of 'racially or religiously aggravated' see **F19**.

┼┼┼┼ 24 month DTO (both basic and racially or religiously aggravated offences)

A1.3.1 *Sentencing*

There is no sentencing guideline specific for youths for this offence. The definitive sentencing guideline *Assault* (2010) provides guidance for sentencing **adult** offenders:

STEP ONE: Determining the offence category

The court should determine the offence category using the table below.

Category 1	Greater harm (serious injury must normally be present) **and** higher culpability
Category 2	Greater harm (serious injury must normally be present) **and** lower culpability; or lesser harm **and** higher culpability
Category 3	Lesser harm **and** lower culpability

The court should determine the offender's culpability and the harm caused, or intended, by reference **only** to the factors identified in the table below (as demonstrated by the presence of one or more). These factors comprise the principal factual elements of the offence and should determine the category.

Factors indicating greater harm	Factors indicating lesser harm
Injury (which includes disease transmission and/or psychological harm) which is serious in the context of the offence (must normally be present)	Injury which is less serious in the context of the offence
Victim is particularly vulnerable because of personal circumstances	**Factors indicating lower culpability**
Sustained or repeated assault on the same victim	Subordinate role in a group or gang
	A greater degree of provocation than normally expected
Factors indicating higher culpability	Lack of premeditation
Statutory aggravating factors:	Mental disorder or learning disability, where linked to commission of the offence
Offence motivated by, or demonstrating, hostility to the victim based on his or her sexual orientation (or presumed sexual orientation)	Excessive self-defence

Offence motivated by, or demonstrating, hostility to the victim based on the victim's disability (or presumed disability)
Other aggravating factors:
A significant degree of premeditation
Use of weapon or weapon equivalent (eg, shod foot, headbutting, use of acid, use of animal)
Intention to commit more serious harm than actually resulted from the offence
Deliberately causes more harm than is necessary for commission of offence
Deliberate targeting of vulnerable victim
Leading role in group or gang
Offence motivated by, or demonstrating, hostility based on the victim's age, sex, gender identity (or presumed gender identity)

STEP TWO: Starting point and category range

Having determined the category, the court should use the corresponding starting points to reach a sentence within the category range below. The starting point applies to all offenders irrespective of plea or previous convictions. A case of particular gravity, reflected by multiple features of culpability in step one, could merit upward adjustment from the starting point before further adjustment for aggravating or mitigating features, set out below.

Offence category	Starting Point (*Applicable to all offenders*)	Category Range (*Applicable to all offenders*)
Category 1	1 year 6 months' custody	1–3 years' custody
Category 2	26 weeks' custody	Low level community order–51 weeks' custody
Category 3	Medium level community order	Band A fine–High level community order

The table below contains a **non-exhaustive** list of additional factual elements providing the context of the offence and factors relating to the offender. Identify whether any combination of these, or other relevant factors, should result in an upward or downward adjustment from the starting point. In some cases, having considered these factors, it may be appropriate to move outside the identified category range.

A1 Offences against the Person

Factors increasing seriousness	Factors reducing seriousness or reflecting personal mitigation
Statutory aggravating factors: Previous convictions, having regard to (a) the nature of the offence to which the conviction relates and its relevance to the current offence; and (b) the time that has elapsed since the conviction Offence committed whilst on bail **Other aggravating factors include:** Location of the offence Timing of the offence Ongoing effect upon the victim Offence committed against those working in the public sector or providing a service to the public Presence of others including relatives, especially children or partner of the victim Gratuitous degradation of victim In domestic violence cases, victim forced to leave their home Failure to comply with current court orders Offence committed whilst on licence An attempt to conceal or dispose of evidence Failure to respond to warnings or concerns expressed by others about the offender's behaviour Commission of offence whilst under the influence of alcohol or drugs Abuse of power and/or position of trust Exploiting contact arrangements with a child to commit an offence Established evidence of community impact Any steps taken to prevent the victim reporting an incident, obtaining assistance, and/or from assisting or supporting the prosecution Offences taken into consideration (TICs)	No previous convictions or no relevant/recent convictions Single blow Remorse Good character and/or exemplary conduct Determination and/or demonstration of steps taken to address addiction or offending behaviour Serious medical conditions requiring urgent, intensive, or long-term treatment Isolated incident Age and/or lack of maturity where it affects the responsibility of the offender Lapse of time since the offence where this is not the fault of the offender Mental disorder or learning disability, where not linked to the commission of the offence Sole or primary carer for dependent relatives

Section 29 offences only:

The court should determine the appropriate sentence for the offence without taking account of the element of aggravation and then make an addition to the sentence, considering the level of aggravation involved. It may be appropriate to move outside the identified category range, taking into account the increased statutory maximum.

Additional steps:

Consider any factors which indicate a reduction, such as: assistance to the prosecution; reduction for guilty plea; dangerousness; totality principle; compensation and ancillary orders; reasons; consideration for remand time.

A1.3.2 Key points

- Harm, which must be more than merely transient or trifling, encompasses not only injury, but also hurt and damage. The concept of bodily harm is wide-ranging, and includes the cutting off of someone's hair (*DPP v Smith* [2006] 1 WLR 157).

- Psychiatric injury, in a medically diagnosed form, can amount to bodily harm, but anything short of this, for example, upset or distress will not (*R v Chan-Fook* [1994] 1 WLR 689, *R v Dhaliwal* [2006] 2 Cr App R 348).

- Where the injury is caused indirectly (eg where a person scares a woman and as a result she injures herself jumping out of the moving car they are travelling in) the proper test was whether the actions of the victim were something that could reasonably have been foreseen as the consequence of what the accused was saying or doing (*R v Roberts* (1971) 56 Cr App R 95).

- Mens rea is intention or subjective recklessness. Note that the mens rea relates to the act of assault or battery, there is no requirement to prove that harm was intended, or that the defendant was reckless as to whether or not harm would be caused (*R v Savage* [1992] 1 AC 699).

- This is an offence of basic intent. Voluntary intoxication cannot be a defence.

A1.4 Assault on constable in execution of duty

> **Police Act 1996 s 89**
>
> (1) Any person who assaults a constable in the execution of his duty, or a person assisting a constable in the execution of his duty, shall be guilty of an offence.

 SO

 6 month DTO

A1.4.1 *Sentencing*

There is no sentencing guideline specific for youths for this offence. The definitive sentencing guideline *Assault* (2010) provides guidance for sentencing **adult** offenders:

A1 Offences against the Person

STEP ONE: Determining the offence category

The court should determine the offence category using the table below.

Category 1	Greater harm **and** higher culpability
Category 2	Greater harm **and** lower culpability; or lesser harm **and** higher culpability
Category 3	Lesser harm **and** lower culpability

The court should determine the offender's culpability and the harm caused, or intended, by reference **only** to the factors below (as demonstrated by the presence of one or more). These factors comprise the principal factual elements of the offence and should determine the category.

Factors indicating greater harm	Factors indicating lesser harm
Sustained or repeated assault on the same victim	Injury which is less serious in the context of the offence
Factors indicating higher culpability	**Factors indicating lower culpability**
Statutory aggravating factors:	Subordinate role in group or gang
Offence racially or religiously aggravated	Lack of premeditation
Offence motivated by, or demonstrating, hostility to the victim based on his or her sexual orientation (or presumed sexual orientation)	Mental disorder or learning disability, where linked to commission of the offence
Offence motivated by, or demonstrating, hostility to the victim based on the victim's disability (or presumed disability)	
Other aggravating factors:	
A significant degree of premeditation	
Use of weapon or weapon equivalent (eg, shod foot, headbutting, use of acid, use of animal)	
Intention to commit more serious harm than actually resulted from the offence	
Deliberately causes more harm than is necessary for commission of offence	
Leading role in group or gang	
Offence motivated by, or demonstrating, hostility based on the victim's age, sex, gender identity (or presumed gender identity)	

STEP TWO: Starting point and category range

Having determined the category, the court should use the corresponding starting points to reach a sentence within the category range below. The starting point applies to all offenders irrespective of plea or previous convictions. A case of particular gravity, reflected by multiple features of culpability in step one, could merit upward adjustment from the starting point before further adjustment for aggravating or mitigating features, set out below.

Offence Category	Starting Point (Applicable to all offenders)	Category Range (Applicable to all offenders)
Category 1	12 weeks' custody	Low level community order–26 weeks' custody
Category 2	Medium level community order	Low level community order–High level community order
Category 3	Band B fine	Band A fine–Band C fine

The table below contains a **non-exhaustive** list of additional factual elements providing the context of the offence and factors relating to the offender. Identify whether any combination of these, or other relevant factors, should result in an upward or downward adjustment from the starting point. In some cases, having considered these factors, it may be appropriate to move outside the identified category range.

Factors increasing seriousness	Factors reducing seriousness or reflecting personal mitigation
Statutory aggravating factors: Previous convictions, having regard to (a) the nature of the offence to which the conviction relates and its relevance to the current offence; and (b) the time that has elapsed since the conviction Offence committed whilst on bail **Other aggravating factors include:** Location of the offence Timing of the offence Ongoing effect upon the victim Gratuitous degradation of victim Failure to comply with current court orders Offence committed whilst on licence An attempt to conceal or dispose of evidence Failure to respond to warnings or concerns expressed by others about the offender's behaviour Commission of offence whilst under the influence of alcohol or drugs Established evidence of community impact Any steps taken to prevent the victim reporting an incident, obtaining assistance, and/or from assisting or supporting the prosecution Offences taken into consideration (TICs)	No previous convictions or no relevant/recent convictions Single blow Remorse Good character and/or exemplary conduct Determination and/or demonstration of steps taken to address addiction or offending behaviour Serious medical conditions requiring urgent, intensive, or long-term treatment Isolated incident Age and/or lack of maturity where it affects the responsibility of the defendant Mental disorder or learning disability, where not linked to the commission of the offence Sole or primary carer for dependent relatives

A1 Offences against the Person

Additional steps:

Consider any factors which indicate a reduction, such as: assistance to the prosecution; reduction for guilty plea; dangerousness; totality principle; compensation and ancillary orders; reasons; consideration for remand time.

A1.4.2 Key points

- The constable must be acting lawfully. In the case of a stop and search the requirements of the PACE 1984 s 2 must be complied with otherwise the search is unlawful (*O (A Juvenile) v DPP* (1999) 163 JP 725).
- If officer A is not acting lawfully in arresting a suspect, officer B who in good faith seeks to assist officer A will not be acting lawfully (*Cumberbatch v Crown Prosecution Service* [2009] EWHC 3353 (Admin)).
- The prosecution does not need to prove that the defendant knew that the person was a police officer (*R v Brightling* [1991] Crim LR 364).
- If a suspect is accused of trying to impede the arrest of a third party, it must be shown that the arrest of that third party was lawful (*Riley v Director of Public Prosecutions* [1990] 91 Cr App R 14).
- An off-duty police officer may act in the course of his duty if a breach of the peace or other incident occurs which justifies immediate action on his part (*Albert v Lavin* [1982] AC 546).
- Where a constable enters premises under the PACE 1984 s 17 having reasonable grounds to believe entry is necessary to save life or limb or to prevent serious damage to property, he is lawfully entitled to remain on the premises until he is reasonably satisfied that life, limb, or property are not or are no longer in danger. While he is thus lawfully on the premises, he is entitled to search for anything which he reasonably believes may be used to endanger life, limb, or property (*Baker v CPS* [2009] EWHC 299 (Admin)).
- The legal right of a police officer to be on a front path or driveway of a house depended on the implied licence of the occupier. Where that implied licence or express permission from the occupier was revoked, the officer had to be given a reasonable opportunity to withdraw before his presence became unlawful (*Robson v Hallett* [1967] 1 QB 939). See also see *R (Fullard) v Woking Magistrates' Court* [2005] EWHC 2922 (Admin)).
- An officer who had not yet established grounds for arrest was acting unlawfully in restraining a suspect (*Wood v Director of Public Prosecutions* [2008] EWHC 1056 (Admin)).
- It is not every interference with a citizen's liberty that will be sufficient to take the officer outside the course of their duty. A police officer may take hold of a person's arm to attract his attention and calm him down (*Mepstead v DPP* (1996) 160 JP 175) but in *Collins v Wilcock* [1984] 1 WLR 1172 it was held to be unlawful to take hold of a woman to question her.

- Section 89(1) does not apply to community support officers unless they are assisting a police constable at the time of the assault. An assault on a community support officer could be charged under the Police Reform Act 2002 s 46 (see **A1.7**).

 See *Blackstone's Criminal Practice 2014* **B2.36–B2.40**

A1.5 Obstructing a constable in execution of duty

Police Act 1996 s 89

(2) Any person who resists or wilfully obstructs a constable in the execution of his duty, or a person assisting a constable in the execution of his duty, shall be guilty of an offence....

 Maximum penalty in case of an adult is 1 month imprisonment therefore DTO not available

A1.5.1 *Sentencing*

There is no sentencing guideline specific for youths for this offence. The *Magistrates' Court Sentencing Guidelines* provide guidance for sentencing **adult** offenders:

Offence seriousness (culpability and harm)

A. Identify the appropriate starting point
Starting points based on first-time offender pleading not guilty

Examples of nature of activity	Starting point	Range
Failure to move when required to do so	Band A fine	Conditional discharge to band B fine
Attempt to prevent arrest or other lawful police action; or giving false details	Band B fine	Band A fine to band C fine
Several people attempting to prevent arrest or other lawful police action	Low level community order	Band C fine to medium level community order

B. Consider the effect of aggravating and mitigating factors (other than those within examples above)
Common aggravating and mitigating factors are identified [elsewhere]—the following may be particularly relevant but these lists are not exhaustive

A1 Offences against the Person

Factors indicating higher culpability	Factors indicating lower culpability
1. Premeditated action 2. Aggressive words/threats 3. Aggressive group action	1. Genuine mistake or misjudgement 2. Brief incident

A1.5.2 Key points

- A person obstructs a police constable if he makes it more difficult for him to carry out his duty (*Hinchcliffe v Sheldon* [1955] 1 WLR 1207).
- There is no legal duty to answer questions put by the police or (unless arrested) to accompany them to the police station, and a refusal to do so could not normally amount to obstruction (*Rice v Connolly* [1966] 2 QB 414).
- A constable must be acting lawfully for there to be an offence of obstruction (*Edwards v DPP* (1993) 97 Cr App R 301).
- For other decisions regarding execution of duty see **A1.4.2**.

 See *Blackstone's Criminal Practice 2014* **B2.41–B2.46**

A1.6 Offences against designated officers

> ### Police Reform Act 2002 s 46
>
> (1) Any person who assaults—
>   - (a) a designated person in the execution of his duty,
>   - (b) an accredited person in the execution of his duty,
>   - (ba) an accredited inspector in the execution of his duty, or
>   - (c) a person assisting a designated or accredited person or an accredited inspector in the execution of his duty, is guilty of an offence.
>
> (2) Any person who resists or wilfully obstructs—
>   - (a) a designated person in the execution of his duty,
>   - (b) an accredited person or an accredited inspector in the execution of his duty,
>   - (ba) an accredited inspector in the execution of his duty, or
>   - (c) a person assisting a designated or accredited person in the execution of his duty, is guilty of an offence.
>
> ...
>
> (4) In this section references to the execution by a designated person, accredited person, or accredited inspector of his duty are references to his exercising any power or performing any duty which is his by virtue of his designation or accreditation.
>
> (5) References in this section to a designated person are to—
>   - (a) a designated person within the meaning given by section 47(1), and
>   - (b) a person in relation to whom a designation under section 38B is for the time being in force.

(assault) 6 month DTO

(obstruct) Maximum penalty for adult is 1 month imprisonment therefore DTO not available

A1.6.1 *Sentencing*

There is no sentencing guideline for these offences but the guidelines for assaulting a constable in the execution of duty (see **A1.4.1**) and obstructing a constable in the execution of duty (see **A1.5.1**) should be considered.

A1.6.2 Key points

- A designated person includes a community support officer and civilian detention officers and investigation officers (Police Reform Act 2002 ss 37 and 47).
- For case law regarding execution of duty see **A1.4.2** and **A1.5.2**.

A1.7 **Wounding or inflicting grievous bodily harm**

Offences Against the Person Act 1861 s 20

Whosoever shall unlawfully and maliciously wound or inflict any grievous bodily harm upon any other person, either with or without any weapon or instrument, shall be guilty of [an offence].

The CDA 1998 s 29 creates a racially or religiously aggravated form of this offence. For the meaning of 'racially or religiously aggravated' see **F19**.

24 month DTO (both basic and racially or religiously aggravated offences)

A1.7.1 *Sentencing*

There is no sentencing guideline specific for youths for this offence. The definitive sentencing guideline *Assault* (2010) provides guidance for sentencing **adult** offenders:

A1 Offences against the Person

STEP ONE: Determining the offence category

Category 1	Greater harm (serious injury must normally be present) **and** higher culpability
Category 2	Greater harm (serious injury must normally be present) **and** lower culpability; or lesser harm **and** higher culpability
Category 3	Lesser harm **and** lower culpability

The court should determine the offender's culpability and the harm caused, or intended, by reference only to the factors below (as demonstrated by the presence of one or more). These factors comprise the principal factual elements of the offence and should determine the category.

Factors indicating greater harm	Factors indicating lesser harm
Injury (which includes disease transmission and/or psychological harm) which is serious in the context of the offence (must normally be present) Victim is particularly vulnerable because of personal circumstances Sustained or repeated assault on the same victim	Injury which is less serious in the context of the offence
Factors indicating higher culpability	**Factors indicating lower culpability**
Statutory aggravating factors:	Subordinate role in group or gang
Offence motivated by, or demonstrating, hostility to the victim based on his or her sexual orientation (or presumed sexual orientation) Offence motivated by, or demonstrating, hostility to the victim based on the victim's disability (or presumed disability)	A greater degree of provocation than normally expected Lack of premeditation Mental disorder or learning disability, where linked to commission of the offence Excessive self-defence
Other aggravating factors:	
A significant degree of premeditation Use of weapon or weapon equivalent (eg, shod foot, headbutting, use of acid, use of animal) Intention to commit more serious harm than actually resulted from the offence Deliberately causes more harm than is necessary for commission of offence Deliberate targeting of vulnerable victim Leading role in group or gang Offence motivated by, or demonstrating, hostility based on the victim's age, sex, gender identity (or presumed gender identity)	

STEP TWO: Starting point and category range

Having determined the category, the court should use the corresponding starting points to reach a sentence within the category range
below. The starting point applies to all offenders irrespective of plea or
previous convictions. A case of particular gravity, reflected by multiple
features of culpability in step one, could merit upward adjustment
from the starting point before further adjustment for aggravating or
mitigating features, set out below.

Offence Category	Starting Point (*Applicable to all offenders*)	Category Range (*Applicable to all offenders*)
Category 1	3 years' custody	2 years 6 months–4 years' custody
Category 2	1 year 6 months' custody	1–3 years' custody
Category 3	High level community order	Low level community order–51 weeks' custody

The table below contains a **non-exhaustive** list of additional factual
elements providing the context of the offence and factors relating to
the offender. Identify whether any combination of these, or other relevant factors, should result in an upward or downward adjustment
from the starting point. In some cases, having considered these factors,
it may be appropriate to move outside the identified category range.

Factors increasing seriousness	Factors reducing seriousness or reflecting personal mitigation
Statutory aggravating factors: Previous convictions, having regard to (a) the nature of the offence to which the conviction relates and its relevance to the current offence; and (b) the time that has elapsed since the conviction Offence committed whilst on bail **Other aggravating factors include:** Location of the offence Timing of the offence Ongoing effect upon the victim Offence committed against those working in the public sector or providing a service to the public Presence of others including relatives, especially children or partner of the victim Gratuitous degradation of victim	No previous convictions or no relevant/recent convictions Single blow Remorse Good character and/or exemplary conduct Determination and/or demonstration of steps taken to address addiction or offending behaviour Serious medical conditions requiring urgent, intensive, or long-term treatment Isolated incident Age and/or lack of maturity where it affects the responsibility of the offender Lapse of time since the offence where this is not the fault of the offender Mental disorder or learning disability, where not linked to the commission of the offence Sole or primary carer for dependent relatives

In domestic violence cases, victim forced to leave their home	
Failure to comply with current court orders	
Offence committed whilst on licence	
An attempt to conceal or dispose of evidence	
Failure to respond to warnings or concerns expressed by others about the offender's behaviour	
Commission of offence whilst under the influence of alcohol or drugs	
Abuse of power and/or position of trust	
Exploiting contact arrangements with a child to commit an offence	
Previous violence or threats to the same victim	
Established evidence of community impact	
Any steps taken to prevent the victim reporting an incident, obtaining assistance, and/or from assisting or supporting the prosecution	
Offences taken into consideration (TICs)	

Section 29 offences only:

The court should determine the appropriate sentence for the offence without taking account of the element of aggravation and then make an addition to the sentence, considering the level of aggravation involved. It may be appropriate to move outside the identified category range, taking into account the increased statutory maximum.

Additional steps:

Consider any factors which indicate a reduction, such as: assistance to the prosecution; reduction for guilty plea; dangerousness; totality principle; compensation and ancillary orders; reasons; consideration for remand time.

A1.7.2 Key Points

- Wounding requires the breaking of the continuity of the whole of the skin. Although this may include relatively minor injuries charging standards indicate that this offence should not be used in such cases.
- Grievous bodily harm has no statutory definition but has been interpreted as really serious harm (*DPP v Smith* [1961] AC 290). It may include psychiatric injury but only if both causation and extent of the disorder is established by expert psychiatric evidence (*R v Ireland* [1998] AC 147).
- To be malicious there must be an intent to inflict some kind of bodily harm or subjective recklessness as to whether any such harm

might be caused. The harm intended or foreseen by the defendant need not be serious; an intent to cause some injury will be sufficient (*R v Mowatt* [1968] 1 QB 421).

- This is a crime of basic intent therefore voluntary intoxication cannot be a defence.

 See *Blackstone's Criminal Practice 2014* **B2.47–B2.61**

A1.8 Wounding or inflicting grievous bodily harm with intent

Offences Against the Person Act 1861 s 18

Whosoever shall unlawfully and maliciously by any means whatsoever wound or cause any grievous bodily harm to any person, with intent, to do some grievous bodily harm to any person, or with intent to resist or prevent the lawful apprehension or detainer of any person, shall be guilty of [an offence].

IO

DO

GC

 24 month DTO/detention for life in Crown Court

A1.8.1 *Sentencing*

There is no sentencing guideline specific for youths for this offence. The definitive sentencing guideline *Assault* (2010) provides guidance for sentencing **adult** offenders:

STEP ONE: Determining the offence category

The court should determine the offence category using the table below.

Category 1	Greater harm (serious injury must normally be present) **and** higher culpability
Category 2	Greater harm (serious injury must normally be present) **and** lower culpability; or lesser harm **and** higher culpability
Category 3	Lesser harm **and** lower culpability

The court should determine the offender's culpability and the harm caused, or intended, by reference only to the factors below (as demonstrated by the presence of one or more). These factors comprise the principal factual elements of the offence and should determine the category.

A1 Offences against the Person

Factors indicating greater harm	Factors indicating higher culpability
Injury (which includes disease transmission and/or psychological harm) which is serious in the context of the offence (must normally be present) Victim is particularly vulnerable because of personal circumstances Sustained or repeated assault on the same victim	**Statutory aggravating factors:** Offence racially or religiously aggravated Offence motivated by, or demonstrating, hostility to the victim based on his or her sexual orientation (or presumed sexual orientation) Offence motivated by, or demonstrating, hostility to the victim based on the victim's disability (or presumed disability)
Factors indicating lesser harm Injury which is less serious in the context of the offence	**Other aggravating factors:** A significant degree of premeditation Use of weapon or weapon equivalent (eg, shod foot, headbutting, use of acid, use of animal) Intention to commit more serious harm than actually resulted from the offence Deliberately causes more harm than is necessary for commission of offence Deliberate targeting of vulnerable victim Leading role in group or gang Offence motivated by, or demonstrating, hostility based on the victim's age, sex, gender identity (or presumed gender identity)
	Factors indicating lower culpability Subordinate role in a group or gang A greater degree of provocation than normally expected Lack of premeditation Mental disorder or learning disability, where linked to commission of the offence Excessive self-defence

STEP TWO: Starting point and category range

Having determined the category, the court should use the corresponding starting points to reach a sentence within the category range below. The starting point applies to all offenders irrespective of plea or previous convictions. A case of particular gravity, reflected by multiple features of culpability in step one, could merit upward adjustment from the starting point before further adjustment for aggravating or mitigating features, set out below.

Offence category	Starting Point (Applicable to all Offenders)	Category Range (Applicable to all Offenders)
Category 1	12 years' custody	9–16 years' custody
Category 2	6 years' custody	5–9 years' custody
Category 3	4 years' custody	3–5 years' custody

Wounding or inflicting grievous bodily harm with intent A1.8

The table below contains a non-exhaustive list of additional factual elements providing the context of the offence and factors relating to the offender. Identify whether any combination of these, or other relevant factors, should result in an upward or downward adjustment from the starting point. In some cases, having considered these factors, it may be appropriate to move outside the identified category range.

Factors increasing seriousness	Exploiting contact arrangements with a child to commit an offence
Statutory aggravating factors:	Previous violence or threats to the same victim
Previous convictions, having regard to (a) the nature of the offence to which the conviction relates and its relevance to the current offence; and (b) the time that has elapsed since the conviction	Established evidence of community impact
	Any steps taken to prevent the victim reporting an incident, obtaining assistance, and/or from assisting or supporting the prosecution
Offence committed whilst on bail	Offences taken into consideration (TICs)
Other aggravating factors include:	**Factors reducing seriousness or reflecting personal mitigation**
Location of the offence	No previous convictions or no relevant/recent convictions
Timing of the offence	Single blow
Ongoing effect upon the victim	Remorse
Offence committed against those working in the public sector or providing a service to the public	Good character and/or exemplary conduct
Presence of others including relatives, especially children and partner of the victim	Determination, and/or demonstration of steps taken to address addiction or offending behaviour
Gratuitous degradation of victim	Serious medical conditions requiring urgent, intensive, or long-term treatment
In domestic violence cases, victim forced to leave their home	Isolated incident
Failure to comply with current court orders	Age and/or lack of maturity where it affects the responsibility of the offender
Offence committed whilst on licence	Lapse of time since the offence where this is not the fault of the offender
An attempt to conceal or dispose of evidence	Mental disorder or learning disability, where not linked to the commission of the offence
Failure to respond to warnings or concerns expressed by others about the offender's behaviour	Sole or primary carer for dependent relatives
Commission of offence whilst under the influence of alcohol or drugs	
Abuse of power and/or position of trust	

Additional steps:

Consider any factors which indicate a reduction, such as: assistance to the prosecution; reduction for guilty plea; dangerousness; totality principle; compensation and ancillary orders; reasons; consideration for remand time.

A1.8.2 Key points

For the definitions of wound and grievous bodily harm see **A1.7.2**.

A1 Offences against the Person

A1.9 False imprisonment

A common law offence—the unlawful and intentional or reckless restraint of a victim's freedom of movement from a particular place (*R v Rahman* (1985) 81 Cr App R 349).

IO

DO

GC

 24 month DTO/detention for life in Crown Court

A1.9.1 *Sentencing*

There is no sentencing guideline for this offence.

- *Att-Gen's Ref Nos 36–7 of 1998* [1999] 2 Cr App R (S) 7—D, aged 17, pleaded guilty to false imprisonment. He with a friend J had forced three teenaged friends to climb over railings into a park at night. Whilst in the park the boys were forced to sit on a park bench. One of them was punched in the face by J who then pushed a lighted cigarette into his face causing a burn. D held the same boy against a tree while J threatened to kill him. The boy managed to escape, cutting his thigh as he climbed back over the railings. He ran away. D and J then forced another of the boys to walk across the park until he also managed to get away. The court identified that the offence was in part racially motivated. At the time of the offence D had no previous convictions but he was on court bail for affray. The youth court committed for sentence [no longer a sentencing option]. The Attorney-General appealed the Recorder's decision to defer sentence. **Held**: If D had been convicted at trial in the youth court, a sentence of fifteen months' detention would have been appropriate for the offence of false imprisonment. As this is a reference a sentence of eight months' detention imposed. No separate penalty for the affray.

A1.9.2 Key points

- The requisite mens rea is intention or subjective recklessness.
- This is an offence of basic intent. Voluntary intoxication is not a defence.

A1.10 Kidnapping

Common law offence—the taking or carrying away of one person by another by force or fraud, without the consent of that person and without lawful excuse.

24 month DTO/detention for life in Crown Court

A1.10.1 *Sentencing*

There is no sentencing guideline for this offence. The guideline case of *R v Spence and Thomas* (1983) 5 Cr App R (S) 413 suggests the following for **adult** offenders:

Circumstances	Guideline sentence
Violence or firearm used, exacerbating features such as detention of victim over long period.	More than 8 years' imprisonment.
Carefully planned abductions, victim used as hostage, or ransom money demanded.	Seldom less than 8 years' imprisonment.
Scarcely kidnapping, perhaps the sequel to a family tiff or lovers' dispute.	Up to 18 months' imprisonment.

A1.11 Harassment (without violence)

A1.11.1 *Prohibition of harassment*

Protection from Harassment Act 1997 s 1

(1) A person must not pursue a course of conduct—
  (a) which amounts to harassment of another, and
  (b) which he knows or ought to know amounts to harassment of the other.

(1A) A person must not pursue a course of conduct—
  (a) which involves harassment of two or more persons, and
  (b) which he knows or ought to know involves harassment of those persons, and
  (c) by which he intends to persuade any person (whether or not one of those mentioned above)—
    (i) not to do something that he is entitled or required to do, or
    (ii) to do something that he is not under any obligation to do.

Protection from Harassment Act 1997, s 2

(1) A person who pursues a course of conduct in breach of section 1(1) or (1A) is guilty of an offence.

A1 Offences against the Person

The CDA 1998 s 32 creates a racially or religiously aggravated form of this offence. For the meaning of 'racially or religiously aggravated' see **F19**.

SO

EW if racially or religiously aggravated

▥ 6 month DTO (24 month DTO if racially or religiously aggravated)

A1.11.2 *Sentencing*

There is no sentencing guideline specific for youths for this offence. The *Magistrates' Court Sentencing Guidelines* provide guidance for sentencing **adult** offenders:

Offence seriousness (culpability and harm)

A. Identify the appropriate starting point

Examples of nature of activity	Starting point	Range
Small number of incidents	Medium level community order	Band C fine to high level community order
Constant contact at night, trying to come into workplace or home, involving others	6 weeks' custody	Medium level community order to 12 weeks' custody
Threatening violence, taking personal photographs, sending offensive material	18 weeks' custody	12 to 26 weeks' custody

Starting points based on first-time offender pleading not guilty.

B. Consider the effect of aggravating and mitigating factors (other than those within examples above)

Common aggravating and mitigating factors are identified [elsewhere]—the following may be particularly relevant but these lists are not exhaustive.

Factors indicating higher culpability	Factors indicating lower culpability
1. Planning 2. Offender ignores obvious distress 3. Offender involves others 4. Using contact arrangements with a child to instigate offence	1. Limited understanding of effect on victim 2. Initial provocation

Factors indicating greater degree of harm	
1. Victim needs medical help/counselling	
2. Action over long period	
3. Children frightened	
4. Use or distribution of photographs	

A1.11.3 Key points

- The question of what constitutes a course of conduct has been considered in a number of cases, and the answer will always be fact-sensitive. In *R v Curtis* [2010] EWCA 123 the court allowed an appeal where the defendant, in the context of there being a volatile relationship, had been responsible for six incidents over a period of nine months. The court held that the conduct must be unacceptable to a degree which would sustain criminal liability and also must be oppressive, and went on to say:

  > Courts are well able to separate the wheat from the chaff at an early stage of the proceedings. They should be astute to do so. In most cases courts should have little difficulty in applying the 'close connection' test. Where the claim meets that requirement, and the quality of the conduct said to constitute harassment is being examined, courts will have in mind that irritations, annoyances, even a measure of upset, arise at times in everybody's day-to-day dealings with other people. Courts are well able to recognise the boundary between conduct which is unattractive, even unreasonable, and conduct which is oppressive and unacceptable. To cross the boundary from the regrettable to the unacceptable the gravity of the misconduct must be of an order which would sustained (*sic*) criminal liability under section 2.

- The naming of two complainants in one charge is not duplicitous, but unlike the charge under s 4 there need only be conduct against at least two people on at least one occasion each (*Director of Public Prosecutions v Dunn* (2008) 165 JP 130).
- A restraining order may be made on conviction (see **F26**).

 See *Blackstone's Criminal Practice 2014* **B2.158–B2.170**

A1.12 Harassment (fear of violence)

Protection from Harassment Act 1997 s 4

(1) A person whose course of conduct causes another to fear, on at least two occasions, that violence will be used against him is guilty of an offence if he knows or ought to know that his course of conduct will cause the other so to fear on each of those occasions.

A1 Offences against the Person

The CDA 1998 s 32 creates a racially or religiously aggravated form of this offence. For the meaning of 'racially or religiously aggravated' see **F19**.

24 month DTO

A1.12.1 *Sentencing*

There is no sentencing guideline specific for youths for this offence. The *Magistrates' Court Sentencing Guidelines* provide guidance for sentencing **adult** offenders:

Offence seriousness (culpability and harm)

A. Identify the appropriate starting point

Starting points based on first-time offender pleading not guilty:

Examples of nature of activity	Starting point	Range
A pattern of two or more incidents of unwanted contact	6 weeks' custody	High level community order to 18 weeks' custody
Deliberate threats, persistent action over a longer period; or Intention to cause fear of violence	18 weeks' custody	12 weeks' custody to Crown Court
Sexual threats, vulnerable person targeted	Crown Court	Crown Court

B. Consider the effect of aggravating and mitigating factors (other than those within examples above)

Common aggravating and mitigating factors are identified [elsewhere]—the following may be particularly relevant but these lists are not exhaustive.

Factors indicating higher culpability	Factors indicating lower culpability
1. Planning 2. Offender ignores obvious distress 3. Visits in person to victim's home or workplace 4. Offender involves others 5. Using contact arrangements with a child to instigate offence **Factors indicating greater degree of harm** 1. Victim needs medical help/counselling 2. Physical violence used	1. Limited understanding of effect on victim 2. Initial provocation

3. Victim aware that offender has history of using violence 4. Grossly violent or offensive material sent 5. Children frightened 6. Evidence that victim changed lifestyle to avoid contact	

A1.12.2 Key points

- References to harassing a person include alarming the person or causing the person distress (Protection from Harassment Act s 7).
- The person whose course of conduct is in question ought to know that it will cause another to fear that violence will be used against him on any occasion if a reasonable person in possession of the same information would think the course of conduct would cause the other so to fear on that occasion (Protection from Harassment Act 1997 s. 4(2)).
- In *R v Haque* [2011] EWCA Crim 1871 the following requirements were identified for there to be proof of harassment
  - (a) The conduct must be targeted at an individual
  - (b) Conduct must be calculated to produce the consequences in s 7 (alarm or distress)
  - (c) Conduct must have been oppressive and unreasonable
  - (d) Provocation may possibly be relevant to causation and reasonableness
  - (e) There must also be proof that the defendant knew or ought to have known that conduct would cause the complainant to fear violence
- In relation to an offence under s 4 the naming of two complainants in one charge is not duplicitous, but at least one of the complainants must have feared violence on at least two occasions (*Caurti v Director of Public Prosecutions* [2002] EWHC 867 (Admin)).
- It is a defence for a person charged with an offence under s 4 to show that:
  - (a) his course of conduct was pursued for the purpose of preventing or detecting crime,
  - (b) his course of conduct was pursued under any enactment or rule of law or to comply with any condition or requirement imposed by any person under any enactment, or
  - (c) the pursuit of his course of conduct was reasonable for the protection of himself or another or for the protection of his or another's property.

• A restraining order may be made on conviction (see **F26**).

 See *Blackstone's Criminal Practice 2014* **B2.174–B2.181**

A1.13 Threats to kill

> ### Offences Against the Person Act 1861 s 16
>
> A person who without lawful excuse makes to another a threat, intending that that other would fear it would be carried out, to kill that other or a third person shall be guilty of an offence . . .

 24 month DTO

A1.13.1 *Sentencing*

There is no sentencing guideline specific for youths for this offence. The *Magistrates' Court Sentencing Guidelines* provide guidance for sentencing **adult** offenders:

Offence seriousness (culpability and harm)

A. Identify the appropriate starting point

Examples of nature of activity	Starting point	Range
One threat uttered in the heat of the moment, no more than fleeting impact on victim	Medium level community order	Low level community order to high level community order
Single calculated threat or victim fears that threat will be carried out	12 weeks' custody	6 to 26 weeks' custody
Repeated threats or visible weapon	Crown Court	Crown Court

Starting points based on first-time offender pleading not guilty:

B. Consider the effect of aggravating and mitigating factors (other than those within examples above)

Common aggravating and mitigating factors are identified [elsewhere]—the following may be particularly relevant but these lists are not exhaustive.

[Sets out the standard sequential sentencing procedure and mentions need to consider football banning order.]

Factors indicating higher culpability	Factor indicating lower culpability
1. Planning	1. Provocation
2. Offender deliberately isolates victim	
3. Group action	
4. Threat directed at victim because of job	
5. History of antagonism towards victim	
Factors indicating greater degree of harm	
1. Vulnerable victim	
2. Victim needs medical help/counselling	

Additional steps:

Consider any factors which indicate a reduction, such as: assistance
to the prosecution; reduction for guilty plea; dangerousness; totality
principle; compensation and ancillary orders; reasons; consideration
for remand time.

A1.13.2 Key points

- Lawful excuse could include a threat made reasonably in self-defence
  (*R v Cousins* [1982] QB 526).

 See *Blackstone's Criminal Practice 2014* **B1.143–B1.147**

A2 Sexual Offences

A2.1 General

A2.1.1 *Consent*

The SOA 2003 provides:

Sexual Offences Act 2003 ss 74–6

74 'Consent'

For the purposes of this Part, a person consents if he agrees by choice, and has the freedom and capacity to make that choice.

75 Evidential presumptions about consent

(1) If in proceedings for an offence to which this section applies it is proved–
   (a) that the defendant did the relevant act,
   (b) that any of the circumstances specified in subsection (2) existed, and
   (c) that the defendant knew that those circumstances existed,
   the complainant is to be taken not to have consented to the relevant act unless sufficient evidence is adduced to raise an issue as to whether he consented, and the defendant is to be taken not to have reasonably believed that the complainant consented unless sufficient evidence is adduced to raise an issue as to whether he reasonably believed it.
(2) The circumstances are that—
   (a) any person was, at the time of the relevant act or immediately before it began, using violence against the complainant or causing the complainant to fear that immediate violence would be used against him;
   (b) any person was, at the time of the relevant act or immediately before it began, causing the complainant to fear that violence was being used, or that immediate violence would be used, against another person;
   (c) the complainant was, and the defendant was not, unlawfully detained at the time of the relevant act;
   (d) the complainant was asleep or otherwise unconscious at the time of the relevant act;
   (e) because of the complainant's physical disability, the complainant would not have been able at the time of the relevant act to communicate to the defendant whether the complainant consented;
   (f) any person had administered to or caused to be taken by the complainant, without the complainant's consent, a substance which, having regard to when it was administered or taken, was capable of causing or enabling the complainant to be stupefied or overpowered at the time of the relevant act.
(3) In subsection (2)(a) and (b), the reference to the time immediately before the relevant act began is, in the case of an act which is one of a continuous series of sexual activities, a reference to the time immediately before the first sexual activity began.

---

76 Conclusive presumptions about consent

(1) If in proceedings for an offence to which this section applies it is proved that the defendant did the relevant act and that any of the circumstances specified in subsection (2) existed, it is to be conclusively presumed—

    (a) that the complainant did not consent to the relevant act, and

    (b) that the defendant did not believe that the complainant consented to the relevant act.

(2) The circumstances are that—

    (a) the defendant intentionally deceived the complainant as to the nature or purpose of the relevant act;

    (b) the defendant intentionally induced the complainant to consent to the relevant act by impersonating a person known personally to the complainant.

A2.1.2 *Sexual in nature*

The SOA 2003 s 78 provides:

Sexual Offences Act 2003 s 78

For the purposes of this Part (except section 71), penetration, touching, or any other activity is sexual if a reasonable person would consider that—

    (a) whatever its circumstances or any person's purpose in relation to it, it is because of its nature sexual, or

    (b) because of its nature it may be sexual and because of its circumstances or the purpose of any person in relation to it (or both) it is sexual.

Acts which are automatically sexual within the meaning of s 78(a) would include penile penetration or oral sex. Where the act is not automatically sexual it was held in *R v H* [2005] EWCA Crim 732, [2005] 2 Cr App R 9 that two requirements must be satisfied: first, that the touching could reasonably be considered to be sexual; and, secondly, that the touching, because of its circumstances or the purpose of any person in relation to it (or both) was sexual.

A2.1.3 *Decision to charge*

General guidance on the decision to prosecute young people for sexual offences is provided in the CPS Legal Guidance *Youth Offenders (Sexual Offences and Child Abuse by Young Offenders)*:

If an allegation of any sexual abuse committed by a youth offender has been fully investigated and there is sufficient evidence to justify instituting proceedings, the balance of the public interest must always be carefully considered before any prosecution is commenced. Positive action may need to be taken at an early stage of offending of this type. Although a reprimand or final warning may provide an acceptable alternative in some cases, in reaching any decision, the police and the CPS will have to take into account

A2 Sexual Offences

fully the view of other agencies involved in the case, in particular the Social Services. The consequences for the victim of the decision whether or not to prosecute, and any views expressed by the victim or the victim's family should also be taken into account.

In child abuse cases, it will be important to have the views of the Social Services on file if at all possible, as well as any background or history of similar conduct, information about the relationship between the two and the effect a prosecution might have on the victim.

Any case referred to the CPS for advice, or in which a prosecution does proceed, must be dealt with as quickly as possible to minimise the delay before the case comes to court.

Irrespective of whether the evidence is sufficient to found a criminal prosecution, the Social Services will consider taking civil action, such as care proceedings, to protect the child. The police and the CPS may well be asked to disclose evidence to assist in this process...

A2.1.4 *Allocation—sexual offences*

Many of the offences created by the Sexual Offences Act 2003 are grave crimes and therefore the youth court will have to determine the mode of trial. A protocol *Sexual Offences in the Youth Court* was issued in 2009 (see **D2.7.4**). The most important requirement is that a district judge should sit to determine the mode of trial decision where penetration of the victim is alleged.

A2.1.5 *Registration as a sex offender*

Registration as a sex offender under the SOA 2003 Part II is required for many of the offences covered in this section (see **F31**).

A2.2 **Rape**

Sexual Offences Act 2003 s 1

(1) A person (A) commits an offence if—
    (a) he intentionally penetrates the vagina, anus, or mouth of another person (B) with his penis,
    (b) B does not consent to the penetration, and
    (c) A does not reasonably believe that B consents.
(2) Whether a belief is reasonable is to be determined having regard to all the circumstances, including any steps A has taken to ascertain whether B consents.
(3) Sections 75 and 76 apply to an offence under this section.

IO

GC

DO

24 month DTO/detention for life in Crown Court

A2.2.1 *Allocation*

Where a youth court is to consider the question of jurisdiction in relation to a sexual offence involving penetration, the case must be listed before a district judge with authorization to hear such cases: *Sexual Offences in the Youth Court* (see **D2.7.4**).

Previously it was said by the Court of Appeal that a youth court should never accept jurisdiction on a rape charge (see *R v Billam* [1986] 1 WLR 349). This pronouncement was made when it was not possible to charge defendants under the age of 14 with this offence. It may be appropriate in the case of very young defendants to accept jurisdiction: *R (W, S and B) v Brent, Enfield and Richmond Youth Courts* [2006] EWHC 95 (Admin).

A2.2.2 *Sentencing*

There is no sentencing guideline specific for youths for this offence. The definitive sentencing guideline *Sexual Offences* (2007) provides guidance for sentencing **adult** offenders:

Type/nature of activity	Starting points	Sentencing ranges
Repeated rape of same victim over a course of time or rape involving multiple victims	15 years' custody	13–19 years' custody
Rape accompanied by any of the following : Abduction or detention; offender aware he is suffering from an STI; more than one offender acting together; abuse of trust; offence motivated by prejudice; sustained attack	13 years' custody if the victim is under 13 10 years' custody if the victim is 13 or over but under 16 8 years' custody if the victim is 16 or over	11–17 years' custody 8–13 years' custody 6–11 years' custody
Single offence of rape	10 years' custody if the victim is under 13 8 years' custody if the victim is 13 or over but under 16 5 years' custody if the victim is 16 or over	8–13 years' custody 6–11 years' custody 4–8 years' custody

A2 Sexual Offences

Additional aggravating factors	Additional mitigating factors
Offender ejaculated or caused victim to ejaculate. Background of intimidation or coercion. Use of drugs, alcohol, or other substance to facilitate the offence. Threats to prevent the victim reporting the incident. Abduction or detention. Offender aware he is suffering from a STD. Pregnancy or infection results.	*Where the victim is aged 16 or over* Victim engaged in consensual sexual activity with the offender on the same occasion and immediately before the offence. *Where the victim is under 16* • Sexual activity between two children (one of whom is the offender) was mutually agreed and experimental. • Reasonable belief (by a young offender) that the victim was age 16 or over.

When sentencing a young offender for rape the appropriate sentence should normally be 'significantly shorter' than the appropriate sentence for an adult offender (*R v Millberry* [2003] 1 Cr App R (S) 25). This is a broadly general observation which was not intended to have invariable and inevitable application. In the gravest of cases, where it cannot be said that the youth of the defendant played a part, it is for the sentencer to decide what reduction to make (*R v Asi-Akram* [2005] EWCA Crim 1543). A court could well have taken the view that 25 per cent or even less of a discount would have been entirely appropriate for a 17-year-old charged with rape who had fathered a child (*CPS v Newcastle-upon-Tyne Youth Court* [2010] EWHC 2773 (Admin)).

Registration as sex offender—automatically required if convicted of this offence (see **F31**).

A2.2.3 Key points

• Penetration is a continuing act from entry to withdrawal (SOA 2003 s 79(2)).
• For consent see **A2.1.1**.

A2.3 Assault by penetration

Sexual Offences Act 2003 s 2

(1) A person (A) commits an offence if—
  (a) he intentionally penetrates the vagina or anus of another person (B) with a part of his body or anything else,
  (b) the penetration is sexual,
  (c) B does not consent to the penetration, and
  (d) A does not reasonably believe that B consents.

(2) Whether a belief is reasonable is to be determined having regard to all the circumstances, including any steps A has taken to ascertain whether B consents.

(3) Sections 75 and 76 apply to an offence under this section.

IO

GC

DO

▦ 24 month DTO/detention for life in Crown Court

A2.3.1 *Allocation*

Where a youth court is to consider the question of jurisdiction in relation to a sexual offence involving penetration, the case must be listed before a district judge with authorization to hear such cases: *Sexual Offences in the Youth Court* (see **D2.7.4**).

A2.3.2 *Sentencing*

There is no sentencing guideline specific for youths for this offence. The definitive sentencing guideline *Sexual Offences* (2007) provides guidance for sentencing **adult** offenders:

Type/nature of activity	Starting points	Sentencing ranges
Penetration with an object or body part, accompanied by any one of the following: abduction or detention; more than one offender acting together; abuse of trust; offence motivated by prejudice; sustained attack	13 years' custody if the victim is under 13 10 years' custody if the victim is 13 or over but under 16 8 years' custody if the victim is 16 or over	11–17 years' custody 8–13 years' custody 6–11 years' custody
Penetration with an object—in general, the larger or more dangerous the object, the higher the sentence should be	7 years' custody if the victim is under 13 5 years' custody if the victim is 13 or over but under 16 3 years' custody if the victim is 16 or over	5–10 years' custody 4–8 years' custody 2–5 years' custody
Penetration with a body part (fingers, toes, or tongue) where no physical harm is sustained by the victim	5 years' custody if the victim is under 13 4 years' custody if the victim is 13 or over but under 16 2 years' custody if the victim is 16 or over	4–8 years' custody 3–7 years' custody 1–4 years' custody

Additional aggravating factors	Additional mitigating factors
Offender ejaculated or caused victim to ejaculate. Background of intimidation or coercion. Use of drugs, alcohol, or other substance to facilitate the offence. Threats to prevent the victim reporting the incident. Abduction or detention. Offender aware he is suffering from a STD. Physical harm arising from the penetration.	Penetration is minimal or for a short duration. *Where the victim is aged 16 or over* Victim engaged in consensual sexual activity with the offender on the same occasion and immediately before the offence. *Where the victim is under 16* • Sexual activity between two children (one of whom is the offender) was mutually agreed and experimental. • Reasonable belief (by a young offender) that the victim was age 16 or over.

See case law discussed under **A2.2**.

Registration as sex offender—automatically required if convicted of this offence: see **F31**.

A2.3.3 Key points

• Penetration is a continuing act from entry to withdrawal (SOA 2008 s 79(2)).
• For the definition of 'sexual' see **A2.1.2**.
• For consent see **A2.1.1**.

A2.4 Sexual assault

Sexual Offences Act 2003 s 3

(1) A person (A) commits an offence if—
   (a) he intentionally touches another person (B),
   (b) the touching is **sexual**,
   (c) B does not consent to the touching, and
   (d) A does not reasonably believe that B consents.
(2) Whether a belief is reasonable is to be determined having regard to all the circumstances, including any steps A has taken to ascertain whether B consents.
(3) Sections 75 and 76 apply to an offence under this section.

EW

GC

DO

24 month DTO/10 years detention in Crown Court

A2.4.1 *Allocation*

For protocol *Sexual Offences in the Youth Court* see **D2.7.4**.

A2.4.2 *Sentencing*

There is no sentencing guideline specific for youths for this offence. The definitive sentencing guideline *Sexual Offences* (2007) provides guidance for sentencing **adult** offenders:

Type/nature of activity	Starting points	Sentencing ranges
Contact between naked genitalia of offender and naked genitalia, face, or mouth of the victim	5 years' custody if the victim is under 13 3 years' custody if the victim is aged 13 or over	4–8 years' custody 2–5 years' custody
Contact between naked genitalia of offender and another part of victim's body. Contact with genitalia of victim by offender using part of his or her body, other than the genitalia, or an object. Contact between either the clothed genitalia of offender and naked genitalia of victim or naked genitalia of offender and clothed genitalia of victim	2 years' custody if the victim is under 13 12 months' custody if the victim is aged 13 or over	1–4 years' custody 26 weeks–2 years' custody
Contact between part of offender's body (other than the genitalia) with part of the victim's body (other than the genitalia)	26 weeks' custody if the victim is under 13 Community order if the victim is aged 13 or over	4 weeks–18 months' custody An appropriate non-custodial sentence*

*'Non-custodial sentence' in this context suggests a [youth rehabilitation order] or a fine. In most instances, an offence will have crossed the threshold for a community order. However, in accordance with normal sentencing practice, a court is not precluded from imposing a financial penalty where that is determined to be the appropriate sentence.

Additional aggravating factors	Additional mitigating factors
Offender ejaculated or caused victim to ejaculate.	*Where the victim is aged 16 or over*
Background of intimidation or coercion.	Victim engaged in consensual sexual activity with the offender on the same occasion and immediately before the offence.
Use of drugs, alcohol, or other substance to facilitate the offence.	*Where the victim is under 16*
Threats to prevent the victim reporting the incident.	• Sexual activity between two children (one of whom is the offender) was mutually agreed and experimental.
Abduction or detention.	• Reasonable belief (by a young offender) that the victim was age 16 or over.
Offender aware he or she is suffering from an STI.	Youth and immaturity of the offender.
Physical harm caused.	Minimal or fleeting contact.
Prolonged activity or contact.	

R v S [2008] EWCA Crim 1059—D was aged 12 at the time of the offence. He pleaded guilty to sexual assault of a 75-year-old woman. D knocked on the door of the victim's bungalow. She let D in mistaking him for her grandson. While inside the bungalow over a thirty-minute period D sucked on her breasts, placed his hand between her legs near to but not on her genitalia, and exposed his penis. Later that day the victim was hospitalized for an unrelated health condition and subsequently died. D was not sentenced on the basis that he had caused the victim's death. D originally pleaded guilty in the youth court and was committed for sentence under the PCCSA 2000 s 3C as the youth court thought that the dangerous offender provisions should be available. In the Crown Court D was held not to present a significant risk of serious harm to the public. He was instead sentenced to four years' s 91 detention. Whilst a custodial sentence upon a 13-year-old boy for an offence of sexual assault would not necessarily be wrong in principle for an offence of sexual assault, the sentence passed was excessive bearing in mind D's age, mitigation, and guilty plea. In the absence of a risk to the public, the need to address D's potential for harm in the future requires a specialist sexual offending treatment programme. **Held**: custodial sentence quashed; three-year supervision order with sexual offending treatment programme substituted.

Sex offender registration—registration will only be required if the sentence condition is satisfied (see **F31**).

A2.4.3 Key points

• The SOA 2003 s 79(8) states that touching includes touching
  (a) with any part of the body,
  (b) with anything else,
  (c) through anything, and in particular includes touching amounting to penetration.

- A person touched another person for the purpose of the offence of sexual assault if he touched the clothes which that person was wearing (*R v H* [2005] EWCA Crim 732, [2005] 2 Cr App R 9).
- For the definition of 'sexual' see **A2.1.2**.
- The touching must be deliberate; reckless touching is not sufficient (*R v Heard* [2008] QB 43).
- Voluntary intoxication will not be a defence to deliberate touching (*R v Heard*, above).
- For consent see **A2.1.1**.

A2.5 Causing a person to engage in sexual activity without consent

> ### Sexual Offences Act 2003 s 4
>
> (1) A person (A) commits an offence if—
>   (a) he intentionally causes another person (B) to engage in an activity,
>   (b) the activity is sexual,
>   (c) B does not consent to engaging in the activity, and
>   (d) A does not reasonably believe that B consents.
> (2) Whether a belief is reasonable is to be determined having regard to all the circumstances, including any steps A has taken to ascertain whether B consents.
> (3) Sections 75 and 76 apply to an offence under this section.

EW **IO** —if penetration involved

GC —only if penetration involved

DO

▦ 24 month DTO (if penetration involved, maximum penalty in Crown Court is detention for life: s 4(4))

A2.5.1 *Allocation*

Where a youth court is to consider the question of jurisdiction in relation to a sexual offence involving penetration, the case must be listed before a district judge with authorization to hear such cases: *Sexual Offences in the Youth Court* (see **D2.7.4**).

A2.5.2 *Sentencing*

There is no sentencing guideline specific for youths for this offence. The definitive sentencing guideline *Sexual Offences* (2007) provides guidance for sentencing **adult** offenders:

A2 Sexual Offences

Type/nature of activity	Starting points	Sentencing ranges
Penetration with one of the following aggravating factors: abduction or detention; offender aware that he or she is suffering from a sexually transmitted infection; more than one offender acting together; abuse of trust; offence motivated by prejudice (race, religion, sexual orientation, physical disability); sustained attack	13 years' custody if the victim is under 13 10 years' custody if the victim is 13 or over but under 16 8 years' custody if the victim is 16 or over	11–17 years' custody 8–13 years' custody 6–11 years' custody
Single offence of penetration of/by single offender with no aggravating or mitigation factors	7 years' custody if the victim is a child under 13 or a person with a mental disorder 5 years' custody if the victim is 13 or over but under 16 3 years' custody if the victim is 16 or over	5–10 years' custody 4–8 years' custody 2–5 years' custody
Contact between naked genitalia of offender and naked genitalia of victim, or causing two or more victims to engage in such activity with each other, or causing victim to masturbate him/herself	5 years' custody if the victim is a child under 13 or a person with a mental disorder 4 years' custody if the victim is 13 or over but under 16 2 years' custody if the victim is 16 or over	4–8 years' custody 3–7 years' custody 1–4 years' custody
Contact between naked genitalia of offender and another part of victim's body, or causing two or more victims to engage in such activity with each other Contact with naked genitalia of victim by offender using part of the body other than the genitalia or an object, or causing two or more victims to engage in such activity with each other Contact between either the clothed genitalia of offender and naked genitalia of victim, between naked genitalia of offender and clothed	2 years' custody if the victim is a child under 13 or a person with a mental disorder 12 months' custody	1–4 years' custody 26 weeks–2 years' custody

genitalia of victim, or causing two or more victims to engage in such activity with each other		
Contact between part of offender's body (other than the genitalia) with part of victim's body (other than genitalia)	26 weeks' custody if the victim is a child under 13 or a person with a mental disorder Community order	4 weeks'–18 months' custody An appropriate non-custodial sentence*

*'Non-custodial sentence' in this context suggests a [youth rehabilitation order] or a fine. In most instances, an offence will have crossed the threshold for a community order. However, in accordance with normal sentencing practice, a court is not precluded from imposing a financial penalty where that is determined to be the appropriate sentence.

Additional aggravating factors	Additional mitigating factors
Offender ejaculated or caused victim to ejaculate. History of intimidation or coercion Use of drugs, alcohol, or other substance to facilitate the offence. Threats to prevent the victim reporting the incident. Abduction or detention. Offender aware he is suffering from a sexually transmitted disease.	

A2.5.3 Key points

- Although there is an overlap with the offence of rape, the scope of the offence under s 4 is wider in that it can be committed by and against persons of either sex.
- For consent see **A2.1.1**.

A2.6 Offences against child under 13

There are three offences under the SOA 2003 ss 5–7. It is not necessary to prove that the defendant knew that the complainant was under the age of 13 (*R v G* [2008] UKHL 37, [2009] 1 AC 92).

A2.6.1 *Rape of child under 13*

> **Sexual Offences Act 2003 s 5**
>
> (1) A person commits an offence if—
>   (a) he intentionally penetrates the vagina, anus, or mouth of another person with his penis, and
>   (b) the other person is under 13.

A2 Sexual Offences

IO

GC

DO

24 month DTO/detention for life in the Crown Court

A2.6.2 *Assault by penetration of a child under 13*

Sexual Offences Act 2003 s 6

(1) A person commits an offence if—
  (a) he intentionally penetrates the vagina or anus of another person with a part of his body or anything else,
  (b) the penetration is sexual, and
  (c) the other person is under 13.

IO

GC

DO

24 month DTO/detention for life in the Crown Court

A2.6.3 *Sexual assault of a child under 13*

Sexual Offences Act 2003 s 7

(1) A person commits an offence if—
  (a) he intentionally touches another person,
  (b) the touching is sexual, and
  (c) the other person is under 13.

EW

GC

DO

24 month DTO/10 years detention in the Crown Court

A2.6.4 *Decision to charge*

The CPS Legal Guidance *Youth Offenders (Rape and other offences against children under 13 (sections 5 to 8 Sexual Offences Act 2003))* states:

CCPs or DCCPs must be notified of any such case where there are both defendants and victims under the age of 13. This includes cases which are diverted from prosecution, whether on evidential or public interest grounds.

All such cases must be reviewed by a prosecutor who is both a rape specialist and a youth specialist. All advocates conducting these cases must have a rape specialism and should also have a youth specialism.

Where the Full Code Test is satisfied in a case in which a youth is suspected of committing a sexual offence involving a child under the age of 13, the appropriate charge will be an offence contrary to sections 5 to 8 Sexual Offences Act 2003, depending on the act, and not the lesser offence contrary to section 13 Sexual Offences Act 2003.

...

When reviewing a case, in which a youth under 18 is alleged to have committed an offence contrary to sections 5 to 8, prosecutors should obtain and consider:

- the views of the local authority Children's and Young People's Service;
- any risk assessment or report conducted by the local authority or youth offending service in respect of sexually harmful behaviour (such as AIM (Assessment, Intervention and Moving On));
- background information and history of the parties;
- the views of the families of all parties.

Careful regard should be paid to the following factors:

- the relative ages of both parties;
- the existence of and nature of any relationship;
- the sexual and emotional maturity of both parties and any emotional or physical effects as a result of the conduct;
- whether the child under 13 in fact freely consented (even though in law this is not a defence) or a genuine mistake as to her age was in fact made;
- whether any element of seduction, breach of any duty of responsibility to the girl or other exploitation is disclosed by the evidence;
- the impact of a prosecution on each child involved.

If the sexual act or activity was in fact genuinely consensual and the youth and the child under 13 concerned are fairly close in age and development, a prosecution is unlikely to be appropriate. Action falling short of prosecution may be appropriate. In such cases, the parents and/or welfare agencies may be able to deal with the situation informally.

However, if a very young child has been seduced by a youth, or a baby-sitter in a position of responsibility has taken advantage of a child under 13 in his/her care, prosecution is likely to be in the public interest. Where a child under 13 has not given ostensible consent to the activity, then a prosecution contrary to sections 5 to 8 is likely to be the appropriate course of action.

There is a fine line between sexual experimentation and offending and in general, children under the age of 13 should not be criminalised for sexual behaviour in the absence of coercion, exploitation or abuse of trust.

The decision to charge a young offender with rape of a child under 13 under s 5 rather than child sexual activity under ss 9 to 13 may exceptionally be the subject of judicial review if the charging decision failed to take into account the Code for Crown Prosecutors and the above guidance. For an unsuccessful attempt to challenge a decision to charge the offender under s 5 see *Tolhurst v DPP* [2008] EWHC 2976 (Admin).

A2.6.5 *Allocation*

Where a youth court is to consider the question of jurisdiction in relation to a sexual offence involving penetration, the case must be listed before a district judge with authorization to hear such cases: *Sexual Offences in the Youth Court* (see **D2.7.4**).

A2.6.6 *Sentencing*

There is no sentencing guideline specific for youths for these offences. The definitive sentencing guideline *Sexual Offences* (2007) provides guidance for sentencing **adult** offenders—see **A2.2** (for rape), **A2.3** (for assault by penetration), and **A2.4** (for sexual assault).

In relation to rape of a child under 13 (SOA 2003 s 5) the following appeal decisions are of significance:

- Although absence of consent was not an ingredient of the offence, presence of consent was material in relation to sentence, particularly with regard to younger defendants. The age of the defendant of itself and when compared with the age of the victim was also an important factor. A very short period of custody was likely to suffice for a teenager where the other party consented. In exceptional cases, a non-custodial sentence might be appropriate for a young defendant (*R v Corran* [2005] EWCA Crim 192, [2005] 2 Cr App R (S) 73). The comments on the appropriate sentence for a young offender remain valuable general guidance even after the implementation of the Sexual Offences Act 2003 and the coming into force of the definitive sentencing guideline *Sexual Offences Act 2003 (Att-Gen Reference Nos 74 and 83 of 2007* [2007] EWCA Crim 2550).

- *R v C* [2009] EWCA Crim 2231—D was 14 years old at the time of the offences. He pleaded guilty to one count of rape of a child under 13, one count of attempted rape of a child under 13, and four counts of causing a child to engage in sexual activity. The victim was D's 8-year-old cousin. The acts had arisen out of challenging each other to 'dares'. Amongst other acts D asked the victim to suck his penis and he also attempted to insert his penis in the victim's anus. The reports before the court outlined strong personal mitigation and concluded that D did not pose a risk to others and such residual risk he might pose was best addressed by a community sentence. The Crown Court judge stated that D had abused a position of influence over his young cousin. The Court of Appeal concluded that in the absence of a risk to others the offences were not so serious that the interests of D's own welfare and the primary aim of preventing offending must come second to the need to punish. **Held**: two-year DTO quashed; three-year supervision order with specified activity requirement to undertake sexual offender courses substituted.

- *R v M* [2010] EWCA Crim 698—D was 17 years old at the time of the offences. He pleaded guilty to two counts of rape of a child under 13 at the earliest opportunity. The 12-year-old victim was staying at D's aunt's house. She told him that she was 14 years old. On two successive nights she came into his bedroom and they had unprotected sexual intercourse. It was accepted that the girl initiated sexual intercourse on both occasions and that D genuinely thought she was 14 years old. Information before the Court of Appeal indicated that the girl's mother thought a warning or suspended sentence was sufficient. Exceptional circumstances of the offence and the attitude of the girl's mother meant a radical departure from the sentencing guidelines called for. **Held**: thirty months' s 91 detention quashed. Twelve-month DTO substituted.

- *R v Q* [2011] EWCA Crim 798—D was 17 years old at the time of the offences. He pleaded guilty to the offence under s 5. He was babysitting for a 12-year-old girl. He allowed her to drink alcohol with him and they eventually had unprotected sexual intercourse. The Court concluded that D knew the family and would therefore have known the approximate age of the girl. The offence was a gross abuse of trust and further aggravated by the fact that the sexual intercourse was unprotected. **Held**: three years' s 91 detention reduced to two years three months.

A2.7 Child sexual offences

Sexual Offences Act 2003 ss 9–13

9 Sexual activity with a child

(1) A person aged 18 or over (A) commits an offence if—
  (a) he intentionally touches another person (B),
  (b) the touching is sexual, and
  (c) either—
    (i) B is under 16 and A does not reasonably believe that B is 16 or over, or
    (ii) B is under 13.

10 Causing or inciting a child to engage in sexual activity

(1) A person aged 18 or over (A) commits an offence if—
  (a) he intentionally causes or incites another person (B) to engage in an activity,
  (b) the activity is sexual, and
  (c) either—

(i) B is under 16 and A does not reasonably believe that B is 16 or over, or

(ii) B is under 13.

11 Engaging in sexual activity in the presence of a child

(1) A person aged 18 or over (A) commits an offence if—

(a) he intentionally engages in an activity,

(b) the activity is sexual,

(c) for the purpose of obtaining sexual gratification, he engages in it—

(i) when another person (B) is present or is in a place from which A can be observed, and

(ii) knowing or believing that B is aware, or intending that B should be aware, that he is engaging in it, and

(d) either—

(i) B is under 16 and A does not reasonably believe that B is 16 or over, or

(ii) B is under 13.

12 Causing a child to watch a sexual act

(1) A person aged 18 or over (A) commits an offence if—

(a) for the purpose of obtaining sexual gratification, he intentionally causes another person (B) to watch a third person engaging in an activity, or to look at an image of any person engaging in an activity,

(b) the activity is sexual, and

(c) either—

(i) B is under 16 and A does not reasonably believe that B is 16 or over, or

(ii) B is under 13.

13 Child sex offences committed by children or young persons

(1) A person under 18 commits an offence if he does anything which would be an offence under any of sections 9 to 12 if he were aged 18.

🏛 24 month DTO/5 years detention in Crown Court

A2.7.1 *Decision to charge*

The CPS Legal Guidance *Youth Offenders (Child Sex Offences)* states:

It should be noted that where both parties to sexual activity are under 16, then they may both have committed a sexual offence. However, the overriding purpose of the legislation is to protect children and it was not Parliament's intention to punish children unnecessarily or for the criminal law to intervene where it was wholly inappropriate. Consensual sexual activity between, for example, a 14- or 15-year-old and a teenage partner would not normally require criminal proceedings in the absence of aggravating features. The relevant considerations include:

- the respective ages of the parties;
- the existence and nature of any relationship;
- their level of maturity;
- whether any duty of care existed;
- whether there was a serious element of exploitation.

A2.7.2 *Allocation*

Where a youth court is to consider the question of jurisdiction in relation to a sexual offence involving penetration, the case must be listed before a district judge with authorization to hear such cases: *Sexual Offences in the Youth Court* (see **D2.7.4**).

A2.7.3 *Sentencing*

The definitive sentencing guideline *Sexual Offences Act 2003* (2007) provides specific guidelines for each of the offences under ss 9–12. These are set out below:

Sexual activity with a child (ss 9 and 13)—The starting points below are based on a first-time offender aged 17 years old who pleaded not guilty. For younger offenders, sentencers should consider whether a lower starting point is justified in recognition of the offender's age or immaturity.

Type/nature of activity	Starting point	Sentencing ranges
Offence involving penetration where one or more aggravating factors exist or where there is a substantial age gap between the parties	Detention and training order 12 months	Detention and training order 6–24 months
CUSTODY THRESHOLD		
Any form of sexual activity that does not involve any aggravating factors	Community order	An appropriate non-custodial sentence*

*'Non-custodial sentence' in this context suggests a [youth rehabilitation order] or a fine. In most instances, an offence will have crossed the threshold for a community order. However, in accordance with normal sentencing practice, a court is not precluded from imposing a financial penalty where that is determined to be the appropriate sentence.

Aggravating factors	Mitigating factors
Background of intimidation or coercion Threats deterring the victim from reporting the incident Offender aware that he or she is suffering from a sexually transmitted disease	Small disparity in age between victim and offender Relationship of genuine affection Youth and immaturity of offender

A2 Sexual Offences

Causing or inciting a child to engage in sexual activity (ss 10 and 13)—The starting points below are based on a first-time offender aged 17 years old who pleaded not guilty. For younger offenders, sentencers should consider whether a lower starting point is justified in recognition of the offender's age or immaturity.

Type/nature of activity	Starting point	Sentencing ranges
Sexual activity involving penetration where on or more aggravating factors exist	Detention and training order 12 months	Detention and training order 6–24 months
CUSTODY THRESHOLD		
Any form of sexual activity (non-penetrative or penetrative) that does not involve any aggravating factors	Community order	An appropriate non-custodial sentence*

*'Non-custodial sentence' in this context suggests a [youth rehabilitation order] or a fine. In most instances, an offence will have crossed the threshold for a community order. However, in accordance with normal sentencing practice, a court is not precluded from imposing a financial penalty where that is determined to be the appropriate sentence.

Aggravating factors	Mitigating factors
Background of intimidation or coercion Use of drugs, alcohol, or other substance Threats deterring the victim from reporting the incident Offender aware that he or she is suffering from a sexually transmitted disease	Small disparity in age between victim and offender Relationship of genuine affection Youth and immaturity of offender

Engaging in sexual activity in the presence of a child (ss 11 and 13)—The starting points below are based on a first-time offender aged 17 years old who pleaded not guilty. For younger offenders, sentencers should consider whether a lower starting point is justified in recognition of the offender's age or immaturity.

Type/nature of activity	Starting point	Sentencing ranges
Sexual activity involving penetration where on or more aggravating factors exist	Detention and training order 12 months	Detention and training order 6–24 months
CUSTODY THRESHOLD		
Any form of sexual activity (non-penetrative or penetrative) that does not involve any aggravating factors	Community order	An appropriate non-custodial sentence*

*'Non-custodial sentence' in this context suggests a [youth rehabilitation order] or a fine. In most instances, an offence will have crossed the threshold for a community order. However, in accordance with normal sentencing practice, a court is not precluded from imposing a financial penalty where that is determined to be the appropriate sentence.

Aggravating factors	Mitigating factors
Background of intimidation or coercion Use of drugs, alcohol, or other substance Threats deterring the victim from reporting the incident Offender aware that he or she is suffering from a sexually transmitted disease	Small disparity in age between victim and offender Relationship of genuine affection Youth and immaturity of offender

Causing a child to watch a sexual act (ss 12 and 13)—The starting points below are based on a first-time offender aged 17 years old who pleaded not guilty. For younger offenders, sentencers should consider whether a lower starting point is justified in recognition of the offender's age or immaturity.

Type/nature of activity	Starting point	Sentencing ranges
Live sexual activity	Detention and training order 8 months	Detention and training order 6–12 months
CUSTODY THRESHOLD		
Moving or still images of people engaged in sexual acts involving penetration	Community order	An appropriate non-custodial sentence*
Moving or still images of people engaged in sexual acts other than penetration	Community order	An appropriate non-custodial sentence*

*'Non-custodial sentence' in this context suggests a [youth rehabilitation order] or a fine. In most instances, an offence will have crossed the threshold for a community order. However, in accordance with normal sentencing practice, a court is not precluded from imposing a financial penalty where that is determined to be the appropriate sentence.

Aggravating factors	Mitigating factors
Background of intimidation or coercion Use of drugs, alcohol, or other substance Threats deterring the victim from reporting the incident Offender aware that he or she is suffering from a sexually transmitted disease	Small disparity in age between victim and offender Relationship of genuine affection Youth and immaturity of offender

Sex offender registration—registration will be required if the sentence condition is satisfied (see **F31**).

A2.8 Familial child sexual offences

Sexual Offences Act 2003 ss 25 and 26

25 Sexual activity with a child family member

(1) A person (A) commits an offence if—

(a) he intentionally touches another person (B),

(b) the touching is sexual,

(c) the relation of A to B is within section 27,

(d) A knows or could reasonably be expected to know that his relation to B is of a description falling within that section, and

(e) either—

(i) B is under 18 and A does not reasonably believe that B is 18 or over, or

(ii) B is under 13.

(2) Where in proceedings for an offence under this section it is proved that the other person was under 18, the defendant is to be taken not to have reasonably believed that that person was 18 or over unless sufficient evidence is adduced to raise an issue as to whether he reasonably believed it.

(3) Where in proceedings for an offence under this section it is proved that the relation of the defendant to the other person was of a description falling within section 27, it is to be taken that the defendant knew or could reasonably have been expected to know that his relation to the other person was of that description unless sufficient evidence is adduced to raise an issue as to whether he knew or could reasonably have been expected to know that it was.

. . .

(6) This subsection applies where the touching involved—

(a) penetration of B's anus or vagina with a part of A's body or anything else,

(b) penetration of B's mouth with A's penis,

(c) penetration of A's anus or vagina with a part of B's body, or

(d) penetration of A's mouth with B's penis.

26 Inciting a child family member to engage in sexual activity

(1) A person (A) commits an offence if—

(a) he intentionally incites another person (B) to touch, or allow himself to be touched by, A,

(b) the touching is sexual,

(c) the relation of A to B is within section 27,

(d) A knows or could reasonably be expected to know that his relation to B is of a description falling within that section, and

(e) either—

(i) B is under 18 and A does not reasonably believe that B is 18 or over, or

(ii) B is under 13.

(2) Where in proceedings for an offence under this section it is proved that the other person was under 18, the defendant is to be taken not to have reasonably believed that that person was 18 or over unless sufficient evidence is adduced to raise an issue as to whether he reasonably believed it.

(3) Where in proceedings for an offence under this section it is proved that the

relation of the defendant to the other person was of a description falling within section 27, it is to be taken that the defendant knew or could reasonably have been expected to know that his relation to the other person was of that description unless sufficient evidence is adduced to raise an issue as to whether he knew or could reasonably have been expected to know that it was.

...

(6) This subsection applies where the touching to which the incitement related involved—

    (a) penetration of B's anus or vagina with a part of A's body or anything else,

    (b) penetration of B's mouth with A's penis,

    (c) penetration of A's anus or vagina with a part of B's body, or

    (d) penetration of A's mouth with B's penis.

EW

GC

DO

 24 month DTO/5 years detention in Crown Court

A2.8.1 *Decision to prosecute*

The CPS Legal Guidance *Youth Offenders (Familial Sexual Offences)* states:

In cases of sexual activity between siblings, care should be taken to balance the public interest in prosecuting such conduct with the interests and welfare of the victim and the family unit. As a general rule, alternatives to prosecution should be sought where the sexual activity was wholly consensual. The welfare agencies will normally intervene.

Prosecution should be considered where there is evidence of:

- seduction;
- coercion;
- exploitation or violence;
- a significant disparity in age;

In all cases the effect of prosecution on a victim and family should be taken into account and if the views of the welfare agencies are not included with the file they should be sought.

A2.8.2 *Allocation*

Where a youth court is to consider the question of jurisdiction in relation to a sexual offence involving penetration, the case must be listed before a district judge with authorization to hear such cases: *Sexual Offences in the Youth Court* (see **D2.7.4**).

A2.8.3 *Sentencing*

The definitive sentencing guideline *Sexual Offences Act 2003* (2007) provides specific guidelines for sentencing youths.

The starting points below are based on a first-time offender aged 17 years old who pleaded not guilty. For younger offenders, sentencers should consider whether a lower starting point is justified in recognition of the offender's age or immaturity.

Type/nature of activity	Starting point	Sentencing ranges
Offence involving penetration where one or more aggravating factors exist or where there is a substantial age gap between the parties	Detention and training order 18 months	Detention and training order 6–24 months
CUSTODY THRESHOLD		
Any form of sexual activity that does not involve any aggravating factors	Community order	An appropriate non-custodial sentence*

*'Non-custodial sentence' in this context suggests a [youth rehabilitation order] or a fine. In most instances, an offence will have crossed the threshold for a community order. However, in accordance with normal sentencing practice, a court is not precluded from imposing a financial penalty where that is determined to be the appropriate sentence.

Aggravating factors	Mitigating factors
Background of intimidation or coercion Use of drugs, alcohol, or other substance Threats deterring the victim from reporting the incident Offender aware that he or she is suffering from a sexually transmitted disease	Small disparity in age between victim and offender Relationship of genuine affection Youth and immaturity of offender

Sex offender registration—registration will be required if the sentence condition is satisfied (see **F31**).

A2.8.4 Key points

- The relevant family relationships covered by these offences are defined in the SOA 2003 s 27.
- Defences exist in the SOA 2003 ss 28 and 29.

A2.9 **Exposure**

> ### Sexual Offences Act 2003 s 66
>
> (1) A person commits an offence if—
>   (a) he intentionally exposes his genitals, and
>   (b) he intends that someone will see them and be caused alarm or distress.

24 month DTO

A2.9.1 *Sentencing*

The definitive sentencing guideline *Sexual Offences* (2007) does not provide specific guidance for sentencing youths in relation to this offence. The guideline provides the following guidance for sentencing **adult** offenders:

Type/nature of activity	Starting point	Sentencing ranges
Repeat offender	12 weeks' custody	4–26 weeks' custody
Basic offence as defined in the SOA 2003, assuming no aggravating or mitigating factors, or some offences with aggravating factors	Community order	An appropriate non-custodial sentence*

*'Non-custodial sentence' in this context suggests a [youth rehabilitation order] or a fine. In most instances, an offence will have crossed the threshold for a community order. However, in accordance with normal sentencing practice, a court is not precluded from imposing a financial penalty where that is determined to be the appropriate sentence.

Additional aggravating factors	Additional mitigating factors
1. Threats to prevent the victim reporting an offence 2. Intimidating behaviour/threats of violence 3. Victim is a child	

Sex offender registration—registration will only be required if the sentence condition is satisfied (see **F31**).

A2.9.2 Key points

- This offence is committed where an offender intentionally exposes his or her genitals and intends that someone will see them and be caused alarm or distress. It is gender neutral, covering exposure of male or female genitalia to a male or female witness.
- The offence has a 'bolted-on' intention, going beyond the intention to expose oneself and therefore is an offence of specific intent; voluntary intoxication may therefore be relied upon as a defence (*R v Heard* [2007] EWCA Crim 125, [2007] 1 Cr App R 37).

A2.10 Voyeurism

Sexual Offences Act 2003 ss 67 and 68

67 Voyeurism

(1) A person commits an offence if—
    (a) for the purpose of obtaining sexual gratification, he observes another person doing a private act, and
    (b) he knows that the other person does not consent to being observed for his sexual gratification.

(2) A person commits an offence if—
    (a) he operates equipment with the intention of enabling another person to observe, for the purpose of obtaining sexual gratification, a third person (B) doing a private act, and
    (b) he knows that B does not consent to his operating equipment with that intention.

(3) A person commits an offence if—
    (a) he records another person (B) doing a private act,
    (b) he does so with the intention that he or a third person will, for the purpose of obtaining sexual gratification, look at an image of B doing the act, and
    (c) he knows that B does not consent to his recording the act with that intention.

(4) A person commits an offence if he installs equipment, or constructs or adapts a structure or part of a structure, with the intention of enabling himself or another person to commit an offence under subsection (1).

68 Voyeurism: interpretation

(1) For the purposes of section 67, a person is doing a private act if the person is in a place which, in the circumstances, would reasonably be expected to provide privacy, and—
    (a) the person's genitals, buttocks, or breasts are exposed or covered only with underwear,
    (b) the person is using a lavatory, or
    (c) the person is doing a sexual act that is not of a kind ordinarily done in public.

(2) In section 67, 'structure' includes a tent, vehicle, or vessel or other temporary or movable structure.

EW

DO

 24 month DTO

A2.10.1 *Sentencing*

The definitive sentencing guideline *Sexual Offences* (2007) does not provide specific guidance for sentencing youths in relation to this offence. The guideline provides the following guidance for sentencing adults:

Type/nature of activity	Starting points	Sentencing ranges
Offence with serious aggravating factors such as recording sexual activity and placing on a website or circulating it for commercial gain	12 months' custody	26 weeks'–2 years' custody
Offence with aggravating factors such as recording sexual activity and showing it to others	26 weeks' custody	4 weeks'–18 months' custody
Basic offence as described in the SOA 2003, assuming no aggravating or mitigating factors, eg the offender spies through a hole he or she has made in a changing room wall	Community order	An appropriate non-custodial sentence*

*'Non-custodial sentence' in this context suggests a [youth rehabilitation order] or a fine. In most instances, an offence will have crossed the threshold for a community order. However, in accordance with normal sentencing practice, a court is not precluded from imposing a financial penalty where that is determined to be the appropriate sentence.

Additional aggravating factors	Additional mitigating factors
1. Threats to prevent the victim reporting an offence 2. Recording activity and circulating pictures/videos 3. Circulating pictures or videos for commercial gain—particularly if victim vulnerable, eg a child or person with a mental or physical disorder 4. Distress to victim, eg where the pictures/videos are circulated to people known to the victim	

Sex offender registration—registration will only be required if the sentence condition is satisfied (see **F31**).

A2.10.2 Key points

- For consent see **A2.1.1**.

A2.11 Indecent photographs of children

Protection of Children Act 1978 s 1

1. Indecent photographs of children

(1) Subject to sections 1A and 1B, it is an offence for a person—
  - (a) to take, or permit to be taken or to make, any indecent photograph or pseudo-photograph of a child; or
  - (b) to distribute or show such indecent photographs or pseudo-photographs; or
  - (c) to have in his possession such indecent photographs or pseudo-photographs, with a view to their being distributed or shown by himself or others; or
  - (d) to publish or cause to be published any advertisement likely to be understood as conveying that the advertiser distributes or shows such indecent photographs or pseudo-photographs, or intends to do so.

(2) For purposes of this Act, a person is to be regarded as distributing an indecent photograph or pseudo-photographs if he parts with possession of it to, or exposes or offers it for acquisition by, another person.

(3) Proceedings for an offence under this Act shall not be instituted except by or with the consent of the Director of Public Prosecutions.

(4) Where a person is charged with an offence under subsection (1)(b) or (c), it shall be a defence for him to prove—
  - (a) that he had a legitimate reason for distributing or showing the photographs or pseudo-photographs or (as the case may be) having them in his possession; or
  - (b) that he had not himself seen the photographs or pseudo-photographs and did not know, nor had any cause to suspect, them to be indecent.

(5) References in the Children and Young Persons Act 1933 (except in sections 15 and 99) to the offences mentioned in Schedule 1 to that Act shall include an offence under subsection (1)(a) above.

Criminal Justice Act 1988 s 160

160 Offence of possession of indecent photograph of child

(1) Subject to section 160A, it is an offence for a person to have any indecent photograph or pseudo-photograph of a child in his possession.

(2) Where a person is charged with an offence under subsection (1) above, it shall be a defence for him to prove—
  - (a) that he had a legitimate reason for having the photograph or pseudo-photograph in his possession; or
  - (b) that he had not himself seen the photograph or pseudo-photograph and did not know, nor had any cause to suspect, it to be indecent; or

> (c) that the photograph or pseudo-photograph was sent to him without
> any prior request made by him or on his behalf and that he did not keep
> it for an unreasonable time.
>
> ...
>
> (4) Sections 1(3), 2(3), 3 and 7 of the Protection of Children Act 1978 shall
> have effect as if any reference in them to that Act included a reference to
> this section.

24 month DTO

A2.11.1 *Sentence*

There is no sentencing guideline specific for youths for this offence.
The definitive sentencing guideline *Sexual Offences* (2007) provides
guidance for sentencing **adult** offenders:

The levels of seriousness (in ascending order) for sentencing for
offences involving pornographic images are:

Level 1   Images depicting erotic posing with no sexual activity
Level 2   Non-penetrative sexual activity between children, or solo
masturbation by a child
Level 3   Non-penetrative sexual activity between adults and children
Level 4   Penetrative sexual activity involving a child or children, or
both children and adults
Level 5   Sadism or penetration of, or by, an animal.

Starting points should be higher where the subject of the indecent
photograph is a child under 13.

Type/nature of activity	Starting points	Sentencing ranges
Offender commission or encouraged the production of level 4 or level 5 images Offender involved in the production of level 4 or 5 images	6 years' custody	4–9 years' custody
Level 4 or 5 images shown or distributed	3 years' custody	2–5 years' custody
Offender involved in the production of, or has traded in, material at levels 1–3	2 years' custody	1–4 years' custody
Possession of a large quantity of level 4 or 5 material for personal use only Large number of level 3 images shown or distributed	12 months' custody	26 weeks'–2 years' custody

A2 Sexual Offences

Possession of large quantity of level 3 material for personal use Possession of a small number of images at level 4 or 5 Large number of level 2 images shown or distributed Small number of level 3 images shown or distributed	26 weeks' custody	4 weeks'–18 months' custody
Offender in possession of a large amount of material at level 2 or a small amount at level 3 Offender has shown or distributed material at level 1 or 2 on a limited scale Offender has exchanged images at level 1 or 2 on a limited scale Offender has exchanged images at level 1 or 2 with other collectors, but with no element of financial gain	12 weeks' custody	4 weeks'–26 weeks' custody
Possession of a large amount of level 1 material and/or no more than a small amount of level 2, and the material is for personal use and has not been distributed or shown to others	Community order	An appropriate non-custodial sentence*

*'Non-custodial sentence' in this context suggests a [youth rehabilitation order] or a fine. In most instances, an offence will have crossed the threshold for a community order. However, in accordance with normal sentencing practice, a court is not precluded from imposing a financial penalty where that is determined to be the appropriate sentence.

Additional aggravating factors	Additional mitigating factors
1. Images shown or distributed to others, especially children 2. Collection is systematically stored or organized, indicating a sophisticated approach to trading or a high level of personal interest 3. Images sorted, made available, or distributed in such a way that they can be inadvertently accessed by others 4. Use of drugs, alcohol, or other substance to facilitate the offence of making or taking 5. Background of intimidation or coercion 6. Threats to prevent victim reporting the activity 7. Threats to disclose victim's activity to friends or relatives 8. Financial or other gain	1. A few images held solely for personal use 2. Images viewed but not stored 3. A few images held solely for personal use and it is established both that the subject is aged 16 or 17 and that he or she was consenting

Sex offender registration—registration will only be required if the sentence condition is satisfied (see **F31**).

A2.11.2 Key points

- Proceedings in relation to either offence requires the consent of the DPP.
- A child is a person under the age of 18 (Protection of Children Act 1978 s 7(6)).
- The definition of a photograph includes a tracing or other image derived in whole or part from a photograph or pseudo-photograph and data stored on a computer disc which is capable of conversion into an image (Protection of Children Act 1978 s 7(4A)).
- Whether a photograph is indecent depends on normally recognized standards of propriety.
- The age of the child may be relevant to the issue of indecency (*R v Owen* (1988) 88 Cr App R 291).
- If a person opens an email attachment knowing it contains an indecent image of a child or is likely to include such an image, then he is guilty of making a photograph for the purposes of the 1978 Act (*R v Smith* [2002] EWCA Crim 683, [2003] 1 Cr App R 13).
- The offence of possession required that the person had possession or control of the images. If the images had been deleted from a computer then it would be a question of fact whether he had control of them. That question could be answered by reference to whether he had the expertise and equipment to retrieve them (*R v Porter* [2006] EWCA Crim 560, [2006] 1 WLR 2633).
- In relation to the offence under the 1978 Act s 1A of that Act creates a defence which applies to images of a child aged 16 or over where the defendant proves that at the time of the offence the child and he were married or lived together as partners in an enduring family relationship. This defence does not extend to more casual sexual relationships (*R v M* [2011] EWCA Crim 2752). A similar defence to the offence under s 160 of the 1988 Act is created by s 160A of that Act.

A2.12 Sexual offenders register—fail to comply with notification requirements

Sexual Offences Act 2003 s 91

(1) A person commits an offence if he—

    (a) fails, without reasonable excuse, to comply with section 83(1), 84(1), 84(4)(b), 85(1), 87(4) or 89(2)(b) or any requirement imposed by regulations made under section 86(1); or

> (b) notifies to the police, in purported compliance with section 83(1), 84(1) or 85(1) or any requirement imposed by regulations made under section 86(1), any information which he knows to be false.

 24 month DTO

A2.12.1 *Sentencing*

There is no sentencing guideline specific for youths for this offence. The *Magistrates' Court Sentencing Guidelines* (2008) provide guidance for sentencing **adult** offenders.

Examples of nature of activity	Starting point	Range
Negligent or inadvertent failure to comply with requirements	Medium level community order	Band C fine to high level community order
Deliberate failure to comply with requirements OR Supply of information known to be false	6 weeks' custody	High level community order to 26 weeks' custody
Conduct as described in box above AND Long period of non-compliance OR Attempts to avoid detection	18 weeks' custody	6 weeks' custody to Crown Court

Factor indicating higher culpability	Factor indicating lower culpability
1. Long period of non-compliance (where not in the examples above) **Factors indicating greater degree of harm** 1. Alarm or distress caused to victim 2. Particularly serious original offence	1. Genuine misunderstanding

A2.12.2 Key points

- For the notification obligations see **F31.3**.
- Where a parental requirement (see **F31.4**) was made, the youth cannot commit an offence under s 91 until he attains 18 when the parental requirement will lapse.

A3 Theft, Fraud, and Other Property Offences

A3.1 Theft

Theft Act 1968 s 1(1)–(2)

(1) A person is guilty of theft if he dishonestly appropriates property belonging to another with the intention of permanently depriving the other of it; and 'thief' and 'steal' shall be construed accordingly.

(2) It is immaterial whether the appropriation is made with a view to gain, or is made for the thief's own benefit.

EW

 24 month DTO

A3.1.1 *Sentencing: theft, breach of trust*

There is no sentencing guideline specific to youths. *The Magistrates' Court Sentencing Guidelines* gives the following guidance for **adult** offenders:

Type/nature of activity	Starting point	Sentencing range
Theft of less than £2,000	Medium level community order	Band B fine to 26 weeks' custody
Theft of £2,000 or more but less than £20,000 OR Theft of less than £20,000 in breach of a high degree of trust	18 weeks' custody	High level community order to Crown Court
Theft of £20,000 or more OR Theft of £20,000 or more in breach of a high degree of trust	Crown Court	Crown Court

---

Additional aggravating factors:

1. Long course of offending
2. Suspicion deliberately thrown on others
3. Offender motivated by intention to cause harm or out of revenge

---

A3 Theft, Fraud, and Other Property Offences

A3.1.2 *Sentencing: theft from the person*

Type/nature of activity	Starting point	Sentencing range
Where the effect on the victim is particularly severe, the stolen property is of high value, or substantial consequential loss results, a sentence higher than the range into which the offence would fall may be appropriate.		
Theft from a vulnerable victim involving intimidation or the use or threat of force (falling short of robbery)	18 months' custody	12 months' to 3 years' custody
Theft from a vulnerable victim	18 weeks' custody	Community order (HIGH) to 12 months' custody
Theft from the person not involving vulnerable victim	Community order (MEDIUM)	Fine Band B to 18 weeks' custody

Additional aggravating factors

1. Offender motivated by intention to cause harm or out of revenge
2. Intimidation or face-to-face confrontation with victim [except where this raises offence into the higher sentencing range]
3. Use of force, or threat of force, against victim (not amounting to robbery) [except where this raises the offence into a higher sentencing range]
4. High level of inconvenience caused to victim, eg replacing house keys, credit cards, etc

A3.1.3 *Sentencing: theft from shop*

Type/nature of activity	Starting point	Sentencing range
Organized gang/group and Intimidation or the use or threat of force (short of robbery)	12 months' custody	36 weeks' to 4 years' custody
Significant intimidation or threats OR Use of force resulting in slight injury OR Very high level of planning OR Significant related damage	6 weeks' custody	Community order (HIGH) to 36 weeks' custody
Low level intimidation or threats OR Some planning, eg a session of stealing on the same day or going equipped OR Some related damage	Community order (LOW)	Fine to community order (MEDIUM)
Little or no planning or sophistication AND Goods stolen of low value	Fine	Conditional discharge to community order (LOW)

Additional aggravating factors:

1. Child accompanying offender is involved in or aware of theft
2. Offender is subject to a banning order that includes the store targeted
3. Offender motivated by intention to cause harm or out of revenge
4. Professional offending
5. Victim particularly vulnerable (eg small independent shop)
6. Offender targeted high value goods

A3.1.4 Key points

- Dishonesty is a two-part test:
  1. Were the accused's actions dishonest according to the ordinary standards of reasonable and honest people?
  2. If so, did the accused know that those actions were dishonest according to those standards? *R v Ghosh* (1982) QB 1058.
- Dishonesty is considered in the Theft Act 1968 s 2:

Theft Act 1968 s 2

(1) A person's appropriation of property belonging to another is not to be regarded as dishonest—
  (a) if he appropriates the property in the belief that he has in law the right to deprive the other of it, on behalf of himself or of a third person; or
  (b) if he appropriates the property in the belief that he would have the other's consent if the other knew of the appropriation and the circumstances of it; or
  (c) (except where the property came to him as trustee or personal representative) if he appropriates the property in the belief that the person to whom the property belongs cannot be discovered by taking reasonable steps.
(2) A person's appropriation of property belonging to another may be dishonest notwithstanding that he is willing to pay for the property.

- Appropriation means the assumption of any of the rights of an owner: *R v Gomez* [1993] AC 442.
- The intention permanently to deprive is considered in the Theft Act 1968 s 6:

Theft Act 1968 s 6

(1) A person appropriating property belonging to another without meaning the other permanently to lose the thing itself is nevertheless to be regarded as having the intention of permanently depriving the other of it if his intention is to treat the thing as his own to dispose of regardless of the other's rights; and a borrowing or lending of it may amount to so treating it if, but only if, the borrowing or lending is for a period and in circumstances making it equivalent to an outright taking or disposal.
(2) Without prejudice to the generality of subsection (1) above, where a person, having possession or control (lawfully or not) of property belonging to another, parts with the property under a condition as to its return which he may not be able to perform, this (if done for purposes of his own and without the other's authority) amounts to treating the property as his own to dispose of regardless of the other's rights...

 See *Blackstone's Criminal Practice 2014* **B4.1–B4.65**

A3.2 Robbery and assault with intent to rob

Theft Act 1968 s 8

(1) A person is guilty of robbery if he steals, and immediately before or at the time of doing so, and in order to do so, he uses force on any person or puts or seeks to put any person in fear of being then and there subjected to force.

(2) A person guilty of robbery, or of an assault with intent to rob, shall on conviction on indictment be liable to imprisonment for life.

24 month DTO/detention for life in Crown Court

A3.2.1 *Sentencing*

The following guideline from the Sentencing Council *Robbery— Definitive Guideline* is specific to youths:

STREET ROBBERY OR 'MUGGING' ROBBERIES OF SMALL BUSINESSES LESS SOPHISTICATED COMMERCIAL ROBBERIES Young Offenders*		
Type/nature of activity	Starting point	Sentencing Range
The offence includes the threat or use of minimal force and removal of property	Community Order	Community Order— 12 months' detention and training order
A weapon is produced and used to threaten, and/or force is used which results in injury to the victim	3 years' detention	1–6 years' detention
The victim is caused serious physical injury by the use of significant force and/or use of a weapon	7 years' detention	6–10 years' detention

*The 'starting points' are based upon a first-time offender aged 17 years old who pleaded not guilty. For younger offenders, sentencers should consider whether a lower starting point is justified in recognition of the offender's age or immaturity.

Additional aggravating factors	Additional mitigating factors
1. More than one offender involved.	1. Unplanned/opportunistic.
2. Being the ringleader of a group of offenders.	2. Peripheral involvement.
3. Restraint, detention, or additional degradation, taken.	3. Voluntary return of property of the victim.
4. Offence was pre-planned.	4. Clear evidence of remorse.
5. Wearing a disguise.	5. Ready cooperation with the police.
6. Offence committed at night.	6. Age of the offender.
7. Vulnerable victim targeted.	7. Immaturity of the offender.
8. Targeting of large sums of money or valuable goods.	8. Peer group pressure.
9. Possession of a weapon that was not used.	

The relative seriousness of each offence will be determined by the following factors:

• Degree of force and/or nature and duration of threats
• Degree of injury to the victim
• Degree of fear experienced by the victim
• Value of property taken

In *R v M* [2011] EWCA Crim 2897 a defendant aged 15 years at the time of the offence had been sentenced with an adult co-defendant in the Crown Court. The youth charged with robbery, and previously of positive good character, was sentenced to a six-month DTO. His adult co-defendant, charged with handling stolen goods, received a twelve-month community order with unpaid work. The offence involved the taking of a mobile phone from a victim who tried to hold on to it. The Court of Appeal said that the offence did not involve minimal force. However, considering the definitive guidelines on *Robbery* and *Overarching Principles—Sentencing Youths,* a custodial sentence must only be imposed as a measure of last resort. A youth rehabilitation order with a short period of supervision was substituted.

A3.2.2 Key points

• Force may be used indirectly, for example wrenching a bag from a victim's hand: *R v Clouden* [1987] Crim LR 56. Snatching a cigarette from the victim's hand was not robbery in *P v DPP* [2012] EWHC 1657 (Admin).
• Force must be used or threatened immediately before or at the time of stealing: *R v Vinall* [2011] EWCA Crim 6252.
• The force must be connected to the stealing: *R v Shendley* [1970] Crim LR 49.

- The elements of theft must be present: dishonesty, an intention to deprive permanently, and appropriation. See **A3.1**.
- There must be intention or at least recklessness as to the use of force.

 See *Blackstone's Criminal Practice 2014* **B4.66–B4.74**

A3.3 Burglary

Theft Act 1968 s 9(1)–(2)

(1) A person is guilty of burglary if—
   (a) he enters any building or part of a building as a trespasser and with intent to commit any such offence as is mentioned in subsection (2) below; or
   (b) having entered any building or part of a building as a trespasser he steals or attempts to steal anything in the building or that part of it or inflicts or attempts to inflict on any person therein any grievous bodily harm.
(2) The offences referred to in subsection (1) (a) above are offences of stealing anything in the building or part of a building in question, of inflicting on any person therein any grievous bodily harm therein, and of doing unlawful damage to the building or anything therein.

EW

IO   If compromises the commission of, or an intention to commit grievous bodily harm or in a dwelling if any person in the dwelling was subjected to violence or the threat of violence (MCA Sch 1 para 28)

DO   Where the burglary is committed with intent to inflict grievous bodily harm or do unlawful damage (CJA 2003 Sch 15)

GC   Dwelling burglary only

▦   24 month DTO/14 years detention in Crown Court (dwelling burglary only)

A3.3.1 *Sentencing—Burglary Dwelling*

There is no sentencing guideline specific to youths. The definitive guideline *Burglary Offences* gives the following guidance for **adult** offenders:

STEP ONE: Determining the offence category

The court should determine the offence category using the table below.

Category 1	Greater harm **and** higher culpability
Category 2	Greater harm **and** lower culpability **or** lesser harm **and** higher culpability
Category 3	Lesser harm **and** lower culpability

The court should determine culpability and harm caused or intended, by reference **only** to the factors below, which comprise the principal factual elements of the offence. Where an offence does not fall squarely into a category, individual factors may require a degree of weighting before making an overall assessment and determining the appropriate offence category.

Factors indicating greater harm	**Factors indicating higher culpability**
Theft of/damage to property causing a significant degree of loss to the victim (whether economic, sentimental, or personal value)	Victim or premises deliberately targeted (eg, due to vulnerability or hostility based on disability, race, sexual orientation)
Soiling, ransacking, or vandalism of property	A significant degree of planning or organization
Occupier at home (or returns home) while offender present	Knife or other weapon carried (where not charged separately)
Trauma to the victim, beyond the normal inevitable consequence of intrusion and theft	Equipped for burglary (eg, implements carried and/or use of vehicle)
Violence used or threatened against victim	Member of a group or gang
Context of general public disorder	**Factors indicating lower culpability**
Factors indicating lesser harm	Offence committed on impulse, with limited intrusion into property
Nothing stolen or only property of very low value to the victim (whether economic, sentimental, or personal)	Offender exploited by others
Limited damage or disturbance to property	Mental disorder or learning disability, where linked to the commission of the offence

STEP TWO: Starting point and category range

Having determined the category, the court should use the corresponding starting points to reach a sentence within the category range below. The starting point applies to all offenders irrespective of plea or previous convictions.

Where the defendant is dependent on or has a propensity to misuse drugs and there is sufficient prospect of success, a community order with a drug rehabilitation requirement under section 209 of the Criminal Justice Act 2003 may be a proper alternative to a short or moderate custodial sentence.

A3 Theft, Fraud, and Other Property Offences

Offence Category	Starting Point (*Applicable to all offenders*)	Category Range (*Applicable to all offenders*)
Category 1	3 years' custody	2–6 years' custody
Category 2	1 year's custody	High level community order—2 years' custody
Category 3	High level Community Order	Low level community order—26 weeks' custody

A case of particular gravity, reflected by multiple features of culpability or harm in step 1, could merit upward adjustment from the starting point before further adjustment for aggravating or mitigating features, set out below.

The table below contains a non-exhaustive list of additional factual elements providing the context of the offence and factors relating to the offender. Identify whether any combination of these, or other relevant factors, should result in an upward or downward adjustment from the starting point. **In particular, relevant recent convictions are likely to result in an upward adjustment**. In some cases, having considered these factors, it may be appropriate to move outside the identified category range.

When sentencing **category 2 or 3** offences, the court should also consider the custody threshold as follows:

- has the custody threshold been passed?
- if so, is it unavoidable that a custodial sentence be imposed?
- if so, can that sentence be suspended?

Factors increasing seriousness	Factors reducing seriousness or reflecting personal mitigation
Statutory aggravating factors: Previous convictions, having regard to (a) the nature of the offence to which the conviction relates and its relevance to the current offence; and (b) the time that has elapsed since the conviction* Offence committed whilst on bail **Other aggravating factors include:** Child at home (or returns home) when offence committed Offence committed at night Gratuitous degradation of the victim Any steps taken to prevent the victim reporting the incident or obtaining assistance and/or from assisting or supporting the prosecution	Offender has made voluntary reparation to the victim Subordinate role in a group or gang No previous convictions or no relevant/recent convictions Remorse Good character and/or exemplary conduct Determination and/or demonstration of steps taken to address addiction or offending behaviour Serious medical conditions requiring urgent, intensive, or long-term treatment Age and/or lack of maturity where it affects the responsibility of the offender Lapse of time since the offence where this is not the fault of the offender

Victim compelled to leave their home (in particular victims of domestic violence)	Mental disorder or learning disability, where not linked to the commission of the offence
Established evidence of community impact	Sole or primary carer for dependent relatives
Commission of offence whilst under the influence of alcohol or drugs	
Failure to comply with current court orders	
Offence committed whilst on licence	
Offences taken into consideration (TICs)	

*Where sentencing an offender for a qualifying third domestic burglary, the court must apply section 111 of the Powers of the Criminal Courts (Sentencing) Act 2000 and impose a custodial term of at least three years, unless it is satisfied that there are particular circumstances which relate to any of the offences or to the offender, which would make it unjust to do so.

Additional steps:

Consider any factors which indicate a reduction, such as: assistance to the prosecution; reduction for guilty plea; dangerousness; totality principle; compensation and ancillary orders; reasons; consideration for remand time.

In *R v W* [2010] EWCA Crim 393 the defendant who was 13 years old at the time of the offence, pleaded guilty to attempting to burgle a dwelling house by trying to force entry. He was a persistent offender with previous convictions for burglary; one of which was a dwelling. He was in breach of a community order. The Court of Appeal noted that the Sentencing Council guideline *Overarching Principles— Sentencing Youths* stressed that the length of a custodial sentence must be the shortest commensurate with the seriousness of the offence. A ten-month DTO was replaced by a six-month DTO.

In *R v McInerney* [2002] EWCA Crim 3003 the Court of Appeal commented that, although the statutory minimum sentence for a third dwelling burglary does not apply to a defendant who is under 18 years, a custodial sentence in excess of twenty-four months will be the likely sentence for such an offender.

A3.3.2 Key points

- Entry can be partial: *R v Brown* [1985] Crim LR 212, and can be effected without any part of the body entering the building (eg, cane and hook burglaries).
- Trespass can be committed knowingly or recklessly: *R v Collins* [1973] QB 100.
- 'Dwelling' is not defined. In *R v Lees* [2007] EWCA Crim 94 a new house which was not yet occupied still belonged to the building contractors and was more akin to commercial premises. Whether a property is a dwelling is a factual issue for the court. In contrast, the Public Order Act 1986, s 8 and the Terrorism Act 2000, s 121 each

define a dwelling as a building that is currently occupied or used as a dwelling.

A3.3.3 *Sentencing—Non-dwelling burglary*

There is no sentencing guideline specific to youths. The Sentencing Council guideline *Burglary Offences* gives the following guidance for **adult** offenders:

STEP ONE: Determine the offence category

Category 1	Greater harm **and** higher culpability
Category 2	Greater harm **and** lower culpability **or** lesser harm **and** higher culpability
Category 3	Lesser harm **and** lower culpability

Factors indicating greater harm	Factors indicating higher culpability
Theft of/damage to property causing a significant degree of loss to the victim (whether economic, commercial, or personal value)	Premises or victim deliberately targeted (to include pharmacy or doctor's surgery and targeting due to vulnerability of victim or hostility based on disability, race, sexual orientation, and so forth)
Soiling, ransacking, or vandalism of property.	
Victim on the premises (or returns) while offender present	A significant degree of planning or organization
Trauma to the victim, beyond the normal inevitable consequence of intrusion and theft	Knife or other weapon carried (where not charged separately)
Violence used or threatened against victim	Equipped for burglary (eg, implements carried and/or use of vehicle)
Context of general public disorder	Member of a group or gang

Factors indicating lesser harm	Factors indicating lower culpability
Nothing stolen or only property of very low value to the victim (whether economic, commercial, or personal)	Offence committed on impulse, with limited intrusion into property
Limited damage or disturbance to property	Offender exploited by others
	Mental disorder or learning disability, where linked to the commission of the offence

STEP TWO: Starting point and category range

Offence category	Starting point	Category range
Category 1	2 years' custody	1–5 years' custody
Category 2	18 weeks' custody	Low level community order to Crown Court (51 weeks' custody)
Category 3	Medium level community order	Band B fine to 18 weeks' custody

Factors increasing seriousness	Factors reducing seriousness or reflecting personal mitigation
Statutory aggravating factors: Previous convictions, having regard to (a) the nature of the offence to which the conviction relates and its relevance to the current offence; and (b) the time that has elapsed since the conviction Offence committed whilst on bail **Other aggravating factors include:** Offence committed at night, particularly where staff present or likely to be present Abuse of a position of trust Gratuitous degradation of the victim Any steps taken to prevent the victim reporting the incident or obtaining assistance and/or from assisting or supporting the prosecution Established evidence of community impact Commission of offence whilst under the influence of alcohol or drugs Failure to comply with current court orders Offence committed whilst on licence Offences taken into consideration (TICs)	Offender has made voluntary reparation to the victim Subordinate role in a group or gang No previous convictions or no relevant/recent convictions Remorse Good character and/or exemplary conduct Determination and/or demonstration of steps taken to address addiction or offending behaviour Serious medical conditions requiring urgent, intensive, or long-term treatment Age and/or lack of maturity where it affects the responsibility of the offender Lapse of time since the offence where this is not the fault of the offender Mental disorder or learning disability, where not linked to the commission of the offence Sole or primary carer for dependent relatives

Additional steps:

Consider any factors which indicate a reduction, such as: assistance to the prosecution; reduction for guilty plea; dangerousness; totality principle; compensation and ancillary orders; reasons; consideration for remand time.

A3.3.4 Key points

- 'Building' is not defined save that it may include an inhabited vehicle or vessel: Theft Act 1968 s 9(4).
- 'Building' is 'a structure of considerable size and intended to be permanent or at least endure for a considerable period': *Stevens v Gourley* (1859) CBNS 99. It will include a garden shed or a portakabin.
- A person who goes into part of a building which he is not entitled to enter, as a trespasser, for example behind a counter in a shop, may be a burglar: *R v Walkington* [1979] 1 WLR 1169.

 See *Blackstone's Criminal Practice 2014* **B4.75-B4.96**

A3.4 Aggravated burglary

> **Theft Act 1968 s 10**
>
> (1) A person is guilty of aggravated burglary if he commits any burglary and at the time has with him any firearm or imitation firearm, any weapon of offence, or any explosive; and for this purpose—
>
>   (a) 'firearm' includes an airgun or air pistol, and 'imitation firearm' means anything which has the appearance of being a firearm, whether capable of being discharged or not; and
>
>   (b) 'weapon of offence' means any article made or adapted for use for causing injury to or incapacitating a person, or intended by the person having it with him for such use; and
>
>   (c) 'explosive' means any article manufactured for the purpose of producing a practical effect by explosion, or intended by the person having it with him for that purpose.

IO

DO

GC

 24 month DTO/detention for life in Crown Court

There is no sentencing guideline specific to youths. The Sentencing Council guideline *Burglary Offences—Definitive Guideline* gives the following guidance for **adult** offenders:

STEP ONE: Determining the offence category

Category 1	Greater harm **and** higher culpability
Category 2	Greater harm **and** lower culpability **or** lesser harm **and** higher culpability
Category 3	Lesser harm **and** lower culpability

The court should determine the offence category using the table below.

The court should determine culpability and harm caused or intended, by reference only to the factors below, which comprise the principal factual elements of the offence. Where an offence does not fall squarely into a category, individual factors may require a degree of weighting before making an overall assessment and determining the appropriate offence category.

Factors indicating greater harm	Factors indicating higher culpability
Theft of/damage to property causing a significant degree of loss to the victim (whether economic, commercial, sentimental, or personal value)	Victim or premises deliberately targeted (eg, due to vulnerability or hostility based on disability, race, sexual orientation)
Soiling, ransacking, or vandalism of property	A significant degree of planning or organization
Victim at home or on the premises (or returns) while offender present	Equipped for burglary (for example, implements carried and/or use of vehicle)
Significant physical or psychological injury or other significant trauma to the victim	
Violence used or threatened against victim, particularly involving a weapon	Weapon present on entry
Context of general public disorder	Member of a group or gang
Factors indicating lesser harm	**Factors indicating lower culpability**
No physical or psychological injury or other significant trauma to the victim	Offender exploited by others
No violence used or threatened and a weapon is not produced	Mental disorder or learning disability, where linked to the commission of the offence

STEP TWO: Starting point and category range

Having determined the category, the court should use the corresponding starting points to reach a sentence within the category range below. The starting point applies to all offenders irrespective of plea or previous convictions. A case of particular gravity, reflected by multiple features of culpability or harm in step 1, could merit upward adjustment from the starting point before further adjustment for aggravating or mitigating features, set out below.

Offence Category	Starting Point (*Applicable to all offenders*)	Category Range (*Applicable to all offenders*)
Category 1	10 years' custody	9–13 years' custody
Category 2	6 years' custody	4–9 years' custody
Category 3	2 years' custody	1–4 years' custody

The table below contains a **non-exhaustive** list of additional factual elements providing the context of the offence and factors relating to the offender. Identify whether any combination of these, or other relevant factors, should result in an upward or downward adjustment from the starting point. **In particular, relevant recent convictions are likely to result in an upward adjustment.** In some cases, having considered these factors, it may be appropriate to move outside the identified category range.

A3 Theft, Fraud, and Other Property Offences

Factors increasing seriousness	Factors reducing seriousness or reflecting personal mitigation
Statutory aggravating factors:	Subordinate role in a group or gang
Previous convictions, having regard to (a) the nature of the offence to which the conviction relates and its relevance to the current offence; and (b) the time that has elapsed since the conviction	Injuries caused recklessly
	Nothing stolen or only property of very low value to the victim (whether economic, commercial, sentimental, or personal)
Offence committed whilst on bail	Offender has made voluntary reparation to the victim
Other aggravating factors include:	No previous convictions or no relevant/recent convictions
Child at home (or returns home) when offence committed	Remorse
Offence committed at night	Good character and/or exemplary conduct
Abuse of power and/or position of trust	Determination, and/or demonstration of steps taken to address addiction or offending behaviour
Gratuitous degradation of victim	
Any steps taken to prevent the victim reporting the incident or obtaining assistance and/or from assisting or supporting the prosecution	Serious medical conditions requiring urgent, intensive, or long-term treatment
Victim compelled to leave their home (in particular victims of domestic violence)	Age and/or lack of maturity where it affects the responsibility of the offender
Established evidence of community impact	Lapse of time since the offence where this is not the fault of the offender
Commission of offence whilst under the influence of alcohol or drugs	Mental disorder or learning disability, where not linked to the commission of the offence
Failure to comply with current court orders	
Offence committed whilst on licence	Sole or primary carer for dependent relatives
Offences Taken Into Consideration (TICs)	

A3.5 Found on enclosed premises

Vagrancy Act 1824 s 4(1)

(i) every person wandering abroad and lodging in any barn or outhouse, or in any deserted or unoccupied building, or in the open air, or under a tent, or in any cart or waggon, and not giving a good account of himself or herself; (ii) every person being found in or upon any dwelling house, warehouse, coach-house, stable, or outhouse, or in any inclosed yard, garden, or area, for any unlawful purpose; commits an offence.

 For an adult maximum 3 months imprisonment. No DTO available for a youth.

A3.5.1 *Sentencing*

There are no sentencing guidelines for this offence.

A3.5.2 Key points

- 'Enclosed yard or area' has a restricted meaning and does not include a university campus or buildings: *Akhurst v DPP* (2009) 173 JP 499.
- 'Unlawful purpose' means for the purpose of committing an offence. Hiding from the police is not enough: *L v CPS* [2007] EWHC 1843 (Admin).

 See *Blackstone's Criminal Practice 2014* **B4.96**

A3.6 Demanding money with menaces/blackmail

Theft Act 1968 s 21

(1) A person is guilty of blackmail if, with a view to gain for himself or another or with intent to cause loss to another, he makes any unwarranted demand with menaces; and for this purpose a demand with menaces is unwarranted unless the person making it does so in the belief—
   (a) that he has reasonable grounds for making the demand; and
   (b) that the use of the menaces is a proper means of reinforcing the demand.
(2) The nature of the act or omission demanded is immaterial, and it is also immaterial whether the menaces relate to action to be taken by the person making the demand.

IO

GC

24 month DTO/14 years detention in Crown Court

A3.6.1 *Sentencing*

There are no sentencing guidelines for this offence.

A3.7 Taking conveyance without authority

Theft Act 1968 s 12

(1) Subject to subsections (5) and (6) below, a person shall be guilty of an offence if, without having the consent of the owner or other lawful authority, he takes any conveyance for his own or another's use or knowing that any conveyance has been taken without such authority, drives it or allows himself to be carried in or on it.

...

(6) A person does not commit an offence under this section by anything done in the belief that he has lawful authority to do it or that he would have the owner's consent if the owner knew of his doing it and the circumstances of it.

(7) For purposes of this section—

(a) 'conveyance' means any conveyance constructed or adapted for the carriage of a person or persons whether by land, water or air, except that it does not include a conveyance constructed or adapted for use only under the control of a person not carried in or on it, and 'drive' shall be construed accordingly; and

(b) 'owner', in relation to a conveyance which is the subject of a hiring agreement or hire-purchase agreement, means the person in possession of the conveyance under that agreement.

SO

 6 month DTO Discretionary disqualification

A3.7.1 *Sentencing*

There is no sentencing guideline specific to youths. *The Magistrates' Court Sentencing Guidelines* gives the following guidance for **adult** offenders:

Offence seriousness (culpability and harm) A. Identify the appropriate starting point Starting points based on first-time offender pleading not guilty		
Examples of nature of activity	**Starting point**	**Range**
Exceeding authorized use of, eg employer's or relative's vehicle; retention of hire car beyond return date	Low level community order	Band B fine to medium level community order
As above with damage caused to lock/ ignition; OR Stranger's vehicle involved but no damage caused	Medium level community order	Low level community order to high level community order
Taking vehicle from private premises; OR Causing damage to, eg lock/ignition of stranger's vehicle	High level community order	Medium level community order to 26 weeks' custody

Offence seriousness (culpability and harm) B. Consider the effect of aggravating and mitigating factors (other than those within examples above) The following may be particularly relevant but **these lists are not exhaustive**	
Factors indicating greater degree of harm	**Factor indicating lower culpability**
1. Vehicle later burnt 2. Vehicle belonging to elderly/disabled person 3. Emergency services vehicle 4. Medium to large goods vehicle 5. Passengers carried	1. Misunderstanding with owner **Factor indicating lesser degree of harm** 1. Offender voluntarily returned vehicle to owner

A3.7.2 Key points

This offence is summary only but subject to the following exception in relation to limitation period. The TA 1968 s 12(4A) to (4C) provides:

Theft Act 1968 s 12(4A)–(4C)

(4A) Proceedings for an offence under subsection (1) above (but not proceedings of a kind falling within subsection (4) above) in relation to a mechanically propelled vehicle—
  (a) shall not be commenced after the end of the period of three years beginning with the day on which the offence was committed; but
  (b) subject to that, may be commenced at any time within the period of six months beginning with the relevant day.

(4B) In subsection (4A)(b) above 'the relevant day' means—
  (a) in the case of a prosecution for an offence under subsection (1) above by a public prosecutor, the day on which sufficient evidence to justify the proceedings came to the knowledge of any person responsible for deciding whether to commence any such prosecution;
  (b) in the case of a prosecution for an offence under subsection (1) above which is commenced by a person other than a public prosecutor after the discontinuance of a prosecution falling within paragraph (a) above which relates to the same facts, the day on which sufficient evidence to justify the proceedings came to the knowledge of the person who has decided to commence the prosecution or (if later) the discontinuance of the other prosecution;
  (c) in the case of any other prosecution for an offence under subsection (1) above, the day on which sufficient evidence to justify the proceedings came to the knowledge of the person who has decided to commence the prosecution.

(4C) For the purposes of subsection (4A)(b) above a certificate of a person responsible for deciding whether to commence a prosecution of a kind mentioned in subsection (4B)(a) above as to the date on which such evidence as is mentioned in the certificate came to the knowledge of any person responsible for deciding whether to commence any such prosecution shall be conclusive evidence of that fact.

- By the TA 1968 s 12(7)(a) 'conveyance' means any conveyance constructed or adapted for the carriage of a person or persons whether by land, water, or air, except that it does not include a conveyance constructed or adapted for use only under the control of a person not carried in or on it, and 'drive' shall be construed accordingly. Pedal cycles are excluded from this definition by s 12(5) but see **A3.9** below.
- There must be movement for a vehicle to be taken: *R v Bogacki* [1973] QB 832.
- The vehicle must be taken for use *as* a conveyance—pushing a car around a corner for a practical joke would not be an offence: *R v Stokes* [1983] RTR 59.
- The burden of proving that the defendant did not have a belief that he had the authority of the owner lies on the Crown, once the defendant has raised the issue by evidence: *R v Gannon* [1987] 87 Cr App R 254.
- The belief must exist at the time of the taking: *R v Ambler* [1979] RTR 217.
- The taking must be intentional: *Blayney v Knight* (1974) 60 Cr App R 269.
- In relation to an offence of 'allowing to be carried', being in the vehicle is not enough. There must be be some movement of the vehicle or the engine running: *R v Miller* [1976] Crim LR 417; *R v Diggin* [1980] 72 Cr App R 204.

A3.8 Aggravated vehicle-taking

Theft Act 1968 s 12A(1)–(3)

(1) Subject to subsection (3) below, a person is guilty of aggravated taking of a vehicle if—

    (a) he commits an offence under section 12(1) above (in this section referred to as a 'basic offence') in relation to a mechanically propelled vehicle; and

    (b) it is proved that, at any time after the vehicle was unlawfully taken (whether by him or another) and before it was recovered, the vehicle was driven, or injury or damage was caused, in one or more of the circumstances set out in paragraphs (a) to (d) of subsection (2) below.

(2) The circumstances referred to in subsection (1)(b) above are—

    (a) that the vehicle was driven dangerously on a road or other public place;

    (b) that, owing to the driving of the vehicle, an accident occurred by which injury was caused to any person;

    (c) that, owing to the driving of the vehicle, an accident occurred by which damage was caused to any property, other than the vehicle;

    (d) that damage was caused to the vehicle.

(3) A person is not guilty of an offence under this section if he proves that, as regards any such proven driving, injury or damage as is referred to in subsection (1)(b) above, either—
   (a) the driving, accident, or damage referred to in subsection (2) above occurred before he committed the basic offence; or
   (b) he was neither in nor on nor in the immediate vicinity of the vehicle when that driving, accident, or damage occurred.

SO If aggravating factor is damage to property of less than £5,000 (MCA 1980 s 22 and Sch 2)

EW If aggravating factor is any other than damage to property of less than £5,000

DO If involves an accident which caused the death of any person (CJA 2003 Sch 15).

GC If accident caused the death of any person (s 12A(4))

▥ 6 month DTO (if aggravating factor is damage to property of less than £5,000)

▥ 24 month DTO/14 years detention if accident caused the death of any person. Must endorse and disqualify for at least 12 months. Must disqualify for at least 2 years if offender has had 2 or more disqualifications for periods of 56 days or more in preceding 3 years

A3.8.1 *Sentencing: dangerous driving or accident causing injury*

There is no sentencing guideline specific to youths. *The Magistrates' Court Sentencing Guidelines* gives the following guidance for **adult** offenders:

Offence seriousness (culpability and harm) B. Identify the appropriate starting point Starting points based on first time offender pleading not guilty		
Example of nature of activity	**Starting point**	**Range**
Taken vehicle involved in single incident of bad driving where little or no damage or risk of personal injury	High level community Order	Medium community order to 12 weeks' custody
Taken vehicle involved in incident(s) involving excessive speed or showing off, especially on busy roads or in built-up area	18 weeks' custody	12 to 26 weeks' custody
Taken vehicle involved in prolonged bad driving involving deliberate disregard for safety of other	Crown Court	Crown Court

A3 Theft, Fraud, and Other Property Offences

Offence seriousness (culpability and harm)

B. Consider the effect of aggravating and mitigating factors (other than those within examples above)

The following may be particularly relevant but **these lists are not exhaustive**

Factors indicating higher culpability

1. Disregarding warnings of others
2. Evidence of alcohol or drugs
3. Carrying out other tasks while driving
4. Tiredness
5. Trying to avoid arrest
6. Aggressive driving, such as driving much too close to vehicle in front, inappropriate attempts to overtake, or cutting in after overtaking

Factors indicating greater degree of harm

1. Injury to others
2. Damage to other vehicle or property

A3.8.2 *Sentencing: damage caused*

Offence seriousness (culpability and harm)

A. Identify the appropriate starting point

Starting points based on first-time offender pleading not guilty

Examples of nature of activity	Starting point	Range
Exceeding authorized use of eg employer's or relative's vehicle; retention of hire car beyond return date; minor damage to taken vehicle	Medium level community order	Low level community order to high level community order
Greater damage to taken vehicle and/or moderate damage to another vehicle and/or moderate damage to another vehicle and/or property	High level community order	Medium level community order to 12 weeks' custody
Vehicle taken as part of burglary or from private premises; severe damage	18 weeks' custody	12 to 26 weeks' custody (Crown Court if damage over £5,000)

Offence seriousness (culpability and harm)

B. Consider the effect of aggravating and mitigating factors (other than those within examples above)

The following may be particularly relevant but **these lists are not exhaustive**

Factors indicating higher culpability	Factors indicating lower culpability
1. Vehicle deliberately damaged/destroyed 2. Offender under influence of alcohol/drugs **Factors indicating greater degree of harm** 1. Passenger(s) carried	1. Misunderstanding with owner 2. Damage resulting from actions of another (where this does not provide a defence)

2. Vehicle belonging to elderly or disabled person	
3. Emergency service vehicle	
4. Medium to large goods vehicle	
5. Damage caused in moving traffic accident	

A3.8.3  Key points

- If the aggravating factor is solely damage and the value does not exceed £5,000, the court has limited sentencing powers.
- A magistrates' court can convict a defendant of the alternative offence of vehicle taking if it does not find the aggravating feature(s): *H v Liverpool Youth Court* [2001] Crim LR 897.

See *Blackstone's Criminal Practice 2014* **B4.128–B4.135**

A3.9 Taking or riding pedal cycle without authority

Theft Act 1968 s 12

(2) Subject to subsections (5) and (6) below, a person shall be guilty of an offence if, without having the consent of the owner or other lawful authority, he takes any conveyance for his own or another's use or knowing that any conveyance has been taken without such authority, drives it or allows himself to be carried in or on it.

...

(8) Subsection (1) above shall not apply in relation to pedal cycles; but, subject to subsection (6) below, a person who, without having the consent of the owner or other lawful authority, takes a pedal cycle for his own or another's use, or rides a pedal cycle knowing it to have been taken without such authority, shall on summary conviction be liable to a fine not exceeding level 3 on the standard scale.

(9) A person does not commit an offence under this section by anything done in the belief that he has lawful authority to do it or that he would have the owner's consent if the owner knew of his doing it and the circumstances of it.

 SO

 Fine level 3

A3.9.1 *Sentencing*

There are no sentencing guidelines for this offence.

A3.9.2 `Key points`

- Formal evidence of ownership may not be necessary where it is possible to infer from the facts that the cycle had not been abandoned: *Sturrock v DPP* [1996] RTR 216.

A3.10 **Interference with vehicles**

Criminal Attempts Act 1981 s 9(1)–(2)

(1) A person is guilty of the offence of vehicle interference if he interferes with a motor vehicle or trailer or with anything carried in or on a motor vehicle or trailer with the intention that an offence specified in subsection (2) below shall be committed by himself or some other person.

(2) The offences mentioned in subsection (1) above are—

    (a) theft of the motor vehicle or trailer or part of it;

    (b) theft of anything carried in or on the motor vehicle or trailer; and

    (c) an offence under section 12 (1) of the Theft Act 1968 (taking and driving away without consent);

and, if it is shown that a person accused of an offence under this section intended that one of those offences should be committed, it is immaterial that it cannot be shown which it was.

`SO`

 For an adult maximum 3 months imprisonment. No DTO available for a youth.

A3.10.1 *Sentencing*

There is no sentencing guideline specific to youths. *The Magistrates' Court Sentencing Guidelines* gives the following guidance for **adult** offenders:

Offence seriousness (culpability and harm)		
A. Identify the appropriate starting point		
Starting points based on first-time offender pleading not guilty		
Examples of nature of activity	**Starting point**	**Range**
Trying door handles; no entry gained to vehicle; no damage caused	Band C fine	Band A fine to low level community order
Entering vehicle, little or no damage caused	Medium level community order	Band C fine to high level community order
Entering vehicle, with damage caused	High level community order	Medium level community order to 12 weeks' custody

Offence seriousness (culpability and harm) B. Consider the effect of aggravating and mitigating factors (other than those within examples above) The following may be particularly relevant but **these lists are not exhaustive**	
Factor indicating higher culpability	
1. Targeting vehicle in dark/isolated location	
Factors indicating greater degree of harm 1. Emergency services vehicle 2. Disabled driver's vehicle 3. Part of series	

A3.10.2 Key points

• There must be interference and intention. Interference is not defined. Looking into cars is probably not enough to found the offence. As to whether touching the door handle is sufficient see *Reynolds and Warren v Metropolitan Police* [1982] Crim LR 831.

 See *Blackstone's Criminal Practice 2014* **B4.137–B4.140**

A3.11 Going equipped

Theft Act 1968 s 25

(1) A person shall be guilty of an offence if, when not at his place of abode, he has with him any article for use in the course of or in connection with any burglary or theft.
(2) A person guilty of an offence under this section shall on conviction on indictment be liable to imprisonment for a term not exceeding three years.
(3) Where a person is charged with an offence under this section, proof that he had with him any article made or adapted for use in committing a burglary or theft shall be evidence that he had it with him for such use.
(4) ...
(5) For purposes of this section an offence under section 12 (1) of this Act of taking a conveyance shall be treated as theft.

EW

 24 month DTO

A3.11.1 *Sentencing*

There is no sentencing guideline specific to youths. *The Magistrates' Court Sentencing Guidelines* gives the following guidance for **adult** offenders:

A3 Theft, Fraud, and Other Property Offences

Offence seriousness (culpability and harm) A. Identify the appropriate starting point Starting points based on first-time offender pleading not guilty		
Examples of nature of activity	**Starting point**	**Range**
Possession of items for theft from shop or of vehicle	Medium level community order	Band C fine to high level community order
Possession of items for burglary, robbery	High level community order	Medium level community order to Crown Court

Offence seriousness (culpability and harm) B. Consider the effect of aggravating and mitigating factors (other than those within examples above) The following may be particularly relevant but **these lists are not exhaustive**	
Factors indicating higher culpability 1. Circumstances suggest offender equipped for particularly serious offence 2. Items to conceal identity	

A3.11.2 Key points

- The article need not be intended for immediate use but it must be intended for future use: *R v Ellames* [1974] 1 WLR 1391.
- Proof of intent is required and not mere contemplation of an offence: *R v Hargreaves* [1985] Crim LR 243.
- 'Has with him' implies a degree of immediate control. Having an item on the person, in a bag or car is sufficient: *R v Kelt* [1977] 1 WLR 1365.

 See *Blackstones Criminal Practice 2014* **B4.151–B4.159**

A3.12 Handling stolen goods

Theft Act 1968 s 22 (1)

(1) A person handles stolen goods if (otherwise than in the course of the stealing) knowing or believing them to be stolen goods he dishonestly receives the goods, or dishonestly undertakes or assists in their retention, removal, disposal or realisation by or for the benefit of another person, or if he arranges to do so.

 EW

 GC

 24 month DTO/14 years detention in Crown Court

EW Either Way   **GC** Grave Crime   Sentence

A3.12.1 *Sentencing*

There is no sentencing guideline specific to youths. *The Magistrates' Court Sentencing Guidelines* gives the following guidance for **adult** offenders:

Offence seriousness (culpability and harm) A. Identify the appropriate starting point Starting points based on first-time offender pleading not guilty		
Examples of nature of activity	**Starting point**	**Range**
Property worth £1,000 or less acquired for offender's own use	Band B fine	Band B fine to low level community order
Property worth £1,000 or less acquired for resale; or property worth more than £1,000 acquired for offender's own use; or presence of at least one aggravating factor listed below—regardless of value	Medium level community order	Low level community order to 12 weeks' custody Note: the custody threshold is likely to be passed if the offender has a record of dishonesty offences
Sophisticated offending; or presence of at least two aggravating factors listed below	12 weeks' custody	6 weeks' custody to Crown Court
Offence committed in context of Offender Acts as organizer/distributor of proceeds of crime; or offender makes self available to other criminals as willing to handle the proceeds of thefts or burglaries; or offending highly organized, professional; or particularly serious original offence, such as armed robbery	Crown Court	Crown Court

Offence seriousness (culpability and harm) B. Consider the effect of aggravating and mitigating factors (other than those within examples above) The following may be particularly relevant but **these lists are not exhaustive**	
Factors indicating higher culpability	**Factors indicating lower culpability**
1. Closeness of offender to primary offence. Closeness may be geographical, arising from presence at or near the primary offence when it was committed, or temporal, where the handler instigated or encouraged the primary offence beforehand, or, soon after, provided a safe haven or route or disposal 2. High level of profit made or expected by offender	1. Little or no benefit to offender 2. Voluntary restitution to victim **Factor indicating lower degree of harm** 1. Low value of goods

Factors indicating greater degree of harm	
1. Seriousness of the primary offence, including domestic burglary	
2. High value of goods to victim, including sentimental value	
3. Threats of violence or abuse of power by offender over others, such as an adult commissioning criminal activity by children, or a drug dealer pressurizing addicts to steal in order to pay for their habit	

A3.12.2 Key points

- Mere suspicion that goods are stolen will not suffice.
- In *R v Hall* [1985] 81 Cr App R 260, belief was said to be present when someone thought: 'I cannot say for certain that those goods are stolen, but there can be no other reasonable conclusion in the light of all the circumstances of all I have heard and seen.' Similarly, if the person admits that 'my brain is telling me [they are stolen] despite what I have heard'.
- If the defendant argues that he has paid an adequate consideration for the goods, it is for the prosecution to disprove: *Hogan v Director of Public Prosecutions* [2007] EWHC 978 (Admin).

 See *Blackstones Criminal Practice 2014* **B4.160–B4.186**

A3.13 Acquisition, use, or possession of criminal property

Proceeds of Crime Act 2002 ss 327–9

327 Concealing etc

(1) A person commits an offence if he—
   (a) conceals criminal property;
   (b) disguises criminal property;
   (c) converts criminal property;
   (d) transfers criminal property;
   (e) removes criminal property from England and Wales or from Scotland or from Northern Ireland.

(2) But a person does not commit such an offence if—
   (a) he makes an authorised disclosure under section 338 and (if the disclosure is made before he does the act mentioned in subsection (1)) he has the appropriate consent;
   (b) he intended to make such a disclosure but had a reasonable excuse for not doing so;
   (c) the act he does is done in carrying out a function he has relating to the enforcement of any provision of this Act or of any other enactment relating to criminal conduct or benefit from criminal conduct.
(3) Concealing or disguising criminal property includes concealing or disguising its nature, source, location, disposition, movement, or ownership or any rights with respect to it.

328 Arrangements

(1) A person commits an offence if he enters into or becomes concerned in an arrangement which he knows or suspects facilitates (by whatever means) the acquisition, retention, use or control of criminal property by or on behalf of another person.
(2) But a person does not commit such an offence if—
   (a) he makes an authorised disclosure under section 338 and (if the disclosure is made before he does the act mentioned in subsection (1)) he has the appropriate consent;
   (b) he intended to make such a disclosure but had a reasonable excuse for not doing so;
   (c) the act he does is done in carrying out a function he has relating to the enforcement of any provision of this Act or of any other enactment relating to criminal conduct or benefit from criminal conduct.

329 Acquisition, use and possession

(1) A person commits an offence if he—
   (a) acquires criminal property;
   (b) uses criminal property;
   (c) has possession of criminal property.
(2) But a person does not commit such an offence if—
   (a) he makes an authorised disclosure under section 338 and (if the disclosure is made before he does the act mentioned in subsection (1)) he has the appropriate consent;
   (b) he intended to make such a disclosure but had a reasonable excuse for not doing so;
   (c) he acquired or used or had possession of the property for adequate consideration;
   (d) the act he does is done in carrying out a function he has relating to the enforcement of any provision of this Act or of any other enactment relating to criminal conduct or benefit from criminal conduct.
(3) For the purposes of this section—
   (a) a person acquires property for inadequate consideration if the value of the consideration is significantly less than the value of the property;
   (b) a person uses or has possession of property for inadequate consideration if the value of the consideration is significantly less than the value of the use or possession;

> (c) the provision by a person of goods or services which he knows or suspects may help another to carry out criminal conduct is not consideration.

 24 month DTO/14 years detention in Crown Court

A3.13.1 *Sentencing*

There are no sentencing guidelines for this offence. The sentencing authorities were reviewed in *R v Greaves* [2010] EWCA Crim 709.

A3.13.2 Key points

- The critical definitions for these offences are contained in the Proceeds of Crime Act 2002 s 340:

Proceeds of Crime Act 2002 s 340

340 Interpretation

(1) This section applies for the purposes of this Part.

(2) Criminal conduct is conduct which—
  (a) constitutes an offence in any part of the United Kingdom, or
  (b) would constitute an offence in any part of the United Kingdom if it occurred there.

(3) Property is criminal property if—
  (a) it constitutes a person's benefit from criminal conduct or it represents such a benefit (in whole or part and whether directly or indirectly), and
  (b) the alleged offender knows or suspects that it constitutes or represents such a benefit.

(4) It is immaterial—
  (a) who carried out the conduct;
  (b) who benefited from it;
  (c) whether the conduct occurred before or after the passing of this Act.

(5) A person benefits from conduct if he obtains property as a result of or in connection with the conduct.

(6) If a person obtains a pecuniary advantage as a result of or in connection with conduct, he is to be taken to obtain as a result of or in connection with the conduct a sum of money equal to the value of the pecuniary advantage.

(7) References to property or a pecuniary advantage obtained in connection with conduct include references to property or a pecuniary advantage obtained in both that connection and some other.

(8) If a person benefits from conduct his benefit is the property obtained as a result of or in connection with the conduct.

(9) Property is all property wherever situated and includes—

(a) money;
(b) all forms of property, real or personal, heritable or moveable;
(c) things in action and other intangible or incorporeal property.

- There must be an intent or suspicion that there is a benefit from criminal conduct for there to be criminal property.
- In *Wilkinson v DPP* [2006] EWHC 3012 (Admin) the court discouraged the use of this offence (with its requirement only for suspicion rather than belief) when a handling charge would adequately have reflected the seriousness of the offence.
- For there to be an offence there must be actual criminal conduct and the proceeds must already be the product of that crime: *R v Gabriel* [2006] EWCA Crim 229.

There are two ways that the Crown can prove the property derives from crime: (a) by showing that it derives from criminal conduct of a specific kind; or (b) by proving that the circumstances in which it was handled create an irresistible inference that it can only have derived from crime: *R v Anwoir* [2008] EWCA Crim 1354.

 See *Blackstones Criminal Practice 2014* **B.21**

A3.14 Fraud by misrepresentation

Fraud Act 2006 ss 1(1)–(2), 2, 3, 4 and 5

1 Fraud

(1) A person is guilty of fraud if he is in breach of any of the sections listed in subsection (2) (which provide for different ways of committing the offence).

(2) The sections are—
    (a) section 2 (fraud by false representation),
    (b) section 3 (fraud by failing to disclose information), and
    (c) section 4 (fraud by abuse of position).

2 Fraud by false representation

(1) A person is in breach of this section if he—
    (a) dishonestly makes a false representation, and
    (b) intends, by making the representation—
        (i) to make a gain for himself or another, or
        (ii) to cause loss to another or to expose another to a risk of loss.

(2) A representation is false if—
    (a) it is untrue or misleading, and
    (b) the person making it knows that it is, or might be, untrue or misleading.

A3 Theft, Fraud, and Other Property Offences

(3) 'Representation' means any representation as to fact or law, including a representation as to the state of mind of—
   (a) the person making the representation, or
   (b) any other person.
(4) A representation may be express or implied.
(5) For the purposes of this section a representation may be regarded as made if it (or anything implying it) is submitted in any form to any system or device designed to receive, convey or respond to communications (with or without human intervention).

3 Fraud by failing to disclose information

(1) A person is in breach of this section if he—
   (a) dishonestly fails to disclose to another person information which he is under a legal duty to disclose, and
   (b) intends, by failing to disclose the information—
      (i) to make a gain for himself or another, or
      (ii) to cause loss to another or to expose another to a risk of loss.

4 Fraud by abuse of position

(1) A person is in breach of this section if he—
   (a) occupies a position in which he is expected to safeguard, or not to act against, the financial interests of another person,
   (b) dishonestly abuses that position, and
   (c) intends, by means of the abuse of that position—
      (i) to make a gain for himself or another, or
      (ii) to cause loss to another or to expose another to a risk of loss.
(2) A person may be regarded as having abused his position even though his conduct consisted of an omission rather than an act.

5 'Gain' and 'loss'.

(1) The references to gain and loss in sections 2 to 4 are to be read in accordance with this section.
(2) 'Gain' and 'loss'—.
   (a) extend only to gain or loss in money or other property;
   (b) include any such gain or loss whether temporary or permanent;
   and 'property' means any property whether real or personal (including things in action and other intangible property).
(3) 'Gain' includes a gain by keeping what one has, as well as a gain by getting what one does not have.
(4) 'Loss' includes a loss by not getting what one might get, as well as a loss by parting with what one has.

EW

 24 month DTO

EW Either Way   Sentence

A3.14.1 *Sentencing*

There is no sentencing guideline specific to youths. The definitive guideline *Sentencing for Fraud–Statutory Offences* gives the following guidance for **adult** offenders:

CONFIDENCE FRAUD

Value of property or consequential loss				
Nature of offence	£500,000 or more *Starting point based on: £750,000**	£100,000 or more and less than £500,000 *Starting point based on: £300,000**	£20,000 or more and less than £100,000 *Starting point based on: £60,000**	Less than £20,000 *Starting point based on: £10,000**
Large-scale advance fee fraud or other confidence fraud involving the deliberate targeting of a large number of vulnerable victims	**Starting point:** 6 years' custody **Range:** 5–8 years' custody	**Starting point:** 5 years' custody **Range:** 4–7 years' custody	**Starting point:** 4 years' custody **Range:** 3–6 years' custody	**Starting point:** 3 years' custody **Range:** 2–5 years' custody
Lower-scale advance fee fraud or other confidence fraud characterized by a degree of planning and/or multiple transactions	**Starting point:** 5 years' custody **Range:** 4–7 years' custody	**Starting point:** 4 years' custody **Range:** 3–6 years' custody	**Starting point:** 3 years' custody **Range:** 2–5 years' custody	**Starting point:** 18 months' custody **Range:** 26 weeks'–3 years' custody
Single fraudulent transaction confidence fraud involving targeting of a vulnerable victim			**Starting point:** 26 weeks' custody **Range:** Community order (HIGH)—18 months' custody	**Starting point:** 6 weeks' custody **Range:** Community order (MEDIUM)—26 weeks' custody
Single fraudulent transaction confidence fraud not targeting a vulnerable victim, and involving no or limited planning			**Starting point:** 12 weeks' custody **Range:** Community order (MEDIUM)—36 weeks' custody	**Starting point:** Community order (MEDIUM) **Range:** Fine–6 weeks' custody

*Where the actual amount is greater or smaller than the figure on which the starting point is based, that is likely to be one of the factors that will move the sentence within the range (see paragraph 6 [above]).

A3 Theft, Fraud, and Other Property Offences

Additional aggravating factors	Additional mitigating factors
1. Number involved in the offence and role of the offender 2. Offending carried out over a significant period of time 3. Use of another person's identity 4. Offence has a lasting effect on the victim	1. Peripheral involvement 2. Behaviour not fraudulent from the outset 3. Misleading or inaccurate advice

The presence of one or more aggravating factors may indicate a more severe sentence within the suggested range while the presence of one or more mitigating factors may indicate a less severe sentence within the suggested range.

The presence of aggravating or mitigating factors of exceptional significance may indicate that the case should move to a higher or lower level of seriousness.

BANKING AND INSURANCE FRAUD, AND OBTAINING CREDIT THROUGH FRAUD

Nature of offence	Amount obtained or intended to be obtained				
	£500,000 or more ***Starting point based on: £750,000***	£100,000 or more and less than £500,000 ***Starting point based on: £300,000****	£20,000 or more and less than £100,000 ***Starting point based on: £60,000****	£5,000 or more and less than £20,000 ***Starting point based on: £12,500****	Less than £5,000 ***Starting point based on: £2,500****
Fraudulent from the outset, professionally planned **and either** fraud carried out over a significant period of time **or** multiple frauds	**Starting point:** 5 years' custody **Range:** 4–7 years' custody	**Starting point:** 4 years' custody **Range:** 3–5 years' custody	**Starting point:** 2 years' custody **Range:** 18 months–3 years' custody		
Fraudulent from the outset **and either** fraud carried out over a significant period of time **or** multiple frauds	**Starting point:** 4 years' custody **Range:** 3–7 years' custody	**Starting point:** 3 years' custody **Range:** 2–4 years' custody	**Starting point:** 15 months' custody **Range:** 18 weeks'–30 months' custody	**Starting point:** 12 weeks' custody **Range:** Community order (HIGH)–12 months' custody	**Starting point:** Community order (HIGH) **Range:** Community order (LOW)–6 weeks' custody

Not fraudulent from the outset **and either** fraud carried out over a significant period of time **or** multiple frauds	**Starting point:** 3 years' custody **Range:** 2–6 years' custody	**Starting point:** 2 years' custody **Range:** 12 months'–3 years' custody	**Starting point:** 36 weeks' custody **Range:** 12 weeks'–18 months' custody	**Starting point:** 6 weeks' custody **Range:** Community order (MEDIUM) –26 weeks' custody	**Starting point:** Community order (MEDIUM) **Range:** Community order (HIGH)
Single fraudulent transaction, fraudulent from the outset			**Starting point:** 26 weeks' custody **Range:** 6 weeks'–12 months' custody	**Starting point:** Community order (HIGH) **Range:** Fine–18 weeks' custody	**Starting point:** Community order (LOW) **Range:** Fine– Community order (MEDIUM)
Single fraudulent transaction, not fraudulent from the outset			**Starting point:** 12 weeks' custody **Range:** Community order (MEDIUM) –36 weeks' custody	**Starting point:** Community order (MEDIUM) **Range:** Fine–6 weeks' custody	**Starting point:** Fine **Range:** Fine– Community order (LOW)

*Where the actual amount is greater or smaller than the figure on which the starting point is based, that is likely to be one of the factors that will move the sentence within the range (see paragraph 4 [above]).

Additional aggravating factors	Additional mitigating factors
1. Number involved in the offence and role of the offender 2. Use of another person's identity	1. Peripheral involvement 2. Misleading or incomplete advice

The presence of one or more aggravating factors may indicate a more severe sentence within the suggested range while the presence of one or more mitigating factors may indicate a less severe sentence within the suggested range.

The presence of aggravating or mitigating factors of exceptional significance may indicate that the case should move to a higher or lower level of seriousness.

 See *Blackstone's Criminal Practice 2014* **B5.4–B5.20**

A3.15 Possession or making of articles for use in fraud

Possessing item for use in fraud.

> ### Fraud Act 2006 s 6
>
> A person is guilty of an offence if he has in his possession or under his control any article for use in the course of or in connection with any fraud.

EW

 24 month DTO

A3.15.1 *Making, adapting, supplying, or offering to supply articles for fraud*

> ### Fraud Act 2006 s 7
>
> (1) A person is guilty of an offence if he makes, adapts, supplies or offers to supply any article—
>
> (a) knowing that it is designed or adapted for use in the course of or in connection with fraud, or intending it to be used to commit, or assist in the commission of, fraud.

EW

 24 month DTO

A3.15.2 *Sentencing*

There is no sentencing guideline specific to youths. *The Magistrates' Court Sentencing Guidelines* gives the following guidance for **adult** offenders:

Nature of offence	Type of offence	
	Making or adapting (ss 1 or 7) **or** Supplying or offering to supply (s 7)	Possessing (s 6)
Article(s) intended for use in an extensive and skilfully planned fraud	**Starting point:** 4 years' custody **Range:** 2–7 years' custody	**Starting point:** 36 weeks' custody **Range:** 6 weeks'–2 years' custody
Article(s) intended for use in a less extensive and less skilfully planned fraud	**Starting point:** 26 weeks' custody **Range:** Community order (HIGH)–2 years' custody	**Starting point:** Community order (MEDIUM) **Range:** Community order (LOW)–26 weeks' custody

Additional aggravating factors	Additional mitigating factors
1. Number involved in the offence and role of the offender 2. Offending carried out over a significant period of time 3. Use of another person's identity 4. Offence has a lasting effect on the victim	1. Peripheral involvement

The presence of one or more aggravating factors may indicate a more severe sentence within the suggested range while the presence of one or more mitigating factors may indicate a less severe sentence within the suggested range.

The presence of aggravating or mitigating factors of exceptional significance may indicate that the case should move to a higher or lower level of seriousness.

A3.15.3 Key points

• 'Article' includes any programme or data held in electronic form: Fraud Act, s 8.

See *Blackstone's Criminal Practice 2014* **B5.23–B5.24**

A3.16 Obtaining services dishonestly

Fraud Act 2006 s 11(1)–(2)

(1) A person is guilty of an offence under this section if he obtains services for himself or another—

    (a) by a dishonest act, and

    (b) in breach of subsection (2).

(2) A person obtains services in breach of this subsection if—

    (a) they are made available on the basis that payment has been, is being or will be made for or in respect of them,

    (b) he obtains them without any payment having been made for or in respect of them or without payment having been made in full, and

    (c) when he obtains them, he knows—

        (i) that they are being made available on the basis described in paragraph (a), or

        (ii) that they might be,

but intends that payment will not be made, or will not be made in full.

24 month DTO

A3.16.1 *Sentencing*

The offence of *obtaining services dishonestly* may be committed in circumstances that otherwise could be charged as an offence contrary to the Fraud Act 2006, s 1 or may be more akin to *making off without payment*, contrary to the Theft Act 1978, s 3. For this reason, it has not been included specifically within any of the guidelines for fraud, and one of the following approaches should be used:

- where it involves conduct which can be characterized as a fraud offence (such as obtaining credit through fraud or payment card fraud), the court should apply the guideline for the relevant type of fraud (see **A3.14**); or

- where the conduct could be characterized as *making off without payment* (ie where an offender, knowing that payment on the spot for any goods supplied or service done is required or expected, dishonestly makes off without having paid and with intent to avoid payment), the guideline for that offence should be used (see **A3.17**).

 See *Blackstone's Criminal Practice 2014* **B5.28–B5.33**

A3.17 Making off without payment

Theft Act 1978 s 3

(1) Subject to subsection (3) below, a person who, knowing that payment on the spot for any goods supplied or service done is required or expected from him, dishonestly makes off without having paid as required or expected and with intent to avoid payment of the amount due shall be guilty of an offence.

(2) For purposes of this section 'payment on the spot' includes payment at the time of collecting goods on which work has been done or in respect of which service has been provided.

(3) Subsection (1) above shall not apply where the supply of the goods or the doing of the service is contrary to law, or where the service done is such that payment is not legally enforceable.

▦ 24 month DTO

A3.17.1 *Sentencing*

There is no sentencing guideline specific to youths. *The Magistrates' Court Sentencing Guidelines* gives the following guidance for **adult** offenders:

Offence seriousness (culpability and harm) A. Identify the appropriate starting point Starting points based on first-time offender pleading not guilty		
Examples of nature of activity	**Starting point**	**Range**
Single offence committed by an offender acting alone with evidence of little or no planning, goods, or services worth less than £200	Band C fine	Band A fine to high level community order
Offence displaying one or more of the following: —offender acting in unison with others —evidence of planning —offence part of a 'spree' —intimidation of victim —goods or services worth £200 or more	Medium level community order	Low level community order to 12 weeks' custody

A3.17.2 Key points

• The intention to avoid making payment means a permanent intention not to pay, so a person who genuinely disputes a bill and challenges someone to bring legal action, cannot be said to have committed an offence.

 See *Blackstones Criminal Practice 2014* **B5.34–B5.41**

A3.18 Railway fare evasion

Regulation of Railways Act 1889 s 5(1) and (3)

Penalty for avoiding payment of fare

(1) Every passenger by a railway shall, on request by an officer or servant of a railway company, either produce, and if so requested deliver up, a ticket showing that his fare is paid, or pay his fare from the place whence he started, or give the officer or servant his name and address; and in case of default shall be liable on summary conviction to a fine not exceeding ~~level 1 on the standard scale~~ level 2 on the standard scale.

(2) . . .[]

(3) If any person—

  (a) Travels or attempts to travel on a railway without having previously paid his fare, and with intent to avoid payment thereof; or

  (b) Having paid his fare for a certain distance, knowingly and wilfully proceeds by train beyond that distance without previously paying the additional fare for the additional distance, and with intent to avoid payment thereof; or

  (c) Having failed to pay his fare, gives in reply to a request by an officer of a railway company a false name or address,

he shall be liable on summary conviction to a fine not exceeding ~~level 2 on the standard scale~~ level 3 on the standard scale, or, in the case of a second or subsequent offence, either to a fine not exceeding ~~level 2 on the standard scale~~ level 3 on the standard scale, or in the discretion of the court to imprisonment for a term not exceeding three months.

 For an adult maximum 3 months imprisonment s5 (3); level 2 fine s 5 (1). No DTO available for a youth

A3.18.1 *Sentencing*

There is no sentencing guideline specific to youths. *The Magistrates' Court Sentencing Guidelines* gives the following guidance for **adult** offenders:

Offence seriousness (culpability and harm) A. Identify the appropriate starting point Starting points based on first-time offender pleading not guilty		
Examples of nature of activity	**Starting point**	**Range**
Failing to produce ticket or pay fare on request	Band A fine	Conditional discharge to band B fine
Travelling on railway without having paid the fare or knowingly and wilfully travelling beyond the distance paid for, with intent to avoid payment	Band B fine	Band A fine to band C fine

Offence seriousness (culpability and harm) B. Consider the effect of aggravating and mitigating factors (other than those within examples above) The following may be particularly relevant but **these lists are not exhaustive**	
Factor indicating higher culpability 1. Offensive or intimidating language or behaviour towards railway staff **Factor indicating greater degree of harm** 1. High level of loss caused or intended to be caused	

A4 **Damage to Property**

A4.1 Definitions and defences

'**Property**' is defined in the Criminal Damage Act 1971 s 10:

> ### Criminal Damage Act 1971, s 10
>
> (1) In this Act 'property' means of a tangible nature, whether real or personal, including money and—
>   (a) including wild creatures which have been tamed or are ordinarily kept in captivity, and any other wild creatures or their carcasses if, but only if, they have been reduced into possession which has not been lost or abandoned or are in the course of being reduced into possession; but
>   (b) not including mushrooms growing wild on any land or flowers, fruit or foliage of a plant growing wild on any land.

Ownership is dealt with in the Criminal Damage Act 1971 s 10:

> ### Criminal Damage Act 1971, s 10
>
> (2) Property shall be treated for the purposes of this Act as belonging to any person—
>   (a) having the custody or control of it;
>   (b) having in it any proprietary right or interest (not being an equitable interest arising only from an agreement to transfer or grant an interest); or
>   (c) having a charge on it.
> (3) Where property is subject to a trust, the persons to whom it belongs shall be so treated as including any person having a right to enforce the trust.
> (4) Property of a corporation sole shall be so treated as belonging to the corporation notwithstanding a vacancy in the corporation.

It is an offence to damage property which is jointly owned: *Seray-Wurie v DPP* [2012] EWHC 208 (Admin).

'**Damage**' is not defined. It is not limited to permanent damage and includes circumstances where the damage can be removed, such as graffiti. If expense or inconvenience is involved in putting right the matter then damage will have been caused, for example erasing computer programmes: *Cox v Riley* (1986) 83 Cr App R 54. Spitting on a police officer's uniform is unlikely to cause damage: *A v R* [1978] Crim LR 689. The soaking of a blanket and the flooding of the floor of a police cell was held to amount to damage in *R v Fiak* [2005] EWCA Crim 2381, as was the daubing of water-soluble paint on a pavement: *Hardman v Chief Constable of Avon and Somerset* [1986] Crim LR 330.

Determining whether something has been damaged is a matter of fact and degree to be determined by the magistrates or jury: *Roe v Kingerlee* [1986] Crim LR 735.

The Act provides for a defence of **lawful excuse**. It is defined in section 5:

Criminal Damage Act 1971, s 5(2)–(5)

(2) A person charged with an offence to which this section applies, shall, whether or not he would be treated for the purposes of this Act as having a lawful excuse apart from this subsection, be treated for those purposes as having a lawful excuse—

    (a) if at the time of the act or acts alleged to constitute the offence he believed that the person or persons whom he believed to be entitled to consent to the destruction of or damage to the property in question had so consented, or would have so consented to it if he or they had known of the destruction or damage and its circumstances; or

    (b) if he destroyed or damaged or threatened to destroy or damage the property in question or, in the case of a charge of an offence under section 3 above, intended to use or cause or permit the use of something to destroy or damage it, in order to protect property belonging to himself or another or a right or interest in property which was or which he believed to be vested in himself or another, and at the time of the act or acts alleged to constitute the offence he believed—

        (i) that the property, right or interest was in immediate need of protection; and

        (ii) that the means of protection adopted or proposed to be adopted were or would be reasonable having regard to all the circumstances.

(3) For the purposes of this section it is immaterial whether a belief is justified or not if it is honestly held.

(4) For the purposes of subsection (2) above a right or interest in property includes any right or privilege in or over land, whether created by grant, licence or otherwise.

(5) This section shall not be construed as casting doubt on any defence recognised by law as a defence to criminal charges.

This does not apply to the aggravated form of the offence under s 1(2).

- The defence of lawful excuse may apply to a belief in consent or a belief in the immediate necessity to protect property.
- The test is subjective; whether the belief is honestly held not whether it is justified or reasonable. A person can avail himself of the defence of lawful excuse notwithstanding the fact that he was intoxicated: *Jaggard v Dickinson* (1981) 72 Cr App R 33. However, whether a person is acting to protect property has an objective element: *R v Hunt* (1977) 66 Cr App R 105.
- There is no definition of 'recklessness'. However, the prosecution will have proved that the defendant was reckless if, having regard to

all the available evidence the court is sure: first, that he was aware of a risk that property would be destroyed/damaged; and secondly that in the circumstances which were known to him it was unreasonable for him to take that risk.

- This test allows for some of the personal characteristics of a defendant to be taken into account: *R v G* [2003] UKHL 50.

A4.2 Destroying or damaging property

Criminal Damage Act 1971, s 1

(1) A person who without lawful excuse destroys or damages any property belonging to another intending to destroy or damage any such property or being reckless as to whether any such property would be destroyed or damaged shall be guilty of an offence.

SO If value does not exceed £5,000 (MCA 1980 s 22 and Sch 2)

EW If value exceeds £5,000

░░ If value does not exceed £5,000—maximum penalty for an adult is 3 months imprisonment. No DTO available for a youth (see **A4.2.1** below)

░░ If value exceeds £5,000—24 month DTO

Racially or religiously aggravated criminal damage: Crime and Disorder Act 1998, s 30

EW

GC

░░ 24 month DTO/14 years detention in Crown Court

For the meaning of 'racially or religiously aggravated' see **F19**.

A4.2.1 *Sentencing*

As the maximum custodial sentence for an adult is a term of three months' imprisonment, a youth convicted of criminal damage to the value of less than £5,000 is not liable to a detention and training order in the youth court: *Pye v Leeds Youth Court* [2006] EWHC 2527 (Admin).

There is no sentencing guideline specific to youths. The *Magistrates' Court Sentencing Guidelines* give the following guidance for **adult** offenders:

Offence seriousness (culpability and harm) A. Identify the appropriate starting point Starting points based on first-time offender pleading not guilty		
Examples of nature of activity	Starting point	Range
Minor damage, eg breaking small window; small amount of graffiti	Band B fine	Conditional discharge to band C fine
Moderate damage, eg breaking large plate-glass or shop window; widespread graffiti	Low level community order	Band C fine to medium level community order
Significant damage up to £5,000, eg damage caused as part of a spree	High level community order	Medium level community order to 12 weeks' custody
Damage between £5,000 and £10,000	12 weeks' custody	6 to 26 weeks' custody
Damage over £10,000	Crown Court	Crown Court

Offence seriousness (culpability and harm) B. Consider the effect of aggravating and mitigating factors (other than those within examples above) The following may be particularly relevant but these lists are not exhaustive	
Factors indicating higher culpability 1. Revenge attack 2. Targeting vulnerable victim Factors indicating greater degree of harm 1. Damage to emergency equipment 2. Damage to public amenity 3. Significant public or private fear caused, eg in domestic context	Factors indicating lower culpability 1. Damage caused recklessly 2. Provocation

A4.3 Aggravated criminal damage

Criminal Damage Act 1971 s 1(2)

(2) A person who without lawful excuse destroys or damages any property, whether belonging to himself or another—
  (a) intending to destroy or damage any property or being reckless as to whether any property would be destroyed or damaged; and

> (b) intending by the destruction or damage to endanger the life of another or being reckless as to whether the life of another would be thereby endangered; shall be guilty of an offence.

 IO

 DO

 GC

24 month DTO/detention for life in Crown Court

A4.3.1 *Sentencing*

There are no sentencing guidelines for this offence.

In *R v T* [2010] 1 Cr App R (S) 377 young persons aged 16, 15, and 13 had been sentenced to four years, three years, and two years. They had thrown stones and bricks at vehicles. Eleven vehicles were damaged and an accident occurred in which two vehicles collided and one of the drivers was killed. The sentences were upheld.

A4.3.2 Key points

- The defence of 'lawful excuse' under the Criminal Damage Act 1971, s 5 does not apply for an offence under section 2(b).

A4.4 Arson

Criminal Damage Act 1971, s 1

(1) A person who without lawful excuse destroys or damages any property belonging to another intending to destroy or damage any such property or being reckless as to whether any such property would be destroyed or damaged shall be guilty of an offence.

(2) ... []

(3) An offence committed under this section by destroying or damaging property by fire shall be charged as arson.

 EW

 DO

 GC

24 month DTO/detention for life in Crown Court

A4.4.1 *Sentencing*

There is no sentencing guideline specific to youths. The *Magistrates' Court Sentencing Guidelines* give the following guidance for **adult** offenders:

Offence seriousness (culpability and harm)		
A. Identify the appropriate starting point		
Starting points based on first-time offender pleading not guilty		
Examples of nature of activity	**Starting point**	**Range**
Minor damage by fire	High level community order	Medium level community order to 12 weeks' custody
Moderate damage by fire	12 weeks' custody	6 to 26 weeks' custody
Significant damage by fire	Crown Court	Crown Court

Offence seriousness (culpability and harm)	
B. Consider the effect of aggravating and mitigating factors (other than those within examples above)	
The following may be particularly relevant but **these lists are not exhaustive**	
Factors indicating higher culpability	**Factor indicating lower culpability**
1. Revenge attack 2. Targeting vulnerable victim	1. Damage caused recklessly
Factors indicating greater degree of harm	
1. Damage to emergency equipment 2. Damage to public amenity 3. Significant public or private fear caused, eg in domestic context	

In *R v Letham* [2000] 1 Cr App R (S) 185 a 16-year-old caused £400,000 worth of damage at a school where he had been a pupil. There had been a guilty plea and he was of good character. Two years' detention was not excessive.

In *R v N* [2007] EWCA Crim 2524 a two-year DTO was substituted for a sentence of three years' detention. A particularly vulnerable 13-year-old of good character with difficult family circumstances and ADHD pleaded guilty to arson. She had set fire to boxes in a shop doorway when under the influence of alcohol, causing damage valued at £1 million. A custodial sentence was necessary despite a good response to a bail package whilst awaiting sentence.

In *R v H* [2011] EWCA Crim 1913 a 13-year-old of good character admitted deliberate damage in business premises where accelerant was used. The damage approximated £750,000 and an exclusion zone had to be imposed around the premises for 24 hours because of the danger of explosion. Others were involved and H made admissions about his own and their involvement. A sentence of two years' detention was replaced by an eighteen-month DTO.

A4.5 Arson with intent to endanger life or being reckless

Criminal Damage Act, s 1

(2) A person who without lawful excuse destroys or damages any property, whether belonging to himself or another—
   (a) intending to destroy or damage any property or being reckless as to whether any property would be destroyed or damaged; and
   (b) intending by the destruction or damage to endanger the life of another or being reckless as to whether the life of another would be thereby endangered; shall be guilty of an offence.
(3) An offence committed under this section by destroying or damaging property by fire shall be charged as arson.

 IO

 DO

 GC

†††† 24 month DTO/detention for life in Crown Court

A4.5.1 *Sentencing*

There are no sentencing guidelines for this offence.

In *R v C* [2001] EWCA Crim 2007 a 14-year-old of good character and suffering from ADHD pushed burning material through the letterbox of an elderly victim on two occasions. The fires were extinguished. He pleaded guilty to two offences of arson being reckless as to whether life was endangered. A sentence of three years' detention was upheld.

In *A-G's Reference No 58 of 2007* [2007] EWCA Crim 2057 a sentence of four years' detention was substituted for the 'unduly lenient' supervision order which had originally been imposed. A 14-year-old with dissimilar previous convictions had set fire to a school building when there were people inside and causing damage valued at approximately £3 million. There was a guilty plea to arson being reckless as to endangering life, entered on the day of trial.

In *R v B* [2010] EWCA Crim 401 the sentence of a DTO of eighteen months was reduced to twelve months on appeal. A 15-year-old pleaded guilty to arson being reckless as to endangering life. He had no convictions but a previous caution for criminal damage. The facts were that he had set fire to an armchair left outside a flat where the sleeping occupant suffered minor burns during his escape.

A4.5.2 Key points

• The defence of 'lawful excuse' under the Criminal Damage Act 1971 s 5 does not apply to an offence under this section.

A4.6 Threats to destroy or damage property

Criminal Damage Act 1971, s 2

A person who without lawful excuse makes to another a threat, intending that that other would fear it would be carried out—

  (a) to destroy or damage any property belonging to that other or a third person; or

  (b) to destroy or damage his own property in a way which he knows is likely to endanger the life of that other or third person; shall be guilty of an offence.

EW

24 month DTO

A4.6.1 *Sentencing*

There are no sentencing guidelines for this offence.

A4.6.2 Key points

• Whether a threat has been made under section 2(a) is to be assessed objectively with reference to the words and actions of the defendant: *R v Cakmak* [2002] EWCA Crim 500.
• The person threatened does not have to actually fear that the threat will be carried out.
• The threat does not have to be immediate.
• The accused does not have to intend to carry out the threat, provided he intends that someone would fear that the threat would be carried out.
• 'Without lawful excuse' is defined in section 5 of the Act: see **A4.1**.

- The defence of 'lawful excuse' under the Criminal Damage Act 1971 s 5 does not apply to an offence under section 2(b).

A4.7 Possession of an item with intent to destroy or damage property

> ### Criminal Damage Act 1971, s 3
>
> A person who has anything in his custody or under his control intending without lawful excuse to use it or cause or permit another to use it—
>   (a) to destroy or damage any property belonging to some other person; or
>   (b) to destroy or damage his own or the user's property in a way which he knows is likely to endanger the life of some other person; shall be guilty of an offence.

|||| 24 month DTO

A4.7.1 *Sentencing*

There are no sentencing guidelines for this offence.

A4.7.2 Key points

- A conditional intent will suffice: *R v Buckingham* (1976) 63 Cr App R 159.
- The defence of 'lawful excuse' under the Criminal Damage Act 1971 s 5 does not apply to an offence under section 3(b).
- The police have powers to search for articles used or intended to be used to cause criminal damage under the Criminal Damage Act 1971 s 6.

See *Blackstone's Criminal Practice 2014* **B8**

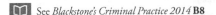

A5 **Public Order Offences**

A5.1 Violent disorder

> ### Public Order Act 1986 s 2
>
> (1) Where three or more persons who are present together use or threaten unlawful violence and the conduct of them (taken together) is such as would cause a person of reasonable firmness present at the scene to fear for his personal safety, each of the persons using or threatening unlawful violence is guilty of violent disorder.
> (2) It is immaterial whether or not the three or more use or threaten unlawful violence simultaneously.
> (3) No person of reasonable firmness need actually be, be likely to be, present at the scene.
> (4) Violent disorder may be committed in private as well as in public places.
>
> ### Public Order Act 1986 s 6
>
> (2) A person is guilty of violent disorder … only if he intends to use or threatens violence or is aware that his conduct may be violent or threatens violence.
>
> …
>
> (5) A person whose awareness is impaired by intoxication shall be taken to be aware of that of which he would be aware if not intoxicated, unless he shows either that his intoxication was not self-induced or that it was caused solely by the taking or administration of a substance in the course of medical treatment.

EW

DO

 24 month DTO

A5.1.1 *Sentencing*

There is no sentencing guideline specific for youths for this offence. The *Magistrates' Court Sentencing Guidelines* (2008) provide very limited guidance on sentencing **adult** offenders for violent disorder. It states that there may be rare cases involving minor violence or threats of violence leading to no or minor injury, with few people involved and no weapon or missiles, in which a custodial sentence of less than six months would be appropriate.

The following decisions of the Court of Appeal may be of more assistance:

- *R v Church* 12 November 1999 unreported. A 19-year-old convicted after trial. He ran as part of a group through streets. Although not

armed himself others in the group were carrying weapons in their hands. No previous convictions. Twelve months' detention reduced to eight months.
- *R v Blackwood and others* [2002] EWCA Crim 3102. Appellants were aged 16 and 17 at the time of the offence. Both were convicted after trial of being part of a 'steaming group' at Notting Hill Carnival. Sentences reduced to fifteen and twelve months' detention in a young offender institution respectively.

A5.1.2 Key points

- The offence of violent disorder does not require a common purpose and the expression 'present together' means no more than being in the same place at the same time; there is no requirement that there is a degree of cooperation between those who are using or offering violence (*R v NW* [2010] EWCA Crim 404).
- In *Allan v Ireland* (1984) 79 Cr App R 206 the Divisional Court held that a defendant's voluntary presence as part of a crowd engaged in threatening behaviour is capable of raising a prima facie case of participation, but mere voluntary presence is not sufficient to convict a defendant unless the court is satisfied that he at least also gave some overt encouragement to the others who were directly involved in the threatening behaviour. In *R v Church* (12 November 1999, unreported) the Court of Appeal declared that this was a correct citation of the law under the Public Order Act 1986, upholding a conviction of a defendant who ran as part of a group where others in the group had weapons in their hands. In such cases the prosecution must also prove that (a) the relevant defendant intended to encourage and did encourage the offence by his presence, and (b) he was aware that his conduct (as opposed to the conduct of the group) might be violent or threatening behaviour (*R v Blackwood* [2002] EWCA Crim 3102).
- A person whose awareness is impaired by intoxication (whether caused by drink, drugs, or other means, or by a combination of means) shall be taken to be aware of that of which he would be aware if not intoxicated, unless he shows either that his intoxication was not self-induced or that it was caused solely by the taking or administration of a substance in the course of medical treatment (s 6(5) and (6)).

See *Blackstone's Criminal Practice 2014* **B11.28–B11.36**

A5.2 **Affray**

Public Order Act 1986 s 3

(1) A person is guilty of affray if he uses or threatens unlawful violence towards another and his conduct is such as would cause a person of reasonable firmness present at the scene to fear for his personal safety.

(2) Where 2 or more persons use or threaten the unlawful violence, it is the conduct of them taken together that must be considered for the purposes of subsection (1).

(3) For the purposes of this section a threat cannot be made by the use of words alone.

(4) No person of reasonable firmness need actually be, or be likely to be, present at the scene.

(5) Affray may be committed in private as well as in public places.

Public Order Act 1986 s 6

...

(2) A person is guilty of affray only if he intends to use or threaten violence or is aware that his conduct may be violent or threaten violence.

...

(5) A person whose awareness is impaired by intoxication shall be taken to be aware of that of which he would be aware if not intoxicated, unless he shows either that his intoxication was not self-induced or that it was caused solely by the taking or administration of a substance in the course of medical treatment.

 EW

 DO

24 month DTO

A5.2.1 *Sentencing*

There is no sentencing guideline specific for youths for this offence. The *Magistrates' Court Sentencing Guidelines* (2008) provide guidance for sentencing **adult** offenders.

Offence seriousness (culpability and harm) A. Identify the appropriate starting point Starting points based on first-time offender pleading not guilty		
Example of nature of activity	**Starting point**	**Range**
Brief offence involving low level violence, no substantial fear created	Low level community order	Band C fine to medium level community order

Degree of fighting or violence that causes substantial fear	High level community order	Medium level community order to 12 weeks' custody
Fight involving a weapon/ throwing objects, or conduct causing risk of serious injury	18 weeks' custody	12 weeks' custody to Crown Court

Offence seriousness (culpability and harm) **B. Consider the effect of aggravating and mitigating factors** **(other than those within examples above)** The following may be particularly relevant but **these lists are not exhaustive**	
Factors indicating higher culpability Group action Threats Lengthy incident	**Factors indicating lower culpability** Did not start the trouble Provocation Stopped as soon as police arrived
Factors indicating greater degree of harm Vulnerable person(s) present Injuries caused Damage to property	

A5.2.2 Key points

- Not all occasions when the defendant offers violence to another should be charged as affray. In *R v Sanchez* (1996) 160 JP 321 the court approved the following academic commentary:

> The offence of affray envisages at least three persons: (i) the person using or threatening unlawful violence; (ii) a person towards whom the violence or threat is directed; and (iii) a person of reasonable firmness who need not actually be, or be likely to be, present at the scene. Thus the question in the present case was not whether a person of reasonable firmness in [the victim's] shoes would have feared for his personal safety but whether this hypothetical person, present in the room and seeing [the defendant's] conduct towards [the victim] would have so feared.... [Affray] is designed for the protection of the bystander. It is a public order offence. There are other offences for the protection of persons at whom the violence is aimed.... The definition of affray is very wide and ... care has to be taken to avoid extending it so widely that it would cover every case of common assault. A common assault may be very trivial, so that it would not cause anyone to fear for his 'personal safety'. But where the assault threatens serious harm to the victim, there may be evidence of affray depending on the circumstances. The person of reasonable firmness present in a small room as in the present case might fear for his

personal safety whereas the same person, observing the same conduct in an open space, would not.

- In an incident involving a one-on-one assault in the street during daylight, the fact that a bystander feared for the safety of the victim of the assault rather than his own safety meant that it was not an affray (*R v Blinkhorn* [2006] EWCA Crim 1416).
- A conviction for affray was quashed in the case of *Leeson v DPP* [2010] EWHC 994 (Admin) when the threat was made by the defendant to her partner in the bathroom of their otherwise unoccupied home. The court held that it was unrealistic to conclude that the hypothetical bystander who for some reason found his way into the bathroom would fear for his own safety rather than the safety of the defendant's partner.
- The carrying of dangerous weapons such as petrol bombs could, in some circumstances, constitute a threat of violence without those weapons being waved or brandished. Whether the carrying of weapons is sufficient to constitute such a threat is a matter for the tribunal of fact to decide. (*I v DPP* [2001] UKHL 10, [2001] 2 WLR 765).

 See *Blackstone's Criminal Practice 2014* **B11.37–B11.46**

A5.3 Threatening behaviour, fear, or provocation of violence

Public Order Act 1986 s 4

(1) A person is guilty of an offence if he—
   (a) uses towards another person threatening, abusive or insulting words or behaviour, or
   (b) distributes or displays to another person any writing, sign or other visible representation which is threatening, abusive or insulting,
   with intent to cause that person to believe that immediate unlawful violence will be used against him or another by any person, or to provoke the immediate use of unlawful violence by that person or another, or whereby that person is likely to believe that such violence will be used or it is likely that such violence will be provoked.
(2) An offence under this section may be committed in a public or a private place, except that no offence is committed where the words or behaviour are used, or the writing, sign or other visible representation is distributed or displayed, by a person inside a dwelling and the other person is also inside that or another dwelling.

Public Order Act 1986 s 6

(3) A person is guilty of an offence under section 4 only if he intends his words or behaviour, or the writing, sign or other visible representation, to be threatening, abusive or insulting, or is aware that it may be threatening, abusive or insulting.

(4) A person is guilty of an offence under section 5 only if he intends his words or behaviour, or the writing, sign or other visible representation, to be threatening, abusive or insulting, or is aware that it may be threatening, abusive or insulting or (as the case may be) he intends his behaviour to be or is aware that it may be disorderly.

SO Basic offence

EW Racially or religiously aggravated offence

▦ 6 month DTO

▦ 24 month DTO if the offence is racially or religiously aggravated

A5.3.1 *Sentencing*

There is no sentencing guideline specific for youths for this offence. The *Magistrates' Court Sentencing Guidelines* (2008) provide guidance for sentencing **adult** offenders.

Offence seriousness (culpability and harm)		
A. Identify the appropriate starting point		
Starting points based on first-time offender pleading not guilty		
Examples of nature of activity	**Starting point**	**Range**
Fear or threat of low level immediate unlawful violence such as push, shove, or spit	Low level community order	Band B fine to medium level community order
Fear or threat of medium level immediate unlawful violence such as punch	High level community order	Low level community order to 12 weeks' custody
Fear or threat of high level immediate unlawful violence such as use of weapon; missile thrown; gang involvement	12 weeks' custody	6 to 26 weeks' custody

Offence seriousness (culpability and harm)	
B. Consider the effect of aggravating and mitigating factors (other than those within examples above)	
The following may be particularly relevant but **these lists are not exhaustive**	
Factors indicating higher culpability 1. Planning 2. Offender deliberately isolates victim 3. Group action 4. Threat directed at victim because of job 5. History of antagonism towards victim	**Factors indicating lower culpability** 1. Impulsive action 2. Short duration 3. Provocation
Factors indicating greater degree of harm 1. Offence committed at school, hospital, or other place where vulnerable persons may be present 2. Offence committed on enclosed premises such as public transport 3. Vulnerable victim(s) 4. Victim needs medical help/counselling	

A5.3.2 Key points

- Subject to the prosecution proving the use of threatening etc words/behaviour and the mens rea there are four ways in which the offence can be committed (*Winn v DPP* [1990] 1 QB 1052):
  - (i) intending the person against whom the conduct is directed to believe that immediate unlawful violence will be used;
  - (ii) intending to provoke the immediate use of unlawful violence by that person;
  - (iii) the person against whom the conduct is directed is likely to believe that immediate unlawful violence will be used; or
  - (iv) it is likely that immediate unlawful violence will be provoked.

- Actions taken in self-defence do not amount to unlawful violence.
- For the conduct to be 'used towards' another they must be physically present (*Atkins v DPP* (1989) 89 Cr App R 199).
- Provocation of immediate unlawful violence does not require the violence to be instantaneous but it cannot be at some uncertain future time (*R v Horseferry Road Stipendiary Magistrate ex parte Siadatan* [1991] 1 QB 260).
- The racially aggravated form of the offence is created by the CDA 1998 s 31. For the meaning of 'racially or religiously aggravated' see **F19**.

 See *Blackstone's Criminal Practice 2014* **B11.47–B11.59**

A5.4 Disorderly behaviour with intent to cause harassment, alarm, or distress

Public Order Act 1986 s 4A

(1) A person is guilty of an offence if, with intent to cause a person harassment, alarm or distress, he—
   (a) uses threatening, abusive or insulting words or behaviour, or disorderly behaviour, or
   (b) displays any writing, sign or other visible representation which is threatening, abusive or insulting,
   thereby causing that or another person harassment, alarm or distress.

SO Basic offence

EW If racially or religiously aggravated offence

▦ 6 month DTO (basic offence)

▦ 24 month DTO (if racially or religiously aggravated)

A5.4.1 *Sentencing*

There is no sentencing guideline specific for youths for this offence. The *Magistrates' Court Sentencing Guidelines* (2008) provide guidance for sentencing **adult** offenders.

Offence seriousness (culpability and harm)		
A. Identify the appropriate starting point		
Starting points based on first-time offender pleading not guilty		
Examples of nature of activity	**Starting point**	**Range**
Threats, abuse, or insults made more than once but on same occasion against the same person, eg while following down the street	Band C fine	Band B fine to low level community order
Group action or deliberately planned action against targeted victim	Medium level community order	Low level community order to 12 weeks' custody
Weapon brandished or used or threats against vulnerable victim—course of conduct over longer period	12 weeks' custody	High level community order to 26 weeks' custody

Offence seriousness (culpability and harm)	
B. Consider the effect of aggravating and mitigating factors (other than those within examples above)	
The following may be particularly relevant but **these lists are not exhaustive**	
Factors indicating higher culpability	**Factors indicating lower culpability**
High degree of planning	Very short period
Offender deliberately isolates victim	Provocation
Factors indicating greater degree of harm	
Offence committed in vicinity of victim's home	
Large number of people in vicinity	
Actual or potential escalation into violence	
Particularly serious impact on victim	

A5.4.2 Key points

- An offence under this section may be committed in a public or a private place, except that no offence is committed where the words or behaviour are used, or the writing, sign, or other visible representation is displayed, by a person inside a dwelling and the person who is harassed, alarmed, or distressed is also inside that or another dwelling (POA 1986 s 4A(2)).
- It is a defence for the accused to prove that he was inside a dwelling and had no reason to believe that the words or behaviour used, or the writing, sign, or other visible representation displayed, would be heard or seen by a person outside that or any other dwelling, or that his conduct was reasonable (POA 1986 s 4A(3)).
- The racially aggravated form of the offence is created by the CDA 1998 s 31. For the meaning of 'racially or religiously aggravated' see **F19**.

 See *Blackstone's Criminal Practice 2014* **B11.60–B11.68**

A5.5 Disorderly behaviour (harassment, alarm, or distress)

Public Order Act 1986 s 5

(1) A person is guilty of an offence if he—
   (a) uses threatening, abusive or insulting words or behaviour, or disorderly behaviour, or displays any writing, sign or other visible representation which is threatening, abusive or insulting,

(b) within the hearing or sight of a person likely to be caused harassment, alarm or distress thereby.

Public Order Act 1986 s 5

(3) It is a defence for the accused to prove—
   (a) that he had no reason to believe that there was any person within hearing or sight who was likely to be caused harassment, alarm or distress, or
   (b) that he was inside a dwelling and had no reason to believe that the words or behaviour used, or the writing, sign or other visible representation displayed, would be heard or seen by a person outside that or any other dwelling, or
   (c) that his conduct was reasonable.

Public Order Act 1986 s 6

(4) A person is guilty of an offence under section 5 only if he intends his words or behaviour, or the writing, sign or other visible representation, to be threatening, abusive or insulting, or is aware that it may be threatening, abusive or insulting or (as the case may be) he intends his behaviour to be or is aware that it may be disorderly.

 Level 3 fine; level 4 fine if racially or religiously aggravated

A5.5.1 *Sentencing*

There is no sentencing guideline specific for youths for this offence. The *Magistrates' Court Sentencing Guidelines* (2008) provide guidance for sentencing **adult** offenders.

Offence seriousness (culpability and harm) A. Identify the appropriate starting point Starting points based on first-time offender pleading not guilty		
Examples of nature of activity	**Starting point**	**Range**
Shouting, causing disturbance for some minutes	Band A fine	Conditional discharge to band B fine
Substantial disturbance caused	Band B fine	Band A fine to band C fine

Offence seriousness (culpability and harm)	
B. Consider the effect of aggravating and mitigating factors (other than those within examples above)	
The following may be particularly relevant but **these lists are not exhaustive**	
Factors indicating higher culpability Group action Lengthy incident **Factors indicating greater degree of harm** Vulnerable person(s) present Offence committed at school, hospital, or other place where vulnerable persons may be present Victim providing public service	**Factors indicating lower culpability** Stopped as soon as police arrived Brief/minor incident Provocation

A5.5.2 Key points

- An offence under this section may be committed in a public or a private place, except that no offence is committed where the words or behaviour are used, or the writing, sign, or other visible representation is displayed, by a person inside a dwelling and the other person is also inside that or another dwelling (POA 1986 s 5(2)).
- A person can be harassed without emotional upset (*Southard v DPP* [2006] EWHC 3449 (Admin)) or an apprehension about personal safety (*Chambers v DPP* [1995] Crim LR 896).
- Using swear words in the presence of a police officer is not in itself an offence under s 5. The Crown must produce evidence of the likelihood of harassment, alarm, or distress. This cannot be implied for police officers or young people for whom they are a regular feature of life (*Harvey v DPP* [2011] EWHC 3992 (Admin), (2012) 176 JP 265). See also *R(R) v DPP* (2006) 170 JP 661 and *Southard v DPP* (above).
- A person whose awareness is impaired by intoxication shall be taken to be aware of that of which he would be aware if not intoxicated, unless he shows either that his intoxication was not self-induced or that it was caused solely by the taking or administration of a substance in the course of medical treatment (POA 1986 s.8(6)).
- The racially aggravated form of the offence is created by the CDA 1998 s 31. For the meaning of 'racially or religiously aggravated' see **F19**.

📖 See *Blackstone's Criminal Practice 2014* **B11.69–B11.83**

A5.6 Drunk and disorderly in a public place

Criminal Justice Act 1967 s 91

(1) Any person who in any public place is guilty, while drunk, of disorderly behaviour ... shall be liable on summary conviction to a fine not exceeding [level 3 on the standard scale].

(2) The foregoing subsection shall have effect instead of any corresponding provision contained in section 12 of the Licensing Act 1872, section 58 of the Metropolitan Police Act 1839, section 37 of the City of London Police Act 1839, and section 29 of the Town Police Clauses Act 1847 (being enactments which authorise the imposition of a short term of imprisonment or of a fine not exceeding £10 or both for the corresponding offence) and instead of any corresponding provision contained in any local Act.

...

(4) In this section 'public place' includes any highway and any other premises or place to which at the material time the public have or are permitted to have access, whether on payment or otherwise.

SO

 Non-imprisonable; level 3 fine

A5.6.1 *Sentencing*

There is no sentencing guideline specific for youths for this offence. The *Magistrates' Court Sentencing Guidelines* (2008) provide guidance for sentencing **adult** offenders.

Offence seriousness (culpability and harm) A. Identify the appropriate starting point Starting points based on first-time offender pleading not guilty		
Examples of nature of activity	**Starting point**	**Range**
Shouting, causing disturbance for some minutes	Band A fine	Conditional discharge to band B fine
Substantial disturbance caused	Band B fine	Band A fine to band C fine

Offence seriousness (culpability and harm)
B. Consider the effect of aggravating and mitigating factors
(other than those within examples above)
The following may be particularly relevant but **these lists are not exhaustive**

Factors indicating higher culpability	Factors indicating lower culpability
Offensive words or behaviour involved	Minor and non-threatening
Lengthy incident	Stopped as soon as police arrived
Group action	
Factors indicating greater degree of harm	
Offence committed at school, hospital, or other place where vulnerable persons may be present	
Offence committed on public transport	
Victim providing public service	

A5.6.2 Key points

• In *Carroll v DPP* [2009] EWHC 554 (Admin) the court held that the offence requires proof of three elements, namely that (1) the defendant was drunk; (2) he was in a public place; and (3) he was guilty of disorderly behaviour. The word 'drunk' should be given its ordinary and natural meaning. In the end, therefore, whether a defendant was drunk is a simple question of fact in each case. On familiar principles it is the voluntary consumption of alcohol which is the requisite mens rea, such as it is, of this most basic offence. If that voluntary consumption results in the defendant becoming drunk then the first element of the offence is proved. As to the third element, there is no requirement for mens rea at all. What is required is proof that objectively viewed the defendant was guilty of disorderly behaviour. Specific drunken intent and recklessness are nothing to the point. The words 'disorderly behaviour' are again to be given their ordinary and natural meaning. In the end, therefore, it is a simple question of fact in each case: whether the defendant is guilty of disorderly behaviour.

 See *Blackstone's Criminal Practice 2014* **B11.202–B11.206**

A5.7 Anti-social behaviour order, breach of

Crime and Disorder Act 1998 s 1(10)

If without reasonable excuse a person does anything which he is prohibited from doing by an anti-social behaviour order, he is guilty of an offence.

EW

 24 month DTO

A5.7.1 *Sentencing*

A conditional discharge may not be imposed for breach of an ASBO (CDA 1998 s 1(11)).

When the Crime and Security Act 2010 s 41 comes into force a parenting order must be made in certain circumstances following a conviction for breaching an anti-social behaviour order (see **J5.4**).

A definitive guideline *Breach of Anti-Social Behaviour Orders* (2009) has been issued. This contains specific guidance on sentencing youths for breach of an ASBO:

7. The principles to be followed when sentencing a youth for breach of an ASBO are as follows:

'First time offender' pleading guilty: the court must make a referral order unless it imposes an absolute discharge, a custodial sentence or a hospital order;

In all other cases:

 (i) in some less serious cases, such as where the breach has not involved any harassment, alarm or distress, a fine may be appropriate if it will be paid by the offender, or otherwise a reparation order;

 (ii) in most cases, the appropriate sentence will be a community sentence;

 (iii) the custody threshold should be set at a significantly higher level than the threshold applicable to adult offenders;

 (iv) the custody threshold usually will not be crossed unless the breach involved serious harassment, alarm or distress through either the use of violence, threats or intimidation or the targeting of individuals/groups in a manner that led to a fear of violence;

 (v) exceptionally, the custody threshold may also be crossed where a youth is being sentenced for more than one offence of breach (committed on separate occasions within a short period) involving a lesser but substantial degree of harassment, alarm or distress;

 (vi) even where the custody threshold is crossed, the court should normally impose a community sentence in preference to a DTO, as custody should be used only as a measure of last resort; and

 (vii) where the court considers a custodial sentence to be unavoidable, the starting point for sentencing should be 4 months detention, with a range of up to 12 months. Where a youth is being sentenced for more than one breach involving serious harassment, alarm or distress, sentence may go beyond that range.

Aggravating and mitigating factors

8. As with adult offenders, factors that are likely to aggravate an offence of breach of an anti-social behaviour order are:

- history of disobedience of court orders
- the breach was committed immediately or shortly after the order was made
- the breach was committed subsequent to earlier breach proceedings arising from the same order
- targeting of a person the order was made to protect or of a witness in the original proceedings.

9. Factors that are likely to mitigate the seriousness of the breach are:
- the breach occurred after a long period of compliance
- the prohibition(s) breached was not fully understood, especially where an interim order was made without notice.

Personal mitigation

10. Offender mitigation is particularly relevant to breach of an ASBO as compliance with the order depends on the ability to understand its terms and make rational decisions in relation to these. Sentence may be mitigated where:
- the offender has a lower level of understanding due to mental health issues or learning difficulties
- the offender was acting under the influence of an older or more experienced offender; or
- there has been compliance with an Individual Support Order or Intervention Order imposed when the ASBO was made.

11. Other offender mitigating factors that may be particularly relevant to young offenders include peer pressure and a lack of parental support.

A5.7.2 Key points

- The prosecution must be in a position to prove that the person before the court is the person in respect of whom the order was made (*Barber v Crown Prosecution Service* [2004] EWHC 2605 (Admin)).
- Forgetfulness, misunderstanding, or ignorance of the terms of the order could amount in law to a reasonable excuse (*R v Nicholson* [2006] EWCA Crim 1518).
- The fact that a person is appealing against the imposition of an order does not give rise to a reasonable excuse (*West Midlands Probation Board v Daly* [2008] EWHC 15 (Admin)).
- A belief that the order has come to an end is capable of amounting to a reasonable excuse (*Barber v Crown Prosecution Service* [2004] EWHC 2605 (Admin)).
- A defendant's state of mind is relevant to the issue of reasonable excuse notwithstanding the fact that the offence is one of strict liability (*JB v Crown Prosecution Service* [2012] EWHC 72 (Admin)).
- The burden of negativing reasonable excuse, once raised by evidence by the defence, falls on the prosecution (*R v Charles* [2009] EWCA Crim 1570).
- Where conduct forming the breach would also be a criminal offence in its own right, a court was not bound by the maximum sentence available for that offence, but should have regard to proportionality. It would be wrong for a prosecutor to proceed with a breach of an anti-social behaviour order simply because it was thought that the penalty for the substantive offence was too lenient (*R v Stevens* [2006] EWCA Crim 255).

See *Blackstone's Criminal Practice 2014* **D25.32–D25.34**

A5.8 Dispersal order, breach of

Anti-social Behaviour Act 2003, s 30

(1) This section applies where a relevant officer has reasonable grounds for believing—

    (a) that any members of the public have been intimidated, harassed, alarmed or distressed as a result of the presence or behaviour of groups of two or more persons in public places in any locality in his police area (the 'relevant locality'), and

    (b) that anti-social behaviour is a significant and persistent problem in the relevant locality.

(2) The relevant officer may give an authorisation that the powers conferred on a constable in uniform by subsections (3) to (6) are to be exercisable for a period specified in the authorisation which does not exceed 6 months.

(3) Subsection (4) applies if a constable in uniform has reasonable grounds for believing that the presence or behaviour of a group of two or more persons in any public place in the relevant locality has resulted, or is likely to result, in any members of the public being intimidated, harassed, alarmed or distressed.

(4) The constable may give one or more of the following directions, namely–

    (a) a direction requiring the persons in the group to disperse (either immediately or by such time as he may specify and in such way as he may specify),

    (b) a direction requiring any of those persons whose place of residence is not within the relevant locality to leave the relevant locality or any part of the relevant locality (either immediately or by such time as he may specify and in such way as he may specify), and

    (c) a direction prohibiting any of those persons whose place of residence is not within the relevant locality from returning to the relevant locality or any part of the relevant locality for such period (not exceeding 24 hours) from the giving of the direction as he may specify;

but this subsection is subject to subsection (5).

(5) A direction under subsection (4) may not be given in respect of a group of persons—

    (a) who are engaged in conduct which is lawful under section 220 of the Trade Union and Labour Relations (Consolidation) Act 1992 (c. 52), or

    (b) who are taking part in a public procession of the kind mentioned in section 11(1) of the Public Order Act 1986 (c. 64) in respect of which—

        (i) written notice has been given in accordance with section 11 of that Act, or

        (ii) such notice is not required to be given as provided by subsections (1) and (2) of that section.

(6) If, between the hours of 9pm and 6am, a constable in uniform finds a person in any public place in the relevant locality who he has reasonable grounds for believing—

    (a) is under the age of 16, and

> (b) is not under the effective control of a parent or a responsible person aged 18 or over,
>
> he may remove the person to the person's place of residence unless he has reasonable grounds for believing that the person would, if removed to that place, be likely to suffer significant harm.
>
> (7) In this section any reference to the presence or behaviour of a group of persons is to be read as including a reference to the presence or behaviour of any one or more of the persons in the group.
>
> **32 Powers under section 30: supplemental**
>
> . . .
>
> (2) A person who knowingly contravenes a direction given to him under section 30(4) commits an offence . . .

 Fine at level 4 and in case of an adult 3 months imprisonment. No power to impose DTO

A5.8.1 *Sentencing*

No sentencing guideline has been issued.

A5.8.2 Key points

- 'Anti-social behaviour' means behaviour by a person which causes or is likely to cause harassment, alarm, or distress to one or more other persons not of the same household as the person (s 36).
- The power to issue dispersal notices has also been given to police community support officers (s 33).
- To prove an offence under s 32(2) it must be established that the officer issuing the dispersal notice was acting lawfully. This means that the prosecution must prove the validity of the authorization (*Carter v DPP* [2009] EWHC 2197 (Admin)) and the reasonableness of the grounds for issuing the notice to the particular defendant (*Buckley v DPP* [2006] 1888 (Admin)).
- Unless there were exceptional circumstances, a reasonable belief under s 30(3) had normally to depend, in part at least, on some behaviour of the group which indicates in some way or other that harassment, alarm, or intimidation had or was likely to occur (*Buckley v DPP*).

 Blackstone's Criminal Practice 2014 **B11.117–B11.121**

A6 Communication Network Offences

A6.1 Improper use of public electronic communications network

> ### Communications Act 2003 s 127(1)–(2)
>
> (1) A person is guilty of an offence if he—
>   (a) sends by means of a public electronic communications network a message or other matter that is grossly offensive or of an indecent, obscene or menacing character; or
>   (b) causes any such message or matter to be so sent.
> (2) A person is guilty of an offence if, for the purpose of causing annoyance, inconvenience or needless anxiety to another, he—
>   (a) sends by means of a public electronic communications network, a message that he knows to be false,
>   (b) causes such a message to be sent; or
>   (c) persistently makes use of a public electronic communications network.

SO

 6 month DTO

A6.1.1 *Sentencing*

There is no sentencing guideline specific to youths. The *Magistrates' Court Sentencing Guidelines* (2008) give the following guidance for sentencing adult offenders:

Offence seriousness (culpability and harm)		
A. Identify the appropriate starting point		
Starting points based on first-time offender pleading not guilty		
Sending grossly offensive, indecent, obscene, or menacing messages (s 127(1))		
Example of nature of activity	**Starting point**	**Range**
Single offensive, indecent, obscene, or menacing call of short duration, having no significant impact on receiver	Band B fine	Band A fine to band C fine
Single call where extreme language used, having only moderate impact on receiver	Medium level community order	Low level community order to high level community order

Single call where extreme language used and substantial distress or fear caused to receiver; OR One of a series of similar calls as described in box above	6 weeks' custody	High level community order to 12 weeks' custody

Sending false message/persistent use of communications network for purpose of causing annoyance, inconvenience, or needless anxiety (s 127(2))		
Example of nature of activity	**Starting point**	**Range**
Persistent silent calls over short period to private individual, causing inconvenience or annoyance	Band B fine	Band A fine to band C fine
Single hoax call to public or private organization resulting in moderate disruption or anxiety	Medium level community order	Low level community order to high level community order
Single hoax call resulting in major disruption or substantial public fear or distress; OR One of a series of similar calls as described in box above	12 weeks' custody	High level community order to 18 weeks' custody

A6.1.2 Key points

- A 'public electronic communications network' means an electronic communications network provided wholly or mainly for the purpose of making electronic communications services available to members of the public (s 151(1)). Messages on Twitter come within this definition even though the website is privately owned as access is through the internet which is plainly a public electronic network provided for the public and paid for by the public through various service providers (*Chambers v DPP* [2012] EWHC 2157).
- The offence under s 127(1) is complete when the message is sent. It makes no difference that the message is never received (*DPP v Collins* [2006] UKHL 40).
- Where the charge under s 127(1)(a) relates to a grossly offensive message the court in *DPP v Collins* held that:
  - (i) The question of whether something is in fact offensive is to be determined by reference to whether or not reasonable persons would find the message grossly offensive, judged by the standards of an open and just multiracial society.
  - (ii) To be guilty the defendant must have intended his words to be offensive to those to whom they related, or be aware that they might be taken to be so.

- Where the charge under s 127(1)(a) relates to a menacing message the court in *Chambers v DPP* [2012] EWHC 2157 held:
  (i) To be menacing a message must create fear or apprehension in those to whom it is communicated, or who may reasonably be expected to see it. Before concluding that a message is menacing its precise terms, and any inferences to be drawn from its precise terms, need to be examined in the context in and the means by which the message was sent.
  (ii) To be guilty a defendant must intend that the message should be of a menacing character or be aware that at the time of sending the message that it may create fear or apprehension in any reasonable member of the public who reads or sees it. If the defendant intended the message as a joke, even if a poor joke in bad taste, it is unlikely that the mens rea will be established.

- European Convention rights to freedom of expression will rarely provide a defence (see *Connolly v Director of Public Prosecutions* [2007] EWHC 237 (Admin), a case concerned with a different statute).

- When dealing with a charge involving messages sent via social media reference should be made to the DPP's *Guidance on Prosecuting Cases Involving Communications via Social Media* (available at <www.cps.gov.uk>).

 See *Blackstone's Criminal Practice 2014* **B18.30**

A6.2 Indecent or offensive or threatening letters etc

Malicious Communications Act 1988 s 1

1 Offence of sending letters etc with intent to cause distress or anxiety

(1) Any person who sends to another person—
    (a) a letter, electronic communication or article of any description which conveys—
        (i) a message which is indecent or grossly offensive;
        (ii) a threat; or
        (iii) information which is false and known or believed to be false by the sender; or
    (b) any article or electronic communication which is, in whole or part, of an indecent or grossly offensive nature, is guilty of an offence if his purpose, or one of his purposes, in sending it is that it should, so far as falling within paragraph (a) or (b) above, cause distress or anxiety to the recipient or to any other person to whom he intends that it or its contents or nature should be communicated.

(2) A person is not guilty of an offence by virtue of subsection (1)(a)(ii) above if he shows—
   (a) that the threat was used to reinforce a demand made by him on reasonable grounds; and
   (b) that he believed, and had reasonable grounds for believing, that the use of the threat was a proper means of reinforcing the demand.
(2A) In this section 'electronic communication' includes—
   (a) any oral or other communication by means of an electronic communications network; and
   (b) any communication (however sent) that is in electronic form.
(3) In this section references to sending include references to delivering or transmitting and to causing to be sent, delivered or transmitted and 'sender' shall be construed accordingly.

 6 month DTO

 Fine level 5/6 months

A6.2.1 *Sentencing*

There is no sentencing guideline for this offence.

A6.2.2 Key points

See *Connolly v Director of Public Prosecutions* [2008] 1 WLR 276 for Articles 9 (religion) and 10 (free speech) considerations. Articles 9(2) and 10(2) allow for restriction on the relevant rights.

See *Blackstone's Criminal Practice 2014* **B18.30**

A7 **Weapons**

A7.1 **Firearms—general**

A7.1.1 *Definitions*

Firearm—defined by the Firearms Act 1968 s 57(1).

> ### Firearms Act 1968 s 57
>
> (1) In this Act, the expression 'firearm' means a lethal barrelled weapon of any description from which any shot, bullet or other missile can be discharged and includes—
>   (a) any prohibited weapon, whether it is such a lethal weapon as aforesaid or not; and
>   (b) any component part of such a lethal or prohibited weapon; and
>   (c) any accessory to any such weapon designed or adapted to diminish the noise or flash caused by firing the weapon;
>   and so much of section 1 of this Act as excludes any description of firearm from the category of firearms to which that section applies shall be construed as also excluding component parts of, and accessories to, firearms of that description.

Imitation firearm—defined by the Firearms Act 1968 s 57(4).

> ### Firearms Act 1968 s 57(4)
>
> 'imitation firearm' means any thing which has the appearance of being a firearm (other than such a weapon as is mentioned in section 5(1)(b) of this Act) whether or not it is capable of discharging any shot, bullet or other missile; ...

An item is an imitation firearm if it 'looked like' a firearm at the time of its use (*R v Morris and King* (1984) 149 JP 60).

An imitation firearm has to be a thing which was separate and distinct from the defendant; putting one's hand inside a jacket pocket and using the fingers to give the impression of a firearm was not enough (*R v Bentham* [2005] UKHL 18).

Ammunition—defined by the Firearms Act 1968 s 57(2).

> ### Firearms Act 1968 s 57(2)
>
> In this Act, the expression 'ammunition' means ammunition for any firearm and includes grenades, bombs and other like missiles, whether capable of use with a firearm or not, and also includes prohibited ammunition.

A7.1.2 *Sentencing*

A sentencing guideline has not been issued in relation to firearms offences. The Court of Appeal decision in *R v Avis* [1998] 1 Cr App R 420 therefore remains the guideline case. This provides the following general guidance:

> The unlawful possession and use of firearms is generally recognised as a grave source of danger to society. The reasons are obvious. Firearms may be used to take life or cause serious injury. They are used to further the commission of other serious crimes. Often the victims will be those charged with the enforcement of the law or the protection of persons or property. In the conflicts which occur between competing criminal gangs, often related to the supply of drugs, the use and possession of firearms provoke an escalating spiral of violence.

> Where imitation firearms are involved, the risk to life and limb is absent, but such weapons can be and often are used to frighten and intimidate victims in order to reinforce unlawful demands. Such imitation weapons are often very hard to distinguish from the real thing—for practical purposes, impossible in the circumstances in which they are used—and the victim is usually as much frightened and intimidated as if a genuine firearm had been used. Such victims are often isolated and vulnerable.

> Sometimes the firearm involved, although genuine, has been disabled from firing, or cannot be fired for want of ammunition. In such cases again the risk to life and limb is absent, but the risk of use to frighten or intimidate remains, and the weapon may be used in earnest on another occasion.

> The appropriate level of sentence for a firearms offence, as for any other offence, will depend on all the facts and circumstances relevant to the offence and the offender, and it would be wrong for this Court to seek to prescribe unduly restrictive sentencing guidelines. It will, however, usually be appropriate for the sentencing court to ask itself a series of questions:
>
> (1) What sort of weapon is involved? Genuine firearms are more dangerous than imitation firearms. Loaded firearms are more dangerous than unloaded firearms. Unloaded firearms for which ammunition is available are more dangerous than firearms for which no ammunition is available. Possession of a firearm which has no lawful use (such as a sawn-off shotgun) will be viewed even more seriously than possession of a firearm which is capable of lawful use.
>
> (2) What (if any) use has been made of the firearm? It is necessary for the court, as with any other offence, to take account of all circumstances surrounding any use made of the firearm: the more prolonged and premeditated and violent the use, the more serious the offence is likely to be.
>
> (3) With what intention (if any) did the defendant possess or use the firearm? Generally speaking, the most serious offences under the Act are those which require proof of a specific criminal intent (to endanger life, to cause fear of violence, to resist arrest, to commit an indictable offence). The more serious the act intended, the more serious the offence.
>
> (4) What is the defendant's record? The seriousness of any firearms offence is inevitably increased if the offender has an established record of committing firearms offences or crimes of violence.

A7.1.3 *Mandatory minimum sentence*

Firearms Act 1968 s 51A

(1) This section applies where—
  (a) an individual is convicted of—
    (i) an offence under section 5(1)(a), (ab), (aba), (ac), (ad), (ae), (af) or (c) of this Act,
    (ii) an offence under section 5(1A)(a) of this Act,
    (iii) an offence under any of the provisions of this Act listed in subsection (1A) in respect of a firearm or ammunition specified in section 5(1)(a), (ab), (aba), (ac), (ad), (ae), (af) or (c) or section 5(1A)(a) of this Act, and
  (b) the offence was committed after the commencement of this section and at a time when he was aged 16 or over.

(1A) The provisions are–
  (a) section 16 (possession of firearm with intent to injure);
  (b) section 16A (possession of firearm with intent to cause fear of violence);
  (c) section 17 (use of firearm to resist arrest);
  (d) section 18 (carrying firearm with criminal intent);
  (e) section 19 (carrying a firearm in a public place);
  (f) section 20(1) (trespassing in a building with firearm).

(2) The court shall impose an appropriate custodial sentence (or order for detention) for a term of at least the required minimum term (with or without a fine) unless the court is of the opinion that there are exceptional circumstances relating to the offence or to the offender which justify its not doing so.

(3) Where an offence is found to have been committed over a period of two or more days, or at some time during a period of two or more days, it shall be taken for the purposes of this section to have been committed on the last of those days.

(4) In this section 'appropriate custodial sentence (or order for detention)' means—
  (a) in relation to England and Wales—
    (i) in the case of an offender who is aged 18 or over when convicted, a sentence of imprisonment, and
    (ii) in the case of an offender who is aged under 18 at that time, a sentence of detention under section 91 of the Powers of Criminal Courts (Sentencing) Act 2000;
    ...

(5) In this section 'the required minimum term' means—
  (a) in relation to England and Wales—
    (i) in the case of an offender who was aged 18 or over when he committed the offence, five years, and
    (ii) in the case of an offender who was under 18 at that time, three years, ...

In a case where s 51A applies there is no provision for a guilty plea to reduce the sentence below the statutory minimum (*R v Jordan* [2005] 2 Cr App R (S) 226).

When determining whether the case involved 'exceptional circumstances', it was necessary to look at the case as a whole. Sometimes there would be a single isolated factor that would amount to exceptional circumstances but in other cases it would be the collective impact of all relevant circumstances (*R v Rehman* [2006] 1 Cr App R (S) 404).

A7.2 Possessing firearm or ammunition without firearm certificate

Firearms Act 1968 s 1

1.— Requirement of firearms certificate

(1) Subject to any exemption under this Act, it is an offence for a person—
   (a) to have in his possession, or to purchase or acquire, a firearm to which this section applies without holding a firearm certificate in force at the time, or otherwise than as authorised by such a certificate;
   (b) to have in his possession, or to purchase or acquire, any ammunition to which this section applies without holding a firearm certificate in force at the time, or otherwise than as authorised by such a certificate, or in quantities in excess of those so authorised.

(2) It is an offence for a person to fail to comply with a condition subject to which a firearm certificate is held by him.

(3) This section applies to every firearm except—
   (a) a shot gun within the meaning of this Act, that is to say a smooth-bore gun (not being an air gun) which—
      (i) has a barrel not less than 24 inches in length and does not have any barrel with a bore exceeding 2 inches in diameter;
      (ii) either has no magazine or has a non-detachable magazine incapable of holding more than two cartridges; and
      (iii) is not a revolver gun; and
   (b) an air weapon (that is to say, an air rifle, air gun or air pistol which does not fall within section 5(1) and which is not of a type declared by rules made by the Secretary of State under section 53 of this Act to be specially dangerous).

(3A) A gun which has been adapted to have such a magazine as is mentioned in subsection (3)(a)(ii) above shall not be regarded as falling within that provision unless the magazine bears a mark approved by the Secretary of State for denoting that fact and that mark has been made, and the adaptation has been certified in writing as having been carried out in a manner approved by him, either by one of the two companies mentioned in section 58(1) of this Act or by such other person as may be approved by him for that purpose.

(4) This section applies to any ammunition for a firearm, except the following articles, namely:—
   (a) cartridges containing five or more shot, none of which exceeds .36 inch in diameter;
   (b) ammunition for an air gun, air rifle or air pistol; and
   (c) blank cartridges not more than one inch in diameter measured immediately in front of the rim or cannelure of the base of the cartridge.

 24 month DTO

A7.2.1 *Sentencing*

There is no statutory minimum sentence for offences under s 1.

There is no sentencing guideline. For general guidance on sentencing firearms offences see **A7.1.2**.

A7.2.2 Key points

- Possession contrary to s 1 is established if the prosecution can prove the defendant knowingly had in his possession an article which was in fact a firearm (*R v Hussain* (1981) 72 Cr App R 143).
- The Firearms Act 1982 s 1(1) applies to any article which has the appearance of being a firearm to which the Firearms Act 1968 s 1 applies and is readily convertible into such a firearm. In such cases it will be an offence under s 1 of the 1968 Act to possess the article without a firearms certificate. It shall be a defence for the accused to show that he did not know and had no reason to suspect that the imitation firearm was so constructed or adapted as to be readily converted into a firearm to which s 1 of the 1968 Act applies (Firearms Act 1982 s 1(5)).

A7.3 Offences relating to air weapons

Firearms Act 1968 s 22(4)

It is an offence for a person under the age of eighteen to have with him an air weapon or ammunition for an air weapon.

Firearms Act 1968 s 23

(1) It is not an offence under section 22(4) of this Act for a person to have with him an air weapon or ammunition while he is under the supervision of a person of or over the age of twenty-one; but where a person has with him an air weapon on any premises in circumstances where he would be

prohibited from having it with him but for this subsection, it is an offence for the person under whose supervision he is to allow him to use it for firing any missile beyond those premises.

(1A) In proceedings against a person for an offence under subsection (1) it shall be a defence for him to show that the only premises into or across which the missile was fired were premises the occupier of which had consented to the firing of the missile (whether specifically or by way of a general consent).

(2) It is not an offence under section 22(4) of this Act for a person to have with him an air weapon or ammunition at a time when—

(a) being a member of a rifle club or miniature rifle club for the time being approved by the Secretary of State for the purposes of this section or section 15 of the Firearms (Amendment) Act 1988, he is engaged as such a member in connection with target shooting; or

(b) he is using the weapon or ammunition at a shooting gallery where the only firearms used are either air weapons or miniature rifles not exceeding .23 inch calibre.

(3) It is not an offence under section 22(4) of this Act for a person of or over the age of fourteen to have with him an air weapon or ammunition on private premises with the consent of the occupier.

Firearms Act 1968 s 21A

21A Firing an air weapon beyond premises

(1) A person commits an offence if—

(a) he has with him an air weapon on any premises; and

(b) he uses it for firing a missile beyond those premises.

(2) In proceedings against a person for an offence under this section it shall be a defence for him to show that the only premises into or across which the missile was fired were premises the occupier of which had consented to the firing of the missile (whether specifically or by way of a general consent).

 Level 3 fine

A7.3.1 *Sentencing*

There is no sentencing guideline for these offences.

A7.3.2 Key points

- Some barrelled air or gas weapons are capable of being firearms within the meaning of the Firearms Act 1968 s 57(1).
- Air weapons are not subject to the certification requirements of the Firearms Act 1968 s 1 unless the device has been declared 'specially dangerous' under the Firearms (Dangerous Air Weapons) Rules 1969 or it falls within the definition of a prohibited weapon (see **A7.4**).

See *Blackstone's Criminal Practice 2014* **B12.17, B12.48–B12.52**

A7.4 Possessing prohibited weapons or ammunition

Firearms Act 1968 s 5

5.— Weapons subject to general prohibition

(1) A person commits an offence if, without the authority of the Secretary of State or the Scottish Ministers (by virtue of provision made under section 63 of the Scotland Act 1998), he has in his possession, or purchases or acquires, or manufactures, sells or transfers—

  (a) any firearm which is so designed or adapted that two or more missiles can be successively discharged without repeated pressure on the trigger;

  (ab) any self-loading or pump-action rifled gun other than one which is chambered for .22 rim-fire cartridges;

  (aba) any firearm which either has a barrel less than 30 centimetres in length or is less than 60 centimetres in length overall, other than an air weapon, a muzzle-loading gun or a firearm designed as signalling apparatus;

  (ac) any self-loading or pump-action smooth-bore gun which is not an air weapon or chambered for .22 rim-fire cartridges and either has a barrel less than 24 inches in length or is less than 40 inches in length overall;

  (ad) any smooth-bore revolver gun other than one which is chambered for 9 mm. rim-fire cartridges or a muzzle-loading gun;

  (ae) any rocket launcher, or any mortar, for projecting a stabilised missile, other than a launcher or mortar designed for line-throwing or pyrotechnic purposes or as signalling apparatus;

  (af) any air rifle, air gun or air pistol which uses, or is designed or adapted for use with, a self-contained gas cartridge system;

  (b) any weapon of whatever description designed or adapted for the discharge of any noxious liquid, gas or other thing; and

  (c) any cartridge with a bullet designed to explode on or immediately before impact, any ammunition containing or designed or adapted to contain any such noxious thing as is mentioned in paragraph (b) above and, if capable of being used with a firearm of any description, any grenade, bomb (or other like missile), or rocket or shell designed to explode as aforesaid.

(1A) Subject to section 5A of this Act, a person commits an offence if, without the authority of the Secretary of State or the Scottish Ministers (by virtue of provision made under section 63 of the Scotland Act 1998), he has in his possession, or purchases or acquires, or sells or transfers—

  (a) any firearm which is disguised as another object;

  (b) any rocket or ammunition not falling within paragraph (c) of subsection (1) of this section which consists in or incorporates a missile designed to explode on or immediately before impact and is for military use;

(c) any launcher or other projecting apparatus not falling within paragraph (ae) of that subsection which is designed to be used with any rocket or ammunition falling within paragraph (b) above or with ammunition which would fall within that paragraph but for its being ammunition falling within paragraph (c) of that subsection;

(d) any ammunition for military use which consists in or incorporates a missile designed so that a substance contained in the missile will ignite on or immediately before impact;

(e) any ammunition for military use which consists in or incorporates a missile designed, on account of its having a jacket and hard-core, to penetrate armour plating, armour screening or body armour;

(f) any ammunition which incorporates a missile designed or adapted to expand on impact;

(g) anything which is designed to be projected as a missile from any weapon and is designed to be, or has been, incorporated in—

   (i) any ammunition falling within any of the preceding paragraphs; or

   (ii) any ammunition which would fall within any of those paragraphs but for its being specified in subsection (1) of this section.

(2) The weapons and ammunition specified in subsections (1) and (1A) of this section (including, in the case of ammunition, any missiles falling within subsection (1A)(g) of this section) are referred to in this Act as 'prohibited weapons' and 'prohibited ammunition' respectively.

…

(7) For the purposes of this section and section 5A of this Act—

(a) any rocket or ammunition which is designed to be capable of being used with a military weapon shall be taken to be for military use;

(b) references to a missile designed so that a substance contained in the missile will ignite on or immediately before impact include references to any missile containing a substance that ignites on exposure to air; and

(c) references to a missile's expanding on impact include references to its deforming in any predictable manner on or immediately after impact.

(8) For the purposes of subsection (1)(aba) and (ac) above, any detachable, folding, retractable or other movable butt-stock shall be disregarded in measuring the length of any firearm.

(9) Any reference in this section to a muzzle-loading gun is a reference to a gun which is designed to be loaded at the muzzle end of the barrel or chamber with a loose charge and a separate ball (or other missile).

24 month DTO (unless 3 year mandatory minimum sentence under s 51A—see **A7.4.2** below)

A7.4.1 *Allocation*

Where the statutory minimum sentence under s 51A applies (see **A7.1.3**) the court must send for trial (see **D2.3**). Otherwise the case must be dealt with in the youth court.

A7.4.2 *Sentence*

A mandatory minimum sentence applies in the case of certain prohibited weapons specified in s 51A (see **A7.1.3**) but only where the youth offender had attained the age of 16 by the date of the offence. Where the statutory minimum sentence does not apply the only custodial penalty would be a detention and training order.

A7.4.3 Key points

- To prove possession contrary to s 5 the prosecution merely had to prove possession of the object and that it was a prohibited weapon. It did not have to prove that the defendant either knew, or could have known, that the object was a weapon prohibited by the 1968 Act (*R v Deyemi* [2007] EWCA 2060, [2008] 1 Cr App R 25).
- It was not a defence to possession of a CS gas canister contrary to s 5(1)(b) that the defendant did not know or could not reasonably have been expected to know that the canister contained CS gas (*R v Bradish* (1990) 90 Cr App R 271).
- A person found in possession of a sawn-off shotgun inside a plastic bag is still in possession of the firearm even if he thought the bag contained a crowbar (*R v Waller* [1991] Crim LR 381).
- Momentary handling of a firearm by the accused followed by his immediate rejection of it, did not constitute possession of it within the meaning of s 5 (*R v T* [2011] EWCA Crim 1646).

A7.5 Possession of firearm with intent to endanger life

> **Firearms Act 1968 s 16**
>
> It is an offence for a person to have in his possession any firearm or ammunition with intent by means thereof to endanger life, or to enable another person by means thereof to endanger life, whether any injury has been caused or not.

 24 month DTO/detention for life (3 year mandatory minimum sentence if s 51A applies – see **A7.5.2** below)

A7.5.1 *Allocation*

Where the statutory minimum sentence under s 51A (see **A7.1.3**) applies the court must send for trial (see **D2.3**). If the minimum sentence does not apply then the youth court must go through a plea before venue and allocation procedure (see **D2.7**).

A7.5.2 *Sentence*

A mandatory minimum sentence applies in the case of certain prohibited weapons specified in s 51A but only where the youth offender had attained the age of 16 by the date of the offence. For s 51A see **A7.1.3**.

There is no sentencing guideline for this offence. For general guidance on sentencing firearms offences see **A7.1.2**.

A7.5.3 Key points

- There is no requirement that the firearm or ammunition is prohibited under the Firearms Act 1968 s 5 (*R v Salih* [2008] 1 WLR 2627).
- Section 16 does not extend to imitation firearms.
- The prosecution are not required to prove an immediate or unconditional intention to endanger life. The intention may last as long as the possession lasts and to possess a firearm ready for use if and when an occasion arises is an offence within s 16 (*R v Bentham* [1973] QB 357).
- It is possible to raise self-defence (*R v Georgiades* [1989] 1 WLR 759) but for the issue to be left to a jury there must be evidence of fear of imminent attack (*R v Stubbs* [2007] EWCA Crim 1714).

A7.6 Possession of firearm with intent to cause fear of violence

Firearms Act 1968 s 16A

It is an offence for a person to have in his possession any firearm or imitation firearm with intent—

(a) by means thereof to cause, or

(b) to enable another person by means thereof to cause,

any person to believe that unlawful violence will be used against him or another person.

IO

DO

GC

---

24 month DTO/10 years (mandatory 3 year minimum sentence applies if s 51A applies—see **A7.1.3**)

A7.6.1 *Allocation*

Where the statutory minimum sentence under s 51A applies the court must send for trial (see **D2.3**). If the minimum sentence does not apply then the youth court must go through a plea before venue and allocation procedure (see **D2.7**).

A7.6.2 *Sentencing*

A mandatory minimum sentence applies in the case of certain prohibited weapons specified in s 51A but only where the youth offender had attained the age of 16 by the date of the offence. For s 51A see **A7.1.3**.

There is no sentencing guideline for this offence. For general guidance on sentencing firearms offences see **A7.1.2**.

A7.6.3 Key points

- For the meaning of firearm and imitation firearm see **A7.1.1**.
- The requirement that the violence must be 'unlawful' allows the defendant to raise the fact that he was acting in reasonable self-defence.
- As long as the defendant intends to cause a fear of unlawful violence, it does not matter that the victim is aware that the item is in fact an imitation firearm (*K v DPP* [2006] EWHC 2183 (Admin)).

A7.7 Use of firearm to resist arrest

Firearms Act 1968 s 17

(1) It is an offence for a person to make or attempt to make any use whatsoever of a firearm or imitation firearm with intent to resist or prevent the lawful arrest or detention of himself or another person.

...

(4) For purposes of this section, the definition of 'firearm' in section 57(1) of this Act shall apply without paragraphs (b) and (c) of that subsection, and 'imitation firearm' shall be construed accordingly.

GC

24 month DTO/detention for life (mandatory 3 year minimum sentence applies if s 51A applies—see **A7.7.2** below)

A7.7.1 *Allocation*

Where the statutory minimum sentence under s 51A applies the court must send for trial (see **D2.3**). If the minimum sentence does not apply then the youth court must go through a plea before venue and allocation procedure (see **D2.7**).

A7.7.2 *Sentencing*

A mandatory minimum sentence applies in the case of certain prohibited weapons specified in s 51A but only where the youth offender had attained the age of 16 by the date of the offence. For s 51A see **A7.1.3**.

There is no sentencing guideline for this offence. For general guidance on sentencing firearms offences see **A7.1.2**.

A7.7.3 Key points

• For the definition of firearm and imitation firearm see **A7.1.1**.

A7.8 Possessing firearm while committing Schedule 1 offence

Firearms Act 1968 s 17(2) and (4)

(2) If a person, at the time of his committing or being arrested for an offence specified in Schedule 1 to this Act, has in his possession a firearm or imitation firearm, he shall be guilty of an offence under this subsection unless he shows that he had it in his possession for a lawful object.

...

(4) For purposes of this section, the definition of 'firearm' in section 57(1) of this Act shall apply without paragraphs (b) and (c) of that subsection, and 'imitation firearm' shall be construed accordingly.

 24 month DTO/detention for life (mandatory 3 year minimum sentence applies if s 51A applies—see **A7.8.2** below)

A7.8.1 *Allocation*

Where the statutory minimum sentence under s 51A applies the court must send for trial (see **D2.3**). If the minimum sentence does not apply then the youth court must go through a plea before venue and allocation procedure (see **D2.7**).

A7.8.2 *Sentence*

A mandatory minimum sentence applies in the case of certain prohibited weapons specified in s 51A but only where the youth offender had attained the age of 16 by the date of the offence. For s 51A see **A7.1.3**.

There is no sentencing guideline for this offence. For general guidance on sentencing firearms offences see **A7.1.2**.

A7.8.3 Key points

- For the definition of firearm and imitation firearm see **A7.1.1**.
- Possession for the purposes of s 17(2) is satisfied by custody and control of the firearm and does not require that the defendant has the firearm with him at the time of his arrest (*R v North* [2001] EWCA Crim 544).
- The Firearms Act 1968 Sch 1 contains the following offences:
  (a) Offences under the Criminal Damage Act 1971 s 1;
  (b) Offences under any of the following provisions of the Offences Against the Person Act 1861: ss 20 to 22 (inflicting bodily injury; garrotting; criminal use of stupefying drugs); s 30 (laying explosive to building etc); s 32 (endangering railway passengers by tampering with track); s 38 (assault with intent to commit felony or resist arrest); s 47 (criminal assaults);
  (c) Offences under Part I of the Child Abduction Act 1984 (abduction of children);
  (d) Theft, robbery, burglary, blackmail, and any offence under the TA 1968 s 12(1);
  (e) Offence under the Police Act 1996 s 89(1) (assaulting constable in execution of his duty);
  (f) Offences under the CJA 1991 s 90(1) (assaulting prisoner custody officer);
  (g) Offences under the Criminal Justice and Public Order Act 1994 s 12(1) (assaulting secure training centre officer);
  (h) Offences under the Immigration and Asylum Act 1999 Sch 11 para 4 (assaulting a detainee custody officer);
  (i) Offences under the SOA 2003 ss 1 (rape), s 2 (assault by penetration), s 4 (causing a person to engage in sexual activity involving penetration without consent), s 5 (rape of child under 13), s 6 (assault by penetration of child under 13), s 30 (sexual

activity involving penetration with a person with a mental disorder impeding choice) and s 31 (causing or inciting a person
with a mental disorder impeding choice to engage in sexual
activity involving penetration);

(j) aiding and abetting the commission of any such offence; and

(k) Attempting to commit any such offence.

• An offence specified in Sch 1 need not have been committed but the
defendant must have been lawfully arrested for one of the offences
specified (*R v Nelson* [2001] 1 QB 55).

A7.9 Possession of firearm with intent to commit indictable offence

> **Firearms Act 1968 s 18**
>
> (1) It is an offence for a person to have with him a firearm or imitation firearm
>   with intent to commit an indictable offence, or to resist arrest or prevent
>   the arrest of another, in either case while he has the firearm or imitation
>   firearm with him.
> (2) In proceedings for an offence under this section proof that the accused had
>   a firearm or imitation firearm with him and intended to commit an offence,
>   or to resist or prevent arrest, is evidence that he intended to have it with him
>   while doing so.

24 month DTO/detention for life (mandatory 3 year minimum
sentence if s 51A applies—see **D7.9.2** below)

A7.9.1 *Allocation*

Where the statutory minimum sentence under s 51A (see **A7.1.3**)
applies the court must send for trial (see **D2.3**). If the minimum sentence does not apply then the youth court must go through a plea
before venue and allocation procedure (see **D2.7**).

A7.9.2 *Sentence*

A mandatory minimum sentence applies in the case of certain prohibited weapons specified in s 51A but only where the youth offender had
attained the age of 16 by the date of the offence. For s 51A see **A7.1.3**.

There is no sentencing guideline for this offence. For general guidance
on sentencing firearms offences see **A7.1.2**.

A7.9.3 Key points

- For the definition of firearm and imitation firearm see **A7.1.1**.
- In *R v Stoddart* [1998] 2 Cr App R 25 the Court of Appeal held that there are three elements to an offence under s 18:
  (a) that the defendant had with him a firearm or imitation firearm;
  (b) that he intended to have it with him; and
  (c) that at the same time he had the intention to commit an indictable offence or to resist or prevent arrest.

The prosecution must prove that the firearm or imitation firearm was with the defendant as opposed to being under his control somewhere else. He may have the firearm with him if it is readily accessible to him at the time of the offence (*R v Pawlicki* [1992] 1 WLR 827).

A7.10 Carrying firearm in public place

> **Firearms Act 1968 s 19**
>
> A person commits an offence if, without lawful authority or reasonable excuse (the proof whereof lies on him) he has with him in a public place—
> (a) a loaded shot gun,
> (b) an air weapon (whether loaded or not),
> (c) any other firearm (whether loaded or not) together with ammunition suitable for use in that firearm, or
> (d) an imitation firearm.

EW Except in case of an imitation firearm or if the firearm is an air weapon

▦ 6 month DTO (in case of an air weapon)

▦ 12 month DTO (in case of an imitation firearm)

▦ 24 month DTO (in case of a loaded shotgun or any other firearm)

A7.10.1 *Allocation*

Where the statutory minimum sentence under s 51A (see **A7.1.3**) applies the court must send for trial (see **D2.3**). If the minimum sentence does not apply then the case will be dealt with summarily.

A7.10.2 *Sentence*

A mandatory minimum sentence applies in the case of certain prohibited weapons specified in s 51A but only where the youth offender had attained the age of 16 by the date of the offence. For s 51A see **A7.1.3**.

The *Magistrates' Court Sentencing Guidelines* contain the following guidance in relation to offences under s 19. It is applicable to **adult** offenders not liable to a statutory minimum sentence.

Offence seriousness (culpability and harm) A. Identify the appropriate starting point Starting points based on first-time offender pleading not guilty		
Examples of nature of activity	**Starting point**	**Range**
Carrying an unloaded air weapon	Low level community order	Band B fine to medium level community order
Carrying loaded air weapon/imitation firearm/ unloaded shotgun without ammunition	High level community order	Medium level community order to 26 weeks' custody (air weapon) Medium level community order to Crown Court (imitation firearm, unloaded shotgun)
Carrying loaded shotgun/ carrying shotgun or any other firearm together with ammunition for it	Crown Court	Crown Court

Offence seriousness (culpability and harm) B. Consider the effect of aggravating and mitigating factors (other than those within examples above) The following may be particularly relevant but **these lists are not exhaustive**	
Factors indicating higher culpability	**Factors indicating lower culpability**
Brandishing firearm	Firearm not in sight
Carrying firearm in a busy place	No intention to use firearm
Planned illegal use	Firearm to be used for lawful purpose (not amounting to defence)
Factors indicating greater degree of harm	
Person or people put in fear	
Offender participating in violent incident	

- *R v M* [2011] EWCA Crim 1371—D, aged 16 at the time, made a rap video filmed at night outside a block of flats on a council estate. The video, which in the opinion of the judge glorified violence, was uploaded to YouTube and later distributed with other rap videos on a DVD. The participants of the video could be seen carrying what appeared to be a sawn-off shotgun. D eventually pleaded guilty aged 18 to possession of an imitation firearm in a public place contrary to s 19. He had previous convictions for wounding, for which he had served a custodial sentence, and burglary. **Held:** The correct starting point was nine months' detention reduced to six months to reflect the guilty plea.

A7.10.3 Key points

- For the definition of firearm and imitation firearm see **A7.1.1**.
- Public place includes any highway and any other premises or place to which at the material time the public have or are permitted to have access, whether on payment or otherwise (Firearms Act 1968 s 57(4)).
- In the case of a shotgun it is not necessary to show that the defendant knew that it was loaded (*R v Harrison* [1996] 1 Cr App R 138).

 See *Blackstone's Criminal Practice 2014* **B12.103–B12.104**

A7.11 Offensive weapon

Prevention of Crime Act 1953 s 1

(1) Any person who without lawful authority or reasonable excuse, the proof whereof shall lie on him, has with him in any public place any offensive weapon shall be guilty of an offence....

(2) Where any person is convicted of an offence under subsection (1) of this section the court may make an order for the forfeiture or disposal of any weapon in respect of which the offence was committed.

...

(4) In this section 'public place' includes any highway and any other premises or place to which at the material time the public have or are permitted to have access, whether on payment or otherwise; and 'offensive weapon' means any article made or adapted for use for causing injury to the person, or intended by the person having it with him for such use by him or by some other person.

EW

 24 month DTO

A7.11.1 *Sentencing*

There is no sentencing guideline specific for youths for this offence. The *Magistrates' Court Sentencing Guidelines* (2008) provide guidance for sentencing **adult** offenders.

Offence seriousness (culpability and harm) A. Identify the appropriate starting point Starting points based on first-time offender pleading not guilty		
Examples of nature of activity	**Starting point**	**Range**
Weapon not used to threaten or cause fear	High level community order	Band C fine to 12 weeks' custody
Weapon not used to threaten or cause fear but offence committed in dangerous circumstances	6 weeks' custody	High level community order to Crown Court
Weapon used to threaten or cause fear and offence committed in dangerous circumstances	Crown Court	Crown Court

Offence seriousness (culpability and harm) B. Consider the effect of aggravating and mitigating factors (other than those within examples above) The following may be particularly relevant but **these lists are not exhaustive**	
Factors indicating higher culpability 1. Particularly dangerous weapon 2. Specifically planned use of weapon to commit violence, threaten violence, or intimidate 3. Offence motivated by hostility towards minority individual or group 4. Offender under influence of drink or drugs 5. Offender operating in group or gang	**Factors indicating lower culpability** 1. Weapon carried only on temporary basis 2. Original possession legitimate, eg in course of trade or business
Factors indicating greater degree of harm 1. Offence committed at school, hospital, or other place where vulnerable persons may be present 2. Offence committed on premises where people carrying out public services 3. Offence committed on or outside licensed premises 4. Offence committed on public transport 5. Offence committed at large public gathering, especially where there may be risk of disorder	

Following the decision of the Court of Appeal in *R v Povey* [2009] 1 Cr App R (S) 228 the above guidelines are to be read in the light of the following:

The guideline provides three categories of seriousness:
- **level 1** is for the situation where a person has a weapon or bladed article, is not in a 'dangerous circumstance' and the weapon or bladed article is not used to threaten or to cause fear; in those circumstances:—

- applying *Povey*, where the offensive weapon is a knife the starting point would be close to 12 weeks custody for a first time adult offender who has pleaded not guilty;
- in relation to an offensive weapon other than a knife, the starting point for a first time adult offender who has pleaded not guilty is a high level community order.

- **level 2** is for the situation where a weapon is in the possession of the offender in 'dangerous circumstances' but is not used to threaten or to cause fear; in those circumstances:
  - applying *Povey*, where the offensive weapon is a knife the starting point for a first time adult offender who has pleaded not guilty is committal to the Crown Court and, therefore, a custodial sentence in excess of 6 months;
  - in relation to an offensive weapon other than a knife, the starting point for a first time adult offender who has pleaded not guilty is a custodial sentence of 6 weeks.

- **level 3** is for the situation where a weapon is used in dangerous circumstances to threaten or cause fear; in those circumstances, both the starting point and range for a first time adult offender who has pleaded not guilty are for sentencing in the Crown Court and, therefore, in excess of 6 months custody.

'Dangerous circumstances' has not been judicially defined but was used in the previous Court of Appeal guideline judgment in *Celaire and Poulton*. In relation to a knife, a circumstance is likely to be dangerous if there is a real possibility that it could be used.

A7.11.2 Key points

- In *R v Simpson* [1983] 1 WLR 1494 the Court of Appeal held there were three possible categories of offensive weapon:
  (a) the weapon made for use for causing injury to the person, that is a weapon offensive *per se*;
  (b) the weapon adapted for such a use; and
  (c) an object not so made or adapted, but one which the person carrying intends to use for the purpose of causing injury to the person.

- Weapons held by the appellate courts to be offensive *per se* include: a bayonet, a stiletto, and a flick knife. It is likely that items prohibited for sale in England and Wales by virtue of the Criminal Justice Act 1988 (Offensive Weapons) Order 1988 are offensive *per se*. These include knuckledusters, butterfly knives, telescopic and friction-lock truncheons, disguised knives, and swordsticks.

- In other cases it is a question for the tribunal of fact whether the item is an offensive weapon (*R v Williamson* (1978) 67 Cr App R 35, CA).

- Items that are inherently dangerous, but manufactured for a lawful purpose, are not offensive *per se* (eg cut-throat razor and kitchen knives).

- A lock knife is not offensive *per se* (*Patterson v Block* (1984) 81 LS Gaz 2458, DC).
- An intention to frighten or intimidate is not an intention to cause injury unless the defendant's intention was to cause injury by shock (*R v Rapier* (1980) 70 Cr App R 17).
- The offence under s 1(1) is not concerned with the actual use of the weapon but the carrying of a weapon with intent to use it if occasion arises (*Ohlson v Hylton* ([1975] 1 WLR 724). In that case a workman was not guilty of an offence under s 1 when he pulled out a hammer from his tool bag and used it to hit another person. See also *C v DPP* [2001] EWHC Admin 1093 where the conviction was quashed when a girl out walking her dog detached the chain and used it to swing at a police officer. The court held that there was no evidence that she had formed the intent to use the dog chain offensively before the occasion of its actual use had arisen. The use of an article picked up and used as a weapon during a fight can be dealt with by charging an assault (*R v Jura* [1954] 1 QB 503).
- 'Public place' includes any highway and any other premises or place to which at the material time the public have or are permitted to have access, whether on payment or otherwise (s 1(4)). In *Knox v Anderson* (1982) 76 Cr App R 156 the Divisional Court held that the upper landing of a block of flats where there were no barriers or notices restricting access was a 'public place'. In contrast, a landing in a block of flats where access to the building is controlled by a locked door and intercom system may not be a public place (cf *Williams v DPP* (1992) 95 Cr App R 415).
- The prosecution must prove that the defendant knew that he was in possession of the offensive weapon (*R v Cugullere* [1961] 2 All ER 343). However, it is not necessary to prove that the defendant was aware that the item was in fact an offensive weapon (see *R v Densu* [1998] 1 Cr App R 4000 where the defendant had found a telescopic baton which he was using as a lever for his trolley jack not knowing that it was a weapon).
- Possession, once established, continued until the accused did something to end it. Merely forgetting was not enough to end possession nor did it of itself amount to a reasonable excuse (*R v McCalla* (1988) 87 Cr App R (S) 372).
- In *R v Glidewell* [1999] EWCA Crim 1221, (1999) 163 JP 557 it was held that depending upon the circumstances of the particular case, forgetfulness could be relevant to whether or not a defendant had a reasonable excuse. In that case involving a cab driver found with offensive weapons which had been left in the car by a passenger a few days before the relevant circumstances included the fact that the defendant had not introduced the weapons into the car, had been in possession of them for a relatively short time, and had given

evidence of how busy he had been since the relevant night. Whether his forgetfulness was relevant to the existence of a reasonable excuse was a matter for the tribunal of fact.

- It may be a reasonable excuse for the carrying of an offensive weapon if the defendant is in anticipation of imminent attack and carrying it for his own personal safety (*Evans v Hughes* [1972] 1 WLR 1452).

 See *Blackstone's Criminal Practice 2014* **B12.136–B12.178**

A7.12 Aggravated possession of offensive weapons

Prevention of Crime Act 1953 s 1A

(1) A person is guilty of an offence if that person—
   (a) has an offensive weapon with him or her in a public place,
   (b) unlawfully and intentionally threatens another person with the weapon, and
   (c) does so in such a way that there is an immediate risk of serious physical harm to that other person.

(2) For the purposes of this section physical harm is serious if it amounts to grievous bodily harm for the purposes of the Offences against the Person Act 1861.

(3) In this section 'public place' and 'offensive weapon' have the same meaning as in section 1.

...

(5) Where a person aged 16 or over is convicted of an offence under this section, the court must impose an appropriate custodial sentence (with or without a fine) unless the court is of the opinion that there are particular circumstances which—
   (a) relate to the offence or to the offender, and
   (b) would make it unjust to do so in all the circumstances.

(6) In this section 'appropriate custodial sentence' means—
   (a) in the case of a person who is aged 18 or over when convicted, a sentence of imprisonment for a term of at least 6 months;
   (b) in the case of a person who is aged at least 16 but under 18 when convicted, a detention and training order of at least 4 months.

(7) In considering whether it is of the opinion mentioned in subsection (5) in the case of a person aged under 18, the court must have regard to its duty under section 44 of the Children and Young Persons Act 1933.

...

(9) In relation to times before the coming into force of paragraph 180 of Schedule 7 to the Criminal Justice and Court Services Act 2000, the reference in subsection (6)(a) to a sentence of imprisonment, in relation to an offender aged under 21 at the time of conviction, is to be read as a reference to a sentence of detention in a young offender institution.

> (10) If on a person's trial for an offence under this section (whether on indict-
> ment or not) the person is found not guilty of that offence but it is proved
> that the person committed an offence under section 1, the person may be
> convicted of the offence under that section.

 24 month DTO (mandatory minimum sentence of 4 month
DTO if offender was 16 or 17 on the date of the offence)

A7.12.1 *Sentencing*

There is no sentencing guideline for this offence. The guideline issued
for offensive weapons will be relevant—see **A7.11.1**.

Where the offender was under the age of 16 on the date of the offence
the minimum sentence does not apply. Where the minimum sentence
does apply, a 20 per cent reduction on that obligatory sentence is available for an early guilty plea (CJA 2003 s 144 (2) and (3)).

The Ministry of Justice Circular 2012/08 at para 36 states:

> In relation to an offender who is 16 or 17, the usual position on a guilty plea
> (that the court is to have regard to it, and must follow any relevant sentencing
> guideline) applies. The detention and training order is only available for fixed
> periods, the shortest of which is 4 months. It follows that a guilty plea will (if
> the 'starting point' is 4 months and credit is given for the plea) have the result
> that a period of detention is not imposed.

A7.12.2 Key points

- For the definition of offensive weapon and public place see **A7.11**.
- For the definition of grievous bodily harm see **A1.7.2.**
- An offence under s 1A has no statutory defence of reasonable excuse
  but the requirement that the violence be unlawful allows the defendant to raise the fact that he was acting in reasonable self-defence.

A7.13 Bladed or pointed article

Criminal Justice Act 1988 s 139

> (1) Subject to subsections (4) and (5) below, any person who has an article to
> which this section applies with him in a public place shall be guilty of an
> offence.
> (2) Subject to subsection (3) below, this section applies to any article which has
> a blade or is sharply pointed except a folding pocketknife.
> (3) This section applies to a folding pocketknife if the cutting edge of its blade
> exceeds 3 inches.

> (4) It shall be a defence for a person charged with an offence under this section to prove that he had good reason or lawful authority for having the article with him in a public place.
>
> (5) Without prejudice to the generality of subsection (4) above, it shall be a defence for a person charged with an offence under this section to prove that he had the article with him—
>   (a) for use at work;
>   (b) for religious reasons; or
>   (c) as part of any national costume.
>   …
>
> (7) In this section 'public place' includes any place to which at the material time the public have or are permitted access, whether on payment or otherwise.

EW

 24 month DTO

A7.13.1 *Sentencing*

See **A7.11.1**.

A7.13.2 Key points

- The prosecution must prove that the person had the item with him and that it falls within the definition in the section. Only then must the defence establish a defence to the civil standard.
- A screwdriver is not a bladed article (*R v Davis* [1998] Crim LR 564).
- A blade does not need to be sharp—a butter knife can be a bladed article (*Brooker v Director of Public Prosecutions* [2005] EWHC 1132).
- To be a folding pocketknife within the meaning of s 139(3) the knife has to be readily and immediately foldable at all times, simply by the folding process (*Harris v DPP* (1993) 96 Cr App R 235). A knife with a locking mechanism does not come within the scope of s 139(3) even when the cutting edge of the blade is less than three inches (*R v Deegan* [1998] 2 Cr App R 121).
- A public place includes any place to which, at the material time, the public have or are permitted to have access, whether on payment or otherwise (s 139(7)). A front garden to a dwelling was not a public place within the meaning of s 139(7) (*R v Roberts* [2004] 1 WLR 181). Unimpeded access to land was not in itself enough to turn private land into public land for the purposes of s 139(7); to become a public place there must be evidence that the access was also invited or tolerated (*Harriot v DPP* [2005] EWHC 965 (Admin)).

- A person has something with him if he knows that he has with him the object in question; a mere belief that a knife was somewhere in the accused's van would not be enough (*R v Daubeney* (2000) 164 JP 519).
- Whilst forgetfulness on its own cannot constitute a good reason, it might do so combined with another reason (*R v Jolie* [2003] EWCA Crim 543, [2004] 1 Cr App R 44). That reason could be the defendant's employment even if only casual (*Chahal v DPP* [2010] EWHC 439 (Admin)).
- Fear of attack may amount to a good reason if the risk is imminent (*R v McAuley* [2009] EWCA Crim 2130, [2010] 1 Cr App R 148).

A7.14 Bladed or pointed article or offensive weapon on school premises

Criminal Justice Act 1988 s 139A

(1) Any person who has an article to which section 139 of this Act applies with him on school premises shall be guilty of an offence.

(2) Any person who has an offensive weapon within the meaning of section 1 of the Prevention of Crime Act 1953 with him on school premises shall be guilty of an offence.

(3) It shall be a defence for a person charged with an offence under subsection (1) or (2) above to prove that he had good reason or lawful authority for having the article or weapon with him on the premises in question.

(4) Without prejudice to the generality of subsection (3) above, it shall be a defence for a person charged with an offence under subsection (1) or (2) above to prove that he had the article or weapon in question with him—
   (a) for use at work,
   (b) for educational purposes,
   (c) for religious reasons, or
   (d) as part of any national costume.
   . . .

(6) In this section and section 139B, 'school premises' means land used for the purposes of a school excluding any land occupied solely as a dwelling by a person employed at the school; and 'school' has the meaning given by section 4 of the Education Act 1996.

EW

|||| 24 month DTO

A7.14.1 *Sentencing*

See **A7.11.1**.

A7.14.2 `Key points`

- For the CJA 1988 s 139 see **A7.13**.
- For offensive weapon see **A7.11**.

A7.15 Aggravated possession of bladed or pointed article

Criminal Justice Act 1988 s 139AA

(1) A person is guilty of an offence if that person—
 (a) has an article to which this section applies with him or her in a public place or on school premises,
 (b) unlawfully and intentionally threatens another person with the article, and
 (c) does so in such a way that there is an immediate risk of serious physical harm to that other person.
(2) In relation to a public place this section applies to an article to which section 139 applies.
(3) In relation to school premises this section applies to each of these—
 (a) an article to which section 139 applies;
 (b) an offensive weapon within the meaning of section 1 of the Prevention of Crime Act 1953.
(4) For the purposes of this section physical harm is serious if it amounts to grievous bodily harm for the purposes of the Offences Against the Person Act 1861.
(5) In this section—
 'public place' has the same meaning as in section 139;
 'school premises' has the same meaning as in section 139A.

. . .

(7) Where a person aged 16 or over is convicted of an offence under this section, the court must impose an appropriate custodial sentence (with or without a fine) unless the court is of the opinion that there are particular circumstances which—
 (a) relate to the offence or to the offender, and
 (b) would make it unjust to do so in all the circumstances.
(8) In this section 'appropriate custodial sentence' means—
 (a) in the case of a person who is aged 18 or over when convicted, a sentence of imprisonment for a term of at least 6 months;
 (b) in the case of a person who is aged at least 16 but under 18 when convicted, a detention and training order of at least 4 months.
(9) In considering whether it is of the opinion mentioned in subsection (7) in the case of a person aged under 18, the court must have regard to its duty under section 44 of the Children and Young Persons Act 1933.

. . .

(12) If on a person's trial for an offence under this section (whether on indictment or not) the person is found not guilty of that offence but it is proved that the person committed an offence under section 139 or 139A, the person may be convicted of the offence under that section.

24 month DTO (4 month mandatory minimum sentence applies if the offender was 16 or 17 on the date of the offence)

A7.15.1 *Sentence*

There is no sentencing guideline for this offence. The guideline issued for offensive weapons will be relevant—see **A7.11.1**.

Where the offender was under the age of 16 on the date of the offence the minimum sentence does not apply. Where the minimum sentence does apply a 20 per cent reduction on that obligatory sentence is available for an early guilty plea (CJA 2003 s 144 (2) and (3))—for the practical effect of this provision see **A7.12.2**.

A7.15.2 Key points

- For the definition of public place see **A7.13.2**.
- The statutory defences of reasonable excuse or good reason do not apply to the aggravated offence under s 139AA. The requirement that the threat be 'unlawful' would allow the defendant to raise the fact that he was acting in reasonable self-defence.

A7.16 Minding a dangerous weapon

> **Violent Crime Reduction Act 2006 s 28**
>
> **28 Using someone to mind a weapon**
>
> (1) A person is guilty of an offence if—
>   (a) he uses another to look after, hide or transport a dangerous weapon for him; and
>   (b) he does so under arrangements or in circumstances that facilitate, or are intended to facilitate, the weapon's being available to him for an unlawful purpose.
> (2) For the purposes of this section the cases in which a dangerous weapon is to be regarded as available to a person for an unlawful purpose include any case where—
>   (a) the weapon is available for him to take possession of it at a time and place; and
>   (b) his possession of the weapon at that time and place would constitute, or be likely to involve or to lead to, the commission by him of an offence.
> (3) In this section 'dangerous weapon' means—
>   (a) a firearm other than an air weapon or a component part of, or accessory to, an air weapon; or
>   (b) a weapon to which section 141 or 141A of the Criminal Justice Act 1988 applies (specified offensive weapons, knives and bladed weapons).

24 month DTO (unless mandatory minimum sentence under s 29 applies)

A7.16.1 *Sentencing*

Violent Crime Reduction Act 2006 s 29

(1) This section applies where a person ('the offender') is guilty of an offence under section 28.

(2) Where the dangerous weapon in respect of which the offence was committed is a weapon to which section 141 or 141A of the Criminal Justice Act 1988 (specified offensive weapons, knives and bladed weapons) applies, the offender shall be liable, on conviction on indictment, to imprisonment for a term not exceeding 4 years or to a fine, or to both.

(3) Where—

    (a) at the time of the offence, the offender was aged 16 or over, and

    (b) the dangerous weapon in respect of which the offence was committed was a firearm mentioned in section 5(1)(a) to (af) or (c) or section 5(1A)(a) of the 1968 Act (firearms possession of which attracts a minimum sentence), the offender shall be liable, on conviction on indictment, to imprisonment for a term not exceeding 10 years or to a fine, or to both.

(4) On a conviction in England and Wales, where—

    (a) subsection (3) applies, and

    (b) the offender is aged 18 or over at the time of conviction,

the court must impose (with or without a fine) a term of imprisonment of not less than 5 years, unless it is of the opinion that there are exceptional circumstances relating to the offence or to the offender which justify its not doing so.

(5) In relation to times before the commencement of paragraph 180 of Schedule 7 to the Criminal Justice and Court Services Act 2000 (c. 43), the reference in subsection (4) to a sentence of imprisonment, in relation to an offender aged under 21 at the time of conviction, is to be read as a reference to a sentence of detention in a young offender institution.

(6) On a conviction in England and Wales, where—

    (a) subsection (3) applies, and

    (b) the offender is aged under 18 at the time of conviction,

the court must impose (with or without a fine) a term of detention under section 91 of the Powers of Criminal Courts (Sentencing) Act 2000 (c. 6) of not less than 3 years, unless it is of the opinion that there are exceptional circumstances relating to the offence or to the offender which justify its not doing so.

(11) Where—

    (a) a court is considering for the purposes of sentencing the seriousness of an offence under section 28, and

    (b) at the time of the offence the offender was aged 18 or over and the person used to look after, hide or transport the weapon was not,

---

the court must treat the fact that that person was under the age of 18 at that time as an aggravating factor (that is to say, a factor increasing the seriousness of the offence).

(12) Where a court treats a person's age as an aggravating factor in accordance with subsection (11), it must state in open court that the offence was aggravated as mentioned in that subsection.

(13) Where—

    (a) an offence under section 28 of using another person for a particular purpose is found to have involved that other person's having possession of a weapon, or being able to make it available, over a period of two or more days, or at some time during a period of two or more days, and

    (b) on any day in that period, an age requirement was satisfied,

the question whether subsection (3) applies or (as the case may be) the question whether the offence was aggravated under this section is to be determined as if the offence had been committed on that day.

(14) In subsection (13) the reference to an age requirement is a reference to either of the following—

    (a) the requirement of subsection (3) that the offender was aged 16 or over at the time of the offence;

    (b) the requirement of subsection (11) that the offender was aged 18 or over at that time and that the other person was not.

A8 Offences against the Administration of Justice

A8.1 Perverting the course of justice

It is an offence at common law to do an act tending and intended to pervert the course of public justice.

IO

GC

▦ 24 month DTO/by detention for life in Crown Court

A8.1.1 *Sentencing*

There is no sentencing guideline for this offence.

The particular factors which the court must have regard to are (a) the seriousness of the substantive offence to which the perverting of the course of justice relates; (b) the degree of persistence during which the deception was maintained; and (c) the seriousness of the consequences (*R v Tunney* [2006] EWCA 2066).

A8.1.2 Key points

- Acts which could amount to perverting the course of justice include destroying or concealing evidence, interfering with jurors or witnesses, and confessing to another's crime.
- Making false allegations against another person, intending that he be prosecuted or knowing that he might be, would constitute an offence (*R v Rowell* [1978] 1 WLR 132).
- Where it is alleged that a false allegation has been made, the prosecution must show that the defendant intended that the police take it seriously. It is not necessary to prove that the defendant intended anyone to be arrested (*R v Cotter* [2002] EWCA Crim 1033).
- False complaints which do not risk the arrest of an innocent person might in certain circumstances be more appropriately charged as wasting police time (see **A8.4**) (*R v Cotter*).
- When dealing with a suspected false sexual allegation reference should be made to the detailed CPS Legal Guidance *Perverting the Course of Justice: Charging in Cases Involving Rape and/or Domestic Violence Allegations*.

📖 See *Blackstone's Criminal Practice 2014* **B14.29–B14.44**

A8.2 Witness intimidation

Criminal Justice and Public Order Act 1994 s 51(1)–(5)

(1) A person commits an offence if—
  (a) he does an act which intimidates, and is intended to intimidate, another person ('the victim'),
  (b) he does the act knowing or believing that the victim is assisting in the investigation of an offence or is a witness or potential witness or a juror or potential juror in proceedings for an offence, and
  (c) he does it intending thereby to cause the investigation or the course of justice to be obstructed, perverted or interfered with.

(2) A person commits an offence if—
  (a) he does an act which harms, and is intended to harm, another person or, intending to cause another person to fear harm, he threatens to do an act which would harm that other person,
  (b) he does or threatens to do the act knowing or believing that the person harmed or threatened to be harmed ('the victim'), or some other person, has assisted in an investigation into an offence or has given evidence or particular evidence in proceedings for an offence, or has acted as a juror or concurred in a particular verdict in proceedings for an offence, and
  (c) he does or threatens to do it because of that knowledge or belief.

(3) For the purposes of subsections (1) and (2) it is immaterial that the act is or would be done, or that the threat is made—
  (a) otherwise than in the presence of the victim, or
  (b) to a person other than the victim.

(4) The harm that may be done or threatened may be financial as well as physical (whether to the person or a person's property) and similarly as respects an intimidatory act which consists of threats.

(5) The intention required by subsection (1)(c) and the motive required by subsection (2)(c) above need not be the only or the predominating intention or motive with which the act is done or, in the case of subsection (2), threatened.

 EW

 24 month DTO

A8.2.1 *Sentencing*

There is no sentencing guideline specific to youths. The *Magistrates' Court Sentencing Guidelines* (2008) give the following guidance on sentencing **adult** offenders:

A8 Offences against the Administration of Justice

Offence seriousness (culpability and harm) A. Identify the appropriate starting point Starting points based on first-time offender pleading not guilty		
Examples of nature of activity	**Starting point**	**Range**
Sudden outburst in chance encounter	6 weeks' custody	Medium level community order to 18 weeks' custody
Conduct amounting to a threat; staring at, approaching, or following witnesses; talking about the case; trying to alter or stop evidence	18 weeks' custody	12 weeks' custody to Crown Court
Threats of violence to witnesses and/ or their families; deliberately seeking out witnesses	Crown Court	Crown Court

Offence seriousness (culpability and harm) B. Consider the effect of aggravating and mitigating factors (other than those within examples above) The following may be particularly relevant but **these lists are not exhaustive**	
Factors indicating higher culpability 1. Breach of bail conditions 2. Offender involves others **Factors indicating greater degree of harm** 1. Detrimental impact on administration of justice 2. Contact made at or in vicinity of victim's home	

 See *Blackstone's Criminal Practice 2014* **B14.46–B14.47**

A8.3 Escape from lawful custody

At common law it is an offence to escape from legal custody.

24 month DTO/detention for life in Crown Court

A8.3.1 *Sentencing*

There is no sentencing guideline applicable to this offence.

IO Indictable Only   **GC** Grave Crime   Sentence

A8.3.2 Key points

- The prosecution must prove that the defendant was in custody, that he knew (or was reckless as to whether he was or not); that the custody was lawful; and that he intentionally escaped from it (*R v Dhillon* [2005] EWCA Crim 2996).
- The escape may be from police custody following arrest (*R v Timmis* [1976] Crim LR 129).
- A prisoner is deemed to be in legal custody while he is confined in, or is being taken to or from, any prison or young offender institution (Prison Act 1952 s 13).
- Whether a person can be said to be in custody at any particular time is a question of fact to be decided by reference to the circumstances of each individual case. For a person to be in custody, his liberty must be subject to such restraint or restriction that he can be said to be confined by another in the sense that that the person's immediate freedom of movement is under the direct control of another (*E v DPP* [2002] EWHC 433(Admin)).
- A youth refused bail and remanded to local authority accommodation with a security requirement (now a remand to youth detention accommodation under an LASPO 2012 s 91(5)) but not placed in such accommodation as no placement was available was in lawful custody when he absented himself from court (*E v DPP*).
- A youth refused bail and remanded to local authority accommodation who had been collected from the cells by a YOT worker and told to wait while she arranged a placement was held to be in lawful custody (*H v DPP* ([2003] EWHC 878 Admin).

A8.4 Wasting police time

Criminal Law Act 1967 s 5

(2) Where a person causes any wasteful employment of the police by knowingly making to any person a false report tending to show that an offence has been committed, or to give rise to apprehension for the safety of any persons or property, or tending to show that he has information material to any police inquiry, he shall be liable on summary conviction to imprisonment for not more than six months or to a fine of not more than two hundred pounds or to both.

SO

▦ 6 month DTO

A8.4.1 *Sentencing*

No sentencing guideline exists.

A8.4.2 Key points

- No proceedings shall be instituted for an offence under this section except by or with the consent of the DPP (s 5(3)).

 See *Blackstone's Criminal Practice 2014* **B14.78**

A8.5 Contempt of court

Magistrates' Court Act 1980 s 97

(4) If any person attending or brought before a magistrates' court refuses without just excuse to be sworn or give evidence, or to produce any document or thing, the court may commit him to custody until the expiration of such period not exceeding one month as may be specified in the warrant or until he sooner gives evidence or produces the document or thing or impose on him a fine not exceeding £2,500 or both.

Contempt of Court Act 1981 s 12

(1) A magistrates' court has jurisdiction under this section to deal with any person who—
  (a) wilfully insults the justice or justices, any witness before or officer of the court or any solicitor or counsel having business in the court, during his or their sitting or attendance in court or in going to or returning from the court; or
  (b) wilfully interrupts the proceedings of the court or otherwise misbehaves in court.
(2) In any such case the court may order any officer of the court, or any constable, to take the offender into custody and detain him until the rising of the court; and the court may, if it thinks fit, commit the offender to custody for a specified period not exceeding one month or impose on him a fine not exceeding £2,500, or both.

A8.5.1 *Sentencing*

Penalties for contempt of court in the Crown Court are governed by the Contempt of Court Act 1981 s 14.

The combined effect of the PCCSA 2000 ss 89 and 108 means that there is no power to impose a custodial sentence on a person under the age of 18 (*R v Byas* (1995) 16 Cr App R (S) 869).

 See *Blackstone's Criminal Practice 2014* **B14.80–B14.128**

A8.6 Breach of non-molestation or restraining order

Family Law Act 1996 s 42A

(1) A person who without reasonable excuse does anything that he is prohibited from doing by a non-molestation order is guilty of an offence.

(2) In the case of a non-molestation order made by virtue of section 45(1), a person can be guilty of an offence under this section only in respect of conduct engaged in at a time when he was aware of the existence of the order.

(3) Where a person is convicted of an offence under this section in respect of any conduct, that conduct is not punishable as a contempt of court.

(4) A person cannot be convicted of an offence under this section in respect of any conduct which has been punished as a contempt of court.

 EW

 24 month DTO

Protection from Harassment Act 1997 s 5

(5) If without reasonable excuse the defendant does anything which he is prohibited from doing by an order under this section, he is guilty of an offence.

(6) A person guilty of an offence under this section is liable—

    (a) on conviction on indictment, to imprisonment for a term not exceeding five years, or a fine, or both, or

    (b) on summary conviction, to imprisonment for a term not exceeding six months, or a fine not exceeding the statutory maximum, or both.

...

(7) A court dealing with a person for an offence under this section may vary or discharge the order in question by a further order.

 EW

 24 month DTO

A8.6.1 *Sentencing*

There is no sentencing guideline specific to youths. The definitive guideline *Breach of a Protective Order* gives the following guidance for sentencing **adult** offenders:

Nature of activity	Starting points
	Custodial sentence
Breach (whether one or more) involving significant physical violence and significant physical or psychological harm to the victim	**More than 12 months** The length of the custodial sentence imposed will depend on the nature and seriousness of the breach(es)

More than one breach involving some violence and/or significant physical or psychological harm to the victim	26–39 weeks' custody
Single breach involving some violence and/or significant physical or psychological harm to the victim	13–26 weeks' custody
	Non-custodial sentence
More than one breach involving no/minimal contact or some direct contact	Medium range community order
Single breach involving no/minimal direct contact	Low range community order

Additional aggravating factors	Additional mitigating factors
1. Victim is particularly vulnerable 2. Impact on children 3. A proven history of violence or threats by the offender 4. Using contact arrangements with a child to instigate an offence 5. Victim is forced to leave home 6. Offence is a further breach, following earlier breach proceedings 7. Offender has a history of disobedience to court orders 8. Breach was committed immediately or shortly after the order was made	1. Breach occurred after a long period of compliance 2. Victim initiated contact

A8.6.2 Key points

- It was necessary for the prosecution properly to prove the order in question. That proof could take a number of different forms, including producing a formal certified copy of the entry in the register. However, it was also open to the prosecution to prove the order in question by means of admissible evidence such as an admission by the defendant (*Barber v CPS* [2004] EWHC 2605 (Admin)).
- A belief that the order had ended is capable of amounting to a reasonable excuse (*Barber v CPS*).

📖 See *Blackstone's Criminal Practice 2014* **B14.138**

A9 **Drugs Offences**

A9.1 **Drugs—general**

Controlled drugs—these are drugs specified in the Misuse of Drugs Act 1971 Sch 2. For the full list of controlled drugs see *Blackstone's Criminal Practice 2014* **B19.7**.

Different controlled drugs will normally be the subject of separate charges.

A9.1.1 *Sentencing*

PCCSA 2000 s 110—The minimum sentence for a third strike Class A drug trafficking conviction does not apply to an offender under the age of 18.
Misuse of Drugs Act 1971 s 4A—The requirement to treat as an aggravating factor the offender's selling of drugs in the vicinity of a school or his use of a person under the age of 18 as a courier does not apply to a person who has not attained the age of 18 by the date of the offence.

The Sentencing Council has issued a definitive guideline *Drugs Offences* (2012). This guideline does not give specific guidance on sentencing youth offenders. For the application of adult sentencing guidelines to youths see **F30**.

In *R v Healey* [2012] EWCA Crim 1005 the Court of Appeal made general comments on the way to approach the guideline:

> The format which is adopted by the Sentencing Council in producing its guidelines is to present the broad categories of offence frequently encountered pictorially in boxes. That is perhaps convenient, especially since it is necessary to condense the presentation as much as possible and to avoid discursive narrative on so wide a range of offending. It may be that the pictorial boxes which are part of the presentation may lead a superficial reader to think that adjacent boxes are mutually exclusive, one of the other. They are not. There is an inevitable overlap between the scenarios which are described in adjacent boxes. In real life offending is found on a sliding scale of gravity with few hard lines. The guidelines set out to describe such sliding scales and graduations. . . . In these guidelines, as in almost all such, there is a recognition that the two principal factors which affect sentencing for crime can broadly be collected together as, first, the harm the offence does, and secondly, the culpability of the offender. . . . Quantity, which is a broad appreciation of harm, may well colour participation, which is a broad appreciation of culpability, and vice versa. What we have just said about sliding scales applies equally to both elements, both to culpability and to harm. In neither case do the boxes have hard edges.

A9.2 Possession of controlled drugs

Misuse of Drugs Act 1971 s 5

(1) Subject to any regulations under section 7 of this Act for the time being in force, it shall not be lawful for a person to have a controlled drug in his possession.

(2) Subject to section 28 of this Act and to subsection (4) below, it is an offence for a person to have a controlled drug in his possession in contravention of subsection (1) above.

. . .

(4) In any proceedings for an offence under subsection (2) above in which it is proved that the accused had a controlled drug in his possession, it shall be a defence for him to prove—

   (a) that, knowing or suspecting it to be a controlled drug, he took possession of it for the purpose of preventing another from committing or continuing to commit an offence in connection with that drug and that as soon as possible after taking possession of it he took all such steps as were reasonably open to him to destroy the drug or to deliver it into the custody of a person lawfully entitled to take custody of it; or

   (b) that, knowing or suspecting it to be a controlled drug, he took possession of it for the purpose of delivering it into the custody of a person lawfully entitled to take custody of it and that as soon as possible after taking possession of it he took all such steps as were reasonably open to him to deliver it into the custody of such a person.

 24 month DTO

A9.2.1 *Sentencing*

There is no guideline specific to youth offenders. The definitive guideline *Drugs Offences* (2012) provides the following guidance for **adult** offenders:

STEP ONE: Determine the offence category

Category 1: class A drug
Category 2: class B drug
Category 3: class C drug

STEP TWO: Starting point and range

Offence category	Starting point	Category range
Category 1 (class A)	Band C fine	Band A fine to 51 weeks' custody
Category 2 (class B)	Band B fine	Discharge to 26 weeks' custody
Category 3 (class C)	Band A fine	Discharge to medium level community order

Factors increasing seriousness	Factors reducing seriousness or reflecting personal mitigation
Statutory aggravating factors: Previous convictions, having regard to (a) nature of the offence to which conviction relates and relevance to current offence; and (b) time elapsed since conviction Offence committed on bail	No previous convictions or no relevant or recent convictions Remorse Good character and/or exemplary conduct Offender is using cannabis to help with a diagnosed medical condition Determination and/or demonstration of steps
Other aggravating factors include: Possession of drug in prison Presence of others, especially children and/ or non-users Possession of drug in school or licensed premises Failure to comply with current court orders Offence committed on licence Attempts to conceal or dispose of evidence, where not charged separately Charged as importation of a very small amount Established evidence of community impact	having been taken to address addiction or offending behaviour Serious medical conditions requiring urgent, intensive, or long-term treatment Isolated incident Age and/or lack of maturity where it affects the responsibility of the offender Mental disorder or learning disability Sole or primary carer for dependent relatives

Additional steps:

Consider any factors which indicate a reduction, such as assistance to the prosecution; reduction for guilty plea; dangerousness; totality principle; compensation and ancillary orders; reasons; consideration for remand time.

A9.2.2 Key points

- Possession has both a physical and a mental element. The physical element involves proof that the thing is in the custody of the defendant or subject to his control; the mental element involves proof that the defendant knows that the thing in question is under his control (*R v Lambert* [2002] 2 AC 545).
- A person does not have possession of drugs which have been put in his pocket or house without his knowledge (*R v McNamara* (1988) 87 Cr App R 246).
- A person who placed drugs in his wallet and then forgot about them is still in possession of the drugs (*R v Martindale* [1986] 3 All ER 25).
- A person need not be in physical possession of a drug provided he is in control (sole or joint): see the MDA 1971 s 37(3). It is not sufficient that the defendant might have knowledge of a confederate's possession of drugs; the test is whether the drugs were

part of a common pool from which all could draw (*R v Searle* [1971] Crim LR 592).

- The fact that the quantity of drug was so minuscule as to be incapable of being used does not amount to a defence; it is merely an indication that the defendant may not have had knowledge of its presence (*R v Boyesen* [1982] AC 768).
- If a person is in possession of a container and he knows there is something inside, he will be in possession of the contents, even if he does not know their characteristics (*R v Lambert* [2002] 2 AC 545).
- Where possession has been established by the prosecution, a person who was not aware of the true nature of the substance, will have to rely on the defences in the MDA 1971 s 28. Section 28 only imposes an evidential burden upon the accused (*R v Lambert* [2002] 2 AC 545).

Misuse of Drugs Act 1971 s 28

(1) This section applies to offences under any of the following provisions of this Act, that is to say section 4(2) and (3), section 5(2) and (3), section 6(2) and section 9.

(2) Subject to subsection (3) below, in any proceedings for an offence to which this section applies it shall be a defence for the accused to prove that he neither knew of nor suspected nor had reason to suspect the existence of some fact alleged by the prosecution which it is necessary for the prosecution to prove if he is to be convicted of the offence charged.

(3) Where in any proceedings for an offence to which this section applies it is necessary, if the accused is to be convicted of the offence charged, for the prosecution to prove that some substance or product involved in the alleged offence was the controlled drug which the prosecution alleges it to have been, and it is proved that the substance or product in question was that controlled drug, the accused—

   (a) shall not be acquitted of the offence charged by reason only of proving that he neither knew nor suspected nor had reason to suspect that the substance or product in question was the particular controlled drug alleged; but

   (b) shall be acquitted thereof—

      (i) if he proves that he neither believed nor suspected nor had reason to suspect that the substance or product in question was a controlled drug; or

      (ii) if he proves that he believed the substance or product in question to be a controlled drug, or a controlled drug of a description, such that, if it had in fact been that controlled drug or a controlled drug of that description, he would not at the material time have been committing any offence to which this section applies.

> (4) Nothing in this section shall prejudice any defence which it is open to a
> person charged with an offence to which this section applies to raise apart
> from this section.

- In considering a defence under s 28(3)(b), self-induced intoxication should not be considered (*R v Young* [1984] 2 All ER 164).
- The defence of necessity (commonly pleaded by sufferers of certain illnesses) is not a defence available in law for this charge (*R v Quayle* [2006] 1 All ER 988).
- Possession of drugs for religious purposes is not afforded any special protection under the European Convention on Human Rights (*R v Taylor* [2002] 1 Cr App R 519).

A9.3 Possession with intent to supply or offering to supply etc controlled drug

Misuse of Drugs Act 1971 s 4

(3) Subject to section 28 of this Act, it is an offence for a person—
  (a) to supply or offer to supply a controlled drug to another in contravention of subsection (1) above; or
  (b) to be concerned in the supplying of such a drug to another in contravention of that subsection; or
  (c) to be concerned in the making to another in contravention of that subsection of an offer to supply such a drug.

Misuse of Drugs Act 1971 s 5

(3) Subject to section 28 of this Act, it is an offence for a person to have a controlled drug in his possession, whether lawfully or not, with intent to supply it to another in contravention of section 4(1) of this Act.

 24 month DTO/detention for life in Crown Court (Class A)

 24 month DTO/14 years detention in Crown Court (Class B or C)

A9.3.1 *Sentencing*

There is no guideline specific to youth offenders. The definitive guideline *Drugs Offences* (2012) provides the following for **adult** offenders:

A9 Drugs Offences

STEP ONE: Determining the offence category

Culpability demonstrated by offender's role. One or more of these characteristics may demonstrate the offender's role. The list is not exhaustive.	Category of harm. Indicative output or potential output (upon which the starting point is based):
LEADING role: • directing or organizing production on a commercial scale; • substantial links to, and influence on, others in a chain; • expectation of substantial financial gain; • uses business as cover; • abuses a position of trust or responsibility.	**Category 1** • heroin, cocaine—5kg; • ecstasy—10,000 tablets; • LSD—250,000 tablets; • amphetamine—20kg; • cannabis—200kg; • ketamine—5kg.
SIGNIFICANT role: • operational or management function within a chain; • involves others in the operation whether by pressure, influence, intimidation, or reward; • motivated by financial or other advantage, whether or not operating alone; • some awareness and understanding of scale of operation.	**Category 2** • heroin, cocaine—1kg; • ecstasy—2,000 tablets; • LSD—25,000 squares; • amphetamine—4kg; • cannabis—40kg; • ketamine—1kg. **Category 3** Where the offence is selling directly to users* ('street dealing'), the starting point is not based on quantity, OR Where the offence is supply of drugs in prison by a prison employee, the starting point is not based on quantity. • heroin, cocaine—150g; • ecstasy—300 tablets; • LSD—2,500 squares; • amphetamine—750g; • cannabis—6kg; • ketamine—150g.
LESSER role: • performs a limited function under direction; • engaged by pressure, coercion, intimidation; • involvement through naivety/exploitation; • no influence on those above in a chain; • very little, if any, awareness or understanding of the scale of operation; • if own operation, solely for own use (considering reasonableness of account in all the circumstances).	**Category 4** • heroin, cocaine—5g; • ecstasy—20 tablets; • LSD—170 squares; • amphetamine—20g; • cannabis—100g; • ketamine—5g. OR Where the offence is selling directly to users* ('street dealing') the starting point is not based on quantity—go to category 3

*Including test purchase officers.

STEP TWO: Starting point and category range

CLASS A	Leading role	Significant role	Lesser role
Category 1	**Starting point** 14 years' custody	**Starting point** 10 years' custody	**Starting point** 7 years' custody
	Category range 12–16 years' custody	**Category range** 9–12 years' custody	**Category range** 6–9 years' custody
Category 2	**Starting point** 11 years' custody	**Starting point** 8 years' custody	**Starting point** 5 years' custody
	Category range 9–13 years' custody	**Category range** 6 years 6 months'–10 years' custody	**Category range** 3 years 6 months'–7 years' custody
Category 3	**Starting point** 8 years 6 months' custody	**Starting point** 5 years' custody	**Starting point** 3 years 6 months' custody
	Category range 6 years 6 months'–10 years' custody	**Category range** 3 years 6 months'–7 years' custody	**Category range** 2–5 years' custody
Category 4	**Starting point** 5 years 6 months' custody	**Starting point** 3 years 6 months' custody	**Starting point** 18 months' custody
	Category range 4 years 6 months'–7 years 6 months' custody	**Category range** 2–5 years' custody	**Category range** High level community order–3 years' custody

CLASS B	Leading role	Significant role	Lesser role
Category 1	**Starting point** 8 years' custody	**Starting point** 5 years 6 months' custody	**Starting point** 3 years' custody
	Category range 7–10 years' custody	**Category range** 5–7 years' custody	**Category range** 2 years 6 months'–5 years' custody
Category 2	**Starting point** 6 years' custody	**Starting point** 4 years' custody	**Starting point** 1 year's custody
	Category range 4 years 6 months'–8 years' custody	**Category range** 2 years 6 months'–5 years' custody	**Category range** 26 weeks'–3 years' custody

A9 Drugs Offences

Category 3	**Starting point** 4 years' custody	**Starting point** 1 year's custody	**Starting point** High level community order
	Category range 2 years 6 months'–5 years' custody	**Category range** 26 weeks'–3 years' custody	**Category range** Low level community order–26 weeks' custody
Category 4	**Starting point** 1 year's custody	**Starting point** High level community order	**Starting point** Band C fine
	Category range High level community order–3 years' custody	**Category range** Medium level community order–26 weeks' custody	**Category range** Discharge–medium level community order

CLASS C	Leading role	Significant role	Lesser role
Category 1	**Starting point** 5 years' custody	**Starting point** 3 years' custody	**Starting point** 18 months' custody
	Category range 4–8 years' custody	**Category range** 2–5 years' custody	**Category range** 1–3 years' custody
Category 2	**Starting point** 3 years 6 months' custody	**Starting point** 18 months' custody	**Starting point** 26 weeks' custody
	Category range 2–5 years' custody	**Category range** 1–3 years' custody	**Category range** High level community order–18 months' custody
Category 3	**Starting point** 18 months' custody	**Starting point** 26 weeks' custody	**Starting point** High level community order
	Category range 1–3 years' custody	**Category range** High level community order–18 months' custody	**Category range** Low level community order–12 weeks' custody
Category 4	**Starting point** 26 weeks' custody	**Starting point** High level community order	**Starting point** Band C fine
	Category range High level community order–18 months' custody	**Category range** Low level community order–12 weeks' custody	**Category range** Discharge–medium level community order

Factors increasing seriousness	Factors reducing seriousness or reflecting personal mitigation
Statutory aggravating factors: Previous convictions, having regard to (a) nature of the offence to which conviction relates and relevance to current offence; and (b) time elapsed since conviction Offender used or permitted a person under 18 to deliver a controlled drug to a third person. Offender 18 or over supplies or offers to supply a drug on, or in the vicinity of, school premises either when school in use as such or at a time between one hour before and one hour after they are to be used **Offence committed on bail** Other aggravating factors include: Targeting of any premises intended to locate vulnerable individuals or supply to such individuals and/or supply to those under 18 Exposure of others to more than usual danger, for example drugs cut with harmful substances Attempts to conceal or dispose of evidence, where not charged separately Presence of others, especially children and/or non-users Presence of weapon, where not charged separately Charged as importation of a very small amount High purity Failure to comply with current court orders Offence committed on licence Established evidence of community impact	Involvement due to pressure, intimidation, or coercion falling short of duress, except where already taken into account at step 1 Supply only of drug to which offender addicted Mistaken belief of the offender regarding the type of drug, taking into account the reasonableness of such belief in all the circumstances. Isolated incident Low purity No previous convictions or no relevant or recent convictions Offender's vulnerability was exploited Remorse Good character and/or exemplary conduct Determination and/or demonstration of steps having been taken to address addiction or offending behaviour Serious medical conditions requiring urgent, intensive, or long-term treatment Age and/or lack of maturity where it affects the responsibility of the offender Mental disorder or learning disability Sole or primary carer for dependent relative

Additional steps:

Consider any factors which indicate a reduction, such as assistance to the prosecution; reduction for guilty plea; dangerousness; totality principle; compensation and ancillary orders; reasons; consideration for remand time.

A9.3.2 Key points

- Supply in its ordinary meaning conveys the idea of providing another something which is wanted or required in order to meet the wants or requirements of that other. It connotes more than the mere transfer of physical control of an object from one person to another. Hence A handing drugs to B for safe keeping would not be supply but B handing the drugs back to A would be (*R v Maginnis* [1987] AC 303).

- Purchasing drugs on behalf of a third party, and passing those drugs to that party, even for no profit, amounts to supply.

- Where friends pool their money to purchase drugs and one of their number goes to the dealer to purchase those drugs, the sharing out of the drugs purchased is supplying (*R v Denslow* [1998] Crim LR 566). However, in *Denslow* the court observed:

> We wonder why it was thought necessary to charge supply in the circumstances of this case. How could it possibly serve the interests of the public that there should be either a trial or if not a trial as conventionally understood a hearing to determine this matter of law? It was inevitable that the appellant would be dealt with at worst as though he were in possession of the drugs and, as turned out in this case, as though he were without any criminal responsibility for that particular part of the transaction. We are told that a plea had been offered to a charge of possession. It ought to have been accepted. We hope that those words will be borne in mind by prosecuting authorities in the future.

- For the purposes of s 5(3) the words 'intent to supply' require the accused in possession of the drugs to have that intent. It is not enough that he is aware that another has the intent to supply the drugs (*R v Greenfield* (1984) 78 Cr App R 179).

- An offer to supply may be made by words or conduct (*R v Mitchell* [1992] Crim LR 723). The offence is complete once the offer is made and it is irrelevant if the offer is subsequently withdrawn (*R v Prior* [2004] EWCA Crim 1147). It is no defence that the offer was a bogus one (*R v Goodard* [1992] Crim LR 588).

- In *R v Hughes* (1985) 81 Cr App R 344 the court held that to prove that a defendant is concerned in the supply of controlled drugs the prosecution must prove that:
  (i) controlled drugs had actually been supplied or that at least there had been an offer to supply;
  (ii) the defendant had participated in the supply or offer to supply; and
  (iii) the defendant knew the nature of the enterprise, that is that it involved the supply or offer to supply drugs.

- To prove a charge of being concerned in the supply there is no requirement that there be direct evidence of supply; reliable circumstantial evidence rather than mere speculation would be sufficient (*R v Akinsete and Prempeh* [2012] EWCA Crim 2377).

- For the MDA 1971 s 28 see **A9.2.2**.

A9.4 Production of controlled drug and cultivation of cannabis

> **Misuse of Drugs Act 1971 s 4(2)**
>
> (2) Subject to section 28 of this Act, it is an offence for a person—
>   (a) to produce a controlled drug in contravention of subsection (1) above; or
>   (b) to be concerned in the production of such a drug in contravention of that subsection by another.

EW

GC

 24 month DTO/detention for life in Crown Court (Class A)

 24 month DTO/14 years detention in Crown Court (Class B or C)

> **Misuse of Drugs Act 1971 s 6**
>
> (1) Subject to any regulations under section 7 of this Act for the time being in force, it shall not be lawful for a person to cultivate any plant of the genus Cannabis.
> (2) Subject to section 28 of this Act, it is an offence to cultivate any such plant in contravention subsection (1) above.

EW

GC

 24 month DTO/14 years detention in Crown Court

A9.4.1 *Sentencing*

There is no guideline specific to youth offenders. The definitive guideline *Drugs Offences* (2012) provides the following for **adult** offenders:

STEP ONE: Determining the offence category

Culpability demonstrated by offender's role. One or more of these characteristics may demonstrate the offender's role. The list is not exhaustive.	Category of harm. Indicative output or potential output (upon which the starting point is based):
LEADING role: directing or organizing production on a commercial scale;	**Category 1** heroin, cocaine—5kg; ecstasy—10,000 tablets;

substantial links to, and influence on, others in a chain;	LSD—250,000 tablets;
expectation of substantial financial gain;	amphetamine—20kg;
uses business as cover;	cannabis—operation capable of producing industrial quantities for commercial use;
abuses a position of trust or responsibility.	ketamine—5kg.
SIGNIFICANT role:	**Category 2**
operational or management function within a chain;	heroin, cocaine—1kg;
	ecstasy—2,000 tablets;
involves others in the operation whether by pressure, influence, intimidation, or reward;	LSD—25,000 squares;
	amphetamine—4kg;
motivated by financial or other advantage, whether or not operating alone;	cannabis—operation capable of producing significant quantities for commercial use;
some awareness and understanding of scale of operation.	ketamine—1kg.
LESSER role:	**Category 3**
performs a limited function under direction;	heroin, cocaine—150g;
engaged by pressure, coercion, intimidation;	ecstasy—300 tablets;
involvement through naivety/exploitation;	LSD—2,500 squares;
no influence on those above in a chain;	amphetamine—750g;
very little, if any, awareness or understanding of the scale of operation;	cannabis—28 plants;*
	ketamine—150g.
if own operation, solely for own use (considering reasonableness of account in all the circumstances).	**Category 4**
	• heroin, cocaine—5g;
	• ecstasy—20 tablets;
	• LSD—170 squares;
	• amphetamine—20g;
	• cannabis—9 plants (domestic operation);*
	• ketamine—5g

*With an assumed yield of 40g per plant.

STEP TWO: Starting point and category range

CLASS A	Leading role	Significant role	Lesser role
Category 1	**Starting point** 14 years' custody	**Starting point** 10 years' custody	**Starting point** 7 years' custody
	Category range 12–16 years' custody	**Category range** 9–12 years' custody	**Category range** 6–9 years' custody
Category 2	**Starting point** 11 years' custody	**Starting point** 8 years' custody	**Starting point** 5 years' custody
	Category range 9–13 years' custody	**Category range** 6 years 6 months'–10 years' custody	**Category range** 3 years 6 months'–7 years' custody

Category 3	**Starting point** 8 years 6 months' custody	**Starting point** 5 years' custody	**Starting point** 3 years 6 months' custody
	Category range 6 years 6 months'–10 years' custody	**Category range** 3 years 6 months'–7 years' custody	**Category range** 2–5 years' custody
Category 4	**Starting point** 5 years 6 months' custody	**Starting point** 3 years 6 months' custody	**Starting point** 18 months' custody
	Category range 4 years 6 months'–7 years 6 months' custody	**Category range** 2–5 years' custody	**Category range** High level community order–3 years' custody

CLASS B	Leading role	Significant role	Lesser role
Category 1	**Starting point** 8 years' custody	**Starting point** 5 years 6 months' custody	**Starting point** 3 years' custody
	Category range 7–10 years' custody	**Category range** 5–7 years' custody	**Category range** 2 years 6 months'–5 years' custody
Category 2	**Starting point** 6 years' custody	**Starting point** 4 years' custody	**Starting point** 1 year's custody
	Category range 4 years 6 months'–8 years' custody	**Category range** 2 years 6 months'–5 years' custody	**Category range** 26 weeks'–3 years' custody
Category 3	**Starting point** 4 years' custody	**Starting point** 1 year's custody	**Starting point** High level community order
	Category range 2 years 6 months'–5 years' custody	**Category range** 26 weeks'–3 years' custody	**Category range** Low level community order–26 weeks' custody
Category 4	**Starting point** 1 year's custody	**Starting point** High level community order	**Starting point** Band C fine
	Category range High level community order–3 years' custody	**Category range** Medium level community order–26 weeks' custody	**Category range** Discharge–medium level community order

A9 Drugs Offences

CLASS C	Leading role	Significant role	Lesser role
Category 1	**Starting point** 5 years' custody	**Starting point** 3 years' custody	**Starting point** 18 months' custody
	Category range 4–8 years' custody	**Category range** 2–5 years' custody	**Category range** 1–3 years' custody
Category 2	**Starting point** 3 years 6 months' custody	**Starting point** 18 months' custody	**Starting point** 26 weeks' custody
	Category range 2–5 years' custody	**Category range** 1–3 years' custody	**Category range** High level community order–18 months' custody
Category 3	**Starting point** 18 months' custody	**Starting point** 26 weeks' custody	**Starting point** High level community order
	Category range 1–3 years' custody	**Category range** High level community order–18 months' custody	**Category range** Low level community order–12 weeks' custody
Category 4	**Starting point** 26 weeks' custody	**Starting point** High level community order	**Starting point** Band C fine
	Category range High level community order–18 months' custody	**Category range** Low level community order–12 weeks' custody	**Category range** Discharge–medium level community order

Factors increasing seriousness	Factors reducing seriousness or reflecting personal mitigation
Statutory aggravating factors: Previous convictions, having regard to (a) nature of the offence to which conviction relates and relevance to current offence; and (b) time elapsed since conviction Offence committed on bail **Other aggravating factors include:** Nature of any likely supply Level of any profit element Use of premises accompanied by unlawful access to electricity/other utility supply of others Ongoing/large-scale operation as evidenced by presence and nature of specialist equipment	Involvement due to pressure, intimidation or coercion falling short of duress, except where already taken into account at step 1 Isolated incident Low purity No previous convictions or no relevant or recent convictions Offender's vulnerability was exploited Remorse Good character and/or exemplary conduct

Exposure of others to more than usual danger, for example drugs cut with harmful substances	Determination and/or demonstration of steps having been taken to address addiction or offending behaviour
Attempts to conceal or dispose of evidence, where not charged separately	
Presence of others, especially children and/or non-users	Serious medical conditions requiring urgent, intensive, or long-term treatment
Presence of weapon, where not charged separately	
High purity or high potential yield	Age and/or lack of maturity where it affects the responsibility of the offender
Failure to comply with current court orders	
Offence committed on licence	
Established evidence of community impact	Mental disorder or learning disability
	Sole or primary carer for dependent relatives

Additional steps:

Consider any factors which indicate a reduction, such as assistance to the prosecution; reduction for guilty plea; dangerousness; totality principle; compensation and ancillary orders; reasons; consideration for remand time.

In *R v Healey* [2012] EWCA Crim 1005 the court stated:

> [T]he quantities which appear in the sentencing guideline pictorial boxes as broad indicators of harm are neither fixed points nor are they thresholds. They are, as the heading to the relevant column says, 'indicative' quantities designed to enable the experienced judge to put the case into the right context on the sliding scale. In the particular context of [cannabis], they are indicators of output or potential output as the preamble to the relevant page (18) explicitly says. In production cases it is the output or the potential output which counts. The guidelines have to provide for all manner of production methods of all manner of drugs. They are not limited to cannabis, nor to plants. Nor can they be revised from month to month as production techniques or cultivation practices or the breeding of plants changes.

A9.4.2 Key points

- The prosecution is not required to prove that the accused knew that the plant he cultivated was in fact cannabis (*R v Champ* (1981) 73 Cr App R 267) but he may have a defence under the MDA 1971 s 28 (see **A9.2.2**).

A9.5 Obstruction of search powers under the MDA 1971

Misuse of Drugs Act s 23

(2) If a constable has reasonable grounds to suspect that any person is in possession of a controlled drug in contravention of this Act or of any regulations or orders made thereunder, the constable may—

    (a) search that person, and detain him for the purpose of searching him;

    (b) search any vehicle or vessel in which the constable suspects that the drug may be found, and for that purpose require the person in control of the vehicle or vessel to stop it;

    (c) seize and detain, for the purposes of proceedings under this Act, anything found in the course of the search which appears to the constable to be evidence of an offence under this Act.

In this subsection 'vessel' includes a hovercraft within the meaning of the Hovercraft Act 1968; and nothing in this subsection shall prejudice any power of search or any power to seize or detain property which is exercisable by a constable apart from this subsection.

(3) If a justice of the peace (or in Scotland a justice of the peace, a magistrate or a sheriff) is satisfied by information on oath that there is reasonable ground for suspecting—

    (a) that any controlled drugs are, in contravention of this Act or of any regulations or orders made thereunder, in the possession of a person on any premises; or

    (b) that a document directly or indirectly relating to, or connected with, a transaction or dealing which was, or an intended transaction or dealing which would if carried out be, an offence under this Act, or in the case of a transaction or dealing carried out or intended to be carried out in a place outside the United Kingdom, an offence against the provisions of a corresponding law in force in that place, is in the possession of a person on any premises,

he may grant a warrant authorising any constable at any time or times within one month from the date of the warrant, to enter, if need be by force, the premises named in the warrant, and to search the premises and any persons found therein and, if there is reasonable ground for suspecting that an offence under this Act has been committed in relation to any controlled drugs found on the premises or in the possession of any such persons, or that a document so found is such a document as is mentioned in paragraph (b) above, to seize and detain those drugs or that document, as the case may be.

...

(4) A person commits an offence if he—

    (a) intentionally obstructs a person in the exercise of his powers under this section; or

    (b) conceals from a person acting in the exercise of his powers under subsection (1) above any such books, documents, stocks or drugs as are mentioned in that subsection; or

(c) without reasonable excuse (proof of which shall lie on him) fails to produce any such books or documents as are so mentioned where their production is demanded by a person in the exercise of his powers under that subsection.

EW

24 month DTO

A9.5.1 *Sentencing*

There is no sentencing guideline for offences under s 23(4).

A9.5.2 Key points

- Conducting a stop and search under the powers of s 23 means that the PACE 1984 s 2 is engaged. Where reasonable steps had not been taken to comply with the requirements of s 2 the search was unlawful and a defendant could not be convicted of obstruction under s 23(4) (*R v Bristol* [2007] EWCA Crim 3214). When a police officer suspects that a person stopped has drugs in his mouth he must at the very least state his name, the police station, 'drugs search' and 'spit it out' in order to comply with those requirements.

A10 **Road Traffic Offences**

A10.1 Age and licence restrictions

A person can apply for a driving licence up to three months before they can start driving.

A10.1.1 *Aged 16 years*

A person aged 16 years can apply for a provisional moped licence and take compulsory basic training (CBT) to start riding category AM and category Q mopeds. They must take a moped test within two years.

- Category AM mopeds have a maximum speed over 25km/h and no more than 45km/h.
- Category Q mopeds are two- or three-wheeled mopeds with a maximum speed of 25km/h.

A10.1.2 *Aged 17 years*

A person aged 17 years can apply for a provisional licence for a small motorbike (category A1). They then need to complete compulsory basic training (CBT) and take the A1 theory and practical tests within two years to get a full A1 licence.

- Category A1 covers motorbikes not exceeding: 125cc engine size/11kW power output/0.1kW/kg power to weight ratio.

A person aged 17 years can apply for a provisional licence to drive a car subject to the restrictions on that licence.

A10.1.3 *Restrictions on the use of a provisional licence*

A provisional licence has certain restrictions on its use.

A person with a provisional licence to drive a moped:

- must not drive a moped that has a maximum speed exceeding 25mph
- must not drive a motorbike on a public road unless they have taken or are in the process of taking a compulsory basic training course
- must not carry a passenger on the motorbike
- must display 'L' plates ('D' plates in Wales) on the front and back of the vehicle
- must not drive on a motorway.

A person with a provisional licence to drive a motorbike:

- must not drive a motorbike that is above 125cc
- must not drive a motorbike on a public road unless they have taken or are in the process of taking a compulsory basic training course

- must not carry a passenger on the motorbike
- must display 'L' plates ('D' plates in Wales) on the front and back of the vehicle
- must not drive on a motorway.

A person who has a provisional licence to drive a car or other vehicle (except a motorbike):

- must display 'L' plates on the front and back of the vehicle (or 'D' plates in Wales)
- must not drive on a motorway
- if the vehicle has more than one seat, must have someone with them whenever they are driving. The person supervising must sit in the front passenger seat and be fit to drive the vehicle, for example, they must not be drunk. They must also be aged 21 or over and have had a full driving licence (for the type of vehicle being driven) for at least three years.

A person who has passed a driving test and is still waiting to receive a full licence is not subject to these restrictions.

A10.1.4 *Full driving licence*

In order to obtain a full licence to drive a moped a person must:

- pass the theory test for motorcycles and
- pass the moped practical test.

In order to obtain a full licence to drive a motorcycle a person must:

- pass the theory test for motorcycles and
- pass the motorcycle practical test.

In order to obtain a full driving licence to drive a car a person must:

- pass the theory test for cars and
- pass the practical driving test.

A10.1.5 *New driver provisions*

A person who builds up six or more penalty points within two years of passing their first driving test will automatically lose their licence. They will have to apply and pay for a new provisional licence and pass both theory and practical parts of the driving test again to obtain a full licence.

However, a period of disqualification does not trigger the new driver provisions.

A10.2 Road traffic offences—definitions

A10.2.1 *Accident*

Accident is to be given its ordinary meaning: *Chief Constable of West Midlands v Billingham* [1979] 1 WLR 747. A deliberate act can amount to an accident: *Chief Constable of Staffordshire v Lees* [1981] RTR 506. A physical impact is not necessary: *R v Currie* [2007] EWCA Crim 927, but the *de minimis* principle applies: *R v Morris* [1972] 1 WLR 228.

A10.2.2 *Causing*

Causing requires a positive act, committed with prior knowledge: *Ross Hillman Ltd v Bond* [1974] QB 435.

A10.2.3 *Driver*

Section 192 of the Road Traffic Act 1988 provides:

Road Traffic Act 1988 s 192(1)

... 'driver', where a separate person acts as a steersman of a motor vehicle, includes (except for the purposes of section 1 of this Act) that person as well as any other person engaged in the driving of the vehicle, and 'drive' is to be interpreted accordingly ...

A person supervising a driver will not be a driver unless they exercise some control over the vehicle (dual controls, for example): *Evans v Walkden* [1956] 1 WLR 1019.

There is no general presumption that the owner of a vehicle is the driver of it at a particular time. All evidence relating to the issue, including circumstantial evidence, can be properly considered together: *McCrombie v Liverpool City Magistrates* [2011] EWHC 758 (Admin).

A10.2.4 *Driving*

R v MacDonagh [1974] QB 448 defined driving as use of the driver's controls for the purpose of directing the movement of the vehicle. The court gave the following guidance:

There are an infinite number of ways in which a person may control the movement of a motor vehicle, apart from the orthodox one of sitting in the driving seat and using the engine for propulsion. He may be coasting down a hill with the gears in neutral and the engine switched off; he may be steering a vehicle which is being towed by another. As has already been pointed out, he may be sitting in the driving seat whilst others push, or half sitting in the driving seat but keeping one foot on the road in order to induce the car to move. Finally, as

in the present case, he may be standing in the road and himself pushing the car
with or without using the steering wheel to direct it. Although the word 'drive'
must be given a wide meaning, the Courts must be alert to see that the net is
not thrown so widely that it includes activities which cannot be said to be driving a motor vehicle in any ordinary use of that word in the English language.

As a person may be driving a stationary vehicle, it is a matter of fact
to be decided in each case and factors such as the reason for the vehicle stopping and the duration of the stop will be relevant: *Planton v
Director of Public Prosecutions* [2002] RTR 107.

Steering a vehicle being towed would amount to driving where there
was an operational breaking system: *McQuaid v Anderton* [1981] 1
WLR 154, as would freewheeling a vehicle down a hill while steering: *Saycell v Bool* [1948] 2 All ER 83. A person steering from the
passenger seat is driving: *Tyler v Whatmore* [1976] RTR 83.

A10.2.5 *In charge*

In cases where the matter is not clear, the case of *Director of Public
Prosecutions v Watkins* (1989) 89 Cr App R 112 should be considered
in detail. The court set out the following guidance:

Broadly there are two distinct classes of case:

(1) If the defendant is the owner or lawful possessor of the vehicle or has
recently driven it, he will have been in charge of it, and the question for the
Court will be whether he is still in charge or whether he has relinquished
his charge. Usually such a defendant will be prima facie in charge unless he
has put the vehicle in someone else's charge. However he would not be so
if in all the circumstances he has ceased to be in actual control and there is
no realistic possibility of his resuming actual control while unfit: eg if he is
at home in bed for the night, if he is a great distance from the car, or if it is
taken by another.

(2) If the defendant is not the owner, the lawful possessor, or recent driver
but is sitting in the vehicle or is otherwise involved with it, the question for
the Court is, as here, whether he has assumed being in charge of it. In this
class of case the defendant will be in charge if, whilst unfit, he is voluntarily
in de facto control of the vehicle or if, in the circumstances, including his
position, his intentions and his actions, he may be expected imminently to
assume control. Usually this will involve his having gained entry to the car
and evinced an intention to take control of it. But gaining entry may not be
necessary if he has manifested that intention some other way, eg by stealing the keys of a car in circumstances which show he means presently to
drive it.

The circumstances to be taken into account will vary infinitely, but the following will be usually relevant:

(i) Whether and where he is in the vehicle or how far he is from it.
(ii) What he is doing at the relevant time.
(iii) Whether he is in possession of a key that fits the ignition.

(iv) Whether there is evidence of an intention to take or assert control of the car by driving or otherwise

(v) Whether any other person is in, at or near the vehicle and if so, the like particulars in respect of that person.

It will be for the Court to consider all the above factors with any others which may be relevant and reach its decision as a question of fact and degree.

A10.2.6 *Motor vehicle*

There is no statutory definition of vehicle and therefore its ordinary meaning of a carriage or conveyance should apply. Where the statute uses the phrase 'motor vehicle', the definition to be found in section 185 of the Road Traffic Act 1988 states that it is a 'mechanically propelled vehicle intended or adapted for use on roads'. The maximum speed of the vehicle is not a relevant factor: *Director of Public Prosecutions v King* [2008] EWHC 447 (Admin). For discussion of segways see *Coates v CPS* [2011] EWHC 2032 (Admin).

A10.2.7 *Permitting*

A person permits use when he allows or authorizes use, or fails to take reasonable steps to prevent use: *Vehicle Inspectorate v Nuttall* [1999] 1 WLR 69, HL. For permitting no insurance the prosecution do not need to show that the person knew the driver to be uninsured. If, however, use is conditional (eg, on the person having insurance) the outcome could be different: *Newbury v Davis* [1974] RTR 367.

A10.2.8 *Public place*

This is a place to which the public have access. However, the law draws a distinction between general public access, and access for a defined group of persons. The law in this area is complex and advocates should seek an adjournment where the answer is not clear.

A10.2.9 *Road*

This is defined as any highway or road to which the public has access. The following have been held to be a road:

• Pedestrian pavement: *Randall v Motor Insurers' Bureau* [1968] 1 WLR 1900.

• Grass verge at the side of a road: *Worth v Brooks* [1959] Crim LR 855.

• Bridges over which a road passes.

It will be a matter of fact and degree as to whether something is a road, and whether or not the public have access. A car park will not generally be a road, even if there are roads running through it. In *Barrett v Director of Public Prosecutions*, unreported, 10 February 2009, the court held that a roadway running through a private caravan park, and facilitating entry to a beach, constituted a road.

A vehicle will be 'on' a road when part of the vehicle protrudes over a road: *Avery v Crown Prosecution Service* [2011] EWHC 2388 (Admin).

A10.2.10 *Highway*

This is defined as land over which there is a right of way on foot, by riding, or with vehicles and cattle. A highway includes: bridleways, footpaths, footways, walkways, carriageways, and driftways.

📖 See *Blackstone's Criminal Practice 2014* **C1**

A10.3 Causing death by dangerous driving

> **Road Traffic Act 1988 s 1**

IO

DO

GC

▦ 24 month DTO/14 years detention in Crown Court. Obligatory disqualification for minimum of 2 years. Mandatory retest by way of extended test

A10.3.1 *Sentencing*

There is no sentencing guideline specific to youths. The sentencing guideline *Causing Death by Driving* gives the following guidance for **adult** offenders:

Nature of offence	Starting point	Sentencing range
Level 1 The most serious offences encompassing driving that involved a deliberate decision to ignore (or a flagrant disregard for) the rules of the road and an apparent disregard for the great danger being caused to others	8 years' custody	7–14 years' custody
Level 2 Driving that created a substantial risk of danger	5 years' custody	4–7 years' custody
Level 3 Driving that created a significant risk of danger [Where the driving is markedly less culpable than for this level, reference should be made to the starting point and range for the most serious level of causing death by careless driving]	3 years' custody	2–5 years' custody

Additional aggravating factors	Additional mitigating factors
1. Previous convictions for motoring offences, particularly offences that involve bad driving or the consumption of excessive alcohol or drugs before driving	1. Alcohol or drugs consumed unwittingly
2. More than one person killed as a result of the offence	2. Offender was seriously injured in the collision
3. Serious injury to one or more victims, in addition to the death(s)	3. The victim was a close friend or relative
4. Disregard of warnings	4. Actions of the victim or a third party contributed significantly to the likelihood of a collision occurring and/or death resulting
5. Other offences committed at the same time, such as driving other than in accordance with the terms of a valid licence; driving while disqualified; driving without insurance; taking a vehicle without consent; driving a stolen vehicle	5. The offender's lack of driving experience contributed to the commission of the offence
6. The offender's irresponsible behaviour such as failing to stop, falsely claiming that one of the victims was responsible for the collision, or trying to throw the victim off the car by swerving in order to escape	6. The driving was in response to a proven and genuine emergency falling short of a defence
7. Driving off in an attempt to avoid detection or apprehension	

In *R v Bennett* [2009] EWCA Crim 591 a 17-year-old of positive good character but with a recent penalty notice for being drunk and disorderly pleaded guilty to causing the death of his best friend by dangerous driving. He had a high level of alcohol in his blood. The Court of Appeal considered the correct starting point to be six years, not eight years as the Crown Court judge had decided. A sentence taking account of plea and mitigation was reduced from 5 years and 4 months' detention to 4 years' detention.

A10.3.2 Key points

- One of the tests for dangerous driving as set out in the Road Traffic Act 1988, s 2A must be satisfied, producing a causal link to the death. See **A10.7.2**.
- CPS policy on prosecuting bad driving can be found on <www.cps.gov.uk>.
- When considering the length of disqualification in death by driving cases the court should have in mind the principles identified in the guideline case of *R v Cooksley* [2004] 1 Cr App R(S) 1.
- A driving ban is designed to protect road users in the future from an offender who, through his conduct on this occasion, and perhaps other occasions, has shown himself to be a real risk on the roads.
- Shorter bans of two years or so will be appropriate where the offender had a good driving record before the offence and where the offence resulted from a momentary error of judgement.

- Longer bans, between three and five years, will be appropriate where, having regard to the circumstances of the offence and the offender's record, it is clear that the offender tends to disregard the rules of the road, or to drive carelessly or inappropriately.
- Bans between five and ten years may be used where the offence itself, and the offender's record, show that he represents a real and continuing danger to other road users.
- Disqualification for life is a highly exceptional course, but may be appropriate in a case where the danger represented by the offender is an extreme and indefinite one.

 See *Blackstone's Criminal Practice 2014* **C3**

A10.4 Causing death by careless driving when under the influence of drink or drugs

Road Traffic Act 1988, section 3A

 24 month DTO/14 years detention in Crown Court. Obligatory disqualification for minimum of 2 years. Mandatory retest by way of extended test

A10.4.1 *Sentencing*

There is no sentencing guideline specific to youths. The sentencing guideline *Causing Death by Driving* gives the following guidance for **adult** offenders:

The legal limit of alcohol is 35 μg breath (80mg in blood and 107mg in urine)	Careless/ inconsiderate driving arising from momentary inattention with no aggravating factors	Other cases of careless/ inconsiderate driving	Careless/inconsiderate driving falling not far short of dangerousness
71 μg or above of alcohol/ high quantity of drugs OR deliberate non-provision of specimen where evidence of serious impairment	Starting point: 6 years' custody Sentencing range: 5–10 years' custody	Starting point: 7 years' custody Sentencing range: 6–12 years' custody	Starting point: 8 years' custody Sentencing range: 7–14 years' custody

51–70 µg of alcohol/ moderate quantity of drugs OR deliberate non-provision of specimen	Starting point: 4 years' custody Sentencing range: 3–7 years' custody	Starting point: 5 years' custody Sentencing range: 4–8 years' custody	Starting point: 6 years' custody Sentencing range: 5–9 years' custody
35–50 µg of alcohol/ minimum quantity of drugs OR test refused because of honestly held but unreasonable belief	Starting point: 18 months' custody Sentencing range: 26 weeks'–4 years' custody	Starting point: 3 years' custody Sentencing range: 2–5 years' custody	Starting point: 4 years' custody Sentencing range: 3–6 years' custody

Additional aggravating factors	Additional mitigating factors
1. Other offences committed at the same time, such as driving other than in accordance with the terms of a valid licence; driving while disqualified; driving without insurance; taking a vehicle without consent; driving a stolen vehicle	1. Alcohol or drugs consumed unwittingly
2. Previous convictions for motoring offences, particularly offences that involve bad driving or the consumption of excessive alcohol before driving	2. Offender was seriously injured in the collision
3. More than one person was killed as a result of the offence	3. The victim was a close friend or relative
4. Serious injury to one or more persons in addition to the death(s)	4. The actions of the victim or a third party contributed significantly to the likelihood of a collision occurring and/or death resulting
5. Irresponsible behaviour such as failing to stop or falsely claiming that one of the victims was responsible for the collision	5. The driving was in response to a proven and genuine emergency falling short of a defence

In *R v Theaker* [2009] EWCA Crim 620 a 17-year-old pleaded guilty to causing death whilst under the influence of alcohol. There was no evidence that she had been over the legal limit. The Court of Appeal stated that the starting point of three years which the Crown Court judge had used was too high. Taking account of the defendant's youth, a starting point of eighteen months was appropriate and the sentence of two years' detention was reduced to twelve months.

A10.4.2 Key points

- The offence can be committed in eight separate ways.
- See **A10.9**, **A10.10**, and **A10.12** for details of constituent offences.

A10.5 Causing death by careless or inconsiderate driving/unlicensed, disqualified, or uninsured drivers

Road Traffic Act 1988 ss 2B and 3ZB

Causing death by:

- careless or inconsiderate driving
- unlicensed, disqualified, or uninsured drivers.

 24 month DTO. Obligatory minimum disqualification of 12 months, discretionary re-test

A10.5.1 *Sentencing*

There is no sentencing guideline specific to youths. The sentencing guideline *Causing Death by Driving* gives the following guidance for **adult** offenders:

Death by careless or inconsiderate driving

Nature of offence	Starting point	Sentencing range
Careless or inconsiderate driving falling not far short of dangerous driving	15 months' custody	36 weeks to 3 years' custody
Other cases of careless or inconsiderate driving	36 weeks' custody	Community order (HIGH) to 2 years' custody
Careless or inconsiderate driving arising from momentary inattention with no aggravating factors	Community order (MEDIUM)	Community order (LOW) to Community order (HIGH)

Additional aggravating factors	Additional mitigating factors
1. Other offences committed at the same time, such as driving other than in accordance with the terms of a valid licence; driving while disqualified; driving without insurance; taking a vehicle without consent; driving a stolen vehicle	1. Offender was seriously injured in the collision 2. The victim was a close friend or relative 3. The actions of the victim or a third party contributed to the commission of the offence

2. Previous convictions for motoring offences, particularly offences that involve bad driving 3. More than one person was killed as a result of the offence 4. Serious injury to one or more persons in addition to the death(s) 5. Irresponsible behaviour, such as failing to stop or falsely claiming that one of the victims was responsible for the collision	4. The offender's lack of driving experience contributed significantly to the likelihood of a collision 5. The driving was in response to a proven and genuine emergency falling short of a defence

Causing death by unlicensed, disqualified, or uninsured drivers

Nature of offence	Starting point	Sentencing range
The offender was disqualified from driving; OR The offender was unlicensed or uninsured plus two or more aggravating factors from the list below	12 months' custody	36 weeks' to 2 years' custody
The offender was unlicensed or uninsured plus at least one aggravating factor from the list below	26 weeks' custody	Community order (HIGH) to 36 weeks' custody
The offender was unlicensed or uninsured—no aggravating factors	Community order (MEDIUM)	Community order (LOW) to Community order (HIGH)

Additional aggravating factors	Additional mitigating factors
1. Previous convictions for motoring offences, whether involving bad driving or involving an offence of the same kind that forms part of the present conviction (ie unlicensed, disqualified, or uninsured driving) 2. More than one person was killed as a result of the offence 3. Serious injury to one or more persons in addition to the death(s) 4. Irresponsible behaviour such as failing to stop or falsely claiming that someone else was driving	1. The decision to drive was brought about by a proven and genuine emergency falling short of a defence 2. The offender genuinely believed that he or she was insured or licensed to drive 3. The offender was seriously injured as a result of the collision 4. The victim was a close friend or relative

In *R v Landon* [2011] EWCA Crim 1755 a defendant who was 17 years old at the time of the offence pleaded guilty to two offences of causing death by careless driving. He was a recently qualified driver who used excessive speed in wet conditions, overtaking another vehicle. His passengers died. His sentence of twenty months' YOI was upheld.

A10.5.2 Key points

- Death must result from the act of driving.
- The driving must be more than a minimal cause of the death.
- It is not necessary for the Crown to prove careless or inconsiderate driving, but there must be something open to proper criticism in the driving of the defendant, beyond the mere presence of the vehicle on the road, and which contributed in some more than minimal way to the death: *R v Hughes* [2013] UKSC 56.
- See *R v Coe* [2009] EWCA Crim 1452 in relation to the admission of samples taken in relation to alcohol.

 See *Blackstone's Criminal Practice 2014* **C3**

A10.6 Causing serious injury by dangerous driving

Section 1A of the Road Traffic Act 1988 states:

> **Road Traffic Act 1988 s 1A**
>
> **1A Causing serious injury by dangerous driving**
> (1) A person who causes serious injury to another person by driving a mechanically propelled vehicle dangerously on a road or other public place is guilty of an offence.
> (2) In this section 'serious injury' means—
>   (a) in England and Wales, physical harm which amounts to grievous bodily harm for the purposes of the Offences against the Person Act 1861 ...

EW

24 month DTO. Obligatory disqualification for 12 months with mandatory extended re-test

Dangerous driving is defined by s 2A of the Road Traffic Act 1988. See **A10.7**.

This provision only applies to driving on or after 3 December 2012.

There is no sentencing guideline in relation to this offence. Reference should be made to the guideline relating to sentences for dangerous driving resulting in serious injury.

See *Blackstone's Criminal Practice 2014* **C3.33**

A10.7 Dangerous driving

> **Road Traffic Act 1988 s 2**
>
> A person who drives a mechanically propelled vehicle dangerously on a road or other public place is guilty of an offence.

 24 month DTO. Must endorse and disqualify for a minimum period of 12 months; mandatory extended re-test; must disqualify for at least 2 years if offender has had two or more disqualifications for periods of 56 days or more in preceding 3 years

A10.7.1 *Sentencing*

There is no sentencing guideline specific to youths. The *Magistrates' Court Sentencing Guidelines* give the following guidance for **adult** offenders:

Offence seriousness (culpability and harm)		
A. Identify the appropriate starting point		
Starting points based on first-time offender pleading not guilty		
Example of nature of activity	**Starting point**	**Range**
Single incident where little or no damage or risk of personal injury	Medium level community order	Low level community order to high level community order Disqualify 12–15 months
Incident(s) involving excessive speed or showing off, especially on busy roads or in built-up area; OR Single incident where little or no damage or risk of personal injury but offender was disqualified driver	12 weeks' custody	High level community order to 26 weeks' custody. Disqualify 15–24 months
Prolonged bad driving involving deliberate disregard for safety of others; OR Incident(s) involving excessive speed or showing off, especially on busy roads or in built-up area, by disqualified driver; OR Driving as described in box above while being pursued by police	Crown Court	Crown Court

Offence seriousness (culpability and harm)	
B. Consider the effect of aggravating and mitigating factors (other than those within examples above)	
The following may be particularly relevant but **these lists are not exhaustive**	
Factors indicating higher culpability	**Factors indicating lower culpability**
1. Disregarding warnings of others	1. Genuine emergency
2. Evidence of alcohol or drugs	2. Speed not excessive
3. Carrying out other tasks while driving	3. Offence due to inexperience rather than irresponsibility of driver
4. Carrying passengers or heavy load	
5. Tiredness	
6. Aggressive driving, such as driving much too close to vehicle in front, racing, inappropriate attempts to overtake, or cutting in after overtaking	
7. Driving when knowingly suffering from a medical condition which significantly impairs the offender's driving skills	
8. Driving a poorly maintained or dangerously loaded vehicle, especially where motivated by commercial concerns	
Factors indicating greater degree of harm	
1. Injury to others	
2. Damage to other vehicles or property	

A10.7.2 Key points

The Road Traffic Act 1988 s 2A, defines what constitutes dangerous driving:

Road Traffic Act 1988 s 2A

(1) For the purposes of sections 1 and 2 above a person is to be regarded as driving dangerously if (and, subject to subsection (2) below, only if)—
   (a) the way he drives falls far below what would be expected of a competent and careful driver, and
   (b) it would be obvious to a competent and careful driver that driving in that way would be dangerous.

(2) A person is also to be regarded as driving dangerously for the purposes of sections 1 and 2 above if it would be obvious to a competent and careful driver that driving the vehicle in its current state would be dangerous.

(3) In subsections (1) and (2) above 'dangerous' refers to danger either of injury to any person or of serious damage to property; and in determining for the purposes of those subsections what would be expected of, or obvious to, a competent and careful driver in a particular case, regard shall be had not only to the circumstances of which he could be expected to be aware but also to any circumstances shown to have been within the knowledge of the accused.

(4) In determining for the purposes of subsection (2) above the state of a vehicle, regard may be had to anything attached to or carried on or in it and to the manner in which it is attached or carried.

- The special skill (or indeed lack of skill) of a driver is an irrelevant circumstance when considering whether the driving is dangerous: *R v Bannister* [2009] EWCA Crim 1571.
- The fact that the defendant had consumed alcohol is an admissible factor: *R v Webster* [2006] 2 Cr App R 103.
- Where a vehicle's dangerous state is due to its official design and not use, it will not usually be appropriate to prosecute: *R v Marchant* [2003] EWCA Crim 2099.
- A vehicle is being driven in a dangerous state if the driver is aware that his ability to control the vehicle might be impaired such that the standard of his driving might fall below the requisite standard: *R v Marison* [1997] RTR 457.

 See *Blackstone's Criminal Practice 2014* **C3.39**

A10.8 Excess alcohol

Road Traffic Act 1988 s 5(1)

(1) If a person—
   (a) drives or attempts to drive a motor vehicle on a road or other public place, or
   (b) is in charge of a motor vehicle on a road or other public place, after consuming so much alcohol that the proportion of it in his breath, blood, or urine exceeds the prescribed limit he is guilty of an offence.

SO

Driving/attempting to drive: 6 month DTO. Must endorse and disqualify for at least 12 months. Must disqualify for at least 2 years if offender has had two or more disqualifications for periods of 56 days or more in preceding 3 years. Must disqualify for at least 3 years if offender has been convicted of a relevant offence in preceding 10 years

In-charge: 3 months imprisonment for an adult. No DTO available for a youth. Must endorse and may disqualify. If no disqualification, impose 10 points

A10.8.1 *Sentencing: driving*

There is no sentencing guideline specific to youths. The *Magistrates' Court Sentencing Guidelines* give the following guidance for **adult** offenders:

Offence seriousness(culpability and harm)						
A. Identify the appropriate starting point						
Starting points based on first-time offender pleading not guilty						
Level of alcohol			Starting point	Range	Disqualification	Disqual. 2nd offence in 10 years—see note above
Breath (mg)	Blood (ml)	Urine (ml)				
36–59	81–137	108–83	Band C fine	Band C fine	12–16 months	36–40 months
60–89	138–206	184–274	Band C fine	Band C fine	17–22 months	36–46 months
90–119	207–75	275–366	Medium level community order	Low level community order to high level community order	23–8 months	36–52 months
120–50 and above	276–345 and above	367–459 and above	12 weeks' custody	High level community order to 26 weeks' custody	29–36 months	36–60 months

Offence seriousness (culpability and harm)
B. Consider the effect of aggravating and mitigating factors (other than those within examples above)
The following may be particularly relevant but **these lists are not exhaustive**

Factors indicating higher culpability	**Factors indicating lower culpability**
1. LGV, HGV, PSV, etc	1. Genuine emergency established*
2. Poor road or weather conditions	2. Spiked drinks*
3. Carrying passengers	3. Very short distance driven*
4. Driving for hire or reward	
5. Evidence of unacceptable standard of driving	
Factors indicating greater degree of harm	
1. Involved in accident	
2. Location, eg near school	
3. High level of traffic or pedestrians in the vicinity	

*even where not amounting to special reasons

A10.8.2 *Sentencing: in charge*

There is no sentencing guideline specific to youths. The *Magistrates' Court Sentencing Guidelines* gives the following guidance for **adult** offenders:

Offence seriousness (culpability and harm) A. Identify the appropriate starting point, Starting points based on first-time offender pleading not guilty				
Level of alcohol			**Starting point**	**Range**
Breath (mg)	Blood (ml)	Urine (ml)	Band B fine	Band B fine 10 points
36–59	81–137	108–83		
60–89	138–206	184–274	Band B fine	Band B fine 10 points OR consider disqualification
90–119	207–75	275–366	Band C fine	Band C fine to medium level community order. Consider disqualification up to 6 months OR 10 points
120–50 and above	276–345 and above	367–459 and above	Medium level community order	Low level community order to 6 weeks' custody. Disqualify 6–12 months

Offence seriousness (culpability and harm) B. Consider the effect of aggravating and mitigating factors (other than those within examples above) The following may be particularly relevant but **these lists are not exhaustive**	
Factors indicating higher culpability	**Factor indicating lower culpability**
1. LGV, HGV, PSV, etc 2. Ability to drive seriously impaired 3. High likelihood of driving 4. Driving for hire or reward	1. Low likelihood of driving

A10.8.3 `Key points`

Section 5(2)–(3) of the Road Traffic Act 1988 provides a statutory defence:

> ### Road Traffic Act 1988, s 5(2)–(3)
>
> (2) It is a defence for a person charged with an offence under subsection (1) (b) above to prove that at the time he is alleged to have committed the offence the circumstances were such that there was no likelihood of his driving

> the vehicle whilst the proportion of alcohol in his breath, blood or urine remained likely to exceed the prescribed limit.
>
> (3) The court may, in determining whether there was such a likelihood as is mentioned in subsection (2) above, disregard any injury to him and any damage to the vehicle.

- The burden of proof falls on the defendant: *Sheldrake v Director of Public Prosecutions* [2005] RTR 2.
- Duress is available as a defence. The defence will only be available for so long as the threat is active and a sober and reasonable person would have driven: *Crown Prosecution Service v Brown* [2007] EWHC 3274 (Admin).
- Where there is post-driving consumption of alcohol the defendant is able to 'back calculate' to obtain a reading at the time of driving, the Road Traffic Offences Act 1988, s 15(3).

 See *Blackstone's Criminal Practice 2014* **C5.57**

A10.9 Fail to provide specimen for analysis

Section 7(6)–(7) of the Road Traffic Act 1988 provides:

Road Traffic Act 1988 s 7(6)–(7)

(6) A person who, without reasonable excuse, fails to provide a specimen when required to do so in pursuance of this section is guilty of an offence.

(7) A constable must, on requiring any person to provide a specimen in pursuance of this section, warn him that a failure to provide it may render him liable to prosecution.

SO

 Driving/attempting to drive: 6 month DTO. Must endorse and disqualify for at least 12 months. Must disqualify for at least 2 years if offender has had two or more disqualifications for periods of 56 days or more in preceding 3 years. Must disqualify for at least 3 years if offender has been convicted of a relevant offence in preceding 10 years

In-charge: For an adult maximum 3 months' imprisonment. No DTO available for a youth. Must endorse and may disqualify. If no disqualification, impose 10 points

---

A10.9.1 *Sentencing: driving or attempting to drive*

There is no sentencing guideline specific to youths. The *Magistrates' Court Sentencing Guidelines* gives the following guidance for **adult** offenders:

Offence seriousness (culpability and harm)				
A. Identify the appropriate starting point				
Starting points based on first-time offender pleading not guilty				
Examples of nature of activity	**Starting point**	**Range**	**Disqual.**	**Disqual. 2nd offence in 10 years**
Defendant refused test when had honestly held but unreasonable excuse	Band C fine	Band C fine	12–16 months	36–40 months
Deliberate refusal or deliberate failure	Low level community order	Band C fine to high level community order	17–28 months	36–52 months
Deliberate refusal or deliberate failure where evidence of serious impairment	12 weeks' custody	High level community order to 26 weeks' custody	29–36 months	36–60 months

Offence seriousness (culpability and harm)	
B. Consider the effect of aggravating and mitigating factors (other than those within examples above)	
The following may be particularly relevant but **these lists are not exhaustive**	
Factors indicating higher culpability	**Factor indicating lower culpability**
1. Evidence of unacceptable standard of driving 2. LGV, HGV, PSV, etc 3. Obvious state of intoxication 4. Driving for hire or reward **Factor indicating greater degree of harm** 1. Involved in accident	1. Genuine but unsuccessful attempt to provide specimen

A10.9.2 *Sentencing: in-charge*

There is no sentencing guideline specific to youths. The *Magistrates' Court Sentencing Guidelines* gives the following guidance for **adult** offenders:

Offence seriousness (culpability and harm) A. Identify appropriate starting point Starting points based on first-time offender pleading not guilty		
Examples of nature of activity	**Starting point**	**Range**
Defendant refused test when had honestly held but unreasonable excuse	Band B fine	Band B fine 10 points
Deliberate refusal or deliberate failure	Band C fine	Band C fine to medium level community order. Consider disqualification OR 10 points
Deliberate refusal or deliberate failure where evidence of serious impairment	Medium level community order	Low level community order to 6 weeks' custody. Disqualify 6–12 months

Offence seriousness (culpability and harm) B. Consider the effect of aggravating and mitigating factors (other than those within examples above) The following may be particularly relevant but **these lists are not exhaustive**	
Factors indicating higher culpability	**Factors indicating lower culpability**
1. Obvious state of intoxication 2. LGV, HGV PSV, etc 3. High likelihood of driving 4. Driving for hire of reward	1. Genuine but unsuccessful attempt to provide specimen 2. Low likelihood of driving

A10.9.3 Key points

- A reasonable excuse for failing to provide must relate to inability due to physical or mental issues: *R v Lennard* [1973] RTR 252.
- The suspect need not in fact be the driver if there is a relevant investigation being conducted by the police.
- Failure to mention a medical reason at the time of refusal does not preclude a court from finding that a reasonable excuse existed, although it was a factor to be taken into account: *Piggott v Director of Public Prosecutions* [2008] RTR 16.
- Once a reasonable excuse is raised it is for the prosecution to disprove it: *McKeon v Director of Public Prosecutions* [2008] RTR 14.
- A failure to understand the statutory warning relating to prosecution may amount to a reasonable excuse if the accused's understanding of English is poor: *Chief Constable of Avon and Somerset v Singh* [1988] RTR 107. If an accredited interpreter is present there is a rebuttable inference that the warning was understood: *Bielecki v*

DPP [2011] EWHC 2245 (Admin). Failure to understand due to intoxication will not suffice.
- The taking of a specimen does not have to be delayed (over and above a couple of minutes) for the purpose of taking legal advice: *R v Gearing* [2008] EWHC 1695 (Admin).

 See *Blackstone's Criminal Practice 2014* **C5.9**

A10.10 Unfit through drink or drugs

Road Traffic Act 1988 s 4(1)–(2) and (5)

(1) A person who, when driving or attempting to drive a mechanically propelled vehicle on a road or other public place, is unfit to drive through drink or drugs is guilty of an offence.
(2) Without prejudice to subsection (1) above, a person who, when in charge of a mechanically propelled vehicle which is on a road or other public place, is unfit to drive through drink or drugs is guilty of an offence.

...

(4) ...a person shall be taken to be unfit to drive if his ability to drive properly is for the time being impaired.

SO

Drive/attempt to drive: 6 month DTO. Must endorse and disqualify for at least 12 months. Must disqualify for at least 2 years if offender has had two or more disqualifications for periods of 56 days or more in preceding years. Must disqualify for at least 3 years if offender has been convicted of a relevant offence in preceding 10 years

In-charge: For an adult maximum 3 months' imprisonment. No DTO available for a youth. Must endorse and may disqualify. If no disqualification, impose 10 points. NB Not imprisonable for a youth

A10.10.1 *Sentencing: driving or attempting to drive*

There is no sentencing guideline specific to youths. The *Magistrates' Court Sentencing Guidelines* gives the following guidance for **adult** offenders:

Offence seriousness (culpability and harm) A. Identify the appropriate starting point Starting points based on first-time offender pleading not guilty				
Examples of nature of activity	Starting point	Range	Disqual.	Disqual. 2nd offence in 10 years
Evidence of moderate level of impairment and no aggravating factors	Band C fine	Band C fine	12–16 months	36–40 months
Evidence of moderate level of impairment and presence of one or more aggravating factors listed below	Band C fine	Band C fine	17–22 months	36–46 months
Evidence of high level of impairment and no aggravating factors	Medium level community order	Low level community order to high level community order	23–8 months	36–52 months
Evidence of high level of impairment and presence of one or more aggravating factors listed below	12 weeks' custody	High level community order to 26 weeks' custody	29–36 months	36–60 months

Offence seriousness (culpability and harm) B. Consider the effect of aggravating and mitigating factors (other than those within examples above) The following may be particularly relevant but these lists are not exhaustive	
Factors indicating higher culpability 1. LGV, HGV PSV, etc 2. Poor road or weather conditions 3. Carrying passengers 4. Driving for hire or reward 5. Evidence of unacceptable standard of driving **Factors indicating greater degree of harm** 1. Involved in accident 2. Location, eg near school 3. High level of traffic or pedestrians in the vicinity	**Factors indicating lower culpability** 1. Genuine emergency established* 2. Spiked drinks* 3. Very short distance driven*

*even where not amounting to special reasons

A10.10.2 *Sentencing: in-charge*

Offence seriousness (culpability and harm) A. Identify the appropriate starting point Starting points based on first-time offender pleading not guilty		
Examples of nature of activity	**Starting point**	**Range**
Evidence of moderate level of impairment and no aggravating factors	Band B fine	Band B fine 10 points
Evidence of moderate level of impairment and presence of one or more aggravating factors listed below	Band B fine	Band B fine 10 points or consider disqualification
Evidence of high level of impairment and no aggravating factors	Band C fine	Band C fine to medium level community order 10 points OR consider disqualification
Evidence of high level of impairment and presence of one or more aggravating factors listed below	High level community order	Medium level community order to 12 weeks' custody. Consider disqualification OR 10 points

Offence seriousness (culpability and harm) B. Consider the effect of aggravating and mitigating factors (other than those within examples above) The following may be particularly relevant but **these lists are not exhaustive**	
Factors indicating higher culpability	**Factor indicating lower culpability**
1. LGV, HGV, PSV, etc 2. High likelihood of driving 3. Driving for hire or reward	1. Low likelihood of driving

A10.10.3 Key points

- No likelihood of driving whilst unfit provides a defence in law to the in-charge offence. Section 4(3) and (4) of the Road Traffic Act 1988 provides:

Road Traffic Act 1988 s 4(3)---(4)

(3) For the purposes of subsection (2) above, a person shall be deemed not to have been in charge of a mechanically propelled vehicle if he proves that at the material time the circumstances were such that there was no likelihood of his driving it so long as he remained unfit to drive through drink or drugs.

(4) The court may, in determining whether there was such a likelihood as is mentioned in subsection (3) above, disregard any injury to him and any damage to the vehicle.

- Drugs include normal medicines.
- Evidence of impairment to drive may be provided by both expert and lay witnesses. Note, however, that a lay witness can give evidence as to a person's demeanour (and how much he drank, for example) but not on the ultimate question of whether the person was 'fit' to drive.
- The results of any evidential specimens are admissible (Road Traffic Offenders Act 1988, ss 15 and 16).

 See Blackstone's Criminal Practice 2014 **C5.57–C5.62**

A10.11 Driving whilst disqualified

> **Road Traffic Act 1988 s 103**
>
> (1) A person is guilty of an offence if, while disqualified for holding or obtaining a licence, he—
>   (a) obtains a licence, or
>   (b) drives a motor vehicle on a road.

SO

 6 month DTO. Must endorse and may disqualify. If no disqualification, must impose 6 points

A10.11.1 *Sentencing*

There is no sentencing guideline specific to youths. The *Magistrates' Court Sentencing Guidelines* give the following guidance for **adult** offenders:

Offence seriousness (culpability and harm) A. Identify the appropriate starting point Starting points based on first-time offender pleading not guilty		
Example of nature of activity	**Starting point**	**Range**
Full period expired but re-test not taken	Low level community order	Band C fine to medium level community order 6 points or disqualify for 3–6 months
Lengthy period of ban already served	High level community order	Medium level community order to 12 weeks' custody. Lengthen disqualification for 6–12 months beyond expiry of current ban
Recently imposed ban	12 weeks' custody	High level community order to 26 weeks' custody. Lengthen disqualification for 12–18 months beyond expiry of current ban

A10.11.2 Key points

- The prosecution do not need to prove that the defendant was aware of the prosecution that led to him being disqualified: *Taylor v Kenyon* [1952] 2 All ER 726.
- Strict proof that the person disqualified by the court is the person charged is required. This will normally arise from (a) admission, (b) fingerprints, (c) evidence of identity from someone in court when the disqualification was made: *R v Derwentside Justices, ex p Heaviside* [1996] RTR 384. Other evidence such as an unusual name will at least raise a prima facie case that the defendant will need to answer in order to avoid conviction: *Olakunori v Director of Public Prosecutions* [1998] COD 443.
- An admission made whilst giving evidence is sufficient to prove a disqualification, even in the absence of a certificate of conviction: *Moran v Crown Prosecution Service* (2000) 164 JP 562.
- A defendant's silence in interview (where he did not later rely on any fact), and his general attitude to the management of the case in accordance with the Criminal Procedure Rules, could not provide sufficient proof: *Mills v Director of Public Prosecutions* [2008] EWHC 3304 (Admin).
- Consistency of personal details will normally be sufficient to raise a prima facie case. If the defendant calls no evidence to contradict that prima facie case, it will be open to the court to be satisfied that identity is proved: *Pattison v Director of Public Prosecutions* [2006] RTR 13.
- A solicitor could be called as a witness to confirm identity although the practice is discouraged: *R (Howe) v South Durham Magistrates' Court* [2005] RTR 4.
- A mistaken belief that he was not driving on a road will not amount to a defence: *R v Miller* [1975] 1 WLR 1222.
- A bad character application in relation to the disqualification is not necessary as it has to do with the facts of the alleged offence (Criminal Justice Act 2003, s 98): *Director of Public Prosecutions v Agyemang* [2009] EWHC 1542 (Admin).
- A person who drives 'whilst disqualified by age' is driving without a licence: see **A12.18.3**.

See *Blackstone's Criminal Practice 2014* **C6.40–C6.45**

A10.12 Careless and inconsiderate driving

Road Traffic Act 1988 s 3

If a person drives a mechanically propelled vehicle on a road or other public place without due care and attention, or without reasonable consideration for other persons using the road or place, he is guilty of an offence.

SO Level 5 fine. Must endorse and may disqualify. If no disqualification, must impose 3–9 points

A10.12.1 *Sentencing*

There is no sentencing guideline specific to youths. The *Magistrates' Court Sentencing Guidelines* give the following guidance for **adult** offenders:

Offence seriousness (culpability and harm)		
A. Identify the appropriate starting point		
Starting points based on first-time offender pleading not guilty		
Example of nature of activity	**Starting point**	**Range**
Momentary lapse of concentration or misjudgement at low speed	Band A fine	Band A fine 3–4 points
Loss of control due to speed, mishandling, or insufficient attention to road conditions, or carelessly turning right across oncoming traffic	Band B fine	Band B fine 5–6 points
Overtaking manoeuvre at speed resulting in collision of vehicles, or driving bordering on the dangerous	Band C fine	Band C fine. Consider disqualification OR 7–9 points

Offence seriousness (culpability and harm)	
B. Consider the effect of aggravating and mitigating factors	
(other than those within examples above)	
The following may be particularly relevant but **these lists are not exhaustive**	
Factors indicating higher culpability	**Factors indicating lower culpability**
1. Excessive speed	1. Minor risk
2. Carrying out other tasks while driving	2. Inexperience of driver
3. Carrying passengers or heavy load	3. Sudden change in road or weather conditions
4. Tiredness	
Factors indicating greater degree of harm	
1. Injury to others	
2. Damage to other vehicles or property	
3. High level of traffic or pedestrians in vicinity	
4. Location, eg near school when children are likely to be present	

A10.12.2 `Key points`

- Careless driving is defined in the Act.
- Section 3ZA of the Road Traffic Act 1988 provides:

> **Road Traffic Act 1988 s 3ZA**
>
> (2) A person is to be regarded as driving without due care and attention if (and only if) the way he drives falls below what would be expected of a competent and careful driver.
>
> (3) In determining for the purposes of subsection (2) above what would be expected of a careful and competent driver in a particular case, regard shall be had not only to the circumstances of which he could be expected to be aware but also to any circumstances shown to have been within the knowledge of the accused.
>
> (4) A person is to be regarded as driving without reasonable consideration for other persons only if those persons are inconvenienced by his driving.

Examples of careless or inconsiderate driving:

Careless driving
- overtaking on the inside or driving inappropriately close to another vehicle
- inadvertent mistakes such as driving through a red light or emerging from a side road into the path of another vehicle
- short distractions such as tuning a car radio

Inconsiderate driving
- flashing of lights to force other drivers in front to give way
- misuse of any lane to avoid queuing or gain some other advantage over other drivers
- driving that inconveniences other road users or causes unnecessary hazards such as unnecessarily remaining in an overtaking lane, unnecessarily slow driving or braking without good cause, driving with undipped headlights which dazzle oncoming drivers, or driving through a puddle causing pedestrians to be splashed.

- Failure to drive in accordance with the Highway Code will generally amount to careless driving.
- If death has resulted from the driving any trial should await the conclusion of any inquest: *Smith v Director of Public Prosecutions* [2000] RTR 36.
- An offence of careless driving can be tried alongside an offence of dangerous driving as an alternative. However, it is not clear as to why this is done in the magistrates' court as the offence is a **statutory alternative** in any event.

- If the facts are such that in the absence of an explanation put forward by the defendant, or that explanation is objectively inadequate, and the only possible conclusion is that he was careless, he should be convicted: *Director of Public Prosecutions v Cox* (1993) 157 JP 1044.
- A court does not need to consider an alternative inference from facts, such as mechanical defect, without hearing evidence of the same: *Director of Public Prosecutions v Tipton* (1992) 156 JP 172.

 See *Blackstone's Criminal Practice 2014* **C6.1–C6.8**

A10.13 Using etc motor vehicle without insurance

Road Traffic Act 1988 s 143

143 Users of motor vehicles to be insured or secured against third-party risks.

(1) Subject to the provisions of this Part of this Act—
   (a) a person must not use a motor vehicle on a road or other public place unless there is in force in relation to the use of the vehicle by that person such a policy of insurance or such a security in respect of third party risks as complies with the requirements of this Part of this Act, and
   (b) a person must not cause or permit any other person to use a motor vehicle on a road or other public place unless there is in force in relation to the use of the vehicle by that other person such a policy of insurance or such a security in respect of third party risks as complies with the requirements of this Part of this Act.

(2) If a person acts in contravention of subsection (1) above he is guilty of an offence.

(3) A person charged with using a motor vehicle in contravention of this section shall not be convicted if he proves—
   (a) that the vehicle did not belong to him and was not in his possession under a contract of hiring or of loan,
   (b) that he was using the vehicle in the course of his employment, and
   (c) that he neither knew nor had reason to believe that there was not in force in relation to the vehicle such a policy of insurance or security as is mentioned in subsection (1) above.

(4) This Part of this Act does not apply to invalid carriages.

SO Level 5 fine/discretionary disqualification/6–8 penalty points

A10.13.1 *Sentencing*

There is no sentencing guideline specific to youths. The *Magistrates' Court Sentencing Guidelines* gives the following guidance for **adult** offenders:

Offence seriousness (culpability and harm)		
A. Identify the appropriate starting point		
Starting points based on first-time offender pleading not guilty		
Examples of nature of activity	**Starting point**	**Range**
Using a motor vehicle on a road or other public place without insurance	Band C fine	Band C fine 6 points to 12 months' disqualification— see notes below

Offence seriousness (culpability and harm)	
B. Consider the effect of aggravating and mitigating factors (other than those within examples above)	
The following may be particularly relevant but **these lists are not exhaustive**	
Factors indicating higher culpability	**Factors indicating lower culpability**
1. Never passed test	1. Responsibility for providing insurance rests with another
2. Gave false details	2. Genuine misunderstanding
3. Driving LGV, HGV, PSV, etc	3. Recent failure to renew or failure to transfer vehicle details where insurance was in existence
4. Driving for hire or reward	4. Vehicle not being driven
5. Evidence of sustained uninsured use	
Factors indicating greater degree of harm	
1. Involved in accident	
2. Accident resulting in injury	

A10.13.2 Key points

- See **A10.2** for definitions.
- Proceedings may be brought within six months of a prosecutor forming the opinion that there is sufficient evidence of an offence having been committed (subject to an overall three-year time bar).
- It is for a defendant to show that he was insured once it is established that a motor vehicle was used on a road or other public place.
- It is not necessary that the vehicle be capable of being driven: *Pumbien v Vines* [1996] RTR 37.
- Employed drivers have a defence available to them under the Road Traffic Act 1988, s 143(3).

 See *Blackstone's Criminal Practice 2014* **C6.46–C6.51**

A10.14 Failing to stop and failing to report accident

Section 170 of the Road Traffic Act 1988 states:

Road Traffic Act 1988 s 170

(1) This section applies in a case where, owing to the presence of a mechanically propelled vehicle on a road or other public place, an accident occurs by which—

    (a) personal injury is caused to a person other than the driver of that mechanically propelled vehicle, or

    (b) damage is caused—

        (i) to a vehicle other than that mechanically propelled vehicle or a trailer drawn by that mechanically propelled vehicle, or

        (ii) to an animal other than an animal in or on that mechanically propelled vehicle or a trailer drawn by that mechanically propelled vehicle, or

        (iii) to any other property constructed on, fixed to, growing in or otherwise forming part of the land on which the road or place in question is situated or land adjacent to such land.

(2) The driver of the mechanically propelled vehicle must stop and, if required to do so by any person having reasonable grounds for so requiring, give his name and address and also the name and address of the owner and the identification marks of the vehicle.

(3) If for any reason the driver of the mechanically propelled vehicle does not give his name and address under subsection (2) above, he must report the accident.

(4) A person who fails to comply with subsection (2) or (3) above is guilty of an offence.

(5) If, in a case where this section applies by virtue of subsection (1)(a) above, the driver of a motor vehicle does not at the time of the accident produce such a certificate of insurance or security, or other evidence, as is mentioned in section 165(2)(a) of this Act—

    (a) to a constable, or

    (b) to some person who, having reasonable grounds for so doing, has required him to produce it,

the driver must report the accident and produce such a certificate or other evidence.

This subsection does not apply to the driver of an invalid carriage.

(6) To comply with a duty under this section to report an accident or to produce such a certificate of insurance or security, or other evidence, as is mentioned in section 165(2)(a) of this Act, the driver—

    (a) must do so at a police station or to a constable, and

    (b) must do so as soon as is reasonably practicable and, in any case, within twenty-four hours of the occurrence of the accident.

(7) A person who fails to comply with a duty under subsection (5) above is guilty of an offence, but he shall not be convicted by reason only of a failure to produce a certificate or other evidence if, within seven days after the occurrence of the accident, the certificate or other evidence is produced at a police station that was specified by him at the time when the accident was reported.

(8) In this section 'animal' means horse, cattle, ass, mule, sheep, pig, goat or dog.

6 month DTO. Must endorse and may disqualify. If no disqualification, must impose 5–10 points

A10.14.1 *Sentencing*

There is no sentencing guideline specific to youths. The *Magistrates' Court Sentencing Guidelines* give the following guidance for **adult** offenders:

Offence seriousness (culpability and harm) A. Identify the appropriate starting point Starting points based on first-time offender pleading not guilty		
Examples of nature of activity	**Starting point**	**Range**
Minor damage/injury or stopped at scene but failed to exchange particulars or report	Band B fine	Band B fine 5–6 points
Moderate damage/injury or failed to stop and failed to report	Band C fine	Band C fine 7–8 points Consider disqualification
Serious damage/injury and/or evidence of bad driving	High level community order	Band C fine to 26 weeks' custody. Disqualify 6–12 months OR 9–10 points

Offence seriousness (culpability and harm) B. Consider the effect of aggravating and mitigating factors (other than those within examples above) The following may be particularly relevant but **these lists are not exhaustive**	
Factors indicating higher culpability	**Factors indicating lower culpability**
1. Evidence of drink or drugs/evasion of test 2. Knowledge/suspicion that personal injury caused (where not an element of the offence) 3. Leaving injured party at scene 4. Giving false details	1. Believed identity known 2. Genuine fear of retribution 3. Subsequently reported

A10.14.2 Key points

A driver who is unaware of the accident cannot commit an offence under these provisions: *Harding v Price* (1948) 1 KB 695. If he later becomes aware of the accident he must report it personally if he becomes aware within 24 hours: *DPP v Drury* [1989] RTR 165.

See *Blackstone's Criminal Practice 2014* **C6.51–C6.55**

A10.15 Failing to provide information as to driver

Road Traffic Act 1988, s 172

(1) This section applies—

    (a) to any offence under the preceding provisions of this Act except—

        (i) an offence under Part V, or

        (ii) an offence under section 13, 16, 51(2), 61(4), 67(9), 68(4), 96 or 120, and to an offence under section 178 of this Act,

    (b) to any offence under sections 25, 26 or 27 of the Road Traffic Offenders Act 1988,

    (c) to any offence against any other enactment relating to the use of vehicles on roads, and

    (d) to manslaughter, or in Scotland culpable homicide, by the driver of a motor vehicle.

(2) Where the driver of a vehicle is alleged to be guilty of an offence to which this section applies—

    (a) the person keeping the vehicle shall give such information as to the identity of the driver as he may be required to give by or on behalf of a chief officer of police, and

    (b) any other person shall if required as stated above give any information which it is in his power to give and may lead to identification of the driver.

(3) Subject to the following provisions, a person who fails to comply with a requirement under subsection (2) above shall be guilty of an offence.

(4) …

(5) …

(6) …

(7) A requirement under subsection (2) may be made by written notice served by post; and where it is so made—

    (a) it shall have effect as a requirement to give the information within the period of 28 days beginning with the day on which the notice is served, and

    (b) the person on whom the notice is served shall not be guilty of an offence under this section if he shows either that he gave the information as soon as reasonably practicable after the end of that period or that it has not been reasonably practicable for him to give it.

(8) …

(9) For the purposes of section 7 of the Interpretation Act 1978 as it applies for the purposes of this section the proper address of any person in relation to the service on him of a notice under subsection (7) above is—

    (a) in the case of the secretary or clerk of a body corporate, that of the registered or principal office of that body or (if the body corporate is the registered keeper of the vehicle concerned) the registered address, and

    (b) in any other case, his last known address at the time of service.

(10) In this section—

    'registered address', in relation to the registered keeper of a vehicle, means the address recorded in the record kept under the Vehicles Excise

> and Registration Act 1994 with respect to that vehicle as being that person's address, and 'registered keeper', in relation to a vehicle, means the person in whose name the vehicle is registered under that Act; and references to the driver of a vehicle include references to the rider of a cycle.

SO Level 3 fine; must endorse 6 points; discretionary disqualification

A10.15.1 Key points

- Section 172(4) of the Road Traffic Act 1988 provides a defence:

Road Traffic Act 1988, s 172(4)

(4) A person shall not be guilty of an offence by virtue of paragraph (a) of subsection (2) above if he shows that he did not know and could not with reasonable diligence have ascertained who the driver of the vehicle was.

- In *Duff v Director of Public Prosecutions* [2009] EWHC 675 (Admin), D's wife was served with a notice under section 172 of the Road Traffic Act 1988 requiring her to identify the name of the driver. D in fact replied to the notice, naming himself as the driver. As a result a further section 172 notice was then served on D. Following legal advice D did not respond to that notice and was subsequently convicted of failing to provide information. It was held that the conviction was sound as the request to which he had in fact responded was a request of D's wife, not D himself.
- A driver is only to be judged in relation to section 172(4) by the actions he did or did not take from the time of the police request to ascertain the identity of the driver, not before: *Atkinson v Director of Public Prosecutions* [2011] EWHC 3363 (Admin).
- For the defences available under section 172(7)(b), see *Purnell v Snaresbrook Crown Court* [2011] EWHC 934 (Admin) and *Whiteside v Director of Public Prosecutions* [2011] EWHC 3471 (Admin). Lack of personal knowledge of the request was not itself a defence, but the defendant may be able to show that it was not reasonably practicable for him to have been aware of the notice and to provide the information sought.

📖 See *Blackstone's Criminal Practice 2014* **C2.20**

A10.16 Speeding

Road Traffic Regulation Act 1984, s 89(10)

SO Level 3 fine (level 4 if motorway); must endorse 3–6 points; discretionary disqualification

A10.16.1 *Sentencing*

There is no sentencing guideline specific to youths. The *Magistrates' Court Sentencing Guidelines* gives the following guidance for **adult** offenders:

Offence seriousness (culpability and harm)			
A. Identify the appropriate starting point			
Starting points based on first-time offender pleading not guilty			
Speed limit (mph)	**Recorded speed (mph)**		
20	21–30	31–40	41–50
30	31–40	41–50	51–60
40	41–55	56–65	66–75
50	51–65	66–75	76–85
60	61–80	81–90	91–100
70	71–90	91–100	101–110
Starting point	Band A fine	Band B fine	Band B fine
Range	Band A fine	Band B fine	Band B fine
Points/disqualification	3 points	4–6 points OR Disqualify 7–28 days	Disqualify 7–56 days OR 6 points

Offence seriousness (culpability and harm)
B. Consider the effect of aggravating and mitigating factors (other than those within examples above)
The following may be particularly relevant but **these lists are not exhaustive**

Factors indicating higher culpability	Factor indicating lower culpability
1. Poor road or weather conditions 2. LGV, HGV, PSV, etc 3. Towing caravan/trailer 4. Carrying passengers or heavy load 5. Driving for hire or reward 6. Evidence of unacceptable standard of driving over and above speed	1. Genuine emergency established

Factors indicating greater degree of harm	
1. Location, eg near school	
2. High level of traffic or pedestrians in the vicinity	

A10.16.2 Key points

- Necessity is available as a defence: *Moss v Howdle* [1997] SLT 782.
- Check that a notice of intended prosecution has been served in time.
- Save where the road is a restricted road, there needs to be signage in accordance with the regulations. A failure to provide adequate signage is fatal to any conviction. In *Jones v Director of Public Prosecutions* [2011] EWHC 50 (Admin), the court held that the relevant question to be answered by the court was:

  Whether by the point on the road where the alleged offence took place (the point of enforcement) the driver by reference to the route taken thereto has been given (or drivers generally have been given) adequate guidance of the speed limit to be observed at that point on the road by the signs on the relevant part of parts of the road in so far as (and thus to the extent that) those traffic signs comply with the 2002 Regulations?

 See *Blackstone's Criminal Practice 2014* **C6.58–C6.62**

A10.17 Other non-imprisonable offences

A10.17.1 *Offences concerning the driver*

Offence	Maximum	Points	Starting point	Special considerations
Fail to cooperate with preliminary (roadside) breath test	L3	4	B	
Fail to produce insurance certificate	L4	–	A	Fine per offence, not per document
Fail to produce test certificate	L3	–	A	
Fail to stop motor vehicle/ cycle when required	L5/L3(cycle)	-	A	
Drive otherwise than in accordance with licence (where could be covered)	L3	-	A	
Drive otherwise than in accordance with licence	L3	3–6	A	Aggravating factor if no licence ever held

 See *Blackstone's Criminal Practice 2014* **C6**

A10.17.2 *Offences concerning the vehicle*

No excise licence	L3 or 5 times annual duty, whichever is greater	—	A (1–3 months unpaid) B (4–6 months unpaid) C (7–12 months unpaid)	Add duty lost
Fail to notify change of ownership to DVLA	L3	—	A	If offence committed in course of business: A (driver) A* (owner-driver) B (owner-company)
No test certificate	L3	—	A	If offence committed in course of business: A (driver) A* (owner-driver) B (owner-company)
Brakes defective Key points: It is sufficient only to prove that any part of the braking system is defective (*Kennett v British Airports Authority* [1975] Crim LR 106). The fact that everything possible (eg servicing) has been done in order to ensure that the vehicle is in good condition does not amount to a defence (*Hawkins v Holmes* [1974] RTR 436), as maintenance of the braking system is an absolute obligation on the driver (*Green v Burnett* [1954] 3 All ER 273)	L4	3	B	If offence committed in course of business: B (driver) B* (owner-driver) C (owner-company) L5 if goods vehicle
Steering defective	L4	3	B	If offence committed in course of business: B (driver) B* (owner-driver) C (owner-company) L5 if goods vehicle

Tyres defective. It is a defence if the vehicle is not being used and there was no intention to use when the tyres were defective, regardless of the fact that the vehicle was on a road (*Eden v Mitchell* [1975] RTR 425). There is no requirement for the prosecution to have had the tyre examined by an authorized examiner as the issue was a simple question of fact (*Phillips v Thomas* [1974] RTR 28)	L4	3	B	If offence committed in course of business: B (driver) B* (owner-driver) C (owner-company) L5 if goods vehicle penalty per tyre
Condition of vehicle/ accessories/equipment involving danger of injury (Road Traffic Act 1988, s 40A)	L4	3	B	Must disqualify for at least 6 months if offender has one or more previous convictions for same offence within 3 years If offence committed in course of business: B (driver) B* (owner-driver) C (owner-company) L5 if goods vehicle
Exhaust defective	L3	—	A	If offence committed in course of business: A (driver) A* (owner-driver) B (owner-company)
Lights defective	L3	—	A	If offence committed in course of business: A (driver) A* (owner-driver) B (owner-company)

See *Blackstone's Criminal Practice 2014* **C6**

A10.17.3 *Offences concerning use of the vehicle*

Offence	Maximum	Points	Starting point	Special considerations
Weight, position, or distribution of load or manner in which load secured involving danger of injury (Road Traffic Act 1988 s 40A). Many cases involve unsecured passengers on the back of vehicles which is objectively often viewed as involving danger of injury (eg *Gray v Director of Public Prosecutions* [1999] RTR 339)	L4	3	B	Must disqualify for at least 6 months if offender has one or more previous convictions for same offence within 3 years. If offence committed in course of business: A (driver) A* (owner-driver) B (owner-company) L5 if goods vehicle
Number of passengers or way carried involving danger of injury (Road Traffic Act 1988 s 40A)	L4	3	B	If offence committed in course of business: A (driver) A* (owner-driver) B (owner-company) L5 if goods vehicle
Position or manner in which load secured (not involving danger) (Road Traffic Act 1988 s 42)	L3		A	L4 if goods vehicle

See *Blackstone's Criminal Practice 2014* **C6**

Youth Justice System

Part 5

Your Trigeminal System

B1 Aim of the Youth Justice System

The legislation relating to children and young persons is contained in many different statutes and it seems unlikely to be codified in the near future. The Crime and Disorder Act 1998 defined the youth justice system and set up some of its current structure. The CDA 1998 s 42(1) states:

Crime and Disorder Act 1998 s 42(1)

The youth justice system is the system of criminal justice insofar as it relates to children and young people.

It also established the principal aim of the youth justice system. The CDA 1998 s 37 states:

Crime and Disorder Act 1998 s 37

(1) It shall be the principal aim of the youth justice system to prevent offending by children and young persons.
(2) In addition to any other duty to which they are subject, it shall be the duty of all persons and bodies carrying out functions in relation to the youth justice system to have regard to that aim.

The purposes of sentencing set out in the CJA 2003 s 142 do not apply to defendants who are under 18 years at the time of conviction. The court must consider the principal aim and the welfare principle.

The Sentencing Council Guideline *Overarching Principles: Sentencing Youths* is essential reading for all those who work in the youth court.

B2 European Convention on Human Rights

The European Convention on Human Rights is embodied in domestic legislation through the Human Rights Act 1998. The most relevant principles applicable to the youth justice system are:

- Article 3 Protection from inhuman degrading treatment
- Article 5 Guarantee of the right to liberty and the security of the person
- Article 6 Guarantee of due process (fair trial, impartial and independent tribunal, etc)
- Article 8 Right to privacy and family life.

The guarantees of Article 6 apply with equal force to juveniles as they do to adults, as was stated in *Nortier v Netherlands* (1993) 17 EHRR 273:

> That minors are as entitled to the same protection of their fundamental rights as adults... but the developing state of their personality—and consequently their limited social responsibility—should be taken into account in applying Article 6 of the Convention

The European Court of Human Rights (ECtHR) rules on Convention Rights when domestic remedies are exhausted. The position of children and young people in relation to Article 6 was extensively discussed, prior to the implementation of the Human Rights Act 1998, in *T v United Kingdom, V v United Kingdom* (2000) 30 EHRR 121 and is important in consideration of issues of effective participation in the criminal process. In *T v United Kingdom* neither the attribution of criminal responsibility to a 10-year-old, nor the three-week trial in public, were thought to constitute inhuman or degrading treatment or punishment in breach of Article 3. However, the appellants were unable to participate effectively in the criminal proceedings and were therefore denied a fair hearing, in breach of Article 6(1). They had a right to hear and follow the proceedings.

In *SC v UK* (2005) 40 EHRR 226 there was a breach of Article 6(1) where an 11-year-old defendant with limited intellectual ability was tried in the Crown Court. The ECtHR held that it was essential in such circumstances that a specialist tribunal should be the trial court.

 See *Blackstone's Criminal Practice 2014* **A7**

B3 UN Convention on the Rights of the Child

B3.1 UN Convention on Human Rights of the Child 1989

The United Kingdom is a signatory to this Convention although it is not part of domestic law. The standards established in the Convention have been increasingly accepted as relevant to decisions regarding the rights of children and young persons under the European Convention on Human Rights. Examples can be seen in the international courts in *V v UK and T v UK*, (2000) 30 EHRR 121 and in the domestic courts in *McKerry v Teesdale & Wear Valley Justices* [2000] All ER (D) 140 QBD.

B3.2 Other international standards

The United Nations has adopted detailed standards for children and young persons involved in the youth justice system and they are contained in:

- The UN Standard Minimum Rules for the administration of juvenile justice 1985 ('The Beijing Rules')
- The UN Rules for the protection of juveniles deprived of their liberty 1990 ('The Havana Rules')
- The UN guidelines for the administration of juvenile delinquency 1990 ('The Riyadh Guidelines').

Although not binding in the United Kingdom, they form part of the international standards that would be relevant to considering any human rights question relating to a child or young person.

The need for a court to consider these provisions is referred to in the SGC Guideline *Overarching Principles: Sentencing Youths* para 1.3 which states:

> a court sentencing a young offender must be aware of obligations under a range of international conventions which emphasise the importance of avoiding 'criminalisation' of young people whilst ensuring that they are held responsible for their actions and, where possible, take part in repairing the damage that they have caused. This includes recognition of the damage caused to the victims and understanding by the young person that the deed was not acceptable. Within a system that provides for both the acknowledgement of guilt and sanctions which rehabilitate, the intention is to establish responsibility and, at the same time, to promote re-integration rather than to impose retribution.

B4 Welfare Principle

B4.1 Welfare of the child or young person

The introduction of the principal aim of the youth justice system did not lead to any lessening in importance of the welfare principal which is set out in the Children and Young Persons Act 1933 s 44 as:

> ### Children and Young Persons Act 1933 s 44
>
> Every court in dealing with a child or young person who is brought before it, either as an offender or otherwise, shall have regard to the welfare of the child or young person and shall in proper cases take steps for removing him from undesirable surroundings and for securing that proper provision is made for his education and training.

There is no statutory definition of 'welfare' but assistance can be found in the SGC Guideline, para 2.9:

> In having regard to the 'welfare' of the young person, a court should ensure that it is alert to:
> * the high incidence of mental health problems amongst young people in the criminal justice system;
> * the high incidence of those with learning difficulties or learning disabilities amongst young people in the criminal justice system;
> * the effect that speech and language difficulties might have on the ability of the young person (or any adult with them) to communicate with the court, to understand the sanction imposed or to fulfil the obligations resulting from that sanction;
> * the extent to which young people anticipate that they will be discriminated against by those in authority and the effect that it has on the way that they conduct themselves during court proceedings;
> * the vulnerability of young people to self-harm, particularly within a custodial environment;
> * the extent to which changes taking place during adolescence can lead to experimentation;
> * the effect on young people of experiences of loss or of abuse.

In making a sentencing decision the court will have regard to the principal aim and the welfare principle. The welfare principle is also relevant when considering bail: *R(B) v Brent Youth Court* [2010] EWHC 1893 (Admin).

B5 Youth Justice Board for England and Wales

The Crime and Disorder Act 1998 s 41 established the Youth Justice Board for England and Wales (YJB). This is a non-departmental government body based in the Ministry of Justice. The Board consists of between ten and twelve members appointed by the Secretary of State for Justice and includes those who have extensive recent experience of the youth justice system. The functions of the Board include:

- monitoring the operation of the youth justice system and the provision of Youth Justice Services;
- advising the Home Secretary on this and the setting of national standards of Youth Justice Services and custodial accommodation;
- advising on how the principal aim of the youth justice system might be most effectively achieved; and
- identifying and promoting and making grants for the development of good practice in the operation of the youth justice system and the preventing of youth offending.

The YJB has powers to require the local authorities, police authorities, probation committees, and health authorities to provide information or reports to the Board on the discharge of their duties. The YJB previously dealt with the commissioning and purchasing of secure facilities, known as 'the secure estate', for youths on remand and serving custodial sentences. Under the provisions of the LASPO 2012 the financial responsibility for children and young people in custody passes to the local authority with responsibility for the child or young person: LASPO 2012 ss 103–4.

The YJB area of the Ministry of Justice website is a useful resource for practitioners.

B6 Youth Offending Teams

The Crime and Disorder Act 1998 s 39 places a duty on local authorities, in consultation with the police, probation, and health authority to establish one or more Youth Offending Team in its area. It is possible for neighbouring local authorities to establish a joint Youth Offending Team.

The Youth Offending Team (YOT) must consist of at least one of each of the following:

- a probation officer
- a social worker of a local authority social services department
- a police officer
- a person nominated by a health authority
- a person nominated by the Chief Education Officer.

It is the duty of the Youth Offending Team to coordinate the provision of the youth justice services 'for all those in the authority's area who need them' and carry out the functions set out in the Youth Justice Plan which sets out how the local authority intends to fulfil its duties in relation to the provision of youth justice services.

The CDA 1998 ss 38–9 place a duty on every local authority with responsibility for education and social services to ensure the availability of appropriate youth justice services within their area. A duty to cooperate with the local authority in the discharge of this obligation is placed on the police, probation committees, and health authorities. These services include:

- Prevention and early intervention work
- Provision of persons to act as appropriate adults
- Assessment and intervention work in support of a final warning
- Support for young persons whilst on bail
- The placement in local authority accommodation of children and young people remanded to such accommodation
- Provision of reports or other information required by the court
- Provision of responsible officers in relation to Parenting Orders and other orders of the court
- Supervision of community sentences and Detention and Training Orders
- Post-release supervision of children and young persons released from custody
- Management of Referral Orders.

B6.1 ASSET

All YOTs use a standardized assessment tool, described by the YJB:

Asset is a structured assessment tool to be used by YOTs in England and Wales on all young offenders who come into contact with the criminal justice system. It aims to look at the young person's offence or offences and identify a multitude of factors or circumstances—ranging from lack of educational attainment to mental health problems—which may have contributed to such behaviour. The information gathered from Asset can be used to inform court reports so that appropriate intervention programmes can be drawn up. It will also highlight any particular needs or difficulties the young person has, so that these may also be addressed. Asset will also help to measure changes in needs and risk of reoffending over time.

Part C
Decision to Prosecute and Diversion

C1 **Introduction**

The key factors which will be relevant in deciding whether to caution, conditionally caution, or charge a youth for an offence are:

- do they admit the offence?
- the seriousness of the offence;
- the age of the person arrested;
- their previous offending history;
- does the proposed disposal adequately address, support, and reduce the risk of re-offending?
- is it in the public interest to prosecute?
- the welfare of the person arrested.

C2 **Cautions**

C2.1 **Cautions**

The Crime and Disorder Act 1998 ss 66ZA and 66ZB give the police the power to administer a caution.

Cautions have replaced the system of reprimands and warnings. A reprimand or warning administered before 8 April 2013 is treated as a caution. The Ministry of Justice and the Youth Justice Board have issued a document entitled *Youth Out-of-Court Disposals: Guidance for Police and Youth Offending Teams*. It is available on the Ministry of Justice and YJB websites.

The police may administer a caution on their own initiative or on the direction of the CPS. The police are permitted to make the decision to offer a simple caution for any offence triable in the case of an adult summarily or either way. Authorization from a Crown Prosecutor should be sought before offering a simple caution for an indictable-only offence.

The decision whether to give an out-of-court disposal or to charge will depend in part on the seriousness of the offence. To help the police assess the seriousness of offences the Association of Chief Police Officers (ACPO) has devised a *Youth Gravity Factor Matrix* under which offences are given a gravity 'score' based on the offence itself and any mitigating or aggravated features. The Gravity Factors will be used to assess whether a young person should be charged for an offence or given an out-of-court disposal. The *ACPO Gravity Factor Matrix* is available on the CPS website.

A youth caution may be given whether or not the youth has a previous youth caution or conviction.

All young people made subject of a caution will be referred to a YOT. The *Guidance* suggests that the first out-of-court disposal for a youth may be a decision for the police but the decision to offer a second such disposal will be taken jointly by the police and YOT after YOT assessment.

Following a youth caution the young person must be assessed by the YOT. The YOT have a duty to assess the young person and put in place a rehabilitation programme unless deemed inappropriate. A 'rehabilitation programme' means a programme with the purpose of rehabilitating participants and preventing them from reoffending.

The offender may be placed on the sex offenders register if a caution is administered for a relevant sexual offence. See **F31**.

A youth caution is spent as soon as it is given, the Rehabilitation of Offenders Act 1974 s 8A and Schedule 2.

Where a defendant who has been made subject of two cautions, or a youth conditional caution followed by a caution, is prosecuted for an offence committed within two years of the last caution, a sentencing court may not impose a conditional discharge unless it is satisfied that there are exceptional circumstances which justify it doing so.

A youth caution and a report on any failure to comply with a rehabilitation programme may be cited in criminal proceedings in the same way as a conviction.

Persons under the age of 18 years cannot be given penalty notices for disorder.

C2.2 Cautions and the *CPS Code for Crown Prosecutors*

The *CPS Code for Crown Prosecutors* states:

7.6 Prosecutors may direct that a simple caution be offered in accordance with CPS and Home Office Guidance.

7.7 Prosecutors must be satisfied that the Full Code Test is met and that there is a clear admission of guilt by the offender in any case in which they authorise or direct a simple caution to be offered by the police.

7.8 The acceptance of a simple caution or other out-of court disposal which is complied with takes the place of a prosecution. If the offer of a simple caution is refused, a prosecution must follow for the original offence. If any other out-of-court disposal is not accepted, prosecutors will apply the Full Code Test, upon receipt of the case from the police or other investigators, and decide whether to prosecute the offender.

C3 **Conditional Cautions**

The CDA 1998 s 66A deals with youth conditional cautions. The statute requires that Guidance be issued by the Secretary of State and by the Director of Public Prosecutions. The *Code of Practice for Youth Conditional Cautions* is available on the Ministry of Justice website. *The Director's Guidance on Youth Conditional Cautions* is available on the CPS website. The Ministry of Justice and the Youth Justice Board have issued non-statutory guidance entitled *Youth Out-of-Court Disposals: Guidance for Police and Youth Offending Teams*. It is available on the Ministry of Justice website.

A youth conditional caution may be administered whether or not the youth has previous cautions, youth conditional cautions, or convictions.

In any case where an authorized person or prosecutor is considering offering a youth conditional caution the local YOT must be consulted to ensure that the youth understands the nature of the proposed caution, is suitable to undertake the required conditions, and that they are likely to have a positive impact on offending behaviour. The YOT will also ascertain whether the offender accepts responsibility for the offending behaviour and is willing to admit the offence and be cautioned. The YOT may also carry out a risk assessment and ascertain the views of the victim and recommend specific conditions for inclusion.

A police officer of the rank of sergeant or above is permitted to make the decision to offer a conditional caution for any offence which for an adult would be summary only or either way. For offences which involve domestic violence or hate crimes a conditional caution may only be offered where the offence scores 3 or less on the ACPO gravity matrix.

The decision whether to give an out-of-court disposal or to charge will depend in part on the seriousness of the offence. To help the police assess the seriousness of offences the Association of Chief Police Officers (ACPO) has devised a *Youth Gravity Factor Matrix* under which offences are given a gravity 'score' based on the offence itself and any mitigating or aggravated features. The Gravity Factors will be used to assess whether a young person should be charged for an offence or given an out-of-court disposal. The *ACPO Gravity Factor Matrix* is available on the CPS website.

Authorization from a Crown Prosecutor must be sought before offering a conditional caution for an indictable-only offence. Only in the most exceptional circumstances will a youth conditional caution be an appropriate way of dealing with such a case. The decision to authorize a youth conditional caution in any indictable-only case must be approved by a Deputy Chief Crown Prosecutor.

Before a conditional caution is made the following requirements must be satisfied:

(a) there is evidence that the offender committed the offence;

(b) there is sufficient evidence to charge the offender with the offence and that a youth conditional caution should be given in respect of that offence;

(c) the offender admits to the authorized person that he committed the offence;

(d) the authorized person explains the effect of the youth conditional caution to the offender and warns him that failure to comply with any of the conditions attached may result in his being prosecuted for the offence (if the offender is 16 or under this must be done in the presence of an appropriate adult);

(e) the offender signs a document containing details of the offence, his admissions, his consent to being given a youth conditional caution, and details of the conditions attached to the caution.

The conditions that can be attached must be rehabilitative, reparative, and punitive. Rehabilitative conditions can include attendance at the local YOT or at a specific treatment course, and reparative conditions can include apologizing to the victim, paying compensation, and making good any damage. Punitive conditions can include unpaid work or a financial penalty. Conditions must always be appropriate, proportionate, and achievable.

The offender may be placed on the sex offenders register if administered for a relevant sexual offence. See **F31**. A youth conditional caution is spent three months from its imposition: Rehabilitation of Offenders Act 1974 s 8A and Schedule 2.

Where a defendant who has been made subject of a youth conditional caution is prosecuted for an offence committed within two years of the date of the conditional caution, a sentencing court may not impose a conditional discharge unless it is satisfied that there are exceptional circumstances which justify its doing so.

If the offender fails, without reasonable excuse, to comply with any of the conditions of the caution, criminal proceedings may be initiated for the offence and the document signed by him confirming his admission of the offence is admissible in evidence.

C3.1 Conditional cautions and the *CPS Code for Crown Prosecutors*

The *CPS Code for Crown Prosecutors* para 7.4 states:

> The offer of a conditional caution which is accepted and complied with takes the place of a prosecution. If the offer of a conditional caution is refused or the suspect does not make the required admission of guilt to the person who seeks to administer the conditional caution, a prosecution must follow for the original offence. If the terms of the conditional caution are not complied with, the prosecutor will reconsider the public interest and decide whether to charge the offender. Usually, a prosecution should be brought for the original offence.

C3.2 Director's guidance on youth conditional cautions

C3.2.1 *Requirement of sufficient evidence to charge*

A youth conditional caution will not be offered unless:

- there has been a clear and reliable admission to the offence by the offender and he has said nothing that could be used as a defence, or
- he has made no admission but has not denied the offence or otherwise indicated it will be contested.

The commission of the offence and the identification of the offender must be capable of being established by reliable evidence, or the suspect can be seen clearly committing the offence on a good quality visual recording.

C3.2.2 *Post-charge review*

Once a case has reached court it is not too late for a youth conditional caution to be offered. The *Guidance* sets out the procedure to be followed where a prosecutor's post-charge review concludes that a youth conditional cautions should have been offered.

> 8.1 Where an offender is charged with an offence, but it appears upon review by a Prosecutor that a Youth Conditional Caution is more appropriate, the reviewing Prosecutor should consult the youth offending team and if it is still considered appropriate should direct an authorised person to offer a youth conditional caution. This includes any case where authorised persons ordinarily make that decision. The current prosecution should be adjourned whilst this action is taken. The authorised person shall then offer a youth caution with conditions as specified by the Prosecutor. If it proves then not to be possible to administer the Youth Conditional Caution an alternative out of court disposal may not be offered and the prosecution must continue.

C3.2.3 *Financial penalty conditions*

Under the CDA s 66C the Secretary of State prescribes the maximum amount which may be specified in a financial penalty condition. The *Guidance*, at Annex A, also suggests a mitigated amount to be imposed as appropriate:

Financial penalty conditions banding

Maximum amount that may be specified where the offender is aged 14 or over but under 18
- Any summary offence: £30
- Any offence triable either way: £50
- Any offence triable only on indictment: £75

Mitigated amount where the offender is aged 14 or over but under 18
- Any summary offence: Between £5 and £20
- Any offence triable either way: Between £5 and £30
- Any offence triable only on indictment: Between £30 and £50

Maximum amount that may be specified where the offender is aged 10 or over but under 14
- Any summary offence: £15
- Any offence triable either way: £25
- Any offence triable only on indictment: £35

Mitigated amount where the offender is aged 10 or over but under 14
- Any summary offence: Between £5 and £10
- Any offence triable either way: Between £5 and £15
- Any offence triable only on indictment: Between £15 and £20

NOTE: A financial penalty condition may not be imposed for loitering or soliciting for the purposes of prostitution, possession of any class of drug or an offence under the Road Traffic Act or Road Traffic Offenders Act 1998.

C3.2.4 *Compensation for personal injuries*

There is assistance as to the level of compensation for injury which can appropriately be made part of the conditions of the caution.

Annex A
Compensation for personal injuries
Graze
- Description: Depending on size
- Award: Up to £75

Bruise
- Description: Depending on size
- Award: Up to £100

Black eye
- Award: Up to £125

C3 Conditional Cautions

Minor cut—no permanent scar
- Description: Depending on size and whether stitched
- Award: £100 to £200

Sprain
- Description: Depending on loss of mobility
- Award: £100 to £200

C4 **Code for Crown Prosecutors**

Special considerations apply to the prosecution of youths under the *Code for Crown Prosecutors*:

> 8.2 Prosecutors must bear in mind in all cases involving youths that the United Kingdom is a signatory to the United Nations 1989 Convention on the Rights of the Child and the United Nations 1985 Standard Minimum Rules for the Administration of Juvenile Justice. In addition, prosecutors must have regard to the principal aim of the youth justice system which is to prevent offending by children and young people. Prosecutors must consider the interests of the youth when deciding whether it is in the public interest to prosecute.
>
> 8.3 Prosecutors should not avoid a decision to prosecute simply because of the suspect's age. The seriousness of the offence or the youth's past behaviour is very important.

The *Directors' Guidance on Charging* states that the police may charge any summary only offence (including criminal damage where the value of the loss or damage is less than £5,000) irrespective of plea and any either way offence anticipated as a guilty plea and suitable for sentence in a magistrates' court, provided it is not:

- a case requiring the consent to prosecute of the DPP or law officer;
- a case involving a death;
- connected with terrorist activity or official secrets;
- classified as hate crime or domestic violence under CPS policies;
- an offence of violent disorder or affray;
- causing grievous bodily harm or wounding, or actual bodily harm;
- a Sexual Offences Act offence committed by or upon a person under 18; or
- an offence under the Licensing Act 2003.

Many cases are brought to court without prior CPS consideration. The decision to prosecute may still be reviewed once a charge or requisition has brought the matter to court.

C4.1 **Representations**

There are two stages in the decision to prosecute, the evidential stage and the public interest stage. Representations can be made in relation to either or both.

As diversion from prosecution is only available if an admission is made, a defendant who made no comment at the investigations stage may now be allowed to make an admission. At the evidential stage, if no admission can be made any representations must be addressed to the admissibility and reliability of the evidence.

Representations in relation to public interest matters will be assisted by the extensive guidance on 'Youth Offenders' in the *CPS Legal Guidance* available on the CPS website.

C4.2 Continuing duty to review

When a decision has been made to bring a youth before the court this can be reviewed, particularly if new information becomes available.

The CPS *Code for Crown Prosecutors* states:

> 2.2 It is the duty of prosecutors to review, to advise on and to prosecute cases or to offer an appropriate out-of-court disposal to the offender. Prosecutors must ensure that the law is properly applied; that all relevant evidence is put before the court; and that obligations of disclosure complied with, in accordance with the principles set out in this Code.
>
> 3.2 The police and other investigators are responsible for conducting enquires into an allegation that a crime may have been committed. Every case that prosecutors receive from the police or other investigators is reviewed. Prosecutors must ensure that they have all the information they need to make an informed decision about how best to deal with the case
>
> 3.6 Review is a continuing process and prosecutors must take account of any change in circumstances that occurs as the case develops. Wherever possible, they should talk to the investigator first if they are thinking about changing the charges or stopping the case. Prosecutors and investigators work closely together, but the final responsibility for the decision whether or not a case should go ahead rests with the prosecution service.

C4.3 Legitimate expectation and abuse of process

The prosecution of a person who has received a promise, undertaking, or representation from the police that he will not be prosecuted is capable of being an abuse of process: *R v Croydon Justices (ex parte Dean)* [1993] QB 769.

The prosecution of a person denied a caution by the failure of the police to make appropriate disclosure to enable legal advice to be given may be an abuse: *DPP v Ara* [2001] EWHC 493 (Admin).

In *R v Guildford Youth Court* [2008] EWHC 506 (Admin) a police officer had indicated, prior to interview, that the case would be dealt with by way of diversion. Subsequent proceedings should have been stayed as an abuse of process.

The administration of a caution may make it an abuse for there to be a later prosecution: *Jones v Whalley* [2007] 1 AC 63.

The Crown may, where there is a proper basis such as fresh evidence, bring proceedings notwithstanding that a caution has been administered: *DPP v Alexander* [2010] EWHC 2266 (Admin).

C5 **CPS Legal Guidance**

The *CPS Legal Guidance on Youth Offenders* is available on the CPS website.

The guidance contains particular reference to the decision whether to prosecute in the following situations:

- Offending behaviour in children's homes
- School bullying
- Sexual offences and child abuse by young offenders (see **A2**)
- Youths with mental disorder including learning disabilities.

CPS Legal Guidance: *Principles Guiding the Decision to Prosecute*:

Prosecutors who are not Youth Offender Specialists must refer the decision to prosecute or divert in any case to a Youth Offender Specialist.

A decision whether to prosecute a youth offender is open to judicial review if it can be demonstrated that the decision was made regardless of, or clearly contrary to a settled policy of the DPP. *R v Chief Constable of Kent and Another ex parte L, R v DPP ex parte B [1991] 93 Cr App R 416*. An application for judicial review could be successful if the decision to prosecute was made without any or sufficient inquiry into the circumstances and general character of the accused. The case highlights the importance in appropriate cases of obtaining sufficient information about the youth's home circumstances and background from sources such as the police, youth offending service, children's services before making the decision whether to prosecute.

It is essential in all youth offender cases to ensure that all of the public interest matters which give rise to the decision are clearly identified, considered and balanced. A note of the factors identified but rejected or outweighed by other considerations should be made. This demonstrates that the decision to prosecute was taken only after a full review of the case and the background information, including that concerning the suspect provided by the youth offending service, police or local authority. Failure to show that the legal guidance has been followed and properly applied to all the information on the case may result in the decision to prosecute being quashed. *R (on the application of E, S and R) v DPP [2011] EWHC 1465 (Admin)*.

When applying the public interest factors in the Full Code Test in a case involving a youth, *paragraph 4.17 b)* will always be a particularly important one. This paragraph provides that:

'A prosecution is less likely to be required if...the seriousness and the consequences of the offending can be appropriately dealt with by an out-of-court disposal which the suspect accepts and with which he or she complies.'

This is a factor which will always carry a special weight in the case of youths who are at a very early stage of their offending, and can be traced back to historic police practice (as set out, for example, in *Home Office Circular*

18/1994) of starting from a presumption of diverting youths away from the courts where possible.

For those youths for whom formal diversion is not an option, it is still important to ensure that a prosecution is only brought in circumstances where this is a proper and proportionate response. The separate Legal Guidance chapter on Minor Offences—Prosecution Guidance and its steer towards the taking of a common sense approach to less serious cases has direct application to a number of youth matters. Alternative options, including restorative interventions, Acceptable Behaviour Contracts and internal sanctions such as school disciplinary measures may be available, and sufficient to satisfy the public interest without a prosecution and the statutory duty to prevent offending (section 37 Crime and Disorder Act 1998).

C5.1 Young people in care

In response to concerns that young people in the care of local authorities are being unfairly criminalized in relation to their behaviour in children's homes, the CPS have issued specific guidance, *Offending Behaviour in Children's Homes.* This is to be considered in conjunction with the Code when deciding whether to prosecute. The guidance requires that there should be evidence, where a prosecution is brought, that written behaviour management plans were followed.

C6 **Notification of prosecutions**

The CYPA 1969 s 5 and s 34(2) provide that before any proceedings are commenced against a young person, notification of the prosecution should be given to the local authority and probation service for the area where the young person resides.

In *DPP v Cottier* [1996] 3 All ER 126 it was stated that the notice could be given orally. In practice the notification is generally sent to the youth offending team. Failure to notify does not invalidate the proceedings: *R v Marsh* [1997] 1 WLR 649.

Part D
Procedure

D1 **Age**

D1.1 **Age of criminal responsibility**

Children and Young Persons Act 1933 s 50

It shall be conclusively presumed that that no child under the age of ten years can be guilty of an offence.

D1.2 **Presumption of *doli incapax***

At common law there was a rebuttable presumption that a person aged under 14 was incapable of committing a crime. This presumption, often termed *doli incapax*, required the prosecution to establish not only that the accused had committed the offence but also that he knew what he had done was seriously wrong rather than merely naughty. The presumption of *doli incapax* was abolished by the CDA 1998 s 34 for all offences committed on or after 30 November 1998. In *R v JTB* [2009] 1 AC 1310 the House of Lords ruled that s 34 abolished both the presumption and the defence of *doli incapax*. It was therefore not open to the defence to argue that the accused had not understood that what had been done was seriously wrong.

D1.3 **Determination of age**

The CYPA 1933 s 99(1) provides:

Children and Young Persons Act 1933 s 99

99.—Presumption and determination of age

(1) Where a person, whether charged with an offence or not, is brought before any court otherwise than for the purpose of giving evidence, and it appears to the court that he is a child or young person, the court shall make due inquiry as to the age of that person, and for that purpose shall take such evidence as may be forthcoming at the hearing of the case, but an order or judgment of the court shall not be invalidated by any subsequent proof that the age of that person has not been correctly stated to the court, and the age presumed or declared by the court to be the age of the person so brought before it shall, for the purposes of this Act, be deemed to be the true age of that person, and, where it appears to the court that the person so brought before it has attained the age of eighteen years, that person shall for the purposes of this Act be deemed not to be a child or young person.

D1.4 Procedure

Age should be dealt with at the first hearing, whether the hearing is in the adult or youth court. The Act does not expressly stipulate what enquiries are appropriate where there is a material dispute as to age. It may be necessary to point out that physical maturity is not a determinant of age. Any documentary evidence or evidence from an adult relative may be of assistance.

D1.5 Determination of age is incorrect

There is no difficulty if a defendant is deemed to be a youth but it subsequently transpires that he is an adult as the CYPA 1933 s 48 states:

Children and Young Persons Act 1933 s 48

Miscellaneous provisions as to powers of juvenile courts

(1) A youth court sitting for the purpose of hearing a charge against a person who is believed to be a child or young person may, if it thinks fit to do so, proceed with the hearing and determination of the charge, notwithstanding that it is discovered that the person in question is not a child or young person.

D2 **Allocation and Sending Proceedings**

D2.1 **Presumption of summary trial**

The MCA 1980 s 24 establishes a presumption that youth defendants will be dealt with summarily.

> **Magistrates' Courts Act 1980 s 24(1)**
>
> Where a person under the age of 18 years appears or is brought before a magistrates' court on an information charging him with an indictable offence he shall, subject to sections 51 and 51A of the Crime and Disorder Act 1998 and to sections 24A and 24B . . . be tried summarily.

A youth defendant will only appear in the Crown Court for trial:

- when charged with homicide;
- when charged with a firearms offence subject to a mandatory minimum sentence;
- when charged with a specified offence and it is considered that the criteria for imposing a sentence of extended detention are met (dangerous offender);
- when charged with a grave crime and a court has determined that it ought to be possible to impose a sentence under the PCCSA 2000 s 91; or
- when charged with an adult offender who has been sent to the Crown Court and it has been determined that the cases should be kept together.

The CDA 1998 ss 51 and 51A set out the procedure for determining the allocation of a youth defendant. This procedure is summarized in the flow chart at Table A.

D2.2 **Homicide**

A youth defendant charged with an offence of homicide must be sent to the Crown Court for trial forthwith: CDA 1998 s 51A(2), (3)(a) and (12). In such cases there will be no plea before venue or allocation procedure.

The term 'offence of homicide' has not been defined in general terms by either statute or case law. There is general agreement that the term will include charges of murder and manslaughter. Attempted murder is subject to the same rules regarding venue of proceedings as the

D2 Allocation and Sending Proceedings

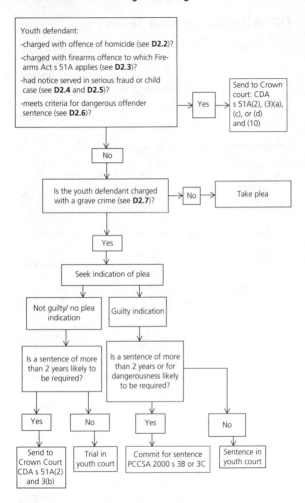

Youth defendant:

- charged with offence of homicide (see **D2.2**)?
- charged with firearms offence to which Firearms Act s 51A applies (see **D2.3**)?
- had notice served in serious fraud or child case (see **D2.4** and **D2.5**)?
- meets criteria for dangerous offender sentence (see **D2.6**)?

→ Yes → Send to Crown court: CDA s 51A(2), (3)(a), (c), or (d) and (10)

↓ No

Is the youth defendant charged with a grave crime (see **D2.7**)? → No → Take plea

↓ Yes

Seek indication of plea

Not guilty/ no plea indication | Guilty indication

Is a sentence of more than 2 years likely to be required?

Is a sentence of more than 2 years or for dangerousness likely to be required?

Yes | No | Yes | No

Send to Crown Court CDA s 51A(2) and 3(b) | Trial in youth court | Commit for sentence PCCSA 2000 s 3B or 3C | Sentence in youth court

Table A Sending for Trial: Crime and Disorder Act 1998 s 51A

offence of murder by virtue of the Criminal Attempts Act 1981 s 2(2) (c). It would therefore seem that a youth defendant charged with this offence should be sent for trial without a plea before venue or allocation procedure.

An offence of causing or allowing the death of a child or vulnerable adult is an offence of homicide for the purposes of the CDA 1998 s 51A (Domestic Violence, Crime and Victims Act 2004 s 6(5)).

It is unclear whether the definition of 'offence of homicide' extends to driving offences where a fatality is caused.

The following offences are punishable with fourteen years' imprisonment in the case of an adult and are therefore grave crimes:

- causing death by dangerous driving—RTA 1988 s 1;
- causing death by careless driving whilst under the influence of drink or drugs or having failed to provide a specimen for analysis or to permit analysis of a blood sample—RTA 1988 s 3A;
- causing death by aggravated vehicle-taking—TA 1968 s 12A(2)(b) and (4).

If these offences are not offences of homicide, a plea before venue procedure must be conducted before an allocation determination is made.

The following offences are not grave crimes and if not offences of homicide only summary trial would be possible:

- causing death by careless or inconsiderate driving—RTA 1988 s 2B (maximum penalty five years' imprisonment);
- causing death by driving (unlicensed, disqualified, or uninsured drivers)—RTA 1988 s 3ZB (maximum penalty two years' imprisonment).

D2.3 Firearms possession

By the CDA 1998 s 51A(2), (3)(a), and (12) a youth defendant must be sent for trial if charged with a firearms offence where on conviction he would be subject to a mandatory minimum sentence of three years under:

- the Firearms Act 1968 s 51A (see **A7.1.3**); or
- the Violent Crime Reduction Act 2006 s 29 (see **A7.16.1**).

In such cases there will be no plea before venue or allocation procedure.

Defendants aged under 16 on the date of the offence are not subject to the mandatory minimum sentence. An allocation decision would still have to be made in relation to offences under the Firearms Act 1968 ss 16, 17, and 18 as they are grave crimes.

D2.4 Notices in serious or complex fraud cases

A youth defendant must be sent for trial forthwith where notice is given under the CDA 1998 s 51B: CDA 1998 s 51A(2) and (3)(c). Where such a notice is served, there will be no plea before venue or allocation procedure.

A notice may be given by a designated authority under s 51B(1) in respect of an indictable offence if the authority is of the opinion that the evidence of the offence charged—

- is sufficient for the person charged to be put on trial for the offence; and
- reveals a case of fraud of such seriousness or complexity that it is appropriate that the management of the case should without delay be taken over by the Crown Court.

A notice under this section must be given to the magistrates' court at which the person charged appears or before which he is brought. Such a notice must be given to the magistrates' court before any summary trial begins: s 51A(4) and (5).

The definition of 'designated authority' includes the following:

- the Director of Public Prosecutions;
- the Director of the Serious Fraud Office; or
- the Secretary of State.

D2.5 Notices in certain cases involving children

A youth defendant must be sent for trial forthwith where notice is given under the CDA 1998 s 51C: CDA 1998 s 51A(2) and (3)(c). Where such a notice is served, there is no plea before venue or allocation procedure.

A notice may be given by the Director of Public Prosecutions under the CDA 1998 s 51C(1) if he is of the opinion:

- that the evidence of the offence would be sufficient for the person charged to be put on trial for the offence;
- that a child would be called as a witness at the trial; and
- that, for the purpose of avoiding any prejudice to the welfare of the child, the case should be taken over and proceeded with without delay by the Crown Court.

By the CDA 1998 s 51C(3) this power applies to an offence:

(a) which involves an assault on, or injury or a threat of injury to, a person;
(b) under section 1 of the Children and Young Persons Act 1933 (cruelty to persons under 16);
(c) under the Sexual Offences Act 1956, the Protection of Children Act 1978, or the Sexual Offences Act 2003;
(d) of kidnapping or false imprisonment, or an offence under section 1 or 2 of the Child Abduction Act 1984;
(e) which consists of attempting or conspiring to commit, or of aiding, abetting, counselling, procuring, or inciting the commission of, an offence falling within paragraph (a), (b), (c), or (d) above.

By the CDA 1998 s 51C(7) 'child' means—

• a person who is under the age of 18; or
• any person of whom a video recording (as defined in the YJCEA 1999 s 63(1)) was made when he was under the age of 18 with a view to its admission as his evidence in chief in the trial.

A notice under s 51C must be given to the magistrates' court before any summary trial begins: s 51B(4) and s 51C(4).

A decision to give notice under s 51C is not subject to appeal or liable to be questioned in any court: s 51C(6).

The CDA 1998 s 51C substantially re-enacts the CJA 1991 s 53. Case law relating to the use of s 53 of the 1991 Act suggest that in the case of a grave crime:

• where the youth court has determined summary trial, the prosecution cannot reverse that decision by issue of a notice—see *R v Fareham Youth Court and Morey ex parte CPS* (1999) 163 JP 812.
• it would be inappropriate for the DPP to use a notice unless satisfied that a magistrates' court would be likely to determine that trial on indictment was required under what is now the CDA 1998 s 51A(2) and (3)(b), ie a sentence substantially in excess of two years required—see *R v T and K* [2001] 1 Cr App R 446, Kay LJ at [37].

D2.6 Dangerousness

By the CDA 1998 s 51A(2) and (3)(d) a youth defendant must be sent for trial forthwith if:

• the offence is a specified offence; and
• it appears to the court that if he is found guilty of the offence the criteria for the imposition of a sentence of extended detention under the CJA 2003 s 226B would be met.

There is no plea before venue procedure.

D2.6.1 *Criteria for imposing extended detention*

The CJA 2003 s 226B is considered in more detail at **H4.3** but in summary it provides that the Crown Court may impose an extended sentence of detention where:

- a person aged under 18 is convicted of a *specified* offence;
- the court considers that there is a significant risk to members of the public of *serious harm* occasioned by the commission by the offender of further specified offences;
- if the court were to impose an extended sentence of detention, the term that it would specify as the appropriate custodial term would be at least four years.

The CJA 2003 s 224(3) provides the following definitions:

- *Specified offence*—a violent or sexual offence listed in the CJA 2003 Schedule 15 (see **Appendix 2**).
- *Serious specified offence*—offence specified in Schedule 15 punishable in the case of an adult with a term of imprisonment of ten years or more.
- *Serious harm*—means death or serious person injury, whether physical or psychological.

D2.6.2 *The assessment of dangerousness*

By the CJA 2003 s 229(2) the court:

- must take into account all such information as is available to it about the nature and circumstances of the offence;
- may take into account any information which is before it about any pattern of behaviour of which the offence forms part; and
- may take into account any information about the offender which is before it.

General advice about assessing dangerousness on sentence was given by Thomas LJ in *R v Lang* [2005] EWCA Crim 2864, [2006] 1 WLR 2509 (for which see **H4.3.2**). For the purposes of allocation the most important points from the judgment are:

- 'significant risk' is more than the possibility of occurrence;
- 'significant risk' must be shown in relation to two matters: first, the commission of further specified, but not necessarily serious, offences; and secondly, the causing thereby of serious harm to a member of the public;
- assessment of risk should include the offending history—the kind of offences, their circumstances, and the sentence imposed.

In *CPS v South East Surrey Youth Court* [2005] EWHC 2929, [2006] 1 WLR 2543 the Administrative Court considered the approach that should be taken by a youth court at the allocation stage and provided the following guidance:

- The policy of the legislature is that those who are under 18 should, wherever possible, be tried in a youth court, which is best designed for their specific needs.
- The guidance given by the Court of Appeal in *R v Lang* is of relevance, particularly in relation to non-serious specified offences.
- The court must be particularly rigorous before concluding that there is a significant risk of serious harm by the commission of further offences: such a conclusion is unlikely to be appropriate in the absence of a pre-sentence report following assessment by a youth offender team.
- In most cases where a non-serious specified offence is charged an assessment of dangerousness will not be appropriate until after conviction, when, if the dangerousness criteria are met, the defendant can be committed to the Crown Court for sentence.

The definitive guideline, *Overarching Principles: Sentencing Youths* (2009) at para 12.14 suggests that where the youth defendant is charged with a specified offence which would not otherwise be sent for trial, it is preferable for the decision on dangerousness to be made after conviction.

D2.6.3 *Co-defendants*

When dealing with youth co-defendants at an allocation hearing the court must address the question of dangerousness for each defendant separately. Where one youth defendant is deemed to satisfy the criteria of s 51A(3)(d) and is sent for trial under s 51A(2), there is no provision to send a youth co-defendant who is not deemed to be dangerous. It would, however, be possible to send an adult co-defendant charged with an either-way offence which is a joint charge or related to the charge which the youth defendant faces: s 51A(6).

D2.6.4 *Related offences*

Where a court sends a youth defendant for trial under s 51A(2), s 51A(4) provides that it may at the same time send him to the Crown Court for trial for any indictable or summary offence with which he is charged and which:

- (if it is an indictable offence) appears to the court to be related to the offence mentioned in s 51A(2); or
- (if it is a summary offence) appears to the court to be related to the offence mentioned in s 51A(2) or to the indictable offence, and which fulfils the 'requisite condition'.

A summary offence fulfils the requisite condition if it is punishable with imprisonment in the case of an adult or involves obligatory or discretionary disqualification from driving: s 51A(9).

D2.6.5 *Post-conviction committal for sentence*

After the summary trial of a specified offence a person under 18 is convicted of the offence, the court must commit the offender to the Crown Court for sentence if it appears to the court that the criteria for the imposition of a dangerous offender sentence would be met (PCCSA 2000 s 3C(2)). For this see **F4.2**.

D2.7 Grave crimes

The term is defined by the PCCSA 2000 s 91. The definition includes:

* **Offences punishable with fourteen years or more**—the definition would include robbery, dwelling burglary, and handling stolen goods. It does not, however, include non-dwelling burglary where the maximum penalty is ten years' imprisonment: *R v Brown* (1995) 16 Cr App R (S) 932.
* **Sexual offences specifically defined as grave crimes**—the following sexual offences may be treated as grave crimes notwithstanding the fact that the maximum sentence is less than fourteen years:
  (a) sexual assault contrary to the SOA 2003 s 3;
  (b) child sex offences committed by children and young persons contrary to the SOA 2003 s 13;
  (c) sexual activity with a child family member contrary to SOA 2003 s 25; and
  (d) inciting a child family member to engage in sexual activity contrary to section 26 of the SOA 2003.
* **Firearms possession**—the mandatory minimum sentence only applies if the accused had attained the age of 16 by the date of the offence. Although grave crimes, these firearms offences must be sent for trial under the CDA 1998 s 51A(1) and (3)(a) if the mandatory minimum sentence applies (see **D2.3** above).

A list of grave crimes may be found in **Appendix 3**. For the offences included in Part **A** the fact that the offence is a grave crime is indicated by the icon **GC** .

D.2.7.1 *Plea before venue*

Before making a decision on allocation of a grave crime the court must deal with plea before venue: MCA 1980 s 24A(1) and (2).

The plea before venue procedure is set out in s 24A and Crim PR rule 9.13:

(a) The procedure must be carried out in the presence of the accused (however, provision exists for the procedure to be carried out in the absence of the accused if his behaviour is disruptive and he is legally represented at the hearing—see the MCA 1980 s 24B).

(b) The court shall cause the charge to be written down (if this has not already been done) and to be read to the accused.

(c) The court shall explain to the accused in ordinary language that he may indicate whether (if the offence were to proceed to trial) he would plead guilty or not guilty, and if he indicates that he would plead guilty, the court will accept that indication as a guilty plea. In the case of a grave crime or a specified offence the court must also warn the accused that committal for sentence could still be possible even after an indication of a guilty plea.

(d) If the accused indicates that he would plead guilty, the court shall proceed as if the indication were a guilty plea.

(e) If the accused indicates that he would plead not guilty, the court shall proceed to make a decision regarding allocation (the 'relevant determination').

(f) If the accused fails to indicate how he would plead, he shall be taken to indicate that he would plead not guilty.

A magistrates' court proceeding under the MCA 1980 s 24A (or s 24B) may adjourn the proceedings at any time, and on doing so on any occasion when the accused is present may remand the accused: MCA 1980 s 24C(1).

D2.7.2 *Committing a grave crime for sentence*

Where a person under 18 charged with a grave crime has indicated a guilty plea at a plea before venue hearing, the court may commit him for sentence if the court is of the opinion that the offence, or the combination of the offence and one or more offences associated with it, was such that the Crown Court should have power to deal with the offender by imposing a sentence under the PCCSA 2000 s 91: PCCSA 2000 s 3B. For this provision see **F4.1**.

An offender cannot be committed for sentence under the PCCSA 2000 s 3B if convicted after a summary trial.

D2.7.3 *Allocation*

If the accused gives a not guilty indication or no indication at all, the court must proceed to determine the allocation of the case.

The criterion for determining allocation: **Ought it be possible to sentence the accused to detention under the PCCSA 2000 s 91(3) for this alleged offence?** (MCA 1980 s 24A and CDA 1998 s 51A(3)(b).)

D2 Allocation and Sending Proceedings

The allocation decision for grave crimes has been the subject of extensive scrutiny by the Administrative Court. Reviewing those authorities Leveson J in *R (H) v Southampton Youth Court* [2004] EWHC 2912 (Admin), [2005] 2 Cr App R (S) summarized the principles as follows:

1. The general policy of the legislature is that those who are under 18 years of age and in particular children of under 15 years of age should, wherever possible, be tried in the youth court. It is that court which is best designed to meet their specific needs. A trial in the Crown Court with the inevitably greater formality and greatly increased number of people involved (including a jury and the public) should be reserved for the most serious cases.

2. It is a further policy of the legislature that, generally speaking, first-time offenders aged 12 to 14 and all offenders under 12 should not be detained in custody and decisions as to jurisdiction should have regard to the fact that the exceptional power to detain for grave offences should not be used to water down the general principle. Those under 15 will rarely attract a period of detention and, even more rarely, those who are under 12.

3. In each case the court should ask itself whether there is a real prospect, having regard to his or her age, that this defendant whose case they are considering might require a sentence of, or in excess of, two years or, alternatively, whether although the sentence might be less than two years, there is some unusual feature of the case which justifies declining jurisdiction, bearing in mind that the absence of a power to impose a detention and training order because the defendant is under 15 is not an unusual feature.

The definitive guideline, *Overarching Principles: Sentencing Youths* (2009) at para 12.11 suggests that a court should only send a youth charged with a grave crime to the Crown Court for trial if the offence is of such a gravity that a sentence substantially beyond the two-year maximum for a detention and training order is a realistic possibility.

D2.7.4 *Allocation procedure*

The allocation decision may be made by a single justice: MCA 1980 s 24D(1).

In relation to sexual offences there are special listing arrangements as set out in *Sexual Offences in the Youth Court*: a Protocol issued by the Senior Presiding Judge on 31 March 2010. Paragraphs 12 and 13 provide:

In the case of sexual offences, the allocation decision should wherever possible be listed before a district judge who has received specific training in dealing with serious sexual offences ('an authorised district judge'). If jurisdiction is retained and the allegation involves actual, or attempted, penetrative activity, the case must be tried by an authorised district judge.

If it is not practicable for an authorised district judge to determine [allocation], any district judge or any youth court bench may consider that issue. If jurisdiction is retained, the case must be referred to an authorised district judge as soon as possible for a decision to be made as to whether the case should be tried by an authorised district judge.

If the youth court is to make a satisfactory decision it must have all the necessary information before it. The facts of the case as alleged, which must be assumed to be true unless manifestly not, should be accurately put before the court. For that reason, the summary of facts must be scrupulously fair and balanced, and it is the duty of both advocates to ensure that is so (*R(W) v Brent Youth Court* [2006] EWHC 95 (Admin), (2006) 170 JP 198).

It is a useful discipline for a youth court declining jurisdiction to give reasons. By doing so, there is a better prospect that the court will consider and apply the appropriate legal test (*R (C) v Balham Youth Court* [2003] EWHC 1332 Admin, [2004] 1 Cr App R (S) 143).

The court is not obliged to consider the evidence but may decide the case is appropriate for trial on indictment after looking at the charges and hearing representations (*R v South Hackney Juvenile Court ex parte RB (a minor) and CB (a minor)* (1983) 77 Cr App R 294).

When considering allocation a court may take into account previous convictions (*R (T) v Medway Magistrates' Court* [2003] EWHC 2279 (Admin), (2003) 167 JP 541).

In making its decision the youth court should take into account undisputed mitigation, for example, good character, but contentious mitigation should be ignored (*R(C&D) v Sheffield Youth Court* [2003] EWHC 35 (Admin)).

Where several defendants are charged together, the court must consider the position of each defendant separately, even if this results in one defendant being tried in the youth court and others in the Crown Court (*R (W) v Brent Youth Court* [2006] EWHC 95 (Admin), (2006) 170 JP 198).

D2.7.5 *Related offences*

By the CDA 1998 s 51A(4) where a court sends a youth defendant for trial under s 51A(2), it may at the same time send him to the Crown Court for trial for any indictable or summary offence with which he is charged and which—

- (if it is an indictable offence) appears to the court to be related to the offence mentioned in s 51A(2); or
- (if it is a summary offence) appears to the court to the offence related to the offence mentioned in s 51A(2) or to the indictable offence, and which fulfils the 'requisite condition'.

A summary offence fulfils the requisite condition if it is punishable in the case of an adult with imprisonment or involves obligatory or discretionary disqualification from driving: s 51A(9).

The CDA 1998 s 51E provides:

- An either-way offence is related to an indictable offence if the charge for the either-way offence could be joined in the same indictment as the charge for the indictable offence.
- A summary offence is related to an indictable offence if it arises out of circumstances which are the same as or connected with those giving rise to the indictable offence.

D2.7.6 *Revisiting the allocation decision*

Prior to the amendments introduced by the CJA 2003 Sch 3 there was a power under the MCA 1980 s 25 for the court to re-examine the allocation decision and by either converting a trial into committal proceedings or, having started to examine the evidence as examining justices, revert to summary trial. With the abolition of committal proceedings s 25 has been substantially amended by the CJA 2003 Sch 3 para 11. The court no longer has a power to revert to summary trial and the power to redetermine trial on indictment may now only be taken in the case of an adult defendant—see the MCA 1980 s 25(1)—(2D). When the original form of s 25 was in force it was held in *R (DPP) v Camberwell Green Youth Court* [2003] EWHC Admin 3217 that a court had no power to reopen the allocation decision other than in circumstances provided for in the MCA 1980 s 25.

D2.7.7 *Challenging the decision to send to the Crown Court for trial*

On judicial review the test is whether the court is satisfied that the original decision was wrong, and not that it would have made a different decision: *R(C&D) v Sheffield Youth Court and R(N) v Sheffield Youth Court* [2003] EWHC 35 (Admin).

D2.7.8 *Prosecution challenge to a decision to try summarily*

The procedure to be used by the prosecution should be judicial review (and not the seeking of a voluntary bill of indictment): *R v (DPP) Camberwell Youth Court* [2004] EWHC 1805 (Admin).

D2.8 Youth charged jointly with an adult

By the CDA 1998 s 51(7) where:

- the court sends an adult defendant A for trial;
- a youth Y appears before the court on the same or a subsequent occasion charged jointly with A with an indictable offence; and
- that offence appears to the court to be related to an offence for which A was sent for trial,

the court shall also send Y to the Crown Court for the indictable offence if it considers it necessary to do so in *the interests of justice*.

Before allocation can be considered under s 51(7) the court must go through a plea before venue procedure (see **D2.8.3**).

D2.8.1 *Jointly charged*

It is not necessary for the charge to specify that the offence was committed 'jointly' or 'together with' the adult concerned (*R v Rowlands* [1972] 1 All ER 306).

A defendant charged with driving a conveyance taken without consent and another defendant charged with allowing to be carried are properly considered to be 'jointly charged' (*R v Peterborough Magistrates' Court ex parte Allgood* (1995) JP 627).

The power to send a youth for trial under s 51(7) is not confined to cases where the adult and youth defendant are before the same adult magistrates' court. In *R v Coventry City Magistrates' Court ex parte M* (1992) JP 809, the Divisional Court held that a youth court could exercise the comparable power under the MCA 1980 s 24(1)(b) in a case where a youth is to be jointly indicted with an adult who has already been sent for trial by an adult magistrates' court.

D2.8.2 *Order of decision-making*

Where a youth is jointly charged with an adult and both appear before the court at the same time, the allocation procedure starts with the adult. The order of decision-making is set out in the CDA 1998 ss 50A, 51, and 51A at **D2.9**. The complex provisions are summarized in three flow charts:

- If the adult is charged with an indictable-only offence see Table B.
- If the adult is charged with an either-way offence and has indicated a guilty plea see Table C.
- If the adult is charged with an either-way offence and has indicated a not guilty plea or given no indication see Table D.

D2.8.3 *Plea before venue*

Before the court determines whether to send the youth with the adult for trial in the Crown Court, it must deal with plea before venue and ask the youth to indicate a plea to the charge (MCA 1980 s 24A).

D2 Allocation and Sending Proceedings

For the prescribed procedure when dealing with plea before venue see **D2.7.1**.

D2.8.4 *Interests of justice*

Every court making an allocation decision must follow any relevant sentencing guideline unless it is satisfied that it would be contrary to the interests of justice to do so (CJA 2003 s 172(1)(b)). The Sentencing Council definitive guideline *Allocation* (2012) states that it is applicable to all defendants in the magistrates' court including youths jointly charged with adults. In relation to the interests of justice test under the CDA 1998 s 51(7) the guideline provides:

> Where a youth and an adult are jointly charged, the youth must be tried summarily unless the court considers it to be in the interest of justice for both the youth and the adult to be committed to the Crown Court for trial. Examples of factors that should be considered when deciding whether to separate the youth and adult defendants include:
> - whether separate trials can take place without causing undue inconvenience to witnesses or injustice to the case as a whole;
> - the young age of the defendant, particularly where the age gap between the adult and youth offender is substantial;
> - the immaturity of the youth;
> - the relative culpability of the youth compared with the adult and whether or not the role played by the youth was minor; and
> - the lack of previous convictions on the part of the youth.

D2.8.5 *Related offences*

The CDA 1998 s 51(8) provides that where the court sends a youth for trial under subsection (7), it may at the same time send him to the Crown Court for trial for any indictable or summary offence with which he is charged and which—

- (if it is an indictable offence) appears to the court to be related to the offence for which he is sent for trial; and
- (if it is a summary offence) appears to the court to be related to the offence for which he is sent for trial or to the indictable offence, and which fulfils the requisite condition.

A summary offence fulfils the requisite condition if it is punishable with imprisonment or involves obligatory or discretionary disqualification from driving (CDA 1998 s 51(11)).

The CDA 1998 s 51E provides:

- An either-way offence is related to an indictable offence if the charge for the either-way offence could be joined in the same indictment as the charge for the indictable offence.
- A summary offence is related to an indictable offence if it arises out of circumstances which are the same as or connected with those giving rise to the indictable offence.

D2.9 **Order of decision-making—flow charts**

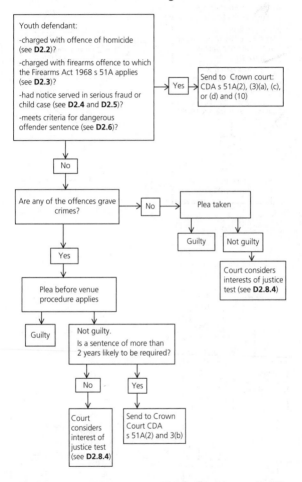

Table B **Youth charged jointly with an adult facing indictable-only offence**

D2 Allocation and Sending Proceedings

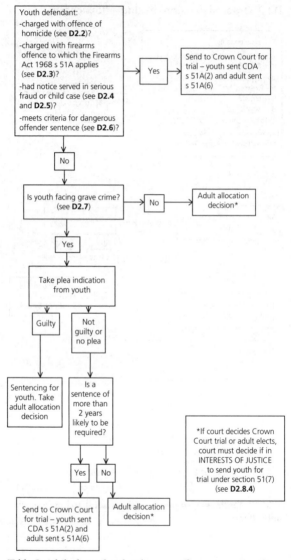

Youth defendant:
- charged with offence of homicide (see **D2.2**)?
- charged with firearms offence to which the Firearms Act 1968 s 51A applies (see **D2.3**)?
- had notice served in serious fraud or child case (see **D2.4** and **D2.5**)?
- meets criteria for dangerous offender sentence (see **D2.6**)?

→ Yes → Send to Crown Court for trial – youth sent CDA s 51A(2) and adult sent s 51A(6)

No

Is youth facing grave crime? (see **D2.7**) → No → Adult allocation decision*

Yes

Take plea indication from youth

Guilty → Sentencing for youth. Take adult allocation decision

Not guilty or no plea → Is a sentence of more than 2 years likely to be required?

Yes → Send to Crown Court for trial – youth sent CDA s 51A(2) and adult sent s 51A(6)

No → Adult allocation decision*

*If court decides Crown Court trial or adult elects, court must decide if in INTERESTS OF JUSTICE to send youth for trial under section 51(7) (see **D2.8.4**)

Table C Adult charged with either-way offence gives not guilty or no plea indication

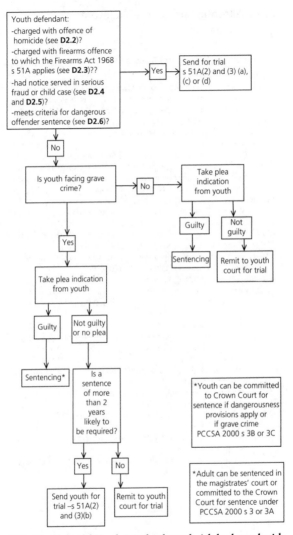

Table D Adult and Youth jointly charged: Adult charged with either-way offence pleads guilty

D2.10 Allocation procedure—relevant legislation

Magistrates Courts Act 1980 s 24A

(1) This section applies where—

  (a) a person under the age of 18 years appears or is brought before a magistrates' court on an information charging him with an offence other than one falling within section 51A(12) of the Crime and Disorder Act 1998 ('the 1998 Act'); and

  (b) but for the application of the following provisions of this section, the court would be required at that stage, by virtue of section 51(7) or (8) or 51A(3)(b), (4) or (5) of the 1998 Act to determine, in relation to the offence, whether to send the person to the Crown Court for trial (or to determine any matter, the effect of which would be to determine whether he is sent to the Crown Court for trial).

(2) Where this section applies, the court shall, before proceeding to make any such determination as is referred to in subsection (1)(b) above (the 'relevant determination'), follow the procedure set out in this section.

(3) Everything that the court is required to do under the following provisions of this section must be done with the accused person in court.

(4) The court shall cause the charge to be written down, if this has not already been done, and to be read to the accused.

(5) The court shall then explain to the accused in ordinary language that he may indicate whether (if the offence were to proceed to trial) he would plead guilty or not guilty, and that if he indicates that he would plead guilty—

  (a) the court must proceed as mentioned in subsection (7) below; and

  (b) (in cases where the offence is one mentioned in section 91(1) of the Powers of Criminal Courts (Sentencing) Act 2000) he may be sent to the Crown Court for sentencing under section 3B or (if applicable) 3C of that Act if the court is of such opinion as is mentioned in subsection (2) of the applicable section.

(6) The court shall then ask the accused whether (if the offence were to proceed to trial) he would plead guilty or not guilty.

(7) If the accused indicates that he would plead guilty, the court shall proceed as if—

  (a) the proceedings constituted from the beginning the summary trial of the information; and

  (b) section 9(1) above was complied with and he pleaded guilty under it, and, accordingly, the court shall not (and shall not be required to) proceed to make the relevant determination or to proceed further under section 51 or (as the case may be) section 51A of the 1998 Act in relation to the offence.

(8) If the accused indicates that he would plead not guilty, the court shall proceed to make the relevant determination and this section shall cease to apply.

(9) If the accused in fact fails to indicate how he would plead, for the purposes of this section he shall be taken to indicate that he would plead not guilty.

(10) Subject to subsection (7) above, the following shall not for any purpose be taken to constitute the taking of a plea—

(a) asking the accused under this section whether (if the offence were to proceed to trial) he would plead guilty or not guilty;

(b) an indication by the accused under this section of how he would plead.

Crime and Disorder Act 1998 ss 50A–51A

50A Order of consideration for either-way offences.

(1) Where an adult appears or is brought before a magistrates' court charged with an either-way offence (the 'relevant offence'), the court shall proceed in the manner described in this section.

(2) If notice is given in respect of the relevant offence under section 51B or 51C below, the court shall deal with the offence as provided in section 51 below.

(3) Otherwise—

(a) if the adult (or another adult with whom the adult is charged jointly with the relevant offence) is or has been sent to the Crown Court for trial for an offence under section 51(2)(a) or 51(2)(c) below—

(i) the court shall first consider the relevant offence under subsection (3), (4), (5) or, as the case may be, (6) of section 51 below and, where applicable, deal with it under that subsection;

(ii) if the adult is not sent to the Crown Court for trial for the relevant offence by virtue of sub-paragraph (i) above, the court shall then proceed to deal with the relevant offence in accordance with sections 17A to 23 of the 1980 Act;

(b) in all other cases—

(i) the court shall first consider the relevant offence under sections 17A to 20 (excluding subsections (8) and (9) of section 20) of the 1980 Act;

(ii) if, by virtue of sub-paragraph (i) above, the court would be required to proceed in relation to the offence as mentioned in section 17A(6), 17B(2)(c) or 20(7) of that Act (indication of guilty plea), it shall proceed as so required (and, accordingly, shall not consider the offence under section 51 or 51A below);

(iii) if sub-paragraph (ii) above does not apply—

(a) the court shall consider the relevant offence under sections 51 and 51A below and, where applicable, deal with it under the relevant section;

> (b) if the adult is not sent to the Crown Court for trial for the relevant offence by virtue of paragraph (a) of this sub-paragraph, the court shall then proceed to deal with the relevant offence as contemplated by section 20(9) or, as the case may be, section 21 of the 1980 Act.

(4) Subsection (3) above is subject to any requirement to proceed as mentioned in subsections (2) or (6)(a) of section 22 of the 1980 Act (certain offences where value involved is small).

(5) Nothing in this section shall prevent the court from committing the adult to the Crown Court for sentence pursuant to any enactment, if he is convicted of the relevant offence.

51 Sending cases to the Crown Court: adults

(1) Where an adult appears or is brought before a magistrates' court ('the court') charged with an offence and any of the conditions mentioned in subsection (2) below is satisfied, the court shall send him forthwith to the Crown Court for trial for the offence.

(2) Those conditions are—
  (a) that the offence is an offence triable only on indictment other than one in respect of which notice has been given under section 51B or 51C below;
  (b) that the offence is an either-way offence and the court is required under section 20(9)(b), 21, 23(4)(b) or (5) or 25(2D) of the Magistrates' Courts Act 1980 to proceed in relation to the offence in accordance with subsection (1) above;
  (c) that notice is given to the court under section 51B or 51C below in respect of the offence.

(3) Where the court sends an adult for trial under subsection (1) above, it shall at the same time send him to the Crown Court for trial for any either-way or summary offence with which he is charged and which—
  (a) (if it is an either-way offence) appears to the court to be related to the offence mentioned in subsection (1) above; or
  (b) (if it is a summary offence) appears to the court to be related to the offence mentioned in subsection (1) above or to the either-way offence, and which fulfils the requisite condition (as defined in subsection (11) below).

(4) Where an adult who has been sent for trial under subsection (1) above subsequently appears or is brought before a magistrates' court charged with an either-way or summary offence which—
  (a) appears to the court to be related to the offence mentioned in subsection (1) above; and
  (b) (in the case of a summary offence) fulfils the requisite condition, the court may send him forthwith to the Crown Court for trial for the either-way or summary offence.

(5) Where—
  (a) the court sends an adult ('A') for trial under subsection (1) or (3) above;
  (b) another adult appears or is brought before the court on the same or a subsequent occasion charged jointly with A with an either-way offence; and
  (c) that offence appears to the court to be related to an offence for which A was sent for trial under subsection (1) or (3) above,

the court shall where it is the same occasion, and may where it is a subsequent occasion, send the other adult forthwith to the Crown Court for
trial for the either-way offence.

(6) Where the court sends an adult for trial under subsection (5) above, it
shall at the same time send him to the Crown Court for trial for any
either-way or summary offence with which he is charged and which—
   (i) (if it is an either-way offence) appears to the court to be related to
   the offence for which he is sent for trial; and
   (ii) (if it is a summary offence) appears to the court to be related
   to the offence for which he is sent for trial or to the either-way
   offence, and which fulfils the requisite condition.

(7) Where—
   (1) the court sends an adult ('A') for trial under subsection (1), (3) or
   (5) above; and
   (2) a child or young person appears or is brought before the court on the
   same or a subsequent occasion charged jointly with A with an indictable offence for which A is sent for trial under subsection (1), (3) or
   (5) above, or an indictable offence which appears to the court to be
   related to that offence,
   the court shall, if it considers it necessary in the interests of justice to do
   so, send the child or young person forthwith to the Crown Court for trial
   for the indictable offence.

(8) Where the court sends a child or young person for trial under subsection (7) above, it may at the same time send him to the Crown Court
for trial for any indictable or summary offence with which he is charged
and which—
   (a) (if it is an indictable offence) appears to the court to be related to the
   offence for which he is sent for trial; and
   (b) (if it is a summary offence) appears to the court to be related to the
   offence for which he is sent for trial or to the indictable offence, and
   which fulfils the requisite condition.

(9) Subsections (7) and (8) above are subject to sections 24A and 24B of the
Magistrates' Courts Act 1980 (which provide for certain cases involving
children and young persons to be tried summarily).

(10) The trial of the information charging any summary offence for which a
person is sent for trial under this section shall be treated as if the court had
adjourned it under section 10 of the 1980 Act and had not fixed the time
and place for its resumption.

(11) A summary offence fulfils the requisite condition if it is punishable with
imprisonment or involves obligatory or discretionary disqualification from
driving.

(12) In the case of an adult charged with an offence—
   (a) if the offence satisfies paragraph (c) of subsection (2) above, the
   offence shall be dealt with under subsection (1) above and not under
   any other provision of this section or section 51A below;
   (b) subject to paragraph (a) above, if the offence is one in respect of
   which the court is required to, or would decide to, send the adult to
   the Crown Court under—
      (i) subsection (5) above; or
      (ii) subsection (6) of section 51A below,

the offence shall be dealt with under that subsection and not under any other provision of this section or section 51A below.

(13) The functions of a magistrates' court under this section, and its related functions under section 51D below, may be discharged by a single justice.

51A Sending cases to the Crown Court: children and young persons

(1) This section is subject to sections 24A and 24B of the Magistrates' Courts Act 1980 (which provide for certain offences involving children or young persons to be tried summarily).

(2) Where a child or young person appears or is brought before a magistrates' court ('the court') charged with an offence and any of the conditions mentioned in subsection (3) below is satisfied, the court shall send him forthwith to the Crown Court for trial for the offence.

(3) Those conditions are—

(a) that the offence falls within subsection (12) below;

(b) that the offence is such as is mentioned in subsection (1) of section 91 of the Powers of Criminal Courts (Sentencing) Act 2000 (other than one mentioned in paragraph (d) below in relation to which it appears to the court as mentioned there) and the court considers that if he is found guilty of the offence it ought to be possible to sentence him in pursuance of subsection (3) of that section;

(c) that notice is given to the court under section 51B or 51C below in respect of the offence;

(d) that the offence is a specified offence (within the meaning of section 224 of the Criminal Justice Act 2003) and it appears to the court that if he is found guilty of the offence the criteria for the imposition of a sentence under section 226B of that Act would be met.

(4) Where the court sends a child or young person for trial under subsection (2) above, it may at the same time send him to the Crown Court for trial for any indictable or summary offence with which he is charged and which—

(a) (if it is an indictable offence) appears to the court to be related to the offence mentioned in subsection (2) above; or

(b) (if it is a summary offence) appears to the court to be related to the offence mentioned in subsection (2) above or to the indictable offence, and which fulfils the requisite condition (as defined in subsection (9) below).

(5) Where a child or young person who has been sent for trial under subsection (2) above subsequently appears or is brought before a magistrates' court charged with an indictable or summary offence which—

(6) appears to the court to be related to the offence mentioned in subsection (2) above; and

(7) (in the case of a summary offence) fulfils the requisite condition,

the court may send him forthwith to the Crown Court for trial for the indictable or summary offence.

(6) Where—

(a) the court sends a child or young person ('C') for trial under subsection (2) or (4) above; and

(b) an adult appears or is brought before the court on the same or a subsequent occasion charged jointly with C with an either-way offence for which C is sent for trial under subsection (2) or (4) above, or an either-way offence which appears to the court to be related to that offence,

the court shall where it is the same occasion, and may where it is a subsequent occasion, send the adult forthwith to the Crown Court for trial for the either-way offence.

(7) Where the court sends an adult for trial under subsection (6) above, it shall at the same time send him to the Crown Court for trial for any either-way or summary offence with which he is charged and which—

(1) (if it is an either-way offence) appears to the court to be related to the offence for which he was sent for trial; and

(2) (if it is a summary offence) appears to the court to be related to the offence for which he was sent for trial or to the either-way offence, and which fulfils the requisite condition.

(8) The trial of the information charging any summary offence for which a person is sent for trial under this section shall be treated as if the court had adjourned it under section 10 of the 1980 Act and had not fixed the time and place for its resumption.

(9) A summary offence fulfils the requisite condition if it is punishable with imprisonment or involves obligatory or discretionary disqualification from driving.

(10) In the case of a child or young person charged with an offence—

(a) if the offence satisfies any of the conditions in subsection (3) above, the offence shall be dealt with under subsection (2) above and not under any other provision of this section or section 51 above;

(b) subject to paragraph (a) above, if the offence is one in respect of which the requirements of subsection (7) of section 51 above for sending the child or young person to the Crown Court are satisfied, the offence shall be dealt with under that subsection and not under any other provision of this section or section 51 above.

(11) The functions of a magistrates' court under this section, and its related functions under section 51D below, may be discharged by a single justice.

(12) An offence falls within this subsection if—

(a) it is an offence of homicide;

(b) each of the requirements of section 51A(1) of the Firearms Act 1968 would be satisfied with respect to—

(i) the offence; and

(ii) the person charged with it,

if he were convicted of the offence; or

(c) section 29(3) of Violent Crime Reduction Act 2006 (minimum sentences in certain cases of using someone to mind a weapon) would apply if he were convicted of the offence....

D3 **Bail**

D3.1 **Introduction**

Under the UN Convention on the Rights of the Child Article 37(1) depriving a child of his liberty during criminal proceedings should be a measure of last resort. To that end there are rules applicable only to defendants under the age of 18 and extra resources are devoted to supporting defendants on bail.

The BA 1976 applies to youth defendants but there are a number of differences which generally narrow the scope of the statutory grounds for refusing bail. In addition if bail is refused there is a further requirement to consider a remand to local authority accommodation before a remand in custody is made (see **D4**).

The main practical difference between applying for bail for a youth as opposed to an adult is the significant role played by the youth offending team. When a court is considering bail in relation to a young defendant, the youth offending team may be involved in the following ways:

* assessing the young defendant;
* providing bail information;
* implementing bail supervision and support; and
* providing a bail Intensive Supervision and Surveillance Programme (bail ISSP).

Assessment Prior to deciding whether to offer any services to the young defendant, the youth offending team will assess him. If the YOT are not already working with the youth defendant an *Asset* Bail Profile will be completed.

Bail information The youth offending team may seek to verify information about the young person (eg regarding school attendance), obtain information from children's services databases, as well as checking out the suitability of a proposed bail address by carrying out child protection and police checks on the address and its occupants.

Bail supervision and support The youth offending team may offer a bail support package to the court. This could be in the form of an oral presentation or in a written report.

If the defendant is at a court outside his own local authority area, the youth offending team workers at the court will contact the 'home' youth offending team.

There will always be a youth offending team worker present at court on a day when there is a scheduled youth court. When dealing with a young defendant who has been refused bail by the police, the advocate should make early contact with the worker to ensure that an early assessment of the young defendant is carried out. Where the defendant is in custody at an adult court, the advocate should ensure that the relevant youth offending team is aware of his presence at court.

D3.2 Right to bail

There is a general right to bail for any person accused of an offence when s/he appears or is brought before a youth court, adult magistrates' court, or the Crown Court in the course of or in connection with proceedings for the offence: BA 1976 s 4(1) and (2).

That presumption does not, however, apply in the following cases:

- following committal to the Crown Court for sentence or for breach of a Crown Court order;
- after conviction, unless the proceedings are adjourned for enquiries to be made or a report to be prepared for sentence;
- on appeal against conviction or sentence; or
- following a breach of bail.

This general right to bail is subject to the CPIA 1996 s 25 which provides that bail may only be granted in exceptional circumstances where a defendant is charged with or convicted of an offence of:

- murder, or
- attempted murder, or
- manslaughter, or
- rape, or
- attempted rape,

and the defendant has been previously convicted in the United Kingdom of any such offence or of culpable homicide. (If the previous conviction was manslaughter or culpable homicide the provision only applies if they received a sentence of imprisonment/long-term detention.) Convictions in EU Member States can be taken into account.

D3.3 Right to apply for bail

An application for bail can be made at the first hearing of the case before a youth court or adult magistrates' court.

The Coroners and Justice Act 2009 s 115 removes the possibility of applying for bail if the defendant is charged with murder. Instead the youth court or adult magistrates' court must commit the defendant to custody to be brought before a judge of the Crown Court: s 115(4). This requirement applies whether or not the defendant is sent for trial at the first hearing. In the case of a youth defendant the duty to 'commit to custody' is still subject to the remand to local authority accommodation provisions of what is now the LASPO 2012 s 91 (for which see **D4**): *R (A) v Lewisham Youth Court* [2011] EWHC 1193 (Admin). A judge of the Crown Court must then make a decision about bail in respect of the person as soon as reasonably practicable and, in any event, within the period of forty-eight hours (excluding weekends and bank holidays) beginning with the day after the day on which the person appears or is brought before the magistrates' court: s 115 (3) and (7).

If bail is refused at the first hearing, the BA 1976 Sch 1 Part IIA provides:

Bail Act 1976 Sch 1 Part IIA

1 If the court decides not to grant the defendant bail, it is the court's duty to consider, at each subsequent hearing while the defendant is a person to whom section 4 above applies and remains in custody, whether he ought to be granted bail.

2 At the first hearing after that at which the court decided not to grant the defendant bail he may support an application for bail with any argument as to fact or law that he desires (whether or not he has advanced that argument previously).

3 At subsequent hearings the court need not hear arguments as to fact or law which it has heard previously.

A refusal of bail on the grounds of insufficient information should not be counted as a decision to refuse bail, thereby exhausting one of the two attempts (*R v Calderdale Justices, ex parte Kennedy* The Times, 18 February 1992). Similarly, a remand in absence should be discounted (*R v Dover and East Kent Justices, ex parte Dean* The Times, 22 August 1991). However, if a fully argued application is not made by the defendant at the first hearing the effect is that one opportunity to argue for bail is lost, meaning that if bail is refused at the subsequent hearing, the two opportunities for bail are spent. Similarly, if an argument is made at the first hearing, but not at a second hearing, there is no right to a second application for bail at the third hearing.

Following two refusals to grant bail, further applications can be made if there has been a change in circumstances, for example:

• Change in the case alleged against the defendant: *R v Reading Crown Court, ex parte Malik* [1981] QB 451 and *R v Slough Justices, ex parte Duncan* [1981] QB 451.
• Increased surety: *R v Isleworth Crown Court, ex parte Commissioners of Customs and Excise* (1990) The Times, 27 July.
• Passage of time (*Neumeister v Austria (No 1)* (1979–80) 1 EHRR 91).

In *R (B) v Brent Youth Court* [2010] EWHC 1893 (Admin) the court held that a different bail address amounted to a change of circumstances. It was not necessary that any new factor be exceptional in nature. The correct test is whether there are any new considerations which were not before the court when the accused was last remanded in custody. Similarly an argument that the prosecution case against the defendant was significantly weaker than at first presented would qualify as a change in circumstance. The court ended by saying:

> [E]ven if the Bench had been entitled to form the view that each and every argument as to fact or law was an argument which it had heard previously, it manifestly failed to go on to consider whether, notwithstanding that, it should nonetheless consider substantively a bail application, given the provisions of [the CYPA 1933 s 44], having regard to the welfare of a child or young person.

D3.4 Grounds to refuse bail

The court may only refuse bail if it can identify one of the prescribed exceptions to that right which are contained in the Bail Act 1976 Schedule 1.

Since the implementation of the CJIA 2008 the BA 1976 Sch 1 is now split into three Parts:

- Part I—Indictable offences;
- Part IA—Imprisonable summary-only offences; and
- Part II—Non-imprisonable offences.

The grounds for refusing bail are different in each category and will be considered separately.

D3.4.1 *Defendants accused of indictable imprisonable offences*

The BA 1976 Sch 1 Part I provides that in the case of indictable offences, bail may be refused if:

- the court is satisfied there are *substantial* grounds for believing that, if released on bail (whether subject to conditions or not) the defendant would:
  - (a) fail to surrender to custody; or
  - (b) commit an offence while on bail; or
  - (c) interfere with witnesses or otherwise obstruct the course of justice, whether in relation to himself or any other person (para 2);
- the court is satisfied that that the defendant should be kept in custody for his own protection or, if he is under 18, for his own welfare (para 3);

- if the defendant is in custody in pursuance of a sentence of a court or a sentence imposed by an officer under the Armed Forces Act 2006 (para 4);
- the court is satisfied that it has not been practicable to obtain sufficient information for the purpose of taking the decisions required regarding bail for want of time since the institution of the proceedings against the defendant (para 5);
- having been released on bail in proceedings for the offence, the defendant has been arrested for breach of bail conditions under the Bail Act 1976 s 7 (para 6);
- (where the case is adjourned for enquiries or a report) it appears to the court that it would be impracticable to complete the enquiries or make the report without keeping the defendant in custody (para 7).

Restrictions on the grant of bail which apply to certain drug users under the BA 1976 Sch 1 Part I paras 6A and 6B do not apply to youth defendants.

If a defendant is charged with murder, the defendant may not be bailed unless the court is of the opinion that there is no significant risk of the defendant committing, while on bail, an offence that would, or would be likely to, cause physical or mental injury to any person other than the defendant (para 6ZA).

When considering if any of the grounds in para 2 are made out, the BA 1976 Sch 1 Part 1 para 9 requires the court to take into account information available to it regarding the following:

- the nature and seriousness of the offence (and the probable means of dealing with the defendant for it);
- the character, antecedents (eg criminal record), associations, and community ties of the defendant;
- the defendant's previous record of complying with the obligation of bail;
- (except in the case of an adjournment for a pre-sentence report) the strength of the evidence against the defendant;
- if the court is satisfied that there are substantial grounds for believing that the defendant, if released on bail (whether subject to conditions or not), would commit an offence while on bail, the risk that the defendant may do so by engaging in conduct that would, or would be likely to, cause physical or mental injury to any person other than the defendant;
- any other factor which the court considers relevant.

The seriousness of the offence (and the likely penalty) cannot of itself justify a refusal of bail on the inference that the person is likely to abscond (*Lettelier v France* (1992) 14 EHRR 83), although a judge is perfectly entitled to regard that as a significant factor (*R (Thompson) v Central Criminal Court* [2005] EWHC 2345). Before bail can be refused on the grounds of interfering with witnesses or obstructing justice the prosecution must point to an identifiable risk and provide supporting evidence (*Clooth v Belgium* (1991) 14 EHRR 717).

The CJA 2003 inserted into the BA 1976 provisions which deal with how the court should approach the decision whether to grant bail when the defendant has committed an offence whilst on bail during the proceedings or has failed to surrender to custody during the proceedings. These provisions are more favourable than the comparable provisions for adult defendants.

Where the defendant has committed an offence on bail during the proceedings, the CJA 2003 s 14(2) inserts a new para 9AA. However, this provision is currently only in force in relation to offences punishable in the case of an adult with life imprisonment: Criminal Justice Act 2003 (Commencement No 14 and Transitional Provision) Order 2006 SI 2006/3217.

Bail Act 1976 Sch 1 para 9AA

(1) This paragraph applies if—
  (a) the defendant is under the age of 18, and
  (b) it appears to the court that he was on bail in criminal proceedings on the date of the offence.
(2) In deciding for the purposes of paragraph 2(1) of this Part of this Schedule whether it is satisfied that there are substantial grounds for believing that the defendant, if released on bail (whether subject to conditions or not), would commit an offence while on bail, the court shall give particular weight to the fact that the defendant was on bail in criminal proceedings on the date of the offence.

Where the defendant has failed to surrender to custody during the proceedings, the CJA 2003 s 15(2) inserts a new para 9AB. However, this provision is currently only in force in relation to offences punishable in the case of an adult with life imprisonment: Criminal Justice Act 2003 (Commencement No 14 and Transitional Provision) Order 2006, SI 2006/3217.

Bail Act 1976 Sch 1 para 9AB

(1) Subject to sub-paragraph (2) below, this paragraph applies if—
  (a) the defendant is under the age of 18, and
  (b) it appears to the court that, having been released on bail in or in connection with the proceedings for the offence, he failed to surrender to custody.

(2) Where it appears to the court that the defendant had reasonable cause for his failure to surrender to custody, this paragraph does not apply unless it also appears to the court that he failed to surrender to custody at the appointed place as soon as reasonably practicable after the appointed time.

(3) In deciding for the purposes of paragraph 2(1) of this Part of this Schedule whether it is satisfied that there are substantial grounds for believing that the defendant, if released on bail (whether subject to conditions or not), would fail to surrender to custody, the court shall give particular weight to—

  (a) where the defendant did not have reasonable cause for his failure to surrender to custody, the fact that he failed to surrender to custody, or

  (b) where he did have reasonable cause for his failure to surrender to custody, the fact that he failed to surrender to custody at the appointed place as soon as reasonably practicable after the appointed time.

(4) For the purposes of this paragraph, a failure to give to the defendant a copy of the record of the decision to grant him bail shall not constitute a reasonable cause for his failure to surrender to custody.

D3.4.2 *Summary-only imprisonable offences*

This category includes not only all imprisonable summary-only offences but also either-way offences specified in the MCA 1980 Sch 2 (criminal damage where the value is less than £5,000). Under the BA 1976 s 9A where a child or young person is charged with such an offence and the court is considering whether to withhold or grant bail it must consider whether, having regard to any representations made by the prosecutor and the defence, the value involved does not exceed £5,000.

Under the BA 1976 Sch 1 Part IA bail need not be granted if:

- it appears to the court that, having been previously granted bail in criminal proceedings, he has failed to surrender to custody in accordance with his obligations under the grant of bail and the court believes that, in view of that failure, that the defendant, if released on bail (whether subject to conditions or not) would fail to surrender to custody (para 2);
- it appears to the court that the defendant was on bail in criminal proceedings on the date of the offence and the court is satisfied that there are substantial grounds for believing that the defendant, if released on bail (whether subject to conditions or not), would commit an offence on bail (para 3);
- the court is satisfied that there are substantial grounds for believing that the defendant, if released on bail (whether subject to conditions or not), would commit an offence while on bail by engaging in conduct which would, or would be likely to, cause:
  (a) physical or mental injury to an associated person; or
  (b) an associated person to fear physical or mental injury (para 4);

- the court is satisfied that the defendant should be kept in custody for his own protection, or if he is a child or young person, for his own welfare (para 5);
- he is in custody serving a sentence of a court or a sentence imposed by an officer under the Armed Forces Act 1996 (para 6);
- having been released on bail in or in connection with the proceedings for the offence, the defendant has been arrested for breach of bail conditions under the BA 1976 s 7 and the court is satisfied that there are substantial grounds for believing that the defendant, if released on bail (whether subject to conditions or not) would fail to surrender to custody, commit an offence while on bail, or interfere with witnesses or otherwise obstruct the course of justice (whether in relation to himself or any other person) (para 7);
- the court is satisfied that it has not been practicable to obtain sufficient information for the purposes of making a decision regarding bail (para 8).

For the purposes of para 4 above 'associated person' means a person associated with the defendant within the meaning of the Family Law Act 1996 s 62. The definition would include parents or children of the defendant as well as spouses, civil partners, cohabitants, or persons who live in the same household otherwise than merely by reason of one being the other's tenant, lodger, or boarder.

Unlike adult defendants there is no proviso in any of the grounds that there be a real prospect that the youth defendant will be sentenced to a custodial sentence.

D3.4.3 *Non-imprisonable offences*

Under the BA 1976 Sch 1 Part II bail need not be granted if:

- it appears to the court that, having been previously granted bail in criminal proceedings, a defendant under the age of 18 has failed to surrender to custody in accordance with his obligations under the grant of bail and the court believes, in view of that failure, that the defendant, if released on bail (whether subject to conditions or not), would fail to surrender to custody (para 2);
- the court is satisfied that the defendant should be kept in custody for his own protection or, if he is a child or young person, for his own welfare (para 3);
- if the defendant is in custody serving a sentence (para 4);
- having been released on bail in or in connection with the proceedings for the offence, a defendant under the age of 18 has been arrested for breach of bail conditions under the BA 1976 s 7 and the court is satisfied that there are substantial grounds for believing that the defendant, if released on bail (whether subject to conditions or not),

would fail to surrender to custody, commit an offence on bail, or interfere with witnesses or otherwise obstruct the courts of justice (whether in relation to himself or any other person) (para 5);
- having been released on bail in or in connection with the proceedings for the offence, the defendant has been arrested for breach of bail conditions under the BA 1976 s 7 and the court is satisfied that there are substantial grounds for believing that the defendant, if released on bail (whether subject to conditions or not), would commit an offence while on bail by engaging in conduct which would, or would be likely to, cause:
  (a) physical or mental injury to an associated person; or
  (b) an associated person to fear physical or mental injury (para 6).

For the purposes of para 6, 'associated person' means a person associated with the defendant within the meaning of the Family Law Act 1976 s 62 (for which see **D3.4.2**).

D3.5 Conditional bail

When granting bail the court may order that:

- a surety or security be taken before the defendant is released on bail; or
- impose conditions which the defendant must comply with either before or after his release on bail.

The power to impose bail conditions is governed by the BA 1976 s 3.

Bail Act 1976 s 3

(3) Except as provided by this section-
  (a) no security for his surrender to custody shall be taken from him,
  (b) he shall not be required to provide a surety or sureties for his surrender to custody, and
  (c) no requirement shall be imposed on him as a condition of bail.
(4) He may be required, before release on bail, to provide a surety or sureties to secure his surrender to custody.
(5) He may be required, before release on bail, to give security for his surrender to custody. The security may be given by him or on his behalf.
(6) He may be required to comply, before release on bail or later, with such requirements as appear to the court to be necessary—
  (a) to secure that he surrenders to custody,
  (b) to secure that he does not commit an offence while on bail,
  (c) to secure that he does not interfere with witnesses or otherwise obstruct the course of justice whether in relation to himself or any other person,
  (ca) for his own protection, or if he is a child or young person, for his own welfare or in his own interests.

(d) to secure that he makes himself available for the purpose of enabling inquiries or a report to be made to assist the court in dealing with him for the offence.

(e) to secure that before the time appointed for him to surrender to custody, he attends an interview with a person who, for the purposes of the Legal Services Act 2007, is an authorised person in relation to an activity which constitutes the exercise of a right of audience or the conduct of litigation (within the meaning of that Act).

A person granted bail on a charge of murder must be required to undergo a psychiatric examination: BA 1976 s 3(6A).

D3.6 Electronic monitoring requirements

The BA 1976 s 3(6ZAA) provides that the power to impose bail conditions includes the power to impose electronic monitoring requirements. These are requirements imposed for the purpose of securing the electronic monitoring of a person's compliance with any other requirement imposed on him as a condition of bail: s 3(6ZAB). The most common electronic monitoring requirement is a tag to monitor compliance with a curfew.

In the case of a youth defendant the use of electronic monitoring requirements is subject to s 3AA.

Bail Act 1976 s 3AA

(1) A court may not impose electronic monitoring requirements on a child or young person unless each of the following conditions is met.

(2) The first condition is that the child or young person has attained the age of 12 years.

(3) The second condition is that-

(a) the child or young person is charged with or has been convicted of a violent or sexual offence, or an offence punishable in the case of an adult with imprisonment for a term of fourteen years or more; or

(b) he is charged with or has been convicted of one or more imprisonable offences which, together with any other imprisonable offences of which he has been convicted in any proceedings-

(i) amount, or

(ii) would, if he were convicted of the offence with which he is charged, amount to a recent history of repeatedly committing imprisonable offences while remanded on bail or to local authority accommodation.

(4) The third condition is that the court is satisfied that the necessary provision for dealing with the person concerned can be made under arrangements for the electronic monitoring of persons released on bail that are currently available in each local justice area which is a relevant area.

(5) The fourth condition is that a youth offending team has informed the court that in its opinion the imposition of electronic monitoring requirements will be suitable in the case of the child or young person.

At the time of introducing electronically monitored bail curfews the Home Office issued a guidance document *Criminal Justice and Police Act 2001: Electronic Monitoring of 12- to 16-year-olds on Bail and on Remand to Local Authority Accommodation*. This guidance includes advice on what steps YOTs should take to assess the suitability of a proposed bail address for electronic monitoring.

At a minimum, contact must be made with a householder (i.e. the person holding the tenancy or the owner/occupier of the proposed bail address), and the parent or carer of the defendant (if different) to ascertain whether s/he consents to the monitoring.

Where the youth offending team has no information about the proposed address, information should be sought from social services departments and other partner agencies. A home visit may be needed before the suitability of an address can be determined. If it is not possible to arrange the home visit on the day of the court hearing then an electronic monitoring requirement may not be used.

For placements in local authority residential accommodation Social Services' consent should be sought for the use of electronic monitoring.

The youth offending team should contact the relevant local authority social services department to ascertain whether there are any current or previous child protection concerns that would indicate that tagging is not advisable in a particular case.

D3.7 Bail supervision and support

Youth offending teams are under a statutory duty to provide support for children and young persons remanded or committed on bail while awaiting trial or sentence: CDA 1998 s 38(4)(c).

Most schemes aim to help the defendants on the programme to comply with their conditions of bail and to provide constructive activities to occupy their time and lessen the risk of further offending.

The contents of bail support programmes vary across the country but may include:

* regular reporting to the youth offending team;
* monitored attendance at youth activities;
* monitoring of school attendance;
* programmes aimed at reintroducing the young defendant to school or to arrange specific educational provision;
* assistance with arranging training or finding employment;

- work with families to resolve conflicts and to ensure a continuing home base for the young defendant and to involve the parents in taking more responsibility for their children's behaviour;
- placements with volunteers during the evening and weekends; and
- Intensive Supervision and Surveillance Programme (see **D3.7.1**).

D3.7.1 *Intensive Supervision and Surveillance Programme (ISSP)*

Bail ISSPs normally involve up to twenty-five hours of activities each week. The programme may include:

- electronic tagging and voice verification;
- tracking of the young offender by YOT staff;
- monitoring of young offenders by police;
- literacy and numeracy programmes;
- work with families; and
- offending behaviour workshops/cognitive behavioural therapy.

Youth offending teams will only advise courts to consider the option of a bail ISSP where:

- the defendant fits the criteria for an ISSP;
- they are not considered to pose an unacceptable risk to the community if placed on an ISSP;
- the current offence before the court is of sufficient gravity for the court to be considering a custodial remand; and
- there is a place available.

D3.8 **Parental surety**

A surety taken under the BA 1976 s 3(4) is to secure that the defendant surrenders to custody. In the case of a defendant under the age of 17 the court may also take a surety from his parent or guardian to ensure the defendant's compliance with other bail conditions.

> **Bail Act 1976 s 3(7)**
>
> If a parent or guardian of a person under the age of 17 consents to be surety for the person for the purposes of this subsection, the parent or guardian may be required to secure that the person complies with any requirement imposed on him by virtue of subsection (6), (6ZAA) or (6A) above, but—
>
> (a) no requirement shall be imposed on the parent or guardian of a person by virtue of this subsection where it appears that the person will attain the age of seventeen before the time to be appointed for him to surrender to custody; and
>
> (b) the parent or guardian shall not be required to secure compliance with any requirements to which his consent does not extend and shall not,

> in respect of those requirements to which his consent does extend, be
> bound in a sum greater than £50.

The words 'parent' and 'guardian' are not specifically defined in the BA 1976. For the definition in other statutory provisions see **J1**.

D3.9 Prosecution appeal against grant of bail

The Bail (Amendment) Act 1993 s 1(1) allows a prosecutor to appeal the grant of bail in any case where the defendant is charged with an offence punishable in the case of an adult with imprisonment.

An appeal may only be made if the prosecutor made representations against the grant of bail before the defendant was granted bail: s 1(3).

Where the prosecutor wishes to appeal the grant of bail, s 1(4) requires that oral notice be given to the court which granted bail at the conclusion of the proceedings in which such bail has been granted and before the defendant is released from custody. A delay of five minutes in giving an oral indication to the court (and after the defendant had been taken from the courtroom) was deemed to comply with the Act in *R v Isleworth Crown Court, ex parte Clarke* [1998] 1 Cr App R 257. Once an oral notice of appeal has been given, the court must remand the defendant until the appeal is determined or otherwise disposed of: s 1(6).

By s 1(5) a written notice of appeal must thereafter be served on the court which has granted bail and the defendant within two hours of the conclusion of the proceedings. Where the prosecution fails, within the period of two hours to serve written notices upon both the court and the defendant, the appeal shall be deemed to be disposed of: s 1(7). In *R v Isleworth Crown Court ex parte Clarke*, above, it was held that there is no requirement to serve the written notice upon the magistrates or the defendant directly. Instead it is valid service to give the notice to the court clerk and have the defendant's copy served via a court gaoler. In *R (Jeffrey) v Crown Court at Warwick* [2002] EWCA 2469 (Admin), a written notice was served three minutes late in circumstances where the court considered the prosecutor had acted with due diligence and there was no prejudice to the defendant. A challenge to the validity of that service failed and the court suggested that s 1(7) should have read into it the following words: 'unless such failure was caused by circumstances outside the control of the prosecution and not due to any fault on its part.'

Where the defendant is under the age of 18, any remand under s 1(6) is still subject to the remand to local authority provisions of the LASPO 2012 s 91: s 1(10)(b).

After written notice has been served, the Crown Court must hear the appeal within forty-eight hours, not counting weekends and public holidays: s 1(8).

The prosecution may also appeal to the High Court against the grant of bail by a Crown Court: s 1(1B). This power does not apply if the grant of bail is made after a prosecution appeal against bail from the youth court or magistrates' court.

D3.10 Appeal against refusal of bail

Following a refusal of bail in the youth court or adult magistrates' court, the defendant may appeal to the Crown Court (Senior Courts Act 1981 s 81(1)).

The Crown Court may only grant bail on appeal if the youth court or adult magistrates' court has certified that it heard full argument on the application for bail before refusing the application: s 81(1J). It is the duty of the youth or adult magistrates' court to issue such certificates under the Bail Act 1976 s 5(6A) and it is important that the advocate requests the certificate at the end of an unsuccessful bail application.

D3.11 Appeal against imposition of a bail condition

The CJA 2003 s 16 allows a defendant to appeal to the Crown Court against the imposition of the following bail conditions:

- that he resides away from a particular place or area;
- that he resides at a particular place other than a bail hostel;
- for the provision of a surety or sureties or the giving of a security;
- that he remains indoors between certain hours;
- any imposed under the BA 1976 s 3 (6ZAA) (requirements with respect to electronic monitoring); or
- that he makes no contact with another person.

The defendant may only appeal if:

- he has previously made an application to the magistrates under the BA 1976 s 3(8) to vary the bail conditions; or
- the conditions were imposed by the magistrates on the application of a constable or prosecutor.

D3.11.1 *Procedure for appealing to the Crown Court*

The procedure for appealing is set out in Crim PR rule 19.8:

- The defendant must apply to the Crown Court in writing as soon as practicable after the magistrates' court decision and serve a copy on the Crown Court officer, the magistrates' court officer, and the prosecutor.

- The application must specify:
  i. the decision that the defendant wants the Crown Court to make;
  ii. the charges;
  iii. why the Crown Court should not withhold bail or why it should vary the conditions under appeal; and
  iv. what further information or legal argument, if any, has become available since the magistrates' court decision;

- Unless the Crown Court otherwise directs, the court officer must arrange for the court to hear the application or appeal as soon as practicable and in any event no later than the business day after it was served.

D3.12 Breach of bail conditions

Breaching bail conditions does not constitute a separate criminal offence. There is, however, a power of arrest to allow the police to enforce bail conditions.

The BA 1976 s 7 provides:

Bail Act 1976 s 7

(3) A person who has been released on bail in criminal proceedings and is under a duty to surrender into the custody of a court may be arrested without warrant by a constable—
   (a) if the constable has reasonable grounds for believing that that person is not likely to surrender to custody;
   (b) if the constable has reasonable grounds for believing that that person is likely to break any of the conditions of his bail or has reasonable grounds for suspecting that that person has broken any of those conditions; or
   (c) in a case where that person was released on bail with one or more surety or sureties, if a surety notifies a constable in writing that that person is unlikely to surrender to custody and that for that reason the surety wishes to be relieved of his obligations as a surety.

(4) a person arrested in pursuance of subsection (3) above—
   (a) shall, except where he was arrested within 24 hours of the time appointed for him to surrender to custody, be brought as soon as practicable and in any event within 24 hours after his arrest before a justice of the peace for the petty sessions area in which he was arrested; and
   (b) in the said excepted case shall be brought before the court at which he was to have surrendered to custody.

In reckoning for the purposes of this subsection any period of 24 hours, no account shall be taken of Christmas Day, Good Friday or any Sunday.

---

(5) A justice of the peace before whom a person is brought under subsection
(4) above may, subject to subsection (6) below, if of the opinion that that
person—
(a) is not likely to surrender to custody, or
(b) has broken or is likely to break any condition of his bail,
remand him in custody or commit him to custody, as the case may require,
or alternatively, grant him bail subject to the same or to different conditions, but if not of that opinion shall grant him bail subject to the same
conditions (if any) as were originally imposed.
...
(6) Where the person so brought before the justice is a child or young person
and the justice does not grant him bail, subsection (5) above shall have
effect subject to the provisions of section 91 of the Legal Aid, Sentencing
and Punishment of Offenders Act 2012 (remands of children otherwise
than on bail).

If the defendant arrested under s 7(3) is charged with murder, then
he must be brought before a Crown Court judge rather than a justice of the peace and in such a case, when reckoning the period of
twenty-four hours, no account shall be taken of any Saturday in addition to the days specified above: s 7(8).

The twenty-four-hour requirement is absolute and requires that the
detainee be brought not merely to the court precincts or cells but actually before a justice of the peace (*R v Governor of Glen Parva Young
Offender Institution ex parte G (A Minor)* [1998] 2 Cr App R 349). The
court's investigation and decision-making in relation to the alleged
breach must be completed within the twenty-four-hour period (*R
(Culley) v Crown Court Sitting at Dorchester* [2007] EWHC 109
(Admin)). A court can, however, bring a defendant into the dock and
then adjourn the hearing until later in the court list or even before a
differently constituted bench, subject to the proviso that the breach
must be resolved within the twenty-four-hour period (*R (Hussein) v
Derby Magistrates' Court* [2001] 1 WLR 254). If a detainee cannot be
brought before a justice of the peace within twenty-four hours then
he should be released.

There is no defence of 'reasonable excuse' in relation to the breaking
of bail conditions (*R (Vickers) v West London Magistrates' Court* [2004]
Crim LR 63), although the reasons for breach would be relevant to the
determination of whether or not to grant bail.

In *R v Liverpool Justices, ex parte Director of Public Prosecutions* (1992)
95 Cr App R 222, the court laid down the following guidance for a
court to follow when considering bail breaches:

• strict rules of evidence did not apply and hearsay was admissible;
• the court must consider the type of evidence called and take account
  of the fact that there had been no cross-examination;

- the prosecution and defence can call witnesses if they so wish, and the other party has the right to cross-examine;
- the defendant has a right to give oral evidence.

If the breach is not proved the defendant must be released on the same conditions as existed previously. If the breach is proved that does not mean an automatic remand into custody, it is simply a factor to be considered when the court decides on whether or not it should rebail.

D3.13 Failing to surrender to custody

A person granted bail in criminal proceedings is under a duty to surrender to custody: BA 1976 s 3(1). Having been granted bail, it is a criminal offence not to surrender to custody at the place and time appointed by the court.

The BA 1976 s 6 creates two separate criminal offences:

Bail Act 1976 s 6

(1) If a person who has been released on bail in criminal proceedings fails without reasonable excuse to surrender to custody he shall be guilty of an offence.

(2) If a person who—
   (a) has been released on bail in criminal proceedings, and
   (b) having reasonable cause therefore, has failed to surrender to custody,
   fails to surrender to custody at the appointed place as soon after the appointed time as is reasonably practicable he shall be guilty of an offence

(3) It shall be for the accused to prove that he had reasonable cause for his failure to surrender to custody.

(4) A failure to give to a person granted bail in criminal proceedings a copy of the record of the decision shall not constitute a reasonable cause for that person's failure to surrender to custody.

. . .

(8) In any proceedings for an offence under subsection (1) or (2) above a document purporting to be a copy of the part of the prescribed record which relates to the time and place appointed for the person specified in the record to surrender to custody and to be duly certified to be a true copy of that part of the record shall be evidence of the time and place appointed for that person to surrender to custody.

(9) For the purposes of subsection (8) above—
   (a) 'the prescribed record' means the record of the decision of the court, officer or constable made in pursuance of section 5(1) of this Act;
   (b) the copy of the prescribed record is duly certified if it is certified by the appropriate officer of the court or, as the case may be, by the constable who took the decision or a constable designated for the purpose by the officer in charge of the police station from which the person to whom the record relates was released; . . .

'Surrender to bail' means, in relation to a person released on bail, surrendering himself into the custody of the court at the time and place for the time being appointed for him to do so (BA 1976 s 2(2)). What precisely constitutes surrendering depends on the procedure followed by a particular court; where a defendant reports to a particular court official in accordance with that court's normal procedure he has surrendered to the court (*DPP v Richards* [1989] QB 701).

A reasonable excuse need only be proved to the civil standard (*R v Carr-Bryant* (1944) 29 Cr App R 76). The mere fact that a defendant is only slightly late cannot afford him a defence: *R v Scott* [2007] EWCA Crim 2757. A genuine, albeit mistaken, belief that bail was to another date would not in itself amount to a reasonable excuse (*Laidlaw v Atkinson* The Times, 2 August 1986). In *R v Liverpool Justices, ex parte Santos* The Times, 23 January 1997 the court held that reliance on mistaken information provided by a solicitor may be found a reasonable excuse for failing to surrender. The court went on to say that all relevant factors would need to be considered and a mistake on the part of a solicitor in calculating the bail date did not automatically excuse the defendant's non-attendance.

The BA 1976 s 6(7) provides that a person who is convicted summarily of an offence under s 6(1) or s 6(2) shall be liable to imprisonment for a term not exceeding three months or to a fine not exceeding level 5 on the standard scale or to both and a person who is dealt with for contempt in the Crown Court shall be liable to imprisonment for a term not exceeding twelve months or to a fine or to both. However, a custodial sentence cannot be imposed on a youth defendant because:

- the minimum term of a detention and training order is four months; and
- a court may not impose detention as a punishment for contempt upon a youth defendant: see *R v Byas* (1995) 16 Cr App R (S) 869.

D4 **Bail Refused**

D4.1 **General**

Where a youth defendant is refused bail, he is not automatically remanded into prison or a remand centre. Instead the court must go on to consider the nature of the remand.

The LASPO 2012 s 91 provides:

Legal Aid, Sentencing and Punishment of Offenders Act 2012 s 91

(1) This section applies where—
   (a) a court deals with a child charged with or convicted of one or more offences by remanding the child, and
   (b) the child is not released on bail.
...
(3) Subject to subsection (4), the court must remand the child to local authority accommodation in accordance with section 92.
(4) The court may instead remand the child to youth detention accommodation in accordance with section 102 where—
   (a) in the case of a child remanded under subsection (1), the first or second set of conditions for such a remand (see sections 98 and 99) is met in relation to the child, or
   (b) [*provision relating to extradition proceedings—not covered in this handbook*].
(5) This section is subject to section 128(7) of the Magistrates' Courts Act 1980 (remands to police detention for periods of not more than 3 days); but that provision has effect in relation to a child as if for the reference to 3 clear days there were substituted a reference to 24 hours.
(6) In this Chapter, 'child' means a person under the age of 18.
(7) References in this Chapter...to the remand of a child include a reference to—
   (a) the sending of a child for trial, and
   (b) the committal of a child for sentence,
   and related expressions are to be construed accordingly.

The LASPO 2012 s 107 provides the following definitions:

- **Child**—a person under the age of 18.
- **Imprisonable offence** means—
   (a) an offence punishable in the case of an adult with imprisonment, or
   (b) in relation to an offence of which a child has been accused or convicted outside England and Wales, an offence equivalent to an offence that, in England and Wales, is punishable in the case of an adult with imprisonment;

- ***Sexual offence*** means an offence specified in Part 2 of Schedule 15 to the Criminal Justice Act 2003 (see **Appendix 2**);
- ***Violent offence*** means murder or an offence specified in Part 1 of Schedule 15 to the Criminal Justice Act 2003 (see **Appendix 2**).

D4.2 Remands to local authority accommodation

A remand to local authority accommodation is a remand to accommodation provided by or on behalf of a local authority (LASPO 2012 s 92(1)).

By s 92(2) a court that remands a child to local authority accommodation must designate the local authority that is to receive the child and by s 92(3) that authority must be—

- in the case of a child who is being looked after by a local authority, that authority, and
- in any other case, the local authority in whose area it appears to the court that the child habitually resides or the offence or one of the offences was committed.

The LASPO 2012 s 92(4) provides that the designated authority must—

- receive the child, and
- provide or arrange for the provision of accommodation for the child whilst the child is remanded to local authority accommodation.

D4.3 Conditions on remands to local authority accommodation

Under the LASPO 2012 s 93(1) a court remanding a child to local authority accommodation may require the child to comply with any conditions that could be imposed under the BA 1976 s 3(6) if the child were then being granted bail.

The BA 1976 s 3(6) allows the court to impose conditions upon a defendant which appear to be necessary to secure that he:

- surrenders to custody;
- does not commit an offence on bail;
- does not interfere with witnesses or otherwise obstruct the course of justice;
- makes himself available for the making of enquiries or a report to assist in sentencing; or
- attends an interview with a legal representative.

Tagging and other forms of electronic monitoring of the youth defendant's compliance with these requirements may be ordered (s 93(2)) but only if the conditions set out in s 94 are satisfied:

- The **first requirement** is that the child has reached the age of 12.
- The **second requirement** is that the youth defendant is charged with one or more imprisonable offences.
- The **third requirement** is that—
    (a) the youth defendant is charged with a violent or sexual offence or an offence punishable in the case of an adult with imprisonment for a term of fourteen years or more, or
    (b) the current charges, together with any other imprisonable offences of which the child has been convicted in any proceedings, amount or would, if the youth were convicted of that offence or those offences, amount to a recent history of committing imprisonable offences while on bail or subject to a custodial remand.

- The **fourth requirement** is that the court is satisfied that the necessary provision for electronic monitoring can be made under arrangements currently available in each local justice area which is a relevant area.
- The **fifth requirement** is that a youth offending team has informed the court that, in its opinion, the imposition of an electronic monitoring condition will be suitable in the youth defendant's case.

By the LASPO 2012 s 93(3) a court remanding a child to local authority accommodation may impose on the designated authority:

- requirements for securing compliance with any conditions imposed on the child under subsection (1) or (2), or
- requirements stipulating that the child must not be placed with a named person.

A court may only impose a condition upon a child or a requirement upon the local authority, after consultation with the designated authority (LASPO 2012 s 92(4)). References to consultation are to such consultation (if any) as is reasonably practical in all the circumstances of the case (s 92(9)).

Where a youth defendant has been remanded to local authority accommodation, the local authority or the defendant may apply to a relevant court to vary or revoke any conditions or requirements made (LASPO 2012 s 93(6)). 'Relevant court' is defined as the court by which the defendant was remanded or any magistrates' court that has jurisdiction in the place where the defendant is for the time being detained (s 93(8)).

D4.4 Breach of remand conditions

By the LASPO 2012 s 97(1) a youth defendant may be arrested without warrant by a police constable if:

- the defendant has been remanded to local authority accommodation;
- conditions on the remand have been imposed upon him under s 93; and
- the constable has reasonable grounds for suspecting that the defendant has broken any of those conditions.

It should be noted that unlike the BA 1976 s 7 a constable may not arrest for breach of remand conditions if he only suspects that the conditions will be broken.

A youth defendant arrested under s 97(1) must be brought before a justice of the peace as soon as is practicable and in any event within the period of twenty-four hours beginning with the youth defendant's arrest: s 97(2). If the defendant is arrested within twenty-four hours of the next court hearing, then he should be taken to the court where the hearing is due to take place whether it is a youth court, other adult magistrates' court, or a Crown Court: s 97(3). In reckoning a period of twenty-four hours, no account is to be taken of Christmas Day, Good Friday, or any Sunday: s 97(4).

If a justice of the peace before whom the youth defendant is brought is of the opinion that the defendant has broken any remand condition imposed on him, the justice of the peace must remand the defendant: s 97(5). Such a remand is still subject to the requirements of s 91: s 97(6). This means that the remand will still be to local authority accommodation unless the court now considers that the criteria for a remand to youth detention accommodation are now satisfied.

If a justice of the peace before whom the youth defendant is brought is not of the opinion that the defendant has broken any remand condition imposed on him, the justice of the peace must remand the defendant to the place to which he had been remanded at the time of his arrest subject to the same conditions as before: s 97(7).

D4.5 Remands to youth detention accommodation

A court may only remand to youth detention accommodation if *either* of the following remand conditions are satisfied:

A. First set of conditions (LASPO 2012 s 98):
- The defendant must have reached the age of 12.
- The offence with which the defendant is charged—

  (a) is a violent or sexual offence, or

  (b) is an offence punishable in the case of an adult with imprisonment for a term of fourteen years or more.

- The court is of the opinion, after considering all the options for the remand of the child, that only remanding the child to youth detention accommodation would be adequate—

  (a) to protect the public from death or serious personal injury (whether physical or psychological) occasioned by further offences committed by the child, or

  (b) to prevent the commission by the child of imprisonable offences.

B. Second set of conditions (LASPO 2012 s 99):

- The defendant must have reached the age of 12.
- It appears to the court that there is a real prospect that the defendant will be sentenced to a custodial sentence for the offence before the court or one or more of those offences.
- The defendant is before the court charged with at least one imprisonable offence.
- The history condition—either:

  (a) the child has a recent history of absconding while subject to a custodial remand and the offence mentioned in section 91(1), or one or more of those offences, is alleged to be or has been found to have been committed while the child was remanded to local authority accommodation or youth detention accommodation; or

  (b) the offence or offences mentioned in section 91(1), together with any other imprisonable offences of which the child has been convicted in any proceedings, amount or would, if the child were convicted of that offence or those offences, amount to a recent history of committing imprisonable offences while on bail or subject to a custodial remand.

- The court is of the opinion, after considering all the options for the remand of the child, that only remanding the youth defendant to youth detention accommodation would be adequate—

  (a) to protect the public from death or serious personal injury (whether physical or psychological) occasioned by further offences committed by him, or

  (b) to prevent the commission by him of imprisonable offences.

For either set of conditions the youth defendant must be legally represented before the court, or, if not legally represented, one of the following must apply:

- representation was provided to the defendant for the purposes of the proceedings, but was withdrawn—

(a) because of the defendant's conduct, or

(b) because it appeared that the defendant's financial resources were such that the defendant was not eligible for such representation,

- the defendant applied for such representation and the application was refused because it appeared that the defendant's financial resources were such that the defendant was not eligible for such representation, or

- having been informed of the right to apply for such representation and having had the opportunity to do so, the defendant refused or failed to apply.

Real prospect of custodial sentence—this means in practice a detention and training order for four months or more is a real prospect. If a guilty plea has been entered, it is arguable that the discount for that plea would have to be taken into account as well.

D4.6 Placement in youth detention accommodation

A remand to youth detention accommodation is a remand to such accommodation as the Secretary of State directs in the child's case: LASPO 2012 s 102(1).

By s 102(2) the accommodation may be any of the following:

- a secure children's home;
- a secure training centre;
- a young offender's institution; or
- accommodation, or accommodation of a description, for the time being specified by order under the PCCSA 2000 s 107(1)(e) (youth detention accommodation for purposes of detention and training order provisions).

The placement decision is the responsibility of the Ministry of Justice but day-to-day management is delegated to the Youth Justice Board (YJB).

A child who is remanded to youth detention accommodation is to be treated as a child who is looked after by the designated local authority: s 104(1). For the duties of local authorities to look after children see **Appendix 4**.

D4.7 Reports on 10- and 11-year-olds

The age threshold for a remand to youth detention accommodation in the LASPO 2012 ss 98 and 99 mean that this type of remand is not available to defendants aged 10 or 11.

By the CYPA 1969 s 23B, where a defendant has been remanded on bail, the court may order a local authority to make an oral or written report specifying where the person is likely to be placed or maintained if he were to be refused bail and remanded to local authority accommodation.

This power to order such a report only exists if the 10- or 11-year-old defendant:

- is charged with or convicted of a serious offence (defined as an offence punishable in the case of an adult with imprisonment for a term of two years or more); or
- in the opinion of the court the person is a persistent offender.

The court must designate the local authority which will prepare the report. This must be the local authority the court would have designated under the LASPO 2012 s 92(2) if the person had been remanded to local authority accommodation (see **D4.2**). The report must be prepared within a maximum period of seven working days.

D4.8 Remand to Youth detention accommodation—flow chart

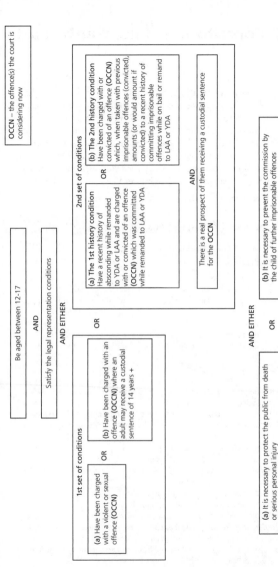

OCCN – the offence(s) the court is considering now

Be aged between 12-17

AND

Satisfy the legal representation conditions

AND EITHER

1st set of conditions

(a) Have been charged with a violent or sexual offence (OCCN)

OR

(b) Have been charged with an offence (OCCN) where an adult may receive a custodial sentence of 14 years +

OR

2nd set of conditions

(a) The 1st history condition
Have a recent history of absconding while remanded to YDA or LAA and are charged with or convicted of an offence (OCCN) which was committed while remanded to LAA or YDA

OR

(b) The 2nd history condition
Have been charged with or convicted of an offence (OCCN) which, when taken with previous imprisonable offences (convicted), amounts (or would amount if convicted) to a recent history of committing imprisonable offences while on bail or remand to LAA or YDA

AND

There is a real prospect of them receiving a custodial sentence for the OCCN

AND EITHER

(a) It is necessary to protect the public from death or serious personal injury

OR

(b) It is necessary to prevent the commission by the child of further imprisonable offences

Table E Remand to Youth Detention Accommodation

D5 **Constitution of the Youth Court**

Magistrates and District Judges sitting in the youth court will have received specialist training and must be authorized to sit. Subject to the limited exceptions set out in the 2007 Youth Court Rules (set out below), the court will consist of at least two justices, who will be a man and a woman. There is a discretion to proceed without a mixed tribunal but the views of the parties should be sought and the matter aired in court before proceeding: *R v Birmingham Justices (ex parte F)* (2000) 164 JP 523. A District Judge (Magistrates' Courts) can sit alone.

The CYPA 1933 s 45 states:

Children and Young Persons Act 1933 s 45

Constitution of the youth court

45 Youth courts

(1) Magistrates' courts—
   (a) constituted in accordance with this section or section 66 of the Courts Act 2003 (judges having powers of District Judges (Magistrates' Courts)), and
   (b) sitting for the purpose of—
      (i) hearing any charge against a child or young person, or
      (ii) exercising any other jurisdiction conferred on youth courts by or under this or any other Act,
   are to be known as youth courts.
(2) A justice of the peace is not qualified to sit as a member of a youth court for the purpose of dealing with any proceedings unless he has an authorisation extending to the proceedings.
(3) He has an authorisation extending to the proceedings only if he has been authorised by the Lord Chief Justice, with the concurrence of the Lord Chancellor, to sit as a member of a youth court to deal with—
   (a) proceedings of that description, or
   (b) all proceedings dealt with by youth courts.
(4) The Lord Chief Justice may, with the concurrence of the Lord Chancellor, by rules make provision about—
   (a) the grant and revocation of authorisations,
   (b) the appointment of chairmen of youth courts, and
   (c) the composition of youth courts.
(5) Rules under subsection (4) may confer powers on the Lord Chancellor or Lord Chief Justice with respect to any of the matters specified in the rules.
(6) Rules under subsection (4) may be made only after consultation with the Criminal Procedure Rule Committee.
(7) Rules under subsection (4) are to be made by statutory instrument.
(8) A statutory instrument containing rules under subsection (4) is subject to annulment in pursuance of a resolution of either House of Parliament.

---

(9) The Lord Chief Justice may nominate a judicial office holder (as defined in section 109(4) of the Constitutional Reform Act 2005) to exercise his functions under subsection (3) or (4) or his powers under rules under subsection (4).

The youth court is also subject to the 2007 rules:

Youth Courts (Constitution of Committees and Right to Preside) Rules 2007 SI 2007/1611 as amended

Constitution of youth courts

10.—(1) A youth court shall consist of either—

    (a) a District Judge (Magistrates' Courts) sitting alone; or

    (b) not more than three justices who shall include a man and a woman.

(2) Paragraph (3) applies if it is not possible to comply with paragraph (1) (b) because—

    (a) no man or no woman is available due to circumstances unforeseen when the justices to sit were chosen; or

    (b) the only man or the only woman present cannot properly sit as a member of the court.

(3) Where this paragraph applies, the court may be constituted without a man, or as the case may be, a woman if the other members of the youth court think it inexpedient in the interests of justice for there to be an adjournment.

(4) Nothing in this rule shall be construed as requiring a youth court to include both a man and a woman in any case where a single justice has by law jurisdiction to act.

Chairmanship of youth courts

11.—(1) A youth court, other than one consisting of a District Judge (Magistrates' Courts)

sitting alone, shall sit under the chairmanship of—

    (a) a District Judge (Magistrates' Courts) if he is sitting as a member of the court; or

    (b) a youth justice who is on the list of approved youth court chairmen.

(2) A youth justice may preside before he has been included on a list of approved youth court

chairmen only if—

    (a) he is under the supervision of a youth justice who is on a list of approved youth court chairmen; and

    (b) he has completed the training courses prescribed by rule 31 of the 2007 Rules.

(3) In this rule 'list of approved youth court chairmen' means a list kept by the ILYTDC or

BTDC as appropriate in accordance with rules 32 and 36 of the 2007 Rules.

D5 Constitution of the Youth Court

Absence of youth justice entitled to preside

12.—(1) The youth justices present may appoint one of their number to preside in a youth court to deal with any case in the absence of a justice
entitled to preside under rule 11 if—

    (a) before making such appointment the youth justices present
are satisfied as to the suitability for this purpose of the justice
proposed; and

    (b) except as mentioned in paragraph (2), the justice proposed has
completed or is undergoing a chairman training course in accordance with rule 31(f) of the 2007 Rules.

  (2) The condition in paragraph (1)(b) does not apply if by reason of illness, circumstances unforeseen when the youth justices to sit were
chosen or other emergency no justice who complies with that condition is present.

D6 Custody Time Limits

The Prosecution of Offences (Custody Time Limits) Regulations 1987 set time limits during which the defendant can be in the custody of a court awaiting the start of his trial. The regulations will apply to any youth defendant refused bail even if he is remanded to local authority accommodation under the LASPO 2012 s 91 (see definition of 'custody' in the Prosecution of Offences Act 1985 s 22(11)).

Category	Time limit
Summary-only offences Either-way offences	56 days to start of summary trial
Indictable-only offences	56 days to start of summary trial Indictable-only cases that are tried summarily in the youth court are subject to the same time limits as either-way cases (*R v Stratford Youth Court, ex parte S (A Minor)* [1998] 1 WLR 1758)
Cases sent to the Crown Court	182 days from the date when the accused is sent for trial less any time spent in custody at the magistrates' court

D6.1 Overview

Custody time limits start at the end of the first day of remand and expire at midnight on the last day. A time limit expiring on a Saturday, Sunday, bank holiday, or on Christmas Day or Good Friday will be treated as having expired on the next preceding day which is not one of those days.

D6.2 Exceptions

Defendants who abscond from prison, or who have been released on bail following expiry of a custody time limit, but are then remanded following a breach of bail, do not enjoy the protections offered by custody time limits.

If a person is granted bail and is then later remanded into custody, the earlier period on remand will count towards the custody time limit.

D6.3 Extending custody time limits

The case law on extending custody time limits is voluminous and since applications will generally be made on notice, this topic is not covered in this book (see instead *Blackstone's Criminal Practice*). In general the following considerations are relevant.

D6 Custody Time Limits

(1) The prosecution should give two days' notice of an intention to apply, but lack of notice is not fatal to the application and the court retains a discretion to extend the time limits (*R v Governor of Canterbury Prison, ex parte Craig* [1991] 2 QB 195).

(2) There is no power to extend once a time limit has lapsed (*R v Sheffield Justices, ex parte Turner* [1991] 2 WLR 987).

(3) The court must be satisfied, on a balance of probabilities, that the need for the extension is due to the illness or absence of the accused, a necessary witness, a judge, or magistrate; or a post-ponement which is occasioned by the ordering of separate trials, or some other good and sufficient cause; and that the prosecution has acted with all due diligence and expedition.

(4) The following have been held to amount to good and sufficient cause: certainly in cases that are not routine (*R(McAuley) v Coventry Crown Court* [2012] EWHC 630 and *R(Raeside) v Luton Crown Court* [2012] EWHC 1064 (Admin) lack of court time, listing difficulties due to the nature of the case, lack of a suitably experienced judge (or lack of any judge at all). Absent exceptional circumstances, resource difficulties do not amount to a good and sufficient case.

 See *Blackstone's Criminal Practice 2014* **D15.7–D15.38**

D7 Jurisdiction of the Youth Court

The CYPA 1933 s 46(1) states:

> **Children and Young Persons Act 1933 s 46**
>
> (1) Subject as hereinafter provided, no charge against a child or young person, and no application whereof the hearing is by rules made under this section assigned to youth courts, shall be heard by a magistrates' court which is not a youth court: …

D7.1 Criminal charges

All criminal charges against a child or young person are assigned to the youth court unless there is an adult co-defendant (see **G1**).

The youth court has power in certain cases to send a youth defendant to the Crown Court for trial (see **D2**) or to commit him for sentence (see **F4**).

D7.2 Applications

Applications involving youths can also be assigned to the youth court under s 46(1). There are no applications currently assigned. The Crime and Courts Act 2013, when in force, will assign applications for gang injunctions to the youth court (see **Appendix 5**).

Applications for orders made under the civil jurisdiction of the summary courts are not specifically assigned to the youth court and therefore are made in the adult magistrates' court. This includes applications for:

- Anti-social behaviour orders (other than on conviction);
- Bind overs under the MCA 1980 s 115;
- Orders relating to dangerous dogs under the Dogs Act 1871 s 2;
- Football banning orders (other than on conviction); and
- Sexual offences prevention orders.

Except in the case of interim orders, all practicable steps should be made for justices on the youth panel to sit when the court is considering an ASBO application in the adult magistrates' court (*Practice Direction (Magistrates' Courts: Anti-Social Behaviour Orders: Composition of Benches*). It is arguable that the same consideration should be applied to any other application relating to a youth.

D8 **Presence of Defendant in Court**

D8.1 **General principles**

If a defendant has been bailed to attend court his presence is mandatory unless and until it is excused by the court. Where a defendant on
bail fails to appear a warrant can be issued for his arrest. On summons
the defendant may be absent but represented by a legal representative: MCA 1980 s 122. This would be unusual in the youth court.

D8.2 **Defendant's presence at trial**

The MCA 1980 s 11 details the court's powers when a defendant does
not appear for trial:

Magistrates' Courts Act 1980 s 11

(1) Subject to the provisions of this Act, where at the time and place appointed for the trial or adjourned trial of an information the prosecutor appears
but the accused does not—
   (a) if the accused is under 18 years of age, the court may proceed in his
   absence; and
   (b) if the accused has attained the age of 18 years, the court shall proceed
   in his absence unless it appears to the court to be contrary to the
   interests of justice to do so.
   This is subject to subsections (2), (2A), (3) and (4).

(2) Where a summons has been issued, the court shall not begin to try the
information in the absence of the accused unless either it is proved to
the satisfaction of the court, on oath or in such other manner as may be
prescribed, that the summons was served on the accused within what
appears to the court to be a reasonable time before the trial or adjourned
trial or the accused has appeared on a previous occasion to answer to the
information.

(2A) The court shall not proceed in the absence of the accused if it considers
that there is an acceptable reason for his failure to appear.

(3) In proceedings to which this subsection applies, the court shall not in a
person's absence sentence him to imprisonment or detention in a detention centre or make a detention and training order or an order under
paragraph 8(2)(a) or (b) of Schedule 12 to the Criminal Justice Act 2003
that a suspended sentence passed on him shall take effect.

(3A) But where a sentence or order of a kind mentioned in subsection (3) is
imposed or given in the absence of the offender, the offender must be
brought before the court before being taken to a prison or other institution to begin serving his sentence (and the sentence or order is not to be
regarded as taking effect until he is brought before the court).

(4) In proceedings to which this subsection applies, the court shall not in
a person's absence impose any disqualification on him, except on

resumption of the hearing after an adjournment under section 10(3) above; and where a trial is adjourned in pursuance of this subsection the notice required by section 10(2) above shall include notice of the reason for the adjournment.

(5) Subsections (3) and (4) apply to—
  (a) proceedings instituted by an information, where a summons has been issued; and
  (b) proceedings instituted by a written charge.

(6) Nothing in this section requires the court to enquire into the reasons for the accused's failure to appear before deciding whether to proceed in his absence.

(7) The court shall state in open court its reasons for not proceeding under this section in the absence of an accused who has attained the age of 18 years; and the court shall cause those reasons to be entered in its register of proceedings.

The distinction between adults and youths in s 11 is important and is emphasized in the Crim PR r 37.11. In deciding whether or not to proceed in the defendant's absence, the Administrative Court in *Shirzadeh v Maidstone Magistrates' Court* [2003] EWHC 2216 (Admin) stated that the trial bench should have regard to all the circumstances of the case including, in particular:

- the conduct of the defendant;
- the extent of the disadvantage to the defendant in not being able to give his account of events, having regard to the nature of the evidence against him;
- the seriousness of the offence, which affects defendant, victim, and public;
- the general public interest and the particular interest of victims and witnesses that a trial should take place within a reasonable time of the events to which it relates;
- the effect of delay on the memories of witnesses;
- the likelihood of obtaining the defendant's attendance on another occasion; and
- where there is more than one defendant and not all have absconded, the undesirability of separate trials, and the prospects of a fair trial for the defendants who are present.

The decision to try a person in their absence must be exercised with great care and only in exceptional circumstances such as cases where the absence was a deliberate absconding: *R (Drinkwater) v Solihull Magistrates' Court* [2012] EWHC 765 (Admin).

D8 Presence of Defendant in Court

The involuntary absence of the defendant is not a reason to proceed in absence: *R v Thames Youth Court* (2002) 166 JP 613 (in this case detained in a police station). It is an important consideration that a youth may not have the same level of understanding as an adult.

See *Blackstone's Criminal Practice 2014* **D22**

D9 **Remand Periods**

D9.1 **Prior to conviction**

- Remand to police cells for twenty-four hours.
- Remand to custody for maximum of eight clear days on first remand.
- Subsequent remand to custody for up to twenty-eight clear days provided the next stage in the proceedings will be dealt with. If it is known that the next stage cannot be dealt with in that period, then eight-day remands will have to follow until such time as completion of the next stage within twenty-eight days is achievable.
- Subsequent remand to custody for twenty-eight clear days if the defendant is already in custody serving a sentence and will not be released before that date.
- Remand on bail for eight days, or longer if the defendant consents.
- Following a sending to the Crown Court, the magistrates have the power to adjourn for a period up to the date of trial (so the normal eight-day limit on first remand does not apply). It is important to note that the expression 'remand' has a particular meaning within the 1980 Act, and the court is not remanding a person when it sends someone for trial—therefore when a court sends a person for trial during their first appearance it can do so in custody for a period in excess of eight days.

The MCA 1980 s 129 allows for the remands of persons not produced before the court due to illness or accident. The court must have 'solid grounds' to justify an opinion that failure to be produced was due to illness or accident (*R v Liverpool Justices, ex parte Grogan* The Times, 8 October 1990).

D9.2 **Post conviction**

- Maximum three weeks if in custody, four weeks if on bail.

 See *Blackstone's Criminal Practice 2014* **D5.21–D5.37**

D10 **Reporting Restrictions in the Youth Court**

Reporting restrictions apply automatically to defendants under the age of 18 appearing in the youth court.

The CYPA 1933 s 49 provides:

Children and Young Persons Act 1933 s 49

49.—Restrictions on reports of proceedings in which children or young persons are concerned.

(1) The following prohibitions apply (subject to subsection (5) below) in relation to any proceedings to which this section applies, that is to say—

    (a) no report shall be published which reveals the name, address or school of any child or young person concerned in the proceedings or includes any particulars likely to lead to the identification of any child or young person concerned in the proceedings; and

    (b) no picture shall be published or included in a programme service as being or including a picture of any child or young person concerned in the proceedings.

(2) The proceedings to which this section applies are—

    (a) proceedings in a youth court;

    (b) proceedings on appeal from a youth court (including proceedings by way of case stated);

    (c) proceedings in a magistrates' court under Schedule 2 to the Criminal Justice and Immigration Act 2008 (proceedings for breach, revocation or amendment of youth rehabilitation orders);

    (d) proceedings on appeal from a magistrates' court arising out of any proceedings mentioned in paragraph (c) (including proceedings by way of case stated).

(3) The reports to which this section applies are reports in a newspaper and reports included in a programme service; and similarly as respects pictures.

(4) For the purposes of this section a child or young person is 'concerned' in any proceedings whether as being the person against or in respect of whom the proceedings are taken or as being a witness in the proceedings.

. . .

(9) If a report or picture is published or included in a programme service in contravention of subsection (1) above, the following persons, that is to say—

    (a) in the case of publication of a written report or a picture as part of a newspaper, any proprietor, editor or publisher of the newspaper;

    (b) in the case of the inclusion of a report or picture in a programme service, any body corporate which provides the service and any person having functions in relation to the programme corresponding to those of an editor of a newspaper,

shall be liable on summary conviction to a fine not exceeding level 5 on the standard scale.

> (10) In any proceedings under Schedule 2 to the Criminal Justice and
> Immigration Act 2008 (proceedings for breach, revocation or amendment
> of youth rehabilitation orders) before a magistrates' court other than a
> youth court or on appeal from such a court it shall be the duty of the
> magistrates' court or the appellate court to announce in the course of the
> proceedings that this section applies to the proceedings; and if the court
> fails to do so this section shall not apply to the proceedings.
> (11) In this section—
> 'programme' and 'programme service' have the same meaning as in the
> Broadcasting Act 1990; . . .

The CYPA 1933 s 49 does not prevent representatives of the press
attending the youth court but merely restricts what can be reported.

The reporting restrictions under s 49 cease to have effect once the
defendant has attained 18 (*T v DPP* [2003] EWHC 2408 (Admin)).

D10.1 Lifting the restrictions during the proceedings

In rare circumstances the court may lift the reporting restriction
before conviction. An application by the defence might be considered
where it is thought that publicizing the case might prompt witnesses
to come forward.

The CYPA 1933 s 49 also provides:

Children and Young Persons Act 1933 s 49

> (5) Subject to subsection (7) below, a court may, in relation to proceedings
> before it to which this section applies, by order dispense to any specified
> extent with the requirements of this section in relation to a child or young
> person who is concerned in the proceedings if it is satisfied—
> (a) that it is appropriate to do so for the purpose of avoiding injustice to the
> child or young person; or
> (b) that, as respects a child or young person to whom this paragraph
> applies who is unlawfully at large, it is necessary to dispense with those
> requirements for the purpose of apprehending him and bringing him
> before a court or returning him to the place in which he was in custody.
> (6) Paragraph (b) of subsection (5) above applies to any child or young person
> who is charged with or has been convicted of—
> (a) a violent offence,
> (b) a sexual offence, or
> (c) an offence punishable in the case of a person aged 21 or over with
> imprisonment for fourteen years or more.
> (7) The court shall not exercise its power under subsection (5)(b) above—
> (a) except in pursuance of an application by or on behalf of the Director of
> Public Prosecutions; and

> (b) unless notice of the application has been given by the Director of Public Prosecutions to any legal representative of the child or young person.
>
> (8) The court's power under subsection (5) above may be exercised by a single justice....
>
> (11) In this section—
>
> 'programme' and 'programme service' have the same meaning as in the Broadcasting Act 1990;
>
> 'sexual offence' means an offence listed in Part 2 of Schedule 15 to the Criminal Justice Act 2003;
>
> 'specified' means specified in an order under this section;
>
> 'violent offence' means an offence listed in Part 1 of Schedule 15 to the Criminal Justice Act 2003;
>
> and a person who, having been granted bail, is liable to arrest (whether with or without a warrant) shall be treated as unlawfully at large.

For the offences listed in the CJA 2003 Sch 15 see **Appendix 2**.

D10.2 Lifting the restrictions on sentence

The youth court has the power to lift the reporting restrictions on conviction. In practice this is unlikely to be considered until the sentencing hearing.

Children and Young Persons Act 1933 s 49

> (4A) If a court is satisfied that it is in the public interest to do so, it may, in relation to a child or young person who has been convicted of an offence, by order dispense to any specified extent with the requirements of this section in relation to any proceedings before it to which this section applies by virtue of subsection (2)(a) or (b) above, being proceedings relating to—
> (a) the prosecution or conviction of the offender for the offence;
> (b) the manner in which he, or his parent or guardian, should be dealt with in respect of the offence;
> (c) the enforcement, amendment, variation, revocation or discharge of any order made in respect of the offence;
> (d) where an attendance centre order is made in respect of the offence, the enforcement of any rules made under section 222(1)(d) or (e) of the Criminal Justice Act 2003; or
> (e) where a detention and training order is made, the enforcement of any requirements imposed under section 103(6)(b) of the Powers of Criminal Courts (Sentencing) Act 2000.
>
> (4B) A court shall not exercise its power under subsection (4A) above without—
> (a) affording the parties to the proceedings an opportunity to make representations; and
> (b) taking into account any representations which are duly made.

D10.3 Judicial guidance

In *McKerry v Teesdale and Wear Valley* (2000) 164 JP 355 Lord Bingham CJ gave the following important guidance to justices on the exercise of the power under s 49(4A):

> It is a hallowed principle that justice is administered in public, open to full and fair reporting of the proceedings in court, so that the public may be informed about the justice administered in their name. That principle comes into collision with another important principle, also of great importance and reflected in international instruments ... that the privacy of a child or young person involved in legal proceedings must be carefully protected, and very great weight must be given to the welfare of such child or young person. It is in my judgment plain that power to dispense with anonymity, as permitted in certain cases by s 49(4A), must be exercised with very great care, caution and circumspection. It would be wholly wrong for any court to dispense with a juvenile's prima facie right to anonymity as an additional punishment. It is also very difficult to see any place for 'naming or shaming'. The court must be satisfied that the statutory criterion that it is in the public interest to dispense with the reporting restrictions is satisfied. This will be very rarely the case, and justices making an order under s 49(4A) must be clear in their minds why it is in the public interest to dispense with the restrictions.

D10.4 Applications for post-conviction order against anti-social behaviour

By the CDA 1998 s 1C(9B) and (9C), when a youth court makes a post-conviction order against anti-social behaviour the automatic reporting restrictions imposed by the CYPA 1933 s 49 do not apply insofar as the proceedings relate to the making of the order. The court does have a discretionary power under the CYPA 1933 s 39 (see **D11**) to impose reporting restrictions in relation to the making of the ASBO. The automatic reporting restrictions under the CYPA 1933 s 49 still apply to the main sentence.

D11 Reporting Restrictions in Other Criminal Courts

D11.1 Discretionary power

In the adult magistrates' court and Crown Court the automatic reporting restrictions imposed by the CYPA 1933 s 49 do not apply. The court has a discretionary power to impose reporting restrictions under the CYPA 1933 s 39. This covers defendants and witnesses, including the alleged victim.

Children and Young Persons Act 1933 s 39

(1) In relation to any proceedings in any court, the court may direct that—
  (a) no newspaper report of the proceedings shall reveal the name, address or school, or include any particulars calculated to lead to the identification, of any child or young person concerned in the proceedings, either as being the person by or against or in respect of whom the proceedings are taken, or as being a witness therein:
  (b) no picture shall be published in any newspaper as being or including a picture of any child or young person so concerned in the proceedings as aforesaid;
  except in so far (if at all) as may be permitted by the direction of the court.
(2) Any person who publishes any matter in contravention of any such direction shall on summary conviction be liable in respect of each offence to a fine not exceeding level 5 on the standard scale.

An order under s 39 may also apply to the contents of a broadcast service such as radio or television (Broadcasting Act 1990 Sch 20) but there is some doubt as to whether an order can extend to social media or the internet (see *MXB v East Sussex Hospitals NHS Trust* [2012] EWHC 3279 (QB)).

The Crim PR Part 16 sets out the procedure to be followed. Applications are rarely opposed and where there is an issue to be determined a short adjournment may be necessary to allow the parties, which may include a representative of the press, to prepare. The Consolidated Criminal Practice Direction Part III.30 (see **Appendix 1**) suggests that a court should be ready to make an order under s 39 at the time of a plea and case management hearing in the Crown Court or a case management hearing in the magistrates' court.

D11.2 Judicial guidance

In *R v Winchester Crown Court* [2000] 1 Cr App R 11 Simon Brown LJ distilled the following propositions from earlier cases:

- In deciding whether to impose or thereafter to lift reporting restrictions, the court will consider whether there are good reasons for naming the defendant;
- In reaching that decision, the court will give considerable weight to the age of the offender and to the potential damage to any young person of public identification as a criminal before the offender has the benefit or burden of adulthood;
- By virtue of section 44 of the 1933 Act, the court must 'have regard to the welfare of the child or young person';
- The prospect of being named in court with the accompanying disgrace is a powerful deterrent and the naming of a defendant in the context of his punishment serves as a deterrent to others. These deterrents are proper objectives for the court to seek;
- There is a strong public interest in open justice and the public knowing as much as possible about what has happened in court, including the identity of those who have committed crime;
- The weight to be attributed to the different factor may shift at different stages of the proceedings and, in particular, after the defendant has been found, or pleads guilty, and is sentenced. It may then be appropriate to place greater weight on the interest of the public in knowing the identity of those who have committed crimes, particularly serious and detestable crimes;
- The fact that an appeal has been made may be a material consideration.

There is authority for the proposition that there have to be exceptional circumstances justifying the refusal to make an order; this is an improper gloss on the language of s 39 (*T v St Alban's Crown Court* [2002] EWHC 1129 (Admin)).

In *R(Y) v Aylesbury Crown Court* [2012] EWHC 1140 (Admin) it was stated that before making an order to restrict reporting under s 39 the court must be satisfied that there is a good reason to impose the restriction. The court must have regard to the welfare of the young person under the CYPA 1933 s 44, to the public interest, and to the right to freedom of expression under ECHR Article 10. Prior to any conviction the defendant's welfare is likely to take precedence over other interests. After conviction the age of the defendant and the seriousness of the crime will be particularly relevant. The court may permit the publication of some details but not all. Where the factors favouring restriction and those favouring publication are finely balanced, the court should make an order restricting publication.

See *Blackstone's Criminal Practice 2014* **D24.78–D24.81**

D12 **Restricted Access to the Youth Court**

The youth court is not a public court to which the public has free access. The CYPA 1933 s 47 provides:

Children and Young Persons Act 1933 s 47

47.— Procedure in juvenile courts

(1) Youth courts shall sit as often as may be necessary for the purpose of exercising any jurisdiction conferred on them by or under this or any other Act.

(2) No person shall be present at any sitting of a youth court except—

(a) members and officers of the court;

(b) parties to the case before the court, their legal representatives, and witnesses and other persons directly concerned in that case;

(c) bona fide representatives of newspapers or news agencies;

(d) such other persons as the court may specially authorise to be present: ...

D13 Secure Accommodation Applications (Children Act 1989 s 25)

D13.1 General power

In addition to the court's power to remand a youth defendant to youth detention accommodation under the LASPO 2012 s 91(4), local authorities may apply to a court under the Children Act 1989 s 25 for permission to place a looked after child into a secure children's home.

Children Act 1989 s 25

(1) Subject to the following provisions of this section, a child who is being looked after by a local authority may not be placed, and, if placed, may not be kept, in accommodation provided for the purpose of restricting liberty ('secure accommodation') unless it appears—
  (a) that—
    (i) he has a history of absconding and is likely to abscond from any other description of accommodation; and
    (ii) if he absconds, he is likely to suffer significant harm; or
  (b) that if he is kept in any other description of accommodation he is likely to injure himself or other persons.

(2) The appropriate national authority may by regulations—
  (a) specify a maximum period—
    (i) beyond which a child may not be kept in secure accommodation without the authority of the court; and
    (ii) for which the court may authorise a child to be kept in secure accommodation;
  (b) empower the court from time to time to authorise a child to be kept in secure accommodation for such further period as the regulations may specify; and
  (c) provide that applications to the court under this section shall be made only by local authorities.

(3) It shall be the duty of a court hearing an application under this section to determine whether any relevant criteria for keeping a child in secure accommodation are satisfied in his case.

(4) If a court determines that any such criteria are satisfied, it shall make an order authorising the child to be kept in secure accommodation and specifying the maximum period for which he may be so kept.

(5) On any adjournment of the hearing of an application under this section, a court may make an interim order permitting the child to be kept during the period of the adjournment in secure accommodation.

(6) No court shall exercise the powers conferred by this section in respect of a child who is not legally represented in that court unless, having been informed of his right to apply for the provision of representation under

> Part 1 of the Legal Aid, Sentencing and Punishment of Offenders Act 2012 and having had the opportunity to do so, he refused or failed to apply.
>
> (7) The appropriate national authority may by regulations provide that—
>   (a) this section shall or shall not apply to any description of children specified in the regulations;
>   (b) this section shall have effect in relation to children of a description specified in the regulations subject to such modifications as may be so specified;
>   (c) such other provisions as may be so specified shall have effect for the purpose of determining whether a child of a description specified in the regulations may be placed or kept in secure accommodation.
>
> (8) The giving of an authorisation under this section shall not prejudice any power of any court in England and Wales or Scotland to give directions relating to the child to whom the authorisation relates.
>
> (9) This section is subject to section 20(8).

'*Being looked after*'—this would include the following:

- a person for whom the local authority has an interim or full care order;
- a person accommodated by the local authority under the Children Act 1989 s 20 (except for persons aged 16 or 17 who are accommodated under s 20(5)—Children (Secure Accommodation) Regulations 1991 reg 5(2)(a));
- a defendant remanded on bail with a condition that he reside as directed by a specified local authority (*Re C (a minor) (secure accommodation: bail*) [1994] 2 FCR 1153); and
- a defendant remanded to local authority accommodation under the LASPO 2012 s 91(3).

The Children Act 1989 s 25 does not apply to defendants remanded to youth detention accommodation even though they are deemed to be looked after by the LASPO 2012 s 104(1) (Children (Secure Accommodation) Regulations 1991 reg 5A).

A child under the age of 13 shall not be placed in secure accommodation in a children's home without the prior approval of the Secretary of State to the placement of that child and such approval shall be subject to such terms and conditions as he sees fit (Children (Secure Accommodation) Regulations 1991 reg 4).

D13.2 Which court?

Applications for secure accommodation orders are normally made to the family proceedings court and an application for civil legal aid would have to be made.

Applications can be made to a criminal court in the circumstances set out in the CJA 1991 s 60(3).

Criminal Justice Act 1991 s 60

(3) In the case of a child or young person who has been remanded to local authority accommodation under section 91(3) of the Legal Aid, Sentencing and Punishment of Offenders Act 2012 by a youth court or a magistrates' court other than a youth court, any application under section 25 of the Children Act 1989 (use of accommodation for restricting liberty) shall, notwithstanding anything in section 92(2) of that Act or section 65 of the 1980 Act, be made to that court.

The reference to 'that court' in s 60(3) is a generic term and allows an application to any court of that type (*Liverpool City Council v B* [1995] 1 WLR 505). When the Crown Court remands to local authority accommodation the CJA 1991 s 60(3) does not apply therefore the secure accommodation application must be made to a family proceedings court. The same is the case if the defendant has been remanded on bail with a condition to reside as directed by the local authority (*Re W (Secure Accommodation Order: Jurisdiction)* [1995] 2 FCR 708).

D13.3 Procedure

An application for a secure accommodation order made to a youth court or adult magistrates' court is governed by the Magistrates' Court (Children and Young Persons) Rules 1992 SI 1992/2071. Notice of the application must be served on the defendant and any parent or guardian whose whereabouts are known to the local authority or can be readily ascertained (r 14). There is no minimum notice period and no provision for the appointment of a litigation guardian in the proceedings.

The maximum period for which a court may make a secure accommodation order for a defendant remanded to local authority accommodation under the LASPO 2012 s 91(3) is the period of the remand (Children (Secure Accommodation) Regulations 1991 reg 13).

An application made to a youth court or adult magistrates' court would be incidental to the criminal proceedings and covered by the criminal legal aid certificate (LASPO 2012 Sch 3 para 5(3)).

An application for a secure accommodation order made to a family proceedings court is governed by Family Procedure Rules Part 12. Such applications are outside the scope of this Handbook.

D13.4 **Placement without court authority**

When the criteria of the Children Act 1989 s 25 are satisfied, a local authority looking after a child may place him in secure accommodation without the authority of a court for a maximum period of seventy-two hours (whether or not consecutive) in any period of twenty-eight consecutive days (Children (Secure Accommodation) Regulations 1991 reg 10).

The Children (Secure Accommodation) Regulations 1991 reg 6 modifies the criteria for the use of secure accommodation in the case of a detained person aged 12 to 16 transferred after charge to local authority accommodation under the PACE s 38(6). In such cases the local authority may not place him in secure accommodation unless it appears that:

- he has a history of absconding and is likely to abscond from any other description of accommodation and, if he absconds, he is likely to suffer significant harm; or
- if he is kept in any other description of accommodation he is likely to injure himself or other persons.

D13.5 **Appeal**

An appeal against the making of a secure accommodation order may be made to the High Court (Children Act 1989 s 94).

D14 Separation of Youth Defendants from Adult Defendants

Children and Young Persons Act 1933 s 31

Arrangements shall be made for preventing a child or young person while detained in a police station, or while being conveyed to or from any criminal court, or while awaiting before or after attendance in any criminal court, from associating with an adult (not being a relative) who is charged with any offence other than an offence with which the child or young person is jointly charged, and for ensuring that a girl (being a child or young person) shall while so detained, being conveyed, or waiting, be under the care of a woman.

The application of s 31 has been considered in *R(T) v Secretary of State* [2013] EWHC 111 (Admin). The court held that the object of s 31 is to prevent the moral risks of contact between young persons and adult defendants. The section does not oblige the use of separate court buildings or even entirely separate custody areas in one court building but arrangements must be in place to ensure that young persons at court are prevented from being able to speak, communicate, or interact with adult defendants. Ensuring that young persons and adults are not afforded the opportunity to speak or socialize by sharing a cell or by associating outside the cell are part of that duty but arrangements may also be needed to address transitory contact or even physical proximity where these give rise to the risks to which the section is directed.

Part E
Case Management

E1 **Case Management**

E1.1 **Criminal procedure rules**

The Crim PR set out the statutory and common law procedural rules that apply to criminal cases. They are revised bi-annually and some parts are yet to be completed. They are available electronically on the Ministry of Justice website. It is intended that the efficiency of the criminal justice system should be enhanced by the rules, particularly Part 1 The Overriding Objective and Part 3 Case Management and subsequent case law has underlined this.

E1.2 **Overriding objective**

Criminal Procedure Rules 2013 rules 1.1 and 1.3

1.1.—(1) The overriding objective of this new code is that criminal cases be dealt with justly.

(2) Dealing with a criminal case justly includes—

(a) acquitting the innocent and convicting the guilty;

(b) dealing with the prosecution and the defence fairly;

(c) recognising the rights of a defendant, particularly those under Article 6 of the European Convention on Human Rights;

(d) respecting the interests of witnesses, victims and jurors and keeping them informed of the progress of the case;

(e) dealing with the case efficiently and expeditiously;

(f) ensuring that appropriate information is available to the court when bail and sentence are considered; and

(g) dealing with the case in ways that take into account—

(i) the gravity of the offence alleged,

(ii) the complexity of what is in issue,

(iii) the severity of the consequences for the defendant and others affected, and

(iv) the needs of other cases.

The application by the court of the overriding objective

1.3. The court must further the overriding objective in particular when—

(a) exercising any power given to it by legislation (including these Rules);

(b) applying any practice direction; or

(c) interpreting any rule or practice direction . . .

The courts will seek to ensure the application of the overriding objective by judicial management and control: *R v Jisl* [2004] EWCA Crim 696.

E1.3 Duties of parties and active case management

The Crim PR r 1.2 sets out the duties of the parties:

Criminal Procedure Rules 2013 rule 1.2

The duty of the participants in a criminal case

1.2.—(1) Each participant, in the conduct of each case, must—
- (a) prepare and conduct the case in accordance with the overriding objective;
- (b) comply with these Rules, practice directions and directions made by the court; and
- (c) at once inform the court and all parties of any significant failure (whether or not that participant is responsible for that failure) to take any procedural step required by these Rules, any practice direction or any direction of the court. A failure is significant if it might hinder the court in furthering the overriding objective.

(2) Anyone involved in any way with a criminal case is a participant in its conduct for the purposes of this rule.

The Crim PR r 3.2 and r 3.3 set out the duties of the court and the parties:

Criminal Procedure Rules 2013 rules 3.2 and 3.3

The duty of the court

3.2.—(1) The court must further the overriding objective by actively managing the case.

(2) Active case management includes—
- (a) the early identification of the real issues;
- (b) the early identification of the needs of witnesses;
- (c) achieving certainty as to what must be done, by whom, and when, in particular by the early setting of a timetable for the progress of the case;
- (d) monitoring the progress of the case and compliance with directions;
- (e) ensuring that evidence, whether disputed or not, is presented in the shortest and clearest way;
- (f) discouraging delay, dealing with as many aspects of the case as possible on the same occasion, and avoiding unnecessary hearings;
- (g) encouraging the participants to co-operate in the progression of the case; and
- (h) making use of technology.

(3) The court must actively manage the case by giving any direction appropriate to the needs of that case as early as possible.

The duty of the parties

3.3. Each party must—

> (a) actively assist the court in fulfilling its duty under rule 3.2, without or if necessary with a direction; and
>
> (b) apply for a direction if needed to further the overriding objective.

The court will expect to progress a case at the first hearing and deal with plea and then venue, if appropriate. Whether this can take place may depend on disclosure. (See **E3**.)

In *R(DDP) v Chorley Justices* [2006] EWHC 1795 (Admin) the role that the defence are expected to play in the early identification of the issues for trial was underlined:

> If a defendant refuses to identify what the issues are, one thing is clear: he can derive no advantage from that or seek . . . to attempt an ambush at trial. The days of ambushing and taking last minute technical points are gone. They are not consistent with the overriding objective of deciding cases justly, acquitting the innocent and convicting the guilty.

In *R (Lawson) v Stratford Magistrates' Court* [2007] EWHC 2490 (Admin) it was held that the court had correctly granted an adjournment to the prosecution in order to address issues raised for the first time in a defence closing speech.

In *Writtle v Director of Public Prosecutions* [2009] EWHC 236 (Admin) it was acknowledged that there may be cases where something arises during the course of the trial which may properly give rise to a new issue which could not have been expected to be disclosed at an earlier stage.

The Crim PR contains the procedure, timetable, and forms relating to applications to admit of bad character evidence, hearsay evidence, or to apply for special measures. (See **E6** Special Measures.) The importance of adhering to the timetable set out in the rules was emphasized in *R (Robinson) v Sutton Coldfield Magistrates' Court* [2006] EWHC 307 (Admin). Any application for an extension of the time limits will be closely scrutinized by the court. Two of the key considerations for the court considering whether to grant an extension to the time limit were whether there was a good explanation for the failure to give notice within the time limit and whether the opposing party had suffered any prejudice by reason of the failure to give notice within the time limit.

E1.4 Case management form and standard directions for case preparation

All youth and magistrates' courts have a Case Management Form which advocates will be required to complete when a case is to be listed for trial. The form deals with duties of the parties to disclose issues and indicate further evidence and applications to be served.

When adjourning the case for trial the court will apply the 'Standard Directions'. The court may vary them and the parties may invite them to do so. The list is not exhaustive.

- Any defence case statement within fourteen days of the prosecutor completing or purporting to complete initial disclosure.
- Defence witness names within fourteen days of the prosecutor completing or purporting to complete initial disclosure.
- Defendant must serve any application for prosecution disclosure when serving any defence statement.
- Prosecutor must serve any representations in response within fourteen days after.
- Defendant must serve any defence witness statement to be read at trial at least fourteen days before the trial.
- Any application for special or other measures must be served within twenty-eight days.
- Any representations in response must be served within fourteen days after.
- Prosecutor must serve any notice to introduce hearsay evidence or bad character evidence within twenty-eight days.
- Defendant must serve any notice to introduce hearsay evidence as soon as reasonably practicable.
- Any application to determine an objection to hearsay evidence or bad character evidence must be served within fourteen days of service of the notice or evidence.
- Any application to introduce evidence of a non-defendant's bad character must be served within fourteen days of prosecution disclosure.
- Any notice of objection to that evidence must be served within fourteen days after that.
- Any skeleton argument must be served at least fourteen days before the trial.
- Any skeleton argument in reply must be served within seven days after that.

E1.5 Binding rulings

An application to adduce evidence of bad character or hearsay evidence may result in the court making a binding ruling. Binding rulings can be made in relation to other issues. Such rulings are made under the MCA 1980, s 8A.

Binding rulings are made at a pre-trial hearing where all the parties have an opportunity to make representations. Unrepresented defendants must be given an opportunity to apply for legal aid to be represented. Although the statute requires there to have been a material change of circumstances before a party to the case can apply to vary or discharge such a ruling, it does not require this for the court to vary or discharge of its own motion. In *R(CPS) v Gloucester Justices* [2008] EWHC 1488 (Admin) it was observed that it would be difficult to accept that it could be in the interests of justice for the court to annul or discharge its own ruling without a compelling reason to do so such as changed circumstances or fresh evidence. It is not sufficient that a different bench reaches a different conclusion on the same material.

In *Jones v South East Surrey Local Justice Area* [2010] EWHC 916 it was said that earlier circumstances not drawn to the court's attention at the first hearing would, infrequently, justify the court later over-turning its decision. The Criminal Procedure rules and particularly the Overriding Objective are relevant to the interests of justice test.

In relation to applications to adduce bad character, in *R v Olu* [2010] EWCA Crim 2975 the situation in relation to police cautions was examined. It may be necessary to examine the circumstances in which the caution was administered and particularly whether the defendant had the benefit of legal advice. This is likely to apply to young defendants and may also be relevant to the admission of reprimands, warnings, youth conditional cautions, and youth cautions.

E1.6 Hearsay and fair trial

The important cases are *R v Horncastle* [2009] UKSC 14 and *Al-Khawaja and Tahery v UK* (2012) 54 EHRR 807, a decision of the Grand Chamber of the European Court of Human Rights. The concern is whether a defendant whose conviction is based 'solely or to a decisive degree' on statements made by a person who there has been no opportunity to examine, has had a fair trial in accordance with Article 6.

The courts have ruled that the statutory framework for admissibility of the evidence of absent witnesses, if properly applied, is sufficient to provide for a fair trial in such cases. The court must be satisfied that there is a sufficient basis for the absence of the witness and that a fair trial will still be possible despite the absence of opportunity to cross-examine. This will be harder to satisfy if the evidence of the absent witness is the sole or decisive evidence against the accused.

E1.7 Trial readiness

Where an application to adjourn, in this case due to unavailability of a witness, was not agreed the application should be heard by the court and not dealt with by a legal adviser under their delegated powers: *R v Lancaster Magistrates' Court* [2010] EWHC 662 (Admin).

E1 Case Management

If the prosecution has failed to carry out its statutory duties in relation to disclosure under the Criminal Procedure and Investigations Act 1996, an adjournment should be granted to the defence: *Swash v Director of Public Prosecutions* [2009] EWHC 803 (Admin).

In *Crown Prosecution Service v Picton* [2006] EWHC 1108 (Admin) the court laid down the following general approach:

(1) A decision whether to adjourn is a decision within the discretion of the trial court. An appellate court will interfere only if very clear grounds for doing so are shown.

(2) Magistrates should pay great attention to the need for expedition in the prosecution of criminal proceedings; delays are scandalous; they bring the law into disrepute; summary justice should be speedy justice; an application for an adjournment should be rigorously scrutinized.

(3) Where an adjournment is sought by the prosecution, magistrates must consider both the interest of the defendant in getting the matter dealt with, and the interest of the public that criminal charges should be adjudicated upon: the guilty convicted as well as the innocent acquitted. With a more serious charge, the public interest that there be a trial will carry greater weight.

(4) Where an adjournment is sought by the accused, the magistrates must consider whether, if it is not granted, the accused will be able fully to present his defence and, if he will not be able to do so, the degree to which his ability to do so is compromised.

(5) In considering the competing interests of the parties, the magistrates should examine the likely consequences of the proposed adjournment, in particular, its likely length, and the need to decide the facts while recollections are fresh.

(6) The reason that the adjournment is required should be examined and, if it arises through the fault of the party asking for the adjournment, that is a factor against granting the adjournment, carrying weight in accordance with the gravity of the fault. If that party was not at fault, then that may favour an adjournment. Likewise, if the party opposing the adjournment has been at fault, then that will favour an adjournment.

(7) The magistrates should take appropriate account of the history of the case, and whether there have been earlier adjournments and at whose request and why.

(8) Lastly, of course, the factors to be considered cannot be comprehensively stated but depend upon the particular circumstances of each case, and they will often overlap. The court's duty is to do justice between the parties in the circumstances as they have arisen.

In *Aravinthan Visvaratnam v Brent Magistrates' Court* [2009] EWHC 3017 (Admin) the court made these observations:

> The prosecution must not think that they are always allowed at least one application to adjourn the case. If that idea were to gain currency, no trial would ever start on the first date set for trial.

> So these are the competing considerations. I have no doubt that there is a high public interest in trials taking place on the date set for trial, and that trials should not be adjourned unless there is a good and compelling reason to do so. The sooner the prosecution understand this—that they cannot rely on their own serious failures properly to warn witnesses—the sooner the efficiency in the Magistrates' Court system improves. An improvement in timeliness and the achievement of a more effective and efficient system of criminal justice in the Magistrates' Court will bring about great benefits to victims and to witnesses and huge savings in time and money.

 See *Blackstone's Criminal Practice 2014* **D4**

E2 **Defendant Evidence Directions**

Special measures directions under Part II of the Youth Justice and Criminal Evidence Act 1999 are not available to the defendant. The court, however, has a wide and flexible inherent power to ensure that the accused receives a fair trial, and this includes a fair opportunity of giving the best evidence he can: *R v SH* [2003] EWCA Crim 1208.

The common law inherent power to order that a witness be shielded by the use of a screen during the giving of evidence is part of the court's armoury in choosing how to regulate a criminal trial. It could, for example, be used to screen a defendant from her co-defendants whilst she is testifying: *R (S) v Waltham Forest Youth Court* [2004] EWHC 715 (Admin).

Amendments to the YJCEA have introduced 'special measures' for defendants which should be referred to as 'defendant evidence directions'.

Youth Justice and Criminal Evidence Act 1999 s 33

33A Live link directions

(1) This section applies to any proceedings (whether in a magistrates' court or before the Crown Court) against a person for an offence.

(2) The court may, on the application of the accused, give a live link direction if it is satisfied—

    (a) that the conditions in subsection (4) or, as the case may be, subsection (5) are met in relation to the accused, and

    (b) that it is in the interests of justice for the accused to give evidence through a live link.

(3) A live link direction is a direction that any oral evidence to be given before the court by the accused is to be given through a live link.

(4) Where the accused is aged under 18 when the application is made, the conditions are that—

    (a) his ability to participate effectively in the proceedings as a witness giving oral evidence in court is compromised by his level of intellectual ability or social functioning, and

    (b) use of a live link would enable him to participate more effectively in the proceedings as a witness (whether by improving the quality of his evidence or otherwise).

(5) Where the accused has attained the age of 18 at that time, the conditions are that—

    (a) he suffers from a mental disorder (within the meaning of the Mental Health Act 1983) or otherwise has a significant impairment of intelligence and social function,

    (b) he is for that reason unable to participate effectively in the proceedings as a witness giving oral evidence in court, and

    (c) use of a live link would enable him to participate more effectively in the proceedings as a witness (whether by improving the quality of his evidence or otherwise).

(6) While a live link direction has effect the accused may not give oral evidence before the court in the proceedings otherwise than through a live link.

(7) The court may discharge a live link direction at any time before or during any hearing to which it applies if it appears to the court to be in the interests of justice to do so (but this does not affect the power to give a further live link direction in relation to the accused).

    The court may exercise this power of its own motion or on an application by a party.

(8) The court must state in open court its reasons for—

    (a) giving or discharging a live link direction, or

    (b) refusing an application for or for the discharge of a live link direction, and, if it is a magistrates' court, it must cause those reasons to be entered in the register of its proceedings.

33B Section 33A: meaning of 'live link'

(1) In section 33A 'live link' means an arrangement by which the accused, while absent from the place where the proceedings are being held, is able—

    (a) to see and hear a person there, and

    (b) to be seen and heard by the persons mentioned in subsection (2), and for this purpose any impairment of eyesight or hearing is to be disregarded.

(2) The persons are—

    (a) the judge or justices (or both) and the jury (if there is one),

    (b) where there are two or more accused in the proceedings, each of the other accused,

    (c) legal representatives acting in the proceedings, and

    (d) any interpreter or other person appointed by the court to assist the accused.

33C Saving

Nothing in this Chapter affects—

    (a) any power of a court to make an order, give directions or give leave of any description in relation to any witness (including an accused), or

    (b) the operation of any rule of law relating to evidence in criminal proceedings.

E2.1 Defendant's evidence direction

The Crim PR r 29.1(c) defines a 'defendant's evidence order' as a direction by the court for the defendant to give evidence—

- via live link, under the YJCEA 1999 s 33A; or
- through an intermediary, under the YJCEA 1999 ss 33BA and 33BB (not in force).

E2.2 Procedure

The Crim PR r 29.14–29.17 states:

Exercise of court's powers

29.14. The court may decide whether to give, vary or discharge a defendant's evidence direction—

(a) at a hearing, in public or in private, or without a hearing;

(b) in a party's absence, if that party—
   (i) applied for the direction, variation or discharge, or
   (ii) has had at least 14 days in which to make representations.

Content of application for a defendant's evidence direction

29.15. An applicant for a defendant's evidence direction must—

(a) explain how the proposed direction meets the conditions prescribed by the Youth Justice and Criminal Evidence Act 1999;

(b) in a case in which the applicant proposes that the defendant give evidence by live link—
   (i) identify a person to accompany the defendant while the defendant gives evidence, and
   (ii) explain why that person is appropriate;

(c) ask for a hearing, if the applicant wants one, and explain why it is needed.

[Note. See sections 33A and 33BA of the Youth Justice and Criminal Evidence Act 1999.]

Application to vary or discharge a defendant's evidence direction

29.16.—(1) A party who wants the court to vary or discharge a defendant's evidence direction must—
   (a) apply in writing, as soon as reasonably practicable after becoming aware of the grounds for doing so; and
   (b) serve the application on—
      (i) the court officer, and
      (ii) each other party.

(2) The applicant must—
   (a) on an application to discharge a live link direction, explain why it is in the interests of justice to do so;
   (b) on an application to discharge a direction for an intermediary, explain why it is no longer necessary in order to ensure that the defendant receives a fair trial;
   (c) on an application to vary a direction for an intermediary, explain why it is necessary for the direction to be varied in order to ensure that the defendant receives a fair trial; and
   (d) ask for a hearing, if the applicant wants one, and explain why it is needed.

[Note. See sections 33A(7) and 33BB of the Youth Justice and Criminal Evidence Act 1999.]

Representations in response

29.17.—(1) This rule applies where a party wants to make representations about—

    (a) an application for a defendant's evidence direction;

    (b) an application for the variation or discharge of such a direction; or

    (c) a direction, variation or discharge that the court proposes on its own initiative.

(2) Such a party must—

    (a) serve the representations on—

        (i) the court officer, and

        (ii) each other party;

    (b) do so not more than 14 days after, as applicable—

        (i) service of the application, or

        (ii) notice of the direction, variation or discharge that the court proposes; and

    (c) ask for a hearing, if that party wants one, and explain why it is needed.

(3) Representations against a direction, variation or discharge must explain why the conditions prescribed by the Youth Justice and Criminal Evidence Act 1999 are not met.

Until s 33BA is in force the court can still be asked to exercise its inherent jurisdiction to direct that the accused be assisted by an intermediary in giving his evidence: see *R(C) v Sevenoaks Youth Court* [2009] EWHC 3088 (Admin) and *R v Head* [2009] EWCA Crim 140.

A youth court acted irrationally in ruling that an accused with ADHD was not entitled to an intermediary: *R (AS) v Great Yarmouth Youth Court* [2011] EWHC 2059.

Where a direction is made that an intermediary should be appointed to assist the accused give evidence but no suitable person can be found, the trial judge must make an informed assessment as to whether it is possible nonetheless to have a fair trial by adapting procedures: *R v Cox* [2012] EWCA Crim 549.

See **E5** Effective Participation.

E3 Disclosure of Evidence

E3.1 First hearing

The extent of initial disclosure required of the prosecution is set out in the Crim PR, r 21:

Criminal Procedure Rules r 21

21.1.—(1) This Part applies in a magistrates' court, where the offence is one that can be tried in a magistrates' court.

(2) The court may direct that, for a specified period, this Part will not apply—

    (a) to any case in that court; or

    (b) to any specified category of case

21.2.—(1) The prosecutor must serve initial details of the prosecution case on the court officer—

    (a) as soon as practicable; and

    (b) in any event, no later than the beginning of the day of the first hearing.

(2) Where a defendant requests those details, the prosecutor must serve them on the defendant—

    (a) as soon as practicable; and

    (b) in any event, no later than the beginning of the day of the first hearing.

(3) Where a defendant does not request those details, the prosecutor must make them available to the defendant at, or before, the beginning of the day of the first hearing

21.3. Initial details of the prosecution case must include—

    (a) a summary of the evidence on which that case will be based; or

    (b) any statement, document or extract setting out facts or other matters on which that case will be based; or

    (c) any combination of such a summary, statement, document or extract; and

    (d) the defendant's previous convictions...

Failure to comply by the prosecution may result in an adjournment. These provisions do not require the service of witness statements at this stage. The witness statements and supporting exhibits (or access to them) will need to be made available before any trial takes place. Prosecutors have a wide discretion as to what is served prior to plea.

Guidance as to the documents which the police should make available to the CPS prior to charge can be found in the *Directors' Guidance on Charging* on the CPS website. Those items should be available as part of the prosecutor's file at court.

There is no jurisdiction to stay proceedings where there is failure in service of such details under Part 21 of the Criminal Procedure Rules. The appropriate remedy was to adjourn: *R v Leeds Youth Court, ex parte P(A)* [2001] EWHC 215 (Admin). Repeated failure to comply with the rules may provide for a stay in truly exceptional circumstances: *R v Willesden Magistrates' Court, ex parte Clemmings* (1988) 152 JPN 46. A threat to stay a prosecution if there were further disclosure breaches did not give rise to any legitimate expectation on the part of the defendant so as to require the court to carry through its threat on the next occasion: *R v Leeds Youth Court, ex parte AP and others* [2001] EWHC 215 (Admin).

Frequent problems arise in relation to the service of video, CCTV, and other recorded evidence. If the Crown is not relying on the undisclosed video evidence then no issue in relation to advance information (initial disclosure) arises. In *R v Calderdale Magistrates' Court, ex parte Donahue and others* [2001] Crim LR 141 it was accepted by the prosecution that a video was a document for the purposes of the then 'advance information rules'. In a later case the prosecution declined to make the same concession and courts are increasingly reluctant to order service of such items: *R v Croydon Magistrates' Court, ex parte Director of Public Prosecutions* [2001] EWHC Admin 552. In any event the prosecution are under a duty only to serve a summary of their case, not the case in its entirety.

Some assistance may be found in the comments of Leveson J in *R (on the application of H, O and A) Southampton Youth Court* [2004] EWHC 2912 (Admin) at para 10:

> the very least one would expect is that each solicitor would have taken careful instructions before permitting the court to embark upon the grave crimes procedure. It is said that there is increasing pressure on advocates to make early decisions and rapidly progress all cases, especially those involving serious charges and young people and, rightly or wrongly, the solicitors did not ask for an adjournment, did not obtain further disclosure and did not consider the case in full prior to this hearing. Suffice it to say, it was for the defence representatives to ensure that they knew enough about the case to make an informed judgment about the submissions to be made.

In appropriate cases an application for an adjournment to consider ABE interviews may be necessary.

E3.2 Pre-trial

In relation to summary trial, which includes all trials in the youth court, the extent of disclosure of the prosecution case which must be made is clearly dealt with in the *A-G's Guidelines on Disclosure*:

> Paragraph 57. The prosecutor should, in addition to complying with the obligations under the Act, provide to the defence all evidence upon which the

Crown proposes to rely in a summary trial. Such provision should allow the accused and their legal advisers sufficient time properly to consider the evidence before it is called.

In the authors' view this would include exhibits. It may be sufficient to provide access to the evidence, such as CCTV, rather than copies.

E4 **Disclosure of Unused Material**

E4.1 **Responsibilities of Investigation Officer and Disclosure Officer**

The duties of the police in relation to the gathering, recording, retention, and disclosure of evidence are set out in the *CPIA Code of Practice* and the *A-G's Guidelines on Disclosure*.

The CPIA 1996, ss 22 and 26 provide:

Criminal Procedure and Investigations Act 1996, ss 22 and 26

22 Introduction

(1) For the purposes of this Part a criminal investigation is an investigation conducted by police officers with a view to it being ascertained—
  (a) whether a person should be charged with an offence, or
  (b) whether a person charged with an offence is guilty of it.

(2) In this Part references to material are to material of all kinds, and in particular include references to—
  (a) information, and
  (b) objects of all descriptions.

(3) In this Part references to recording information are to putting it in a durable or retrievable form (such as writing or tape).

26 Effect of code

(1) A person other than a police officer who is charged with the duty of conducting an investigation with a view to it being ascertained—
  (a) whether a person should be charged with an offence, or
  (b) whether a person charged with an offence is guilty of it, shall in discharging that duty have regard to any relevant provision of a code which would apply if the investigation were conducted by police officers.

(2) A failure—
  (a) by a police officer to comply with any provision of a code for the time being in operation by virtue of an order under section 25, or
  (b) by a person to comply with subsection (1), shall not in itself render him liable to any criminal or civil proceedings.

(3) In all criminal and civil proceedings a code in operation at any time by virtue of an order under section 25 shall be admissible in evidence.

(4) If it appears to a court or tribunal conducting criminal or civil proceedings that—
  (a) any provision of a code in operation at any time by virtue of an order under section 25, or
  (b) any failure mentioned in subsection (2)(a) or (b), is relevant to any question arising in the proceedings, the provision or failure shall be taken into account in deciding the question.

E4.2 Prosecution disclosure duties

The prosecution disclosure duties in relation to unused material are dealt with in the CPIA 1996, its *Code of Practice* and the Crim PR, rule 22.

Criminal Procedure and Investigations Act 1996 s 3

(1) The prosecutor must—
   (a) disclose to the accused any prosecution material which has not previously been disclosed to the accused and which might reasonably be considered capable of undermining the case for the prosecution against the accused or of assisting the case for the accused, or
   (b) give to the accused a written statement that there is no material of a description mentioned in paragraph (a).

(2) For the purposes of this section prosecution material is material—
   (a) which is in the prosecutor's possession, and came into his possession in connection with the case for the prosecution against the accused, or
   (b) which, in pursuance of a code operative under Part II, he has inspected in connection with the case for the prosecution against the accused.

(3) Where material consists of information which has been recorded in any form the prosecutor discloses it for the purposes of this section—
   (a) by securing that a copy is made of it and that the copy is given to the accused, or
   (b) if in the prosecutor's opinion that is not practicable or not desirable, by allowing the accused to inspect it at a reasonable time and a reasonable place or by taking steps to secure that he is allowed to do so;and a copy may be in such form as the prosecutor thinks fit and need not be in the same form as that in which the information has already been recorded.

(4) Where material consists of information which has not been recorded the prosecutor discloses it for the purposes of this section by securing that it is recorded in such form as he thinks fit and—
   (a) by securing that a copy is made of it and that the copy is given to the accused, or
   (b) if in the prosecutor's opinion that is not practicable or not desirable, by allowing the accused to inspect it at a reasonable time and a reasonable place or by taking steps to secure that he is allowed to do so.

(5) Where material does not consist of information the prosecutor discloses it for the purposes of this section by allowing the accused to inspect it at a reasonable time and a reasonable place or by taking steps to secure that he is allowed to do so.

(6) Material must not be disclosed under this section to the extent that the court, on an application by the prosecutor, concludes it is not in the public interest to disclose it and orders accordingly.

(7) Material must not be disclosed under this section to the extent that it is material the disclosure of which is prohibited by section 17 of the Regulation of Investigatory Powers Act 2000.

(8) The prosecutor must act under this section during the period which, by virtue of section 12, is the relevant period for this section.

The standard directions in place in the magistrates' court usually require disclosure of unused material by the prosecution within twenty-eight days of pleas being taken. Disclosure is either by way of provision of a copy to the defence or allowing inspection of the material at a reasonable time or place. The test in the CPIA s 3(1) is an objective one. In *R v Barkshire* [2011] EWCA Crim 1885 it was stated that the statutory test extends to anything available to the prosecution which might undermine confidence in the accuracy of the evidence called by the prosecution, or which might provide a measure of support for the defence at trial.

E4.3 Continuing duty to review

Criminal Procedure and Investigations Act 1996 s 7A

(1) This section applies at all times—
   (a) after the prosecutor has complied with section 3 or purported to comply with it, and
   (b) before the accused is acquitted or convicted or the prosecutor decides not to proceed with the case concerned.

(2) The prosecutor must keep under review the question whether at any given time (and, in particular, following the giving of a defence statement) there is prosecution material which—
   (a) might reasonably be considered capable of undermining the case for the prosecution against the accused or of assisting the case for the accused, and
   (b) has not been disclosed to the accused.

(3) If at any time there is any such material as is mentioned in subsection (2) the prosecutor must disclose it to the accused as soon as is reasonably practicable (or within the period mentioned in subsection (5)(a), where that applies).

(4) In applying subsection (2) by reference to any given time the state of affairs at that time (including the case for the prosecution as it stands at that time) must be taken into account.

(5) Where the accused gives a defence statement under section 5, 6 or 6B—
   (a) if as a result of that statement the prosecutor is required by this section to make any disclosure, or further disclosure, he must do so during the period which, by virtue of section 12, is the relevant period for this section;
   (b) if the prosecutor considers that he is not so required, he must during that period give to the accused a written statement to that effect.

(6) For the purposes of this section prosecution material is material—
   (a) which is in the prosecutor's possession and came into his possession in connection with the case for the prosecution against the accused, or
   (b) which, in pursuance of a code operative under Part 2, he has inspected in connection with the case for the prosecution against the accused.

(7) Subsections (3) to (5) of section 3 (method by which prosecutor discloses) apply for the purposes of this section as they apply for the purposes of that.

(8) Material must not be disclosed under this section to the extent that the court, on an application by the prosecutor, concludes it is not in the public interest to disclose it and orders accordingly.

(9) Material must not be disclosed under this section to the extent that it is material the disclosure of which is prohibited by section 17 of the Regulation of Investigatory Powers Act 2000 (c 23).

E4.4 Defence applications for disclosure and defence statements

A defence statement is not required to be served in summary cases but the defence must do so before making an application to the court for an order that the prosecution should disclose any material which might reasonably be expected to assist the defence. When serving a defence statement the time limit for service in summary proceedings is within **fourteen days** of the date on which the prosecutor complies or purports to comply with the initial duty of disclosure. The court has power to extend this time limit on application of the defence. There is no provision to abridge this period.

Criminal Procedure and Investigations Act 1996 s 8

(1) This section applies where the accused has given a defence statement under section 5, 6 or 6B and the prosecutor has complied with section 7A(5) or has purported to comply with it or has failed to comply with it.

(2) If the accused has at any time reasonable cause to believe that there is prosecution material which is required by section 7A to be disclosed to him and has not been, he may apply to the court for an order requiring the prosecutor to disclose it to him.

(3) For the purposes of this section prosecution material is material—
   (a) which is in the prosecutor's possession and came into his possession in connection with the case for the prosecution against the accused,
   (b) which, in pursuance of a code operative under Part II, he has inspected in connection with the case for the prosecution against the accused, or
   (c) which falls within subsection (4).

(4) Material falls within this subsection if in pursuance of a code operative under Part II the prosecutor must, if he asks for the material, be given a copy of it or be allowed to inspect it in connection with the case for the prosecution against the accused.

(5) Material must not be disclosed under this section to the extent that the court, on an application by the prosecutor, concludes it is not in the public interest to disclose it and orders accordingly.

(6) Material must not be disclosed under this section to the extent that it is material the disclosure of which is prohibited by section 17 of the Regulation of Investigatory Powers Act 2000.

The procedure to be followed is set out in the Crim PR r 22.5. There is also a prescribed form to be used.

Where the defendant has served a defence statement given under the Criminal Procedure and Investigations Act 1996; and wants the court to require the prosecutor to disclose material:

- the defendant must serve an application on the court officer and the prosecutor.

The application must:

- describe the material that the defendant wants the prosecutor to disclose;
- explain why the defendant thinks there is reasonable cause to believe that—
  (i) the prosecutor has that material, and
  (ii) it is material that the Criminal Procedure and Investigations Act 1996 requires the prosecutor to disclose; and
- ask for a hearing, if the defendant wants one, and explain why it is needed.

The court may determine an application under this rule:

- at a hearing, in public or in private; or
- without a hearing.

The court must not require the prosecutor to disclose material unless the prosecutor is present; or has had at least fourteen days in which to make representations.

E4.5 Consequences of non-disclosure

In *Brants v DPP* [2011] EWHC 754(Admin) it was stated that the public interest in prosecuting cases transcended any notion of punishing the prosecution for delay. If delay by the prosecution does not cause prejudice to the defence, then normally it would not be appropriate to stay proceedings for abuse of process where there has been delay in complying with court directions to disclose.

E4.6 Third-party disclosure

See **E7**.

E5 **Effective Participation**

E5.1 Introduction

The question of fairness of trial in the Crown Court for young defendants was considered by the European Court of Human Rights in *V v UK* (2000) 30 EHRR 121. The inability of a defendant to effectively participate in the criminal proceedings against them will be a breach of the right to a fair trial under Article 6(1). The right of the accused to effectively participate in his criminal trial includes the right to hear and follow the proceedings. In the case of a child it is essential that he be dealt with in a manner which takes account of his age, level of maturity, and intellectual and emotional capacities, and that steps are taken to promote his ability to understand and participate in the proceedings, including conducting the hearing in such a way so as to reduce as far as possible his feelings of intimidation and inhibition.

A child may be at risk of not being able to participate effectively because of his young age and/or limited intellectual capacity. The importance of the existence of a specialist tribunal, the youth court, was emphasized in *SC v UK* (2005) 40 EHRR 226.

E5.2 Adapting the trial process

The Consolidated Criminal Practice Direction III.30 (see **Appendix 1**) sets out the steps to be taken to assist a young defendant to understand and participate in criminal proceedings, adapting the trial process where appropriate and necessary. The Direction applies in all criminal courts.

In *R(TP) v West London Youth Court* [2005] EWHC 2583 (Admin) the minimum requirements for a fair trial were stated to be:

(i) the defendant had to understand what he is said to have done wrong;

(ii) the court had to be satisfied that the defendant when he had done wrong by act or omission had the means of knowing that was wrong;

(iii) he had to understand what, if any, defences were available to him;

(iv) he had to have a reasonable opportunity to make relevant representations if he wished; and

(v) he had to have the opportunity to consider what representations he wished to make once he had understood the issues involved.

He had therefore to be able to give proper instructions and to participate by way of providing answers to questions and suggesting questions to his lawyers in the circumstances of the trial as they arose. The
case involved a defendant aged 15 with a mental age of 8. It was crucial
that the tribunal hearing the case, in this case a youth court, was able
to adapt its procedures so that the defendant could effectively participate in the proceedings. Emphasis was again placed on the specialist
nature of the tribunal and legal representatives.

In *R(C) v Sevenoaks Youth Court* [2009] EWHC 3088 (Admin) the
youth court dealing with a mentally disordered defendant was directed to assist his effective participation in the proceedings by the use of
its inherent powers to provide an intermediary 'to befriend and to help
him', during the trial and in preparation for it.

Where a direction is made that an intermediary should be appointed
to assist the accused give evidence but no suitable person can be found,
the trial judge must make an informed assessment as to whether it is
possible nonetheless to have a fair trial by adapting procedures: *R v
Cox* [2012] EWCA Crim 549.

See **E2** Defendants Evidence Directions.

E5.3 Mental Health Act procedures

In *R (P) v Barking Youth Court* [2002] EWHC 734 (Admin) the question of fitness to plead was raised in the youth court in relation to a
young person aged 12 years with a history of learning difficulties and
mental health problems. The High Court stated that the procedure for
dealing with matters of this kind in the magistrates' court is specifically provided for by a combination of section 37(3) of the Mental
Health Act 1983 when read in conjunction with the PCCSA 2000
s 11(1). An order can be made on a finding that the defendant 'did the
act alleged' without conviction and disposals are then available under
the Mental Health Act. 'Fitness to plead' can be decided in the Crown
Court but not in the youth or magistrates' court.

The Mental Health Act 1983 s 37(3) provides that:

Mental Health Act 1983 s 37(3)

(3) Where a person is charged before a magistrates' court with any act or omission as an offence and the court would have power, on convicting him of that
offence, to make an order under subsection (1) above in his case, then, if the
court is satisfied that the accused did the act or made the omission charged,
the court may, if it thinks fit, make such an order without convicting him.

The PCCSA 2000 s 11(1) sets out the procedure which the court can use to get medical reports to determine how to proceed further:

Powers of Criminal Courts (Sentencing) Act 2000 s 11

Remand by magistrates' court for medical examination.

(1) If, on the trial by a magistrates' court of an offence punishable on summary conviction with imprisonment, the court—

    (a) is satisfied that the accused did the act or made the omission charged, but

    (b) is of the opinion that an inquiry ought to be made into his physical or mental condition before the method of dealing with him is determined,

    the court shall adjourn the case to enable a medical examination and report to be made, and shall remand him.

(2) An adjournment under subsection (1) above shall not be for more than three weeks at a time where the court remands the accused in custody, nor for more than four weeks at a time where it remands him on bail.

(3) Where on an adjournment under subsection (1) above the accused is remanded on bail, the court shall impose conditions under paragraph (d) of section 3(6) of the Bail Act 1976 and the requirements imposed as conditions under that paragraph shall be or shall include requirements that the accused—

    (a) undergo medical examination by a registered medical practitioner or, where the inquiry is into his mental condition and the court so directs, two such practitioners; and

    (b) for that purpose attend such an institution or place, or on such practitioner, as the court directs and, where the inquiry is into his mental condition, comply with any other directions which may be given to him for that purpose by any person specified by the court or by a person of any class so specified.

E5.4 A hybrid approach?

In *CPS v P* [2007] EWHC 946 (Admin) the court gave specific guidance as to how these issues should be approached by a youth court. The case involved a defendant against whom proceedings in the Crown Court had previously been stayed on the basis of a number of medical reports. Smith LJ at para [61] stated:

(i) The fact that a court of 'higher authority' has previously held that a person is unfit to plead does not make it an abuse of process to try that person for subsequent criminal acts. The issue of the child's ability to participate effectively must be decided afresh.

(ii) Where the court decides to proceed to decide whether the person did the acts alleged, the proceedings are not a criminal trial.

(iii) The court may consider whether to proceed to decide the facts at any stage. It may decide to do so before hearing any evidence or it may stop the criminal procedure and switch to the fact-finding procedure at any stage.

(iv) The DJ should not have stayed the proceedings at the outset as he did without considering the alternative of allowing the trial to proceed while keeping P's situation under constant review.

(v) If the court proceeds with fact-finding only, the fact that the defendant does not or cannot take any part in the proceedings does not render them unfair or in any way improper; the defendant's Article 6 rights are not engaged by that process.

The court clearly stated that there would be a very small number of cases where it would be right to stay proceedings at the outset. This would only be where the child was clearly so severely impaired as to be unable to participate in the trial and where there is no useful purpose in finding the facts.

It is likely that applications to adapt the trial process or to proceed under the PCCSA 2000 s 11(1) will need the support of specialist reports. It may be possible to obtain guidance from professionals who are already involved with the young person. Where proceedings take the form of a finding of the facts, rather than a conviction, an order under the Mental Health Act does not have to be made.

See **H** Youths in the Crown Court and **F14** Mentally Disordered Offenders.

E6 Special Measures for Young and Vulnerable Witnesses

The Youth Justice and Criminal Evidence Act 1999 ss 16 and 17 provide:

Youth Justice and Criminal Evidence Act 1999 ss 16 and 17

16 Witnesses eligible for assistance on grounds of age or incapacity

(1) For the purposes of this Chapter a witness in criminal proceedings (other than the accused) is eligible for assistance by virtue of this section—

    (a) if under the age of 18 at the time of the hearing; or

    (b) if the court considers that the quality of evidence given by the witness is likely to be diminished by reason of any circumstances falling within subsection (2).

(2) The circumstances falling within this subsection are—

    (a) that the witness—

        (i) suffers from mental disorder within the meaning of the Mental Health Act 1983, or

        (ii) otherwise has a significant impairment of intelligence and social functioning;

    (b) that the witness has a physical disability or is suffering from a physical disorder.

(3) In subsection (1)(a) 'the time of the hearing', in relation to a witness, means the time when it falls to the court to make a determination for the purposes of section 19(2) in relation to the witness.

(4) In determining whether a witness falls within subsection (1)(b) the court must consider any views expressed by the witness.

(5) In this Chapter references to the quality of a witness's evidence are to its quality in terms of completeness, coherence and accuracy; and for this purpose 'coherence' refers to a witness's ability in giving evidence to give answers which address the questions put to the witness and can be understood both individually and collectively.

17 Witnesses eligible for assistance on grounds of fear or distress about testifying

(1) For the purposes of this Chapter a witness in criminal proceedings (other than the accused) is eligible for assistance by virtue of this subsection if the court is satisfied that the quality of evidence given by the witness is likely to be diminished by reason of fear or distress on the part of the witness in connection with testifying in the proceedings.

(2) In determining whether a witness falls within subsection (1) the court must take into account, in particular—

    (a) the nature and alleged circumstances of the offence to which the proceedings relate;

(b) the age of the witness;

(c) such of the following matters as appear to the court to be relevant, namely—

   (i) the social and cultural background and ethnic origins of the witness,

   (ii) the domestic and employment circumstances of the witness, and

   (iii) any religious beliefs or political opinions of the witness;

(d) any behaviour towards the witness on the part of—

   (i) the accused,

   (ii) members of the family or associates of the accused, or

   (iii) any other person who is likely to be an accused or a witness in the proceedings.

(3) In determining that question the court must in addition consider any views expressed by the witness.

(4) Where the complainant in respect of a sexual offence is a witness in proceedings relating to that offence (or to that offence and any other offences), the witness is eligible for assistance in relation to those proceedings by virtue of this subsection unless the witness has informed the court of the witness's wish not to be so eligible by virtue of this subsection.

(5) A witness in proceedings relating to a relevant offence (or to a relevant offence and any other offences) is eligible for assistance in relation to those proceedings by virtue of this subsection unless the witness has informed the court of the witness's wish not to be so eligible by virtue of this subsection.

(6) For the purposes of subsection (5) an offence is a relevant offence if it is an offence described in Schedule 1A.

(7) The Secretary of State may by order amend Schedule 1A.

E6.1 Special measures in force

The following special measures are available in the youth and adult magistrates' courts:

- screening witness from accused, s 23
- evidence via live link, s 24
- evidence given in private, s 25
- video-recorded evidence in chief, s 27
- examination through an intermediary, s 29
- aids to communication, s 30.

See **E6.8** Special measures.

E6.2 Witnesses under the age of 18

Child witnesses are automatically eligible for special measures as provided in s 16 without having to satisfy any other tests. The YJCEA 1999 s 21 provides:

Youth Justice and Criminal Evidence Act 1999 s 21

21(1) For the purposes of this section—

    (a) a witness in criminal proceedings is a 'child witness' if he is an eligible witness by reason of section 16(1)(a) (whether or not he is an eligible witness by reason of any other provision of section 16 or 17);

    (b) ...and

    (c) a 'relevant recording', in relation to a child witness, is a video recording of an interview of the witness made with a view to its admission as evidence in chief of the witness.

(2) Where the court, in making a determination for the purposes of section 19(2), determines that a witness in criminal proceedings is a child witness, the court must—

    (a) first have regard to subsections (3) to (4C) below; and

    (b) then have regard to section 19(2);

and for the purposes of section 19(2), as it then applies to the witness, any special measures required to be applied in relation to him by virtue of this section shall be treated as if they were measures determined by the court, pursuant to section 19(2)(a) and (b)(i), to be ones that (whether on their own or with any other special measures) would be likely to maximise, so far as practicable, the quality of his evidence.

(3) The primary rule in the case of a child witness is that the court must give a special measures direction in relation to the witness which complies with the following requirements—

    (a) it must provide for any relevant recording to be admitted under section 27 (video recorded evidence in chief); and

    (b) it must provide for any evidence given by the witness in the proceedings which is not given by means of a video recording (whether in chief or otherwise) to be given by means of a live link in accordance with section 24.

(4) The primary rule is subject to the following limitations—

    (a) the requirement contained in subsection (3)(a) or (b) has effect subject to the availability (within the meaning of section 18(2)) of the special measure in question in relation to the witness;

    (b) the requirement contained in subsection (3)(a) also has effect subject to section 27(2);

    (ba) if the witness informs the court of the witness's wish that the rule should not apply or should apply only in part, the rule does not apply to the extent that the court is satisfied that not complying with the rule would not diminish the quality of the witness's evidence; and

    (c) the rule does not apply to the extent that the court is satisfied that compliance with it would not be likely to maximise the quality of the witness's evidence so far as practicable (whether because the application to that evidence of one or more other special measures available in relation to the witness would have that result or for any other reason).

(4A) Where as a consequence of all or part of the primary rule being disapplied under subsection (4)(ba) a witness's evidence or any part of it would fall to be given as testimony in court, the court must give a special measures direction making such provision as is described in section 23 for the evidence or that part of it.

(4B) The requirement in subsection (4A) is subject to the following limitations—

    (a) if the witness informs the court of the witness's wish that the requirement in subsection (4A) should not apply, the requirement does not apply to the extent that the court is satisfied that not complying with it would not diminish the quality of the witness's evidence; and

    (b) the requirement does not apply to the extent that the court is satisfied that making such a provision would not be likely to maximise the quality of the witness's evidence so far as practicable (whether because the application to that evidence of one or more other special measures available in relation to the witness would have that result or for any other reason).

(4C) In making a decision under subsection (4)(ba) or (4B)(a), the court must take into account the following factors (and any others it considers relevant)—

    (a) the age and maturity of the witness;

    (b) the ability of the witness to understand the consequences of giving evidence otherwise than in accordance with the requirements in subsection (3) or (as the case may be) in accordance with the requirement in subsection (4A);

    (c) the relationship (if any) between the witness and the accused;

    (d) the witness's social and cultural background and ethnic origins;

    (e) the nature and alleged circumstances of the offence to which the proceedings relate.

Where a witness is eligible by reason of age, there may be agreement between the prosecution and defence as to the making of a special measures direction at an early stage in the proceedings, avoiding the making of a formal written application. The court may raise the issue on completion of the case management form.

The provisions apply to prosecution and defence witnesses. They do not apply to the defendant.

The Crim PR 2012 r 29.9 states:

Criminal Procedure Rules 2012 r 29.9

29.9.—(1) This rule applies where, under section 21 or section 22 of the Youth Justice and Criminal Evidence Act 1999, the primary rule requires the court to give a direction for a special measure to assist a child witness or a qualifying witness—

    (a) on an application, if one is made; or

    (b) on the court's own initiative, in any other case.

(2) A party who wants to introduce the evidence of such a witness must as soon as reasonably practicable—

    (a) notify the court that the witness is eligible for assistance;

> (b) provide the court with any information that the court may need
>   to assess the witness's views, if the witness does not want the
>   primary rule to apply; and
> (c) serve any video recorded evidence on—
>   (i) the court officer, and
>   (ii) each other party.

E6.2.1 *Disapplying a special measures direction*

The YJCEA 1999 s 21(4) allows the court to disapply all or part of
a special measures direction if the witness informs the court that he
does not wish to have the benefit of them. The court must also be
satisfied that the quality of the evidence given by the witness will not
be affected by the removal of the special measure. In considering the
application the court must take account of the following factors and
any others it considers relevant:

* the age and maturity of the witness;
* the ability of the witness to understand the consequences of giving
  evidence without the assistance of the special measure;
* the relationship (if any) between the witness and the accused;
* the witness's social and cultural background and ethnic origins; and
* the nature and alleged circumstances of the offence to which the
  proceedings relate.

E6.3 Adult witness with physical or mental impairment

The YJCEA 1999 s 16(2) applies and any application is likely to need
supporting evidence.

E6.4 Witness in fear or distress

The YJCEA 1999 s 17(2) sets out the factors which the court will take
into account in considering an application.

E6.5 Sexual offences

The YJCEA 1999 s 17(4) applies to the complainant in an allegation
of a sexual offence. The entitlement to special measures includes the
admission of any recorded evidence in chief where the trial takes place
in the Crown Court. That particular special measure does not apply
where a trial takes place in the youth and adult magistrates' court.

E6.6 Other relevant offences involving knives or guns

The YJCEA 1999 s 17(5) applies to the offences set out in the YJCEA 1999 Sch 1A. Entitlement to special measures is given to all witnesses, which would include police officers, unless they do not wish to have them.

The YJCEA 1999 Sch 1A states:

Youth Justice and Criminal Evidence Act 1999 Sch 1A

Relevant Offences for the Purposes of Special Measures Direction

Relevant offences for the purposes of s 17

Murder and manslaughter

1 Murder in a case where it is alleged that a firearm or knife was used to cause the death in question.
2 Manslaughter in a case where it is alleged that a firearm or knife was used to cause the death in question.
3 Murder or manslaughter in a case (other than a case falling within paragraph 1 or 2) where it is alleged that—
    (a) the accused was carrying a firearm or knife at any time during the commission of the offence, and
    (b) a person other than the accused knew or believed at any time during the commission of the offence that the accused was carrying a firearm or knife.

Offences against the Person Act 1861 (c 100)

4 An offence under section 18 of the Offences against the Person Act 1861 (wounding with intent to cause grievous bodily harm etc) in a case where it is alleged that a firearm or knife was used to cause the wound or harm in question.
5 An offence under section 20 of that Act (malicious wounding) in a case where it is alleged that a firearm or knife was used to cause the wound or inflict the harm in question.
6 An offence under section 38 of that Act (assault with intent to resist arrest) in a case where it is alleged that a firearm or knife was used to carry out the assault in question.
7 An offence under section 47 of the Offences against the Person Act 1861 (assault occasioning actual bodily harm) in a case where it is alleged that a firearm or knife was used to inflict the harm in question.
8 An offence under section 18, 20, 38 or 47 of the Offences against the Person Act 1861 in a case (other than a case falling within any of paragraphs 4 to 7) where it is alleged that—
    (a) the accused was carrying a firearm or knife at any time during the commission of the offence, and
    (b) a person other than the accused knew or believed at any time during the commission of the offence that the accused was carrying a firearm or knife.

Prevention of Crime Act 1953 (c 14)

9 An offence under section 1 of the Prevention of Crime Act 1953 (having an offensive weapon in a public place).

Firearms Act 1968 (c 27)

10 An offence under section 1 of the Firearms Act 1968 (requirement of firearm certificate).

11 An offence under section 2(1) of that Act (possession etc of a shot gun without a certificate).

12 An offence under section 3 of that Act (business and other transactions with firearms and ammunition).

13 An offence under section 4 of that Act (conversion of weapons).

14 An offence under section 5(1) of that Act (weapons subject to general prohibition).

15 An offence under section 5(1A) of that Act (ammunition subject to general prohibition).

16 An offence under section 16 of that Act (possession with intent to injure).

17 An offence under section 16A of that Act (possession with intent to cause fear of violence).

18 An offence under section 17 of that Act (use of firearm to resist arrest).

19 An offence under section 18 of that Act (carrying firearm with criminal intent).

20 An offence under section 19 of that Act (carrying firearm in a public place).

21 An offence under section 20 of that Act (trespassing with firearm).

22 An offence under section 21 of that Act (possession of firearms by person previously convicted of crime).

23 An offence under section 21A of that Act (firing an air weapon beyond premises).

24 An offence under section 24A of that Act (supplying imitation firearms to minors).

Criminal Justice Act 1988 (c 33)

25 An offence under section 139 of the Criminal Justice Act 1988 (having article with blade or point in public place).

26 An offence under section 139A of that Act (having article with blade or point (or offensive weapon) on school premises).

Violent Crime Reduction Act 2006 (c 38)

27 An offence under section 28 of the Violent Crime Reduction Act 2006 (using someone to mind a weapon).

28 An offence under section 32 of that Act (sales of air weapons by way of trade or business to be face to face).

29 An offence under section 36 of that Act (manufacture, import and sale of realistic imitation firearms).

General

30 A reference in any of paragraphs 1 to 8 to an offence ('offence A') includes—

(a) a reference to an attempt to commit offence A in a case where it is alleged that it was attempted to commit offence A in the manner or circumstances described in that paragraph,

(b) a reference to a conspiracy to commit offence A in a case where it is alleged that the conspiracy was to commit offence A in the manner or circumstances described in that paragraph,

(c) a reference to an offence under Part 2 of the Serious Crime Act 2007 in relation to which offence A is the offence (or one of the offences) which the person intended or believed would be committed in a case where it is alleged that the person intended or believed offence A would be committed in the manner or circumstances described in that paragraph, and

(d) a reference to aiding, abetting, counselling or procuring the commission of offence A in a case where it is alleged that offence A was committed, or the act or omission charged in respect of offence A was done or made, in the manner or circumstances described in that paragraph.

31 A reference in any of paragraphs 9 to 29 to an offence ('offence A') includes—

(a) a reference to an attempt to commit offence A,

(b) a reference to a conspiracy to commit offence A,

(c) a reference to an offence under Part 2 of the Serious Crime Act 2007 in relation to which offence A is the offence (or one of the offences) which the person intended or believed would be committed, and

(d) a reference to aiding, abetting, counselling or procuring the commission of offence A.

Interpretation

32 In this Schedule—

'firearm' has the meaning given by section 57 of the Firearms Act 1968;

'knife' has the meaning given by section 10 of the Knives Act.

E6.7 Procedure and time limits

The issue of special measures may arise on application by the prosecution, the defence, or on the courts' own motion.

The YJCEA 1999 s 19 provides:

Youth Justice and Criminal Evidence Act 1999 s 19

19 Special measures direction relating to eligible witness

(1) This section applies where in any criminal proceedings—

(a) a party to the proceedings makes an application for the court to give a direction under this section in relation to a witness in the proceedings other than the accused, or

(b) the court of its own motion raises the issue whether such a direction should be given.

(2) Where the court determines that the witness is eligible for assistance by virtue of section 16 or 17, the court must then—

(a) determine whether any of the special measures available in relation to the witness (or any combination of them) would, in its opinion, be likely to improve the quality of evidence given by the witness; and

(b) if so—

    (i) determine which of those measures (or combination of them) would, in its opinion, be likely to maximise so far as practicable the quality of such evidence; and

    (ii) give a direction under this section providing for the measure or measures so determined to apply to evidence given by the witness.

(3) In determining for the purposes of this Chapter whether any special measure or measures would or would not be likely to improve, or to maximise so far as practicable, the quality of evidence given by the witness, the court must consider all the circumstances of the case, including in particular—

    (a) any views expressed by the witness; and

    (b) whether the measure or measures might tend to inhibit such evidence being effectively tested by a party to the proceedings.

(4) A special measures direction must specify particulars of the provision made by the direction in respect of each special measure which is to apply to the witness's evidence.

(5) In this Chapter 'special measures direction' means a direction under this section.

(6) Nothing in this Chapter is to be regarded as affecting any power of a court to make an order or give leave of any description (in the exercise of its inherent jurisdiction or otherwise)—

    (a) in relation to a witness who is not an eligible witness, or

    (b) in relation to an eligible witness where (as, for example, in a case where a foreign language interpreter is to be provided) the order is made or the leave is given otherwise than by reason of the fact that the witness is an eligible witness.

Application must be made in the form prescribed in the Crim PR r 29.3(a):

Making an application for a direction or order

29.3. A party who wants the court to exercise its power to give or make a direction or order must—

    (a) apply in writing as soon as reasonably practicable, and in any event not more than—

        (i) 28 days after the defendant pleads not guilty, in a magistrates' court, or

        (ii) 14 days after the defendant pleads not guilty, in the Crown Court; and

    (b) serve the application on—

        (i) the court officer, and

        (ii) each other party.

E6.8 Special measures

E6.8.1 *Recorded evidence in chief*

Where a witness has made a statement in the form of a recording, that evidence will be admitted as evidence in chief and their cross examination will take place on the live link.

The YJCEA 1999 s 27 states:

Youth Justice and Criminal Evidence Act 1999 s 27

27 Video recorded evidence in chief

(1) A special measures direction may provide for a video recording of an interview of the witness to be admitted as evidence in chief of the witness.

(2) A special measures direction may, however, not provide for a video recording, or a part of such a recording, to be admitted under this section if the court is of the opinion, having regard to all the circumstances of the case, that in the interests of justice the recording, or that part of it, should not be so admitted.

(3) In considering for the purposes of subsection (2) whether any part of a recording should not be admitted under this section, the court must consider whether any prejudice to the accused which might result from that part being so admitted is outweighed by the desirability of showing the whole, or substantially the whole, of the recorded interview.

(4) Where a special measures direction provides for a recording to be admitted under this section, the court may nevertheless subsequently direct that it is not to be so admitted if—

    (a) it appears to the court that—

        (i) the witness will not be available for cross-examination (whether conducted in the ordinary way or in accordance with any such direction), and

        (ii) the parties to the proceedings have not agreed that there is no need for the witness to be so available; or

    (b) any rules of court requiring disclosure of the circumstances in which the recording was made have not been complied with to the satisfaction of the court.

(5) Where a recording is admitted under this section—

    (a) the witness must be called by the party tendering it in evidence, unless—

        (i) a special measures direction provides for the witness's evidence on cross-examination to be given otherwise than by testimony in court, or

        (ii) the parties to the proceedings have agreed as mentioned in subsection (4)(a)(ii); and

    (b) the witness may not without the permission of the court give evidence in chief otherwise than by means of the recording as to any matter which, in the opinion of the court, is dealt with in the witness's recorded testimony.

---

(6) Where in accordance with subsection (2) a special measures direction provides for part only of a recording to be admitted under this section, references in subsections (4) and (5) to the recording or to the witness's recorded testimony are references to the part of the recording or testimony which is to be so admitted.

(7) The court may give permission for the purposes of subsection (5)(b) if it appears to the court to be in the interests of justice to do so, and may do so either—
    (a) on an application by a party to the proceedings or
    (b) of its own motion.

(8) Repealed

(9) The court may, in giving permission for the purposes of subsection (5)(b), direct that the evidence in question is to be given by the witness by means of a live link; and, if the court so directs, subsections (5) to (7) of section 24 shall apply in relation to that evidence as they apply in relation to evidence which is to be given in accordance with a special measures direction.

(9A) If the court directs under subsection (9) that evidence is to be given by live link, it may also make such provision in that direction as it could make under section 24(1A) in a special measures direction.

(10) A magistrates' court inquiring into an offence as examining justices under section 6 of the Magistrates' Courts Act 1980 may consider any video recording in relation to which it is proposed to apply for a special measures direction providing for it to be admitted at the trial in accordance with this section.

(11) Nothing in this section affects the admissibility of any video recording which would be admissible apart from this section.

Important guidance is contained in *Achieving Best Evidence in Criminal Proceedings, Guidance on Interviewing Victims and Witnesses, and Guidance on Using Special Measures* which is available on the CPS website. It is of particular use if there is to be a challenge to the admissibility of all or part of recorded evidence in chief.

E6.8.2 *Live links*

The YJCEA 1999 s 24 states:

Youth Justice and Criminal Evidence Act 1999 s 24

24 Evidence by live link

(1) A special measures direction may provide for the witness to give evidence by means of a live link.

(1A) Such a direction may also provide for a specified person to accompany the witness while the witness is giving evidence by live link.

(1B) In determining who may accompany the witness, the court must have regard to the wishes of the witness.

(2) Where a direction provides for the witness to give evidence by means of a live link, the witness may not give evidence in any other way without the permission of the court.

(3) The court may give permission for the purposes of subsection (2) if it appears to the court to be in the interests of justice to do so, and may do so either—

    (a) on an application by a party to the proceedings, if there has been a material change of circumstances since the relevant time, or

    (b) of its own motion.

(4) In subsection (3) 'the relevant time' means—

    (a) the time when the direction was given, or

    (b) if a previous application has been made under that subsection, the time when the application (or last application) was made.

(5) Where in proceedings before a magistrates' court—

    (a) evidence is to be given by means of a live link in accordance with a special measures direction, but

    (b) suitable facilities for receiving such evidence are not available at any petty-sessional court-house in which that court can (apart from this subsection) lawfully sit,

the court may sit for the purposes of the whole or any part of those proceedings at a place where such facilities are available and which has been appointed for the purposes of this subsection by the justices acting for the petty sessions area for which the court acts.

(6) A place appointed under subsection (5) may be outside the petty sessions area for which it is appointed; but (if so) it is to be regarded as being in that area for the purpose of the jurisdiction of the justices acting for that area.

(7) In this section 'petty-sessional court-house' has the same meaning as in the Magistrates' Courts Act 1980 and 'petty sessions area' has the same meaning as in the Justices of the Peace Act 1997.

(8) In this Chapter 'live link' means a live television link or other arrangement whereby a witness, while absent from the courtroom or other place where the proceedings are being held, is able to see and hear a person there and to be seen and heard by the persons specified in section 23(2)(a) to (c).

E6.8.3 *Intermediaries for witnesses*

The YJCEA 1999 s 29 states:

Youth Justice and Criminal Evidence Act 1999 s 29

29 Examination of witness through intermediary

(1) A special measures direction may provide for any examination of the witness (however and wherever conducted) to be conducted through an interpreter or other person approved by the court for the purposes of this section ('an intermediary').

(2) The function of an intermediary is to communicate—

    (a) to the witness, questions put to the witness, and

    (b) to any person asking such questions, the answers given by the witness in reply to them, and to explain such questions or answers so far as necessary to enable them to be understood by the witness or person in question.

(3) Any examination of the witness in pursuance of subsection (1) must take place in the presence of such persons as rules of court or the direction may provide, but in circumstances in which—

(a) the judge or justices (or both) and legal representatives acting in the proceedings are able to see and hear the examination of the witness and to communicate with the intermediary, and

(b) (except in the case of a video recorded examination) the jury (if there is one) are able to see and hear the examination of the witness.

(4) Where two or more legal representatives are acting for a party to the proceedings, subsection (3)(a) is to be regarded as satisfied in relation to those representatives if at all material times it is satisfied in relation to at least one of them.

(5) A person may not act as an intermediary in a particular case except after making a declaration, in such form as may be prescribed by rules of court, that he will faithfully perform his function as intermediary.

(6) Subsection (1) does not apply to an interview of the witness which is recorded by means of a video recording with a view to its admission as evidence in chief of the witness; but a special measures direction may provide for such a recording to be admitted under section 27 if the interview was conducted through an intermediary and—

(a) that person complied with subsection (5) before the interview began, and

(b) the court's approval for the purposes of this section is given before the direction is given.

E7 Witnesses: Issue of Summons or Warrant

Magistrates' Courts Act 1980 s 97

Where a justice of the peace is satisfied that—

- (a) any person in England or Wales is likely to be able to give material evidence, or produce any document or thing likely to be material evidence, at the summary trial of an information or hearing of a complaint or of an application under the Adoption and Children Act 2002 (c 38) by a magistrates' court, and
- (b) it is in the interests of justice to issue a summons under this subsection to secure the attendance of that person to give evidence or produce the document or thing, the justice shall issue a summons directed to that person requiring him to attend before the court at the time and place appointed in the summons to give evidence or to produce the document or thing.

(2) If a justice of the peace is satisfied by evidence on oath of the matters mentioned in subsection (1) above, and also that it is probable that a summons under that subsection would not procure the attendance of the person in question, the justice may instead of issuing a summons issue a warrant to arrest that person and bring him before such a court as aforesaid at a time and place specified in the warrant; but a warrant shall not be issued under this subsection where the attendance is required for the hearing of a complaint or of an application under the Adoption and Children Act 2002 (c 38).

(2A) A summons may also be issued under subsection (1) above if the justice is satisfied that the person in question is outside the British Islands but no warrant shall be issued under subsection (2) above unless the justice is satisfied by evidence on oath that the person in question is in England or Wales

(2B) A justice may refuse to issue a summons under subsection (1) above in relation to the summary trial of an information if he is not satisfied that an application for the summons was made by a party to the case as soon as reasonably practicable after the accused pleaded not guilty.

(2C) In relation to the summary trial of an information, subsection (2) above shall have effect as if the reference to the matters mentioned in subsection (1) above included a reference to the matter mentioned in subsection (2B) above.

(3) On the failure of any person to attend before a magistrates' court in answer to a summons under this section, if—

- (a) the court is satisfied by evidence on oath that he is likely to be able to give material evidence or produce any document or thing likely to be material evidence in the proceedings; and
- (b) it is proved on oath, or in such other manner as may be prescribed, that he has been duly served with the summons, and that a reasonable sum has been paid or tendered to him for costs and expenses; and

> (c) it appears to the court that there is no just excuse for the failure, the
> court may issue a warrant to arrest him and bring him before the court
> at a time and place specified in the warrant.
> (4) If any person attending or brought before a magistrates' court refuses
> without just excuse to be sworn or give evidence, or to produce any docu-
> ment or thing, the court may commit him to custody until the expiration of
> such period not exceeding one month as may be specified in the warrant
> or until he sooner gives evidence or produces the document or thing or
> impose on him a fine not exceeding £2,500 or both.
> (5) A fine imposed under subsection (4) above shall be deemed, for the pur-
> poses of any enactment, to be a sum adjudged to be paid by a conviction.

The procedure for issue and withdrawal is set out in the Crim PR, Part 28. Application is made on the prescribed form. Where disclosure of evidence held by a third party is required application to the court must be made in accordance with these rules.

In *R v Reading Justices, ex parte Berkshire County Council* [1996] Cr App R 239 the nature of 'material evidence' was considered. The court gave the following guidance where the application is to produce a document or thing:

- To be material evidence documents must be relevant to the issues in the criminal proceedings and admissible as such in evidence;
- This does not apply to documents desired solely for the purpose of possible cross-examination;
- The party making the application must show that the documents are 'likely to be material' which involves a real possibility, although not necessarily a probability;
- This procedure should not be used as a disguised attempt at discovery.

This was illustrated in *R (Cunliffe) v Hastings Magistrates' Court & Others* [2006] EWHC 2081 (Admin) where the court said that a wit-ness summons to produce documents relating to the function and design of breath-testing machines should not have been issued as 'the documents requested could not be "material evidence" as they were not admissible without interpretation by other expert witnesses and would not have constituted evidence in the case per se'.

Part F
Sentencing

F1 Age of Offender

F1.1 Relevant age

The powers of the court on sentence depend on the age of the offender. The relevant age is the age on the date of conviction, that is the date on which the defendant pleads guilty or is found guilty (*R v Danga* [1992] 13 Cr App R (S) 408).

This principle applies to detention and training orders (*R v Cassidy* (2000) The Times, 13 October) and detention under the PCCSA 2000 s 91 (*R v Robinson* (1993) 14 Cr App R (S) 448).

F1.2 Age at date of offence

Where an offender crosses a significant age threshold between the date of the commission of the offence and the date of conviction, the starting point is the sentence that the defendant would have been likely to receive if he had been sentenced at the date of the commission of the offence; where the date of conviction is only a few months after the date of the offence it would rarely be appropriate to pass a longer sentence that that which could have been passed on the date of offence (*R v Ghafoor* [2002] EWCA Crim 1857, [2003] 1 Cr App R (S) 428). In *Ghafoor* a 17-year-old was involved in a serious public disturbance. He was jointly charged with adults on a charge of riot. Riot is not a grave crime for which detention under the PCCSA 2000 s 91(3) is available but the appellant was sent to the Crown Court for trial as he was jointly charged with adults. He pleaded guilty in the Crown Court after he had attained 18. His sentence of four years' detention in a young offender institution was quashed and eighteen months' detention in a young offender institution substituted. The court held that if he had been sentenced at the time of the offence the maximum sentence would have been a twenty-four-month detention and training order. With the discount for a guilty plea, the sentence passed would not have been more than eighteen months and that should have been the sentence passed in the Crown Court notwithstanding the fact that the appellant had attained 18. The fact that the sentence available to a 17-year-old is deemed to be inadequate to reflect the gravity of the offence is not in itself a reason for departing from that starting point (*R v Britton* [2006] EWCA Crim 2875, [2007] 1 Cr App R (S) 121).

The relevant case law is usefully summarized in the definitive sentencing guideline *Overarching Principles: Sentencing Youths* (2009):

F1 Age of Offender

5.1 There will be occasions when an increase in the age of an offender will result in the maximum sentence on the date of *conviction* being greater than that available on the date on which the offence was *committed*.

5.2 In such circumstances, the approach should be:
- where an offender crosses a relevant age threshold between the date on which the offence was committed and the date of conviction or sentence, a court should take as its starting point the sentence likely to have been imposed on the date on which the offence was committed;
- where an offender attains the age of 18 after committing the offence but before conviction, section 142 of the Criminal Justice Act 2003 applies (whilst section 37 of the 1998 Act and section 44 of the 1933 Act...apply to those aged under 18) and the sentencing disposal has to take account of the matters set out in that section;
- it will be rare for a court to have to consider passing a sentence more severe than the maximum it would have had jurisdiction to pass at the time the offence was committed even where an offender has subsequently attained the age of 18;
- however, a sentence at or close to that maximum may be appropriate, especially where a serious offence was committed by an offender close to the age threshold.

For the application of this principle to the age thresholds relevant to detention and training orders see **F7.2.1**.

F1.3 Determining age

If there is any doubt about the age of the offender this will normally have been resolved at the start of the proceedings (see **D1**). If any doubt about the offender's real age is raised for the first time at the sentencing hearing the court must make a determination before proceeding to sentence.

The PCCSA 2000 s 164(1) provides:

> ### Powers of Criminal Courts (Sentencing) Act 2000 s 164(1)
>
> For the purposes of any provision of this Act which requires the determination of the age of a person by the court or the Secretary of State, his age shall be deemed to be that which it appears to the court or (as the case may be) the Secretary of State to be after considering any available evidence.

This provision will apply to detention and training orders as well as detention under the PCCSA 2000 s 91. It will also apply to discharges, referral orders, and reparation orders. Similar statutory provisions apply to youth rehabilitation orders (CJIA 2008 s 7(2)) and dangerous offender sentences (CJA 2003 s 305(2)).

Where all the evidence before a sentencing court indicates a particular age, the sentence is not invalidated by the later discovery of the correct date of birth of the offender (*R v Brown* (1989) 11 Cr App R (S) 263). However, where a sentencing court does have evidence of the offender's correct date of birth but that is overlooked and the court proceeds to pass an invalid sentence on the basis of an incorrect age, the sentence will not be allowed to stand (*R v Harris* (1989) 12 Cr App R (S) 318).

F2 Anti-social Behaviour Order on Conviction

This section deals with the making of an order against anti-social behaviour on conviction in the youth, adult magistrates', or Crown Court under the provisions of the CDA 1998 s 1C. Applications on complaint in the adult magistrates' court for an anti-social behaviour order under the CDA 1998 s 1, sometimes known as 'stand-alone' orders, are beyond the scope of this book.

F2.1 Notice

The Crim PR r 50.3 requires the prosecutor to give notice, on a prescribed form, of the intention to apply for an anti-social behaviour order following conviction.

The notice must:

• summarize the relevant facts;
• identify the evidence in support on which the prosecutor relies;
• attach any evidence not previously served; and
• specify the terms of the proposed order.

The court may also make an order of its own motion. There is power to adjourn the proceedings for consideration of the issues to another date. A warrant may be issued if the young person does not then attend.

F2.2 Interim orders

If the court decides to adjourn the proceedings it may make an interim order if it considers that it is just to do so.

F2.3 Criteria

The CDA 1998 s 1C provides:

> ### Crime and Disorder Act 1998 s 1C
>
> (1) This section applies where a person (the 'offender') is convicted of a relevant offence.
> (2) If the court considers—
>   (a) that the offender has acted, at any time since the commencement date, in an anti-social manner, that is to say in a manner that caused or was likely to cause harassment, alarm or distress to one or more persons not of the same household as himself, and

    (b) that an order under this section is necessary to protect persons in any place in England and Wales from further anti-social acts by him, it may make an order which prohibits the offender from doing anything described in the order.

(3) The court may make an order under this section—
    (a) if the prosecutor asks it to do so, or
    (b) if the court thinks it is appropriate to do so.

(3A) For the purpose of deciding whether to make an order under this section the court may consider evidence led by the prosecution and the defence.

(3B) It is immaterial whether evidence led in pursuance of subsection (3A) would have been admissible in the proceedings in which the offender was convicted.

(4) An order under this section shall not be made except—
    (a) in addition to a sentence imposed in respect of the relevant offence; or
    (b) in addition to an order discharging him conditionally.

(4A) The court may adjourn any proceedings in relation to an order under this section even after sentencing the offender.

(4B) If the offender does not appear for any adjourned proceedings, the court may further adjourn the proceedings or may issue a warrant for his arrest.

(4C) But the court may not issue a warrant for the offender's arrest unless it is satisfied that he has had adequate notice of the time and place of the adjourned proceedings.

(5) An order under this section takes effect on the day on which it is made, but the court may provide in any such order that such requirements of the order as it may specify shall, during any period when the offender is detained in legal custody, be suspended until his release from that custody.
    ...

(9A) The council for the local government area in which a person in respect of whom an anti-social behaviour order has been made resides or appears to reside may bring proceedings under section 1(10) (as applied by subsection (9) above) for breach of an order under subsection (2) above.

(9AA) Sections 1AA and 1AB apply in relation to orders under this section, with any necessary modifications, as they apply in relation to anti-social behaviour orders.

(9AB) In their application by virtue of subsection (9AA), sections 1AA(1A)(b) and 1AB(6) have effect as if the words 'by complaint' were omitted.

(9AC) ...

(9B) Subsection (9C) applies in relation to proceedings in which an order under subsection (2) is made against a child or young person who is convicted of an offence.

(9C) In so far as the proceedings relate to the making of the order—
    (a) section 49 of the Children and Young Persons Act 1933 (c 12) (restrictions on reports of proceedings in which children and young persons are concerned) does not apply in respect of the child or young person against whom the order is made;

(b) section 39 of that Act (power to prohibit publication of certain matter) does so apply.

(9) In this section—

'child' and 'young person' have the same meaning as in the Children and Young Persons Act 1933 (c 12);

'the commencement date' has the same meaning as in section 1 above;

'the court' in relation to an offender means—

(a) the court by or before which he is convicted of the relevant offence; or

(b) if he is committed to the Crown Court to be dealt with for that offence, the Crown Court; and

'relevant offence' means an offence committed after the coming into force of section 64 of the Police Reform Act 2002 (c 30).

Before making an order the court must be satisfied that:

- the offender has acted in a manner that has caused or is likely to cause harassment, alarm or distress to one or more persons not of the same household as himself, and
- that an order is necessary to protect persons in any place in England and Wales from further anti-social acts by him.

F2.4 Procedure

The court will already have heard evidence in relation to the offence and it may hear evidence under the civil evidence provisions as part of the application. The standard of proof is to the criminal standard.

Evidence of post-complaint behaviour is admissible both to show whether a person has acted in an anti-social manner and whether an order is necessary: *Birmingham City Council v Dixon* [2009] EWHC 761 (Admin).

The findings of fact which give rise to the making of the order must be recorded by the court: *R v W and F* [2006] EWCA Crim 686. The findings of fact are likely to form the basis of the terms of the order.

In *R v Dyer* [2010] EWCA Crim 2096 it was suggested that assistance in considering the making of an order should be sought from the Judicial Studies Board guide *Anti-Social Behaviour Orders: A Guide for the Judiciary*, available at <www.judiciary.gov.uk>.

F2.5 Necessity of an order

The sentence imposed by the court on conviction will be a relevant consideration.

The court should not make an order where the underlying objective was to give the court higher sentencing powers in the event of future similar offending: *R v Sunderland Youth Court* [2003] EWHC 2385.

It is not necessary to make an order not to commit a specified criminal offence if the sentence which could be passed on conviction for the offence should be sufficient deterrence: *R v Boness and others* [2005] EWCA Crim 2395.

F2.6 Length of the order

The minimum length is two years and there is no maximum. The court may suspend any requirements of the order until release from a period of custody. The age of the offender is a consideration in considering the appropriate length: *R v H, Stevens and Lovegrove* [2006] EWCA Crim 255.

F2.7 Terms of the order

The terms of the order must be:

- clear and easily understood;
- enforceable;
- commensurate with the seriousness of the offence;
- commensurate with the risk of future conduct; and
- the prohibitions must be tailor-made to the facts of the case and the circumstances of the offender.

Whilst an order may last a minimum of two years, not all the terms in the order need do so: *R (Lonergan) v Lewes Crown Court* [2005] 2 All ER 362.

In *R v McGrath* [2005] EWCA Crim 353 an order containing provisions preventing a prolific offender from entering any car park in three counties, from trespassing, and from having in his possession tools or implements capable of being used for breaking into cars was too wide and not justified.

In *R v H, Stevens and Lovegrove* [2006] EWCA Crim 255 an order excluding a young offender from entering an area which included his home was said to be likely to reduce his prospects of successful rehabilitation.

In *T v CPS* [2006] EWHC 728 (Admin) the terms of an order made on a 13-year-old which prevented him from 'acting in an anti-social manner in the City of Manchester' were said to be too vague and lacking in clarity. It was important that the offender would be able understand the terms of the order.

In *R (Cooke) v Director of Public Prosecutions* [2008] EWHC 2703 (Admin) the court held that an order was not appropriate in relation to an offender who due to mental incapacity was not able to understand its terms, as such an order would fail to protect the public and could therefore not be said to be necessary to protect others.

A condition not to cause harassment, alarm, or distress was too imprecise; conditions should be clear as to what behaviour the order was seeking to discourage: *Heron v Plymouth City Council* [2009] EWHC 3562 (Admin).

F2.8 Review

An order made in respect of a youth under the age of 17 years must be reviewed by the police and local authority on an annual basis. The review period begins on the day in which the order is made. The YOT should be involved in any review. The review must consider:

- the extent of compliance;
- the adequacy of support available to the offender; and
- any other matters relevant as to whether the order should be varied or discharged.

F2.9 Reporting restrictions

The reporting restrictions which automatically apply in the youth court do not apply to the making of an order under the CDA s 1C. The court has a discretionary power to impose an order under the CYPA 1933 s 39 for which see **D11**.

F2.10 Appeal

Appeal is to the Crown Court. The Crown Court will consider the necessity of an order and can also consider the terms of the order.

 See *Blackstone's Criminal Practice 2014* **D25.1–D25.44**

F3 **Bind Over**

F3.1 **Criteria**

Any person before the court, as defendant or witness (provided that they have given evidence), can be bound over. The court has common law powers to do this of its own motion as a measure of preventive justice where the person's conduct amounts to a breach of the peace involving violence or an imminent threat of violence or that there is a real risk of violence in the future. The violence feared may be from the person being bound over or a third party as a result of their conduct.

The MCA 1980 s 115 contains the provisions relating to bind overs following a complaint. This is not a matter assigned to the youth court under the CYPA 1933 s 46 and would therefore be heard in the adult magistrates' court.

A bind over can only be made by consent and the court should give the person who may be subject to the bind over the opportunity to make representations. Refusal to consent can result in committal to prison in the case of an adult but there is no such power for a youth. In *Veater v Glennan* [1981] 2 All ER 307 it was confirmed that there was no sanction to compel a binding over where youths aged 14 and 15 years refused to consent. The order is to keep the peace. The previously used term 'to be of good behaviour' has been held to be too imprecise to be enforceable: *Hashman and Harrup v UK* [2000] Crim LR 185. Where a youth consents the court still has power to bind over: *Conlan v Oxford* [1983] 79 Cr App R 157.

F3.2 **Practice direction**

The Consolidated Criminal Practice Direction at paragraph III.31 states:

> ### **Consolidated Criminal Practice Direction paras III.31.2, III.31.3, III.31.4, and III.31.8**
>
> **Binding over to keep the peace**
>
> III.31.2
> Before imposing a binding over order, the court must be satisfied that a breach of the peace involving violence, or an imminent threat of violence, has occurred, or that there is a real risk of violence in the future.
> Such violence may be perpetrated by the individual who will be subject to the order, or by a third party as a natural consequence of the individual's conduct.

III.31.3
In light of the judgment in Hashman and Harrup, courts should no longer bind an individual over 'to be of good behaviour'. Rather than binding an individual over to 'keep the peace' in general terms, the court should identify the specific conduct or activity from which the individual must refrain.

Written order
III.31.4
When making an order binding an individual over to refrain from specified types of conduct or activities, the details of that conduct or those activities should be specified by the court in a written order served on all relevant parties. The court should state its reasons for the making of the order, its length and the amount of the recognisance. The length of the order should be proportionate to the harm sought to be avoided and should not generally exceed 12 months.

Burden of proof
III.31.8
The court should be satisfied beyond reasonable doubt of the matters complained of before a binding over order may be imposed. Where the procedure has been commenced on complaint, the burden of proof rests on the complainant. In all other circumstances the burden of proof rests on the prosecution.

The court will set a recognizance to be forfeit on breach. If the sum set is more than trivial, enquiry should be made in relation to means; a failure to do so may give rise to a successful challenge: *R v Lincoln Crown Court, ex parte Jude* [1997] 3 All ER 737.

In *R v Middlesex Crown Court, ex parte Khan* (1997) 161 JP 240 the court held:

> if a judge is going to require a man to be bound over in circumstances where he has been acquitted, it is particularly important that he should be satisfied beyond a reasonable doubt that the man poses a potential threat to other persons and that he is a man of violence.

 See *Blackstone's Criminal Practice 2014* **E13**

F4 Committal for Sentence

There is no general power to commit a youth defendant to the Crown Court for sentence. There are, however, a number of provisions which allow committal in limited circumstances. These are:

- Committal for sentence for grave crime after guilty plea at plea before venue procedure: PCCSA 2000 s 3B
- Committal of specified offence for sentence (dangerous youth offender): PCCSA 2000 s 3C
- Committal because offender subject to existing Crown Court order
- Committal for sentence for confiscation procedure: Proceeds of Crime Act 2002 s 70.

If a defendant attains 18 before the date of conviction then the committal powers applicable to adults apply (see **I6.3**).

F4.1 Committal of grave crime for sentence

Where a person under 18 charged with a grave crime has indicated a guilty plea at a plea before venue hearing, the court may commit him for sentence if the court is of the opinion that the offence, or the combination of the offence and one or more offences associated with it, was such that the Crown Court should have power to deal with the offender by imposing a sentence under the PCCSA 2000 s 91: PCCSA 2000 s 3B.

Where an offender is committed for sentence under s 3B, s 5A provides that the Crown Court shall inquire into the circumstances of the case and may deal with the offender in any way in which it could deal with him if he had just been convicted of the offence on indictment before the court.

Where the court commits an offender under this provision, the PCCSA 2000 s 6 shall also apply. This permits the court to commit the offender to the Crown Court to be dealt with in respect of any other offence whatsoever in respect of which the committing court has power to deal with him (being an offence of which he has been convicted by that or any other court).

An offender cannot be committed for sentence under this provision if convicted after a summary trial.

F4.2 Committal of specified offence for sentence

After the summary trial of a specified offence a person under 18 is convicted of the offence, the court must commit the offender to the Crown Court for sentence if it appears to the court that the criteria for the imposition of a dangerous offender sentence would be met: PCCSA 2000 s 3C(2).

The criteria as set out in the CJA 2003 s 228B are that:

- the court considers that there is a significant risk to members of the public of serious harm occasioned by the commission by the offender of further specified offences;
- if the court were to impose an extended sentence of detention, the term that it would specify as the appropriate custodial term would be at least four years.

These criteria are considered in more detail at **H5.3**.

Where an offender is committed for sentence under s 3C, s 5A provides that the Crown Court shall inquire into the circumstances of the case and may deal with the offender in any way in which it could deal with him if he had just been convicted of the offence on indictment before the court.

Where the court commits an offender under this provision, the PCCSA 2000 s 6 shall also apply. This permits the court to commit the offender to the Crown Court to be dealt with in respect of any other offence whatsoever in respect of which the committing court has power to deal with him (being an offence of which he has been convicted by that or any other court).

F4.3 Committal where offender already subject to certain Crown Court orders

The youth court or adult magistrates' court has the power to commit a youth defendant to the Crown Court for sentence where he:

- is subject to a conditional discharge imposed by the Crown Court and the new offence was committed during the period of the discharge: PCCSA 2000 s 13(5); and
- is convicted of the new offence whilst subject to a youth rehabilitation order imposed by the Crown Court: CJIA 2008 Sch 2 para 18 (see **F34.9**).

When the Crown Court deals with the new offence under either of these provisions it only has the sentencing powers available to the youth court.

F4.4 Committal for sentence under the Proceeds of Crime Act 2002 s 70

A youth court or adult magistrates' court has no power to make a confiscation order. A youth court or adult magistrates' court may commit a youth offender to the Crown Court for the purposes of activating the confiscation regime under the Proceeds of Crime Act 2002. For youth defendants this is most likely to arise in drug dealing cases. This power exists even where a discharge is considered the proper sentence (see *R v Varma* [2012] UKSC 42 above).

In the event that the prosecution wishes to proceed with confiscation proceedings the court *must* commit the offender to the Crown Court for sentence.

Proceeds of Crime Act 2002 s 70

(1) This section applies if—
  (a) a defendant is convicted of an offence by a magistrates' court, and
  (b) the prosecutor asks the court to commit the defendant to the Crown Court with a view to a confiscation order being considered under section 6.
(2) In such a case the magistrates' court—
  (a) must commit the defendant to the Crown Court in respect of the offence, and
  (b) may commit him to the Crown Court in respect of any other offence falling within subsection (3).
(3) An offence falls within this subsection if—
  (a) the defendant has been convicted of it by the magistrates' court or any other court, and
  (b) the magistrates' court has power to deal with him in respect of it.
(4) If a committal is made under this section in respect of an offence or offences—
  (a) section 6 applies accordingly, and
  (b) the committal operates as a committal of the defendant to be dealt with by the Crown Court in accordance with section 71.
(5) If a committal is made under this section in respect of an offence for which (apart from this section) the magistrates' court could have committed the defendant for sentence under section 3(2) of the Sentencing Act (offences triable either way) the court must state whether it would have done so.
(6) A committal under this section may be in custody or on bail.

When committal for sentence is under s 70, the Crown Court must enquire into the circumstances of the case and may deal with the youth defendant in any way in which the youth court could deal with him if it had just convicted him of the offence: s 71(3).

F5 **Compensation Order**

Powers of Criminal Courts (Sentencing) Act 2000 s 130(1)–(10)

(1) A court by or before which a person is convicted of an offence, instead of or in addition to dealing with him in any other way, may, on application or otherwise, make an order (in this Act referred to as a 'compensation order') requiring him—

   (a) to pay compensation for any personal injury, loss or damage resulting from that offence or any other offence which is taken into consideration by the court in determining sentence; or

   (b) to make payments for funeral expenses or bereavement in respect of a death resulting from any such offence, other than a death due to an accident arising out of the presence of a motor vehicle on a road; but this is subject to the following provisions of this section and to section 131 below.

(2) Where the person is convicted of an offence the sentence for which is fixed by law or falls to be imposed under 110(2) or 111(2) above, section 51A(2) of the Firearms Act 1968, section 225, 226, 227 or 228 of the Criminal Justice Act 2003 or section 29(4) or (6) of the Violent Crime Reduction Act 2006, subsection (1) above shall have effect as if the words 'instead of or' were omitted.

(3) A court shall give reasons, on passing sentence, if it does not make a compensation order in a case where this section empowers it to do so.

(4) Compensation under subsection (1) above shall be of such amount as the court considers appropriate, having regard to any evidence and to any representations that are made by or on behalf of the accused or the prosecutor.

(5) In the case of an offence under the Theft Act 1968 or Fraud Act 2006, where the property in question is recovered, any damage to the property occurring while it was out of the owner's possession shall be treated for the purposes of subsection (1) above as having resulted from the offence, however and by whomever the damage was caused.

(6) A compensation order may only be made in respect of injury, loss or damage (other than loss suffered by a person's dependants in consequence of his death) which was due to an accident arising out of the presence of a motor vehicle on a road, if—

   (a) it is in respect of damage which is treated by subsection (5) above as resulting from an offence under the Theft Act 1968 or Fraud Act 2006; or

   (b) it is in respect of injury, loss or damage as respects which—

      (i) the offender is uninsured in relation to the use of the vehicle; and

      (ii) compensation is not payable under any arrangements to which the Secretary of State is a party.

(7) Where a compensation order is made in respect of injury, loss or damage due to an accident arising out of the presence of a motor vehicle on a road, the amount to be paid may include an amount representing the whole or part of any loss of or reduction in preferential rates of insurance attributable to the accident.

(8) A vehicle the use of which is exempted from insurance by section 144 of the Road Traffic Act 1988 is not uninsured for the purposes of subsection (6) above.

(9) A compensation order in respect of funeral expenses may be made for the benefit of any one who incurred the expenses.

(10) A compensation order in respect of bereavement may be made only for the benefit of a person for whose benefit a claim for damages for bereavement could be made under section 1A of the Fatal Accidents Act 1976; and the amount of compensation in respect of bereavement shall not exceed the amount for the time being specified in section 1A (3) of that Act.

F5.1 Principles

A magistrates' court, which includes the youth court, can order compensation up to a maximum of £5,000 for each offence, and may also award compensation in relation to offences taken into consideration (but may not exceed the total arrived at by multiplying offences × £5,000).

In relation to motor vehicle damage the maximum payable will generally be the excess not paid by the Motor Insurers Bureau (currently £300), save where it is in respect to a vehicle stolen or taken without consent and there is damage to that vehicle, or the claim is not covered by the MIB.

If the amount of compensation is not agreed, the prosecution must be in a position to call evidence. In cases where the loss is unclear or subject to complex argument, the best course of action is to leave the matter to the civil courts to resolve (*R v Horsham Justices, ex parte Richards* [1985] 2 All ER 1114). In *R v Bewick* [2007] EWCA Crim 3297 the court observed that it would generally not be appropriate to resolve compensation applications where it was necessary to hear from a third party in evidence. A court can, however, make a common sense determination (eg £50 for a small broken window).

F5.2 Assessment of means

In determining whether to make a compensation order against any person, and in determining the amount to be paid by any person under such an order, the court shall have regard to his means so far as they appear or are known to the court. An order made in the absence of a means enquiry is at risk of being ruled unlawful (*R v Gray* [2011] EWCA 225).

Where the court considers:

- that it would be appropriate both to impose a fine and to make a compensation order; but
- that the offender has insufficient means to pay both an appropriate fine and appropriate compensation, the court shall give preference to compensation (though it may impose a fine as well).

Save where a sentence of custody impacts on the offender's ability to pay, there is nothing wrong in principle with imposing compensation in addition to a custodial penalty.

F5.3 Power to order payment by a parent or guardian

The court may order a parent or guardian to pay the compensation. For the exercise of this power see **J3.1**.

F5.4 Suggested levels of compensation

The *Magistrates' Court Sentencing Guidelines* (2008) set out scales for the award of compensation. The limited financial resources of most youth defendants mean that the suggested levels of compensation are only likely to be relevant if a parent or guardian has the necessary financial resources.

 See *Blackstone's Criminal Practice 2014* **E16**

F6 **Deferment of Sentence**

F6.1 **Criteria**

The court can defer sentence, on one occasion, for a maximum period of six months to enable the court to assess the offender's capacity to change or carry out reparation to the victim.

F6.2 **Power to defer**

The power to defer under the PCCSA 2000 ss 1–1D shall be exercisable only if:

(a) the offender consents;
(b) the offender undertakes to comply with any requirements as to his conduct during the period of the deferment that the court considers it appropriate to impose; and
(c) the court is satisfied, having regard to the nature of the offence and the character and circumstances of the offender, that it would be in the interests of justice to exercise the power.

F6.3 **Requirements**

The court may include a residence requirement during the whole or part of the period of deferment: PCCSA 2000 s1A(1).

The court may appoint a supervisor to monitor the offender's compliance with any requirements and to report to the court: PCCSA 2000 s 1A(3)–(5). This is likely to be a member of the YOT.

F6.4 **Sentencing Council Guidance**

The current regime was introduced by the CJA 2003 and the Sentencing Council issued guidance on their use:

- The conditions imposed could be specific requirements as set out in the provisions for community sentences, or requirements that are drawn more widely. They should be specific, measurable conditions so that the offender knows exactly what is required and the court can assess compliance; the restriction on liberty should be limited to ensure that the offender has a reasonable expectation of being able to comply.
- The use of deferred sentences should be predominantly for a small group of cases close to a significant threshold where, should the defendant be prepared to adapt his behaviour in a way clearly

specified by the sentencer, the court may be prepared to impose a lesser sentence.

- Given the need for clarity in the mind of the offender and the possibility of sentence by another court, the court should give a clear indication (and make a written record) of the type of sentence it would be minded to impose if it had not decided to defer and ensure that the offender understands the consequences of failure to comply with the court's wishes during the deferral period.
- A court may impose any conditions during the period of deferment that it considers appropriate.
- When deferring sentence, the sentencer must make clear the consequence of not complying with any requirements and should indicate the type of sentence it would be minded to impose. Sentencers should impose specific, measurable conditions that do not involve a serious restriction on liberty.

F6.5 Failing to attend

Where sentence is deferred the case is adjourned and the offender is not on bail. A warrant can be issued, PCC(S)A 2000 s 1(7), if the offender fails to attend for sentence. The court also has the option of issuing a summons.

F6.6 Failing to comply

If the offender fails to comply with any of the terms of the deferment he may be dealt with before the end of the period of deferment.

If the offender reoffends before the period of deferment has expired he may be dealt with for the deferred matter before the end of the period of the deferment.

 See *Blackstone's Criminal Practice 2014* **D20.103–D20.109**

F7 **Detention and Training Order**

F7.1 **Introduction**

The detention and training order is the only custodial sentence that can be imposed in the youth court. It is also available in the Crown Court.

The order may be imposed on a defendant who has attained the age of 12 by the date of conviction but in the case of offenders under the age of 15 the court must determine that they are persistent offenders.

By the PCCSA 2000 s 83 a detention and training order cannot be imposed by a youth court or a Crown Court if the offender is not legally represented unless the youth offender has refused to apply for legal aid or the legal aid has been withdrawn as a result of his conduct. An offender is only deemed to be legally represented for the purposes of s 83 if he has a solicitor or barrister to represent him in the court at some time after he is found guilty and before he is sentenced.

The PCCSA 2000 s 100 provides:

> ### Powers of Criminal Courts (Sentencing) Act 2000 s 100
>
> (1) Subject to sections 90 and 91 above, sections 226 and 226B of the Criminal Justice Act 2003, and subsection (2) below, where—
>   (a) a child or young person (that is to say, any person aged under 18) is convicted of an offence which is punishable with imprisonment in the case of a person aged 21 or over, and
>   (b) the court is of the opinion that subsection (2) of section 152 of the Criminal Justice Act 2003 applies or the case falls within subsection (3) of that section,
>   the sentence that the court is to pass is a detention and training order.
> (1A) Subsection (1) applies with the omission of paragraph (b) in the case of an offence the sentence for which falls to be imposed under these provisions—
>   (a) section 1A(5) of the Prevention of Crime Act 1953 (minimum sentence for offence of threatening with offensive weapon in public);
>   (b) section 139AA(7) of the Criminal Justice Act 1988 (minimum sentence for offence of threatening with article with blade or point or offensive weapon).
> (2) A court shall not make a detention and training order—
>   (a) in the case of an offender under the age of 15 at the time of the conviction, unless it is of the opinion that he is a persistent offender;
>   (b) in the case of an offender under the age of 12 at that time, unless—
>   (i) it is of the opinion that only a custodial sentence would be adequate to protect the public from further offending by him; and
>   (ii) the offence was committed on or after such date as the Secretary of State may by order appoint.

> (3) A detention and training order is an order that the offender in respect of whom it is made shall be subject, for the term specified in the order, to a period of detention and training followed by a period of supervision.

For the purposes of a detention and training order the relevant age is the age on the date of conviction, that is when the offender pleads guilty or is found guilty at trial: *R v Cassidy* (2000) The Times, 13 October. Where an offender attains 18 between the date of conviction and the date of sentence the appropriate custodial sentence would therefore be a detention and training order rather than detention in a young offender institution. For the position where the offender attains 18 before conviction see **I6.2.2**.

F7.1.1 *Offenders under the age of 12 at the time of conviction*

At the time of writing no order has been made pursuant to s 100(2)(b)(ii) therefore a detention and training order is not available for this age group.

F7.2 Custody threshold

Where a mandatory sentence is not applicable, the CJA 2003 s 156 provides:

> **Criminal Justice Act 2003 s 156**
>
> (2) The court must not pass a custodial sentence unless it is of the opinion that the offence, or the combination of the offence and one or more offences associated with it, was so serious that neither a fine alone nor a community sentence can be justified for the offence.

A written pre-sentence report must be considered before a detention and training order can be imposed on an offender aged under 18 (see **F24.2**).

The definitive sentencing guideline *Overarching Principles: Sentencing Youths* at paras 11.5–11.18 considers the custody threshold when sentencing young offenders. In summary the guidance suggests the following general principles:

- a custodial sentence must be imposed only as a 'measure of <u>last resort</u>' (para 11.5);
- for a first-time offender who has pleaded guilty, in most circumstances a referral order will be the most appropriate sentence (para 11.6);

- a custodial sentence is most likely to be unavoidable where it is necessary to protect the public from serious harm (para 11.8);
- even where the threshold is crossed, a court is not required to impose a custodial sentence (para 11.10).

The guideline at para 11.11 states:

> Before deciding to impose a custodial sentence on a young offender, the court must ensure that all the statutory tests are satisfied—namely:
>
> (i) that the offender cannot properly be dealt with by a fine alone or by a youth rehabilitation order,
>
> (ii) that a youth rehabilitation order with intensive supervision and surveillance or with fostering cannot be justified, and
>
> (iii) that custody is the last resort and in doing so should take account of the circumstances, age and maturity of the young offender.

F7.2.1 *Persistent offender*   ✗ 3 in past 12 months.

In the case of offenders aged 12 to 14 at the time of conviction, a detention and training order may only be imposed if the custody threshold is met and the court deems the offender to be a persistent offender (PCCSA 2000 s 100(2)). There is no statutory definition of a 'persistent offender'. A court may take into account not only convictions but also cautions (*R v B* [2001] Cr App R (S) 113). The definitive sentencing guideline *Overarching Principles: Sentencing Youths* (2009) considers the meaning of 'persistent offender' at paras 6.4–6.6. It suggests that the term is likely to be satisfied where the offender has been convicted of, or made subject to a pre-court disposal that involves an admission or finding of guilt in relation to, imprisonable offences on at least three occasions in the past twelve months.

In the case of *R v Ghafoor* [2002] EWCA Crim 1857, [2003] 1 Cr App R (S) 428 it was held that where an offender crosses a significant age threshold between the date of the commission of the offence and the date of conviction, the starting point for determining the sentence is the sentence that he would have been likely to receive if he had been sentenced at the date of the offence (see **F1.2**). The Court of Appeal has held that the principle in *Ghafoor* means that a detention and training order should not be imposed on a youth offender who was 14 on the date of the offence but 15 on the date of conviction if he could not be deemed to be a persistent offender at the time of the offence (see *R v LM* [2002] EWCA Crim 3047, [2003] 2 Cr App R (S) 26, and *R v NH* [2004] EWCA 2674). The contrary view was taken by the Court of Appeal in *R v Jahmarl* [2004] EWCA Crim 2199, [2005] 1 Cr App R (S) 96. The appeal concerned an offence of robbery for which the court had decided that twelve months' detention under the PCCSA 2000 s 91 could properly be imposed. Having received advice that the regime under a detention and training order would be more appropriate for the 15-year-old appellant the court considered that a detention and training order should be imposed rather than a period of s 91 detention. It is arguable that this decision is based on its particular facts and in any event has no application to cases where s 91 detention is not a sentencing option.

F7.2.2 *Length of order*

The PCCSA 2000 s 101 provides:

Powers of Criminal Courts (Sentencing) Act 2000 s 101

(1) Subject to subsection (2) below, the term of a detention and training order made in respect of an offence (whether by a magistrates' court or otherwise) shall be 4, 6, 8, 10, 12, 18 or 24 months.

(2) The term of a detention and training order may not exceed the maximum term of imprisonment that the Crown Court could (in the case of an offender aged 21 or over) impose for the offence.

The minimum order applies to each offence not the aggregate sentence: *R v Ganley* (unreported, 9 April 2000). The minimum term therefore creates a much higher custody threshold for young offenders than that applicable to adult offenders. As the maximum custodial sentence for an adult is a term of three months' imprisonment, a youth convicted of criminal damage to the value of less than £5,000 is not liable to a custodial sentence in the youth court: *Pye v Leeds Youth Court* [2006] EWHC 2527 (Admin). The same principle also applies to (amongst others) the following offences:

- failure to surrender (Bail Act 1976 s 6—maximum penalty: three months);
- being found on enclosed premises (Vagrancy Act 1824 s 4—three months);
- motor vehicle interference (Criminal Attempts Act 1981 s 9—three months);
- obstructing a police officer (Police Act 1996 s 89(2)—one month);
- refusing to give COZART drugs sample (Police and Criminal Evidence Act 1984 s 63C—one month); and
- refusing to leave dispersal area (Anti-Social Behaviour Act 2003 s 32—one month).

F7.2.3 *Consecutive orders*

A court may impose a consecutive detention and training order. The PCCSA 2000 s 101 provides:

Powers of Criminal Courts (Sentencing) Act 2000 s 101

(3) Subject to subsections (4) and (6) below, a court making a detention and training order may order that its term shall commence on the expiry of the term of any other detention and training order made by that or any other court.

(4) A court shall not make in respect of an offender a detention and training order the effect of which would be that he would be subject to detention and training orders for a term which exceeds 24 months.

(5) Where the term of the detention and training orders to which an offender would otherwise be subject exceeds 24 months, the excess shall be treated as remitted.

(6) A court making a detention and training order shall not order that its term shall commence on the expiry of the term of a detention and training order under which the period of supervision has already begun (under section 103(1) below).

(7) Where a detention and training order ('the new order') is made in respect of an offender who is subject to a detention and training order under which the period of supervision has begun ('the old order'), the old order shall be disregarded in determining—

(a) for the purposes of subsection (4) above whether the effect of the new order would be that the offender would be subject to detention and training orders for a term which exceeds twenty-four months; and

(b) for the purposes of subsection (5) above whether the term of the detention and training orders to which the offender would (apart from that subsection) be subject exceeds twenty-four months.

Where consecutive orders are imposed, the term of each order must be of a length specified in s 101(1), however, there is no further requirement that the aggregate sentence must also be of a length specified in that subsection: *R v Norris* [2001] 1 Cr App (S) 401, (2000) 164 JP 689. This is the case whether the orders are imposed on the same occasion or on different occasions.

A court imposing detention and training orders for summary offences is not restricted by the MCA 1980 s 133, and therefore may impose a series of consecutive detention and training orders amounting in aggregate to more than six months (*C v DPP* [2001] EWHC 453 (Admin), [2002] 1 Cr App R (S) 189).

F7.3 Taking remand time into account

Remand time will not be deducted from the time to be served by the custodial institution as happens with adult offenders. Instead the court is required to take into account the time spent on remand in custody when calculating the length of the order.

F7 Detention and Training Order

The PCCSA s 101 provides:

Powers of Criminal Courts (Sentencing) Act 2000 s 101

(8) In determining the term of a detention and training order for an offence, the court shall take account of any period for which the offender has been remanded—

    (a) in custody, or

    (b) on bail subject to a qualifying curfew condition and an electronic monitoring condition (within the meaning of section 240A of the Criminal Justice Act 2003), in connection with the offence, or any other offence the charge for which was founded on the same facts or evidence.

(9) Where a court proposes to make detention and training orders in respect of an offender for two or more offences—

    (a) subsection (8) above shall not apply; but

    (b) in determining the total term of the detention and training orders it proposes to make in respect of the offender, the court shall take account of the total period (if any) for which he has been remanded as mentioned in that subsection in connection with any of those offences, or any other offence the charge for which was founded on the same facts or evidence.

(10) Once a period of remand has, under subsection (8) or (9) above, been taken account of in relation to a detention and training order made in respect of an offender for any offence or offences, it shall not subsequently be taken account of (under either of those subsections) in relation to such an order made in respect of the offender for any other offence or offences.

(11) Any reference in subsection (8) or (9) above to an offender's being remanded in custody is a reference to his being—

    (a) held in police detention;

    (b) remanded in or committed to custody by an order of a court;

    (c) remanded to youth detention accommodation under s 94(1) of the Legal Aid, Sentencing and Punishment of Offenders Act 2012; or

    (d) remanded, admitted or removed to hospital under section 35, 36, 38 or 48 of the Mental Health Act 1983.

(12) A person is in police detention for the purposes of subsection (11) above—

    (a) at any time when he is in police detention for the purposes of the Police and Criminal Evidence Act 1984; and

    (b) at any time when he is detained under section 41 of the Terrorism Act 2000; and in that subsection 'secure accommodation' has the same meaning as in section 23 of the Children and Young Persons Act 1969.

(12A) Section 243 of the Criminal Justice Act 2003 (persons extradited to the United Kingdom) applies in relation to a person sentenced to a detention and training order as it applies in relation to a fixed-term prisoner, with the reference in subsection (2) of that section to section 240 being read as a reference to subsection (8) above.

(13) For the purpose of any reference in sections 102 to 105 below to the term of a detention and training order, consecutive terms of such orders and terms of such orders which are wholly or partly concurrent shall be treated as a single term if—

    (a) the orders were made on the same occasion; or

    (b) where they were made on different occasions, the offender has not been released (by virtue of subsection (2), (3), (4) or (5) of section 102 below) at any time during the period beginning with the first and ending with the last of those occasions.

F7.3.1 *Remand in custody*

The adult rules for remand time contained in the CJA 2003 s 240ZA do not apply to detention and training orders. In order to achieve the same effect which the operation of this section would have for adult offenders, it is necessary for the sentencer to double the number of days spent on remand before determining what deduction should be made to the length of the order to take account of the remand time (*R v Eagles* [2006] EWCA Crim 2368, [2007] 1 Cr App R (S) 612).

F7.3.2 *Qualifying curfew condition*

Under the CJA 2003 s 240A time spent remanded on bail with a curfew must be taken into account where the bail:

- is subject to a qualifying curfew condition (currently a condition which requires the person granted bail to remain at one or more specified places for a total of not less than nine hours in any given day); and
- an electronic monitoring condition is imposed under the BA 1976 s 3(6ZAA).

The CJA 2003 s 240A(3) sets out the way that the number of days subject to a qualifying curfew should be calculated:

- The first day that the defendant is subject to a qualifying curfew should be counted; the last day should not be counted if he spends the last part of it in custody.
- Days when the defendant is also subject to a curfew requirement as part of a sentence or in breach of the bail curfew requirement should not be counted.
- When calculating the credit period for an adult offender the period subject to a qualifying curfew is halved. By analogy with the reasoning set out in *Eagles* (see **F7.3.1** above) the court should then double the figure again to establish the equivalent remand time which should be taken into account before passing a detention and training order (*R v J* [2012] EWCA Crim 1570, [2013] 1 Cr App R (S) 412).

The CJA 2003 s 240A only refers to crediting periods of remand on bail. There is no statutory requirement to take into account time spent remanded to local authority accommodation with a electronically monitored curfew of at least nine hours a day. However, it is arguable that it is open to the sentencing court to take such time into account should it wish to (cf *R v Secretary of State for the Home Office ex parte A (a juvenile)* [2000] UKHL 4, [2000] 2 AC 276).

In *R v Inner London Crown Court ex parte N and S (Minors)* [2001] 1 Cr App R (S) 89 Rose LJ gave general guidance on how a court should approach the task of taking remand time into account:

> It is not appropriate or desirable that any precise reflection should be sought to be given, in making detention and training orders, of a day or two spent in custody. Of course if a significant time has been spent in custody, a matter of weeks or months, the proper approach of the court, taking such a period into account, is to reduce, if possible, the sentence otherwise appropriate to reflect that period. But, in my judgement, it is impossible for courts to fine tune, by reference to a few days in custody, the sentence which is appropriate in making detention and training orders.

In *R v Fieldhouse and Watts* [2001] 1 Cr App R (S) 104 Rose LJ gave more detailed guidance:

> [T]he proper approach can perhaps best be illustrated by taking by way of example a defendant who has spent four weeks in custody on remand—that is the equivalent of a two month term. The court is likely to take such a period into account in different ways according to the length of the detention and training order which initially seems appropriate for the particular offence and offender. If that period is four months, the court may conclude that a non-custodial sentence is appropriate. If that period is six, eight, 10 or 12 months, the court is likely to impose a period of four, six, eight or 10 months respectively. If that period is 18 or 24 months, the court may well conclude that no reduction can properly be made from 18 or 24 months, although the court will of course bear in mind in such a case, as in all others involving juveniles, the continuing importance of limiting the period of custody to the minimum necessary.

F7.4 Taking account of a guilty plea

In determining the sentence to pass on an offender who has pleaded guilty, a court must take into account the stage in the proceedings at which the offender indicated his intention to plead guilty and the circumstances in which the indication was made: CJA 2003 s 144(1). Detailed guidance on the amount of the discount and the limited grounds for refusing to give a discount is contained in the definitive guideline *Reduction in a Sentence for a Guilty Plea* (2007) for which see **F.12**.

Previous appeal decisions relating to sentences in the Crown Court have established the following principles:

- where an offender has pleaded guilty to an offence and detention under the PCCSA 2000 s 91 is not a sentencing option, the court should not impose the maximum twenty-four-month detention and training order unless there are proper grounds for withholding a discount for an offender's plea (*R v Kelly* [2001] EWCA 1030, *R v March* [2002] EWCA Crim 551);
- where the offence is a grave crime and the option of s 91 detention exists, a maximum twenty-four-month detention and training order may be imposed after a guilty plea if the sentencing judge decides in light of the guilty plea not to impose a sentence of s 91 detention (*R v Fieldhouse and Watts* [2001] 1 Cr App R (S) 104).

These principles will now apply in the youth court in the case of a grave crime where the offender indicated a guilty plea prior to allocation being determined. The discount for pleading guilty could be choosing not to exercise the power to commit for sentence under the PCCSA 2000 s 3B (for which see **F4.1**). Where a committal for sentence under s 3B is not an option, credit for a guilty plea should normally be granted from the twenty-four-month maximum.

Where the court is dealing with two or more offences in circumstances where consecutive sentences are justified, the guilty plea discount should result in a reduction of the aggregate sentence from the twenty-four-month maximum (*R v Dunkley* [2012] EWCA Crim 619).

F7.5 Interaction with other custodial sentences

Powers of Criminal Courts (Sentencing) Act 2000 ss 106 and 106A

106. (1) Where a court passes a sentence of detention in a young offender institution in the case of an offender who is subject to a detention and training order, the sentence shall take effect as follows—

    (a) if the offender has been released by virtue of subsection (2), (3), (4) or (5) of section 102 above, at the beginning of the day on which it is passed;

    (b) if not, either as mentioned in paragraph (a) above or, if the court so orders, at the time when the offender would otherwise be released by virtue of subsection (2), (3), (4) or (5) of section 102.

    . . .

(4) Subject to subsection (5) below, where at any time an offender is subject concurrently—

    (a) to a detention and training order, and

    (b) to a sentence of detention in a young offender institution,

he shall be treated for the purposes of sections 102 to 105 above and of section 98 above (place of detention), Chapter IV of this Part (return to detention) and Part II of the Criminal Justice Act 1991 (early release) as if he were subject only to the one of them that was imposed on the later occasion.

(5) Nothing in subsection (4) above shall require the offender to be released in respect of either the order or the sentence unless and until he is required to be released in respect of each of them.

(6) Where, by virtue of any enactment giving a court power to deal with a person in a way in which a court on a previous occasion could have dealt with him, a detention and training order for any term is made in the case of a person who has attained the age of 18, the person shall be treated as if he had been sentenced to detention in a young offender institution for the same term.

106A. (1) In this section—

'the 2003 Act' means the Criminal Justice Act 2003;

'sentence of detention' means—

(a) a sentence of detention under section 91 above or section 209 of the Armed Forces Act 2006, or

(b) a sentence of detention under section 228 of the 2003 Act (extended sentence for certain violent or sexual offences: persons under 18)

and references in this section to a sentence of detention under section 228 of the 2003 Act include such a sentence passed as a result of section 222 of the Armed Forces Act 2006.

(2) Where a court passes a sentence of detention in the case of an offender who is subject to a detention and training order, the sentence shall take effect as follows—

(a) if the offender has at any time been released by virtue of subsection (2), (3), (4) or (5) of section 102 above, at the beginning of the day on which the sentence is passed, and

(b) if not, either as mentioned in paragraph (a) above or, if the court so orders, at the time when the offender would otherwise be released by virtue of subsection (2), (3), (4) or (5) of section 102.

(3) Where a court makes a detention and training order in the case of an offender who is subject to a sentence of detention, the order shall take effect as follows—

(a) if the offender has at any time been released under Chapter 6 of Part 12 of the 2003 Act (release on licence of fixed-term prisoners), at the beginning of the day on which the order is made, and

(b) if not, either as mentioned in paragraph (a) above or, if the court so orders, at the time when the offender would otherwise be released under that Chapter.

(4) Where an order under section 102(5) above is made in the case of a person in respect of whom a sentence of detention is to take effect as mentioned in subsection (2)(b) above, the order is to be expressed as an order that the period of detention attributable to the detention and training order is to end at the time determined under section 102(5)(a) or (b) above.

(5) In determining for the purposes of subsection (3)(b) the time when an offender would otherwise be released under Chapter 6 of Part 12

of the 2003 Act, section 246 of that Act (power of Secretary of State to release prisoners on licence before he is required to do so) is to be disregarded.

(6) Where by virtue of subsection (3)(b) above a detention and training order made in the case of a person who is subject to a sentence of detention under section 228 of the 2003 Act is to take effect at the time when he would otherwise be released under Chapter 6 of Part 12 of that Act, any direction by the Parole Board under subsection (2)(b) of section 247 of that Act in respect of him is to be expressed as a direction that the Board would, but for the detention and training order, have directed his release under that section.

(7) Subject to subsection (9) below, where at any time an offender is subject concurrently—

(a) to a detention and training order, and

(b) to a sentence of detention,

he shall be treated for the purposes of the provisions specified in subsection (8) below as if he were subject only to the sentence of detention.

(8) Those provisions are—

(a) sections 102 to 105 above,

(b) section 92 above, section 235 of the 2003 Act and section 210 of the Armed Forces Act 2006 (place of detention etc),

(c) Chapter 6 of Part 12 of the 2003 Act, and

(d) section 214 of the Armed Forces Act 2006 (offences committed during a detention and training order under that Act).

(9) Nothing in subsection (7) above shall require the offender to be released in respect of either the order or the sentence unless and until he is required to be released in respect of each of them.

F7.6 Placement and release from detention

The PCCSA 2000 s 102 provides:

Powers of Criminal Courts (Sentencing) Act 2000 s 102

(1) An offender shall serve the period of detention and training under a detention and training order in such youth detention accommodation as may be determined by the Secretary of State.

(2) Subject to subsections (3) to (5) below, the period of detention and training under a detention and training order shall be one-half of the term of the order.

(3) The Secretary of State may at any time release the offender if he is satisfied that exceptional circumstances exist which justify the offender's release on compassionate grounds.

(4) The Secretary of State may release the offender—

(a) in the case of an order for a term of 8 months or more but less than 18 months, at any time during the period of one month ending with the half-way point of the term of the order; and

> (b) in the case of an order for a term of 18 months or more, at any time during the period of two months ending with that point.
> (5) If a youth court so orders on an application made by the Secretary of State for the purpose, the Secretary of State shall release the offender—
>   (a) in the case of an order for a term of 8 months or more but less than 18 months, one month after the half-way point of the term of the order; and
>   (b) in the case of an order for a term of 18 months or more, one month or two months after that point.
> (6) An offender detained in pursuance of a detention and training order shall be deemed to be in legal custody.

The choice of placement is not made by the court but by the YJB via its Secure Placements Clearinghouse. The youth offending team is required to forward details of the young offender to the YJB highlighting any disability or other reason to consider him or her exceptionally vulnerable. Boys aged under 15 will be placed in a secure children's home or secure training centre; those aged 15 or over can still be placed in such places but are more usually placed in a young offender institution. Girls will generally be placed in secure children's homes or secure training centres. Placement in a female young offender institution unit is only possible for 17-year-olds.

There is a presumption in favour of trainees being granted early release under s 102(4). All trainees released early under s 102(4) will be subject to an electronically monitored curfew from the date of early release until the halfway point of the order: Home Office/Youth Justice Board Guidance—*The Detention and Training Order: Revised Guidance on Electronically-Monitored Early Release* (2002).

F7.7 Supervision after release

No matter the length of the order, the young offender will be subject to supervision upon release for the remainder of the order.

The PCCSA 2000 s 103 provides:

> ### Powers of Criminal Courts (Sentencing) Act 2000 s 103
>
> (1) The period of supervision of an offender who is subject to a detention and training order—
>   (a) shall begin with the offender's release, whether at the half-way point of the term of the order or otherwise; and
>   (b) subject to subsection (2) below, shall end when the term of the order ends.

(2) The Secretary of State may by order provide that the period of supervision shall end at such point during the term of a detention and training order as may be specified in the order under this subsection.

(3) During the period of supervision, the offender shall be under the supervision of—
   (a) an officer of a local probation board or an officer of a provider of probation services;
   (b) a social worker of a local authority; or
   (c) a member of a youth offending team;
   and the category of person to supervise the offender shall be determined from time to time by the Secretary of State.

(4) Where the supervision is to be provided by an officer of a local probation board, the officer of a local probation board shall be an officer appointed for or assigned to the local justice area within which the offender resides for the time being.

(4A) Where the supervision is to be provided by an officer of a provider of probation services, the officer of a provider of probation services shall be an officer acting in the local justice area within which the offender resides for the time being.

(5) Where the supervision is to be provided by—
   (a) a social worker of a local authority, or
   (b) a member of a youth offending team,
   the social worker or member shall be a social worker of, or a member of a youth offending team established by, the local authority within whose area the offender resides for the time being.

(6) The offender shall be given a notice from the Secretary of State specifying—
   (a) the category of person for the time being responsible for his supervision; and
   (b) any requirements with which he must for the time being comply.

(7) A notice under subsection (6) above shall be given to the offender—
   (a) before the commencement of the period of supervision; and
   (b) before any alteration in the matters specified in subsection (6)(a) or (b) above comes into effect.

F7.8 Breach of supervision requirements

Unlike in the case of adult offenders enforcement action is not carried out administratively by notifying the Ministry of Justice of any breach of the requirements; instead the young offender must be taken back to court. Enforcement is by a youth court whatever court passed the original sentence or whatever the age of the offender at the time of the breach proceedings.

The LASPO 2012 s 80 substantially amended the provisions relating to breach of supervision requirements. The previous law still applies to any breach found to have occurred before 3 December 2012 (for which see *Blackstone's Criminal Practice 2014*, **E7.25**).

For breaches found to have occurred on 3 December 2012 or after the PCCSA 2000 s 104 provides:

Powers of Criminal Courts (Sentencing) Act 2000 s 104

(1) Where a detention and training order is in force in respect of an offender and it appears on information to a justice of the peace that the offender has failed to comply with requirements under section 103(6)(b) above, the justice—

    (a) may issue a summons requiring the offender to appear at the place and time specified in the summons; or

    (b) if the information is in writing and on oath, may issue a warrant for the offender's arrest.

(2) Any summons or warrant issued under this section shall direct the offender to appear or be brought—

    (a) before a youth court acting in the local justice in which the offender resides; or

    (b) if it is not known where the offender resides, before a youth court acting in the same local justice area as the justice who issued the summons or warrant.

(3) If it is proved to the satisfaction of the youth court before which an offender appears or is brought under this section that he has failed to comply with requirements under section 103(6)(b) above, that court may—

    (a) order the offender to be detained, in such youth detention accommodation as the Secretary of State may determine, for such period, not exceeding the maximum period found under subsection (3A) below, as the court may specify;

    (aa) order the offender to be subject to such period of supervision, not exceeding the maximum period found under subsection (3A) below, as the court may specify; or

    (b) impose on the offender a fine not exceeding level 3 on the standard scale.

(3A) The maximum period referred to in subsection (3)(a) and (aa) above is the shorter of—

    (a) three months, and

    (b) the period beginning with the date of the offender's failure and ending with the last day of the term of the detention and training order.

(3B) For the purposes of subsection (3A) above a failure that is found to have occurred over two or more days is to be taken to have occurred on the first of those days.

(3C) A court may order a period of detention or supervision, or impose a fine, under subsection (3) above before or after the end of the term of the detention and training order.

(3D) A period of detention or supervision ordered under subsection (3) above—

    (a) begins on the date the order is made, and

    (b) may overlap to any extent with the period of supervision under the detention and training order.

(4) An offender detained in pursuance of an order under subsection (3)(a) above shall be deemed to be in legal custody.

(4A) Where an order under subsection (3)(a) above is made in the case of a person who has attained the age of 18, the order has effect to require the person to be detained in prison for the period specified by the court.

(5) A fine imposed under subsection (3)(b) above shall be deemed, for the purposes of any enactment, to be a sum adjudged to be paid by a conviction.

(5A) Sections 104A and 104B below make further provision about the operation of orders under subsection (3) above.

(6) An offender may appeal to the Crown Court against any order made under subsection (3)(a), (aa) or (b) above.

The law and procedure of proceedings for breach of the supervision requirements under s 103 was considered in *S v Doncaster Youth Offending Team* [2003] EWHC 1128 (Admin), (2003) 167 JP 381. In his judgment Scott Baker LJ gave the following guidance:

- Where several detention and training orders are made on the same occasion the effect of s 101(13) is that they are to be treated as a single term and therefore the information laid to institute breach proceedings should only allege breach of one order.
- Failing to attend four separate supervision appointments is a manifestation of the offender's failure to keep in touch with his supervising officer and it would be entirely artificial to split this up into four quite separate offences.
- Breach of quite separate licence conditions (eg failing to keep in touch with the supervisor and failure to live at the address approved by the supervisor) should not be the subject of the same information.
- Proof of service upon the young offender of the supervision requirements under s 103(7) is required. Proof by inference is sufficient but, for the future, it seems desirable that when an offender is given notice under s 103(7) he should be asked to sign a copy so that there can be no dispute that he has been given it.
- Where a failure is alleged of a requirement to comply with a specific order such as to live at a specified address or attend on a specified occasion, the person who gave the order should, if it is disputed, be at court to give evidence about it.

By the PCCSA 2000 s 104A where a further period of supervision is imposed under s 104(3)(aa), a written notice of the supervision requirements must be given to the offender as soon as practicable after the court hearing. The PCCSA 2000 s 104 applies to any proceedings for breach of the requirements of this further period of supervision.

The PCCSA 2000 s 104B makes detailed provision for the interaction between a period of recall ordered under s 104(3)(a) and another sentence.

F7.9 Offences during currency of the order

When a young offender commits an offence whilst still subject to a detention and training order supervision, the court dealing with the new offence has a power to recall the young offender.

The PCCSA 2000 s 105 provides:

> ### Powers of Criminal Courts (Sentencing) Act 2000 s 105
>
> (1) This section applies to a person subject to a detention and training order if—
>   (a) after his release and before the date on which the term of the order ends, he commits an offence punishable with imprisonment in the case of a person aged 21 or over ('the new offence'); and
>   (b) whether before or after that date, he is convicted of the new offence.
> (2) Subject to section 8(6) above (duty of adult magistrates' court to remit young offenders to youth court for sentence), the court by or before which a person to whom this section applies is convicted of the new offence may, whether or not it passes any other sentence on him, order him to be detained in such youth detention accommodation as the Secretary of State may determine for the whole or any part of the period which—
>   (a) begins with the date of the court's order; and
>   (b) is equal in length to the period between the date on which the new offence was committed and the date mentioned in subsection (1) above.
> (3) The period for which a person to whom this section applies is ordered under subsection (2) above to be detained in youth detention accommodation—
>   (a) shall, as the court may direct, either be served before and be followed by, or be served concurrently with, any sentence imposed for the new offence; and
>   (b) in either case, shall be disregarded in determining the appropriate length of that sentence.
> (4) Where the new offence is found to have been committed over a period of two or more days, or at some time during a period of two or more days, it shall be taken for the purposes of this section to have been committed on the last of those days.
> (5) A person detained in pursuance of an order under subsection (2) above shall be deemed to be in legal custody.

F8 Discharges (Absolute and Conditional)

F8.1 Criteria

By the PCCSA 2000 s 12(1) where an offender is convicted of an offence (not being an offence where the sentence is fixed by law or subject to a mandatory minimum sentence) and the court is of the opinion, having regard to the circumstances including the nature of the offence and the character of the offender, that it is inexpedient to inflict punishment, the court may make an order either:

- discharging him absolutely; or
- discharging him subject to the condition that he commits no offence during such period, not exceeding three years from the date of the order as may be specified in the order.

F8.2 Combining discharge with other sentences or orders

Only the orders mentioned in the PCC(S)A 2000 s 12(7) can be combined with a discharge for the same offence. These are:

- Order to pay prosecution costs;
- Compensation order;
- Deprivation order;
- Restitution order; and
- Any disqualification.

F8.3 Restrictions on use of conditional discharge

The CDA 1998 s 65ZB imposes restrictions on the use of conditional discharges if:

- a person who has received two or more youth cautions is convicted of an offence committed within two years beginning with the date of the last of those cautions; or
- a person who has received a youth conditional caution followed by a youth caution is convicted of an offence committed within two years beginning with the date of the youth caution.

In the above circumstances the court by or before which the offender is so convicted:

- shall not impose a conditional discharge in respect of the offence unless it is of the opinion that there are exceptional circumstances relating to the offence or the offender which justify its doing so; and

- where it does so, shall state in open court that it is of that opinion and why it is.

For the purposes of this provision a reprimand or warning under the CDA 1998 s 65 is to be treated as a youth caution given under s 65ZA(1)—see the LASPO 2012 s 135(5).

An offender convicted of breaching the requirements of an anti-social behaviour order may not be conditionally discharged in any circumstances: CDA 1998 s 1(11).

F8.4 Effect of a discharge

By the PCCSA 2000 s 14 a conviction for an offence for which the offender is discharged either absolutely or conditionally shall be deemed not to be a conviction for any purpose other than the purpose of proceedings in which the order is made and of any subsequent proceedings for breach which may be taken under s 13.

F8.5 Breach of a conditional discharge

The PCCSA 2000 s 13 provides that, if a person commits an offence during the life of a conditional discharge, he may be resentenced for that original offence, even if the period of discharge has expired at the date of sentence. The offender will be sentenced with reference to his age at the date of sentence, not the date of the previous offence, and can be sentenced in any way as if he had just been convicted of the offence. If the conditional discharge was imposed by the Crown Court the offender can be committed to that court for re-sentence.

There is no requirement to re-sentence and a court could sentence for a new offence and leave the conditional discharge in place if it saw fit to do so.

Where an order for conditional discharge has been made by a magistrates' court in the case of an offender under 18 years of age in respect of an indictable-only offence the powers on re-sentence after the offender attains 18 are:

- to impose a fine not exceeding £5,000; and
- to impose a term of detention in a young offender institution not exceeding six months.

 See *Blackstone's Criminal Practice 2014* **E12**

F9 **Disqualification from Driving**

F9.1 **Criteria**

Disqualification may arise in one of five ways:

- Offence carrying obligatory disqualification (see **F9.3**).
- Offence carrying discretionary disqualification (see **F9.5**).
- As a result of accumulating twelve or more penalty points (see **F9.6**).
- As a result of conviction for any offence, or an offence where a vehicle was used for crime: (PCC(S)A 2000, ss 146 and 147) (see **F9.7**).
- As a result of a 'new driver' accumulating six penalty points (Revocation) (see **9.8**).

F9.2 **Interim disqualification**

An interim disqualification under the Road Traffic Offenders Act 1988 s 26 can be imposed when the court:

- commits an offender for sentence to the Crown Court,
- remits the case to another court,
- defers or adjourns sentence.

The interim disqualification lasts until the defendant is sentenced. More than one interim disqualification can be imposed but the total term must not exceed six months.

F9.3 **Obligatory disqualification**

Obligatory disqualification is dealt with by the Road Traffic Offenders Act 1988 s 34.

Where a person is convicted of an offence involving obligatory disqualification, the court must order him to be disqualified for such period not less than twelve months as the court thinks fit unless the court finds special reasons (see **F9.4**) to order him to be disqualified for a shorter period or not to order him to be disqualified.

A person disqualified for dangerous driving must also be ordered to undertake an extended driving test.

A mandatory disqualification does not have the effect of removing any penalty points existing on the licence.

There are exceptions to the minimum twelve-month period:

- A minimum three-year disqualification follows where within the ten years immediately preceding the commission of the offence, a person has been convicted of any such offence, and is again convicted of an offence under any of the following provisions of the Road Traffic Act 1988, that is:

(a) s 3A (causing death by careless driving when under the influence of drink or drugs);

(b) s 4(1) (driving or attempting to drive while unfit);

(c) s 5(1)(a) (driving or attempting to drive with excess alcohol);

(d) s 7(6) (failing to provide a specimen) where that is an offence involving obligatory disqualification; or

(e) s 7A(6) (failing to allow a specimen to be subjected to laboratory test) where that is an offence involving obligatory disqualification.

- A minimum two-year disqualification follows in relation to a person on whom more than one disqualification for a fixed period of fifty-six days or more has been imposed within the three years immediately preceding the commission of the offence.

- A minimum six months' disqualification follows where a person convicted of an offence of using a vehicle in dangerous condition has, within the three years immediately preceding the commission of the offence, been convicted of any such offence: RTA 1988 s 40A.

F9.4 Special reasons

There is no statutory definition of 'special reasons', but it will fulfil the following criteria:

- It will be a mitigating or extenuating circumstance
- It will not be a legal defence to the charge
- It will be directly connected with the commission of the offence
- It will be a matter which the court ought properly take in to consideration.

The burden, to the civil standard, falls on the defendant. Good character, financial hardship as a result of a disqualification, and the fact the offence was not particularly serious have all been held not to amount to special reasons. In the case of aggravated vehicle taking, the fact that the offender did not actually drive the car will not be regarded as a special reason: *R v Callister* [1993] RTR 70.

Common special reasons are:

- shortness of distance driven;
- medical or other emergencies;
- spiked drinks or mistake as to item drunk.

F9.4.1 *Shortness of distance driven*

Chatters v Burke [1986] 3 All ER 168 details the seven factors relevant to a shortness of distance driven argument:

- distance;
- manner of driving;
- state of the vehicle;
- whether there was an intention to drive further;
- road and traffic conditions;
- possibility of danger to road users and pedestrians; and
- reason for the driving.

In *Director of Public Prosecutions v Oram* [2005] EWHC 964 (Admin) the court held that special reasons would not be arguable to a drunk driver who relied upon shortness of distance driven alone.

F9.4.2 *Medical or other emergencies*

In *Warring-Davies v Director of Public Prosecutions* [2009] EWHC 1172 (Admin) the court emphasized the need to find a causal link between any alleged medical condition and the driving in question.

In *DPP v Heathcote* [2011] EWHC 2536 (Admin) it was concluded that when deciding whether an 'emergency' justified driving the court should ask whether a sober, reasonable, and responsible friend would have advised the defendant to drive.

Relevant factors included:

- amount drunk
- threat to others
- state of the roads
- distance to be driven
- nature of the emergency
- what alternatives were available.

The defence was not limited to life and limb cases but to chase the thieves of a relative's car was not acceptable.

F9.4.3 *Spiked drinks or mistake as to item drunk*

It will be necessary to prove:

- that the drink was laced,
- the defendant did not know it was laced, and
- that but for the lacing of the drink his alcohol level would not have exceeded the legal limit.

It will normally be necessary to call expert evidence in relation to the last point. The higher the reading, the less likely it is that a defendant will be able to prove he had no knowledge. If a court is of the view that the defendant ought to have realized his drink was spiked it will not find special reasons: *Pridige v Grant* [1985] RTR 196.

F9.4.4 *Effect of finding special reasons*

If 'special reasons' are found the court has a discretion not to endorse points, and to reduce or not impose a mandatory period of disqualification. Note, however, that for an offence involving mandatory disqualification, where special reasons are found and the court does not disqualify, it must impose points, unless it finds special reasons also for not doing so.

 See *Blackstone's Criminal Practice 2014* **C7.8** and **C7.55**

F9.5 Discretionary disqualification

Where an offence carries discretionary disqualification, the court must consider disqualification before it considers the imposition of penalty points. This is the case even if the offender would be liable to disqualification under the 'totting-up' provisions. The benefit of a discretionary disqualification is that it can be for as short a period as the court directs; the negative side is that any previous points remain on the licence. The period of disqualification can be for any period the court thinks proper.

F9.5.1 *Length of disqualification*

In *R v Aspen* [1975] RTR 456 the court considered that where there is a real chance that the ability to drive will improve a young offender's employment prospects, disqualification should be kept to a minimum.

In *R v Russell* [1993] RTR 249 it was stated that a lengthy period of disqualification should be avoided, particularly when imposed at the same time as a custodial sentence, as it may have an adverse effect on the offender's chances of rehabilitation.

In *R v Thomas* [1983] 1 WLR 1490 two years' disqualification under the totting-up procedure was reduced to twelve months. The court suggested that lengthy periods of disqualification for those who seem incapable of leaving motor vehicles alone would be counterproductive.

F9.6 As a result of accumulating twelve or more penalty points 'totting-up'

In calculating the points on the licence, the court will have regard to:

- the points to be imposed for the new offence, and
- any points on the licence for offences committed no longer than three years from the date of commission of the new offence (therefore, points run from date of old offence to date of new offence).

The minimum period of disqualification is:

- six months if no previous disqualification;
- twelve months if one previous disqualification (for fifty-six days or more);
- two years if two or more previous disqualifications (for fifty-six days or more).

The previous disqualifications must have been imposed within three years of the date of the new offence to count.

F9.6.1 *Mitigating circumstances*

'Mitigating circumstances' in relation to the offender or the offence can be argued in order to prevent disqualification as a result of totting-up. The burden of establishing mitigating circumstances is on the defendant and will generally need to be proved by way of evidence rather than submission. Most mitigating circumstances relate to 'exceptional hardship', for example the loss of employment as a result of disqualification.

 See *Blackstone's Criminal Practice 2014* **C7.28**

F9.7 As a result of conviction for any offence, or an offence where a vehicle was used for crime

The PCC(S)A 2000 s 146 gives a court the power to disqualify an offender from holding a driving licence following a conviction for any offence. There need be no nexus between driving and the offence in question. This allows a court to use the provision whenever it feels it to be appropriate in all of the circumstances: *R v Sofekun* [2008] EWCA Crim 2035.

The PCC(S)A 2000 s 147 gives courts a narrower power to disqualify where a motor vehicle was involved in the commission of an offence of assault.

 See *Blackstone's Criminal Practice 2014* **E 21.11–E21.12**

F9.8 Road Traffic (New Drivers) Act 1995

Newly qualified drivers are subject to a two-year probationary period. If at any time during that period the points to be endorsed on a driving licence amount to six or more, the licence will be automatically revoked. The relevant date is the date of offence not conviction, so revocation cannot be avoided by delaying court proceedings.

F9 Disqualification from Driving

In appropriate cases, advocates may seek to invite courts to disqualify instead of endorse points in order to try to avoid the draconian consequences of accumulating six or more penalty points.

See *Blackstone's Criminal Practice 2014* **C7.44**

F10 **Financial Order Enforcement**

F10.1 **Payment**

Where a court has ordered financial penalties against the offender it will enforce the order against him. The court will, depending on the age of the offender, consider making the financial penalties the responsibility of the parent or guardian (for which see **J3**).

F10.2 **Enforcement**

- The CYPA 1933, s 46 assigns charges against children and young persons to the youth court. It does not deal with enforcement of financial penalties. As the orders were made as part of the proceedings in the youth court, there is an argument that it is that court which should deal with subsequent enforcement.
- Welfare issues are relevant.
- Where payment is not made as ordered at the sentencing hearing a warrant with or without bail may be issued.

F10.3 **Powers of the court**

The court may deal with a fine defaulter in the following ways:

- Conduct a means enquiry: MCA 1980 s 86(1)
- Allow further time to pay: MCA 1980 s 85A
- Remit of all or part of the fine: MCA 1980 s 85 & CJA 2003, s 165
- Make an attachment of earnings order
- Make a money payment supervision order: MCA 1980 s 88
- Attendance centre order: PCCSA 2000 s 60
- Youth default order: CJIA 2008 (not in force)
- Order parents to pay or bind them over to ensure payment by the youth.

There is no power to make a Fines Collection Order, a Deduction from Benefit Order, or to order time in custody in default of payment.

F10.4 **Attendance centre order**

Where there has been 'wilful refusal or culpable neglect' to pay a financial penalty the court can make an attendance centre order.

- Where the offender is aged under 14 years the maximum length of the order is twelve hours.

- Where the offender is aged under 16 years the order may be for twelve to twenty-four hours.
- Where the offender is aged 16 years or over the order may be for twelve to thirty-six hours.

The financial penalty will be reduced or considered paid in proportion to the number of hours completed.

F11 **Fines**

F11.1 **Criteria**

The *Magistrates' Court Sentencing Guidelines* sets out the approach to fines in relation to **adult** offenders. There is no specific guidance in relation to youths.

F11.2 **Power to fine**

The maximum fine in the magistrates' court for a youth depends on age:

Aged 10–13 years inclusive	£250
Aged 14–17 years inclusive	£1,000

A fine must not exceed the statutory limit. Where this is expressed in terms of a 'level', the maximum fines for adults are:

Level 1	£200
Level 2	£500
Level 3	£1,000
Level 4	£2,500
Level 5	£5,000

Where the maximum fine for an adult is less than the limit for a youth, the adult maximum will apply.

There is no statutory limit on the amount of fine which may be imposed in the Crown Court.

F11.3 **Assessment of fines**

- The amount of a fine must reflect the seriousness of the offence.
- Account should be taken of any guilty plea.
- The court must take into account the financial circumstances of the offender.
- Normally a fine should be of an amount that is capable of being paid within twelve months.
- Priority should be given to payment of compensation and surcharge.

F11.4 **Assessment of financial circumstances**

The court may require a defendant to provide details of their financial circumstances. Most youth defendants are unlikely to have income aside from money provided by their parents or guardians. It is important to establish whether any weekly allowance includes travel to school or college and any lunch money whilst there. In the case of young defendants who live independently, their benefits will be taken into account.

F11.5 **Surcharge**

See **F33**.

F11.6 **Payment**

The payment in full of any financial order is due on the day it is made. The court will ordinarily consider allowing time to pay. It will set payment terms allowing payment in full within a specified period or payment by instalments. The court will consider whether parents or guardians should be ordered to make payment (for which see **J3**).

See *Blackstone's Criminal Practice 2014* **E15**

F12 **Guilty Plea Discounts**

F12.1 **Criteria**

The CJA 2003 s 153(2) provides:

> ### Criminal Justice Act 2003 s 153(2)
>
> In determining what sentence to pass on an offender who has pleaded guilty to an offence in proceedings before that or another court, a court must take into account—
> (a) the stage in the proceedings for the offence at which the offender indicated his intention to plead guilty, and
> (b) the circumstances in which this indication was given.

There is a definitive sentencing guideline *Reduction in Sentence for a Guilty Plea* (2007). The current application of this guideline in the light of various procedural changes has been considered in detail in *R v Caley* [2012] EWCA Crim 2821.

A reduction in sentence is appropriate because a guilty plea avoids the need for a trial, saving cost, and, in the case of an early guilty plea, saves victims and witnesses from the concern of having to give evidence. The reduction principle derives from the need for the effective administration of justice and not as an aspect of mitigation.

The level of reduction should reflect the stage at which the offender indicated a willingness to admit guilt to the offence for which he is eventually sentenced. The SGC guideline suggests a sliding scale:

In each category, there is a presumption that the recommended reduction will be given unless there are good reasons for a lower amount		
First reasonable opportunity	After a trial date is set	Door of the court/after trial has begun
recommended 1/3	**recommended** 1/4	**recommended** 1/10

F12.2 **First reasonable opportunity**

The discussion about determining the first reasonable opportunity contained in the definitive guideline has been largely superseded by the guidance contained in *R v Caley*. This can be summarized as follows:

- The question of when the defendant's first reasonable opportunity arose is a matter for the sentencing court.

- The first reasonable opportunity will not normally be during the police interview. A defendant who frankly admits in police interview what he did will, however, have additional mitigation which should normally be recognized in sentencing.
- The first reasonable opportunity for the defendant to indicate his guilt is not the same as the first opportunity for his lawyers to assess the strength of the evidence against him. Whilst it is perfectly proper for a defendant to require advice from his lawyers on the strength of the evidence, he does not require it in order to know whether he is guilty or not.
- There will be cases when the defendant genuinely does not know whether he is guilty or not and needs sight of the evidence in order to decide. This might arise when even if the facts are known there is need for legal advice as to whether an offence is constituted by them, or cases where the defendant genuinely has no recollection of events.
- Where a case is sent for trial at the Crown Court, the first reasonable opportunity for the defendant to indicate his plea of guilty is not the PCMH. It is normally either at the first hearing in the youth court or immediately on arrival in the Crown Court, whether at a preliminary hearing or by way of a locally approved system for indicating plea through his solicitors.

F12.3 **Reasons to reduce or withhold the suggested discount**

Where the prosecution case is overwhelming it may not be appropriate to give the full discount. There will, however, often be some public benefits in giving some discount. A sentencing court should also be wary of concluding that a case is 'overwhelming' when that evidence has not yet been tested in a trial. Where the court is satisfied that it is appropriate to give a lower discount for this reason a reduction of 20 per cent is likely to be appropriate where the guilty plea was indicated at the first reasonable opportunity. It will very rarely be appropriate to withhold the discount completely (*R v Wilson* [2012] EWCA Crim 386).

If there is a *Newton* hearing and the offender's version of the circumstances of the offence is rejected, this should be taken into account in determining the level of reduction. The reduction for plea which should survive an adverse *Newton* finding depends on all the circumstances of the case, including the extent of the issue determined, whether lay witnesses had to give evidence, and the extra public time and money that has been involved. Although the great bulk of the reduction for a guilty plea will be dissipated by advancing a false basis of plea, it was said in *Caley* that in Crown Court proceedings there should still be some limited reduction to reflect the fact that the guilty plea avoided the extra cost of a jury trial.

The sentencer is bound to sentence for the offence with which the offender has been charged, and to which he has pleaded guilty. The sentence cannot remedy perceived defects (eg an inadequate charge or maximum penalty) by refusal of the appropriate discount. Courts must resist the temptation to withhold a discount for this reason. The practical relevance of this principle is most often seen in the context of the twenty-four-month maximum for detention and training orders for which see **F7.4**.

F12.4 Residual flexibility

In *R v Caley* the court accepted that there was a residual discretion to deal with the facts of individual cases. This might include:

- Poor legal advice, if clearly demonstrated, might be relevant to the issue of first reasonable opportunity, especially in the case of a young or inexperienced defendant particularly in need of advice. Establishing this might involve full waiver of legal privilege as the question may well be raised what (if anything) the defendant had said to his lawyers about his actions.
- The avoidance of an exceptionally long or complex trial may also lead to an exceptional discount even at a late stage. Care must, however, be taken to ensure that such an approach should not become routine otherwise the incentive to plead at an early stage is lost.

F13 Hospital and Guardianship Orders

A youth court or a Crown Court may impose a hospital order or guardianship order upon a youth defendant when the requirements of the MHA 1983 s 37 are satisfied.

Mental Health Act 1983 s 37

(1) Where a person is convicted before the Crown Court of an offence punishable with imprisonment other than an offence the sentence for which is fixed by law, or is convicted by a magistrates' court of an offence punishable on summary conviction with imprisonment, and the conditions mentioned in subsection (2) below are satisfied, the court may by order authorise his admission to and detention in such hospital as may be specified in the order or, as the case may be, place him under the guardianship of a local social services authority or of such other person approved by a local social services authority as may be so specified.

(1A) In the case of an offence the sentence for which would otherwise fall to be imposed—...

    (a) under section 51A(2) of the Firearms Act 1968,

    (aa) under section 139AA(7) of the Criminal Justice Act 1988,

    ...

    (c) under [section 225(2) or 226(2) of the Criminal Justice Act 2003, or

    (d) under section 29(4) or (6) of the Violent Crime Reduction Act 2006 (minimum sentences in certain cases of using someone to mind a weapon).

nothing in those provisions shall prevent a court from making an order under subsection (1) above for the admission of the offender to a hospital.

(1B) References in subsection (1A) above to a sentence falling to be imposed under any of the provisions mentioned in that subsection are to be read in accordance with section 305(4) of the Criminal Justice Act 2003.

(2) The conditions referred to in subsection (1) above are that—

    (a) the court is satisfied, on the written or oral evidence of two registered medical practitioners, that the offender is suffering from mental disorder and that either—

        (i) the mental disorder from which the offender is suffering is of a nature or degree which makes it appropriate for him to be detained in a hospital for medical treatment and appropriate medical treatment is available for him; or

        (ii) in the case of an offender who has attained the age of 16 years, the mental disorder is of a nature or degree which warrants his reception into guardianship under this Act; and

    (b) the court is of the opinion, having regard to all the circumstances including the nature of the offence and the character and antecedents of the offender, and to the other available methods of dealing

---

with him, that the most suitable method of disposing of the case is by means of an order under this section.

(3) Where a person is charged before a magistrates' court with any act or omission as an offence and the court would have power, on convicting him of that offence, to make an order under subsection (1) above in his case, then, if the court is satisfied that the accused did the act or made the omission charged, the court may, if it thinks fit, make such an order without convicting him.

(4) An order for the admission of an offender to a hospital (in this Act referred to as 'a hospital order') shall not be made under this section unless the court is satisfied on the written or oral evidence of the approved clinician who would have overall responsibility for his case or of some other person representing the managers of the hospital that arrangements have been made for his admission to that hospital, and for his admission to it within the period of 28 days beginning with the date of the making of such an order; and the court may, pending his admission within that period, give such directions as it thinks fit for his conveyance to and detention in a place of safety.

(5) If within the said period of 28 days it appears to the Secretary of State that by reason of an emergency or other special circumstances it is not practicable for the patient to be received into the hospital specified in the order, he may give directions for the admission of the patient to such other hospital as appears to be appropriate instead of the hospital so specified; and where such directions are given—

(a) the Secretary of State shall cause the person having the custody of the patient to be informed, and

(b) the hospital order shall have effect as if the hospital specified in the directions were substituted for the hospital specified in the order.

(6) An order placing an offender under the guardianship of a local social services authority or of any other person (in this Act referred to as 'a guardianship order') shall not be made under this section unless the court is satisfied that that authority or person is willing to receive the offender into guardianship.

...

(8) Where an order is made under this section, the court shall not—

(a) pass sentence of imprisonment or impose a fine or make a community order (within the meaning of Part 12 of the Criminal Justice Act 2003) or a youth rehabilitation order (within the meaning of Part 1 of the Criminal Justice and Immigration Act 2008) in respect of the offence,

(b) if the order under this section is a hospital order, make a referral order (within the meaning of [the Powers of Criminal Courts (Sentencing) Act 2000) in respect of the offence, or

(c) make in respect of the offender an order under section 150 of that Act (binding over of parent or guardian),

but the court may make any other order which it has power to make apart from this section; and for the purposes of this subsection 'sentence of imprisonment' includes any sentence or order for detention.

For the definition of mentally disordered see **F14.1**.

Under the MHA 1983 s 37(3) a hospital order may also be imposed without a formal conviction. A youth court is a magistrates' court for the purposes of s 37(3) (*R (P) v Barking Youth Court* [2002] EWHC 734 (Admin), [2002] 2 Cr App R 294). For the use of this provision where the court considers that the youth defendant is unable to participate effectively in the proceedings see **E5.3**.

F13.1 Restriction order

A restriction order is a hospital order where the court orders that the offender's release shall be subject to special restrictions. It may only be made if it appears to the court, having regard to the nature of the offence, the antecedents of the offender, and the risk of his committing further offences if set at large, that it is necessary for the protection of the public from serious harm from him (Mental Health Act 1983 s 41).

A restriction order may only be made by a Crown Court judge. An offender who has attained the age of 14 may be committed to the Crown Court for such an order to be considered. This power is exercisable by a youth court.

Mental Health Act 1983 s 43

(1) If in the case of a person of or over the age of 14 years who is convicted by a magistrates' court of an offence punishable on summary conviction with imprisonment—

    (a) the conditions which under section 37(1) above are required to be satisfied for the making of a hospital order are satisfied in respect of the offender; but

    (b) it appears to the court, having regard to the nature of the offence, the antecedents of the offender and the risk of his committing further offences if set at large, that if a hospital order is made a restriction order should also be made,

the court may, instead of making a hospital order or dealing with him in any other manner, commit him in custody to the Crown Court to be dealt with in respect of the offence.

F14 **Mentally Disordered Offenders**

F14.1 **Definition of mentally disordered**

The Mental Health Act 1983 s 1 provides:

Mental Health Act 1983 s 1

(2) In this Act—
'mental disorder' means any disorder or disability of the mind; and
'mentally disordered' shall be construed accordingly;
…

(2A) But a person with learning disability shall not be considered by reason of that disability to be—
  (a) suffering from mental disorder for the purposes of the provisions mentioned in subsection (2B) below; or
  (b) requiring treatment in hospital for mental disorder for the purposes of sections 17E and 50 to 53 below,
  unless that disability is associated with abnormally aggressive or seriously irresponsible conduct on his part.

(2B) The provisions are—
  (a) sections 3, 7, 17A, 20 and 20A below;
  (b) sections 35 to 38, 45A, 47, 48 and 51 below; and
  (c) section 72(1)(b) and (c) and (4) below.

(3) Dependence on alcohol or drugs is not considered to be a disorder or disability of the mind for the purposes of subsection (2) above.

(4) In subsection (2A) above, 'learning disability' means a state of arrested or incomplete development of the mind which includes significant impairment of intelligence and social functioning.

F14.2 **Restrictions on imposing a custodial sentence**

The CJA 2003 s 157 provides:

Criminal Justice Act 2003 s 157

(1) Subject to subsection (2), in any case where the offender is or appears to be mentally disordered, the court must obtain and consider a medical report before passing a custodial sentence other than one fixed by law.

(2) Subsection (1) does not apply if, in the circumstances of the case, the court is of the opinion that it is unnecessary to obtain a medical report.

(3) Before passing a custodial sentence other than one fixed by law on an offender who is or appears to be mentally disordered, a court must consider—

(a) any information before it which relates to his mental condition (whether given in a medical report, a pre-sentence report or otherwise), and

(b) the likely effect of such a sentence on that condition and on any treatment which may be available for it.

(4) No custodial sentence which is passed in a case to which subsection (1) applies is invalidated by the failure of a court to comply with that subsection, but any court on an appeal against such a sentence—

(a) must obtain a medical report if none was obtained by the court below, and

(b) must consider any such report obtained by it or by that court.

(5) In this section 'mentally disordered', in relation to any person, means suffering from a mental disorder within the meaning of the Mental Health Act 1983.

(6) In this section 'medical report' means a report as to an offender's mental condition made or submitted orally or in writing by a registered medical practitioner who is approved for the purposes of section 12 of the Mental Health Act 1983 by the Secretary of State, or by another person by virtue of section 12ZA or 12ZB of that Act, as having special experience in the diagnosis or treatment of mental disorder.

F14.3 Possible disposals

If there are concerns regarding the mental health of a youth offender the following disposals may be available:

• youth rehabilitation order with mental health treatment requirement (see **F34.5.12**);

• guardianship order (see **F13**); or

• hospital order (see **F13**).

F15 *Newton* Hearings

The rule in *R v Newton* (1982) 77 Cr App R 13 indicates that an offender will be sentenced on the prosecution's version of the facts unless the defence make clear that they are pleading on an alternative basis. In that situation the Crown must prove its version of the facts by admissible evidence to the criminal standard of proof.

F15.1 Criteria

Updated guidance in relation to the holding of *Newton* hearings were set down in *R v Underwood* [2004] EWCA Crim 2256:

(1) The starting point has to be the defendant's instructions. His advocate will appreciate whether any significant facts about the prosecution evidence are disputed and the factual basis on which the defendant intends to plead guilty. Responsibility for taking initiative and alerting the prosecutor to the disputed areas rests with the defence.

(2) Where the Crown accepts the defendant's account of the disputed facts, the agreement should be written down and signed by both advocates. It should then be made available to the judge. If pleas have already been accepted and approved then it should be available before the sentencing hearing begins. If the agreed basis of plea is not signed by both advocates, the judge is entitled to ignore it. The Crown might reject the defendant's version. If so, the areas of dispute should be identified in writing, focusing the court's attention on the precise facts in dispute.

(3) The prosecution's position might be that they have no evidence to contradict the defence's assertions. In those circumstances, particularly if the facts relied on by the defendant arise from his personal knowledge and depend on his own account of the facts, the Crown should not normally agree the defendant's account unless supported by other material. The court should be notified at the outset in writing of the points in issue and the Crown's responses.

(4) After submissions, the judge will decide how to proceed. If not already decided, he would address the question of whether he should approve the Crown's acceptance of pleas. Then he would address the proposed basis of plea. It should be emphasized that whether or not the basis of plea is agreed, the judge is not bound by any such agreement and is entitled of his own motion to insist that any evidence relevant to the facts in dispute should be called before him, paying appropriate regard to any agreement

reached by the advocates and any reasons which the Crown, in particular, might advance to justify him proceeding immediately to sentence. The judge is responsible for the sentencing decision and may order a *Newton* hearing to ascertain the truth about disputed facts.

(5) Relevant evidence should be called by prosecution and defence, particularly where the issue arises from facts which are within the exclusive knowledge of the defendant. If the defendant is willing to give evidence he should be called and, if not, subject to any explanation offered, the judge may draw such inference as he sees fit. The judge can reject the evidence called by the prosecution or by the defendant or his witnesses even if the Crown has not called contradictory evidence. The judge's conclusions should be explained in the judgment.

(6) There are occasions when a *Newton* hearing would be inappropriate. Some issues require a jury's verdict; if a defendant denies that a specific criminal offence has been committed, the tribunal for deciding whether the offence has been proved is the jury. At the end of a *Newton* hearing the judge cannot make findings of fact and sentence on a basis which is inconsistent with the pleas to counts which have already been accepted and approved by the court. Particular care is needed in relation to a multi-count indictment involving one defendant or an indictment involving a number of defendants. Where there are a number of defendants to a joint enterprise, the judge, while reflecting on the individual basis of pleas, should bear in mind the relative seriousness of the joint enterprise on which the defendants were involved.

(7) Normally, matters of mitigation are not dealt with by way of a *Newton* hearing but it is always open to the court to allow a defendant to give evidence on matters of mitigation which are within his own knowledge. The judge is entitled to decline to hear evidence about disputed facts if the case advanced is, for good reason, to be regarded as absurd or obviously untenable.

(8) If the issues at the *Newton* hearing are wholly resolved in the defendant's favour, mitigation for guilty pleas should not be reduced. If the defendant is disbelieved or obliges the prosecution to call evidence from the victim, who is then subjected to cross-examination which, because it is entirely unfounded, causes unnecessary and inappropriate distress, or if the defendant conveys that he has no insight into the consequences of his offence, and no genuine remorse, the judge might reduce the discount for the guilty pleas. There may be a few exceptional cases in which the

normal entitlement to credit for a plea of guilty is wholly dissipated by the *Newton* hearing, and, in such cases, the judge should explain his reasons.

 See *Blackstone's Criminal Practice 2014* **D20.8–D20.29**

F16 Offences Taken into Consideration

The Sentencing Council has issued a definitive guideline *Offences Taken into Consideration* (2012). The guidance is intended to reflect the existing case law (eg *R v Miles* [2006] EWCA Crim 256). The guideline provides a useful summary of the principles.

- When sentencing an offender who requests offences to be taken into consideration, courts should pass a total sentence which reflects all the offending behaviour. The sentence must be just and proportionate and must not exceed the statutory maximum for the conviction offence.
- The court is likely to consider that the fact that the offender has assisted the police (particularly if the offences would not otherwise have been detected) and avoided the need for further proceedings demonstrates a genuine determination by the offender to wipe the slate clean.
- The sentence imposed on the offender should, in most circumstances, be increased to reflect the fact that other offences have been taken into consideration.

The court should:

1. Determine the sentencing starting point for the conviction offence.
2. Consider aggravating and mitigating circumstances. The presence of TICs should generally be treated as an aggravating feature that justifies an upward adjustment from the starting point. Where there is a large number of TICs it may be appropriate to move outside the category range although this must be considered in the context of the case and subject to the principle of totality. The court is limited to the statutory maximum for the conviction offence.
3. Consider whether the frank admission of a number of offences is an indication of a defendant's remorse or determination and/ or demonstration of steps taken to address addiction or offending behaviour.
4. Any reduction for guilty plea should be applied to the total sentence as should the totality principle.
5. Ancillary orders may take account of TICs to the limit allowed by the offences for which there is a conviction.

 See *Blackstone's Criminal Practice 2014* **D20**

F17 Penalty Points for Driving Offences

F17.1 Criteria

Penalty points must be imposed for all offences that are subject to obligatory endorsement, unless the court finds special reasons for not imposing points. If an offender is too young to drive or does not have a driving licence, the court should still impose the relevant penalty points for the offence.

See **A10** for penalty points applicable to individual offences.

F17.2 More than one offence

If a person is found guilty of more than one offence committed on the same occasion, the range of penalty points is taken as being whichever is the highest available for any one offence (eg a person convicted of speeding (3–6 points) and no insurance (6–8 points) is liable to receive up to 8 points). A court does, however, have discretion to disapply this rule if reasons are given: Road Traffic Act 1988 s 28.

Where a court orders obligatory disqualification and there are further offences to be sentenced it should not order points for the further offences.

F17.3 Special reasons not to endorse

A 'special reason' will fulfil the following criteria:

- It will be a mitigating or extenuating circumstance
- It will not be a legal defence to the charge
- It will be directly connected with the commission of the offence
- It will be a matter which the court ought properly take into consideration.

An example might be where a young defendant, who was a qualified driver, had been misled by a parent into believing that he was insured to drive.

See **F9.4** for special reasons.

F17.4 Secondary parties

A person who acts as a secondary party to an offence carrying obligatory disqualification is liable to ten penalty points.

See **F9.8** for New Driver provisions.

 See *Blackstone's Criminal Practice 2014* **C7.10–C7.23**

F18 **Previous Convictions**

F18.1 **Criteria**

The CJA 2003 s 143 provides:

Criminal Justice Act 2003 s 143

(1) In considering the seriousness of any offence, the court must consider the offender's culpability in committing the offence and any harm which the offence caused, was intended to cause or might foreseeably have caused.

(2) In considering the seriousness of an offence ('the current offence') committed by an offender who has one or more previous convictions, the court must treat each previous conviction as an aggravating factor if (in the case of that conviction) the court considers that it can reasonably be so treated having regard, in particular, to—

  (a) the nature of the offence to which the conviction relates and its relevance to the current offence, and

  (b) the time that has elapsed since the conviction.

(3) In considering the seriousness of any offence committed while the offender was on bail, the court must treat the fact that it was committed in those circumstances as an aggravating factor.

(4) Any reference in subsection (2) to a previous conviction is to be read as a reference to—

  (a) a previous conviction by a court in the United Kingdom,

  (aa) a previous conviction by a court in another member State of a relevant offence under the law of that State,

  (b) a previous conviction of a service offence within the meaning of the Armed Forces Act 2006 ('conviction' here including anything that under section 376(1) and (2) of that Act is to be treated as a conviction), or

  (c) a finding of guilt in respect of a member State service offence.

(5) Subsections (2) and (4) do not prevent the court from treating—

  (a) a previous conviction by a court outside both the United Kingdom and any other member State, or

  (b) a previous conviction by a court in any member State (other than the United Kingdom) of an offence which is not a relevant offence,

    as an aggravating factor in any case where the court considers it appropriate to do so.

(6) For the purposes of this section—

  (a) an offence is 'relevant' if the offence would constitute an offence under the law of any part of the United Kingdom if it were done in that part at the time of the conviction of the defendant for the current offence,

  (b) 'member State service offence' means an offence which—

    (i) was the subject of proceedings under the service law of a member State other than the United Kingdom, and

    (ii) would constitute an offence under the law of any part of the United Kingdom, or a service offence (within the meaning of the

> Armed Forces Act 2006), if it were done in any part of the United Kingdom, by a member of Her Majesty's forces, at the time of the conviction of the defendant for the current offence,
> (c) 'Her Majesty's forces' has the same meaning as in the Armed Forces Act 2006, and
> (d) 'service law', in relation to a member State other than the United Kingdom, means the law governing all or any of the naval, military or air forces of that State.

Whilst a court is required to aggravate the seriousness of an offence where there are previous convictions, a sentence that follows re-offending does not need to be more severe than the previous sentence solely because there had been a previous conviction (definitive guideline, *Overarching Principles: Sentencing Youths* (2009), para 2.4).

 See *Blackstone's Criminal Practice 2014* **D20.45 and D20.51**

F19 Racially and Religiously Aggravated Crimes

F19.1 Criteria

The CJA 2003 s 145 provides:

Criminal Justice Act 2003 s 145

(1) This section applies where a court is considering the seriousness of an offence other than one under sections 29 to 32 of the Crime and Disorder Act 1998 (c 37) (racially or religiously aggravated assaults, criminal damage, public order offences and harassment etc).

(2) If the offence was racially or religiously aggravated, the court—
   (a) must treat that fact as an aggravating factor, and
   (b) must state in open court that the offence was so aggravated.

(3) Section 28 of the Crime and Disorder Act 1998 (meaning of 'racially or religiously aggravated') applies for the purposes of this section as it applies for the purposes of sections 29 to 32 of that Act. An offence is racially or religiously aggravated if—
   (a) at the time of committing the offence, or immediately before or after doing so, the offender demonstrates towards the victim of the offence hostility based on the victim's membership (or presumed membership) of a racial or religious group; or
   (b) the offence is motivated (wholly or partly) by hostility towards members of a racial or religious group based on their membership of that group.

Following the guidance given by the court in *R v Kelly and Donnelly* [2001] 2 Cr App R (S) 73 (p 341), the court should follow a two-stage process, identifying first the sentence it would have passed if the offence had not been racially aggravated and then adding an appropriate uplift to reflect the racial element so that the sentencing process is transparent and the public could see to what extent the racial element had been reflected. There is no fixed uplift, but in *Kelly and Donnelly*, an uplift of 50 per cent was applied.

For other aggravating factors see **F30.2.2**.

 See *Blackstone's Criminal Practice 2014* **B11.149–B11.158; E1.16**

F20 **Referral Order**

F20.1 **Referral orders**

A referral order is the primary sentence for first-time offenders under the age of 18 who plead guilty. The order is unique in the criminal justice system in that the sentencing court determines the length of the referral but the requirements of the order are subsequently determined by a youth offender panel convened by the youth offending team.

A referral order is not a community sentence within the meaning of the CJA 2003 s 147 so there is no requirement to consider a pre-sentence report before imposing it.

F20.1.1 *Availability of a referral order*

The PCCSA 2000 s 16 provides that a referral order may be made by a youth court or other magistrates' court. It is also available in the Crown Court if the sentencing judge decides to proceed under the Courts Act 2003 s 66 and exercise the powers of a district judge when sentencing. The referral order conditions set out below apply where a court is dealing with a person aged under 18. The relevant age is the offender's age on the date of conviction (see **F1.1**) and therefore the conditions still apply where the court adjourns the case and the offender attains 18 before the sentence date.

Compulsory referral order conditions—By the PCCSA 2000 s 17(1) a court **must** make a referral order if:

- the youth defendant has not previously been convicted of an offence; and
- he has pleaded guilty to an imprisonable offence (and any associated offences)

unless the sentence is one which is fixed by law or the court proposes to give the defendant a custodial sentence, an absolute or conditional discharge, or hospital order. A conditional discharge is not available for offences committed before 3 December 2012.

Discretionary referral order conditions—By the PCCSA 2000 s 17(2), where the compulsory referral order conditions are not met and the defendant pleads guilty to at least one offence the court may make a referral order.

If the defendant is to be sentenced for one or more offences but he has not pleaded guilty to any of them, then a referral order is not an option available to the court.

An offence is connected with another if the offender falls to be dealt with for it at the same time as he is dealt with for the other offence (whether or not he is convicted of the offences at the same time or by or before the same court).

More restrictive discretionary referral conditions apply to offences committed before 3 December 2012 (for which see *Blackstone's Criminal Practice 2014*, **E10.4**).

Powers of Criminal Courts (Sentencing) Act 2000

16.—Duty and power to refer certain young offenders to youth offender panels

(1) This section applies where a youth court or other magistrates' court is dealing with a person aged under 18 for an offence and—
   (a) neither the offence nor any connected offence is one for which the sentence is fixed by law;
   (b) the court is not, in respect of the offence or any connected offence, proposing to impose a custodial sentence on the offender or make a hospital order (within the meaning of the Mental Health Act 1983) in his case; and
   (c) the court is not proposing to discharge him, whether absolutely or conditionally, in respect of the offence.

(2) If—
   (a) the compulsory referral conditions are satisfied in accordance with section 17 below, and
   (b) referral is available to the court,
   the court shall sentence the offender for the offence by ordering him to be referred to a youth offender panel.

(3) If—
   (a) the discretionary referral conditions are satisfied in accordance with section 17 below, and
   (b) referral is available to the court,
   the court may sentence the offender for the offence by ordering him to be referred to a youth offender panel.

(4) For the purposes of this Part an offence is connected with another if the offender falls to be dealt with for it at the same time as he is dealt with for the other offence (whether or not he is convicted of the offences at the same time or by or before the same court).

(5) For the purposes of this section referral is available to a court if—
   (a) the court has been notified by the Secretary of State that arrangements for the implementation of referral orders are available in the area in which it appears to the court that the offender resides or will reside; and
   (b) the notice has not been withdrawn.

(6) An order under subsection (2) or (3) above is in this Act referred to as a 'referral order'.

17.—The referral conditions.

(1) For the purposes of section 16(2) above and subsection (2) below the compulsory referral conditions are satisfied in relation to an offence if the offence is an offence punishable with imprisonment and the offender—

> (a) pleaded guilty to the offence and to any connected offence; and
> (b) has never been—
>   (i) convicted by or before a court in the United Kingdom of any offence other than the offence and any connected offence, or
>   (ii) convicted by or before a court in another member State of any offence.
> (2) For the purposes of section 16(3) above, the discretionary referral conditions are satisfied in relation to an offence if—
>   (a) the compulsory referral conditions are not satisfied in relation to the offence; and
>   (b) the offender pleaded guilty—
>   (i) to the offence; or
>   (ii) if the offender is being dealt with by the court for the offence and any connected offence, to at least one of those offences.

F20.2 Length of referral order

The court must specify the length of the referral. A referral order may be for a period not less than three nor more than twelve months (PCCSA 2000 s 18(1)(c)). The definitive guideline *Overarching Principles: Sentencing Youths* (2009) at paras 8.4–8.5 states that in general orders of ten to twelve months should only be made for the more serious offences and suggests the following bands:

Offence seriousness	Length of referral
Low	3–5 months
Medium	5–7 months
High	7–9 months

The order does not start on the day of sentence but instead on the date when the youth offender contract is signed (PCCSA 2000 s 24(2)). The order ends when that contract is successfully completed (s 27(2) and (3)).

F20.3 Custody threshold cases and intensive referral orders

Before a custodial sentence can be considered, the court will have to order a pre-sentence report: CJA 2003 s 156(3) and (5).

The statutory guidance *Referral Order Guidance* (2012) issued by the Ministry of Justice and YJB (available at <www.justice.gov.uk>) states:

7.4 'Custody threshold' cases are those where the court has indicated that custody is being considered but, as a first time guilty plea case, a referral order is the only available non-custodial alternative and cases where the court may choose to make a referral order instead of a custodial sentence. The latter will include, for example, where a referral order is made on second conviction when a Detention and Training Order was given on first conviction. In these cases, it is essential that a pre-sentence report proposal for a referral order is presented as a robust and credible sentencing option which should involve a referral order **intensive contract**.

7.5 The YOT should consider convening an informal 'pre-sentence panel' involving all parties and youth offender panel volunteers to consider the likely content of a Referral Order intensive contract and use it to inform the pre-sentence report proposal. A provisional date for the first formal panel meeting should be set within 5 working days of the court hearing.

7.6 The young person and parents/carers will need to understand fully that a pre-sentence panel does not create a presumption as to likely sentence, but provides an option for consideration by the court as an alternative to custody: the sentencing decision rests with the court alone and custody **may** still be given. Where a pre-sentence panel is not able to be convened, the YOT should consider including within the report proposal an outline of the areas (based on the ASSET assessment) that the YOT will be presenting to the youth offender panel for consideration in determining a Referral Order intensive contract. YOTs should consider commissioning similar resources to those available for other community sentences in custody threshold cases; the full range of intensive community intervention options, including non-electronic curfews and restrictions, should be considered to match the requirements of the case.

F20.4 Mixing referral orders with other sentences or orders (PCCSA 2000 s 19)

When imposing a referral order upon a young offender the court may not, for that offence or a connected offence, also:

- impose a community sentence on him;
- order him to pay a fine;
- make a reparation order in respect of him; or
- conditionally discharge him.

The court may not make, in connection with the conviction of the offender for the offence or a connected offence:

- an order binding him over to keep the peace or to be of good behaviour; or
- an order binding over a parent or guardian.

When making a referral order a court would still be able to make the following:

- a compensation order;
- a restitution order;
- a deprivation order; and
- a parenting order.

F20.5 Procedural requirements (PCCSA 2000 s 18)

A referral order shall:

- specify the youth offending team responsible for implementing the order;
- require the offender to attend each of the meetings of a youth offender panel to be established for the offender; and
- specify the 'compliance period', that is the period for which any offender contract taking effect between the offender and the panel is to have effect (which must not be less than three months nor more than twelve months).

The youth offending team specified shall be the team having the function of implementing referral orders in the area in which it appears to the court that the offender resides or will reside.

On making a referral order the court shall explain to the offender in ordinary language the effect of the order and the consequences of failure to agree a contract or breach of the requirements of contract made.

F20.6 Ordering attendance of parent/guardian at panel meetings

The PCCSA 2000 s 20 provides:

Powers of Criminal Courts (Sentencing) Act 2000 s 20

20.—Making of referral orders: attendance of parents etc.

(1) A court making a referral order may make an order requiring—
  (a) the appropriate person, or
  (b) in a case where there are two or more appropriate persons, any one or more of them,
  to attend the meetings of the youth offender panel.
(2) Where an offender is aged under 16 when a court makes a referral order in his case—
  (a) the court shall exercise its power under subsection (1) above so as to require at least one appropriate person to attend meetings of the youth offender panel; and
  (b) if the offender falls within subsection (6) below, the person or persons so required to attend those meetings shall be or include a representative of the local authority mentioned in that subsection.

---

(3) The court shall not under this section make an order requiring a person to attend meetings of the youth offender panel—

    (a) if the court is satisfied that it would be unreasonable to do so; or

    (b) to an extent which the court is satisfied would be unreasonable.

(4) Except where the offender falls within subsection (6) below, each person who is a parent or guardian of the offender is an 'appropriate person' for the purposes of this section.

(5) Where the offender falls within subsection (6) below, each of the following is an 'appropriate person' for the purposes of this section—

    (a) a representative of the local authority mentioned in that subsection; and

    (b) each person who is a parent or guardian of the offender with whom the offender is allowed to live.

(6) An offender falls within this subsection if he is (within the meaning of the Children Act 1989) a child who is looked after by a local authority.

(7) If, at the time when a court makes an order under this section—

    (a) a person who is required by the order to attend meetings of a youth offender panel is not present in court, or

    (b) a local authority whose representative is so required to attend such meetings is not represented in court,

    the court must send him or (as the case may be) the authority a copy of the order forthwith.

F20.7 Establishing a youth offender panel (PCCSA 2000 ss 21–2)

It is the duty of the specified youth offending team to establish a panel for the offender and to arrange meetings of that panel. At each of its meetings a panel shall consist of at least one representative of the youth offending team and two other panel members who are not members of the team. National Standard 8.18 requires the first panel meeting to be convened within twenty working days of the court hearing.

The specified youth offender team must notify the offender and any appropriate person of the time and place at which they are required to attend the meeting.

The panel may also allow the following to attend:

- a person over 18 chosen by the offender;
- a person who is capable of having a good influence one the offender; and
- a victim of the offence (accompanied to the meeting by one person chosen by the victim with the agreement of the panel).

If the offender fails to attend any part of a meeting the panel may:

- adjourn the meeting to such place and time as it may specify; or
- end the meeting and refer the offender back to the appropriate court.

F20.8 Youth offender contract (PCCSA 2000 ss 23–5)

At the first meeting of the panel, the members of the panel shall seek to reach agreement with the offender on a programme of behaviour. The aim of this programme is the prevention of re-offending by the offender.

The programme may include provision for any of the following:

- financial or other reparation to any person who appears to the panel to be a victim of, or otherwise affected by, the offence or any of the offences, for which the offender was referred to the panel;
- the offender to attend mediation sessions with any such victim or other person;
- the offender to carry out unpaid work or service in or for the community;
- the offender to be at home at times specified in the programme;
- attendance by the offender at a school or other educational establishment or at a place of work;
- the offender to participate in specified activities;
- the offender to present him/herself to specified persons at times and places specified in or determined under the programme;
- the offender to stay away from specified places or persons (or both);
- enabling the offender's compliance with the programme to be supervised and recorded.

The programme may not, however, provide:

- for the monitoring of the offender's whereabouts (electronically or otherwise); or
- for the offender to have imposed on him/her any physical restriction on his/her movements.

No condition requiring anything to be done to or with any victim or other person affected by the offence(s) may be included in the programme with the consent of the victim or other person.

When a programme has been agreed it should be confirmed in writing and signed by a representative of the panel and the young offender. This written record becomes the youth offender contract. The contract starts on the day it is signed and lasts for the length of the compliance period specified by the court (unless revoked earlier).

F20.9 Progress meetings (PCCSA 2000 s 26)

At any time after a youth offender contract has taken effect and before the expiry of the period for which the contract has effect, the panel may request the specified youth offending team to arrange a further meeting of the panel.

A progress meeting may be requested if it appears to the panel to be expedient to review:

- the offender's progress in implementing the programme of behaviour contained in the contract; or
- any other matter arising in connection with the contract.

A progress meeting must be requested if it appears to the panel that the offender is in breach of any terms of the contract.

The panel must request a progress meeting if the offender has notified the panel that:

- he wishes to seek the panel's agreement to a variation in the terms of the contract, or
- he wishes the panel to refer him/her back to the appropriate court with a view to the referral order (or orders) being revoked on account of a significant change in his/her circumstances making compliance with any youth offender contract impractical.

F20.10 Final meeting (PCCSA 2000 s 27)

Where the compliance period of a youth offender contract is due to expire, the youth offending team must arrange a final meeting of the panel.

At the final meeting the panel shall:

- review the extent of the offender's compliance with the terms of the contract; and
- decide, in the light of that review, whether the offender's compliance with those terms justifies the conclusion that, by the time the contract expires, he will have satisfactorily completed the contract.

If the panel determines that the offender's compliance has been satisfactory, it shall give him written confirmation of its decision. This decision shall have the effect of discharging the referral order (or orders) as from the end of the compliance period.

F20.11 Further convictions while referral order in force

When a young offender under the age of 18 is convicted of an offence whilst subject to a referral order, the court may consider:

- discharging him absolutely;
- extending the compliance period of the referral order (up to a maximum order of twelve months); or

- passing another sentence which will automatically revoke the referral order.

There is no statutory requirement that the offender has pleaded guilty to the new offence before the court can consider extending the compliance period.

The detailed statutory provisions relating to the powers of the court on a further conviction are set out in the PCCSA 2000 Sch 1 Part 2.

Powers of Criminal Courts (Sentencing) Act 2000 Sch 1 Part 2

10.—Extension of referral for further offences

(1) Paragraphs 11 and 12 below apply where, at a time when an offender aged under 18 is subject to referral, a youth court or other magistrates' court ('the relevant court') is dealing with him for an offence in relation to which paragraphs (a) to (c) of section 16(1) of this Act are applicable.

(2) But paragraphs 11 and 12 do not apply unless the offender's compliance period is less than twelve months.

11. Extension where further offences committed pre-referral

If—
  (a) the occasion on which the offender was referred to the panel is the only other occasion on which it has fallen to a court in the United Kingdom to deal with the offender for any offence or offences, and
  (b) the offender committed the offence mentioned in paragraph 10 above, and any connected offence, before he was referred to the panel,
  the relevant court may sentence the offender for the offence by making an order extending his compliance period.

12.—Extension where further offence committed after referral

(1) If—
  (a) paragraph 11(a) above applies, but
  (b) the offender committed the offence mentioned in paragraph 10 above, or any connected offence, after he was referred to the panel,
  the relevant court may sentence the offender for the offence by making an order extending his compliance period, but only if the requirements of sub-paragraph (2) below are complied with.

(2) Those requirements are that the court must—
  (a) be satisfied, on the basis of a report made to it by the relevant body, that there are exceptional circumstances which indicate that, even though the offender has re-offended since being referred to the panel, extending his compliance period is likely to help prevent further re-offending by him; and
  (b) state in open court that it is so satisfied and why it is.

(3) In sub-paragraph (2) above 'the relevant body' means the panel to which the offender has been referred or, if no contract has yet taken effect between the offender and the panel under section 23 of this Act, the specified team.

13.—Provisions supplementary to paragraphs 11 and 12

(1) An order under paragraph 11 or 12 above, or two or more orders under one or other of those paragraphs made in respect of connected offences, must not so extend the offender's compliance period as to cause it to exceed twelve months.

(2) Sub-paragraphs (3) to (5) below apply where the relevant court makes an order under paragraph 11 or 12 above in respect of the offence mentioned in paragraph 10 above; but sub-paragraphs (3) to (5) do not affect the exercise of any power to deal with the offender conferred by paragraph 5 or 14 of this Schedule.

(3) The relevant court may not deal with the offender for that offence in any of the prohibited ways specified in section 19(4) of this Act.

(4) The relevant court—
   (a) shall, in respect of any connected offence, either—
      (i) sentence the offender by making an order under the same paragraph; or
      (ii) make an order discharging him absolutely; and
   (b) may not deal with the offender for any connected offence in any of those prohibited ways.

(5) The relevant court may not, in connection with the conviction of the offender for the offence or any connected offence, make any such order as is mentioned in section 19(5) of this Act.

(6) For the purposes of paragraphs 11 and 12 above any occasion on which the offender was discharged absolutely in respect of the offender, or each of the offences, for which he was being dealt with shall be disregarded.

(7) Any occasion on which, in criminal proceedings in England and Wales or Northern Ireland, the offender was bound over to keep the peace or to be of good behaviour shall be regarded for those purposes as an occasion on which it fell to a court in the United Kingdom to deal with the offender for an offence.

...

14.—Further convictions which lead to revocation of referral

(1) This paragraph applies where, at a time when an offender is subject to referral, a court in England and Wales deals with him for an offence (whether committed before or after he was referred to the panel) by making an order other than—
   (a) an order under paragraph 11 or 12 above; or
   (b) an order discharging him absolutely.

(2) In such a case the order of the court shall have the effect of revoking—
   (a) the referral order (or orders); and
   (b) any related order or orders under paragraph 9ZD, 11 or 12 above.

(3) Where any order is revoked by virtue of sub-paragraph (2) above, the court may, if appears to the court that it would be in the interests of justice to do so, deal with the offender for the offence in respect of which the revoked order was made in any way in which (assuming section 16 of this Act had not applied) he could have been dealt with for that offence by the court which made the order.

(4) When dealing with the offender under sub-paragraph (3) above the court shall, where a contract has taken effect between the offender and the

panel under section 23 of this Act, have regard to the extent of his compliance with the terms of the contract.

15.—Interpretation

(1) For the purposes of this Part of this Schedule an offender is for the time being subject to referral if—

(a) a referral order has been made in respect of him and that order has not, or

(b) two or more referral orders have been made in respect of him and any of those orders has not,

been discharged (whether by virtue of section 27(3) of this Act or under paragraph 7(3) or 8 above) or revoked (whether under paragraph 5(2) above or by virtue of paragraph 14(2) above).

(2) In this Part of this Schedule 'compliance period', in relation to an offender who is for the time being subject to referral, means the period for which (in accordance with section 24 of this Act) any youth offender contract taking effect in his case under section 23 of this Act has (or would have) effect.

F20.12 Referral back to court

Under the PCCSA 2000 the panel may refer the young offender back to court by one of three statutory routes. These are for:

- breach of the requirements of the order;
- early revocation (s 27A); and
- an extension of the contract period (s 27B).

Each of these referral routes confer distinct powers upon the court and are therefore considered separately.

F20.12.1 *Referral back for breach of order*

A youth offending panel may refer an offender back to the appropriate court if:

- the offender fails to attend any panel meeting: s 22(2);
- it appears that there is no prospect of agreement being reached with the offender within a reasonable time after the making of the referral order: s 25(2);
- the offender unreasonably refuses to sign a contract which has been agreed at a meeting: s 25(3);
- the offender unreasonably refuses to sign an amended contract: s 26(8);
- the panel considers that the offender is in breach of the terms of the contract: s 26(4)(b) and (5)(b); or
- the panel considers that the offender's compliance does not justify the conclusion that he has successfully completed the contract: s 27(2) and (4).

Where there is a referral back to court for breach of the order the following provisions of the PCCSA 2000 Sch 1 Part 1 apply.

Powers of Criminal Courts (Sentencing) Act 2000 Sch 1 Part 1

1.—Introductory

(1) This Part of this Schedule applies where a youth offender panel refers an offender back to the appropriate court under section 22(2), 25(2) or (3), 26(5), (8) or (10), 27(4) or 27A(2) of this Act.

(2) For the purposes of this Part of this Schedule and the provisions mentioned in sub-paragraph (1) above the appropriate court is—

    (a) in the case of an offender aged under 18 at the time when (in pursuance of the referral back) he first appears before the court, a youth court acting in the local justice area in which it appears to the youth offender panel that the offender resides or will reside; and

    (b) otherwise, a magistrates' court (other than a youth court) acting in that area.

2. Mode of referral back to court

The panel shall make the referral by sending a report to the appropriate court explaining why the offender is being referred back to it.

3.—Bringing the offender before the court

(1) Where the appropriate court receives such a report, the court shall cause the offender to appear before it.

(2) For the purpose of securing the attendance of the offender before the court, a justice acting in the local justice area in which the court acts may—

    (a) issue a summons requiring the offender to appear at the place and time specified in it; or

    (b) if the report is substantiated on oath, issue a warrant for the offender's arrest.

(3) Any summons or warrant issued under sub-paragraph (2) above shall direct the offender to appear or be brought before the appropriate court.

4.—Detention and remand of arrested offender

(1) Where the offender is arrested in pursuance of a warrant under paragraph 3(2) above and cannot be brought immediately before the appropriate court—

    (a) the person in whose custody he is may make arrangements for his detention in a place of safety (within the meaning given by section 107(1) of the Children and Young Persons Act 1933) for a period of not more than 72 hours from the time of the arrest (and it shall be lawful for him to be detained in pursuance of the arrangements); and

    (b) that person shall within that period bring him before a court which—

        (i) if he is under the age of 18 when he is brought before the court, shall be a youth court; and

        (ii) if he has then attained that age, shall be a magistrates' court other than a youth court.

(2) Sub-paragraphs (3) to (5) below apply where the court before which the offender is brought under sub-paragraph (1)(b) above ('the alternative court') is not the appropriate court.

(3) The alternative court may direct that he is to be released forthwith or remand him.

(4) Section 128 of the Magistrates' Courts Act 1980 (remand in custody or on bail) shall have effect where the alternative court has power under sub-paragraph (3) above to remand the offender as if the court referred to in subsections (1)(a), (3), (4)(a) and (5) were the appropriate court.

(5) That section shall have effect where the alternative court has power so to remand him, or the appropriate court has (by virtue of sub-paragraph (4) above) power to further remand him, as if in subsection (1) there were inserted after paragraph (c)

'or

(d) if he is aged under 18, remand him to accommodation provided by or on behalf of a local authority (within the meaning of the Children Act 1989) and, if it does so, shall designate as the authority who are to receive him the local authority for the area in which it appears to the court that he resides or will reside'.

5.—Power of court where it upholds panel's decision

(1) If it is proved to the satisfaction of the appropriate court as regards any decision of the panel which resulted in the offender being referred back to the court—

(a) that, so far as the decision relied on any finding of fact by the panel, the panel was entitled to make that finding in the circumstances, and

(b) that, so far as the decision involved any exercise of discretion by the panel, the panel reasonably exercised that discretion in the circumstances,

the court may exercise the power conferred by sub-paragraph (2) below.

(2) That power is a power to revoke the referral order (or each of the referral orders).

(3) The revocation under sub-paragraph (2) above of a referral order has the effect of revoking any related order under paragraph 9ZD, 11, or 12 below.

(4) Where any order is revoked under sub-paragraph (2) above or by virtue of sub-paragraph (3) above, the appropriate court may deal with the offender in accordance with sub-paragraph (5) below for the offence in respect of which the revoked order was made.

(5) In so dealing with the offender for such an offence, the appropriate court—

(a) may deal with him in any way in which (assuming section 16 of this Act had not applied) he could have been dealt with for that offence by the court which made the order; and

(b) shall have regard to—

(i) the circumstances of his referral back to the court; and

(ii) where a contract has taken effect under section 23 of this Act between the offender and the panel, the extent of his compliance with the terms of the contract.

(6) The appropriate court may not exercise the powers conferred by sub-paragraph (2) or (4) above unless the offender is present before it; but

those powers are exercisable even if, in a case where a contract has taken effect under section 23, the period for which the contract has effect has expired (whether before or after the referral of the offender back to the court).

6. Appeal

Where the court in exercise of the power conferred by paragraph 5(4) above deals with the offender for an offence, the offender may appeal to the Crown Court against the sentence.

7.—Court not revoking referral order or orders

(1) This paragraph applies—
  (a) where the appropriate court decides that the matters mentioned in paragraphs (a) and (b) of paragraph 5(1) above have not been proved to its satisfaction; or
  (b) where, although by virtue of paragraph 5(1) above the appropriate court—
      (i) is able to exercise the power conferred by paragraph 5(2) above, or
      (ii) would be able to do so if the offender were present before it,
  the court (for any reason) decides not to exercise that power.

(2) If either—
  (a) no contract has taken effect under section 23 of this Act between the offender and the panel, or
  (b) a contract has taken effect under that section but the period for which it has effect has not expired,
  the offender shall continue to remain subject to the referral order (or orders) in all respects as if he had not been referred back to the court.

(3) If—
  (a) a contract had taken effect under section 23 of this Act, but
  (b) the period for which it has effect has expired (otherwise than by virtue of section 24(6)),
  the court shall make an order declaring that the referral order (or each of the referral orders) is discharged.

8. Exception where court satisfied as to completion of contract

If, in a case where the offender is referred back to the court under section 27(4) of this Act, the court decides (contrary to the decision of the panel) that the offender's compliance with the terms of the contract has, or will have, been such as to justify the conclusion that he has satisfactorily completed the contract, the court shall make an order declaring that the referral order (or each of the referral orders) is discharged.

9. Discharge of extension orders

The discharge under paragraph 7(3) or 8 above of a referral order has the effect of discharging any related order under paragraph 9ZD, 11 or 12 below.

9ZA Power to adjourn hearing and remand offender

(1) This paragraph applies to any hearing relating to an offender held by a youth court or other magistrates' court in proceedings under this Part of this Schedule.

(2) The court may adjourn the hearing, and, where it does so, may—
   (a) direct that the offender be released forthwith, or
   (b) remand the offender.

(3) Where the court remands the offender under sub-paragraph (2)—
   (a) it must fix the time and place at which the hearing is to be resumed, and
   (b) that time and place must be the time and place at which the offender is required to appear or be brought before the court by virtue of the remand.

(4) Where the court adjourns the hearing under sub-paragraph (2) but does not remand the offender—
   (a) it may fix the time and place at which the hearing is to be resumed, but
   (b) if it does not do so, it must not resume the hearing unless it is satisfied that the persons mentioned in sub-paragraph (5) have had adequate notice of the time and place for the resumed hearing.

(5) The persons referred to in sub-paragraph (4)(b) are—
   (a) the offender,
   (b) if the offender is aged under 14, a parent or guardian of the offender, and
   (c) a member of the youth offending team specified under section 18(1)(a) as responsible for implementing the order.

(6) If a local authority has parental responsibility for an offender who is in its care or provided with accommodation by it in the exercise of any social services functions, the reference in sub-paragraph (5)(b) to a parent or guardian of the offender is to be read as a reference to that authority.

(7) In sub-paragraph (6)—
   'local authority' has the same meaning as it has in Part 1 of the Criminal Justice and Immigration Act 2008 by virtue of section 7 of that Act,
   'parental responsibility' has the same meaning as it has in the Children Act 1989 by virtue of section 3 of that Act, and
   'social services functions' has the same meaning as it has in the Local Authority Social Services Act 1970 by virtue of section 1A of that Act.

(8) The powers of a magistrates' court under this paragraph may be exercised by a single justice of the peace, notwithstanding anything in the Magistrates' Courts Act 1980.

(9) This paragraph—
   (a) applies to any hearing in proceedings under this Part of this Schedule in place of section 10 of the Magistrates' Courts Act 1980 (adjournment of trial) where that section would otherwise apply, but
   (b) is not to be taken to affect the application of that section to hearings of any other description.

F20.12.2 *Referral back to court for early revocation of order*

The PCCSA 2000 s 27A provides that, having regard to circumstances which have arisen since a youth offender contract took effect, it appears to the youth offender panel to be in the interests of justice for the referral order (or each of the referral orders) to be revoked, the panel may refer the young offender back to the appropriate court requesting it

- to revoke the referral order (or each of the referral orders); or
- to revoke the referral order and deal with the offender for the offence in respect of which the revoked order was made.

When so dealing with the offender, the PCCSA 2000 Sch 1 para 5(4) and (5) provides that:

- the appropriate court may deal with him in any way in which (assuming s 16 had not applied) he could have been dealt with for that offence by the court which made the order; and
- the court shall have regard to the circumstances of his referral back to the court and,
- where a contract has taken effect, the extent of his compliance with the terms of the contract.

The circumstances in which the panel may make a referral under s 27A(2) include the offender's making good progress under the contract: s 27A(3).

Where the panel makes a referral under s 27A(2) in relation to any offender and any youth offender contract, and the appropriate court decides not to revoke the order, the panel may not make a further referral for early revocation within the relevant period except with the consent of the appropriate court: s 27A(4). The 'relevant period' means the period of three months beginning with the date on which the appropriate court made the decision not to revoke the order: s 27A(5).

F20.12.3 *Referral back to court to extend period of order*

The PCCSA 2000 s 27B provides that the panel may refer the offender back to the appropriate court requesting it to extend the length of the contract period by up to three months where:

- a youth offender contract has taken effect for a period which is less than twelve months;
- that period has not ended; and
- having regard to circumstances which have arisen since the contract took effect, it appears to the youth offender panel to be in the interests of justice for the length of that period to be extended.

When the panel refers the case to court under s 27B the powers of the court are set out in the PCCSA 2000 Sch 1 Part 1ZA which is set out below.

Powers of Criminal Courts (Sentencing) Act 2000
Sch 1 Part 1ZA

9ZB Introductory

(1) This Part of this Schedule applies where a youth offender panel refers an offender back to the appropriate court under section 27B of this Act with a view to the court extending the period for which the offender's youth offender contract has effect.

(2) For the purposes of this Part of this Schedule and that section the appropriate court is—

    (a) in the case of an offender aged under 18 at the time when (in pursuance of the referral back) the offender first appears before the court, a youth court acting in the local justice area in which it appears to the youth offender panel that the offender resides or will reside; and

    (b) otherwise, a magistrates' court (other than a youth court) acting in that area.

9ZC Mode of referral back to court

The panel shall make the referral by sending a report to the appropriate court explaining why the offender is being referred back to it.

9ZD Power of court

(1) If it appears to the appropriate court that it would be in the interests of justice to do so having regard to circumstances which have arisen since the contract took effect, the court may make an order extending the length of the period for which the contract has effect.

(2) An order under sub-paragraph (1) above—

    (a) must not extend that period by more than three months; and

    (b) must not so extend that period as to cause it to exceed twelve months.

(3) In deciding whether to make an order under sub-paragraph (1) above, the court shall have regard to the extent of the offender's compliance with the terms of the contract.

(4) The court may not make an order under sub-paragraph (1) above unless—

    (a) the offender is present before it; and

    (b) the contract has effect at the time of the order.

9ZE Supplementary

The following paragraphs of Part 1 of this Schedule apply for the purposes of this Part of this Schedule as they apply for the purposes of that Part—

    (a) paragraph 3 (bringing the offender before the court);

    (b) paragraph 4 (detention and remand of arrested offender); and

    (c) paragraph 9ZA (power to adjourn hearing and remand offender).

F20.12.4 *Amendment of referral order because of offender's change of address*

The court which made the referral order may vary the order to specify a different youth offending team if it appears that the young offender has moved or is about to move to an address outside the area covered by the current youth offending team: PCCSA 2000 s 21(5).

F20.13 Amendment or revocation of the referral order at request of young offender

The PCCSA 2000 s 26(3) provides that the young offender may request that a progress meeting be held if:

- he wishes to seek the panel's agreement to a variation of the terms of the contract; or
- he wishes the panel to refer him back to the appropriate court with a view to the referral order (or orders) being revoked on account of a significant change in his circumstances (such as his being taken to live abroad) making compliance with a youth offender contract impractical.

There is no provision for the young offender to apply directly to the court for the order to be revoked.

F21 **Rehabilitation of Offenders Act 1974**

The LASPO 2012 s 139 makes significant changes to the 1974 Act and in particular the rehabilitation periods. These changes have not been implemented at the time of writing. Implementation is now expected at the end of 2013 but as this is not certain both the current law and the LASPO amendments will be covered below. When implemented the LASPO amendments will have retrospective effect.

The 1974 Act establishes a scheme whereby a person convicted of a criminal offence can be rehabilitated for most official purposes. This is achieved by deeming that offences are 'spent' after a certain period of time. Once a conviction is spent the Act deems that the person concerned shall be treated as if he were never convicted of the offence. This means that spent convictions do not need to be declared when applying for employment or for financial services. Convictions are never spent for the purposes of criminal proceedings.

The length of time before a conviction is spent depends on the sentence passed not the offence.

F21.1 Sentences excluded from rehabilitation

Certain sentences may never be rehabilitated. These include:

- detention under the PCCSA 2000 s 91(3) for terms exceeding thirty months (forty-eight months after LASPO 2012 s 139 implemented);
- extended detention under the CJA 2003 s 226B;
- detention for life under the CJA 2003 s 226; and
- detention during Her Majesty's pleasure.

F21.2 Excluded occupations

The Rehabilitation of Offenders Act 1974 (Exceptions) Order 1975 lists professions and occupations which are excluded from the operation of the Act. These include

- all health professionals;
- veterinary surgeons;
- pharmacists;
- solicitors and barristers;
- accountants;
- probation officers;
- prison staff;

- police officers;
- traffic wardens;
- teachers;
- employees of social services departments (or voluntary organizations) who in the course of ordinary duties would have access to various vulnerable groups (eg elderly, mentally ill, disabled, etc); and
- any employment concerned with the provision of services to persons under the age of 18.

F21.3 Rehabilitation periods

Below are the rehabilitation periods for an offender aged under 18 on the date of conviction.

Sentence/disposal	Current period	Period on implementation of LASPO 2012 s 139
Youth caution (includes reprimands and warnings)		Spent as soon as issued
Youth conditional caution		Spent once conditions have been met
Absolute discharge	6 months	Spent on day of sentence
Conditional discharge	1 year or until the order expires, whichever is the longer	The last day of the period of discharge
Fine	2 and a half years	6 months after the date of conviction
Compensation order	2 and a half years	The day on which the payment is made in full
Reparation order	2 and a half years	Spent on day of sentence
Referral order	The date the contract ceases to have effect	The last day on which the order is to have effect (ie the day the youth offending contract is successfully completed)
Youth rehabilitation order	2 and a half years	The end of the period of 6 months beginning with the day specified on sentence as the last day on which the order is to have effect

Detention and training order of 6 months or less	*If aged 15 or over on date of conviction:* 3 and a half years *If aged less than 15 on date of conviction:* 1 year after the date on which the order ceases to have effect	The end of the period of 18 months beginning with the day on which the sentence (including any supervision period) is completed
Detention and training order of more than 6 months	*If aged 15 or over on date of conviction:* 5 years *If aged less than 15 on date of conviction:* 1 year after the date on which the order ceases to have effect	The end of the period of 24 months beginning with the day on which the sentence (including any supervision period) is completed
Detention under the PCCSA 2000 s 91(3) of more than 6 months and up to 30 months	5 years	The end of the period of 24 months beginning with the day on which the sentence (including any licence period) is completed
Detention under the PCCSA 2000 s 91(3) of more than 30 months and up to 48 months	5 years (excluded sentence if sentence is more than 30 months)	The end of the period of 42 months beginning with the day on which the sentence (including any licence period) is completed

F21.4 Effect of further convictions

If a person is convicted of further offences whilst a conviction is unspent, the rehabilitation period is extended until the end of the rehabilitation period for the new offence(s).

F22 **Remittal to Youth Court for Sentence**

The PCCSA 2000 s 8 allows for a youth defendant to be remitted to a youth court for sentence. The provision permits:

- a youth court to remit him to a different youth court acting for the local justice area where he habitually resides; the local youth court acting for his local youth court;
- an adult magistrates' court to remit him to the youth court acting for the same local justice area or the area where the offender habitually resides;
- the Crown Court to remit him to the youth court acting for the local justice area from which he was sent for trial.

Remittal for sentence by the Crown Court is considered in more detail at **H3**.

The power of a youth court to remit to the youth offender's local youth court is of considerable practical benefit. Not only will it usually be more convenient and less expensive for the youth defendant to attend his local youth court but it also means that the youth offending team which will be writing any pre-sentence report will be present at court when the matter comes up for sentence.

It should be noted that the power to remit to a local youth court is not subject to the same preconditions as the power under s 10 to remit an adult offender to a different magistrates' court. The power under s 8 can be exercised without the need for another matter to be listed for sentence at the local court. There is also no requirement to seek the consent of the local court before remitting the case for sentence.

The youth court receiving the case under s 8 may hear an application to vacate a guilty plea and if it considers it appropriate proceed to try the defendant (*R v Stratford Youth Court ex parte Conde* [1997] 1 WLR 113).

Powers of Criminal Courts (Sentencing) Act 2000 s 8

(1) Subsection (2) below applies where a child or young person (that is to say, any person aged under 18) is convicted by or before any court of an offence other than homicide.

(2) The court may and, if it is not a youth court, shall unless satisfied that it would be undesirable to do so, remit the case—

    (a) if the offender was sent to the Crown Court for trial under section 51 or 51A of the Crime and Disorder Act 1998 to a youth court acting for the place where he was sent to the Crown Court for trial;

    (b) in any other case, to a youth court acting either for the same place as the remitting court or for the place where the offender habitually resides;

but in relation to a magistrates' court other than a youth court this subsection has effect subject to subsection (6) below.

(3) Where a case is remitted under subsection (2) above, the offender shall be brought before a youth court accordingly, and that court may deal with him in any way in which it might have dealt with him if he had been tried and convicted by that court.

(4) A court by which an order remitting a case to a youth court is made under subsection (2) above—

    (a) may, subject to section 25 of the Criminal Justice and Public Order Act 1994 (restrictions on granting bail), give such directions as appear to be necessary with respect to the custody of the offender or for his release on bail until he can be brought before the youth court; and

    (b) shall cause to be transmitted to the designated officer for the youth court a certificate setting out the nature of the offence and stating—

        (i) that the offender has been convicted of the offence; and

        (ii) that the case has been remitted for the purpose of being dealt with under the preceding provisions of this section.

(5) Where a case is remitted under subsection (2) above, the offender shall have no right of appeal against the order of remission, but shall have the same right of appeal against any order of the court to which the case is remitted as if he had been convicted by that court.

(6) Without prejudice to the power to remit any case to a youth court which is conferred on a magistrates' court other than a youth court by subsections (1) and (2) above, where such a magistrates' court convicts a child or young person of an offence it must exercise that power unless the case falls within subsection (7) or (8) below.

(7) The case falls within this subsection if the court would, were it not so to remit the case, be required by section 16(2) below to refer the offender to a youth offender panel (in which event the court may, but need not, so remit the case).

(8) The case falls within this subsection if it does not fall within subsection (7) above but the court is of the opinion that the case is one which can properly be dealt with by means of—

    (a) an order discharging the offender absolutely or conditionally, or

    (b) an order for the payment of a fine, or

    (c) an order (under section 150 below) requiring the offender's parent or guardian to enter into a recognizance to take proper care of him and exercise proper control over him,

with or without any other order that the court has power to make when absolutely or conditionally discharging an offender.

(9) In subsection (8) above 'care' and 'control' shall be construed in accordance with section 150(11) below.

(10) A document purporting to be a copy of an order made by a court under this section shall, if it purports to be certified as a true copy by the designated officer for the court, be evidence of the order.

F23 **Reparation Order**

A reparation order requires the youth defendant to perform direct or indirect reparation for up to twenty-four hours.

A reparation order is not a community sentence within the meaning of the CJA 2003 s 147. Whilst there is no requirement for the court to consider a pre-sentence report, the court must consider a written specific sentence report before imposing the order.

Powers of Criminal Courts (Sentencing) Act 2000 ss 73 and 74

73.—Reparation orders

(1) Where a child or young person (that is to say, any person aged under 18) is convicted of an offence other than one for which the sentence is fixed by law, the court by or before which he is convicted may make an order requiring him to make reparation specified in the order—
   (a) to a person or persons so specified; or
   (b) to the community at large;
      and any person so specified must be a person identified by the court as a victim of the offence or a person otherwise affected by it.

(2) An order under subsection (1) above is in this Act referred to as a 'reparation order'.

(3) In this section and section 74 below 'make reparation', in relation to an offender, means make reparation for the offence otherwise than by the payment of compensation; and the requirements that may be specified in a reparation order are subject to section 74(1) to (3).

(4) The court shall not make a reparation order in respect of the offender if it proposes—
   (a) to pass on him a custodial sentence; or
   (b) to make in respect of him a youth rehabilitation order or a referral order.

(4A) The court shall not make a reparation order in respect of the offender at a time when a youth rehabilitation order is in force in respect of him unless when it makes the reparation order it revokes the youth rehabilitation order.

(4B) Where a youth rehabilitation order is revoked under subsection (4A), paragraph 24 of Schedule 2 to the Criminal Justice and Immigration Act 2008 (breach, revocation or amendment of youth rehabilitation order) applies to the revocation.

(5) Before making a reparation order, a court shall obtain and consider a written report by an officer of a local probation board, an officer of a provider of probation services, a social worker of a local authority or a member of a youth offending team indicating—
   (a) the type of work that is suitable for the offender; and
   (b) the attitude of the victim or victims to the requirements proposed to be included in the order.

(6) The court shall not make a reparation order unless it has been notified by the Secretary of State that arrangements for implementing such orders are available in the area proposed to be named in the order under section 74(4) below and the notice has not been withdrawn....

(8) The court shall give reasons if it does not make a reparation order in a case where it has power to do so.

74.—Requirements and provisions of reparation order, and obligations of person subject to it

(1) A reparation order shall not require the offender—
   (a) to work for more than 24 hours in aggregate; or
   (b) to make reparation to any person without the consent of that person.

(2) Subject to subsection (1) above, requirements specified in a reparation order shall be such as in the opinion of the court are commensurate with the seriousness of the offence, or the combination of the offence and one or more offences associated with it.

(3) Requirements so specified shall, as far as practicable, be such as to avoid—
   (a) any conflict with the offender's religious beliefs or with the requirements of any youth community order to which he may be subject; and
   (b) any interference with the times, if any, at which he normally works or attends school or any other educational establishment.

(4) A reparation order shall name the local justice area in which it appears to the court making the order (or to the court amending under Schedule 8 to this Act any provision included in the order in pursuance of this subsection) that the offender resides or will reside.

(5) In this Act 'responsible officer', in relation to an offender subject to a reparation order, means one of the following who is specified in the order, namely—
   (a) an officer of a local probation board or an officer of a provider of probation services (as the case may be);
   (b) a social worker of a local authority;
   (c) a member of a youth offending team.

(6) Where a reparation order specifies an officer of a local probation board under subsection (5) above, the officer specified must be an officer appointed for or assigned to the local justice area named in the order.

(6A) Where a reparation order specifies an officer of a provider of probation services under subsection (5) above, the officer specified must be an officer acting in the local justice area named in the order.

(7) Where a reparation order specifies under that subsection—
   (a) a social worker of a local authority, or
   (b) a member of a youth offending team,
   the social worker or member specified must be a social worker of, or a member of a youth offending team established by, the local authority within whose area it appears to the court that the offender resides or will reside.

(8) Any reparation required by a reparation order—
   (a) shall be made under the supervision of the responsible officer; and
   (b) shall be made within a period of three months from the date of the making of the order.

Breach, revocation, and amendment of reparation orders are governed by the PCCSA 2000 Sch 8. The 'appropriate court' is the youth court acting in the local justice area named in the order. This would seem to be the case even if the offender has attained 18.

Where a reparation order is in force and it is proved to the satisfaction of the appropriate court that the offender has failed to comply with any requirement included in the order, the court may:

- order the offender to pay a fine not exceeding £1,000;
- if the order was made by a youth court, revoke the order and deal with the offender for the offence in respect of which the order was made, in any way in which he could have been dealt with for that offence by the court which made the order if the order had not been made; or
- if the order was made by the Crown Court, commit him in custody or release him on bail until he can be brought or appear before the Crown Court.

When re-sentencing an offender the court must take into account the extent to which the offender has complied with the requirements of the order.

Where a reparation order is in force, on the application of the responsible officer or offender, the appropriate court may:

- revoke the order; or
- amend the order by cancelling any provision or by inserting in it (either in addition to or in substitution for any of its provisions) any provision which could have included in the order if the court had then had power to make it and were exercising the power.

If revoking the order when the offender has not been found to be in breach of the requirements there would seem to be no power to re-sentence.

F24 **Reports**

F24.1 **Duty to provide information about the youth defendant**

Local authorities are under a statutory duty to provide information about a youth charged with a criminal offence. Although the duty extends to children's services departments and education departments, the information is generally provided by the youth offending team. Information is most commonly provided through sentencing reports.

The CYPA 1969 s 9 provides:

Children and Young Persons Act 1969 s 9

(1) Where a local authority bring proceedings for an offence alleged to have been committed by a young person or are notified that any such proceedings are being brought, it shall be the duty of the authority, unless they are of opinion that it is unnecessary to do so, to make such investigations and provide the court before which the proceedings are heard with such information relating to the home surroundings, school record, health and character of the person in respect of whom the proceedings are brought as appear to the authority likely to assist the court.

(2) If the court mentioned in subsection (1) of this section requests the authority aforesaid to make investigations and provide information or to make further investigations and provide further information relating to the matters aforesaid, it shall be the duty of the authority to comply with the request.

F24.2 **Pre-sentence reports**

The statutory requirement to obtain and consider a pre-sentence report before deciding on sentence is much tighter in the case of a youth defendant. In particular a court may not impose a custodial sentence without considering a pre-sentence report.

The CJA 2003 s 156 provides:

Criminal Justice Act 2003 s 156

(1) In forming any such opinion as is mentioned in section 148(1) or (2)(b), section 152(2) or section 153(2), or in section 1 (4)(b) or (c) of the Criminal Justice and Immigration Act 2008 (youth rehabilitation orders with intensive supervision and surveillance or fostering), a court must take into account all such information as is available to it about the circumstances of the offence or (as the case may be) of the offence and the offence or offences associated with it, including any aggravating or mitigating factors.

---

(2) In forming any such opinion as is mentioned in section 148(2)(a), the court may take into account any information about the offender which is before it.

(3) Subject to subsection (4), a court must obtain and consider a pre-sentence report before—

(a) in the case of a custodial sentence, forming any such opinion as is mentioned in section 152(2), section 153(2), section 225(1)(b), section 226(1)(b), section 227(1)(b) or section 228(1)(b)(i), or

(b) in the case of a community sentence, forming any such opinion as is mentioned in section 148(1) or (2)(b), or in section 1(4)(b) or (c) of the Criminal Justice and Immigration Act 2008, or any opinion as to the suitability for the offender of the particular requirement or requirements to be imposed by the community order or youth rehabilitation order.

(4) Subsection (3) does not apply if, in the circumstances of the case, the court is of the opinion that it is unnecessary to obtain a pre-sentence report.

(5) In a case where the offender is aged under 18, the court must not form the opinion mentioned in subsection (4) unless—

(a) there exists a previous pre-sentence report obtained in respect of the offender, and

(b) the court has had regard to the information contained in that report, or, if there is more than one such report, the most recent report.

(6) No custodial sentence or community sentence is invalidated by the failure of a court to obtain and consider a pre-sentence report before forming an opinion referred to in subsection (3), but any court on an appeal against such a sentence—

(a) must, subject to subsection (7), obtain a pre-sentence report if none was obtained by the court below, and

(b) must consider any such report obtained by it or by that court.

(7) Subsection (6)(a) does not apply if the court is of the opinion—

(a) that the court below was justified in forming an opinion that it was unnecessary to obtain a pre-sentence report, or

(b) that, although the court below was not justified in forming that opinion, in the circumstances of the case at the time it is before the court, it is unnecessary to obtain a pre-sentence report.

(8) In a case where the offender is aged under 18, the court must not form the opinion mentioned in subsection (7) unless—

(a) there exists a previous pre-sentence report obtained in respect of the offender, and

(b) the court has had regard to the information contained in that report, or, if there is more than one such report, the most recent report.

By the CJA 2003 s 158(1) a 'pre-sentence report' means a report which:

- with a view to assisting the court in determining the most suitable method of dealing with an offender, is made or submitted by a YOT or local probation service; and

- contains information as to such matters, presented in such manner, as may be prescribed by rules made by the Secretary of State.

A pre-sentence report may be presented orally in open court (often called a stand-down report) but in the case of an offender aged under 18 a written report must be obtained and considered before a court may form the opinion that a custodial sentence should be imposed (CJA 2003 s 158(1A) and (1B)).

National Standards for Youth Justice 2013 require that reports by the YOT are balanced, impartial, timely, focused, free from discriminatory language and stereotypes, verified, factually accurate, understandable to the youth defendant and his parents/carers, and provide the required level of information and analysis to enable sentencers to make informed decisions regarding sentencing.

National Standard 5.3 states that a pre-sentence report must be based on:

- at least one interview with the youth defendant;
- where possible, an interview with the parents/carers;
- a home visit where appropriate; and
- an assessment using the *Asset* standardized assessment tool.

National Standard 5.9 states that a stand-down report should be based on youth justice assessment information gathered within the last three months and other relevant reports. It must be based upon at least one interview with the youth defendant and, where relevant, his parents/carers.

The CJA 2003 2003 s 158(2) requires the court to provide a copy of any written pre-sentence report to:

- the offender or his legal representative;
- if the offender is aged under 18, any parent or guardian of his who is present in court; and
- the prosecutor.

In the case of an offender aged under 18 the court may order that a complete copy of the report need not be given to the offender or his parent or guardian, if it appears to the court that the disclosure of information contained in the report would be likely to create a risk of significant harm to the offender (CJA 2003 s 158(3)).

F24.3 Specific sentence reports

Before imposing a reparation order the PCCSA 2000 s 73(5) requires the court to obtain and consider a specific sentence report. The report must be in writing and prepared by a YOT or local probation service. It must indicate:

- the type of work that is suitable for the offender; and

- the attitude of the victim or victims to the requirements proposed to be included in the order.

National Standard 5.6 states that a specific sentence report must be based on:

- a recent YOT assessment which is up to date and relevant; and
- any relevant information contained in any other local assessment.

 See *Blackstone's Criminal Practice 2014* **E1.27–E1.28**

F25 **Restraining Order**

F25.1 **Criteria**

A court may impose a restraining order following conviction or acquittal of any offence. Acquittal includes where the prosecution offers no evidence on a charge. The Protection from Harassment Act ss 5 and 5A provide:

> ### **Protection from Harassment Act 1997 s 5**
>
> (1) ...
> (2) The order may, for the purpose of protecting the victim or victims of the offence, or any other person mentioned in the order, from further conduct which—
>   (a) amounts to harassment, or
>   (b) will cause a fear of violence,
>   prohibit the defendant from doing anything described in the order.
> (3) The order may have effect for a specified period or until further order.
> (4) The prosecutor, the defendant or any other person mentioned in the order may apply to the court which made the order for it to be varied or discharged by a further order.
>
> ### **5A Restraining orders on acquittal**
>
> (1) A court before which a person ('the defendant') is acquitted of an offence may, if it considers it necessary to do so to protect a person from harassment by the defendant, make an order prohibiting the defendant from doing anything described in the order.
> (2) Subsections (3) to (7) of section 5 apply to an order under this section as they apply to an order under that one.
> (3) ...
> (4) ...
> (5) A person made subject to an order under this section has the same right of appeal against the order as if—
>   (a) he had been convicted of the offence in question before the court which made the order, and
>   (b) the order had been made under section 5.

F25.2 **Evidence**

Guidance as to the circumstances in which an order is made is found in *R v Major* [2010] EWCA Crim 3016:

- The court should set out the factual basis for making an order.
- The civil standard of proof applies.

- There is no contradiction in making an order post-acquittal as the standard of proof required for a conviction is higher than that for making a restraining order.
- The evidence does not have to establish on the balance of probabilities that there had been harassment; it is enough if the evidence establishes conduct which falls short of harassment but which might well, if repeated in the future, amount to harassment and so make an order necessary.

F25.3 Procedure

By the Crim PR r 50.4 where a court can make a restraining order on its own initiative, a party who wants the court to take account of evidence not already introduced must—

(a) serve notice in writing on—
    (i) the court officer, and
    (ii) every other party,
    as soon as practicable (without waiting for the verdict); and
(b) in the notice, identify that evidence; and
(c) attach any written statement containing such evidence.

F25.4 Terms

- In making an order on acquittal the court must ensure that the defendant is not denied the opportunity to make submissions on the propriety and the terms of an order: *R v Trott* [2011] EWCA Crim 2395.
- The terms of the order must be clear and precise.
- The terms of the order must be proportionate and not violate the offender's human rights. However, a person can harass someone by publishing truthful things (eg that someone is gay), and an order can be made preventing publication of information that is the truth, and such an order will not violate a person's right of freedom of expression under the European Convention: *R v Debnath* [2006] 2 Cr App R (S) 25.
- An order must name the person that it is seeking to protect but there is no reason in principle why an order cannot be made to protect a group of individuals or a company: *R v Buxton* [2010] EWCA Crim 2023.
- A court should not make an order preventing contact with a complainant who had capacity to decide and who genuinely (and not in fear) wished, notwithstanding a course of violence against her, the relationship to continue: *R v Brown* [2012] EWCA Crim 1152.
- Even though the defendant had been convicted of a sexual offence against a neighbour, an order excluding him for five years from his

home, where he cared for elderly parents, could not be justified. The order already prevented him from contacting the neighbour directly or indirectly and the mere fact of knowing he was living next door, or the anxiety from knowing there might be a sighting of him, did not make this part of the order necessary for the protection of the victim from conduct of the defendant which would cause fear of violence: *R v M* [2012] EWCA Crim 1144.

- The order can be made for a specified period or until further order. There is no minimum period.

F25.5 Variation and discharge

The prosecutor, defendant, or any other person mentioned in the order may apply to the court which made the order for the order to be varied or discharged. This applies to orders made on conviction or acquittal.

F25.6 Breach of the order

Breach of the order without a reasonable excuse is a criminal offence—see **A8.6**.

See *Blackstone's Criminal Practice 2014* **E21.28–E21.29**

F26 **The Scaled Approach**

In 2009 the YJB introduced a tiered approach to interventions by youth offending teams in order to reduce the likelihood of re-offending and risk of serious harm. This is called the Scaled Approach.

Under the Scaled Approach the YOT will assess the young person using the standardized assessment tool *Asset*. An initial assessment will calculate the risk of re-offending; where necessary an additional assessment will consider the risk of serious harm likely to be involved in further offending.

On the basis of this assessment the YOT will identify a level of intervention:

- **Standard level**—for those who show a low likelihood of re-offending and a low risk of serious harm; in those circumstances, the order primarily will seek to repair the harm caused by the offence—typically, this will involve interventions to meet the requirements of the order and the engagement of parents in those interventions to meet the requirements of the order and the engagement of parents in those interventions and/or in supporting the young person.
- **Enhanced level**—for those who show a medium likelihood of re-offending or a medium risk of serious harm; in those circumstances, the order will, in addition, seek to enable help or change as appropriate—typically this will involve greater activity in motivating the young person and in addressing the reasons for non-compliance with the law and may involve external interventions.
- **Intensive level**—for those with a high likelihood of re-offending or a high or very high risk of serious harm; in these circumstances, the order will, in addition, seek to ensure control of the young person as necessary to minimize the risk of further offending or of serious harm—typically this will involve additional control, restrictions, and monitoring.

The definitive guideline *Overarching Principles: Sentencing Youths* (2009) gives the following guidance on the Scaled Approach:

10.14 For the broad generality of offences where a youth rehabilitation order is to be imposed, this approach will enable the writer of a pre-sentence report to make proposals that match the obligations on the court to balance the various statutory obligations that apply.

10.15 Where a young person is assessed as presenting a **high risk of re-offending or of causing serious harm** despite having committed a relatively less serious offence, the emphasis is likely to be on requirements that are primarily rehabilitative or for the protection of the public. Care will need to be taken to ensure both that the requirements are 'those most suitable for the offender' and that the restrictions on liberty are commensurate with the seriousness of the offence.

10.16 Where a young person is assessed as presenting a **low risk despite having committed a relatively high seriousness offence**, the emphasis is likely to be on requirements that are primarily punitive, again ensuring that restrictions on liberty are commensurate with the seriousness of the offence. In relation to young offenders, the primary purpose of punitive sanctions is to achieve acknowledgement by the young person of responsibility for his or her actions and, where possible, to take a proper part in repairing the damage caused.

Under the *National Standards for Youth Justice 2013* a YOT is required to supervise the following orders in line with Scaled Approach model contacts as set out in the table below:

- YRO with a supervision requirement and other requirements where appropriate;
- Referral orders; and
- Community element of detention and training order.

Scaled Approach model

Intervention level	Minimum contact for 1st 12 weeks (per month)	Minimum contact after 12 weeks (per month)
Intensive	8	4
Enhanced	4	2
Standard	2	1

F27 **Sentence: Procedure in the Youth Court**

By the CYPA 1933 s 59 the words 'conviction' and 'sentence' should not be used in relation to a youth defendant dealt with in the youth court or adult magistrates' court. Instead the terms 'finding of guilt' and 'order on a finding of guilt' should be used. In practice this provision is rarely observed. It does not apply in any event to youth defendants tried on indictment at the Crown Court.

The procedure for the sentencing hearing in the youth court is governed by the Crim PR r 37.10.

The prosecutor must:

- summarize the prosecution case, if the sentencing court has not heard evidence;
- identify any offence to be taken into consideration in sentencing;
- provide information relevant to sentence (usually no more than details about previous findings of guilt or cautions); and
- where it is likely to assist the court, identify any other matter relevant to sentence, including:
  (a) aggravating and mitigating factors,
  (b) the legislation applicable, and
  (c) any sentencing guidelines or guideline cases.

The defendant must provide information relevant to sentence, including details of financial circumstances.

Before the court passes sentence it must give the defendant an opportunity to make representations and introduce evidence relevant to sentence. Where the defendant is under 18, the court must give the defendant's parents, guardian, or other supporting adult, if present, such an opportunity as well.

When the court has taken into account all the evidence, information, and any report available, the general rule is that the court will:

- pass sentence there and then;
- explain the sentence, the reasons for it, and its effect, in terms the defendant can understand (with help, if necessary); and
- consider exercising any power it has to make a costs or other order.

F28 **Sentences Available in the Youth Court**

For offenders aged under 18 on the date of conviction the court may impose the following:

- Absolute discharge
- Conditional discharge (for restrictions see **F8.3**)
- Fine
- Compensation order
- Referral order (where referral conditions apply—see **F20.11**)
- Reparation order.
- Youth rehabilitation order
- Detention and training order

A court may not suspend a custodial sentence if the offender was under the age of 18 on the date of conviction.

For sentences available to the youth court when the offender has attained 18 by the date of conviction see **I3**.

F29 Sentencing Guidelines Issued by the Sentencing Council

On 5 April 2010 the Sentencing Council took over the role previously carried out by the Sentencing Guidelines Council and Sentencing Advisory Panel. A court must follow sentencing guidelines issued by the Sentencing Council unless it is contrary to the interests of justice to do so.

The CJA 2003 s 174(2) provides:

> ### Criminal Justice Act 2003 s 174(2)
>
> . . . the court must—
> (a) identify any definitive sentencing guidelines relevant to the offender's case and explain how the court discharged any duty imposed on it by section 125 of the Coroners and Justice Act 2009,
> (aa) where the court did not follow any such guidelines because it was of the opinion that it would be contrary to the interests of justice to do so, state why it was of that opinion, . . .

Very few sentencing guidelines issued by the Sentencing Council (or its predecessor the Sentencing Guidelines Council) deal specifically with sentencing youths. The specific guidelines for sentencing youths are contained in the robbery guideline and for some sexual offences. These specific guidelines are reproduced in the relevant offence section.

Where there is no specific youth guideline the SGC definitive guideline *Overarching Principles: Sentencing Youths* (2009) suggests at para 16.11:

> Where the offender is aged 15, 16 or 17, the court will need to consider the maturity of the offender as well as chronological age. Where there is no offence specific guideline, it may be appropriate, depending on maturity, to consider a starting point from half to three quarters of that which would have been identified for an adult offender. . . . The closer an offender was to age 18 when the offence was committed and the greater the maturity of the offender or the sophistication of the offence, the closer the starting point is likely to be to that appropriate for an adult. Some offenders will be extremely mature, more so than some offenders who are over 18, whilst others will be significantly less mature.
>
> For younger offenders, greater flexibility will be required to reflect the potentially wide range of culpability. Where an offence shows considerable

planning or sophistication, a court may need to adjust the approach upwards. Where the offender is particularly immature, the court may need to adjust the approach downwards.

 See *Blackstone's Criminal Practice 2014* **E1.3–E1.6**

F30 Sentencing Youth Offenders: General Approach

F30.1 General principles

The definitive guideline *Overarching Principles: Sentencing Youths* (2009) summarizes the approach to sentencing youth offenders as follows:

- Offence seriousness is the starting point.
- A court must have regard to the principal aim of the youth justice system to prevent offending by children and young persons (see **B1**) and to the welfare of the offender (see **B4**).
- A court must also be aware of obligations under a range of international conventions which emphasize the importance of avoiding 'criminalization' of young people whilst ensuring that they are held responsible for their actions and, where possible, take part in repairing the damage they have caused (for international standards issued by the United Nations see **B3**).
- The approach to sentence will be individualistic.
- The youth of the offender is widely recognized as requiring a different approach from that which would be adopted in relation to an adult. The response to an offence is likely to be very different depending on whether the offender is at the lower end of the youth court age bracket, in the middle, or towards the top end; in many instances, the maturity of the offender will be at least as important as the chronological age.
- A custodial sentence must be imposed only as a 'measure of last resort'.

F30.2 Seriousness

Criminal Justice Act 2003 s 143(1)

In considering the seriousness of any offence, the court must consider the offender's culpability in committing the offence and any harm which the offence caused, was intended to cause or might foreseeably have caused.

F30.2.1 *Culpability*

The definitive guideline *Seriousness* (2005) identifies four levels of culpability. These are where the offender:

- has the **intention** to cause harm, with the highest culpability when an offence is planned. The worse the harm intended, the greater the seriousness.

- is **reckless** as to whether harm is caused, that is, where the offender appreciates at least some harm would be caused but proceeds giving no thought to the consequences even though the extent of the risk would be obvious to most people.
- has **knowledge** of the specific risks entailed by his actions even though he does not intend to cause the harm that results.
- is guilty of **negligence**.

F30.2.2 *Aggravating and mitigating factors of the offence*

Many guidelines relating to offences will identify specific factors relating to culpability or harm. The definitive guideline *Seriousness* (2005) also identifies general factors.

General factors indicating higher culpability:

- Offence committed whilst on bail for other offences (CJA 2003 s 143(3))
- Failure to respond to previous sentences
- Offence was racially or religiously aggravated (see **F19**)
- Offence motivated by, or demonstrating, hostility to the victim based on his or her sexual orientation (or presumed sexual orientation) (see **F32**)
- Offence motivated by, or demonstrating, hostility based on the victim's disability (or presumed disability) (**F32**)
- Previous conviction(s), particularly where a pattern of repeat offending is disclosed (**F18**)
- Planning of an offence
- An intention to commit more serious harm than actually resulted from the offence
- Offenders operating in groups or gangs
- 'Professional' offending
- Commission of the offence for financial gain (where this is not inherent in the offence itself)
- High level of profit from the offence
- An attempt to conceal or dispose of evidence
- Failure to respond to warnings or concerns expressed by others about the offender's behaviour
- Offence committed whilst on licence
- Offence motivated by hostility towards a minority group, or a member or members of it
- Deliberate targeting of vulnerable victim(s)
- Commission of an offence while under the influence of alcohol or drugs
- Use of a weapon to frighten or injure victim
- Deliberate and gratuitous violence or damage to property, over and above what is needed to carry out the offence

- Abuse of power
- Abuse of a position of trust.

General factors indicating a more than usually serious degree of harm:

- Multiple victims
- An especially serious physical or psychological effect on the victim, even if unintended
- A sustained assault or repeated assaults on the same victim
- Victim is particularly vulnerable
- Location of the offence (eg, in an isolated place)
- Offence is committed against those working in the public sector or providing a service to the public
- Presence of others, for example relatives, especially children or partner of the victim
- Additional degradation of the victim (eg taking photographs of a victim as part of a sexual offence)
- In property offences, high value (including sentimental value) of property to the victim, or substantial consequential loss (eg where the theft of equipment causes serious disruption to a victim's life or business).

F30.3 Mitigating factors

Some factors may indicate that an offender's culpability is unusually low, or that the harm caused by an offence is less than usually serious. The definitive guideline *Seriousness* (2005) identifies the following:

- A greater degree of provocation than normally expected
- Mental illness or disability
- Youth or age, where it affects the responsibility of the individual defendant
- The fact that the offender played only a minor role in the offence.

The definitive guideline *Overarching Principles: Sentencing Youths* (2009) at para 3.1 notes that there is an expectation that, in general, a young person will be dealt with less severely than an adult offender, although this distinction diminishes as the offender approaches the age of 18 (subject to an assessment of maturity and criminal sophistication). The guideline at paras 3.1–3.7 gives reasons for mitigating the sentence because of youth and these can be summarized as follows:

- offending by a young person is frequently a phase which passes fairly rapidly and therefore the reaction to it needs to be kept well balanced in order to avoid alienating the young person from society;
- a criminal conviction at this stage of a person's life may have a disproportionate impact on the ability of the young person to gain meaningful employment and play a worthwhile role in society;

- the impact of punishment is felt more heavily by young people in the sense that any sentence will seem to be far longer in comparison with their relative age compared with adult offenders;
- young people may be more receptive to changing the way they conduct themselves and be able to respond more quickly to interventions;
- young people should be given greater opportunity to learn from their mistakes;
- young people will be no less vulnerable than adults to the contaminating influences that can be expected within a custodial context and probably more so.

F30.4 Personal mitigation

The CJA 2003 s 166(1) provides that a sentencing court may take into account any matters that, in the opinion of the court, are relevant in mitigation of sentence. The CJA 2003 s 166(2) expressly confirms that personal mitigation can result in a court imposing a community order where the seriousness of the offence crosses the custody threshold.

F31 Sexual Offences Notification Requirements

F31.1 Criteria

The law relating to notification as a sex offender is contained in the SOA 2003 Part II. The regime applicable to offenders who were under the age of 18 at the time of the offence is substantially different to that applicable to adult offenders. The most significant differences are:

- the notification requirements are triggered in a narrower set of circumstances; and
- the notification period is half that applicable to adult offenders.

An offender becomes subject to the notification requirements if he is convicted of or cautioned for an offence listed in the SOA 2003 (s 80). The date when the offender is convicted of or receives a caution is referred to as the 'relevant date' (s 82(6)).

Where the offender was under 18 years at the time of the offence there is automatic registration if he is convicted of or cautioned for the following offences in the SOA 2003:

- Rape (s 1);
- Assault by penetration (s 2);
- Causing sexual activity without consent (s 4);
- Rape of child under 13 (s 5);
- Assault of child under 13 by penetration (s 6);
- Causing or inciting a child under 13 to engage in sexual activity (s 8);
- Offences against persons with a mental disorder (ss 30–7);
- Administering a substance with intent (s 61).

In the case of the offences listed above the offender must register within three days of the relevant date, that is the date of conviction or the administering of the caution. For the purposes of the SOA 2003 Part II an offence which is dealt with by way of a conditional discharge is to be treated as a conviction notwithstanding the PCCSA 2000 s 14 (s 134).

In the case of youth offenders other offences under the SOA 2003 as well as offences relating to possession of indecent photographs of children have a sentencing condition which must be met before the offender is subject to the notification requirements. The relevant age is the age on the date of the offence (Sch 3 para 95).

The sentencing condition is that the notification requirements only apply if the offender is sentenced to a term of imprisonment of twelve months or more. By the SOA 2003 s 131 'sentence of imprisonment' is to be construed to include reference to:

- a period of detention which a person is liable to serve under a detention and training order;
- a sentence of detention under the PCCSA 2000 ss 90 or 91;
- a sentence of extended detention under the CJA 2003 s 226.

In the case of a detention and training order the 'term of imprisonment' has been held to mean the length of the period served in custody and not the full length of the order (*R v Slocombe* [2005] EWCA Crim 2997). This would seem to mean that no detention and training order for less than the twenty-four-month maximum would satisfy the sentencing condition.

Where the offence has a sentencing condition, the offender is not deemed to be convicted of the offence for the purposes of notification requirements until the sentence is passed (SOA 2003 s 132). The time limits for registration would therefore run from the date of sentence.

F31.2 Notification period

The length of the notification period depends on the sentence or other disposal. The relevant periods are set out in the SOA 2003 s 82. When the offender is under the age of 18 on the date of conviction the applicable period is half that of an adult offender (s 82(2)). These reduced periods are set out in the table below:

Disposal	Applicable period
Sentence of imprisonment for a term of 30 months or more	An indefinite period beginning with the relevant date
A person admitted to hospital under a restriction order	An indefinite period beginning with that date
Sentence of imprisonment for a term of more than 6 months but less than 30 months	5 years beginning with that date
Sentence of imprisonment for a term of 6 months or less	3 and a half years beginning with that date
A person made subject to a hospital order without a restriction requirement	3 and a half years beginning with that date
A person who has received a youth caution or youth conditional caution for the offence	1 year beginning with that date
A person in whose case an order for conditional discharge is made in respect of the offence	The period of conditional discharge
A person of any other description	2 and a half years beginning with that date

If a detention and training order is imposed the length of the applicable period is determined by the length of the custodial part of the order (*R v Slocombe*, see above).

F31.3 Notification obligations

By the SOA 2003 s 83 within three days of the relevant date, the offender must provide to the police the following information:

* his/her name;
* any other names used;
* date of birth;
* National Insurance number (where the offender has attained 16);
* home address; and
* any other premises in the United Kingdom at which he regularly resides or stays.

The last requirement would mean that where an offender spends part of the week with one parent and part of the week with the other, then both addresses would have to be provided.

Whilst subject to notification requirements the offender must also:

* notify the police of any change of circumstances including, a stay of seven days or more at a temporary address (s 84);
* renew registration annually (s 85); and
* notify the police of any proposed travel outside the United Kingdom for a period of three days or longer (s 86).

Failure without reasonable excuse to comply with the notification requirements is a criminal offence punishable in the case of an adult with five years' imprisonment (s 91).

F31.4 Parental directions

By the SOA 2003 s 89 a court sentencing a defendant under the age of 18 for an offence where the notification requirements apply may make a parental direction against an individual who has parental responsibility for the defendant. The direction takes immediate effect and applies until the offender attains the age of 18 or for such shorter period as the court may, at the time the direction is given, direct.

The effect of a parental direction is that the notification obligations normally imposed on the offender are to be treated instead as obligations of the parent. The parent must still ensure that the young offender attends at the police station with him, when a notification is being given. Failure by the parent without a reasonable excuse to ensure that the notification requirements are satisfied is a criminal offence (s 91).

See *Blackstone's Criminal Practice 2014* **E23**

F32 Sexual Orientation, Disability, or Transgender Identity

The CJA 2003 s 146 provides:

Criminal Justice Act 2003 s 146

(1) This section applies where the court is considering the seriousness of an offence committed in any of the circumstances mentioned in subsection (2).

(2) Those circumstances are—

    (a) that, at the time of committing the offence, or immediately before or after doing so, the offender demonstrated towards the victim of the offence hostility based on—

        (i) the sexual orientation (or presumed sexual orientation) of the victim, or

        (ii) a disability (or presumed disability) of the victim,

        (iii) the victim being or being presumed to be transgender; or

    (b) that the offence is motivated (wholly or partly)—

        (i) by hostility towards persons who are of a particular sexual orientation, or

        (ii) by hostility towards persons who have a disability or a particular disability

        (iii) by hostility to persons who are transgender.

(3) The court—

    (a) must treat the fact that the offence was committed in any of those circumstances as an aggravating factor, and

    (b) must state in open court that the offence was committed in such circumstances.

(4) It is immaterial for the purposes of paragraph (a) or (b) of subsection (2) whether or not the offender's hostility is also based, to any extent, on any other factor not mentioned in that paragraph.

(5) In this section 'disability' means any physical or mental impairment.

(6) In this section references to being transgender include references to being transsexual, or undergoing, proposing to undergo or having undergone a process or part of a process of gender reassignment.

 See *Blackstone's Criminal Practice 2014* **E1.17**

F33 **Surcharge**

There are different rates of surcharge applicable depending on the age of the offender on the date of the commission of the offence.

F33.1 **Criteria**

In any case relating to an offence committed on or after 1 October 2012, the court must impose a surcharge order. The surcharge may be reduced if the offender is not able to pay both the surcharge and compensation.

The CJA 2003, s 161A states:

Criminal Justice Act s 161A

(1) A court when dealing with a person for one or more offences must also (subject to subsections (2) and (3)) order him to pay a surcharge.
(2) Subsection (1) does not apply in such cases as may be prescribed by an order made by the Secretary of State.
(3) Where a court dealing with an offender considers—
  (a) that it would be appropriate to make a compensation order, but
  (b) that he has insufficient means to pay both the surcharge and appropriate compensation,
the court must reduce the surcharge accordingly (if necessary to nil).
(4) For the purposes of this section a court does not 'deal with' a person if it—
  (a) discharges him absolutely, or
  (b) makes an order under the Mental Health Act 1983 in respect of him.

Surcharge rates where offender was under 18 when the offence was committed:

Conditional discharge	£10
Fine, youth rehabilitation order, or community order	£15
Suspended sentence or custodial sentence imposed by the Crown Court	£20

At present no surcharge may be imposed if a custodial sentence is imposed in the youth court or adult magistrates' court.

For offences committed before 1 October 2012 a surcharge of £15 is only payable if the court imposes a fine (Criminal Justice Act (Surcharge No 2) Order 2007).

F33.2 Payment by parent or guardian

The PCCSA s 137(1A) provides that where the offender is under the age of 16 on the date of conviction the court must order the parent or guardian to pay the surcharge in place of the youth offender unless the court is satisfied that:

- the parent or guardian cannot be found; or
- it would be unreasonable to make an order for payment having regard to the circumstances of the case.

In the case of an offender aged 16 or 17 the court may order the parent or guardian to pay the surcharge duty: s 137(3).

A Ministry of Justice circular issued on 18 January 2013 suggests that it would normally be unreasonable to order a parent or guardian to pay the surcharge where he was the victim of the offence.

See **J3**.

 See *Blackstone's Criminal Practice 2014* **E15.24**

F34 Youth Rehabilitation Order

Where a person under 18 is convicted of an offence, he may be sentenced to a youth rehabilitation order (CJIA 2008 s 1(1)).

As part of the order the court may impose any of the following requirements specified in s 1(1):

- an activity requirement;
- a supervision requirement;
- an unpaid work requirement (only available for offenders aged 16 or 17 on the date of conviction);
- a programme requirement;
- an attendance centre requirement;
- a prohibited activity requirement,
- a curfew requirement;
- an exclusion requirement,
- a residence requirement (only available for offenders aged 16 or 17 on the date of conviction);
- a local authority residence requirement;
- a fostering requirement;
- a mental health treatment requirement;
- a drug treatment requirement (with or without drug testing);
- an intoxicating substance treatment requirement;
- an education requirement; and
- an intensive supervision and surveillance (ISS) requirement.

A youth rehabilitation order is a community order within the meaning of the CJA 2003 s 147. A court must not pass a youth rehabilitation order on an offender unless it is of the opinion that the offence, or the combination of the offence and one or more offences associated with it, was serious enough to warrant such a sentence (CJA 2003 s 148(1)).

F34.1 Date of taking effect

Normally a youth rehabilitation order takes effect on the day on which the order is made (CJIA 2008 Sch 1 para 30(1)).

A court making a youth rehabilitation order may order that it is to take effect instead on a later date (Sch 1 para 30(1A)). If a detention and training order is in force in respect of an offender, a court making a youth rehabilitation order in respect of the offender may order that it is to take effect instead either when the period of supervision begins in relation to the detention and training order or on the expiry of the term of the detention and training order (Sch 1 para 30(2)).

F34.2 Existing orders

A court must not make a youth rehabilitation order in respect of an offender at a time when another youth rehabilitation order or a reparation order is in force, unless when it makes the new order it revokes the earlier order (CJIA 2008 Sch 1 para 30(4)).

When a youth rehabilitation order already exists the sentencing court may revoke and re-sentence for the original offence (CJIA 2008 Sch 2 para 18—see **F34.9**). Where the existing youth rehabilitation order was made by the Crown Court and no direction under the CJIA 2008 Sch 1 para 36 was made, the youth court has no power to revoke the existing order. Instead, if the court wishes to make a youth rehabilitation order for the new offence, it must commit the case to the Crown Court under Sch 2 para 18(11) (see **F34.9** and **H4.1.1**).

Where a reparation order already exists the sentencing court may revoke the order but only if it is a youth court acting in the local justice area named in the order (PCCSA 2000 Sch 8 para 1 [see **F23**]).

F34.3 Concurrent and consecutive orders

Where the court is dealing with an offender for two or more associated offences on the same occasion it may impose youth rehabilitation orders for each offence but the court cannot combine Intensive Supervision and Surveillance and Intensive Fostering requirements nor combine any intensive activity requirement with other requirements (CJIA 2008 Sch 1 para 31(1)).

Under the CJIA 2008 Sch 1 para 31(6) the court may impose two youth rehabilitation orders with a combination of requirements (other than Intensive Supervision and Surveillance or fostering). Where this is done the court must indicate whether the requirements are to run concurrently or consecutively. Where the same requirement is included in different orders, the court must direct if the requirements of the different orders are to run consecutively or concurrently, and if consecutive, the cumulative number of hours/days must not exceed the maximum specified for that particular requirement. For example, if two unpaid work requirements are to run consecutively, the aggregate length of the requirement must not exceed 240 hours.

F34.4 Procedural requirements

Before making a youth rehabilitation order, the court must obtain and consider information about the offender's family circumstances and the likely effect of such an order on those circumstances (CJIA 2008 Sch 1 para 28).

The sentencing court must specify the end date (not more than three years after the date the order takes effect) for compliance with the requirements of the order. Different deadlines may be specified for different requirements and the last of those dates must be the same as the end date (CJIA 2008 Sch 1 para 32).

A youth rehabilitation order must specify the local justice area in which the offender resides or will reside (CJIA 2008 Sch 1 para 33).

Where the youth rehabilitation order is made by the Crown Court the judge may authorize a youth court or other magistrates' court to deal with breach proceedings and any applications to amend or revoke the order (CJIA 2008 Sch 1 para 36). Without a direction under Sch 1 para 36 the Crown Court will be the only court able to deal with such proceedings.

F34.5 Requirements of the order

By the CJA 2003 s 148(2) where a court passes a youth rehabilitation order:

- the particular requirement or requirements forming part of the order must be such as, in the opinion of the court, is, or taken together are, the most suitable for the offender; and
- the restrictions on liberty imposed by the order must be such as in the opinion of the court are commensurate with the seriousness of the offence, or the combination of the offence and one or more offences associated with it.

By the CJIA 2008 Sch 1 para 29(1) before making:

- a youth rehabilitation order imposing two or more requirements, or
- two or more youth rehabilitation orders in respect of associated offences,

the court must consider whether, in the circumstances of the case, the requirements to be imposed by the order or orders are compatible with each other.

By the CJIA 2008 Sch 1 para 29(3) the court must ensure, as far as practicable, that any requirement imposed by a youth rehabilitation order is such as to avoid:

- any conflict with the offender's religious beliefs,
- any interference with the times, if any, at which the offender normally works or attends school or any other educational establishment, and
- any conflict with the requirements of any other youth rehabilitation order to which the offender may be subject.

The detailed provisions relating to the requirements which may be imposed as part of a youth rehabilitation order are contained in the CJIA 2008 Sch 1.

F34.5.1 *Activity requirement (CJIA 2008 s 1(1)(a) and Sch 1 paras 6 to 8)*

This requires the young offender to comply with any or all of the following:

- participate on such number of days as may be specified in the order, in activities at a place, or places, so specified;
- participate in an activity, or activities, specified in the order on such number of days as may be so specified;
- participate in one or more residential exercises for a continuous period or periods comprising such number or numbers of days as may be specified in the order;
- engage in activities in accordance with instructions of the responsible officer on such number of days as may be specified in the order (if this includes a residential activity this must be for no longer than seven days and be specified in the order).

The number of days contained in the activity requirement must not exceed in aggregate ninety days (unless imposed as part of an ISS requirement for which see **F34.5.18**).

A court may not impose an activity requirement unless:

- it has consulted with the YOT or local probation services;
- it is satisfied that it is feasible to secure compliance with the requirement; and
- it is satisfied that there are adequate provisions for the offender to participate in the activities proposed to be specified in the order in the local justice area in which the offender resides or is to reside.

A court may not include an activity requirement in a youth rehabilitation order if compliance with that requirement would involve the cooperation of a person other than the offender and the responsible officer, unless that other person consents to its inclusion.

The activity requirement may consist of or include an activity whose purpose is that of reparation, such as an activity involving contact between an offender and persons affected by the offences in respect of which the order was made.

F34.5 2 *Supervision requirement (CJIA 2008 s 1(1)(b) and Sch 1 para 9)*

This requires an offender to attend appointments with the responsible officer or another person determined by the responsible officer, at such times and places as may be determined by the responsible officer.

The requirement lasts for the length of the youth rehabilitation order. The frequency of the appointments will be determined by the responsible officer in accordance with the Scaled Approach (see **F26**).

F34.5.3 *Unpaid work requirement (CJIA 2008 s 1(1)(c) and Sch 1 para 10)*

This requirement may only be imposed where the offender is aged 16 or 17 at the time of the conviction for the offence.

The number of hours which a person may be required to work under an unpaid work requirement must be specified in the order and must be, in aggregate:

• not less than 40; and
• not more than 240.

A court may not impose an unpaid work requirement unless it is satisfied that:

• the offender is a suitable person to perform work under such a requirement as notified by the YOT or probation service; and
• provision for the offender to work under such a requirement is available in the local justice area in which the offender resides or is to reside.

The offender must perform for the number of hours specified in the order such work at such times as the responsible officer may specify in instructions.

The unpaid work must normally be performed during the period of twelve months beginning with the day on which the order takes effect. However, this period may be extended, on application to the court by either the responsible officer or the offender, where it appears to the court that it would be in the interests of justice to do so having regard to the circumstances which have arisen since the order was made (see CJIA 2008 Sch 2 para 17).

Unless revoked, a youth rehabilitation order imposing an unpaid work requirement remains in force until the offender has completed the hours specified in the order.

Youth offenders sentenced to an unpaid work requirement will often carry out any work placement in the company of adult offenders. The YRO Guidance advises YOTs to consider carefully the circumstances of the young person concerned before proposing an unpaid work requirement and it suggests that in general an unpaid work requirement will only be suitable for young people with reasonable levels of maturity.

F34.5.4 *Programme requirement (CJIA 2008 s 1(1)(d) and Sch 1 para 11)*

This requires the offender to participate in a systematic set of activities ('a programme') specified in the order at a place or places so specified on such number of days as may be so specified.

The offender may be required to reside at any place specified in the youth rehabilitation order for any period so specified if it is necessary for the offender to reside there for that period in order to participate in the programme.

A court may not include a programme requirement in a youth rehabilitation order unless:

- the programme which the court proposes to specify in the order has been recommended to the court by the YOT or the local probation service as being suitable for the offender; and
- the court is satisfied that the programme is available at the place or places proposed to be specified.

A court may not include a programme requirement in a youth rehabilitation order if compliance with that requirement would involve the cooperation of a person other than the offender and the offender's responsible officer, unless that other person consents to its inclusion.

A requirement to participate in a programme operates to require the offender:

- in accordance with instructions given by the responsible officer to participate in the programme at the place or places specified in the order on the number of days so specified, and
- while at any of those places, to comply with instructions given by, or under the authority of, the person in charge of the programme.

F34.5.5 *Attendance centre requirement (CJIA 2008 s 1(1) (e) and Sch 1 para 12)*

This requires the offender to attend at an attendance centre specified in the order for a specified number of hours.

For an offender aged 16 or 17 at the date of conviction the aggregate number of hours for which the offender may be required to attend must be:

- not less than twelve, and
- not more than thirty-six.

For an offender aged 16 or 17 at the date of conviction the aggregate number of hours for which the offender may be required to attend must be:

- not less than twelve, and
- not more than twenty-four.

For an offender aged under 14 at the time of conviction, the aggregate number of hours for which he may be required to attend must not be more than twelve.

A court may not include an attendance centre requirement in a youth rehabilitation order unless it—

- has been notified by the Secretary of State that an attendance centre is available for persons of the offender's description and provision can be made at the centre for the offender; and
- is satisfied that the attendance centre proposed to be specified is reasonably accessible to the offender, having regard to the means of access available to the offender and any other circumstances.

The responsible officer will notify the offender of the first time that he is required to attend at the attendance centre. The subsequent hours are to be fixed by the officer in charge of the centre:

- in accordance with arrangements made by the responsible officer, and
- having regard to the offender's circumstances.

An offender may not be required to attend at an attendance centre:

- on more than one occasion on any day, or
- for more than three hours on any occasion.

A requirement to attend at an attendance centre for any period on any occasion operates as a requirement:

- to attend at the centre at the beginning of the period, and
- during that period, to engage in occupation, or receive instruction, under the supervision of and in accordance with instructions given by, or under the authority of, the officer in charge of the centre, whether at the centre or elsewhere.

F34.5.6 *Prohibited activity requirement (CJIA 2008 s 1(1) (f) and Sch 1 para 13)*

This requires the offender to refrain from participating in activities specified in the order:

- on a day or days so specified, or
- during a period so specified.

A court may not include a prohibited activity requirement in a youth rehabilitation order unless it has consulted the YOT or the local probation service.

The requirements that may by virtue of this paragraph be included in a youth rehabilitation order include a requirement that the offender does not possess, use, or carry a firearm within the meaning of the Firearms Act 1968.

F34.5.7 *Curfew requirement (CJIA 2008 s 1(1)(g) and Sch 1 para 14)*

This requires the offender to remain in a specified place for the period specified in the order. The order may specify different places or different periods for different days.

The curfew period cannot be for less than two hours a day or for more than sixteen hours a day. The order may not specify periods which fall outside the period of twelve months beginning with the day on which the requirement first takes effect.

Before making a youth rehabilitation order imposing a curfew requirement, the court must obtain and consider information about the place proposed to be specified in the order (including information as to the attitude of persons likely to be affected by the enforced presence there of the offender).

By the CJIA 2008 Sch 1 paras 2 and 26(3) the curfew must be electronically monitored unless:

- in the particular circumstances of the case, the court considers it inappropriate; or
- the court does not have the consent of any person (other than the offender) without whose cooperation it will not be practicable to secure that the monitoring takes place.

In November 2012 the Ministry of Justice and YJB issued the following guidance to youth offending teams (available at <www.justice. gov.uk>).

Proportionality

Care should be taken when proposing YRO requirements to ensure that they are proportionate to the level of assessed risk of serious harm to others and the likelihood of reoffending, that they are achievable and that they take into account the possibility of further YROs. Longer curfews should therefore only be used for the highest risk cases

When is it appropriate?

A Curfew Requirement should be considered where there is a clear identified time-based pattern of offending behaviour by the young person and a curfew during that period of time would contribute to preventing further offending. Longer curfews can become part of a strategic plan to keep the use of custody to a minimum. Stand alone curfews should therefore only be used in exceptional circumstances.

However, safeguarding aspects (i.e. domestic violence, mental health issues, impact on siblings) need to be identified and addressed as part of the sentence plan prior to recommending longer curfews to court.

Maturity and likelihood of compliance are key considerations when recommending longer curfew hours and these may be best reserved for 16 to 18 year olds.

Consideration could also be given to flexible use i.e. longer curfew periods at the weekend than on week days.

F34.5.8 *Exclusion requirement (CJIA 2008 s 1(1)(h) and Sch 1 para 13)*

This means that the youth offender is prohibited from entering a place or area specified in the order for a specified period. The specified period must not be more than three months.

The requirement may:

- provide for the prohibition to operate only during the periods specified in the order; and
- may specify different places for different periods or days.

By the CJIA 2008 Sch 1 paras 2 and 26(3) the exclusion requirement must be electronically monitored unless:

- in the particular circumstances of the case, the court considers it inappropriate; or
- the court does not have the consent of any person (other than the offender) without whose cooperation it will not be practicable to secure that the monitoring takes place.

F34.5.9 *Residence requirement (CJIA 2008 s 1(1)(i) and Sch 1 para 16)*

This requires the youth offender to reside for a specified period:

- with a specified person (that person's consent must be obtained); or
- at a specified place (known as a 'place of residence requirement').

A place of residence requirement may not be imposed unless the offender was 16 or over at the time of conviction. Before making such a requirement the court must consider the home surroundings of the offender. The court may not specify a hostel or other institution except on the recommendation of YOT worker, probation officer, or local authority social worker. On making the place of residence requirement the court may provide that the offender may reside in a place not specified in the order with the prior approval of the responsible officer. If this provision is not made then any change of address will require an application to the court to vary the requirements of the youth rehabilitation order.

F34.5.10 *Local authority accommodation requirement (CJIA 2008 s 1(1)(j) and Sch 1 paras 17 and 19)*

This requires the offender, during the period specified in the order, to reside in accommodation provided by or on behalf of a local authority specified in the order.

The court may also may also stipulate that the offender is not to reside with a person specified in the order.

A court may not include a local authority residence requirement in a youth rehabilitation order made in respect of an offence unless it is satisfied that:

- the behaviour which constituted the offence was due to a significant extent to the circumstances in which the offender was living; and
- the imposition of that requirement will assist in the offender's rehabilitation.

A court may not include a local authority residence requirement in a youth rehabilitation order unless it has consulted:

- a parent or guardian of the offender (unless it is impracticable to do so); and
- the local authority which is to receive the offender (ie the authority in whose area the offender resides or is to reside).

The period for which the offender must reside in local authority accommodation must:

- not be longer than six months, and
- not include any period after the offender has reached the age of 18.

A court may not include a local authority residence requirement in a youth rehabilitation order in respect of an offender unless the offender was legally represented at the relevant time in court. This requirement does not apply if a representation order was originally granted for the proceedings but it was withdrawn because of the offender's conduct or if the offender failed to apply for a representation order at all.

F34.5.11 *Fostering requirement (CJIA 2008 s 1(3)(b) and (4) and Sch 1 paras 4 and 19)*

A fostering requirement is intended to be a community alternative to custody. A court may only impose the requirement if:

- the court is dealing with the offender for an offence which is punishable in the case of an adult with imprisonment;
- the court is of the opinion that the offence, or the combination of the offence and one or more offences associated with it, was so serious that, but for a fostering requirement (or Intensive Supervision and Surveillance requirement), a custodial sentence would be appropriate;
- if the offender was aged under 15 at the time of conviction, the court is of the opinion that the offender is a persistent offender (for definition of persistent offender see **F7.2.1**).

Under a fostering requirement (often called intensive fostering) the offender must reside with a local authority foster parent for a period specified in the order.

The period specified in the order must:

• end no later than the end of the period of twelve months beginning with the date on which the requirement first has effect;

• not include any period after the offender has reached the age of 18.

The court must specify the local authority which is to place the offender with a local authority foster parent under the Children Act 1989 s 23C. The authority so specified must be the local authority in whose area the offender resides or is to reside.

A fostering requirement may be imposed if the court is satisfied—

• that the behaviour which constituted the offence was due to a significant extent to the circumstances in which the offender was living, and

• that the imposition of a fostering requirement would assist in the offender's rehabilitation.

A court may not impose a fostering requirement unless—

• it has consulted the offender's parents or guardians (unless it is impracticable to do so), and

• it has consulted the local authority which is to place the offender with a local authority foster parent.

A youth rehabilitation order which imposes a fostering requirement must also impose a supervision requirement. A youth rehabilitation order may not include an intensive supervision and surveillance requirement at the same time as a fostering requirement.

By the CJIA 2008 Sch 1 para 19 a court may not include a fostering requirement in a youth rehabilitation order in respect of an offender unless the offender was legally represented at the relevant time in court. This requirement does not apply if a representation order was originally granted for the proceedings but it was withdrawn because of the offender's conduct or if the offender failed to apply for a representation order at all.

A court may not include a fostering requirement in a youth rehabilitation order unless the court has been notified by the Secretary of State that arrangements for implementing such a requirement are available in the area of the local authority which is to place the offender with a local authority foster parent.

'Local authority foster parent' has the same meaning as it has in the Children Act 1989.

F34.5.12 *Mental health treatment requirement (CJIA 2008 s 1(1)(k) and Sch 1 paras 20 and 21)*

This requires the offender to submit, during a period or periods specified in the order, to treatment by or under the direction of a registered medical practitioner or a chartered psychologist (or both, for different periods) with a view to the improvement of the offender's mental condition.

The treatment required during the specified period must be one of the following kinds of treatment:

- treatment as a resident patient in an independent hospital or care home within the Mental Health Act 1983, but not in hospital premises where high security psychiatric services within the meaning of that Act are provided;
- treatment as a non-resident patient at such institution or place as may be specified in the order;
- treatment by or under the direction of such registered medical practitioner or chartered psychologist (or both) as may be so specified;

but the order must not otherwise specify the nature of the treatment.

A court may not include a mental health treatment requirement in a youth rehabilitation order unless:

- the court is satisfied that the mental condition of the offender is such as requires and may be susceptible to treatment, but is not such as to warrant the making of a hospital order or guardianship order within the meaning of the Mental Health Act 1983; and
- the court is satisfied that arrangements have been or can be made for the treatment intended to be specified in the order.

The LASPO 2012 s 82 removed the requirement that the court must have a report from a medical practitioner authorized under the Mental Health Act 1983 s 12. The YJB now anticipates that assessments will be carried out by mental health workers seconded to the youth offending team or by medical practitioners from the local Child and Adolescent Mental Health Service (CAMHS). A standardized screening tool *Comprehensive Health Assessment Tool* (CHAT) has been developed and is due to be rolled out during 2013.

A mental health requirement cannot be made unless the offender expresses his willingness to comply with the requirement. The YJB non-statutory guidance *Youth Rehabilitation Order and the Criminal Justice and Immigration Act 2008* (2010) at page 36 states:

> It is important to note that the child or young person is not admitted under the Mental Health Act 1983 and therefore cannot be compulsorily treated in accordance with the provisions of that Act. Whether the child or young person is resident in hospital or not, they can only be treated if they consent.

Having made the YRO with the Mental Health Treatment Requirement, the child or young person must expressly consent to any treatment. The Code of Practice for the Mental Health Act 1983 at paragraph 23.31 states:

'Consent is the voluntary and continuing permission of a patient to be given . . . treatment, based on a sufficient knowledge of the purpose, nature, likely effects and risks of that treatment, including the likelihood of its success and any alternatives to it. Permission given under any unfair or undue pressure is not consent.'

Not only must all this be clearly explained to the child or young person, but the child or young person must be able to understand all this when s/he expresses willingness.

A lack of consent to a particular form of treatment being provided by the medical practitioner once the requirement is in place does not itself constitute an unwillingness to comply with the requirement and is not therefore a potential breach. The medical practitioner will approach the matter of consent to treatment with their patient in the legally accepted way.

While the offender is under treatment as a resident patient in pursuance of a mental health treatment requirement of a youth rehabilitation order, the responsible officer is to carry out the supervision of the offender to such extent only as may be necessary for the purpose of the revocation or amendment of the order.

F34.5.13 *Drug treatment requirement (CJIA 2008 s 1(1)(l) and Sch 1 para 22)*

This requires the offender to submit, during a period or periods specified in the order, to treatment, by or under the direction of a person so specified having the necessary qualifications or experience ('the treatment provider'), with a view to the reduction or elimination of the offender's dependency on, or propensity to misuse, drugs.

A court may not include a drug treatment requirement in a youth rehabilitation order unless it is satisfied—

- that the offender is dependent on, or has a propensity to misuse, drugs, and
- that the offender's dependency or propensity is such as requires and may be susceptible to treatment.

The treatment required during a period specified in the order must be such one of the following kinds of treatment as may be specified in the youth rehabilitation order—

- treatment as a resident in such institution or place as may be specified in the order, or
- treatment as a non-resident at such institution or place, and at such intervals, as may be so specified,

but the order must not otherwise specify the nature of the treatment.

F34 Youth Rehabilitation Order

A court may not include a drug treatment requirement in a youth rehabilitation order unless—

- the court has been notified by the Secretary of State that arrangements for implementing drug treatment requirements are in force in the local justice area in which the offender resides or is to reside,
- the court is satisfied that arrangements have been or can be made for the treatment intended to be specified in the order (including, where the offender is to be required to submit to treatment as a resident, arrangements for the reception of the offender),
- the requirement has been recommended to the court as suitable for the offender by the YOT or local probation service; and
- the offender has expressed willingness to comply with the requirement.

'Drug' means a controlled drug as defined by the Misuse of Drugs Act 1971 s 2.

F34.5.14 *Drug testing requirement (CJIA 2008 s 1(1)(m) and Sch 1 para 23)*

This requires the offender, for the purpose of ascertaining whether there is any drug in his body during any treatment period, to provide samples during the treatment period in accordance with instructions given by the responsible officer or the treatment provider.

A court may not include a drug testing requirement in a youth rehabilitation order unless:

- the court has been notified by the Secretary of State that arrangements for implementing drug testing requirements are in force in the local justice area in which the offender resides or is to reside,
- the order also imposes a drug treatment requirement, and
- the offender has expressed willingness to comply with the requirement.

A youth rehabilitation order which imposes a drug testing requirement:

- must specify for each month the minimum number of occasions on which samples are to be provided, and
- may specify times at which and circumstances in which the responsible officer or treatment provider may require samples to be provided, and descriptions of the samples which may be so required.

F34.5.15 *Intoxicating substance treatment requirement (CJIA 2008 s 1(1)(n) and Sch 1 para 24)*

This requires the offender to submit, during a period or periods specified in the order, to treatment, by or under the direction of a person so specified having the necessary qualifications or experience, with a view to the reduction or elimination of the offender's dependency on or propensity to misuse intoxicating substances.

'Intoxicating substance' means:

- alcohol, or
- any other substance or product (other than a controlled drug within the meaning of the Misuse of Drugs Act 1971) which is, or the fumes of which are, capable of being inhaled or otherwise used for the purpose of causing intoxication.

A court may not include an intoxicating substance treatment requirement in a youth rehabilitation order unless it is satisfied—

- that the offender is dependent on, or has a propensity to misuse, intoxicating substances, and
- that the offender's dependency or propensity is such as requires and may be susceptible to treatment.

The treatment required must be specified in the order and may be one of the following kinds of treatment:

- treatment as a resident in such institution or place as may be specified in the order, or
- treatment as a non-resident at such institution or place, and at such intervals, as may be so specified.

A court may not include an intoxicating substance treatment requirement in a youth rehabilitation order unless—

- the court is satisfied that arrangements have been or can be made for the treatment intended to be specified in the order (including, where the offender is to be required to submit to treatment as a resident, arrangements for the reception of the offender),
- the requirement has been recommended to the court as suitable for the offender by a member of a youth offending team, an officer of a local probation board, or an officer of a provider of probation services, and
- the offender has expressed willingness to comply with the requirement.

F34.5.16 *Education requirement (CJIA 2008 s 1(1)(o) and Sch 1 para 25)*

This requires the offender to comply, during a period or periods specified in the order, with approved education arrangements.

'Approved education arrangements' means arrangements for the offender's education:

- made for the time being by the offender's parent or guardian, and
- approved by the local education authority specified in the order.

The specified local education authority must be the authority for the area in which the offender resides or is to reside.

A court may not include an education requirement in a youth rehabilitation order unless:

- it has consulted the local education authority proposed to be specified in the order with regard to the proposal to include the requirement: and
- it is satisfied—
  - (i) that, in the view of that local education authority, arrangements exist for the offender to receive efficient full-time education suitable to the offender's age, ability, aptitude, and special educational needs (if any), and
  - (ii) that, having regard to the circumstances of the case, the inclusion of the education requirement is necessary for securing the good conduct of the offender or for preventing the commission of further offences.

Any period specified in a youth rehabilitation order as a period during which an offender must comply with approved education arrangements must not include any period after the offender has ceased to be of compulsory school age.

F34.5.17. *Intensive supervision and surveillance (ISS) requirement (CJIA 2008 s 1(3)(a) and (4) and Sch 1 paras 3 and 5)*

An ISS requirement is intended to be a community alternative to custody. A court may only impose the requirement if:

- the court is dealing with the offender for an offence which is punishable in the case of an adult with imprisonment;
- the court is of the opinion that the offence, or the combination of the offence and one or more offences associated with it, was so serious that, but for an ISS (or fostering requirement) a custodial sentence would be appropriate;
- if the offender was aged under 15 at the time of conviction, the court is of the opinion that the offender is a persistent offender (for definition of persistent offender see **F7.2.1**).

An ISS requirement must include the following:

- an extended activity requirement (specified number of days more than 90 but not more than 180);
- a supervision requirement; and
- a curfew requirement.

By the CJIA 2008 Sch 1 paras 2 and 26(3) the curfew must be electronically monitored unless:

- in the particular circumstances of the case, the court considers it inappropriate; or
- the court does not have the consent of any person (other than the offender) without whose cooperation it will not be practicable to secure that the monitoring takes place.

A youth rehabilitation order with an ISS requirement may also include other requirements with the exception of a fostering requirement.

The pre-sentence report will propose a level of ISS in accordance with the Scaled Approach. *National Standards for Youth Justice 2013* (para 8.22) require the following number of contacts:

ISS type	Contacts per week		
Extended ISS (180 days)	1–4 months	5–6 months	7–12 months
	25 hours	15 hours	5 hours
Band 1 ISS (91 days)	1–3 months 4–6 months		
	25 hours 5 hours		
Band 2 ISS (91 days)	1–2 months	month 3	4–6 months
	20 hours	10 hours	5 hours

Where a high intensity ISS is considered appropriate, *National Standards* (para 8.23) allow the requirement to be adjusted in the following cases:

- ***ISS Junior version***—offender aged 13 years or younger—12.5 hours programmed contact time each week (of which seven and a half hours can be education) for three months followed by a minimum of five hours a week for the next three months.
- ***ISS Education, training, and employment version***—minimum of one programmed contact each day totalling seven hours of contact per week for three months, followed by a minimum of three hours a week for the next three months.

F34.6 Management of the order

There will be a responsible officer to manage each youth rehabilitation order. The CJIA 2008 s 4(1) and (2) defines this as:

- in a case where only a curfew or exclusion requirement is imposed with electronic monitoring, a representative of the relevant monitoring company;
- in a case where the only requirement imposed by the order is an attendance centre requirement, the officer in charge of the attendance centre in question;
- in any other case, the qualifying officer who, as respects the offender, is for the time being responsible for discharging the functions conferred on the responsible officer.

'Qualifying officer', in relation to a youth rehabilitation order, means—

- a member of a youth offending team established by a local author- ity for the time being specified in the order for the purposes of this section, or
- an officer of a local probation board appointed for or assigned to the local justice area for the time being so specified or (as the case may be) an officer of a provider of probation services acting in the local justice area for the time being so specified.

F34.7 Duties of responsible officer

By the CJIA 2008 s 5(1) where a youth rehabilitation order has effect, it is the duty of the responsible officer—

- to make any arrangements that are necessary in connection with the requirements imposed by the order,
- to promote the offender's compliance with those requirements, and
- where appropriate, to take steps to enforce those requirements.

By s 5(3) when giving instructions in pursuance of a youth rehabilita- tion order relating to an offender, the responsible officer must ensure, as far as practicable, that any instruction is such as to avoid:

- any conflict with the offender's religious beliefs,
- any interference with the times, if any, at which the offender normally works or attends school or any other educational establishment, and
- any conflict with the requirements of any other youth rehabilitation order to which the offender may be subject.

F34.8 Duties of offender

By the CJIA 2008 s 5(5) an offender in respect of whom a youth reha- bilitation order is in force:

- must keep in touch with the responsible officer in accordance with such instructions as the offender may from time to time be given by that officer; and
- must notify the responsible officer of any change of address.

These obligations are enforceable as if they were a requirement imposed by the order.

F34.9 Further convictions while youth rehabilitation order in force

If an offender is convicted of an offence while a youth rehabilitation order is in force, the requirement that a new order cannot be made while another youth rehabilitation order is in force means that that provision has to be made for the convicting court to deal with the existing order. That power is set out in the CJIA 2008 Sch 2 para 18:

Criminal Justice and Immigration Act 2008 Sch 2 para 18

(1) This paragraph applies where—
   (a) a youth rehabilitation order is in force in respect of an offender, and
   (b) the offender is convicted of an offence (the 'further offence') by a youth court or other magistrates' court ('the convicting court').
(2) Sub-paragraphs (3) and (4) apply where—
   (a) the youth rehabilitation order—
      (i) was made by a youth court or other magistrates' court, or
      (ii) was made by the Crown Court and contains a direction under paragraph 36 of Schedule 1, and
   (b) the convicting court is dealing with the offender for the further offence.
(3) The convicting court may revoke the order.
(4) Where the convicting court revokes the order under sub-paragraph (3), it may deal with the offender, for the offence in respect of which the order was made, in any way in which it could have dealt with the offender for that offence (had the offender been before that court to be dealt with for the offence).
(5) The convicting court may not exercise its powers under sub-paragraph (3) or (4) unless it considers that it would be in the interests of justice to do so, having regard to circumstances which have arisen since the youth rehabilitation order was made.
(6) In dealing with an offender under sub-paragraph (4), the sentencing court must take into account the extent to which the offender has complied with the order.
(7) A person sentenced under sub-paragraph (4) for an offence may appeal to the Crown Court against the sentence.
(8) Sub-paragraph (9) applies where—
   (a) the youth rehabilitation order was made by the Crown Court and contains a direction under paragraph 36 of Schedule 1, and
   (b) the convicting court would, but for that sub-paragraph, deal with the offender for the further offence.
(9) The convicting court may, instead of proceeding under sub-paragraph (3)—
   (a) commit the offender in custody, or
   (b) release the offender on bail,
   until the offender can be brought before the Crown Court.
(10) Sub-paragraph (11) applies if the youth rehabilitation order was made by the Crown Court and does not contain a direction under paragraph 36 of Schedule 1.
(11) The convicting court may—
   (a) commit the offender in custody, or
   (b) release the offender on bail,
   until the offender can be brought or appear before the Crown Court.

(12) Where the convicting court deals with an offender's case under sub-paragraph (9) or (11), it must send to the Crown Court such particulars of the case as may be desirable.

F34.10 Breach of a youth rehabilitation order

Proceedings for breach of the requirements of the youth rehabilitation order normally start in the youth court (or adult magistrates' court if the offender has attained 18) unless the order was made in the Crown Court.

On breach of the requirements of a youth rehabilitation order a court has the following options:

* take no action and allow the order to continue;
* fine the offender for the breach and allow the order to continue;
* amend the requirements of the order; or
* revoke the order and re-sentence the offender for the original offence.

If the youth rehabilitation order was made by a Crown Court and no direction under the CJIA 2008 Sch 1 para 36 (see **F34.4**) was made then the youth court must commit the offender to the Crown Court.

Where the offender has 'wilfully and persistently' failed to comply with the order, and the court proposes to sentence again for the offence(s) in respect of which the order was made, additional powers are available. These additional powers include:

* the making of a youth rehabilitation order with intensive supervision and surveillance even though the offence is not imprisonable or a custodial sentence would not have been imposed if the order had not been available;
* even though the offence is not imprisonable, the imposition of a detention and training order for four months for breach of a youth rehabilitation order with intensive supervision and surveillance imposed following wilful and persistent breach of an order made for a non-imprisonable offence.

The definitive sentencing guideline *Overarching Principles: Sentencing Youths* (2009) at para 10.42 summarizes the approach to dealing with young offenders for breach of the requirements of a youth rehabilitation order:

The primary objective when sentencing for breach of a youth rehabilitation order is to ensure that the young person completes the requirements imposed by the court.

Where the failure arises primarily from non-compliance with reporting or other similar obligations, where a sanction is necessary, the most appropriate is likely to be the inclusion of (or increase in) a primarily punitive requirement.

A court must ensure that it has sufficient information to enable it to understand why the order has been breached and that all steps have been taken by the YOT and other local authority services to give the young person appropriate opportunity and support. This will be particularly important if the court is considering imposing a custodial sentence as a result of the breach.

Where a court is determining whether the young person has 'wilfully and persistently' breached an order, it should apply the same approach as when determining whether an offender is a 'persistent offender'. In particular, almost certainly a young person will have 'persistently breached' a youth rehabilitation order where there have been three breaches (each resulting in an appearance before a court) demonstrating a lack of willingness to comply with the order.

The detailed provisions are contained in the CJIA 2008 Sch 2 which provides:

Criminal Justice and Immigration Act 2008 Sch 2

3 Duty to give warning

(1) If the responsible officer is of the opinion that the offender has failed without reasonable excuse to comply with a youth rehabilitation order, the responsible officer must give the offender a warning under this paragraph unless under paragraph 4(1) or (3) the responsible officer causes an information to be laid before a justice of the peace in respect of the failure.

(2) A warning under this paragraph must—
   (a) describe the circumstances of the failure,
   (b) state that the failure is unacceptable, and
   (c) state that the offender will be liable to be brought before a court—
      (i) in a case where the warning is given during the warned period relating to a previous warning under this paragraph, if during that period the offender again fails to comply with the order, or
      (ii) in any other case, if during the warned period relating to the warning, the offender fails on more than one occasion to comply with the order.

(3) The responsible officer must, as soon as practicable after the warning has been given, record that fact.

(4) In this paragraph, 'warned period', in relation to a warning under this paragraph, means the period of 12 months beginning with the date on which the warning was given.

4 Breach of order

(1) If the responsible officer—
   (a) has given a warning ('the first warning') under paragraph 3 to the offender in respect of a youth rehabilitation order,
   (b) during the warned period relating to the first warning, has given another warning under that paragraph to the offender in respect of a failure to comply with the order, and
   (c) is of the opinion that, during the warned period relating to the first warning, the offender has again failed without reasonable excuse to comply with the order,

the responsible officer must cause an information to be laid before a justice of the peace in respect of the failure mentioned in paragraph (c).

(2) But sub-paragraph (1) does not apply if the responsible officer is of the opinion that there are exceptional circumstances which justify not causing an information to be so laid.

(3) If—
  (a) the responsible officer is of the opinion that the offender has failed without reasonable excuse to comply with a youth rehabilitation order, and
  (b) sub-paragraph (1) does not apply (in a case not within subparagraph (2)), the responsible officer may cause an information to be laid before a justice of the peace in respect of that failure.

(4) In this paragraph, 'warned period' has the same meaning as in paragraph 3.

5 Issue of summons or warrant by justice of the peace

(1) If at any time while a youth rehabilitation order is in force it appears on information to a justice of the peace that an offender has failed to comply with a youth rehabilitation order, the justice may—
  (a) issue a summons requiring the offender to appear at the place and time specified in it, or
  (b) if the information is in writing and on oath, issue a warrant for the offender's arrest.

(2) Any summons or warrant issued under this paragraph must direct the offender to appear or be brought—
  (a) if the youth rehabilitation order was made by the Crown Court and does not include a direction under paragraph 36 of Schedule 1, before the Crown Court, and
  (b) in any other case, before the appropriate court.

(3) In sub-paragraph (2), 'appropriate court' means—
  (a) if the offender is aged under 18, a youth court acting in the relevant local justice area, and
  (b) if the offender is aged 18 or over, a magistrates' court (other than a youth court) acting in that local justice area.

(4) In sub-paragraph (3), 'relevant local justice area' means—
  (a) the local justice area in which the offender resides, or
  (b) if it is not known where the offender resides, the local justice area specified in the youth rehabilitation order.

(5) Sub-paragraphs (6) and (7) apply where the offender does not appear in answer to a summons issued under this paragraph.

(6) If the summons required the offender to appear before the Crown Court, the Crown Court may—
  (a) unless the summons was issued under this sub-paragraph, issue a further summons requiring the offender to appear at the place and time specified in it, or
  (b) in any case, issue a warrant for the arrest of the offender.

(7) If the summons required the offender to appear before a magistrates' court, the magistrates' court may issue a warrant for the arrest of the offender.

6 Powers of magistrates' court

(1) This paragraph applies where—

    (a) an offender appears or is brought before a youth court or other magistrates' court under paragraph 5, and

    (b) it is proved to the satisfaction of the court that the offender has failed without reasonable excuse to comply with the youth rehabilitation order.

(2) The court may deal with the offender in respect of that failure in any one of the following ways—

    (a) by ordering the offender to pay a fine of an amount not exceeding £2,500.—

    (b) by amending the terms of the youth rehabilitation order so as to impose any requirement which could have been included in the order when it was made—

        (i) in addition to, or

        (ii) in substitution for,

        any requirement or requirements already imposed by the order;

    (c) by dealing with the offender, for the offence in respect of which the order was made, in any way in which the court could have dealt with the offender for that offence (had the offender been before that court to be dealt with for it).

(3) Sub-paragraph (2)(b) is subject to sub-paragraphs (6) to (9).

(4) In dealing with the offender under sub-paragraph (2), the court must take into account the extent to which the offender has complied with the youth rehabilitation order.

(5) A fine imposed under sub-paragraph (2)(a) is to be treated, for the purposes of any enactment, as being a sum adjudged to be paid by a conviction.

(6) Subject to sub-paragraph (6A) any requirement imposed under sub-paragraph (2)(b) must be capable of being complied with before the date specified under paragraph 32(1) of Schedule 1.

(6A) When imposing a requirement under sub-paragraph (2)(b), the court may amend the order to substitute a later date for that specified under paragraph 32(1) of Schedule 1.

(6B) A date substituted under sub-paragraph (6A)—

    (a) may not fall outside the period of six months beginning with the date previously specified under paragraph 32(1) of Schedule 1;

    (b) subject to that, may fall more than three years after the date on which the order took effect.

(6C) The power under sub-paragraph (6A) may not be exercised in relation to an order if that power or the power in paragraph 8(6A) has previously been exercised in relation to that order.

(6D) A date substituted under sub-paragraph (6A) is to be treated as having been specified in relation to the order under paragraph 32(1) of Schedule 1.

(7) Where—

    (a) the court is dealing with the offender under sub-paragraph (2)(b), and

    (b) the youth rehabilitation order does not contain an unpaid work requirement, paragraph 10(2) of Schedule 1 applies in relation to the inclusion of such a requirement as if for '40' there were substituted '20'.

(8) The court may not under sub-paragraph (2)(b) impose—

(a) an extended activity requirement, or

(b) a fostering requirement,

if the order does not already impose such a requirement.

(9) Where—

(a) the order imposes a fostering requirement (the 'original requirement'), and

(b) under sub-paragraph (2)(b) the court proposes to substitute a new fostering requirement ('the substitute requirement') for the original requirement,

paragraph 18(2) of Schedule 1 applies in relation to the substitute requirement as if the reference to the period of 12 months beginning with the date on which the original requirement first had effect were a reference to the period of 18 months beginning with that date.

(10) Where—

(a) the court deals with the offender under sub-paragraph (2)(b), and

(b) it would not otherwise have the power to amend the youth rehabilitation order under paragraph 13 (amendment by reason of change of residence),

that paragraph has effect as if references in it to the appropriate court were references to the court which is dealing with the offender.

(11) Where the court deals with the offender under sub-paragraph (2)(c), it must revoke the youth rehabilitation order if it is still in force.

(12) Sub-paragraphs (13) to (15) apply where—

(a) the court is dealing with the offender under sub-paragraph (2)(c), and

(b) the offender has wilfully and persistently failed to comply with a youth rehabilitation order.

(13) The court may impose a youth rehabilitation order with intensive supervision and surveillance notwithstanding anything in section 1(4)(a) or (b).

(14) If—

(a) the order is a youth rehabilitation order with intensive supervision and surveillance, and

(b) the offence mentioned in sub-paragraph (2)(c) was punishable with imprisonment,

the court may impose a custodial sentence notwithstanding anything in section 152(2) of the Criminal Justice Act 2003 (c. 44) (general restrictions on imposing discretionary custodial sentences).

(15) If—

(a) the order is a youth rehabilitation order with intensive supervision and surveillance which was imposed by virtue of sub-paragraph (13) or paragraph 8(12), and

(b) the offence mentioned in sub-paragraph (2)(c) was not punishable with imprisonment,

for the purposes of dealing with the offender under sub-paragraph (2)(c), the court is to be taken to have had power to deal with the offender for that offence by making a detention and training order for a term not exceeding 4 months.

(16) An offender may appeal to the Crown Court against a sentence imposed under sub-paragraph (2)(c).

7 Power of magistrates' court to refer offender to Crown Court

(1) Sub-paragraph (2) applies if—
  (a) the youth rehabilitation order was made by the Crown Court and contains a direction under paragraph 36 of Schedule 1, and
  (b) a youth court or other magistrates' court would (apart from that sub-paragraph) be required, or has the power, to deal with the offender in one of the ways mentioned in paragraph 6(2).
(2) The court may instead—
  (a) commit the offender in custody, or
  (b) release the offender on bail,
  until the offender can be brought or appear before the Crown Court.
(3) Where a court deals with the offender's case under sub-paragraph (2) it must send to the Crown Court—
  (a) a certificate signed by a justice of the peace certifying that the offender has failed to comply with the youth rehabilitation order in the respect specified in the certificate, and
  (b) such other particulars of the case as may be desirable;
  and a certificate purporting to be so signed is admissible as evidence of the failure before the Crown Court.

. . .

9 Restriction of powers in paragraphs 6 and 8 where treatment required

(1) Sub-paragraph (2) applies where a youth rehabilitation order imposes any of the following requirements in respect of an offender—
  (a) a mental health treatment requirement;
  (b) a drug treatment requirement;
  (c) an intoxicating substance treatment requirement.
(2) The offender is not to be treated for the purposes of paragraph 6 or 8 as having failed to comply with the order on the ground only that the offender had refused to undergo any surgical, electrical or other treatment required by that requirement if, in the opinion of the court, the refusal was reasonable having regard to all the circumstances.

F34.11 Revocation of a youth rehabilitation order

Criminal Justice and Immigration Act 2008 Sch 2

11 Revocation of order with or without re-sentencing: powers of appropriate court

(1) This paragraph applies where—
  (a) a youth rehabilitation order is in force in respect of any offender,
  (b) the order—
    (i) was made by a youth court or other magistrates' court, or

      (ii) was made by the Crown Court and contains a direction under paragraph 36 of Schedule 1, and

(c) the offender or the responsible officer makes an application to the appropriate court under this sub-paragraph.

(2) If it appears to the appropriate court to be in the interests of justice to do so, having regard to circumstances which have arisen since the order was made, the appropriate court may—

    (a) revoke the order, or

    (b) both—

      (i) revoke the order, and

      (ii) deal with the offender, for the offence in respect of which the order was made, in any way in which the appropriate court could have dealt with the offender for that offence (had the offender been before that court to be dealt with for it).

(3) The circumstances in which a youth rehabilitation order may be revoked under sub-paragraph (2) include the offender's making good progress or responding satisfactorily to supervision or treatment (as the case requires).

(4) In dealing with an offender under sub-paragraph (2)(b), the appropriate court must take into account the extent to which the offender has complied with the requirements of the youth rehabilitation order.

(5) A person sentenced under sub-paragraph (2)(b) for an offence may appeal to the Crown Court against the sentence.

(6) No application may be made by the offender under sub-paragraph (1) while an appeal against the youth rehabilitation order is pending.

(7) If an application under sub-paragraph (1) relating to a youth rehabilitation order is dismissed, then during the period of three months beginning with the date on which it was dismissed no further such application may be made in relation to the order by any person except with the consent of the appropriate court.

(8) In this paragraph, 'the appropriate court' means—

    (a) if the offender is aged under 18 when the application under sub-paragraph (1) was made, a youth court acting in the local justice area specified in the youth rehabilitation order, and

    (b) if the offender is aged 18 or over at that time, a magistrates' court (other than a youth court) acting in that local justice area.

F34.12   Amendment of a youth rehabilitation order

Criminal Justice and Immigration Act 2008 Sch 2

13   Amendment by appropriate court

(1) This paragraph applies where—

    (a) a youth rehabilitation order is in force in respect of an offender,

    (b) the order—

      (i) was made by a youth court or other magistrates' court, or

      (ii) was made by the Crown Court and contains a direction under paragraph 36 of Schedule 1, and

(c) an application for the amendment of the order is made to the appropriate court by the offender or the responsible officer.

(2) If the appropriate court is satisfied that the offender proposes to reside, or is residing, in a local justice area ('the new local justice area') other than the local justice area for the time being specified in the order, the court—

(a) must, if the application under sub-paragraph (1)(c) was made by the responsible officer, or

(b) may, in any other case,

amend the youth rehabilitation order by substituting the new local justice area for the area specified in the order.

(3) Sub-paragraph (2) is subject to paragraph 15.

(4) The appropriate court may by order amend the youth rehabilitation order—

(a) by cancelling any of the requirements of the order, or

(b) by replacing any of those requirements with a requirement of the same kind which could have been included in the order when it was made.

(5) Sub-paragraph (4) is subject to paragraph 16.

(6) In this paragraph, 'the appropriate court' means—

(a) if the offender is aged under 18 when the application under sub-paragraph (1) was made, a youth court acting in the local justice area specified in the youth rehabilitation order, and

(b) if the offender is aged 18 or over at that time, a magistrates' court (other than a youth court) acting in that local justice area.

15 Exercise of powers under paragraph 13(2) or 14(2): further provisions

(1) In sub-paragraphs (2) and (3), 'specific area requirement', in relation to a youth rehabilitation order, means a requirement contained in the order which, in the opinion of the court, cannot be complied with unless the offender continues to reside in the local justice area specified in the youth rehabilitation order.

(2) A court may not under paragraph 13(2) or 14(2) amend a youth rehabilitation order which contains specific area requirements unless, in accordance with paragraph 13(4) or, as the case may be, 14(4), it either—

(a) cancels those requirements, or

(b) substitutes for those requirements other requirements which can be complied with if the offender resides in the new local justice area mentioned in paragraph 13(2) or (as the case may be) 14(2).

(3) If—

(a) the application under paragraph 13(1)(c) or 14(1)(c) was made by the responsible officer, and

(b) the youth rehabilitation order contains specific area requirements, the court must, unless it considers it inappropriate to do so, so exercise its powers under paragraph 13(4) or, as the case may be, 14(4) that it is not prevented by sub-paragraph (2) from amending the order under paragraph 13(2) or, as the case may be, 14(2).

(4) The court may not under paragraph 13(2) or, as the case may be, 14(2) amend a youth rehabilitation order imposing a programme requirement unless the court is satisfied that a programme which—

(a) corresponds as nearly as practicable to the programme specified in the order for the purposes of that requirement, and

(b) is suitable for the offender,

is available in the new local justice area.

16 Exercise of powers under paragraph 13(4) or 14(4): further provisions

(1) Subject to sub-paragraph (16A) any requirement imposed under paragraph 13(4)(b) or 14(4)(b) must be capable of being complied with before the date specified under paragraph 32(1) of Schedule 1.

(2) Where—

    (a) a youth rehabilitation order imposes a fostering requirement (the 'original requirement'), and

    (b) under paragraph 13(4)(b) or 14(4)(b) a court proposes to substitute a new fostering requirement ('the substitute requirement') for the original requirement,

    paragraph 18(2) of Schedule 1 applies in relation to the substitute requirement as if the reference to the period of 12 months beginning with the date on which the original requirement first had effect were a reference to the period of 18 months beginning with that date.

(3) The court may not under paragraph 13(4) or 14(4) impose—

    (a) a mental health treatment requirement,

    (b) a drug treatment requirement, or

    (c) a drug testing requirement,

    unless the offender has expressed willingness to comply with the requirement.

(4) If an offender fails to express willingness to comply with a mental health treatment requirement, a drug treatment requirement or a drug testing requirement which the court proposes to impose under paragraph 13(4) or 14(4), the court may—

    (a) revoke the youth rehabilitation order, and

    (b) deal with the offender, for the offence in respect of which the order was made, in any way in which that court could have dealt with the offender for that offence (had the offender been before that court to be dealt with for it).

(5) In dealing with the offender under sub-paragraph (4)(b), the court must take into account the extent to which the offender has complied with the order.

F34.13 Extension of a youth rehabilitation order

On application by the responsible officer or the offender a court may extend the length of a youth rehabilitation order by up to six months if the requirements of the order have not been completed. This power may only be exercised once.

In the case of an unpaid work requirement the court may extend the period in which the work must be completed. In this case only the extension is not limited to six months.

Criminal Justice and Immigration Act 2008 Sch 2

16A Extension of order

(1) The appropriate court may, on the application of the offender or the responsible officer, amend a youth rehabilitation order by substituting a later date for that specified under paragraph 32(1) of Schedule 1.

(2) A date substituted under sub-paragraph (1)—

   (a) may not fall outside the period of six months beginning with the date previously specified under paragraph 32(1) of Schedule 1;

   (b) subject to that, may fall more than three years after the date on which the order took effect.

(3) The power under sub-paragraph (1) may not be exercised in relation to an order if it has previously been exercised in relation to that order.

(4) A date substituted under sub-paragraph (1) is to be treated as having been specified in relation to the order under paragraph 32(1) of Schedule 1.

(5) In this paragraph 'the appropriate court' means—

   (a) if the order was made by a youth court or other magistrates' court, or was made by the Crown Court and contains a direction under paragraph 36 of Schedule 1, the court determined under sub-paragraph (6), and

   (b) if the order was made by the Crown Court and does not contain a direction under paragraph 36 of Schedule 1, the Crown Court.

(6) The court referred to in sub-paragraph (5)(a) is—

   (a) if the offender is aged under 18 when the application is made, a youth court acting in the local justice area specified in the youth rehabilitation order, and

   (b) if the offender is aged 18 or over at that time, a magistrates' court (other than a youth court) acting in that local justice area.

17 Extension of unpaid work requirement

Where—

   (a) a youth rehabilitation order imposing an unpaid work requirement is in force in respect of an offender, and

   (b) on the application of the offender or the responsible officer, it appears to the appropriate court that it would be in the interests of justice to do so having regard to circumstances which have arisen since the order was made,

the court may, in relation to the order, extend the period of 12 months specified in paragraph 10(6) of Schedule 1.

F34.14 Requiring attendance of offender (revocation, amendment, extension)

Where a court is considering revocation, amendment, or an extension of the youth rehabilitation order in circumstances where it is not on the application of the offender, the court must require the attendance of the offender. The CJIA 2008 Sch 2 provides:

Criminal Justice and Immigration Act 2008 Sch 2

20 Appearance of offender before court

(1) Subject to sub-paragraph (2), where, otherwise than on the application of the offender, a court proposes to exercise its powers under Part 3, 4 or 5 of this Schedule, the court—

    (a) must summon the offender to appear before the court, and

    (b) if the offender does not appear in answer to the summons, may issue a warrant for the offender's arrest.

(2) Sub-paragraph (1) does not apply where a court proposes to make an order—

    (a) revoking a youth rehabilitation order,

    (b) cancelling, or reducing the duration of, a requirement of a youth rehabilitation order, or

    (c) substituting a new local justice area or place for one specified in a youth rehabilitation order.

21 Warrants

(1) Sub-paragraph (2) applies where an offender is arrested in pursuance of a warrant issued by virtue of this Schedule and cannot be brought immediately before the court before which the warrant directs the offender to be brought ('the relevant court').

(2) The person in whose custody the offender is—

    (a) may make arrangements for the offender's detention in a place of safety for a period of not more than 72 hours from the time of the arrest, and

    (b) must within that period bring the offender before a magistrates' court.

(3) In the case of a warrant issued by the Crown Court, section 81(5) of the Supreme Court Act 1981 (c. 54) (duty to bring person before magistrates' court) does not apply.

(4) A person who is detained under arrangements made under sub-paragraph (2)(a) is deemed to be in legal custody.

(5) In sub-paragraph (2)(a) 'place of safety' has the same meaning as in the Children and Young Persons Act 1933.

(6) Sub-paragraphs (7) to (10) apply where, under sub-paragraph (2), the offender is brought before a court ('the alternative court') which is not the relevant court.

(7) If the relevant court is a magistrates' court—

    (a) the alternative court may—

        (i) direct that the offender be released forthwith, or

        (ii) remand the offender, and

    (b) for the purposes of paragraph (a), section 128 of the Magistrates' Courts Act 1980 (c. 43) (remand in custody or on bail) has effect as if the court referred to in subsections (1)(a), (3), (4)(a) and (5) were the relevant court.

(8) If the relevant court is the Crown Court, section 43A of that Act (functions of magistrates' court where a person in custody is brought before it with a view to appearance before the Crown Court) applies as if, in subsection (1)—

(a) the words 'issued by the Crown Court' were omitted, and

(b) the reference to section 81(5) of the Supreme Court Act 1981 were a reference to sub-paragraph (2)(b).

(9) Any power to remand the offender in custody which is conferred by section 43A or 128 of the Magistrates' Courts Act 1980 is to be taken to be a power—

(a) if the offender is aged under 18, to remand the offender to accommodation provided by or on behalf of a local authority, and

(b) in any other case, to remand the offender to a prison.

(10) Where the court remands the offender to accommodation provided by or on behalf of a local authority, the court must designate, as the authority which is to receive the offender, the local authority for the area in which it appears to the court that the offender resides.

22 Adjournment of proceedings

(1) This paragraph applies to any hearing relating to an offender held by a youth court or other magistrates' court in any proceedings under this Schedule.

(2) The court may adjourn the hearing, and, where it does so, may—

(a) direct that the offender be released forthwith, or

(b) remand the offender.

(3) Where the court remands the offender under sub-paragraph (2)—

(a) it must fix the time and place at which the hearing is to be resumed, and

(b) that time and place must be the time and place at which the offender is required to appear or be brought before the court by virtue of the remand.

(4) Where the court adjourns the hearing under sub-paragraph (2) but does not remand the offender—

(a) it may fix the time and place at which the hearing is to be resumed, but

(b) if it does not do so, must not resume the hearing unless it is satisfied that the offender, the responsible officer and, if the offender is aged under 14, a parent or guardian of the offender have had adequate notice of the time and place of the resumed hearing.

(5) The powers of a magistrates' court under this paragraph may be exercised by a single justice of the peace, notwithstanding anything in the Magistrates' Courts Act 1980 (c 43).

(6) This paragraph—

(a) applies to any hearing in any proceedings under this Schedule in place of section 10 of the Magistrates' Courts Act 1980 (adjournment of trial) where that section would otherwise apply, but

(b) is not to be taken to affect the application of that section to hearings of any other description.

F34.15 Youth Rehabilitation Order requirements

Requirement	Age on conviction	Possible range	Consent required	Preconditions	Other comments
Activity **F34.5.1**	10–17	Up to 90 days	No	Court must consult with YOT or probation service. It must be feasible to secure compliance with the requirement.	
Supervision **F34.5.2**	10–17	Up to 3 years	No	–	
Unpaid work **F34.5.3**	16–17	Minimum 40 hours Maximum 240 hours	No	The court must be satisfied that the offender is suitable to perform the work.	
Programme **F34.5.4**	10–17	Up to 90 days	No	The programme must have been recommended by the YOT or probation service.	
Attendance centre **F34.5.5**	10–17	*16–17years* Min 12 hours Max 36 hours *14–15years* Min 12 hours Max 24 hours *Under 14 years* Max 12 hours	No	The court must be satisfied that the centre is reasonably accessible for the offender.	
Prohibited activity **F34.5.6**	10–17		No	Court must consult with YOT or probation service.	

Curfew **F34.5.7**		Max 12 months Min 2 hours a day Max 16 hours a day	No	Court must obtain and consider information about the proposed curfew address.	Electronic monitoring requirement should normally be imposed as well
Exclusion **F34.5.8**	10–17	Max 3 months	No		Electronic monitoring requirement should normally be imposed as well
Residence with specified person **F34.5.9**	10–17		No	The specified person must consent.	
Place of residence **F34.5.9**	16–17		No	Court must consider the offender's home surroundings. Residence specified must be recommended by YOT or probation service.	
Residence in local authority accommodation **F34.5.10**		Max 6 months (must not include any period after offender has reached age of 18)	No	The behaviour which led to the offence was, to a significant extent, due to the living conditions of the young person. The addition of the requirement will assist the rehabilitation of the young person.	

				The court must consult with parent/guardian and local authority. Offender must be legally represented.
Fostering **F34.5.11**	10–17	Max 12 months (must not include any period after offender has reached age of 18)	No	Statutory threshold—see **F34.5.11** The behaviour which led to the offence was, to a significant extent, due to the living conditions of the young person. The imposition of the requirement would assist in the offender,'s rehabilitation. The court must consult with parent/guardian and local authority. Offender must be legally represented.
Mental health treatment **F34.5.12**	10–17		Yes	The mental condition of the young person is such that it requires and may be susceptible to treatment, but is not such as to warrant the making of a hospital order or guardianship order under the MHA 1983.

Drug treatment **F34.5.13**	10–17		Yes	Offender is dependent on, or has the propensity to misuse, drugs and that their dependency or propensity is such that it requires and may be susceptible to treatment. Requirement recommended by YOT or probation service has recommended treatment.	Drug testing requirement may also be imposed— See **F34.5.14**
Intoxicating substance treatment **F34.5.15**	10–17		Yes	The young person is dependent on, or has the propensity to misuse, intoxicating substances and that their dependency or propensity is such that it requires and may be susceptible to treatment. Requirement recommended by YOT or probation service has recommended treatment.	

F34 Youth Rehabilitation Order

Education **F34.5.16**	Compulsory school age	Length of YRO	No	In the view of the local authority, arrangements exist for the young person to receive efficient full-time education suitable to the young person's age, ability, aptitude, and special educational need (if any). Requirement is necessary for securing the good conduct of the young person or for preventing reoffending.	
Intensive supervision and surveillance (ISS) **F34.5.17**	10–17		No	Statutory threshold—see **F34.5.17**	Electronic monitoring requirement should normally be imposed as well

Youths in the Adult Magistrates' Court

G1 Jurisdiction of the Adult Magistrates' Court

G1.1 Jointly charged with an adult

A child or young person **must** appear before the adult court if jointly charged with an adult.

A child or young person **may** appear before the adult court if:

- charged with aiding or abetting an adult
- an adult is charged with aiding or abetting the child or young person
- charged with an offence arising out of the same circumstances as those giving rise to proceedings against an adult.

The CYPA 1933 s 46 states:

Children and Young Persons Act 1933 s 46

(1) Subject as hereinafter provided, no charge against a child or young person, and no application whereof the hearing is by rules made under this section assigned to youth courts, shall be heard by a magistrates' court which is not a youth court:

Provided that—

(a) a charge made jointly against a child or young person and a person who has attained the age of eighteen years **shall** be heard by a magistrates' court other than a youth court; and

(b) where a child or young person is charged with an offence, the charge **may** be heard by a magistrates' court which is not a youth court if a person who has attained the age of eighteen years is charged at the same time with aiding, abetting, causing, procuring, allowing or permitting that offence; and

(c) where, in the course of any proceedings before any magistrates' court other than a youth court, it appears that the person to whom the proceedings relate is a child or young person, nothing in this subsection shall be construed as preventing the court, if it thinks fit so to do, from proceeding with the hearing and determination of those proceedings.

The CYPA 1963 s 18 states:

Children and Young Persons Act 1963 s 18

Notwithstanding section 46(1) of the principal Act (which restricts the jurisdiction of magistrates' courts which are not youth courts in cases where a child or young person is charged with an offence) a magistrates' court which is not a youth court **may** hear an information against a child or young person if he is charged—

(a) with aiding, abetting, causing, procuring, allowing or permitting an offence with which a person who has attained the age of eighteen is charged at the same time; or

(b) with an offence arising out of circumstances which are the same as or connected with those giving rise to an offence with which a person who has attained the age of eighteen is charged at the same time.

G1.2 Youth in adult court alone

The CYPA 1933 s 46(2) states:

Children and Young Persons Act 1933 s 46(2)

S46(2) No direction, whether contained in this or any other Act, that a charge shall be brought before a youth court shall be construed as restricting the powers of any justice or justices to entertain an application for bail or for a remand, and to hear such evidence as may be necessary for that purpose.

There are many places where the youth court does not sit every day. This provision enables an adult magistrates' court to deal with an application for a remand or bail in relation to a youth. The court must then remand the defendant to appear in the youth court for that area. In these circumstances the adult court will not deal with any issues relating to allocation or plea.

A child or young person will appear in an adult magistrates' court where an application is made under the CDA 1998 s 1 for an anti-social behaviour order. This is also known as a 'stand-alone' order as it is an application made other than on conviction. Applications for similar orders may also be made in the county court. Such applications are outside the scope of this book.

See **D7**.

G2 **Allocation and Plea before Venue**

Where the adult and/or youth face indictable-only or either-way offences there is a complex procedure for deciding which court should deal with the allegations.

These provisions are dealt with in detail at **D2**.

G3 Case Management

G3.1 Reporting restrictions

There are no automatic reporting restrictions and the provisions of the CYPA 1933 s 39 apply. The court will usually make an order restricting reporting.

See **D11**.

G3.2 Adapting the proceedings

The Consolidated Criminal Practice Direction III.30 applies in the adult court and the court will need to consider making provisions to assist the youth defendant. The Practice Direction states that such amendments to the trial process that may be necessary should be considered at a case management hearing.

See **Appendix 1** and **E5**.

G3.3 Defendant evidence directions

In some cases application may be made for the defendant to give evidence via a live link.

See **E2**.

G4 Remittal to the Youth Court for Trial

The Consolidated Criminal Practice Direction III.30.4 states that at a case management hearing the court should consider whether a young defendant should be tried on his own and should direct a separate trial unless it is of the opinion that a joint trial would be in accordance with the overriding objective and in the interests of justice. However, a youth and adult who are to be tried summarily are likely to be tried together in the adult court.

The magistrates' court may remit to:

- a youth court acting for the same place as the remitting court, or
- a youth court acting for the place where the young offender habitually resides.

If the youth is charged with an offence which is a 'grave crime', the court must decide whether the case should proceed to the Crown Court for trial before the matter can be remitted to the youth court: *R v Tottenham Youth Court ex parte Fawzy* [1998] 1 All ER 365, QBD. See **D2**.

The MCA 1980 s 29 states:

Magistrates' Courts Act 1980 s 29

(1) Where—

    (a) a person under the age of 18 years ('the juvenile') appears or is brought before a magistrates' court other than a youth court on an information jointly charging him and one or more other persons with an offence; and

    (b) that other person, or any of those other persons, has attained that age, subsection (2) below shall have effect notwithstanding proviso (a) in section 46(1) of the Children and Young Persons Act 1933 (which would otherwise require the charge against the juvenile to be heard by a magistrates' court other than a youth court).

In the following provisions of this section 'the older accused' means such one or more of the accused as have attained the age of 18 years.

(2) If—

    (a) the court proceeds to the summary trial of the information in the case of both or all of the accused, and the older accused or each of the older accused pleads guilty; or

    (b) the court—

        (i) in the case of the older accused or each of the older accused, sends him to the Crown Court for trial under section 51 or 51A of the Crime and Disorder Act 1998; and

      (ii) in the case of the juvenile, proceeds to the summary trial of the information,

then, if in either situation the juvenile pleads not guilty, the court may before any evidence is called in his case remit him for trial to a youth court acting for the same place as the remitting court or for the place where he habitually resides.

(3) A person remitted to a youth court under subsection (2) above shall be brought before and tried by a youth court accordingly.

(4) Where a person is so remitted to a youth court—

    (a) he shall have no right of appeal against the order of remission; and

    (b) the remitting court may, subject to section 25 of the Criminal Justice and Public Order Act 1994, give such directions as appear to be necessary with respect to his custody or for his release on bail until he can be brought before the youth court.

G5 Remittal to the Youth Court for Sentence

The sentencing powers of an adult magistrates' court in relation to a youth are limited and the court will usually remit the youth for sentence. The magistrates' court may remit to:

- a youth court acting for the same place as the remitting court, or
- a youth court acting for the place where the young offender habitually resides.

The power to remit is set out in the PCCSA 2000, s 8. See **F22**.

G6 Sentencing Powers of the Adult Magistrates' Court

An adult magistrates' court can (subject to any legislative restrictions) make the following orders in relation to a youth:

- an absolute discharge
- a conditional discharge
- a fine
- a referral order
- a parental bind over.

The courts' sentencing powers are set out in the PCCSA 2000 s 8. See **F23**.

If the court wishes to consider dealing with the defendant in any other way the case will be remitted to the youth court. See **G5**.

Part H
Youths in the Crown Court

H1 **Routes to Trial on Indictment**

The circumstances when a youth may be sent to the Crown Court for trial on indictment are set out in the CDA 1998 ss 51 and 51A. A youth will only appear in the Crown Court for trial:

- when charged with homicide: s 51A(3)(a) and (12);
- when charged with a firearms offence subject to a mandatory minimum sentence: s 51A(3)(a) and (12);
- when charged with a grave crime and a court has determined that it ought to be possible to impose a sentence under the PCCSA 2000 s 91: s 51A(3)(b);
- when notice is served in serious or complex fraud cases or cases involving children: s 51A(3)(c);
- when charged with a specified offence and it is considered that the criteria for imposing a sentence of extended detention are met: s 51A(3)(a) and (12)—sent for trial under s 51A(2);
- when charged with an adult offender who has been sent to the Crown Court and it has been determined that the cases should be kept together in the interests of justice: s 51(7).

In the case of the first five routes the ending for trial will be under the CDA 1998 s 51A(2); in the case of the last route the sending for trial will be under s 51(7).

H1.1 **Changes of charge after sending for trial**

Where an adult is sent for trial for an indictable-only offence and that charge is withdrawn and in its place an either-way offence is preferred, the CDA 1998 Sch 3 paras 7–12 require the court to deal with plea before venue.

This requirement does not apply to youth defendants. Instead Sch 3 para 13 provides:

Crime and Disorder Act 1998 Schedule 3 para 13

(1) This paragraph applies in place of paragraphs 7 to 12 above, in the case of a child or young person who—
  (a) has been sent for trial under section 51 or 51A of this Act but has not been arraigned; and
  (b) is charged on an indictment which (following amendment of the indictment, or as a result of an application under paragraph 2 above [dismissal application], or for any other reason) includes no main offence.

---

(2) The Crown Court shall remit the child or young person for trial to a magistrates' court acting for the place where he was sent to the Crown Court for trial.

(3) In this paragraph, a 'main offence' is—

    (a) an offence for which the child or young person has been sent to the Crown Court for trial under section 51A(2) of this Act; or

    (b) an offence—

        (i) for which the child or young person has been sent to the Crown Court for trial under subsection (7) of section 51 of this Act; and

        (ii) in respect of which the conditions for sending him to the Crown Court for trial under that subsection (as set out in paragraphs (a) and (b) of that subsection) continue to be satisfied.

The CDA 1998 s 51(7) provides:

Crime and Disorder Act 1998 s 51(7)

Where-

    (a) the court sends an adult ('A') for trial under subsection (1), (3) or (5) above; and

    (b) a child or young person appears or is brought before the court on the same or a subsequent occasion charged jointly with A is sent for trial under subsection (1), (3) or (5) above, or an indictable offence which appears to be related to that offence,

    the court shall, if it considers it necessary in the interests of justice to do so, send the child or young person forthwith to the Crown Court for trial for the indictable offence.

H1.2 Remittal for trial

Except in the circumstances of the CDA 1998 Sch 3 para 13 above, there is no other power to remit a youth defendant for summary trial.

Where a youth has been validly committed for trial with an adult, he has to be tried in the Crown Court even if the adult pleaded guilty. There was therefore no power to remit the youth defendant to the youth court under the PCCSA 2000 s 8 or under any inherent power (*R (W) v Leeds Crown Court* [2011] EWHC 2326 (Admin)).

H2 Case Management and Effective Participation

H2.1 Fair trial

The fair trial guarantee of ECHR Article 6 includes the ability of the youth defendant to participate effectively in the trial process (*V v United Kingdom* (2000) EHRR 121—see **E5**).

The demands of a trial on indictment are considerably greater than those of a summary trial. It is therefore in the Crown Court that concerns regarding effective participation arise in a higher proportion of cases. It would be good practice for a defence lawyer to collect background information about a youth defendant's educational history as well as any information about any mental disorder. If significant doubts exist about his ability to participate effectively, consideration should be given to instructing a chartered psychologist to carry out psychometric testing and to advise on the defendant's ability to participate effectively in the proceedings.

Careful consideration should be given to the guidance contained in Consolidated Criminal Practice Direction Part III.30 *Treatment of Vulnerable Defendants* (see **Appendix 1**). The guidance applies to all defendants under the age of 18. It advises that all possible steps should be taken to assist a youth defendant to understand and participate in criminal proceedings and the ordinary trial process should, so far as necessary, be adapted to meet those needs. The appropriate time to address these issues is at the plea and case management hearing (III.30.5) and the appropriate trial modifications should be raised in the case management form.

H2.2 Fitness to plead

In *R v Pritchard* (1836) 7 C& P 303 it was held that the test was

Whether he is of sufficient intellect to comprehend the course of proceedings on the trial, so as to make a proper defence—to know that he might challenge [any jurors] to whom he may object—and to comprehend the details of the evidence . . . if you think that there is no certain mode of communicating the details of the trial to the prisoner, so that he can clearly understand them, and be able properly to make his defence to the charge; you ought to find that he is not of sane mind. It is not enough, that he may have a general capacity of communicating on ordinary matters.

The test has been further considered in *R v Podola* [1960] 1 QB 325 where the court held that the test was whether:

> He is of sufficient intellect to comprehend the course of proceedings on the trial, so as to make a proper defence—to know that he might challenge (the jurors) to whom he may object—and to comprehend the details of the evidence, which in a case of this nature must constitute a minute investigation, upon this issue, therefore, if you think that there is no certain mode of communicating details of the trial to the prisoner, so that he can clearly understand them, and be able properly to make his defence to the charge; you ought to find that he is not of sane mind.

Although not stated in either of the formulations of the test, it is generally accepted that the defendant must also be able to give coherent and reliable evidence in his own defence if he so wishes.

In the case of youth defendants the reason for being unfit to plead could be because of any one or more of:

- mental illness;
- learning disability or other mental disorder; or
- developmental immaturity.

H2.2.1 *Procedure*

The procedure is covered by the Criminal Procedure (Insanity) Act 1964 as amended by the Domestic Violence, Crime and Victims Act 2004.

- The question of fitness to plead may be raised by any party to the proceedings, but is normally raised by the defence.
- If raised by the defence, the burden of proof rests upon the defendant on a balance of probabilities.
- If the question of fitness to plead is raised before the defendant is asked to plead, a judge sitting without a jury will determine whether the defendant is unfit to stand trial. The court shall not make a finding of unfitness except on the written or oral evidence of two or more registered medical practitioners at least one of whom is approved under the MHA 1983 s 12.
- If the judge finds the defendant fit to plead, a jury is empanelled to try him/her.
- If the judge finds the defendant unfit to plead, a jury shall be empanelled to determine whether the defendant did the act or omission alleged.

This statutory procedure is compatible with the ECHR as it strikes a proper balance between the rights of those accused of crime and the victims of the crime, as well as the general public (*R v H* [2003] UKHL 1, [2003] 1 WLR 411).

H2.2.2 *Possible disposals in the Crown Court*

Where an accused has been found both unfit to plead and to have done the act or omission alleged, the court may make one of the following orders:

- a hospital order (with or without a restriction order); or
- a supervision order; or
- an order for his/her absolute discharge.

Hospital orders and restriction orders may only be made if the criteria of the MHA 1983 ss 37 and 41 are satisfied (for which see **F13**). There will therefore need to be medical evidence that justifies detention on the grounds of the accused's mental state.

H2.2.3 *Fitness to plead as measure of last resort*

In *R v Walls* [2011] EWCA Crim 443 Thomas LJ stressed that the adequacy of measures such as intermediaries to assist the defendant in the trial process should be carefully considered before embarking on the statutory fitness to plead procedure. He pointed out the disadvantages of the statutory procedure both for the defendant (who is not able to testify in his own defence) and for the protection of the general public (limited range of disposals, for which see below). Therefore where the procedure is invoked Thomas LJ said that courts must rigorously examine the evidence of psychiatrists adduced before them and then subject that evidence to careful analysis against the *Pritchard* criteria as interpreted in *Podola*. Save in cases where the unfitness is clear, the fact that psychiatrists agree is not enough, as this case demonstrates; a court would be failing in its duty to both the public and a defendant if it did not rigorously examine the evidence and reach its own conclusion.

H2.3 **Reporting restrictions**

In proceedings on indictment or committal for sentence, the automatic reporting restrictions applicable in the youth court under the CYPA 1933 s 49 do not apply.

Instead the court may make an order under the CYPA 1933 s 39 imposing reporting restrictions (see **D11**).

The Consolidated Criminal Practice Direction Part III.30.8 suggests that at the plea and case management hearing the court should be ready, if it has not already done so, to make an order under s 39 (see **Appendix 1**).

H3 **Remittal for Sentence**

The power to remit to the youth court for sentence is contained in the PCCSA 2000 s 8 (see **F22**). It should be noted that when exercised by the Crown Court remittal can only be to a youth court acting for the place where the youth was sent to the Crown Court for trial.

The wording of s 8 would seem to create a presumption in favour of remittal for sentence but this is not how the power is exercised in practice. When considering the similar provision in the Children and Young Persons Act 1933 s 56 in *R v Lewis* (1984) 79 Cr App R 94, Lord Lane identified the following reasons for not remitting:

- that, in a case where the youth pleaded not guilty and was convicted, the Crown Court judge who presided at the trial will be better informed about the facts of the offence and general nature of the case than the youth court could hope to be;
- that, in a case where an adult and juvenile have been jointly tried on indictment and both convicted, sentencing the youth in the Crown Court will avoid the risk of unacceptable disparity in sentencing that would arise if he were to be remitted to the youth court;
- that remitting would cause delay, unnecessary duplication of proceedings, and extra expense.

It was suggested by the Court of Appeal in the case of *R v Allen* (1999) 163 JP 841 that in the case of a grave crime it will generally be undesirable for the Crown Court to remit the case to the youth court for sentence, since the youth court has already determined that the case is too serious for its powers. It is submitted that this principle would not necessarily apply if the youth defendant has been convicted of the offence on a less serious basis or where not all of the original charges have resulted in convictions.

The definitive guideline, *Overarching Principles: Sentencing Youths* (2009) at paras 12.19 and 12.20 suggest that when considering whether to remit to the youth court for sentence the Crown Court judge should balance the need for expertise in the sentencing of young offenders with the benefits of sentence being imposed by the court which had determined guilt. Particular attention should be paid to the statutory presumption where a young person appears before the Crown Court only because he or she is jointly charged with an adult offender.

H4 Sentences Available to Crown Court

The following sentences are available:

- Absolute and conditional discharge (see **F8**)
- Fine (see **F11**)
- Reparation order (see **F23**)
- Youth rehabilitation order (see **F34** for the general principles and **H4.1** below for its application in the Crown Court)
- Detention and training order (see **F7**)
- Section 91 detention (see **H4.2** below)
- Extended detention under the CJA 2003 s 226B (see **H4.3.4** below)
- Detention for life (see **H4.3.2** below)
- Detention during Her Majesty's pleasure (see **H4.4** below).

Referral orders may only be made by a youth court or other magistrates' court: PCCSA 2000 s 16(1). It would seem possible that a Crown Court judge could make such an order if he exercised his power under the Courts Act 2003 s 66 to sit as a district judge.

It has been the practice of some youth courts to adjourn sentence on summary-only matters where the youth is due to appear at the Crown Court on other matters and inviting the Crown Court to deal with the summary offence at the same time (by sitting as a district judge). In the case of *R v Iles* [2012] EWCA Crim 1610 it was said that before this is done the youth court must carefully consider whether this is in the interests of justice and ensure there is a power to do so. Moreover before sitting as a district judge the Crown Court judge must consider whether it is appropriate in the light of submissions from both prosecution and defence. If this route is followed the judge's powers for the summary-only offences would be limited to those of the magistrates' court and sentences imposed by a judge sitting as a district judge would have a different route of appeal.

H4.1 Youth rehabilitation order

When a Crown Court judge is imposing a youth rehabilitation order, it is important to draw the court's attention to the following provision:

> ### Criminal Justice and Immigration Act 2008 Sch 1 para 36
>
> (1) Where the Crown Court makes a youth rehabilitation order, it may include in the order a direction that further proceedings relating to the order be

> in a youth court or other magistrates' court (subject to paragraph 7 of
> Schedule 2).
> (2) In sub-paragraph (1), 'further proceedings', in relation to a youth rehabili-
> tation order, means proceedings—
> (a) for any failure to comply with the order within the meaning given by
> paragraph 1(2)(b) of Schedule 2, or
> (b) on any application for amendment or revocation of the order under
> Part 3 or 4 of that Schedule.

Without such a direction the youth court dealing with any matter for
sentence while the youth defendant is subject to the Crown Court
order will have to commit the young offender to the Crown Court if
it considers that the new matter can properly be dealt with by a new
youth rehabilitation order (for which see **H4.1.1** below).

H4.1.1 *Subsequent conviction*

Where a defendant is convicted of an offence whilst he is subject to a
youth rehabilitation order made in the Crown Court the CJIA 2008
Sch 2 provides that the convicting court may commit him to the
Crown Court for sentence (CJIA 2008 Sch 2 para 18). When such a
committal takes place the CJIA 2008 Sch 2 para 19 provides:

Criminal Justice and Immigration Act 2008 Sch 2

19 Powers of Crown Court following subsequent conviction

(1) This paragraph applies where—
   (a) a youth rehabilitation order is in force in respect of an offender, and
   (b) the offender—
      (i) is convicted by the Crown Court of an offence, or
      (ii) is brought or appears before the Crown Court by virtue of para-
         graph 18(9) or (11) or having been committed by the magistrates'
         court to the Crown Court for sentence.
(2) The Crown Court may revoke the order.
(3) Where the Crown Court revokes the order under sub-paragraph (2), the
   Crown Court may deal with the offender, for the offence in respect of
   which the order was made, in any way in which the court which made the
   order could have dealt with the offender for that offence.
(4) The Crown Court must not exercise its powers under sub-paragraph (2) or
   (3) unless it considers that it would be in the interests of justice to do so,
   having regard to circumstances which have arisen since the youth rehabilitation order was made.
(5) In dealing with an offender under sub-paragraph (3), the Crown Court
   must take into account the extent to which the offender has complied with
   the order.
(6) If the offender is brought or appears before the Crown Court by virtue of
   paragraph 18(9) or (11), the Crown Court may deal with the offender for

the further offence in any way which the convicting court could have dealt with the offender for that offence.

(7) In sub-paragraph (6), 'further offence' and 'the convicting court' have the same meanings as in paragraph 18.

H4.1.2 *Breach of Crown Court order*

Where an offender is to be breached in relation to a youth rehabilitation order made by the Crown Court, the proceedings are initiated by the responsible officer applying to the relevant youth court (or magistrates' court if the offender has attained 18) for the issue of a summons directing attendance at the Crown Court (see **F34.10**). Once the offender is before the Crown Court the CJIA 2008 Sch 2 provides:

Criminal Justice and Immigration Act 2008 Sch 2

8 Powers of Crown Court

(1) This paragraph applies where—
   (a) an offender appears or is brought before the Crown Court under paragraph 5 or by virtue of paragraph 7(2), and
   (b) it is proved to the satisfaction of that court that the offender has failed without reasonable excuse to comply with the youth rehabilitation order.

(2) The Crown Court may deal with the offender in respect of that failure in any one of the following ways—
   (a) by ordering the offender to pay a fine of an amount not exceeding £2,500;
   (b) by amending the terms of the youth rehabilitation order so as to impose any requirement which could have been included in the order when it was made—
      (i) in addition to, or
      (ii) in substitution for,
      any requirement or requirements already imposed by the order;
   (c) by dealing with the offender, for the offence in respect of which the order was made, in any way in which the Crown Court could have dealt with the offender for that offence.

(3) Sub-paragraph (2)(b) is subject to sub-paragraphs (6) to (9).

(4) In dealing with the offender under sub-paragraph (2), the Crown Court must take into account the extent to which the offender has complied with the youth rehabilitation order.

(5) A fine imposed under sub-paragraph (2)(a) is to be treated, for the purposes of any enactment, as being a sum adjudged to be paid by a conviction.

(6) Subject to sub-paragraph (6A) any requirement imposed under sub-paragraph (2)(b) must be capable of being complied with before the date specified under paragraph 32(1) of Schedule 1.

(6A) When imposing a requirement under sub-paragraph (2)(b), the Crown Court may amend the order to substitute a later date for that specified under paragraph 32(1) of Schedule 1.

(6B) A date substituted under sub-paragraph (6A)—
  (a) may not fall outside the period of six months beginning with the date previously specified under paragraph 32(1) of Schedule 1;
  (b) subject to that, may fall more than three years after the date on which the order took effect.

(6C) The power under sub-paragraph (6A) may not be exercised in relation to an order if that power or the power in paragraph 6(6A) has previously been exercised in relation to that order.

(6D) A date substituted under sub-paragraph (6A) is to be treated as having been specified in relation to the order under paragraph 32(1) of Schedule 1.

(7) Where—
  (a) the court is dealing with the offender under sub-paragraph (2)(b), and
  (b) the youth rehabilitation order does not contain an unpaid work requirement,
  paragraph 10(2) of Schedule 1 applies in relation to the inclusion of such a requirement as if for '40' there were substituted '20'.

(8) The court may not under sub-paragraph (2)(b) impose—
  (a) an extended activity requirement, or
  (b) a fostering requirement,
  if the order does not already impose such a requirement.

(9) Where—
  (a) the order imposes a fostering requirement (the 'original requirement'), and
  (b) under sub-paragraph (2)(b) the court proposes to substitute a new fostering requirement ('the substitute requirement') for the original requirement,
  paragraph 18(2) of Schedule 1 applies in relation to the substitute requirement as if the reference to the period of 12 months beginning with the date on which the original requirement first had effect were a reference to the period of 18 months beginning with that date.

(10) Where the Crown Court deals with an offender under sub-paragraph (2) (c), it must revoke the youth rehabilitation order if it is still in force.

(11) Sub-paragraphs (12) to (14) apply where—
  (a) an offender has wilfully and persistently failed to comply with a youth rehabilitation order; and
  (b) the Crown Court is dealing with the offender under sub-paragraph (2) (c).

(12) The court may impose a youth rehabilitation order with intensive supervision and surveillance notwithstanding anything in section 1(4)(a) or (b).

(13) If—
  (a) the order is a youth rehabilitation order with intensive supervision and surveillance, and
  (b) the offence mentioned in sub-paragraph (2)(c) was punishable with imprisonment,
  the court may impose a custodial sentence notwithstanding anything in section 152(2) of the Criminal Justice Act 2003 (c. 44) (general restrictions on imposing discretionary custodial sentences).

(14) If—
  (a) the order is a youth rehabilitation order with intensive supervision and surveillance which was imposed by virtue of paragraph 6(13) or sub-paragraph (12), and
  (b) the offence mentioned in sub-paragraph (2)(c) was not punishable with imprisonment,
  for the purposes of dealing with the offender under sub-paragraph (2) (c), the Crown Court is to be taken to have had power to deal with the offender for that offence by making a detention and training order for a term not exceeding 4 months.
(15) In proceedings before the Crown Court under this paragraph any question whether the offender has failed to comply with the youth rehabilitation order is to be determined by the court and not by the verdict of a jury.

H4.2 Section 91 detention

Detention under the PCCSA 2000 s 91(3) (often referred to as 'section 91 detention') is only available if:

• the offender was aged under 18 on the date of conviction;
• the offender was convicted on indictment; and
• the offence is one specified in subsections (1), (1A), or (1B) ('grave crimes').

Powers of Criminal Courts (Sentencing) Act 2000 s 91

(1) Subsection (3) below applies where a person aged under 18 is convicted on indictment of—
  (a) an offence punishable in the case of a person aged 21 or over with imprisonment for 14 years or more, not being an offence the sentence for which is fixed by law; or
  (b) an offence under section 3 of the Sexual Offences Act 2003 (in this section, 'the 2003 Act') (sexual assault); or
  (c) an offence under section 13 of the 2003 Act (child sex offences committed by children or young persons); or
  (d) an offence under section 25 of the 2003 Act (sexual activity with a child family member); or
  (e) an offence under section 26 of the 2003 Act (inciting a child family member to engage in sexual activity).
(1A) Subsection (3) below applies also where—
  (a) a person aged under 18 is convicted on indictment of an offence—
    (i) under subsection (1)(a), (ab), (aba), (ac), (ad), (ae), (af) or (c) of section 5 of the Firearms Act 1968 (prohibited weapons), or
    (ii) under subsection (1A)(a) of that section,
  (b) the offence was committed after the commencement of section 51A of that Act and [for the purposes of subsection (3) of that section] 3 at a time when he was aged 16 or over, and
  (c) the court is of the opinion mentioned in section 51A(2) of that Act (exceptional circumstances which justify its not imposing required custodial sentence).

(1B) Subsection (3) below also applies where—

  (a) a person aged under 18 is convicted on indictment of an offence under the Firearms Act 1968 that is listed in section 51A(1A)(b), (e) or (f) of that Act and was committed in respect of a firearm or ammunition specified in section 5(1)(a), (ab), (aba), (ac), (ad), (ae), (af) or (c) or section 5(1A)(a) of that Act;

  (b) the offence was committed after the commencement of section 30 of the Violent Crime Reduction Act 2006 and for the purposes of section 51A(3) of the Firearms Act 1968 at a time when he was aged 16 or over; and

  (c) the court is of the opinion mentioned in section 51A(2) of the Firearms Act 1968.

(1C) Subsection (3) below also applies where–

  (a) a person aged under 18 is convicted of an offence under section 28 of the Violent Crime Reduction Act 2006 (using someone to mind a weapon);

  (b) section 29(3) of that Act applies (minimum sentences in certain cases); and

  (c) the court is of the opinion mentioned in section 29(6) of that Act (exceptional circumstances which justify not imposing the minimum sentence).

  …

(3) If the court is of the opinion that neither a youth rehabilitation order nor a detention and training order is suitable, the court may sentence the offender to be detained for such period, not exceeding the maximum term of imprisonment with which the offence is punishable in the case of a person aged 21 or over, as may be specified in the sentence.

(4) Subsection (3) above is subject to (in particular) sections 152 and 153 of the Criminal Justice Act 2003.

(5) Where —

  (a) subsection (2) of section 51A of the Firearms Act 1968, or

  (b) subsection (6) of section 29 of the Violent Crime Reduction Act 2006,

  requires the imposition of a sentence of detention under this section for a term of at least the term provided for in that section, the court shall sentence the offender to be detained for such period, of at least the term so provided for but not exceeding the maximum term of imprisonment with which the offence is punishable in the case of a person aged 18 or over, as may be specified in the sentence.

The principles for the sentencing power now enacted in s 91(3) were originally set out by Lane LCJ in *R v Fairhurst* (1986) 8 Cr App R (S) 346. These principle were later expressly endorsed by Bingham LCJ in *R v Mills* [1998] 1 WLR 363. Below is a summary of the principles outlined in these two cases.

H4.2.1 *General principles*

On the one hand there exists the desirability of keeping youths under the age of 18 out of long terms of custody. On the other hand it is necessary that serious offences committed by youths of this age should be met with sentences sufficiently substantial to provide both the appropriate punishment and also the necessary deterrent effect, and in certain cases to provide a measure of protection to the public. A balance has to be struck between these objectives. It is not necessary, in order to invoke the provisions of s 91, that the crime committed should be one of exceptional gravity, such as attempted murder, manslaughter, wounding with intent, armed robbery, or the like.

H4.2.2 *Offenders aged 15 to 17*

Section 91 may be properly invoked where the crime committed is one within the scope of the section, and is one that not only calls for a sentence of detention but detention for a longer period than twenty-four months. The court should not exceed the twenty-four-month limit for a detention and training order without much careful thought; but if it concludes that a longer sentence, even if not a much longer sentence, is called for, then the court should impose whatever it considers the appropriate period of detention under s 91.

H4.2.3 *Offenders aged under 15*

Section 91 detention will be the only custodial option for the Crown Court in relation to offenders under 15, unless the offender is aged 12 to 14 and is deemed to be a persistent offender, in which case a detention and training order will also be available.

Where the seriousness of the offence warrants a sentence of over two years, there is no doubt that a sentence of s 91 detention may be imposed. There are, however, conflicting lines of authority regarding the Crown Court's powers in relation to an offender aged under 15 years who cannot be deemed to be a persistent offender.

In *R v Gaskin* (1985) 7 Cr App R (S) 28 it was held that where no other custodial sentence was available because of the offender's age, a sentence under the Children and Young Persons Act 1933 s 53(2) (the predecessor of s 91 detention) could be imposed for a period shorter than two years. This approach was later endorsed by Lord Bingham CJ in *Mills* and, after the introduction of detention and training orders, followed by the Court of Appeal in *R v S.J-R and D.G* [2001] 1 Cr App R (S) 109.

This line of authorities was not followed in the cases of *R (D) v Manchester City Youth Court* [2001] EWHC 860 (Admin); and *R (W) v Thetford Youth Court* [2002] EWHC 1252 (Admin). Judgments in both cases were delivered by Gage J. In *Thetford Youth Court*, having reviewed the above line of authorities, Gage J said:

> There is no statutory restriction on a court, using its powers under section 91, passing a sentence of less than two years. But it seems to me that it will only

be in very exceptional and restricted circumstances that it will be appropriate to do so, rather than making a detention and training order. The fact that an offender...does not qualify for a detention and training order because he is not a persistent offender does not seem to me such an exceptional circumstance as to justify the passing of a period of detention of less that two years under section 91 of the Act of 2000.

My conclusion is that the authorities...do not alter my conclusions already expressed on the relationship between [the statutory provisions relating to section 91 detention and detention and training orders]...I remain of the opinion that where an offence or offences are likely to attract a sentence of less than two years' custody the appropriate sentence will be a detention and training order. In the case of an offender under 15, who is not a persistent offender or a child under 12, the most likely sentence will be a non-custodial sentence....

However, I accept that there may be cases, where despite the fact that the offender is under 15, and no detention and training order can be made, the only appropriate sentence is a custodial sentence pursuant to section 91 and possibly for a period of less than two years. In expressing my views, as I did, in *D v Manchester City Youth Court*, my use of the expression 'very exceptional' may be more restrictive than was strictly necessary or justified...Perhaps it would be better to say that cases involving offenders under 15 for whom a detention and training order is not available will only rarely attract a period of detention under section 91; the more rarely if the offender is under 12.

This judgment of Gage J was expressly endorsed by Lord Woolf CJ and Sedley LJ in *R (W) v Southampton Youth Court* [2002] EWHC 1252 (Admin), at [28]–[30]. The reasoning of Gage J was, however, rejected by the Court of Appeal in *R v Thomas* [2004] EWCA Crim 2199 where Hooper LJ held that the Administrative Court decisions following on from the *Manchester City* case were not binding on the Court of Appeal and only in fact applied to the youth court decision regarding jurisdiction.

H4.2.4 Sentencing for more than one grave crime together

Where more than one offence is involved for which s 91 detention is available, but the offences vary in seriousness, provided that at least one offence is sufficiently serious to merit section 91 detention, detention sentences of under two years' duration, whether concurrent or consecutive, may properly be imposed in respect of the other offences.

H4.2.5 Sentencing grave crimes together with non-grave crime

Where there are two offences committed by a youth offender and one of them (A) carries a maximum sentence of fourteen years and the other (B) carries a lower maximum, then generally speaking it is not proper to pass a sentence of section 91 detention in respect of offence

A which would not otherwise merit it in order to compensate for the fact that a twenty-four-month detention and training order is grossly inadequate for offence B.

Where, however, it can be truly said that the defendant's behaviour giving rise to offence B is part and parcel of the events giving rise to offence A such a sentence may properly be passed. See for example *R v Walsh* [1997] 2 Cr App R (S) 210.

The non-grave crime would also be an associated offence which could be taken into account when determining the seriousness of the grave crime. See for example *R v McKay* [2000] 1 Cr App R (S) 17.

H4.2.6 *Light at the end of the tunnel*

Even when dealing with serous offences, consideration should still be given to the youth of the offender. In *R v Storey* (1984) 6 Cr App R (S) 104 Mustill J gave general guidance which has been referred to in many subsequent appeal decisions:

> There is another principle to which effect must, in our opinion, be given. These are young men not of outstanding intellectual attainments, and perhaps not very gifted in imagination. It is important, when using the powers under the Act, that the court should not impose a sentence, which, the far end of it, would to young men like this seem completely out of sight.... The court must take care to select a duration for the order upon which the offender can fix his eye, so that he could buckle down to taking advantage of the structured environment [in detention], with a view to emerging from it in the foreseeable future improved by his study there.

H4.2.7 *Remand time*

By the CJA 2003 s 240(10) provisions regarding remand time in the CJA 2003 ss 240 and 240A apply to s 91 detention.

H4.2.8 *Interaction with detention and training orders*

It has been held that a detention and training order cannot be ordered to run consecutively to an order of detention under s 91 (*R v Hayward* [2001] 2 Cr App R (S) 149), nor vice versa (*R v Lang* [2001] 2 Cr App R (S) 175).

Both of these cases were decided before implementation of the PCCSA 2000 s 106A (see **F7.5**) which would seem to permit consecutive orders to be imposed.

H4.3 Sentences for dangerous offenders under the CJA 2003

When a Crown Court concludes that a youth defendant should be deemed a dangerous offender, there are two sentencing options:

- detention for life under the CJA 2003 s 226; and
- extended detention under s 226B.

The mandatory life sentence for a second listed offence under the CJA 2003 s 224A does not apply to a person aged under 18 on the date of conviction.

H4.3.1 *Definitions*

The CJA 2003 s 224(3) provides the following definitions:

- *Specified offence*—violent or sexual offence listed in the CJA 2003 Sch 15 (see **Appendix 2**).
- *Serious offence*—a specified offence punishable in the case of a person aged 18 or over by imprisonment for life or imprisonment for a determinate period of ten years or more.
- *Serious harm*—means death or serious personal injury, whether physical or psychological.

H4.3.2 *The assessment of dangerousness*

The CJA 2003 s 229(2) provides that the court:

- must take into account all such information as is available to it about the nature and circumstances of the offence;
- may take into account any information which is before it about any pattern of behaviour of which the offence forms part; and
- may take into account any information about the offender which is before it.

The legislation regarding dangerous offenders was originally implemented in 2005 in a substantially different form. Nevertheless the general guidance provided by the Court of Appeal in relation to the original legislation is still of assistance. In *R v Lang* [2005] EWCA Crim 2864 the court said:

- 'Significant risk' is more than the possibility of occurrence.
- Significant risk must be shown in relation to two matters: first, the commission of further specified, but not necessarily serious,

offences; and secondly, the causing thereby of serious harm to a member of the public.
- Assessment of risk should include the offending history—the kind of offences, their circumstances, and the sentence imposed.
- The defendant's attitude to offending and supervision are also relevant.
- When sentencing young offenders, it is necessary to bear in mind that, within a shorter time than adults, they might change and develop. This and their level of maturity might be highly pertinent when assessing what their future conduct might be and whether it might give rise to significant risk of serious harm.
- In relation to a particularly young offender, an indeterminate sentence might be inappropriate even where a serious offence has been committed and there was a significant risk of serious harm from further offences.

H4.3.3 *Detention for life*

The CJA 2003 s 226 provides:

Criminal Justice Act 2003 s 226

(1) This section applies where—
   (a) a person aged under 18 is convicted of a serious offence committed after the commencement of this section, and
   (b) the court is of the opinion that there is a significant risk to members of the public of serious harm occasioned by the commission by him of further specified offences.

(2) If—
   (a) the offence is one in respect of which the offender would apart from this section be liable to a sentence of detention for life under section 91 of the [Powers of Criminal Courts (Sentencing) Act 2000], and
   (b) the court considers that the seriousness of the offence, or of the offence and one or more offences associated with it, is such as to justify the imposition of a sentence of detention for life,
   the court must impose a sentence of detention for life under that section.

...

(5) An offence the sentence for which is imposed under this section is not to be regarded as an offence the sentence for which is fixed by law.

When the court finds that the defendant satisfies the criteria for dangerousness, a life sentence should be reserved for those cases where the culpability of the offender is particularly high or the offence itself particularly grave (*R v Kehoe* [2008] EWCA Crim 819).

When imposing detention for life the PCCSA 2000 s 82A requires the court to set a minimum term which must be served in custody before the offender can be released at the direction of the Parole Board. This minimum term shall be such as the court considers appropriate taking into account:

- the seriousness of the offence, or the combination of the offence and one or more offences associated with it; and
- time spent on remand or subject to a qualifying curfew.

A person sentenced to detention for life is liable to be detained in such place, and under such conditions, as may be determined by the Secretary of State or by such other person as may be authorized by him for the purpose (CJA 2003 s 235). Release at the expiry of the minimum term is subject to the Crime (Sentences) Act 1997 s 28.

H4.3.4 *Extended detention*

The court may impose a sentence of extended detention if:

- a person aged under 18 is convicted of a specified offence;
- the court considers that there is a significant risk to members of the public of serious harm occasioned by the commission by the offender of further specified offences;
- if the court were to impose an extended sentence of detention, the term that it would specify as the appropriate custodial term would be at least four years.

Criminal Justice Act 2003 s 226B

(1) This section applies where—
   (a) a person aged under 18 is convicted of a specified offence (whether the offence was committed before or after this section comes into force),
   (b) the court considers that there is a significant risk to members of the public of serious harm occasioned by the commission by the offender of further specified offences,
   (c) the court is not required by section 226(2) to impose a sentence of detention for life under section 91 of the Sentencing Act, and
   (d) if the court were to impose an extended sentence of detention, the term that it would specify as the appropriate custodial term would be at least 4 years.
(2) The court may impose an extended sentence of detention on the offender.
(3) An extended sentence of detention is a sentence of detention the term of which is equal to the aggregate of—
   (a) the appropriate custodial term, and
   (b) a further period (the 'extension period') for which the offender is to be subject to a licence.
(4) The appropriate custodial term is the term of detention that would (apart from this section) be imposed in compliance with section 153(2).
(5) The extension period must be a period of such length as the court considers necessary for the purpose of protecting members of the public from serious harm occasioned by the commission by the offender of further specified offences, subject to subsections (6) and (7).

---

(6) The extension period must not exceed—
  (a) 5 years in the case of a specified violent offence, and
  (b) 8 years in the case of a specified sexual offence.
(7) The term of an extended sentence of detention imposed under this section in respect of an offence may not exceed the term that, at the time the offence was committed, was the maximum term of imprisonment permitted for the offence in the case of a person aged 21 or over.

A person sentenced to extended detention is liable to be detained in such place, and under such conditions, as may be determined by the Secretary of State or by such other person as may be authorized by him for the purpose (CJA 2003 s 235).

An offender sentenced to extended detention will generally be released on licence when he has served two-thirds of the custodial term. If the custodial term is ten years or more the offender may have to apply to the Parole Board before release. The detailed provisions are set out in the CJA s 246A.

H4.4 Detention during Her Majesty's pleasure

This is the mandatory sentence for a person convicted of a murder committed when he was under the age of 18.

The PCCSA 2000 s 90 provides:

Powers of Criminal Courts (Sentencing) Act 2000 s 90

Where a person convicted of murder appears to the court to have been aged under 18 at the time the offence was committed, the court shall (notwithstanding anything in this or any other Act) sentence him to be detained during Her Majesty's pleasure.

When detaining an offender under s 90 the judge must set a minimum term. In the case of an offender aged under 18 on the date of the murder the starting point for the minimum term is twelve years (CJA 2003 s 269(5) and Sch 21 para 7).

A person sentenced to be detained under s 90 shall be liable to be detained in such place and under such conditions as the Secretary of State may direct or arrange with any person (PCCSA 2000 s 92).

H5 **Appeal Cases**

H5.1 **Case management**

When the Crown Court is dealing with a youth appellant regard should be had to the Consolidated Criminal Practice Direction Part III.30 (see **Appendix 1**). Advice on how to modify the court procedure during the appeal hearing is set out in paras III.30.9–III.30.18.

H5.2 **Reporting restrictions**

When the Crown Court is acting in its appellate role reporting restrictions under the CYPA 1933 s 49 apply:

> ### Children and Young Persons Act 1933 s 49
>
> (10) In any proceedings under Schedule 7 to the Powers of Criminal Courts (Sentencing) Act 2000 (proceedings for varying or revoking supervision orders) before a magistrates' court other than a youth court or on appeal from such a court it shall be the duty of the magistrates' court or the appellate court to announce in the course of the proceedings that this section applies to the proceedings; and if the court fails to do so this section shall not apply to the proceedings.

Reporting restrictions under the CYPA 1933 s 49 cannot continue after the young person attains the age of 18: *T v DPP* [2003] EWHC 2408 (Admin).

Part I
Attaining 18

I1 Cautions

Youth cautions and youth conditional cautions may only be administered to a person under the age of 18. If the offender attains 18 before the final decision on disposal is made then an adult caution or adult conditional caution should be administered.

12 **Before First Appearance**

If a youth attains 18 before the first court appearance the youth court has no jurisdiction to deal with the case (*R v Amersham Juvenile Court, ex parte Wilson* [1981] 2 All ER 315).

If a youth is going have his 18th birthday before a first appearance he should be bailed or summonsed to the adult magistrates' court.

If a youth fails to attend the first appearance and attains 18 before he appears or is brought before the court, the youth court will have no jurisdiction to deal with the case. There is no power to remit the case to an adult magistrates' court so proceedings will have to be re-started in the adult magistrates' court (*R v Uxbridge Youth Court, ex parte Howard* [1998] EWHC (Admin) 341).

13 **After the First Court Hearing**

Once a defendant has appeared before it, the youth court does not lose jurisdiction to deal with the case simply because the defendant attains 18. In the case of an indictable offence the defendant who attains the age of 18 will now have the right to elect jury trial (*Re Daley* [1983] 1AC 327; *R v West London Justices, ex parte Siley-Winditt* [2000] Crim LR 926).

Any new charges laid after the defendant has attained 18 must be in the adult court even if the new charge arises out of the same facts as charges currently before the youth court (*R v Chelsea Justices ex parte DPP* [1963] 3 All ER 657).

14 Remand to Youth Detention Accommodation

Where the defendant turns 18 during a remand to youth detention accommodation he will remain in the youth detention accommodation until he is released or returned to court. The YJB will not invoice a local authority for any time remanded to local authority accommodation after the defendant has attained 18.

If the case is adjourned again after the defendant has attained 18, any refusal of bail will not be subject to the LASPO 2002 s 91 and the remand will be to a remand centre or prison.

15 Remittal to Adult Magistrates' Court for Trial

Crime and Disorder Act 1998 s 47

(1) Where a person who appears or is brought before a youth court charged with an offence subsequently attains the age of 18, the youth court may, at any time—

    (a) before the start of the trial;

    ...

    remit the person for trial or, as the case may be, for sentence to a magistrates' court (other than a youth court).

    In this subsection 'the start of the trial' shall be construed in accordance with section 22(11B) of the 1985 Act.

(2) Where a person is remitted under subsection (1) above—

    (a) he shall have no right of appeal against the order of remission;

    (b) the remitting court shall adjourn proceedings in relation to the offence; and

    (c) subsections (3) and (4) below shall apply.

(3) The following, namely—

    (a) section 128 of the 1980 Act; and

    (b) all other enactments (whenever passed) relating to remand or the granting of bail in criminal proceedings,

    shall have effect in relation to the remitting court's power or duty to remand the person on the adjournment as if any reference to the court to or before which the person remanded is to be brought or appear after remand were a reference to the court to which he is being remitted ('the other court').

(4) The other court may deal with the case in any way in which it would have power to deal with it if all proceedings relating to the offence which took place before the remitting court had taken place before the other court.

I6 **Sentence**

The relevant age for sentence is the age on the date of conviction (whether guilty plea or conviction after trial)—see **F1.1**.

If the offender was 17 on the date of conviction the court has the range of sentences set out at **F28**. If the offender has attained 18 before conviction, the youth court may still proceed to sentence (see **I6.2** below).

Where an offender crosses a significant age threshold between the date of the commission of the offence and the date of conviction, the starting point for determining the length of sentence is the sentence that he would have been likely to receive if he had been sentenced at the date of the offence (*R v Ghafoor* [2002] EWCA Crim 1857, [2003] 1 Cr App R (S) 428). See **F1.2**.

I6.1 **Purpose of sentencing**

For offenders under the age of 18 on the date of conviction there are no statutory purposes of sentencing and the court will have regard to the principal aim of the youth justice system of preventing further offending and to the welfare of the youth defendant.

If an offender has attained 18 by the date of conviction the adult purposes of sentencing will apply. The CJA 2003 s 142 provides:

Criminal Justice Act 2003 s 142

(1) Any court dealing with an offender in respect of his offence must have regard to the following purposes of sentencing—
  (a) the punishment of offenders,
  (b) the reduction of crime (including its reduction by deterrence),
  (c) the reform and rehabilitation of offenders,
  (d) the protection of the public, and
  (e) the making of reparation by offenders to persons affected by their offences.
(2) Subsection (1) does not apply—
  (a) in relation to an offender who is aged under 18 at the time of conviction,
  ...

I6.2 **Available sentences**

The sentences available to any court dealing with an offender who has attained 18 by the date of conviction are:

- Discharge (absolute or conditional)
- Fine

- Community order under the CJA 2003
- Detention in a young offender institution
- Suspended sentence order.

I6.2.1 *Community order*

When the offender has attained 18 before conviction the appropriate community sentence is a community order under the CJA 2003 rather than a youth rehabilitation order. When imposing requirements on the offender as part of the community order, a court should balance the requirements, or combination of requirements, with the offender's personal circumstances, and avoid conflict with work, schooling, or religious beliefs.

The available requirements are contained in the CJA 2003 ss 199–215. They are:

- unpaid work of between 40 and 300 hours;
- activity for up to 60 days;
- programme;
- prohibited activity;
- curfew for up to 16 hours a day for up to 12 months;
- exclusion, normally with electronic monitoring;
- residence;
- mental health treatment;
- drug treatment;
- alcohol treatment;
- supervision;
- (if under 25) attendance centre;
- foreign travel restriction for up to 12 months; or
- alcohol abstinence and monitoring (not fully in force) if alcohol an element of the offence or a factor contributing to it.

I6.2.2 *Detention in a young offender institution*

The usual custodial sentence for an offender who has attained the age of 18 but is under the age of 21 on the date of conviction is detention in a young offender institution under the PCCSA 2000 s 96.

The minimum term of the order is three weeks (s 97(2)). This applies to the sentence passed for each offence and not just to the total aggregate sentence (*R v Dover Youth Court ex parte K* [1998] 4 All ER 24). When imposing detention in a young offender institution upon an offender who attained 18 between the date of the offence and the date of conviction, the court should have regard to the terms permitted for a detention and training order (ie 4, 6, 8, 10, 12, 18, or 24 months) (*R v Jones* [2003] EWCA Crim 1609, [2004] 1 Cr App R (S) 18).

I6.2.3 *Suspended sentence order*

A term of detention in a young offender institution may be suspended. When a suspended sentence order is made the community requirements listed in **I6.2.1** may be imposed.

I6.3 Committal for sentence

When an offender has attained 18 before being convicted of an *offence triable either way* in the case of an adult, the youth court or adult magistrates' court may commit the offender to the Crown Court for sentence under the PCCSA 2000 s 3 if the court is of the opinion that the offence or the combination of the offence and one or more offences associated with it was so serious that greater punishment should be inflicted for the offence than the court has power to impose.

Where an offender has attained 18 before being convicted of an *indictable-only* offence committal for sentence under the PCCSA 2000 s 3 is not available.

I6.4 Remittal to adult court for sentence

The PCCSA 2000 s 9 provides:

Powers of Criminal Courts (Sentencing) Act 2000 s 9

(1) Where a person who appears or is brought before a youth court charged with an offence subsequently attains the age of 18, the youth court may, at any time after conviction and before sentence, remit him for sentence to a magistrates' court (other than a youth court).

(2) Where an offender is remitted under subsection (1) above, the youth court shall adjourn proceedings in relation to the offence, and—

(a) section 128 of the Magistrates' Courts Act 1980 (remand in custody or on bail) and all other enactments, whenever passed, relating to remand or the granting of bail in criminal proceedings shall have effect, in relation to the youth court's power or duty to remand the offender on that adjournment, as if any reference to the court to or before which the person remanded is to be brought or appear after remand were a reference to the court to which he is being remitted; and

(b) subject to subsection (3) below, the court to which the offender is remitted ('the other court') may deal with the case in any way in which it would have power to deal with it if all proceedings relating to the offence which took place before the youth court had taken place before the other court.

---

(3) Where an offender is remitted under subsection (1) above, section 8(6) above (duty of adult magistrates' court to remit young offenders to youth court for sentence) shall not apply to the court to which he is remitted.

(4) Where an offender is remitted under subsection (1) above he shall have no right of appeal against the order of remission (but without prejudice to any right of appeal against an order made in respect of the offence by the court to which he is remitted).

(5) In this section—

    (a) 'enactment' includes an enactment contained in any order, regulation or other instrument having effect by virtue of an Act; and

    (b) 'bail in criminal proceedings' has the same meaning as in the Bail Act 1976.

A youth court should never remit under s 9 an offence which is indictable only in the case of an adult (*R (Denny) v Acton Youth Court* [2004] EWHC 94 (Admin), [2004] 2 All ER 961).

Remitting to the adult magistrates' court under s 9 does not mean that the receiving court will have any extra powers of sentence but it can be a useful power if the offender already has other matters for sentence in the adult court.

16.5 Discretion to ignore fact offender has attained 18

The CYPA 1963 s 29 provides:

Children and Young Persons Act 1963 s 29

(1) Where proceedings in respect of a young person are begun for an offence and he attains the age of eighteen before the conclusion of the proceedings, the court may deal with the case and make any order which it could have made if he had not attained that age.

For the purposes of s 29 proceedings have not commenced until the defendant appears or is brought before the court (*R v Uxbridge Youth Court ex parte Howard* (1998) 162 JP 327).

In general youth offending teams will not want to supervise offenders who have attained 18, so this provision will be rarely used. The use of the provision to impose a detention and training order on an offender who had attained 18 before conviction was upheld in the case of *Aldis v DPP* [2002] EWHC 403 (Admin), [2002] 2 Cr App R (S) 88. In that case the defendant was 17 when the youth court accepted jurisdiction in relation to a charge of wounding with intent. Invoking s 29 the magistrates sentenced him to an eighteen-month detention and training order. The sentence was upheld by the Administrative Court. It must have been plain to everyone that the possibility of a two-year detention and training order was a factor, if not the crucial factor, in the magistrates' decision to try the case summarily.

17 Reporting Restrictions in Youth Court

- The provisions of the CYPA 1933 s 49 no longer apply if the defendant attains 18 during the proceedings (*T v DPP* [2003] EWHC 2408 (Admin)).

18 Breach Proceedings

18.1 Conditional discharges

An adult offender convicted of a new offence committed during the period of a conditional discharge made by a youth court may be re-sentenced for the original offence by the convicting adult magistrates' court or, if no action is taken by that court, the youth court which gave the original sentence may summons the offender for the breach to be dealt with (CYPA 1933 s 48(2)).

If the original offence is indictable only, the court may impose a fine not exceeding £5,000 or impose a term of detention in a young offender institution not exceeding six months (PCCSA 2000 s 13(9)).

18.2 Referral orders

The breach proceedings must be dealt with by the adult magistrates' court if the offender has attained 18 by the first court hearing (PCCSA 2000 Sch 1 para 5(5)). If the order is revoked the court's sentencing powers are limited to those available at the time of the original sentence (see **F20.12.1**).

18.3 Reparation orders

Proceedings for breach of a reparation order can only be dealt with in the youth court even when the offender has attained 18 (PCCSA 2000 Sch 8 para 1). For the court's powers on breach see **F23**.

18.4 Youth rehabilitation orders

The breach proceedings must be dealt with by the adult magistrates' court if the offender has attained 18 by the first court hearing (CJIA 2008 Sch 2 para 5). For the court's powers on breach see **F34.10**.

18.5 Detention and training order

Proceedings for breach of the supervision requirements can only be dealt with in the youth court even when the offender has attained 18 (PCCSA 2000 s 104(1)). For the court's powers on breach see **F7.8**.

19 Applying to Amend or Revoke a Sentence

19.1 Referral orders

If the panel wishes to refer an offender who has attained 18 back to court to request early revocation under the PCCSA 2000 s 27A or at the request of the offender, the appropriate court is the adult magistrates' court acting in the local justice area in which it appears to the panel that the offender resides or will reside (PCCSA 2000 Sch 1 para 1(2)). For the court's powers see **F20.12.2**.

If the panel wishes to refer an offender who has attained 18 back to court to extend the period of the order, the appropriate court is again the adult magistrates' court acting in the local justice area in which it appears to the panel that the offender resides or will reside (PCCSA 2000 Sch 1 para 9ZB(1)(2)). For the court's powers see **F20.12.3**.

19.2 Reparation orders

Applications to amend or revoke a reparation order can only be dealt with in the youth court even when the offender has attained 18 (PCCSA 2000 Sch 8 para 1). For the court's powers when dealing with such an application see **F23**.

19.3 Youth rehabilitation orders

Applications to revoke or amend a youth rehabilitation order in the case of an offender who has attained the age of 18 by the date of the first court hearing must be made to the adult magistrates' court (CJIA 2008 Sch 2 paras 11 and 13). For the powers of the court when dealing with such an application see **F34.11** for revocation of the order and **F34.12** for amendment of the order.

I10 Sexual Offences Registration Requirement

- When determining whether there is a requirement to register the relevant age is the age on the date of the offence (see **F31.1**).
- If there is a requirement to register, the reduced applicable period does not apply if the offender has attained 18 by the date of conviction (see **F31.2**).

I11 Rehabilitation of Offenders Act 1974

- The relevant age is the age on the date of conviction. The reduced rehabilitation periods do not apply if the offender has attained 18 by the date of conviction.

Part J
Parents and Guardians

J1 Definition of Parent/Guardian

J1.1 Parent

There is no definition of who is a 'parent' but it is likely to include a person with parental responsibility under the Children Act 1989.

J1.2 Guardian

The CYPA 1933 s 107(1) states:

Children and Young Persons Act 1933 s 107(1)

'Guardian', in relation to a child or young person, includes any person who, in the opinion of the court having cognisance of any case in relation to the child or young person or in which the child or young person is concerned, has for the time being the care of the child or young person.

J2 Requiring Attendance at Court

The CYPA 1933 s 34A states:

Children and Young Persons Act 1933 s 34A

(1) Where a child or young person is charged with an offence or is for any other reason brought before a court, the court—
   (a) may in any case; and
   (b) shall in the case of a child or a young person who is under the age of sixteen years,
   require a person who is a parent or guardian of his to attend at the court during all the stages of the proceedings, unless and to the extent that the court is satisfied that it would be unreasonable to require such attendance, having regard to the circumstances of the case.
(2) In relation to a child or young person for whom a local authority have parental responsibility and who—
   (a) is in their care; or
   (b) is provided with accommodation by them in the exercise of any functions (in particular those under the Children Act 1989) which are social service functions within the meaning of the Local Authority Social Services Act 1970,
   the reference in subsection (1) above to a person who is a parent or guardian of his shall be construed as a reference to that authority or, where he is allowed to live with such a person, as including such a reference.

In this subsection 'local authority' and 'parental responsibility' have the same meanings as in the Children Act 1989.

The Crim PR rule 7.4(9) sets out two options:

A summons or requisition issued to a defendant under 18 may require that defendant's parent or guardian to attend the court with the defendant, or a separate summons or requisition may be issued for that purpose.

The Sentencing Guideline *Overarching Principles: Sentencing Youths* provides the following guidance:

7.2 The statutory framework clearly envisages the attendance of an adult with a degree of responsibility for the young person; this obligation reflects the principal aim of reducing offending, recognising that that is unlikely to be achieved by the young person alone. A court must be aware of a risk that a young person will seek to avoid this requirement either by urging the court to proceed in the absence of an adult or in arranging for a person to come to court who purports to have (but in reality does not have) the necessary degree of responsibility.

7.3 Insistence on attendance may produce a delay in the case before the court; however, it is important that this obligation is maintained and that it is widely recognised that a court will require such attendance, especially when ~osing sentence. If a court proceeds in the absence of a responsible adult, ·ld ensure that the outcome of the hearing is properly communicated.

J3 Responsibility for Financial Orders

There are different considerations in relation to the position of parents and guardians and that of local authorities with parental responsibilities.

J3.1 Parents and guardians

The PCCSA 2000 s 137 states that where the defendant is aged under 16 years the court **must** order the parent or guardian to pay the fine, costs, surcharge, and compensation if ordered unless

- s/he cannot be found or
- it would be unreasonable to make an order for payment having regard to the circumstances of the case.

Where the defendant is aged 16 or 17 years the court **may** order the parent or guardian to pay the fine, costs, surcharge, and compensation if ordered unless

- s/he cannot be found or
- it would be unreasonable to make an order for payment having regard to the circumstances of the case.

The PCCSA 2000 ss 136 and 138 state that before making a financial order against a parent or guardian the court may require details of their circumstances through a financial circumstances order. If there is no cooperation with this inquiry the court may make such determination as it thinks fit.

The question of when it is 'unreasonable' to make a financial order has been considered by the courts.

- A compensation order payable by a mother who 'had done what she could to keep her son from criminal ways' was quashed. She was also of limited means and the order meant that it would have taken her more than two years to pay: *R v Sheffield Crown Court ex parte Clarkson* [1986] Cr App R (S) 454.
- The parent of a child accommodated by the local authority under s 20 of the Children Act 1989 was not reasonably to be ordered to pay a financial penalty: *TA v DPP* [1997] 1 Cr App R (S) 1, [1996] Crim LR 606, QBD.
- The policy underlying the legislation meant that it was in the public interest that the financial order be recovered from the parent unless there were special circumstances which made that

inappropriate: *R(M) v Inner London Crown Court* [2003] EWHC 301 (Admin).

- In *R v JB* [2004] EWCA Crim 14 there seems to be an assumption that in the absence of parental fault it would be unreasonable to order the parent to pay.

J3.2 Local authorities

The PCCSA 2000 s 137(8) states that a local authority is responsible for payment of financial orders where the authority has parental responsibility for the defendant and the defendant is in the authority's care or is accommodated by it.

An order remanding a young person to the care of the local authority does not confer parental responsibility on the local authority. Parental responsibility is only acquired with a full care order: *North Yorkshire County Council v Selby Youth Court* [1994] 1All ER 991, QBD.

The question of when it is 'unreasonable' to make a financial order has been considered by the courts.

- A local authority that had done everything it reasonably and properly could to protect the public from the criminal behaviour of a young person in its care could not be expected to assume responsibility for financial orders: *D and R v DPP* [1995] 16 Cr App R (S) 1040, [1995] Crim LR 748.
- A causal link between the authority's lack of care and the offending needs to be established before the court should order payment of the financial penalty by the authority: *Bedfordshire County Council v DPP* [1996] 1 Cr App R (S) 322; [1995] Crim LR 962.
- A company contracted by the local authority to look after the young person could not be ordered to pay a financial order: *Marlowe Child and Family Services Ltd v DPP* [1998] Crim LR 594.

See **F10**.

J4 Parental Bind Overs

Since the introduction of parenting orders the imposition of parental bind overs has declined. The making of a bind over requires consideration of its terms and the consent of the person being bound over.

The PCCSA 2000 s 150 states:

Powers of the Criminal Courts (Sentencing) Act 2000 s 150

(1) Where a child or young person (that is to say, any person aged under 18) is convicted of an offence, the powers conferred by this section shall be exercisable by the court by which he is sentenced for that offence, and where the offender is aged under 16 when sentenced it shall be the duty of that court—

   (a) to exercise those powers if it is satisfied, having regard to the circumstances of the case, that their exercise would be desirable in the interests of preventing the commission by him of further offences; and

   (b) if it does not exercise them, to state in open court that it is not satisfied as mentioned in paragraph (a) above and why it is not so satisfied;

but this subsection has effect subject to section 19(5) above and paragraph 13(5) of Schedule 1 to this Act (cases where referral orders made or extended).

(2) The powers conferred by this section are as follows—

   (a) with the consent of the offender's parent or guardian, to order the parent or guardian to enter into a recognizance to take proper care of him and exercise proper control over him; and

   (b) if the parent or guardian refuses consent and the court considers the refusal unreasonable, to order the parent or guardian to pay a fine not exceeding £1,000;

and where the court has passed a community sentence on the offender, it may include in the recognizance a provision that the offender's parent or guardian ensure that the offender complies with the requirements of that sentence.

(3) An order under this section shall not require the parent or guardian to enter into a recognizance for an amount exceeding £1,000.

(4) An order under this section shall not require the parent or guardian to enter into a recognizance—

   (a) for a period exceeding three years; or

   (b) where the offender will attain the age of 18 in a period shorter than three years, for a period exceeding that shorter period.

Article 8 Convention rights are engaged and the procedure set out in the Consolidated Criminal Practice Direction Part III.31 must be followed. This includes:

> III.31.17 Where a court is considering binding over a parent or guardian under section 150 of the Powers of Criminal Courts (Sentencing) Act 2000 to enter into a recognisance to take proper care of and exercise proper control over a child or young person, the court should specify the actions which the parent or guardian is to take.

Where a bind over is not made the court must explain in open court its reasons.

Where the court makes a referral order it cannot impose a parental bind over. PCCSA 2000 s 19.

The parent who is made subject to a bind over has the right of appeal to the Crown Court from the youth court or adult magistrates' court and to the Court of Appeal from the Crown Court.

J5 Parenting Orders

A parenting order may be made by any criminal court—youth court, adult magistrates' court, or Crown Court. They may also be made by a Family Proceedings Court and an adult magistrates' court in the exercise of its civil jurisdiction.

The Crime and Disorder Act 1998 s 8 states:

Crime and Disorder Act 1998 s 8

8 Parenting orders

(1) This section applies where, in any court proceedings—
  (a) a child safety order is made in respect of a child;
  (b) an anti-social behaviour order or sex offender order is made in respect of a child or young person;
  (c) a child or young person is convicted of an offence; or
  (d) a person is convicted of an offence under section 443 (failure to comply with school attendance order) or section 444 (failure to secure regular attendance at school of registered pupil) of the Education Act 1996.

(2) Subject to subsection (3) and section 9(1) below and to section 19(5) of, and paragraph 13(5) of Schedule 1 to, the Powers of Criminal Courts (Sentencing) Act 2000, if in the proceedings the court is satisfied that the relevant condition is fulfilled, it may make a parenting order in respect of a person who is a parent or guardian of the child or young person or, as the case may be, the person convicted of the offence under section 443 or 444 ('the parent').

(3) A court shall not make a parenting order unless it has been notified by the Secretary of State that arrangements for implementing such orders are available in the area in which it appears to the court that the parent resides or will reside and the notice has not been withdrawn.

(4) A parenting order is an order which requires the parent—
  (a) to comply, for a period not exceeding twelve months, with such requirements as are specified in the order; and
  (b) subject to subsection (5) below, to attend, for a concurrent period not exceeding three months and not more than once in any week, such counselling or guidance sessions as may be specified in directions given by the responsible officer;

and in this subsection 'week' means a period of seven days beginning with a Sunday.

(5) A parenting order may, but need not, include such a requirement as is mentioned in subsection (4)(b) above in any case where such an order has been made in respect of the parent on a previous occasion.

(6) The relevant condition is that the parenting order would be desirable in the interests of preventing—
  (a) in a case falling within paragraph (a) or (b) of subsection (1) above, any repetition of the kind of behaviour which led to the child safety order, anti-social behaviour order or sex offender order being made;

(b) in a case falling within paragraph (c) of that subsection, the commission of any further offence by the child or young person;

(c) in a case falling within paragraph (d) of that subsection, the commission of any further offence under section 443 or 444 of the Education Act 1996.

(7) The requirements that may be specified under subsection (4)(a) above are those which the court considers desirable in the interests of preventing any such repetition or, as the case may be, the commission of any such further offence.

(8) In this section and section 9 below 'responsible officer', in relation to a parenting order, means one of the following who is specified in the order, namely—

(a) an officer of a local probation board;

(b) a social worker of a local authority social services department; and

(bb) a person nominated by a person appointed as chief education officer under section 532 of the Education Act 1996

(c) a member of a youth offending team.

A parenting order is an order requiring a parent or guardian to comply with requirements that the court considers desirable:

- in criminal proceedings, in the interests of preventing the commission of further offences;
- in civil proceedings, to prevent the behaviour which led to the making of a particular order.

Where an offender is aged under 16 years, the court must make a parenting order if it considers it desirable as above. If the court is not so satisfied it must state this in open court and give reasons.

Where an offender is aged 16 or 17 years, the court has a discretionary power to make an order.

Before making an order the court shall obtain and consider information about the family circumstances and the likely effect of the order on them. Where the court is considering making a referral order and a parenting order, this information shall be in a report by an appropriate officer.

J5.1 Terms of the order

The order will last for up to twelve months and must include a requirement to attend a parenting programme for a period not exceeding three months and not more than once a week. It may be a residential course if it is likely to be more effective than a non-residential course and the likely interference with family life is proportionate.

The order must specify a responsible officer who may be:

- a probation officer
- a social worker
- a person nominated by the local education authority
- a member of the youth offending team.

J5.2 Breach

Breach of the order, without reasonable excuse, is punishable on conviction by a fine not exceeding level 3.

J5.3 Variation, discharge, and appeal

The responsible officer or parent may apply to the court which made the order to vary or discharge the order.

Appeal against an order made in the youth or adult magistrates' courts is to the Crown Court and to the Court of Appeal if the order is made in the Crown Court. If the order is imposed following the making of a child safety order, appeal is to the High Court by way of case stated.

J5.4 Breach of ASBO

When brought into force, the Crime and Security Act 2010 s 41 will insert s 8A into the CDA 1998. Under that provision, where a person aged under 16 years is convicted of an offence of breach of an ASBO the court must make a parenting order in respect of the parent or guardian unless it is of the opinion that there are exceptional circumstances that would make a parenting order inappropriate. If an order is not made the circumstances must be stated in open court.

J6 Referral Order: Requiring Attendance at Panel

The Powers of Criminal Courts (Sentencing) Act 2000 s 20 states:

Powers of Criminal Courts (Sentencing) Act 2000 s 20

(1) A court making a referral order may make an order requiring—
   (a) the appropriate person, or
   (b) in a case where there are two or more appropriate persons, any one or more of them,

   to attend the meetings of the youth offender panel.

(2) Where an offender is aged under 16 when a court makes a referral order in his case—
   (a) the court shall exercise its power under subsection (1) above so as to require at least one appropriate person to attend meetings of the youth offender panel; and
   (b) if the offender falls within subsection (6) below, the person or persons so required to attend those meetings shall be or include a representative of the local authority mentioned in that subsection.

(3) The court shall not under this section make an order requiring a person to attend meetings of the youth offender panel—
   (a) if the court is satisfied that it would be unreasonable to do so; or
   (b) to an extent which the court is satisfied would be unreasonable.

(4) Except where the offender falls within subsection (6) below, each person who is a parent or guardian of the offender is an 'appropriate person' for the purposes of this section.

(5) Where the offender falls within subsection (6) below, each of the following is an 'appropriate person' for the purposes of this section—
   (a) a representative of the local authority mentioned in that subsection; and
   (b) each person who is a parent or guardian of the offender with whom the offender is allowed to live.

(6) An offender falls within this subsection if he is (within the meaning of the Children Act 1989) a child who is looked after by a local authority.

(7) If, at the time when a court makes an order under this section—
   (a) a person who is required by the order to attend meetings of a youth offender panel is not present in court, or
   (b) a local authority whose representative is so required to attend such meetings is not represented in court, the court must send him or (as the case may be) the authority a copy of the order forthwith.

Where a parent who has been required to do so does not attend meetings of the referral order panel, the panel can refer the parent to the youth court for consideration of the making of a parenting order.

The PCCSA 2000 Schedule 1 Part 1A states:

Powers of Criminal Courts (Sentencing) Act 2000 Sch 1

Part 1A referral of parent or guardian for breach of section 20 order

Introductory

9A(1) This Part of this Schedule applies where, under section 22(2A) of this Act, a youth offender panel refers an offender's parent or guardian to a youth court.

(2) In this Part of this Schedule—

   (a) 'the offender' means the offender whose parent or guardian is referred under section 22(2A);

   (b) 'the parent' means the parent or guardian so referred; and

   (c) 'the youth court' means a youth court as mentioned in section 22(2A).

Mode of referral to court

9B The panel shall make the referral by sending a report to the youth court explaining why the parent is being referred to it.

Bringing the parent before the court

9C(1) Where the youth court receives such a report it shall cause the parent to appear before it.

(2) For the purpose of securing the attendance of the parent before the court, a justice acting for the petty sessions area for which the court acts may—

   (a) issue a summons requiring the parent to appear at the place and time specified in it; or

   (b) if the report is substantiated on oath, issue a warrant for the parent's arrest.

(3) Any summons or warrant issued under sub-paragraph (2) above shall direct the parent to appear or be brought before the youth court.

Power of court to make parenting order: application of supplemental provisions

9D(1) Where the parent appears or is brought before the youth court under paragraph 9C above, the court may make a parenting order in respect of the parent if—

   (a) it is proved to the satisfaction of the court that the parent has failed without reasonable excuse to comply with the order under section 20 of this Act; and

   (b) the court is satisfied that the parenting order would be desirable in the interests of preventing the commission of any further offence by the offender.

(2) A parenting order is an order which requires the parent—

   (a) to comply, for a period not exceeding twelve months, with such requirements as are specified in the order, and

   (b) subject to sub-paragraph (4) below, to attend, for a concurrent period not exceeding three months, such counselling or guidance programme as may be specified in directions given by the responsible officer.

(3) The requirements that may be specified under sub-paragraph (2)(a) above are those which the court considers desirable in the interests of preventing the commission of any further offence by the offender.

(4) A parenting order under this paragraph may, but need not, include a requirement mentioned in subsection (2)(b) above in any case where a parenting order under this paragraph or any other enactment has been made in respect of the parent on a previous occasion.

(5) A counselling or guidance programme which a parent is required to attend by virtue of subsection (2)(b) above may be or include a residential course but only if the court is satisfied—

    (a) that the attendance of the parent at a residential course is likely to be more effective than his attendance at a non-residential course in preventing the commission of any further offence by the offender, and

    (b) that any interference with family life which is likely to result from the attendance of the parent at a residential course is proportionate in all the circumstances.

(6) Before making a parenting order under this paragraph where the offender is aged under 16, the court shall obtain and consider information about his family circumstances and the likely effect of the order on those circumstances.

(7) Sections 8(3) and (8), 9(3) to (7) and 18(3) and (4) of the Crime and Disorder Act 1998 apply in relation to a parenting order made under this paragraph as they apply in relation to any other parenting order.

Appeal

9E(1) An appeal shall lie to the Crown Court against the making of a parenting order under paragraph 9D above.

(2) Subsections (2) and (3) of section 10 of the Crime and Disorder Act 1998 (appeals against parenting orders) apply in relation to an appeal under this paragraph as they apply in relation to an appeal under subsection (1)(b) of that section.

Effect on section 20 order

9F(1) The making of a parenting order under paragraph 9D above is without prejudice to the continuance of the order under section 20 of this Act.

(2) Section 63(1) to (4) of the Magistrates' Courts Act 1980 (power of magistrates' court to deal with person for breach of order, etc) apply (as well as section 22(2A) of this Act and this Part of this Schedule) in relation to an order under section 20 of this Act.

See **F20**.

Appendix 1

Consolidated Criminal Practice Direction Part III.30

III.30 **Treatment of Vulnerable Defendants**

III.30.1 This direction applies to proceedings in the Crown Court and in magistrates' courts on the trial, sentencing or (in the Crown Court) appeal of (a) children and young persons under 18 or (b) adults who suffer from a mental disorder within the meaning of the Mental Health Act 1983 or who have any significant impairment of intelligence and social function. In this direction, such defendants are referred to collectively as 'vulnerable defendants'. The purpose of this direction is to extend to proceedings in relation to such persons in the adult courts procedures analogous to those in use in youth courts.

III.30.2 The steps which should be taken to comply with paragraphs III.30.3 to III.30.17 should be judged, in any given case, taking account of the age, maturity and development (intellectual, social and emotional) of the defendant concerned and all other circumstances of the case.

The overriding principle

III.30.3 A defendant may be young and immature, or may have a mental disorder within the meaning of the Mental Health Act 1983, or some other significant impairment of intelligence and social function such as to inhibit his understanding of and participation in the proceedings. The purpose of criminal proceedings is to determine guilt, if that is in issue, and decide on the appropriate sentence if the defendant pleads guilty or is convicted. All possible steps should be taken to assist a vulnerable defendant to understand and participate in those proceedings. The ordinary trial process should, so far as necessary, be adapted to meet those ends. Regard should be had to the welfare of a young defendant as required by section 44 of the Children and Young Persons Act 1933, and generally to Parts 1 and 3 of The Criminal Procedure Rules (the overriding objective and the court's powers of case management).

Before the trial, sentencing or appeal

III.30.4 If a vulnerable defendant, especially one who is young, is to be tried jointly with one who is not, the court should consider at the plea and case management hearing, or at a case management hearing in a magistrates' court, whether the vulnerable defendant should be tried on his own and should so order unless of the opinion that a joint trial would be in accordance with Part 1 of The Criminal Procedure Rules (the overriding objective) and in the interests of justice. If a vulnerable defendant is tried jointly with one who is not, the court should consider whether any of the modifications set out in this direction should apply in the circumstances of the joint trial and, so far as practicable, make orders to give effect to any such modifications.

III.30.5 At the plea and case management hearing, or at a case management hearing in a magistrates' court, the court should consider and so far as practicable give directions on the matters covered in paragraphs III.30.9 to III.30.17.

III.30.6 It may be appropriate to arrange that a vulnerable defendant should visit, out of court hours and before the trial, sentencing or appeal hearing, the courtroom in which that hearing is to take place so that he can familiarise himself with it.

III.30.7 If any case against a vulnerable defendant has attracted or may attract widespread public or media interest, the assistance of the police should be enlisted to try and ensure that the defendant is not, when attending the court, exposed to intimidation, vilification or abuse. Section 41 of the Criminal Justice Act 1925 prohibits the taking of photographs of defendants and witnesses (among others) in the court building or in its precincts, or when entering or leaving those precincts. A direction informing media representatives that the prohibition will be enforced may be appropriate.

III.30.8 The court should be ready at this stage, if it has not already done so, where relevant to make a reporting restriction under section 39 of the Children and Young Persons Act 1933 or, on an appeal to the Crown Court from a youth court, to remind media representatives of the application of section 49 of that Act. Any such order, once made, should be reduced to writing and copies should on request be made available to anyone affected or potentially affected by it.

The trial, sentencing or appeal hearing

III.30.9 Subject to the need for appropriate security arrangements, the proceedings should, if practicable, be held in a courtroom in which all the participants are on the same or almost the same level.

III.30.10 A vulnerable defendant, especially if he is young, should normally, if he wishes, be free to sit with members of his family or others in a like relationship, and with some other suitable supporting adult such as a social worker, and in a place which permits easy, informal communication with his legal representatives. The court should ensure that a suitable supporting adult is available throughout the course of the proceedings.

III.30.11 At the beginning of the proceedings, the court should ensure that what is to take place has been explained to a vulnerable defendant in terms he can understand and, at trial in the Crown Court, it should ensure in particular that the role of the jury has been explained. It should remind those representing the vulnerable defendant and the supporting adult of their responsibility to explain each step as it takes place and, at trial, to explain the possible consequences of a guilty verdict. Throughout the trial the court should continue to ensure, by any appropriate means, that the defendant understands what is happening and what has been said by those on the bench, the advocates and witnesses.

III.30.12 A trial should be conducted according to a timetable which takes full account of a vulnerable defendant's ability to concentrate. Frequent and regular breaks will often be appropriate. The court should ensure, so far as practicable, that the trial is conducted in simple, clear language that the defendant can understand and that cross-examination is conducted by questions that are short and clear.

III.30.13 A vulnerable defendant who wishes to give evidence by live link, in accordance with section 33A of the Youth Justice and Criminal Evidence Act 1999, may apply for a direction to that effect. Before making such a direction, the court must be satisfied that it is in the interests of justice to do so and that the use of a live link would enable the defendant to participate more effectively as a witness in the proceedings. The direction will need to deal with the practical arrangements to be made, including the room from which the defendant will give evidence, the identity of the person or persons who will accompany him, and how it will be arranged for him to be seen and heard by the court.

III.30.14 In the Crown Court, robes and wigs should not be worn unless the court for good reason orders that they should. It may be appropriate for the court to be robed for sentencing in a grave case, even though it has sat without robes for trial. It is generally desirable that those responsible for the security of a vulnerable defendant who is in custody, especially if he is young, should not be in uniform, and that there should be no recognisable police presence in the courtroom save for good reason.

III.30.15 The court should be prepared to restrict attendance by members of the public in the court room to a small number, perhaps limited to those with an immediate and direct interest in the outcome. The court should rule on any challenged claim to attend.

III.30.16 Facilities for reporting the proceedings (subject to any restrictions under section 39 or 49 of the Children and Young Persons Act 1933) must be provided. But the court may restrict the number of reporters attending in the courtroom to such number as is judged practicable and desirable. In ruling on any challenged claim to attend in the court room for the purpose of reporting, the court should be mindful of the public's general right to be informed about the administration of justice.

III.30.17 Where it has been decided to limit access to the courtroom, whether by reporters or generally, arrangements should be made for the proceedings to be relayed, audibly and if possible visually, to another room in the same court complex to which the media and the public have access if it appears that there will be a need for such additional facilities. Those making use of such a facility should be reminded that it is to be treated as an extension of the court room and that they are required to conduct themselves accordingly.

III.30.18 Where the court is called upon to exercise its discretion in relation to any procedural matter falling within the scope of this practice direction but not the subject of specific reference, such direction should be exercised having regard to the principles in paragraph III.30.3.

Appendix 2

Dangerous Offenders: Specified Offences

For the purposes of the Criminal Justice Act 2003 s 224 the following offences are listed in Schedule 15 as specified offences.

Specified violent offences

1. Manslaughter.
2. Kidnapping.
3. False imprisonment.
4. An offence under section 4 of the Offences Against the Person Act 1861 (soliciting murder).
5. An offence under section 16 of that Act (threats to kill).
6. An offence under section 18 of that Act (wounding with intent to cause grievous bodily harm).
7. An offence under section 20 of that Act (malicious wounding).
8. An offence under section 21 of that Act (attempting to choke, suffocate, or strangle in order to commit or assist in committing an indictable offence).
9. An offence under section 22 of that Act (using chloroform, etc to commit or assist in the committing of any indictable offence).
10. An offence under section 23 of that Act (maliciously administering poison etc so as to endanger life or inflict grievous bodily harm).
11. An offence under section 27 of that Act (abandoning children).
12. An offence under section 28 of that Act (causing bodily injury by explosives).
13. An offence under section 29 of that Act (using explosives etc with intent to do grievous bodily harm)
14. An offence under section 30 of that Act (placing explosives with intent to do bodily injury).
15. An offence under section 31 of that Act (setting spring guns etc with intent to do grievous bodily harm).
16. An offence under section 32 of that Act (endangering the safety of railway passengers).
17. An offence under section 35 of that Act (injuring persons by furious driving).
18. An offence under section 37 of that Act (assaulting officer preserving wreck).

19. An offence under section 38 of that Act (assault with intent to resist arrest).

20. An offence under section 47 of that Act (assault occasioning actual bodily harm).

21. An offence under section 2 of the Explosive Substances Act 1883 (causing explosion likely to endanger life or property).

22. An offence under section 3 of that Act (attempt to cause explosion, or making or keeping explosive with intent to endanger life or property).

23. An offence under section 1 of the Infant Life (Preservation) Act 1929 (child destruction).

24. An offence under section 1 of the Children and Young Persons Act 1933 (cruelty to children).

25. An offence under section 1 of the Infanticide Act 1938 (infanticide).

26. An offence under section 16 of the Firearms Act 1968 (possession of firearm with intent to endanger life).

27. An offence under section 16A of that Act (possession of firearm with intent to cause fear of violence).

28. An offence under section 17(1) of that Act (use of firearm to resist arrest).

29. An offence under section 17(2) of that Act (possession of firearm at time of committing or being arrested for offence specified in Schedule 1 to that Act).

30. An offence under section 18 of that Act (carrying a firearm with criminal intent).

31. An offence under section 8 of the Theft Act 1968 (robbery or assault with intent to rob).

32. An offence under section 9 of that Act of burglary with intent to— (a) inflict grievous bodily harm on a person; or (b) do unlawful damage to a building or anything in it.

33. An offence under section 10 of that Act (aggravated burglary).

34. An offence under section 12A of that Act (aggravated vehicle-taking) involving an accident which caused the death of any person.

35. An offence of arson under section 1 of the Criminal Damage Act 1971.

36. An offence under section 1(2) of that Act (destroying or damaging property with intent to endanger life).

37. An offence under section 1 of the Taking of Hostages Act 1982 (hostage taking).

38. An offence under section 1 of the Aviation Security Act 1982 (hijacking).

39. An offence under section 2 of that Act (destroying, damaging, or endangering safety of aircraft).

40. An offence under section 3 of that Act (other acts endangering or likely to endanger safety of aircraft).

41. An offence under section 4 of that Act (offences in relation to certain dangerous articles).

42. An offence under section 127 of the Mental Health Act 1983 (ill-treatment of patients).

43. An offence under section 1 of the Prohibition of Female Circumcision Act 1985 (prohibition of female circumcision).

44. An offence under section 1 of the Public Order Act 1986 (riot).

45. An offence under section 2 of that Act (violent disorder).

46. An offence under section 3 of that Act (affray).

47. An offence under section 134 of the Criminal Justice Act 1988 (c 33) (torture).

48. An offence under section 1 of the Road Traffic Act 1988 (c 52) (causing death by dangerous driving).

49. An offence under section 3A of that Act (causing death by careless driving when under influence of drink or drugs).

50. An offence under section 1 of the Aviation and Maritime Security Act 1990 (endangering safety at aerodromes).

51. An offence under section 9 of that Act (hijacking of ships).

52. An offence under section 10 of that Act (seizing or exercising control of fixed platforms).

53. An offence under section 11 of that Act (destroying fixed platforms or endangering their safety).

54. An offence under section 12 of that Act (other acts endangering or likely to endanger safe navigation).

55. An offence under section 13 of that Act (offences involving threats).

56. An offence under Part II of the Channel Tunnel (Security) Order 1994 (SI 1994/570) (offences relating to Channel Tunnel trains and the tunnel system).

57. An offence under section 4 of the Protection from Harassment Act 1997 (putting people in fear of violence).

58. An offence under section 29 of the Crime and Disorder Act 1998 (racially or religiously aggravated assaults).

59. An offence falling within section 31(1)(a) or (b) of that Act (racially or religiously aggravated offences under section 4 or 4A of the Public Order Act 1986).

59A. An offence under section 54 of the Terrorism Act 2000 (weapons training).

59B. An offence under section 56 of that Act (directing terrorist organization).

59C. An offence under section 57 of that Act (possession of article for terrorist purposes).

59D. An offence under section 59 of that Act (inciting terrorism overseas).

60. An offence under section 51 or 52 of the International Criminal Court Act 2001 (genocide, crimes against humanity, war crimes, and related offences), other than one involving murder.

60A. An offence under section 47 of the Anti-terrorism, Crime, and Security Act 2001 (use etc of nuclear weapons).

60B. An offence under section 50 of that Act (assisting or inducing certain weapons-related acts overseas).

60C. An offence under section 113 of that Act (use of noxious substance or thing to cause harm or intimidate).

61. An offence under section 1 of the Female Genital Mutilation Act 2003 (female genital mutilation).

62. An offence under section 2 of that Act (assisting a girl to mutilate her own genitalia).

63. An offence under section 3 of that Act (assisting a non-UK person to mutilate overseas a girl's genitalia).

63A. An offence under section 5 of the Domestic Violence, Crime, and Victims Act 2004 (causing or allowing a child or vulnerable adult to die or suffer serious physical harm).

63B. An offence under section 5 of the Terrorism Act 2006 (preparation of terrorist acts).

63C. An offence under section 6 of that Act (training for terrorism).

63D. An offence under section 9 of that Act (making or possession of radioactive device or material).

63E. An offence under section 10 of that Act (use of radioactive device or material for terrorist purposes etc).

63F. An offence under section 11 of that Act (terrorist threats relating to radioactive devices etc).

64. An offence of: (a) aiding, abetting, counselling, procuring or inciting the commission of an offence specified in this Part of this appendix, (b) conspiring to commit an offence so specified, or (c) attempting to commit an offence so specified.

65. An attempt to commit murder or a conspiracy to commit murder.

Specified sexual offences

The offences listed at paragraphs 66–98 are not reproduced as they only apply to offences committed before 1 May 2004.

...

99. An offence under section 1 of the Protection of Children Act 1978 (indecent photographs of children).

100. An offence under section 170 of the Customs and Excise Management Act 1979 (penalty for fraudulent evasion of duty etc) in relation to goods prohibited to be imported under section 42 of the Customs Consolidation Act 1876 (indecent or obscene articles).

101. An offence under section 160 of the Criminal Justice Act 1988 (possession of indecent photograph of a child).

102 An offence under section 1 of the Sexual Offences Act 2003 (rape).

103. An offence under section 2 of that Act (assault by penetration).

104. An offence under section 3 of that Act (sexual assault).

105. An offence under section 4 of that Act (causing a person to engage in sexual activity without consent).

106. An offence under section 5 of that Act (rape of a child under 13).

107. An offence under section 6 of that Act (assault of a child under 13 by penetration).

108. An offence under section 7 of that Act (sexual assault of a child under 13).

109. An offence under section 8 of that Act (causing or inciting a child under 13 to engage in sexual activity).

110. Not applicable.

111. Not applicable.

112. Not applicable.

113. Not applicable.

114. An offence under section 13 of that Act (child sex offences committed by children or young persons).

115. An offence under section 14 of that Act (arranging or facilitating commission of a child sex offence).

116. Not applicable.

117. Not applicable.

118. Not applicable.

119. Not applicable.

120. Not applicable.

121. An offence under section 25 of that Act (sexual activity with a child family member).

122. An offence under section 26 of that Act (inciting a child family member to engage in sexual activity).

123. An offence under section 30 of that Act (sexual activity with a person with a mental disorder impeding choice).

124. An offence under section 31 of that Act (causing or inciting a person with a mental disorder impeding choice to engage in sexual activity).

125. An offence under section 32 of that Act (engaging in sexual activity in the presence of a person with a mental disorder impeding choice).

126. An offence under section 33 of that Act (causing a person with a mental disorder impeding choice to watch a sexual act).
127. An offence under section 34 of that Act (inducement, threat, or deception to procure sexual activity with a person with a mental disorder).
128. An offence under section 35 of that Act (causing a person with a mental disorder to engage in or agree to engage in sexual activity by inducement, threat, or deception).
129. An offence under section 36 of that Act (engaging in sexual activity in the presence, procured by inducement, threat, or deception, of a person with a mental disorder).
130. An offence under section 37 of that Act (causing a person with a mental disorder to watch a sexual act by inducement, threat, or deception).
131. An offence under section 38 of that Act (care workers: sexual activity with a person with a mental disorder).
132. An offence under section 39 of that Act (care workers: causing or inciting sexual activity).
133. An offence under section 40 of that Act (care workers: sexual activity in the presence of a person with a mental disorder).
134. An offence under section 41 of that Act (care workers: causing a person with a mental disorder to watch a sexual act).
135. An offence under section 47 of that Act (paying for sexual services of a child).
136. An offence under section 48 of that Act (causing or inciting child prostitution or pornography).
137. An offence under section 49 of that Act (controlling a child prostitute or a child involved in pornography).
138. An offence under section 50 of that Act (arranging or facilitating child prostitution or pornography).
139. An offence under section 52 of that Act (causing or inciting prostitution for gain).
140. An offence under section 53 of that Act (controlling prostitution for gain).
141. An offence under section 57 of that Act (trafficking into the UK for sexual exploitation).
142. An offence under section 58 of that Act (trafficking within the UK for sexual exploitation).
143. An offence under section 59 of that Act (trafficking out of the UK for sexual exploitation).
144. An offence under section 61 of that Act (administering a substance with intent).
145. An offence under section 62 of that Act (committing an offence with intent to commit a sexual offence).

146. An offence under section 63 of that Act (trespass with intent to commit a sexual offence).
147. An offence under section 64 of that Act (sex with an adult relative: penetration).
148. An offence under section 65 of that Act (sex with an adult relative: consenting to penetration).
149. An offence under section 66 of that Act (exposure).
150. An offence under section 67 of that Act (voyeurism).
151. An offence under section 69 of that Act (intercourse with an animal).
152. An offence under section 70 of that Act (sexual penetration of a corpse).
153. An offence of: (a) aiding, abetting, counselling, procuring, or inciting the commission of an offence specified in this part of this appendix (b) conspiring to commit an offence so specified (c) attempting to commit an offence so specified.

Appendix 3

Grave Crimes

Detention under section 91(3) of the Powers of Criminal Courts (Sentencing) Act 2000 is available for the following offences:

Aggravated burglary (s 10 Theft Act 1968—life)

Aiding suicide (s 2 Suicide Act 1961—14 years)

Arranging commission of a child sex offence (s 14 Sexual Offences Act 2003—14 years)

Arson (s 1 Criminal Damage Act 1971—life)

Assault by penetration (s 2 Sexual Offences Act 2003—life)

Assault of a child under 13 by penetration (s 6 Sexual Offences Act 2003—life)

Assault with intent to rob (s 8 Theft Act 1968—life)

Attempted murder (s 4(1) Criminal Attempts Act 1981—life)

Attempting to strangle with intent to endanger life (s 21 Offences Against the Person Act 1861—life)

Blackmail (s 21 Theft Act 1968—14 years)

Burglary of dwelling (s 9(3)(a) Theft Act 1968—14 years) *NB does not include non-dwelling burglaries*

Causing child under 13 to engage in sexual activity (s 8 Sexual Offences Act 2003—14 years/life if subsection (2) applies)

Causing death by aggravated vehicle-taking (s 12A(5) Theft Act 1968—14 years)

Causing death by careless driving while under the influence of alcohol or drugs (s 3 Road Traffic Act 1988—14 years)

Causing death by dangerous driving (s 1 Road Traffic Act 1988—14 years)

Causing a person with a mental disorder impeding choice to engage in sexual activity (s 31 Sexual Offences Act 2003—14 years/life if subsection (3) applies)

Causing a person with a mental disorder to engage in or agree to engage in sexual activity by inducement, threat, or deception (s 35 Sexual Offences Act 2003—14 years/life if subsection (2) applies)

Child destruction (s 1 Infant Life (Preservation) Act 1929—life)

Child prostitution or pornography

- Paying for sexual services of a child (s 47 Sexual Offences Act 2003—14 years if child under 14/life if child under 13)

- Causing or inciting child prostitution or pornography (s 48 Sexual Offences Act 2003—14 years)
- Controlling a child prostitute or a child involved in pornography (s 49 Sexual Offences Act 2003—14 years)
- Arranging or facilitating child prostitution or pornography (s 50 Sexual Offences Act 2003—14 years)

Child sex offences (s 13 Sexual Offences Act 2003—5 years)

Criminal damage with intent to endanger life (s 1(2) Criminal Damage Act 1971—life)

Criminal property

- Concealing etc criminal property (s 327 Proceeds of Crime Act 2002—14 years)
- Entering into an arrangement etc about criminal property—(s 328 Proceeds of Crime Act 2002—14 years)
- Acquiring, using, or possessing criminal property (s 329 Proceeds of Crime Act 2002—14 years)

Demanding money with menaces (s 21 Theft Act 1968—14 years)

Destroying property with intent to endanger life (s 1 Criminal Damage Act 1971—life)

Drugs

- Production (s 4(2) Misuse of Drugs Act 1971: class A—life; class B—14 years)
- Supplying/offering to supply/being concerned in the supply (s 4(3) Misuse of Drugs Act 1971: class A—life; class B and C—14 years)
- Possession with intent to supply (s 5(3) Misuse of Drugs Act 1971: class A—life; class B and C—14 years)
- Cultivation of cannabis (s 6(2) Misuse of Drugs Act 1971—14 years)
- Fraudulent evasion of prohibition by importing/exporting controlled drugs (s 3 Misuse of Drugs Act 1971 and s 170(2) and (4) Customs and Excise Management Act 1979 s 50: class A—life; class B and C—14 years)

Endangering safety of aircraft (s 3 Aviation Security Act 1982—life)

Endangering safety of railway passengers (s 32 Offences Against the Person Act 1961—life)

Escape from custody (police or prison detention)—(common law—life)

Explosives

- causing explosion likely to endanger life (s 1 Explosive Substances Act 1883—life)
- attempting to cause explosion (s 2 Explosive Substances Act 1883—life)

- possession of explosive substance with intent (s 2 Explosive Substances Act 1883—life)
- making or possessing explosive substance (s 4 Explosive Substances Act 1883—14 years)
- Facilitating commission of a child sex offence (s 14 Sexual Offences Act 2003—14 years)

False imprisonment (common law—life)

Female genital mutilation (ss 1 to 3 Female Genital Mutilation Act 2003—14 years)

Firearms

- possession of prohibited weapon (subsections (1)(a), (ab), (aba), (ac), (ad), (af) or (c) or subsection (1A)(a) of Firearms Act 1968— only for offenders who have attained 16 by the date of offence and are subject to the minimum mandatory sentence under s 51A Firearms Act 1968)
- possession with intent to endanger life (s 16 Firearms Act 1968—life)
- using a firearm with intent to resist arrest (s 17(1) Firearms Act 1968—life)
- possession of a firearm at time of commission of offence or arrest for scheduled offence (s 17(2) Firearms Act 1968—14 years)
- possession with intent to commit an indictable offence or to resist arrest (s 18 Firearms Act 1968—14 years)
- using a person to mind a prohibited firearm (s 28(1) Violent Crime Reduction Act 2006—only for offenders who have attained 16 by the date of offence and are subject to the minimum mandatory sentence under s 29(3) and (6) of the 2006 Act)

GBH with intent (s 18 Offences Against the Person Act 1861—life)

Handling stolen goods (s 22 Theft Act 1968—14 years)

Hijacking (s 1 Aviation Security Act 1982—life)

Inciting a child under 13 to engage in sexual activity (s 8 Sexual Offences Act 2003—14 years/life if subsection (2) applies)

Inciting a person with a mental disorder impeding choice to engage in sexual activity (s 31 Sexual Offences Act 2003—14 years/life if subsection (3) applies)

Inducement, threat, or deception to procure sexual activity with a person with a mental disorder (s 34 Sexual Offences Act 2003— 14 years/life if subsection (2) applies)

Infanticide (s 1 Infanticide Act 1938—life)

Kidnapping (common law—life)

Manslaughter (s 5 Offences Against the Person Act 1861—life)

Money laundering—see criminal property above

Perverting the course of justice (common law—life)

Placing object on railway with intent to obstruct or overthrow any engine (s 35 Malicious Damage Act 1861—life)

Racially aggravated criminal damage (s 30 Crime and Disorder Act 1998—14 years)

Rape (s 1 Sexual Offences Act 2003—life)

Rape of a child under 13 (s 5 Sexual Offences Act 2003—life)

Robbery (s 8 Theft Act 1968—life)

Sexual activity with a child family member (s 25 Sexual Offences Act 2003—5 years)

Sexual activity with a person with a mental disorder impeding choice (s 30 Sexual Offences Act 2003—14 years/life, if subsection (3) applies)

Sexual assault (s 3 Sexual Offences Act 2003—10 years)

Sexual assault of a child under 13 (s 7 Sexual Offences Act 2003—14 years)

Soliciting to murder (s 4 Offences Against the Person Act 1861—life)

Throwing corrosive liquid with intent to endanger life (s 29 Offences Against the Person Act 1861—life)

Throwing object with intent to endanger rail passenger (s 33 Offences Against the Person Act 1861—life)

Torture (s 134 Criminal Justice Act 1988—life)

Trafficking for sexual exploitation (ss 57 to 59 Sexual Offences Act 2003—14 years)

Wounding with intent (s 18 Offences Against the Person Act 1861—life)

Note: an attempt or conspiracy to commit any of the above offences will also be a grave crime (s 1 Criminal Attempts Act 1981 and s 1 Criminal Law Act 1977 respectively).

Appendix 4

Children Act 1989

The Children Act 1989 is of considerable practical importance for practitioners working with youth defendants in the criminal courts. This appendix aims to provide an overview of the relevant provisions applicable to England. The statutory framework and statutory instruments for Wales are different.

1 Definitions

Child—a person under the age of 18 (Children Act 1989 s 105(1)).

Parental responsibility—defined as 'all the rights, duties, powers, responsibilities and authority which by law a parent of a child has in relation to the child and his property' (Children Act 1989 s 3).

Care order—order made by family proceedings court under Children Act 1989 s 31. Interim care orders may also be made. While a care order is in force the local authority shall have parental responsibility for the child (Children Act 1989 s 33(3)).

Looked after child—a child who is in the care of a local authority or who is provided accommodation by the authority. Defendants remanded to local authority accommodation under the LASPO 2012 s 91(3) are looked after children. Defendants remanded to youth detention accommodation under the LASPO 2012 s 91(4) are deemed to be looked after children no matter where they are placed by the YJB (LASPO 2012 s 104). A local authority does not acquire parental responsibility for looked after children unless a care order is in force.

Accommodated child—a child placed in accommodation by a local authority under a voluntary arrangement under the Children Act 1989 s 20. This is often termed 'voluntary care'.

Eligible child—a child who is

- looked after,
- aged 16 or 17, and
- has been looked after by a local authority for a period of 13 weeks, or periods amounting in total to 13 weeks, which began after he reached 14 and ended after he reached 16.

Relevant child—a child who:

- is not being looked after by any local authority;
- was, before last ceasing to be looked after, an eligible child; and
- is aged 16 or 17.

2 **Children in need**

There is a general duty of every local authority to safeguard and promote the welfare of children within their area who are in need and, so far as is consistent with that duty, to promote the upbringing of such children by their families (Children Act 1989 s 17). Children's services departments of local authorities are under an obligation to carry out child in need assessments to determine what help or support may be required. This duty will apply to children serving a custodial sentence. Detailed guidance is provided in the Department of Education statutory guidance *Framework for the Assessment of Children in Need and their Families* (2010).

3 **Provision of accommodation for children**

3.1 General provisions

Under the Children Act 1989 s 20(1) every local authority shall provide accommodation for any child in need within their area who appears to them to require accommodation as a result of:

- there being no person who has parental responsibility for him;
- his being lost or having been abandoned; or
- the person who has been caring for him being prevented (whether or not permanently, and for whatever reason) from providing him with suitable accommodation or care.

There is a duty under the Children Act 1989 s 20(3) to provide accommodation for any child in need within their area who has reached the age of 16 and whose welfare the authority consider is likely to be seriously prejudiced if they do not provide him with accommodation. There is also a discretionary power to provide accommodation for any child within the area (even though a person who has parental responsibility for him is able to provide him with accommodation) if they consider that to do so would safeguard or promote the child's welfare (Children Act 1989 s 20(4)).

3.2 Provisions relating to criminal proceedings

The designated local authority must provide accommodation for a defendant refused bail and remanded to local authority accommodation (LASPO 2012 s 92(4)).

In addition to this provision there are a number of other specific duties to provide accommodation which arise in the context of criminal proceedings. These are where:

- the police have refused bail and request that the local authority receive the child under the PACE 1984 s 38(6);

- the child is remanded to accommodation provided by or on behalf of a local authority by virtue of the PCCSA 2000 Sch 1 para 4 or Sch 8 para 6 (breach etc of referral orders and reparation orders);
- the child is remanded to accommodation provided by or on behalf of a local authority by virtue of CJIA 2008 Sch 2 para 21 (breach etc of youth rehabilitation orders); or
- the child is the subject of a youth rehabilitation order imposing a local authority residence requirement or a youth rehabilitation order with fostering.

3.3 Type of accommodation

The Children Act 1989 s 22C lays down the ways in which looked after children are to be accommodated and maintained in England (in Wales s 23 of the 1989 Act applies).

In the first instances the local authority must make arrangements for the child to live with:

(a) a parent;
(b) a person who is not a parent but who has parental responsibility for him;
(c) a person with a residence order in respect of him.

If the local authority does not think that placement with one of the above persons would be consistent with the child's welfare or would not be reasonably practicable, then it may make arrangements to place the child:

(a) with a relative, friend, or other person connected with the child who is also a local authority foster parent;
(b) with a local authority foster parent who does not fall into (a):
(c) in a children's home; or
(d) in a placement in accordance with other arrangements which comply with the Care Planning, Placement, and Case Review (England) Regulations 2010.

Before placing a child in an unregulated setting under s 22C(6)(d) the local authority must be satisfied that the accommodation is suitable for the child. In making that assessment the Care Planning, Placement, and Care Review (England) Regulations 2010 reg 26 and Sch 6 requires the local authority to have regard to:

- in respect of the accommodation, the facilities and services provided, state of repair, safety, location, support, tenancy status, and the financial commitments involved for the child and their affordability.
- in respect of the child, his views about the accommodation, his understanding of his rights and responsibilities in relation to the accommodation, and his understanding of funding arrangements.

The local authority may apply to a court under the Children Act 1989 s 25 for permission to place a looked after child in secure accommodation. For more see **D13**.

4 Duties to looked after children

Under the Children Act 1989 s 22(3) it shall be the duty of a local authority looking after any child:

- to safeguard and promote his welfare; and
- to make such use of services available for children cared for by their own parents as appears to the authority reasonable in his case.

The duty of a local authority to safeguard and promote the welfare of a child looked after by them includes in particular a duty to promote the child's educational achievement (s 22(3A)).

The duties of a local authority in relation to a looked after child are set out in the Care Planning, Placement, and Case Review (England) Regulations 2010 (separate regulations apply in Wales). A social worker must:

- assess the needs of the child for services to maintain a reasonable standard of health or development;
- prepare a care plan (which should include a health plan and a personal education plan); and
- prepare a placement plan.

A social worker should visit the child within seven days of the placement and at least every six weeks thereafter. This duty should not be performed by a YOT worker in place of the social worker.

The child's case should be reviewed regularly. The first review must be within twenty days of placement; the next review must be no more than three months later. Subsequent reviews must take place at least every six months.

A local authority looking after a child has a duty to appoint a person to be a child's independent visitor where it appears to be in the child's interest to do so (Children Act s 23ZB(1)(b)).

5 Duties to care leavers

A local authority must provide leaving care services to children who meet the definition of eligible or relevant children. Defendants remanded to local authority accommodation or youth detention accommodation for more than thirteen weeks will qualify as eligible or relevant children.

The duties of the local authority are set out in detail in the Care Leavers (England) Regulations 2010 (separate regulations apply in Wales).

In the case of an *eligible* child the local authority, in addition to the general duties owed to a looked after child, must:

- prepare an assessment of the eligible child's needs with a view to determining what advice, assistance, and support it would be appropriate to provide him (both while he is looked after and after he stops being looked after);
- as soon as possible after the assessment of needs is completed prepare a pathway plan;
- keep the pathway plan under regular review; and
- appoint a personal adviser for the child.

In the case of a *relevant child* the local authority which last looked after him must:

- take reasonable steps to keep in touch with him;
- prepare an assessment of his needs with a view to determining what advice, assistance, and support it would be appropriate for them to provide him;
- as soon as possible after any assessment of needs is completed, prepare a pathway plan;
- keep the pathway plan under regular review;
- appoint a personal adviser for the child;
- safeguard and promote his welfare by maintaining him, providing him with, or maintaining him in suitable accommodation and providing assistance in order to meet his needs in relation to education, training, or employment.

6 Children serving custodial sentences

Children subject to care orders will remain looked after children while they serve a custodial sentence. The local authority will continue to be responsible for planning and reviewing their care.

If the person is a relevant child (see above) then they are entitled to support and services as a care leaver whilst in custody and on release.

Children accommodated by the local authority before their sentence lose their looked after status while serving the sentence. The Children Act 1989 s 23ZA imposes a duty on the local authority to ensure that a child who was looked after by that local authority, but has ceased to be so as a result of certain circumstances, is visited by a representative of the authority. The local authority also has a duty to arrange for appropriate advice, support, and assistance to be available to those children. The Visits to Former Looked After Children in Detention (England) Regulations 2010 provide that these duties will apply to children who have ceased to be looked after as a result of being detained in a young offender institution, secure training centre, or a secure children's home and who are not 'relevant' children. The role of appointed representative should not be performed by a YOT worker. The first visit should be made within ten working days of the child entering custody, unless not reasonably practicable. The appointed representative should then visit the child when reasonably requested by the child, a parent, a member of staff at the custodial institution, or a YOT worker.

7 Child protection

Local authorities have duties to carry out child protection investigations in relation to children who live or are found in their area if they have reasonable cause to suspect that the child is suffering, or is likely to suffer significant harm (Children Act 1989 s 47). This duty also applies to children in custodial institutions run by the Prison Service (*R (Howard League for Penal Reform) v Secretary of State for the Home Department* [2002] EWHC 2497 (Admin)).

Appendix 5

Gang Injunctions

Gang injunctions are governed by the Policing and Crime Act 2009 Part 4. The Home Office has issued statutory guidance *Injunctions to Prevent Gang-Related Violence* (December 2011).

They are civil orders and at the time of writing, application for an injunction may only be made to a county court. Upon implementation of the Crime and Courts Act 2013 s 18 applications against respondents under the age of 18 will be made to the youth court.

What follows is a summary of the law upon implementation of s 18 of the 2013 Act. Statutory references are to the Policing and Crime Act 2009.

1 Consultation (ss 37 and 38)

Applications for a gang injunction may be made by the police or a local authority. Before applying for an injunction, the applicant must consult—

- any local authority, and any chief police officer, that the applicant thinks it appropriate to consult, and
- where the respondent is under the age of 18 (and will be under that age when the application is made), the youth offending team in whose area it appears to the applicant that the respondent resides, and
- any other body or individual that the applicant thinks it appropriate to consult.

If it appears to the applicant that the respondent resides in the area of two or more youth offending teams, it must consult such of those teams as the applicant thinks appropriate.

2 Grounds for an injunction (s 34)

A court may grant an injunction against a respondent aged 14 or over if:

- the court is satisfied on the balance of probabilities that the respondent has engaged in, or has encouraged or assisted, gang-related violence; and
- the court thinks it is necessary to grant the injunction for either or both of the following purposes—

(a) to prevent the respondent from engaging in, or encouraging or assisting, gang-related violence;

(b) to protect the respondent from gang-related violence.

'Gang-related violence' means violence or a threat of violence which occurs in the course of, or is otherwise related to, the activities of a group that:

- consists of at least three people,
- uses a name, emblem, or colour or has any other characteristic that enables its members to be identified by others as a group, and
- is associated with a particular area.

3 Contents of injunctions (ss 35 and 36)

An injunction may include both prohibitions and requirements. It may not include either a prohibition or a requirement that has effect after the end of the period of two years beginning with the day on which the injunction is granted ('the injunction date').

The prohibitions included in the injunction may, in particular, have the effect of prohibiting the respondent from—

- being in a particular place;
- being with particular persons in a particular place;
- being in charge of a particular species of animal in a particular place;
- wearing particular descriptions of articles of clothing in a particular place;
- using the internet to facilitate or encourage violence.

The requirements included in the injunction may, in particular, have the effect of requiring the respondent to:

- notify the person who applied for the injunction of the respondent's address and of any change to that address;
- be at a particular place between particular times on particular days;
- present himself or herself to a particular person at a place where he or she is required to be between particular times on particular days;
- participate in particular activities between particular times on particular days.

A curfew requirement may not be such as to require the respondent to be at a particular place for more than eight hours in any day.

The prohibitions and requirements included in the injunction must, so far as practicable, be such as to avoid—

- any conflict with the respondent's religious beliefs, and
- any interference with the times, if any, at which the respondent normally works or attends any educational establishment.

4 **Arrest power (s 36(6) and (7))**

The court may attach a power of arrest in relation to—

- any prohibition in the injunction, or
- any requirement in the injunction, other than one which has the effect of requiring the respondent to participate in particular activities.

If the court attaches a power of arrest, it may specify that the power is to have effect for a shorter period than the prohibition or requirement to which it relates.

5 **Review hearings (s 36)**

A review hearing is a hearing held for the purpose of considering whether the injunction should be varied or discharged. The youth court may order the applicant and the respondent to attend one or more review hearings on a specified date or dates.

If any prohibition or requirement in the injunction is to have effect after the end of the period of one year beginning with the injunction date, the court must order the applicant and the respondent to attend a review hearing on a specified date within the last four weeks of the one-year period (whether or not the court orders them to attend any other review hearings).

Where:

- the respondent is under the age of 18 on the injunction date, and
- any prohibition or requirement in the injunction is to have effect after the respondent reaches that age and for at least the period of four weeks beginning with the respondent's 18th birthday,

the court must order the applicant and the respondent to attend a review hearing on a specified date within that period.

6 **Applications without notice (s 39)**

An application for an injunction may be made without the respondent being given notice.

If an application without notice is made the court must either—

- dismiss the application, or
- adjourn the proceedings.

If the court adjourns the proceedings, the applicant must comply with the consultation requirement before the date of the first full hearing.

7 Interim injunctions (ss 40 and 41)

Where the application was made on notice and the court adjourns the application, an interim injunction may be made if the court thinks that it is just and convenient to do so.

An interim order made after an application on notice may include any provision the court could have made in relation to a full injunction (including a power of arrest).

Where an application was made without notice and the court adjourns the application, the youth court may make an interim injunction but only if it thinks it is necessary to do so.

An interim order made after an application on notice may include any provision the court could have made in relation to a full injunction (including a power of arrest) except for a requirement to participate in particular activities.

8 Variation or discharge of injunctions (s 42)

The youth court may vary or discharge an injunction:

* a review hearing is held, or
* an application to vary or discharge the injunction is made.

An application to vary or discharge the injunction may be made by—

* the person who applied for the injunction; or
* the respondent.

The power to vary an injunction includes power to—

* include an additional prohibition or requirement in the injunction;
* extend the period for which a prohibition or requirement in the injunction has effect; and
* attach a power of arrest or extend the period for which a power of arrest attached to the injunction has effect.

9 Breach of injunction—arrest without warrant (s 43)

Where a power of arrest is attached to a provision of the gang injunction, a constable may arrest a person whom the constable has reasonable cause to suspect to be in breach of that provision.

If a constable arrests a person for breach of the injunction, the constable must inform the person who applied for the injunction.

A person arrested for breach must be brought before a relevant judge within the period of twenty-four hours beginning with the time of the arrest. In calculating when the period of twenty-four hours ends, Christmas Day, Good Friday, and any Sunday are to be disregarded.

If the matter is not disposed of when the person is brought before the judge, the judge may remand the person.

'Relevant judge', in relation to an injunction, means a judge of the court that granted the injunction, except where the respondent is now aged 18 or over and the injunction was made by a youth court, it means a judge of the county court. In relation to a youth court it means a person qualified to sit as a member of that court (s 49(1)).

10 Warrant of arrest (ss 43–45)

If the injunction applicant considers that the respondent is in breach of any of its provisions, the applicant may apply to a relevant judge for the issue of a warrant for the arrest of the respondent.

A relevant judge may not issue a warrant unless the judge has reasonable grounds for believing that the respondent is in breach of any provision of the injunction.

If a person is brought before a court by virtue of a warrant, but the matter is not disposed of, the court may remand the person.

11 Remand of the defaulter (Sch 5)

An alleged defaulter under the age of 18 may only be remanded on bail. The youth court may remand him:

- with a recognizance
- with such requirements as appear to the court to be necessary to secure that the person does not interfere with witnesses or otherwise obstruct the course of justice.

12 Powers of court on breach of an injunction (s 46A and Sch 5A)

Where a gang injunction was granted against a person under the age of 18 and that person is still under the age of 18, and on an application made by the injunction applicant, the youth court is satisfied beyond reasonable doubt that the person is in breach of any provision of the injunction, the court may make:

- a supervision order;
- a detention order.

Before the court makes either order it must consider a report written by the YOT. Neither order may be made against a person who has attained the age of 18.

12.1 Supervision order (Sch 5A paras 2–13)

This imposes on the defaulter one or more of the following requirements:

- a supervision requirement (keeping appointments with a YOT worker for a specified period up to maximum of six months);
- an activity requirement (participation in specified activities for a specified number of days which in aggregate must not be less than twelve nor more than twenty-four days);
- a curfew requirement (for a specified period not less than two hours and not more than eight hours a night).

Before making a supervision order the court must obtain and consider information about the defaulter's family circumstances and the likely effect of such an order on those circumstances. Before making a supervision order imposing two or more requirements, the court must consider their mutual compatibility.

The court must ensure, as far as practicable, that any requirement imposed by a supervision order is such as to avoid:

- any conflict with the defaulter's religious beliefs,
- any interference with the times, if any, at which the defaulter normally works or attends school or any other educational establishment, and
- any conflict with the requirements of any other court order or injunction to which the defaulter may be subject.

The court must specify the maximum period for the operation of any requirement in the order. This period may not exceed six months.

The order must also specify the YOT which will work with the defaulter. This must be the YOT in whose area it appears to the court that the respondent will reside during the period of the supervision order.

A court may only include an activity requirement in a supervision order if—

- it has consulted the youth offending team which is to be, or is, specified in the order,
- it is satisfied that it is feasible to secure compliance with the requirement or requirement as varied,
- it is satisfied that provision for the defaulter to participate in the activities proposed can be made under the arrangements for persons to participate in such activities which exist in the area of the youth offending team which is to be or is specified in the order, and
- in a case where the requirement or requirement as varied would involve the cooperation of a person other than the defaulter and the responsible officer, that person consents to its inclusion or variation.

The youth court, on application by the injunction applicant or the defaulter, may:

- vary the operation period;
- amend the order on change of area of residence; or
- revoke the order.

If the responsible officer considers that the defaulter has failed to comply with any requirement of the supervision order, the responsible officer must inform the injunction applicant.

On being informed by the responsible officer, the injunction applicant may apply to the appropriate court. Before making such an application the injunction applicant must consult with the YOT specified in the order and any person consulted before the making of the original application.

Where an application is made by the injunction applicant and the court is satisfied beyond reasonable doubt that the defaulter has without reasonable excuse failed to comply with any requirement of the supervision order, the court may:

- revoke the supervision order and make a new one; or
- revoke the order and make a detention order.

These powers may not be exercised at any time after the defaulter reaches the age of 18.

12.2 Detention orders (Sch 5A paras 14 and 15)

A detention order is an order that the defaulter be detained for a specified period not exceeding three months beginning with the day after the day the order was made.

The court may not make a detention order unless it is satisfied, in view of the severity or extent of the breach, that no other power available to the court is appropriate.

Before making a detention order the injunction applicant must consult the YOT previously consulted and any other person consulted before the original application.

The order may be served in a youth offender institution, secure training centre, or secure accommodation. There is no provision for early release so a defaulter would serve the whole of the period specified in the order.

The injunction applicant or the defaulter may apply to the court to revoke the order. The court may revoke the order if it appears to be in the interests of justice to do so, having regard to circumstances which have arisen since the detention order was made.

13 Breach of injunction when defaulter has attained 18

The proceedings for breach of the injunction will be dealt with in the county order. The court will have a power to remand in custody if the proceedings are adjourned and if the breach is proved beyond reasonable doubt the county court has the power to deal with the breach as a civil contempt of court punishable by up to two years in prison and/or an unlimited fine.

14 Appeals (s 46B)

An appeal lies to the Crown Court against a decision of a youth court made under Part 4 of the Act.

On appeal the Crown Court may make:

- whatever orders are necessary to give effect to its determination of the appeal;
- whatever incidental or consequential order appear to it to be just.

Index

Index

Index

Index

Index

Index

Index

Index

Index

Index

Index

Index

Index

Index

Index

Index

2014

	January				
M		6	13	20	27
T		7	14	21	•28
W	1	8	15	22	29
T	2	9	16	23	30
F	3	10	17	24	31
S	4	11	18	25	
S	5	12	19	26	

	February				
M		3	10	17	24
T		4	11	18	25
W		5	12	19	26
T		6	13	20	27
F		7	14	21	28
S	1	8	15	22	
S	2	9	16	23	

	March				
M	31	3	10	17	24
T		4	11	18	25
W		5	12	19	26
T		6	13	20	27
F		7	14	21	28
S	1	8	15	22	29
S	2	9	16	23	30

	April				
M		7	14	21	28
T	1	8	15	22	29
W	2	9	16	23	30
T	3	10	17	24	
F	4	11	18	25	
S	5	12	19	26	
S	6	13	20	27	

	May				
M		5	12	19	26
T		6	13	20	27
W		7	14	21	28
T	1	8	15	22	29
F	2	9	16	23	30
S	3	10	17	24	31
S	4	11	18	25	

	June				
M	30	2	9	16	23
T		3	10	17	24
W		4	11	18	25
T		5	12	19	26
F		6	13	20	27
S		7	14	21	28
S	1	8	15	22	29

	July				
M		7	14	21	28
T	1	8	15	22	29
W	2	9	16	23	30
T	3	10	17	24	31
F	4	11	18	25	
S	5	12	19	26	
S	6	13	20	27	

	August				
M		4	11	18	25
T		5	12	19	26
W		6	13	20	27
T		7	14	21	28
F	1	8	15	22	29
S	2	9	16	23	30
S	3	10	17	24	31

	September				
M	1	8	15	22	29
T	2	9	16	23	30
W	3	10	17	24	
T	4	11	18	25	
F	5	12	19	26	
S	6	13	20	27	
S	7	14	21	28	

	October				
M		6	13	20	27
T		7	14	21	28
W	1	8	15	22	29
T	2	9	16	23	30
F	3	10	17	24	31
S	4	11	18	25	
S	5	12	19	26	

	November				
M		3	10	17	24
T		4	11	18	25
W		5	12	19	26
T		6	13	20	27
F		7	14	21	28
S	1	8	15	22	29
S	2	9	16	23	30

	December				
M	1	8	15	22	29
T	2	9	16	23	30
W	3	10	17	24	31
T	4	11	18	25	
F	5	12	19	26	
S	6	13	20	27	
S	7	14	21	28	